PUBLICATIONS OF

THE COLONIAL SOCIETY OF MASSACHUSETTS

VOLUME LXXV

PORTRAIT OF A PATRIOT

THE MAJOR POLITICAL AND LEGAL PAPERS OF JOSIAH QUINCY JUNIOR

PORTRAIT OF A PATRIOT

The Major Political and Legal Papers of Josiah Quincy Junior

EDITORS

DANIEL R. COQUILLETTE

J. Donald Monan, S.J. University Professor, Boston College
Lester Kissel Visiting Professor, Harvard Law School

NEIL LONGLEY YORK

Karl G. Maeser Professor of General Education
Chair, History Department, Brigham Young University

VOLUME TWO

The Law Commonplace Book

BOSTON · 2007

The Colonial Society of Massachusetts

Distributed by the University of Virginia Press

ACKNOWLEDGMENTS FOR THE QUINCY PAPERS

This series of volumes represents the tireless and invaluable work of our research and administrative assistants: Brandon Bigelow, Kevin Cox, Jane Downing, Natalia Fekula, Michael Hayden, Elizabeth Kamali, Christina Nolan, Nicole Scimone, Brian Sheppard, Susannah Tobin, and Elisa Underwood, with special recognition to the Editorial Assistants to the Boston College Monan Chair, Brendan Farmer, Charles Riordan, and Patricia Tarabelsi, and to Inge Burgess at Harvard. Their intelligence and enthusiasm are visible on every page. Of course, we are deeply in debt to John W. Tyler, Editor of Publications of the Colonial Society of Massachusetts, as well as to the Committee of Publications, without whose guidance and support this project would have been impossible. Finally, special thanks are also due to the guardians of the Quincy heritage: the Massachusetts Historical Society with its enormously helpful Librarian, Peter Drummey, and his staff, the Museum of Fine Arts, Boston, and the Quincy family itself.

FRONTISPIECE:

Old State House, by James Brown Marston (1775–1817). Oil on Panel, Boston, 1801. For many years, this was the seat of the Massachusetts Superior Court of Judicature. Josiah Quincy Jr., John Adams, Robert Treat Paine, James Otis Jr. and many others learned and practiced law in this neighborhood. See *Witness to America's Past: Two Centuries of Collecting by the Massachusetts Historical Society* (Boston, 1991), p. 135. Image courtesy of the Massachusetts Historical Society.

ISBN 978-0-9620737-8-6

Printed from the income of the Sarah Louise Edes Fund

JOSIAH QUINCY JR.
Political and Legal Works

VOLUME TWO

THE LAW COMMONPLACE
(COMMENCED, 1763)

CO-EDITORS:
Daniel R. Coquillette
Neil Longley York

VOLUME EDITOR:
Daniel R. Coquillette

"From LAW arises Security: From Security Curiosity: And from Curiosity Knowledge. The latter Steps of this Progress may be more accidental; but the former are altogether necessary."

From the first page of Josiah Quincy Jr.'s *Law Commonplace*, (1763) n.p., p. [1], Quoting David Hume, "Of the Rise and Progress of the Arts and Sciences," vol. 2, *Hume's Essays, Moral and Political* (1742). See note 3, p. [81], *infra*.

To The Memory of My Mother

CONTENTS

VOLUME 2

*

ACKNOWLEDGMENTS

VOLUME TWO

THIS VOLUME has been a true team effort. Appropriately enough, Quincy's *Law Commonplace* appeals, more than two centuries later, to new lawyers and law students, like Quincy himself. I must begin with my law student research assistants, now successful members of the bar. Jane Downing and Natalia Fekula prepared the first transcription with saintly patience, and Susannah Tobin prepared the initial Latin translations. Next came Kevin Cox and Elizabeth Kamali, whose exceptional contributions are represented by Appendices I and II, plus much more. Their hard work and intellectual originality has improved every page. Three Editorial Assistants to the Monan Chair worked tirelessly at these most complicated manuscripts: Brendon Farmer, Charles Riordan and Patricia Tarabelsi, together with Inge Burgess at Harvard Law School. Charles Riordan also safeguarded this volume through publication with great skill.

Complicated legal history also requires teamwork between institutions. First, the original text is reproduced courtesy of the Massachusetts Historical Society. Peter Drummey and his staff at the Massachusetts Historical Society have been invaluable, as have Karen Beck and Mark Sullivan at the Boston College Law School Library, David Warrington at the Harvard Law School Library, and David Whitesell at Harvard's Houghton Library, who is responsible for Appendix III. My learned colleagues Mary Sarah Bilder at Boston College and Charles Donahue Jr. at Harvard have always been available, although the errors remaining are certainly not theirs. Of course, there has been the exceptional support of the Colonial Society of Massachusetts, including its sterling Publication Committee and its inspirational Editor of Publications, John W. Tyler. For wise advice and assistance I have always been able to look to my co-editor, Neil York, to my loyal colleagues at Boston College and Harvard, and, of course, to my wife Judith and my wonderful family.

DANIEL R. COQUILLETTE
Volume Editor

JOSIAH QUINCY JR.

The Law Commonplace

(COMMENCED, 1763)

Transcribed and Annotated by
DANIEL R. COQUILLETTE
Volume Editor
J. Donald Monan, S.J. University Professor,
Boston College Law School,
Lester Kissel Visiting Professor,
Harvard Law School

With many thanks for the extraordinary and invaluable assistance of Jane G. Downing and Natalia Fekula, both J.D. Boston College Law School, Class of 1997, who skillfully and patiently prepared the initial transcript; Susannah Tobin, J.D. Harvard Law School, Class of 2004, Kevin Willoughby Cox, Harvard Law School, Class of 2006, and Elizabeth Papp Kamali, Harvard Law School Class of 2007, unparalleled Latin translators and research assistants; Mark Sullivan, reference librarian extraordinaire, and Brendan Farmer, Charles Riordan, Patricia Tarabelsi, and Laurie Tautkas, the simply invaluable Editorial Assistants to the Monan Chair.

ILLUSTRATION 1. Quincy's pupil master, Oxenbridge Thacher (1719–1765) by Robert Feke, or In the manner of Robert Feke (c. 1748 or 1749). Thacher was a leading member of the Boston bar. At only twenty-one, Quincy assumed Thacher's law practice upon his teacher's death in 1765. See "The Making of a Patriot," by Neil Longley York in *Quincy Papers*, vol. 1, p. 17. Image courtesy of Yale University Art Gallery, Gift of Thomas Thacher, B.A. 1938. See also note 42, *infra*. My thanks to Kevin Cox for tracking down the original portrait at Yale University, and to David Warrington, for locating a copy at Harvard Law School.

INTRODUCTION

The Legal Education of a Patriot: Josiah Quincy Jr.'s *Law Commonplace*

*Daniel R. Coquillette**

MUCH HAS BEEN WRITTEN about the history of American legal education. And almost all of it is about law schools. Literally hundreds of volumes have described the hundreds of professional law schools established in North America, from the prototype Litchfield Law School (1784 to 1833) to the newly published account of the "Dark Ages" of the 1960s through the early 1980s at Yale Law School.[1] Even the different, but related, phenomenon of teaching law to undergraduates as a "liberal art," symbolized Thomas Jefferson's establishment of the Professorship of Law and Police at The College of William and Mary in 1779, has been carefully chronicled.[2] But the lawyers who founded this nation and defended the early Republic, famous lawyers, learned most of their law a very different way. Take Massachusetts as an example. John Adams, Robert Treat Paine and James Otis Jr. were great lawyers, but they never attended a law school. Neither did Patrick Henry, Joseph Story, James Monroe or Thomas Jefferson. John Marshall was another, if one overlooks a brief tuition from George Wythe while Wythe was at William and Mary.[3] Story and Jefferson established great law schools, but they did not learn law that way themselves.

* A version of this introduction first appeared in volume 39 of the *Arizona State Law Journal* (Summer, 2007), 11, 317. I am most grateful to the talented student editors of that law review.

1. See Robert Stevens's classic *Law School: Legal Education in America from the 1850s to the 1980s* (Chapel Hill, N.C., 1983). (Hereafter, "Stevens.") For both Litchfield and Yale in the 1960s see the fine essays of John H. Langbein and Laura Kalman, respectively, in *History of Yale Law School: The Tercentennial Lectures* (New Haven, Conn., 2004), pp. 17–52, 154–237.

2. See Paul D. Carrington, "The Revolutionary Idea of University Legal Education," 31 *William & Mary L. Rev.* 527 (1990). (Hereafter, Carrington, "University Legal Education.")

3. Wythe, a great law teacher, did most of his teaching outside of a college, taking pupils in his chambers. Wythe taught at William and Mary from only 1780 to 1790, when he resigned "in anger." See Carrington, "University Legal Education," *supra*, p. 537. Jefferson and Monroe were educated by Wythe privately. Interestingly, Wythe refused to sign Patrick Henry's license, leav-

Of course, the primary method for learning law in the American colonial period was apprenticeship. That would be true for much of the next century, too. Perhaps because most books about legal education are written by law professors, apprenticeship as a pedagogy and a course of study has been widely overlooked and belittled.[4] The popular conception is that apprentices were educated by chance, picking up whatever learning they could while copying documents and running errands for their indifferent masters.[5] Possibly there

---

ing it to the other two examinees to admit him. See Charles Warren, *A History of the American Bar* (Boston, 1911), p. 165. (Hereafter, "Warren.")

4. See the standard accounts in Anton-Hermann Chroust, *The Rise of the Legal Profession in America*, Volume 1: *The Colonial Experience* (Norman, Okla., 1965), pp. 30–33. ("This kind of training or apprenticeship . . . had many serious defects." p. 33); Warren, *supra*, pp. 165–87 ("As a rule, the lawyer was too busy a man to pay much attention to his students . . ." p. 166). See also Robert Lefcourt's 1983 Ph.D. thesis, "Democratic Influences on Legal Education from Colonial Times to the Civil War," University Microfilms International, Ann Arbor, which argues that the primary purpose of the apprenticeship method, described as "irrelevant and impractical," was the "monopolistic tendency" of "ruling lawyers." *Id.*, pp. 72–79. Even Lawrence M. Friedman emphasized the negative aspects of apprenticeship. "At worst, an apprentice went through a haphazard course of drudgery and copy-work, with a few glances, catch-or-catch can, at the law books." Lawrence M. Friedman, *A History of American Law* (2d ed., New York, 1985), p. 98. Of course there were some well publicized bad experiences, such as that of William Livingston's 1745 "invective" against his pupil master, James Alexander of New York. See Warren, pp. 167–69. But, as we will see, there was another side to the story. The best and most balanced account is Charles R. McKirdy's "The Lawyer As Apprentice: Legal Education in Eighteenth Century Massachusetts," 28 *J. of Legal Education* (1976), p. 124. McKirdy astutely observes that "Sir William Blackstone took the opportunity offered in his introductory Vinerian Lecture at Oxford [1758] to blame most of the ills besetting the legal profession on the 'pernicious' custom of apprenticeship." *Id.*, p. 135. See William Blackstone, *A Discourse on the Study of Law* (Oxford, 1758), p. 28. As the first teacher of English common law within a university setting, Blackstone's conflict of interest was apparent. And Blackstone inspired other university law teachers to attack the apprenticeship method. Conspicuous among these was Daniel Mayes at the important Transylvania University Law Department in Lexington, Kentucky, who cited Blackstone while attacking apprenticeship in an introductory lecture in 1833. See M. H. Hoeflich, "Plus Ça Change, Plus C'est La Même Chose: The Integration of Theory and Practice in Legal Education," 66 *Temple Law Review*, pp. 123, 133–34 (1993). See also Paul D. Carrington's excellent essay, "Teaching Law and Virtue at Transylvania University: The George Wythe Tradition in the Antebellum Years," 41 *Mercer Law Review* 673 (1989–1990), pp. 691–96, 697–99. As Hoeflich observes, "One of the 'hot' topics in legal education has been the debate over the extent to which it is desirable and possible to integrate a more practical approach into the predominantly theoretical classroom model of legal education used in most American law schools." *Id.*, p. 123. Indeed, nothing changes.

5. Warren actually tried to make the argument that apprenticeship was such a bad system that it made good lawyers because they had so much to overcome, an argument I would like to try on my law students! "When all is said, however, as to the meagerness of a lawyer's education,

would be useful books in their masters' libraries, possibly not. Possibly they would have the chance to browse in whatever books there were, but it would all be happenstance. Certainly, whatever instruction there was would be practical, not theoretical, and would focus on local, not national, law and certainly not—even more inconceivable—international law!

But the history of the pre-revolutionary bar seems most odd if this was truly the case. Take, for example, the legal world of 1773 described in Quincy's *Southern Journal*, set out Volume 3. While there was an occasional lawyer who had "experience" at the remarkably lax Inns of Court in London, particularly in the South, most of Quincy's professional acquaintances in South Carolina, North Carolina, Virginia, Delaware and Pennsylvania were taught by apprenticeship.[6] Yet there was a clear sense of a legal elite, with a firmly established professional identity. John Adams's *Diary* paints a similar picture—a self-defined and small professional elite, set apart by education and skill from a host of "petty foggers."[7] It is true Quincy had a low opinion of the training of

---

one fact must be strongly emphasized—that this very meagerness was a source of strength. *Multum in parvo* was particularly applicable to the training for the Bar of that era." Warren, *supra*, p. 187. Of course, what else could be expected from the great historian of the Harvard Law School! See Charles Warren, *History of the Harvard Law School and of Early Legal Conditions in America* (New York, 1908), 3 vols.

6. See E. Alfred Jones, *American Members of the Inns of Court* (London, 1924), pp. ix–xxx. Between 1674 to 1776 over sixty Virginians attended the Inns of Court, "but only twenty engaged in practice once they got home," and of these "some never practiced." W. Hamilton Bryson, *Legal Education in Virginia 1779–1979* (Charlottesville, 1982), p. 9. Formal educational programs had deteriorated in the Inns of Court by this time. "The essence of membership in an English Inn was that it was a prestigious place to do a legal apprenticeship," usually by "an apprenticeship to a practicing lawyer in London with residence in the Inn." *Id.*, p. 9. "In fact, many Virginians who were members of an Inn had no intention of ever practicing law but joined for purely social purposes." *Id.*, p. 9. On the "marked decay" in the "'system' of legal education" in the Inns of Court, see David Lemmings, *Gentlemen and Barristers: The Inns of Court and The English Bar 1686–1730* (Oxford, 1980), pp. 75–109.

7. See *Diary and Autobiography of John Adams* (L. H. Butterfield ed., Cambridge, Mass., 1964), vol. 1, pp. 136–37, vol. 2, p. 274. (Hereafter, "Adams, *Diary*.") See also Daniel R. Coquillette, "Justinian in Braintree: John Adams, Civilian Learning, and Legal Elitism, 1758–1775" in *Law in Colonial Massachusetts 1630–1800* (eds. D. R. Coquillette, R. J. Brink, C. S. Menand, Boston, 1984), pp. 395–400. (Hereafter, "Coquillette, Adams.") For the highly comparable history of medical apprenticeship or pupilage and the "professionalization of Boston medicine during the last half of the eighteenth century," see Philip Cash, "The Professionalization of Boston Medicine, 1760–1803" in *Medicine in Colonial Massachusetts* (eds. P. Cash, E. H. Christianson, J. W. Estes, Boston, 1980), pp. 69–100. The "Harvard Medical Institution," the area's first medical school, was not founded until 1782. *Id.*, p. 89.

some of the Southern lawyers he met, particularly in South Carolina, but that, in itself, speaks of professional standards.

My thesis is that, at its best, elite legal apprenticeship had both a pedagogy and a curricular structure that was far from random. It was neither "local" nor necessarily "practical" in its forms, and it could include comparative study, particularly of Roman law. This education may not have been ideal, nor uniformly excellent, but given a good tutor and a good student it was rigorous enough to explain the strong sense of legal professionalism to be found in America before the Revolution.

Why has this been so overlooked? First, the institutional records of this type of legal education are relatively scarce. The few that have survived tend to be the legal commonplace books of the apprentices, and these, although not rare, have rarely been published. This alone makes Quincy's *Law Commonplace* of 1763 an important document, and it has never been transcribed or published until now. Unless included in the papers of an Adams or a Jefferson, such records have usually been inaccessible to all but a handful of scholars.[8]

8. One of these exceptions is John Adams's law "Commonplace Book." See *Legal Papers of John Adams* (eds. L. Kinvin Wroth, Hiller B. Zobel, Cambridge, Mass., 1976), vol. 1, pp. 4–25. This dates from ca. 1759 and is a very rudimentary affair compared to Quincy's *Law Commonplace*. See discussion at Section I, "The Manuscript," *infra*. Another exception is Thomas Jefferson's Legal Commonplace Book, which was edited by Gilbert Chinard in 1926. See *The Commonplace Book of Thomas Jefferson: A Repertory of his Ideas on Government* (G. Chinard ed., Baltimore, 1926) and the discussion in Douglas L. Wilson, "Thomas Jefferson's Early Notebooks," 42 *William and Mary Quarterly* (1985), pp. 433–52. Jefferson also had an Equity Commonplace Book which is in the Huntington Library. See the discussion in Douglas L. Wilson's fine edition of *Jefferson's Literary Commonplace Book* (D. L. Wilson ed., Princeton, N.J., 1989), p. 195, n. 195 and in his article cited above. Wilson sets the date for the beginning of Jefferson's Legal Commonplace Book as "the period 1765–1766" which makes it almost exactly a contemporary of Quincy's book. *Id.*, p. 198, n. 14.

See also the remarkable commonplace collection, spanning the 17th century to 1935, found in the Bounds Law Library at the University of Alabama School of Law and described in Paul M. Pruitt Jr., David I. Durham, *Commonplace Book of Law: A Selection of Related Notebooks from the Seventeenth Century to the Mid-Twentieth Century* (Tuscaloosa, Ala., 2005). Another important exception was the exhibit at the Beinecke Rare Book and Manuscript Library at Yale, organized by Earle Havens in 2001. See Earle Havens, *Commonplace Books: A History of Manuscripts and Printed Books from Antiquity to the Twentieth Century* (New Haven, Conn., 2001). My own distinguished colleague, Karen Beck, organized an equally important exhibit of law student notebooks at the Boston College Law School Rare Books Room in 1999. See Karen Beck, *Notable Notes: A Collection of Law Student Notebooks*, Boston, 1999; Karen Beck, "One Step at a Time: The Research Value of Student Notebooks," 91 *Law Library*, p. 29 (1999). The latter arti-

But there is a further reason. Most American legal historians, even those who are not trained as lawyers, have been subconsciously "brainwashed" by two powerful, and complementary, visions of legal education, which have been superimposed on each other. The first was the vision of Joseph Story, and the second of Christopher Columbus Langdell.

Joseph Story (1779–1845) was, at age thirty-two, the youngest Justice of the Supreme Court ever appointed and, at age forty-nine, the "Savior of Harvard Law School." Founded by the proceeds of the will of Isaac Royall in 1817, the Harvard Law School had previously failed to compete effectively with apprenticeship and was down to one student in 1829.[9] A generous donor, Nathan Dane, agreed to establish a newly endowed professorship, but only on the condition that Story would take it. Without abandoning his judicial career, Story took this position as well.

He had a simple formula for success. Harvard Law School must become an elite, national institution, drawing students from all states. To do that, it must offer broad instruction in legal theory, legal history, comparative and international law, and constitutional law.[10] Its graduates would be the meritocrats of the new Republic, displacing both the hereditary oligarchy of the Federalists and the egalitarianism of the Jacksonian Democrats.[11] The cornerstone of the pedagogy would be well-organized treatises, which Story himself would write as part of his duties. Readings from these would be required for each class, and the teacher would reinforce each section by lecturing, backed up further by a second teacher, who was called a "crammer." (This was initially John Ashmun.) The "crammer" would drill the class in the lessons learned. The competition

---

cle emphasizes the importance of the law commonplace of Theophilius Parsons Sr. (1750–1813), created in 1773. *Id.*, p. 32. See Theophilius Parsons Jr., *Memoir of Theophilius Parsons* (Boston, 1859), p. 137.

9. See Arthur E. Sutherland, *The Law at Harvard* (Cambridge, Mass., 1967), pp. 79–92. (Hereafter, "Sutherland.")

10. See Daniel R. Coquillette, "'Mourning Venice and Genoa': Joseph Story, Legal Education, and the *Lex Mercatoria*" in *From Lex Mercatoria to Commerical Law* (ed. Vito Piergiovanni, Berlin, 2005), pp. 14–26. (Hereafter, "Coquillette, *Joseph Story*.") See also Sutherland, *supra*, pp. 92–139; R. Kent Newmyer, *Supreme Court Justice Joseph Story: Statesman of the Old Republic* (Chapel Hill, N.C., 1985), pp. 237–70. (Hereafter, "Newmyer.")

11. See Coquillette, *Joseph Story*, *supra*, pp. 14–26; Newmyer, *supra*, pp. 269–71. Newmyer observes that "much of Story's grand plan for a cadre of conservative lawyer-statesmen went unrealized." *Id.*, p. 269. This may be a fair statement in the short run, but the future of Harvard Law School surely provided such a "cadre"!

was, throughout, with apprenticeship. Story and his intellectual heirs at Harvard had every incentive to describe the apprenticeship process as haphazard and parochial.

Harvard Law School and its peers have remained national and elitist, just as Story had hoped. But the Civil War greatly damaged the very sense of "nation" that Story extolled.[12] A returning veteran, Oliver Wendell Holmes Jr., found the School in shambles, and said so publicly.[13] Once again a savior was needed. In a brilliant move, the newly appointed President of Harvard, Charles Eliot, turned to a practicing lawyer with no educational experience, and made Christopher Columbus Langdell the Dean in 1871.

Langdell (1826–1906) had impressed Eliot, a chemist, with the idea that law could be taught as a science, "dissecting" appellate cases to discover the underlying principles of the law, just as chemistry is taught through experiments, or biology through dissection of organisms. Langdell published the first casebook in 1871,[14] and began teaching courses by the "Socratic" method, questioning students on the assigned cases, rather than lecturing from treatises. Despite early protests, this "interactive" pedagogy became a great success. Langdell also organized the curriculum into the required first year courses familiar today, the ideological "cubbyholes" of contract, tort, property, procedure, and, in some instances, criminal law. The power of this first year "boot camp" on the intellectual development of modern American lawyers has been profound. "Thinking like a lawyer" has been defined by this educational experience for more than a century.

Those conditioned by the legal pedagogy of Story and Langdell look at the elite apprenticeships of the pre-revolutionary period and see nothing familiar, and, therefore, are inclined to see nothing. Quincy's *Law Commonplace* does not use the intellectual "cubbyholes" of Story's treatises or of Langdell's cur-

12. See Sutherland, *supra*, pp. 140–61.

13. See the *American Law Review* (October, 1870), "Summary of Events," set out at Sutherland, *supra*, p. 140. See also Warren, *supra*, pp. 342–78.

14. Christopher Columbus Langdell, *Cases on Contracts* (Cambridge, Mass., 1871). The most insightful commentator on Langdell today is my esteemed colleague, Bruce Kimball. See, for example, Bruce A. Kimball, "'Warn Students That I Entertain Heretical Opinions, Which They Are Not to Take as Law': The Inception of Case Method Teaching in the Classrooms of the Early C. C. Langdell, 1870–1885," 17 *Law and History Review* 56 (1999), pp. 91–93, 124–25; Bruce A. Kimball, Pedro Reyes, "The 'First Modern Civil Procedure Course' as Taught by C. C. Langdell, 1870–78," 47 *American Journal of Legal History* (2005), pp. 257–58, 289–95.

riculum. But it is highly structured in its own way. Apprenticeship was not taught by lecture or by the Socratic method, but it had its own pedagogy and its own theory of learning, and it was a fairly formal theory, at that.

Leading intellectuals of the seventeenth-century profession, including Francis Bacon, Mathew Hale, and John Locke, advocated a "two-pronged" approach to learning law: learning by "maxims" and learning by "commonplacing." As we will see in Quincy's *Law Commonplace*, these were closely related pedagogies, and each had an extensive common law literature.[15] It was Bacon's belief that all education was based on four "rational arts": "the Art of Custody or Memory," the "Art of Elocution [or Transmission]," the "Art of Inquiry or Invention" and the "Art of Examination or Judgment."[16] The first two "arts" are appropriate to basic education. You need to "memorize" the vocabulary and the structure of a science, or a language, before you can progress, and you need to know how the science or language is transmitted, by books or other sources, and how to find what you need to know. The second two "rational arts" are more appropriate for advanced study—how to design original research, the "art of inquiry," and how to exercise mature judgment, and distinguish between the foolish and the wise. The latter art, Bacon maintained, had to be taught by experience.

Bacon, like many of his contemporaries of the Enlightenment, saw "maxims" as an ideal way to memorize and to store legal knowledge. Often based on Roman models, such maxims would be a "search engine" for relevant precedents and authorities, in a day long before word searchable texts. Mathew Hale, and other less well-known contemporaries, linked learning by maxims with keeping commonplace books, both for students and practitioners. The commonplace book was usually organized around alphabetical topics, but these topics often were suggested by, or contained, maxims.

Keeping a law commonplace was not "interactive" in the same way as being interrogated by a "crammer" after one of Story's lectures, or being cross-examined by a "Socratic" law professor pursuing Langdell's case method. But it was

15. See Section II, "Pedagogy," *supra*.

16. See discussion in Daniel R. Coquillette, "'The Purer Fountains': Bacon and Legal Education," in *Francis Bacon and the Refiguring of Early Modern Thought: Essays to Commemorate the Advancement of Learning (1605–2005)* (J. R. Solomon, C. G. Martin, eds., London, 2005), pp. 145–72.

an active, and often creative and critical process, in which the student interrogated the basic sources of the law and distilled, for the student's own purposes, the essence of the law. And this process was hardly unstructured. As we shall see, Quincy was very much aware of John Locke's "A New Method of a Common-place book," first published in French as "Methode nouvelle de dresser des Recueils" in the *Bibliothèque Universelle et Historique* in July, 1686, and then translated into English in 1697, as well as Mathew Hale's Preface to *Rolle's Abridgment* of 1668, which specifically addressed legal "commonplacing."[17] Not only did he follow these guides, but he created both an initial index and a sophisticated final cross-index that linked comparable subjects and ideas. Finally, he did not just copy the relevant sections of cases and treatises, but condensed and arranged them in a highly individual way, using both American and English sources, and cross-citing to his own manuscript *Law Reports* of cases in the Massachusetts Superior Court of Judicature. (Hereafter, "*Reports.*")[18] He also, on occasion, criticized these sources, marking "query" in the margins and noting inconsistencies. Indeed, compared to the passive, painstaking note-taking and copying of a Litchfield student and the treatise-based lectures of Story's Harvard Law School, Quincy's *Law Commonplace* seems original and analytical, not unlike the interactive pedagogical goals of Langdell's "Socratic" method, the "modern" approach that evolved more than a century later.

There was one final surprise. In Volumes 3 and 4 (1764–1765) of Quincy's four original notebooks there were 22 pages of Latin Maxims, now brilliantly translated and annotated by Elizabeth Papp Kamali and included as Appendix I to this volume. These maxims, in turn, were hardly random, and reflected a letter of advice on Roman law by Professor Francis Dickins, who taught Roman Law at Cambridge from 1714–1755 as the 16th Regius Professor of Civil Law. This letter, originally addressed to Jeremy Gridley, law tutor to John Adams and dean of the Boston bar, was copied into Quincy's Note Book, Volume 4, at pages 148–150, by another hand. So learning by maxims and commonplacing extended, at least in Quincy's case, to comparative legal studies. Roman Law was the common denominator within the continental legal system of the day, as well as the basis of the Admiralty proceedings so important

17. See Section II, "Pedagogy," *infra.*
18. See Section I, "The Manuscript," *infra.*

to New England, not to mention the law of the Spanish and French possessions in the New World, including Louisiana.[19] The Latin Maxims were hardly an archaic exercise, but rather a link between Quincy's legal studies and the world beyond the seas.

In short, Quincy's *Law Commonplace* is important. It is not just important because its author was a courageous patriot and, by all accounts, a brilliant man. It is also a particularly complete and convincing evidence of how the elites of the pre-revolutionary bar learned law, by apprenticeship, structured and focused by a pedagogy of maxims and commonplacing. It may not be our modern idea of legal education, but it was serious legal education nevertheless. To the extent that it offered a very different pedagogy to that which dominates modern American legal education, it remains fascinating to innovators and reformers.[20] To the extent such an education strengthened and molded the legal elite of the pre-revolution, it remains important to the history of our nation.

I. THE MANUSCRIPT

Josiah Quincy's *Law Commonplace* occupies most of "Volume I" of a three-volume set of yellowed leather-bound notebooks. This notebook is marked "Vol. 1 1763" on the cover and "Vol. 1" on the spine. It is exactly 20.0 cm. in height and 16.1 cm. in width. There are two other such volumes, each measuring exactly 20.0 cm. in height, and 16.1 cm. in width. They are marked "Vol. 3, 1764" and "Vol. 4." There is another volume, with a new binding, which also has identical paper. The notebooks marked "Vol. 1," Vol. 3" and "Vol. 4" are about the same breadth, 2.2 cm., 2.0 cm., and 2.1 cm. respectively. The remaining volume with the modern binding is much thinner, 0.8 cm. For the exact contents of each volume, see Appendix A, *infra*. Roughly speaking, however, "Vol. 1" contains the *Law Commonplace* plus the *Legis Miscellanea*, which is indexed to the *Law Commonplace*, together with various incidental items. The thin, unmarked volume is something of a mystery. It contains the reports of

19. John Adams appreciated this fact, and not only trained himself in Roman law, but used it systematically in his Vice-Admiralty practice. See Coquillette, *Adams*, *supra*, pp. 382–95.

20. See M. H. Hoeflich, pp. 123–27. William R. Trail, William D. Underwood, "The Decline of Professional Legal Training and a Proposal for its Revitalization in Professional Law Schools," 48 *Baylor L. Rev.* 201 (1996), pp. 201–08, 210–11, 244–45.

the "Middlesex Cases" of 1771–1772. These are not in Quincy's hand.[21] Is it "Volume 2," or a fragment of "Volume 2"? Or is it something else altogether? In which case, "Volume" 2 is lost.[22]

The top of the first page of the *Law Commonplace*, which is the first page of "Vol. 1," bears the inscription "Pretium 20/09." This could represent the price of all four of the volumes, twenty shillings, nine pence. Though not cheap, this would be a reasonable price for four bound volumes. (Approximate 2005 equivalent, $25 each volume. See the discussion of currency equivalents in the *Introduction to the Southern Journal*, *Quincy Papers*, Volume 3.) All four volumes have been microfilmed by the Massachusetts Historical Society. "Vol. 1," containing the *Law Commonplace*, is Call No. 347, Reel 4, QP56. "Vol. 3" and "Vol. 4" are Call No. 347, Reel 4, QP57 and QP58, respectively, while the unmarked volume is Call No. 347, Reel 4, QP54.[23]

The physical notebooks are particularly important in understanding Quincy's "commonplacing." There was no such thing as a "three-ring loose-leaf binder," much less a laptop computer that permits easy insertions or amendments. It was necessary, therefore, to plan ahead. Quincy did this by dividing up his notebook in advance, allocating a certain number of pages for each subject. This "preliminary" list, which Quincy described as an "Index . . . to ye following Little Abridgment for private use," is highly instructive in itself, because it necessarily indicated what subjects Quincy felt were of principal importance in legal study. But, as you might imagine in the exercise, he made inevitable misjudgments, and these too are very instructive.

For example, under "A," the headings are "Arbitramt: arbitrors + awards," "Accord" and "Apprentices + Servants." The first was not only out of alphabetical order, it was an afterthought—stuck in after "Bailment" and, then, as there was inadequate room there, added further after "Estates." See *Law Commonplace*, pp. 18 [23] and 29 [33]. (The first page number is Quincy's in the manuscript. The second is that of the transcription page. Double numbering was required in this edition because Quincy not only left numbered pages blank and skipped over page numbers, but also forgetfully repeated page num-

21. See *Reports*, pp. 318–40, and annotations.

22. See the discussion at note 34, *infra*. See also *The Law Commonplace*, p. [21], n. 10, *infra*.

23. I am particularly grateful to my research assistant, Kevin Willoughby Cox, Harvard Law School Class of 2006, for his invaluable and careful work on the manuscripts. See Appendix II, *infra*, the "Cox Chart."

bers!) The first entry, "Attachments," was omitted from the preliminary "Index" altogether! In short, the preliminary "Index" was Quincy's initial idea of what a law curriculum should look like, and the amendments to it reflect his actual experience once the study began.

Quincy's original scheme consisted of twenty-two captions: 1) Arbitration ("Arbitramt"), 2) Accord, 3) Apprentices + Servants, 4) Bailment, 5) Baron + Feme (Domestic Law), 6) Bills (Treated under "Notes"), 7) Demurrer, 8) Estates, 9) Estopells, 10) Evidence, 11) Executors and Co-Executors, 12) Insurance, 13) Jury, 14) Lands, 15) Laws (Treated with "Statutes,") 16) Lease, Lessor + Lessee, 17) Legacy, 18) Notes, 19) Pleading, 20) Releases, 21) Statute + Acts, and 22) Trespass. These take up the first 98 pages of "Vol. 1" of his four notebooks. Following this, Quincy inserted "A copy of Mr. Prat's Minutes" [Benjamin Prat, 1711–1763] of the case of *Banister* v. *Cunningham*, a 1754 case which is not reported directly in *Quincy's Reports*, though he reports a case regarding contest over the same will, *Banister* v. *Henderson*, in volume 3 of his notebooks, page 12. (Quincy's great-grandson and reports editor, Samuel M. Quincy, notes an independent account of *Banister* v. *Cunningham*. See *Reports*, *Quincy Papers*, Volume 4, pp. 156–59.) Following this are a list of legal records stored by Quincy in his "Law-file C," and then major gaps, with pages 108 to 113 cut out, followed by Quincy's copy of *Hale's Advice on the Study of Common Law* and other copied "advice," not transcribed in this edition.[24] But, beginning on Quincy's page 150 (our 93), Quincy adds a section called "Legis Miscellanea Cursim, libris exscripta" or "Miscellaneous Laws Cursorily Copied Out of Books." This is a hodgepodge of legal notes, but it is carefully indexed by Quincy beginning on his journal page 175 (our 118) continuing to the end of the volume, his page 182 (our 125), using the captions of the initial index, together with others added. Thus, to the original three captions under "A" ("Arbitration," "Accord," and "Apprentices + Servants") he added "Account," "Actions," and "Administrator."

In short, Quincy's method was as ingenious as possible, given the fixed format of the pre-bound notebooks. The initial "Index" sets out a preliminary "scheme" of study, which divided the notebook into reasonable "guesses" as to the importance and length of the subjects studied. Then there were some necessary "additions" of popular subjects, whereas other subjects used fewer pages

24. See p. 347, Reel 4, QP56, "Vol. 1 1763," pp. 122–41.

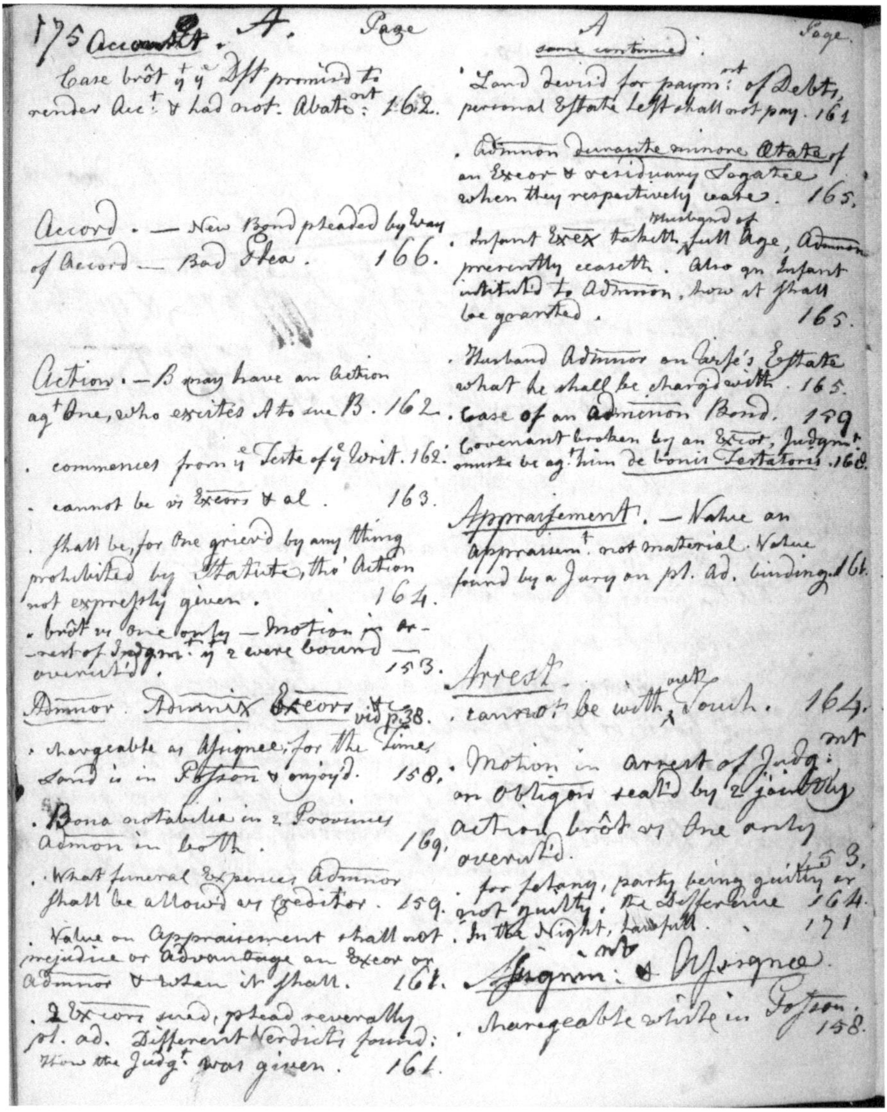

ILLUSTRATION 2. Page 175 [118] of the *Law Commonplace*, where Quincy begins a retroactive alphabetical index. Image courtesy of the Massachusetts Historical Society.

than anticipated. Finally, there was the "Legis Miscellanea Cursim" section, in which Quincy recorded everything he read of interest in chronological order. This he retroactively indexed to the alphabetical structure of the original scheme. Very clever!

Quincy did not get this idea in a vacuum. In his *Diary* for October 11, 1758, John Adams described a conversation he had with Quincy's brothers, Edmund ("Ned") and Samuel, and a very bright young man called Peter Chardon.

> Rode to Boston. Conversed with Ned Quincy and Saml., Peter Chardon &c. By the Way Peter Chardon is a promising Youth. He aspires, and will reach to a considerable Height. He has a sense of the Dignity and Importance of his Profession, that of the Law. He has a just Contempt of the idle, incurious, Pleasure hunting young fellows of the Town, who pretend to study Law. He scorns the Character, and he aims at a nobler. He talks of exulting in an unlimited field of natural, civil and common Law, talks of nerving, sharpening the mind by the Study of Law and Mathematicks, quotes Locks Conducts of the Understanding and transcribes Points of Law into a Common-Place Book on Locks Modell. This fellows Thoughts are not employed on Songs and Girls, nor his Time, on flutes, fiddles, Concerts and Card Tables. He will make something.[25]

Unfortunately, Peter Chardon died young in Barbados in 1766, but John Adams particularly remarked on how Chardon "transcribes Points of Law into a Common-Place Book on Locks Modell."[26] This is a reference to the great John Locke (1632–1704) and his "A New Method of a Common-Place book," first translated into English in 1697.[27] While Locke's method was technically more complex than Quincy's—using an index of both alphabetical headings and subheadings based on the first vowel of the head word ("a," "e," "i," "o," "u")—it is essentially the same, including leaving a margin "of about the largeness of an inch" on every page for special annotation, which Quincy carefully did.[28]

Of course, Locke's system was designed for any type of commonplacing. The leading inspiration for *law* commonplacing was Matthew Hale (1609–1676), Chief Justice of the Court of King's Bench from 1671–1676. Originally published as a "Publisher's Preface to the Young Students of the Common Law" to Henry Rolle's *Un Abridgment Des Plusieurs Cases . . . Del Common Ley*

25. Adams, *Diary*, vol. 1, p. 47.
26. *Id.*, vol. 1, p. 47.
27. John Locke, *Works* (London, 1823), vol. 3, pp. 331 ff.
28. *Id.*, p. 336.

. . . (London, 1668) ("*Rolle's Abridgment*"). Hale's advice was widely known as a basic introduction to legal study.[29] Quincy certainly knew of it because he copied it in his "Vol. 1" notebook at pages 122–41. According to Hale, after "two or three years of systematic study of the legal classics," a student should

> get a large Common-place Book, divide it into Alphabetical Titles, which he may easily gather up, by observing the Titles of Brooks Abridgment, and some Tables of Law-Books, and possibly (as shall be shewn) this book now published may be the basis of his Common-place Book . . . What he reads in the course of his Reading, let him enter the abstract or substance thereof, especially of cases or points resolved into his Common-place-Book, under their proper Titles; and if one case falls aptly under several titles, and it can be conveniently Broken, let him enter each part under its proper title; if it cannot be well broken, let him enter the abstract of the entire case under the Title most proper for it, and make references from the other Titles unto it.[30]

Hale admits that this method could be inherently repetitious. "It is true, a student will waste much Paper this way . . ."[31] And, at least at the beginning, there would be mistakes which—before loose-leaf notebooks and "delete" keys—would remain in the commonplace. The student "possibly in two or three years will see many Errors and Impertinencies in what he hath formerly done, and much irregularity and disorder in the disposing of his matter under proper Heads."[32] But, as will be seen in the next section on pedagogy, Hale saw "infallible advantages attending his [the student's] course." The very process of trial and error in assembling the commonplace, like the painstaking case analysis of Langdell's "Socratic Method," taught the student. This, too, was a pedagogy of struggle and interaction.

29. Hale's advice was one of the first readings assigned by Jeremy Gridley to his new apprentice, John Adams. "Then he took his [Gridley's] Common Place Book and [illegible] gave me Ld. Hales Advice to a Student of the Common law." Adams, *Diary*, October 25, 1758, vol. 1, p. 55. The prestige and influence of Hale's *Preface* was doubtless bolstered by the posthumous publication of his *Analysis of the Law*, an immensely influential and important book. It was originally written around 1670 and not published until 1713 as *The History and Analysis of the Common Law of England; by a Learned Hand* (London, 1713). For the importance of this "pathbreaking work," this "comprehensive method of analysis," see Harold J. Berman, Charles J. Reid Jr., "The Transformation of English Legal Science: From Hale to Blackstone," 45 *Emory Law Journal* 437 (1996), pp. 486–89.

30. *Rolle's Abridgment* (London, 1668), "Publisher's Preface," n.p. [8].

31. *Id.*

32. *Id.*, n.p. [8].

Quincy followed Hale's directions precisely, making careful cross-references between his "Alphabetical Titles," and an extensive cross-referencing index of his *Legis Miscellanea*. See *Law Commonplace*, pages 175 [118]–182 [125]. In this he was superior to John Adams, whose 1759 Commonplace Book is far more rudimentary in structure, with little or no cross-referencing and indexing.[33] This was not just a question of style, it was a question of learning. By following the advice and methodologies of Locke and Hale, including Locke's "one inch" margin for annotation and critique and Hale's system of cross-references, Quincy maximized the potential of his bound notebook. In addition, Quincy cross-referenced his *Law Commonplace* to the first volume of his manuscript *Reports*, which he called the "Red Reports" because of the color of the cover. See the references to *Angier* v. *Jackson* "*vid.* Red Rep. 70" and *Baker* v. *Mattocks* "*vid.* Red Rep. 57" at *Law Commonplace*, pp. 105 [90] and 106 [91], which are in the 1865 edition of the *Reports* at pages 84 and 69, respectively.[34] He also cross-referenced topics on the same pages of his *Law Commonplace* to his "Law file A" and his "Law file C." Thus, Quincy took the techniques of Locke and Hale one step further, integrating his *Law Commonplace* to his own *Reports* and to a filing system of precedents! Given the constraints of pen and paper, it was a "data retrieval" system of real sophistication.

33. *Legal Papers of John Adams* (L. Kinvin Wroth, Hiller B. Zobel, eds., Cambridge, Mass., 1965), vol. 1, pp. 4–25.

34. I am most indebted to Kevin W. Cox for deciphering the "Red Reports" cross citations. According to Samuel M. Quincy the manuscripts of the *Reports* "consist of three volumes: one with paper covers (from the original color of which it is referred to as "Red Reports") and two others bound in parchment, and numbered "3" and "4." The first two volumes of this set are missing, and were probably destroyed in a fire by which the reporter's law library was lost." *Reports*, "Preface," pp. iii–iv. But Samuel M. Quincy is at least partly wrong, as the volume containing the *Law Commonplace* is identical in binding and paper page size (20.0 cm. by 16.1. cm.) to "Vol. 3" and "Vol. 4" containing the *Reports*, and is marked "Vol. 1." There are also citations from the *Reports* to "Vol. 1" which clearly connect to the *Law Commonplace* substantively. So, at most, only one volume is missing. But there is a fourth volume, also of identical paper and page size (20.0 cm. by 16.1 cm.), which has a new cover. This is P 347 Reel 4 QP54. It is much thinner than the other three, and was dismissed by Samuel M. Quincy as "the fragment of another volume apparently just commenced." It contained the "Middlesex Cases" (1771–1772) detailed at *Reports*, pp. 318–40, which were not in Quincy's hand. Could it be the missing "Vol. 2"? Or a fragment of the volume? Most likely, Samuel M. Quincy was correct in dismissing the thin volume, but the identical paper and page size causes one to pause. Otherwise, "Vol. 2" was lost. It could have perished in the fire. A happier thought is that it may be discovered someday. What a fascinating find that would be.

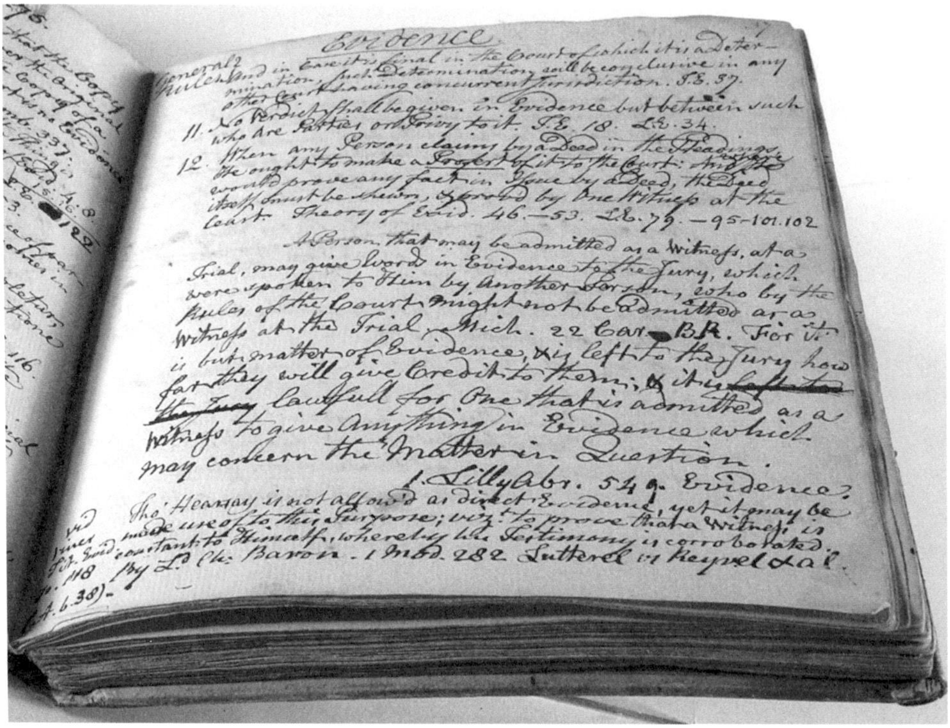

ILLUSTRATION 3. Pages 36 [37] and 37 [38] of the *Law Commonplace*, presenting rules of "Evidence." This shows Quincy's notebook, open. The marginal notes and tight fitting of text are characteristic of the *Law Commonplace*'s general style. Image courtesy of the Massachusetts Historical Society. My thanks to Kevin Cox.

II. THE PEDAGOGY

Quincy began his *Law Commonplace* on September 24, 1763. At the time, legal education in the common law world was in a state of flux, and dramatic changes were on the horizon. Only five years before, in 1758, William Blackstone had taken the Vinerian Chair at Oxford. There, he had commenced his famous annual lectures that introduced, for the first time, common law study to an English university.[35] And only two years before Quincy began his work, in 1761, Francis Stoughton Sullivan published his revolutionary *A Plan for the Study of the Feudal and English Laws in the University of Dublin* (hereafter, "*A Plan*") outlining a complete two-year method of learning law, emphasizing "the elementary parts" and developing "the Outlines of the remaining Heads of the Law, with the necessary Definitions, Divisions, Maxims and Illustrations, such as the young Gentleman may receive with Ease, and retain without Confusion, and may afterwards fill up at their leisure by their subsequent heading, and their Attendance at *Westminster*."[36]

Now let us look forward just two years in the future. In 1765, Blackstone would publish the first volume of his famous *Commentaries on the Laws of England* (1765–1770), whose success in the American colonies would be phenomenal.[37] Had Quincy only been permitted an ordinary adult life, he would have

35. See F. H. Lawson, *The Oxford Law School 1850–1965* (Oxford, 1968), pp. 4–5 (hereafter,"Lawson"); Sutherland, *supra*, pp. 19–25. Lawson was certainly right in observing that "Blackstone exerted a greater influence in the North American colonies and subsequently in the United States than in England . . ." *Lawson*, p. 4. But both the theoretical style and the politics of his *Commentaries* earned Blackstone powerful enemies, such as Thomas Jefferson. Jefferson, writing to Madison in 1826, observed that when "the honied Mansfieldism of Blackstone became the student's hornbook, from that moment, that profession (the nursery of our Congress), began to slide into toryism . . ." Thomas Jefferson, *Works* (P. L. Ford, ed., New York, 1905), vol. 12, pp. 455–56. See Sutherland, p. 13. Blackstone still has his pedagogical enemies. See Duncan Kennedy, "The Structure of Blackstone's Commentaries," 28 *Buffalo Law Review* 205 (1979). In addition, a good deal of the practiced legal training in England was outside both the Inns of Court and the universities, and remained more practical than formal. See David Lemmings, *Professors of the Law, Barristers and English Legal Culture in the Eighteenth Century* (Oxford, 2000), pp. 107–48.

36. Francis Stoughton Sullivan, *A Plan For the Study of the Feudal and English Laws in the University of Dublin* (Dublin, 1761), p. 4.

37. At least one thousand sets were exported to America before 1771, when a pirated edition was published in Philadelphia by Robert Bell. One thousand and four hundred copies were subscribed in advance, with one New York dealer taking two hundred and thirty-nine. See Suther-

witnessed Thomas Jefferson's establishment of a professorship of "Law and Police" at William and Mary in 1779 and the beginning of George Wythe's teaching career.[38] He also would have witnessed James Wilson's appointment in 1789 as professor of law at the University of Pennsylvania, and James Kent's appointment to a similar position at Columbia in 1794. Had Quincy lived to be only forty, he would have seen Judge Tapping Reeve establish the nation's first professional law school, the famous Litchfield School of Law, in 1784, and had Quincy lived to seventy-three he would have witnessed the founding of the Harvard Law School in 1817, America's first university professional school of law.

John Langbein has demonstrated that these historical forces were about pedagogy, how law was taught and learned.[39] Langbein argues that Litchfield succeeded because of its system of lecturing, "which had been such an advance over the apprenticeship in the 1780s." But that system became "retrograde" by the 1830s, and was surpassed by a "different and superior technique, the so-called text-and-recitation system" established by the university professional schools, including Harvard and Yale.[40]

But this is what makes Quincy's *Law Commonplace* so important. Because it was begun before Blackstone and these major institutional pedagogies, it remains a largely "pure" example of the ancestral learning from which these dramatic innovations evolved. And, because its author was a brilliant—if very young—lawyer, it presents this pedagogical heritage at its best. Finally, this document challenges Langbein's assumption that pedagogical evolution was

---

land, p. 25. Although Blackstone's *Commentaries* were not available to Quincy when he began the *Law Commonplace*, he owned a set at his death in 1775. See Quincy's *Reports*, Appendix 9, "Catalogue of Books Belonging to the Estate of Josiah Quincy Jun: Esq: Deceas'd," Item 67. At least one volume of this set survived, for a time, in the library of Phillips Andover. It is now gone. Again, many thanks to Mark Sullivan, superb reference librarian. In addition, there is one citation to the first volume (1765) of Blackstone's *Commentaries* at *Law Commonplace*, p. 94 [82], which may be a later addition, although apparently in Quincy's hand. See page 281, n. 2, *infra*. There are several citations to Blackstone's earlier *Analysis of the Laws of England* (Oxford, 1756). See *Law Commonplace*, pp. n.p. [6], n.p. [10] and 89 [77]. See also n. 46, *infra*.

38. See Carrington, *supra*, pp. 527–38 and note 3 *supra*.

39. See John H. Langbein, "Blackstone, Litchfield, and Yale: The Founding of the Yale Law School," *History of the Yale Law School* (ed. Anthony T. Kronman, New Haven, Conn., 2004), pp. 17–36. (Hereafter, "Langbein, The Founding.")

40. *Id.*, p. 30.

inherently an "advance."[41] At its best, apprenticeship, and its attendant learning techniques of commonplacing and instruction by maxims, could be a sophisticated and effective way to learn.

To begin, Quincy's *Law Commonplace* was a "system" with three separate elements. The "core" was the pre-indexed commonplace contained in his notebook "Vol. 1," pp. 1–98 (P347, Reel 4, QP56). This was obviously a pre-designed project, following the methodologies of John Locke and Mathew Hale discussed in Section A, "The Manuscript," *supra*. It could have been designed by Quincy's pupil master, Oxenbridge Thacher, but there were plenty of other possible sources.[42] This was analogous to the "elementary parts" of the law, emphasized by Francis Stoughton Sullivan's *Plan* of 1761.

Then there was the second element, the *Legis Miscellanea* contained in Quincy's notebook "Vol. 1," pp. 150–82 and in "Vol. 4," pp. 5–10, indexed retroactively and cross referenced to the "core" commonplace. This would be analogous to the "afterwards fill up at their Leisure" outlines of Sullivan's *Plan*. It would be an ongoing project, to be continued by the apprentice or student. While Quincy's *Legis Miscellanea* lacked the prearranged "outlines of the remaining Heads of the Law, with the necessary Definitions, Divisions, Maxims and Illustrations" prescribed by Sullivan's method, the index prepared retroactively by Quincy did supply the principal "Heads of the Law," arranged alphabetically, which also provided easy cross-referencing to the "core" commonplace.

Finally, there was Quincy's unique contribution to his "system," his *Law Reports*. Discussed at length in the "Introduction" to Volume 4 of this series, these were begun in 1761, two years before the *Law Commonplace*. The *Reports*

41. *Id.*, p. 30.

42. Oxenbridge Thacher (1719–1765) was one of Boston's most "eminent lawyers of the period." See the biography set out in Appendix 6 to the *Reports*, vol. 5, *infra*. He was Quincy's law tutor from 1763 to Thacher's death in July, 1765. See Josiah Quincy, *Memoir of the Life of Josiah Quincy, Jr.* (2d ed., Boston, 1874), pp. 6–7. (Hereafter, "*Memoir*.") See also Clifford K. Shipton, *Sibley's Harvard Graduate, vol. xv: Biographical Sketches of Those Who Attended Harvard College in the Classes 1761–1763* (Boston, 1970), p. 479. On Thacher's death in 1765, Quincy "took over the office and as much of the practice as he could handle." *Id.*, p. 479. According to John Adams, Thacher believed strongly in commonplacing. "He [Thacher] says He is sorry that he neglected to keep a Common Place Book when he began to study Law, and he is half a mind to begin now." Adams, *Diary*, vol. 1, p. 55 (October 25, 1758).

were actively continued throughout the creation of the *Law Commonplace*, until the first gap in the August Term, 1768. The *Legis Miscellanea* sections of the *Law Commonplace* cross-referenced the *Reports*.[43] The *Reports* also occasionally cited to related materials in the *Law Commonplace*. For instance, one such cross-reference appears in the case of *Banister* v. *Henderson*, which begins on page 12 of Quincy's volume 3 (page 119 of the 1865 published *Reports*). At the beginning of the case, Quincy cross-referenced to page 103 [89] of volume 1, the *Law Commonplace*, though this cross-reference was not included in the 1865 publication. Page 103 [89] of the *Law Commonplace* includes the minutes of *Banister* v. *Cunningham*, an earlier case which dealt with a controversy over the same estate contested in *Banister* v. *Henderson*, and demonstrates that the two volumes are interconnected by Quincy's method.

These cross-references were largely gathered in a separate section which followed the alphabetized "core" *Law Commonplace* after three blank pages, Quincy pp. 99–102, and went from Quincy page 103 up to page 107, Transcription pp. [87]–[92]. For convenience, this section will be called the "Case Notes Section," although Quincy did not label it at all. This "Case Notes Section" also contained cross-references to Quincy's "Law file C" and "Law file A," which contained notes of legal arguments, decided cases, and methods for studying law, like Chief Justice Mathew Hale's "Method of studying the Common Law from Rolls's Abr.g Preface" and Chief Justice Thomas Reeve's "To his Nephew, Directions for beginning the Study of Law." See *Law Commonplace*, Quincy n.p., [transcription p. 7] and n.p. [transcription p. 9].

It is easier to appreciate this sophisticated system of information retrieval using a diagram:

43. See, for example, the citation at *Law Commonplace*, p. 105 [transcript 90] to "Red Rep. 70 *Angier* v. *Jackson*." That is a citation to Quincy's "red" notebook, P347 Reel 4 QP55 (now rebound in brown), which contained the manuscript of his report of *Angier* v. *Jackson*, *Reports*, p. 84. As Samuel M. Quincy observed in his "Preface" to the *Reports*, this volume had "paper covers, (from the original color of which it is referred to as 'Red Reports,')." See *Reports*, p. iii. Quincy also cross-referenced the important case of *Baker* v. *Mattocks* at *Law Commonplace*, p. 106 [transcript 91]. *Baker* v. *Mattocks* was in the "Red Reports" at page 57, and in the *Reports* at page 69. I am most grateful to Kevin Cox, my brilliant research assistant, for deciphering these cross-references!

QUINCY'S "SYSTEMS" OF LEARNING

The "Pre-Index" plan of alphabetical categories
"Vol. 1," pp. 4–8
[11]–[15]

pp. 9–10 Blank

Legis Miscellanea
"Vol. 1," pp. 150–74
[93]–[117]

Input New Additions here!

"Core Commonplace"
"Vol. 1," pp. 11–98
[16]–[86]

Created by alphabetical categories

Both use Alphabetical Categories for easy access

Retroactive Index
"Vol. 1," pp. 175–82
[118]–[125]

Created by alphabetical categories

Look up points of law by alphabetical category here!

pp. 99–102 Blank

"Case Note Section"
"Vol. 1," pp. 103–07
[87]–[92]

Cross-reference *Law Reports* here!
Quincy's Law Reports "vol. 3" and "vol. 4," 1761–1768

NOTE: Citations are to Quincy's Volumes "1," "3," and "4." See Cox Chart, Appendix II, p. 429, *infra*. These correspond to Volumes 2, 4 and 5 of Quincy's *Works* in this series.

Cross-reference your research file here! Quincy "Law File A," "Law File C"

ILLUSTRATION 4. Sir Matthew Hale (1609–1676) was one of the dominant jurists of the English Restoration, serving as Chief Baron of the Exchequer (1660–1671) and Chief Justice (1671–1676). Noted for his moral character and his learning, he was the author of many books, including the famous *Summary of the Pleas of the Crown* (London, 1678), published in a better edition in 1736 as *Historia Placitorum Coronae* (London, 1736). Hale's "Preface Directed to the Young Students of the Common Law," which appeared at the beginning of Henry Rolle's *Un Abridgement des plusiers Cases . . . del Common Ley* . . . (London, 1668), had a huge influence on legal pedagogy, and was carefully referred to by Quincy. See "Vol. 1," p. 547, Reel 4, QP56, Quincy's pages 122–41. See also Alan Cromartie, *Sir Matthew Hale 1609–1676: Law, religion and natural philosophy* (Cambridge, 1995). Courtesy Harvard Law School Library. My thanks to David Warrington.

If Quincy wished to update his "core commonplace," he could add to the *Legis Miscellanea* or to the "Case Note Section." The "Case Note Section" was cross-referenced to his *Law Reports*. Both the "core" commonplace and the retroactive index to the *Legis Miscellanea*, which was updated, were organized in alphabetical headings. And there were cross-references to his "Law file A" and "Law file C." All he needed to do was remember the right alphabetical heading, and he could locate anything in the commonplace!

But this was not just a way of storing and cross-referencing information. It was a program to teach law. Setting up and compiling a commonplace was hard work. Updating it and cross-referencing the categories was even harder. Creating reports of argued cases and referencing *those* reports to the commonplace was harder still. It was a process that required "trial and error." It taught by requiring the student to do the analysis and classification for himself. Again, this is the same way that the Socratic method and the case method taught law, by interaction between the student and the material.

We do not have to speculate on the sources of Quincy's pedagogy, because he carefully copied them into the *Law Commonplace* itself. The most important was Chief Justice Mathew Hale's (1609–1676) "Publisher's Preface Directed to the Young Students of the Common Law" appearing at the beginning of Henry Rolle's *Un Abridgment Des Plusieurs Cases . . . del Common Ley* . . . (London, 1668) (hereafter, "Hale's *Preface*"). This was carefully copied by Quincy into "Vol. 1," P 347, Reel 4, QP56, Quincy's pages 122–41 (not transcribed in this series as not original Quincy).

We have already discussed, in Section A, *supra*, Hale's influence on the structure of Quincy's *Law Commonplace*. But equally important was Hale's theory of legal education. He certainly believed that direct interaction between the student and the undigested mass of the law was necessary and desirable, and that struggle was a part of learning. According to Hale,

> It is true, a student will waste much Paper this way, and possibly in two or three years will see many Errors and Impertinencies in what he hath formerly done, and much irregularity and disorder in the disposing of his matter under proper Heads. But he will have these infallible Advantages attending his course. 1. In process of time he will be more perfect and dexterous in this business. 2. Those imperfect and disordered essays will by frequent returns upon them, be intelligible, at least, to himself, and refresh his memory. 3. He will by this means keep together under apt titles whatsoever he hath read. 4. By often

> returning upon every title, as occasions of search or new intentions require, he will strangely revive and imprint in his memory what he hath formerly read. 5. He will be able at one view to feel the substance of whatsoever he hath read concerning any one Subject, without turning to every Book (only when he hath particular occasion of Advice, or Argument, then it will be necessary to look upon that Book at large, which he findes useful to his purpose. 6. He will be able upon any occasion suddenly to find anything hc hath read, without recoursing to Tables or other Repertories, which are oftentimes short, and give a lame account of the subject sought for . . .[44]

Also important to Quincy was Chief Justice Thomas Reeve's (1672/73–1737) "Directions [to his Nephews] for beginning the study of Law," which Quincy copied into the beginning of his *Law Commonplace* on unnumbered pages (transcription pages [7]–[9]) (hereafter, "Reeve's *Directions to his Nephew*"). See "Vol. 1," P347, Reel 4, QP56, unnumbered Quincy introduction. Reeve emphasized the effort of commonplacing, using Thomas Wood's *An Institute of the Laws of England*; or *Laws of England in their natural order according to Common use* (1st ed., London, 1720) (hereafter, "Wood's *Institute of the Laws of England*") "to understand the several Divisions of the Law, + obtain the precise Ideas used in it."[45] Reeve went on:

> My whole scheme without naming Books, is no more than this. 1.st Obtain precise ideas of the Terms + several meanings of the Law. 2.dly Learn the general Reasons whereon the Law is founded. 3.dly Find some authentic system, collect the great heading Points of the Laws, in their natural order, as the first Heads + Divisions of your future enquiry; 4.thly Collect the several <u>particular</u> Points + arrange them under their <u>generals</u>, as they occur + as you find you can best digest them.
>
> And whereas Law must be consider'd in a two-fold Respect. 1.st As a Rule of Action. 2.dly As the art of procuring redress when this Rule is violated; the study in each of them may be regulated by the foregoing method. And the Books so recommended will so carry on your Joint Work, that with this course so finish'd, the student may pursue each Branch of either, to its uttermost Extent, or return to his Center of Knowledge without confusion, which is the only way of rendering Things easily to the memory.[46]

44. Hale's *Preface*, n.p. [page 8].

45. *Law Commonplace*, Quincy n.p., Transcription p. [7].

46. *Id.*, n.p., Transcription p. [9]. Quincy followed Reeve's advice and relied on Wood's *Institute of the Laws of England* for his preliminary "heads + divisions." As J. L. Barton observed

Interestingly enough, Hale's *Advice to a Student* and Reeve's *Direction to his Nephew* were two of the sources recommended by Jeremiah Gridley to John Adams in 1758, five years before, along with Dr. Dickins's "Method of Studying the Civil Law," which we will discuss later in connection with Quincy's collection of Latin maxims.[47] John Adams also met in 1758 with Oxenbridge Thacher, who, as noted above, would become Quincy's pupil master. Thacher also emphasized commonplacing, stating that he was "sorry that he neglected to keep a Common Place Book when he began to study Law, and he is half a mind to begin now."[48]

This was no casual, haphazard course of study. The university lectures of Blackstone, to be followed by Wilson, Kent, and many others, doubtless were an easier path to legal theory. Tapping Reeve's lectures at Litchfield and Story's "text-and-recitation" system at Harvard may have been better structured professional training, but commonplacing had its own virtues as a way to learn. You had to discover the structure of the law for yourself. It was analogous to the "rite of passage" of having to study *Coke on Littleton*, remarked on by both Adams and Story, who "wept bitterly."[49] It is also comparable to the student effort required by Langdell's casebooks and the Socratic

---

of Wood's *Institute*, "Its success was certainly due in part to the fact that it was the only book of its kind in print until Blackstone's *Commentaries* was published, but it is only fair to say that the tenth edition appeared as late as 1772, when the *Commentaries* had been in circulation for some years." J. L. Barton, "Legal Studies" in *The History of the University of Oxford* (ed. T. H. Ashton), vol. 5, *The Eighteenth Century* (eds. L. S. Sutherland, L. C. Mitchell, Oxford, 1986), p. 600.

The first volume of Blackstone's *Commentaries* did not appear until 1765, and there is only one mention of it in Quincy's *Law Commonplace*, which may be a later addition. See note 37 *supra*. There are several citations to Blackstone's more rudimentary *Analysis of the Laws of England* [with] *Introductory discourse on the Study of the Law* (Oxford, 1756) and just preceding Reeve's *Directions to his Nephew*, at *Law Commonplace*, Quincy n.p., Transcription, p. [6], but Quincy made little use of it, apparently preferring Wood's "divisions" and Hale's system. See further citations to Blackstone's *Analysis* at p. n.p. [10] and p. 89 [77] of the *Law Commonplace*. John Adams was also aware of Blackstone's *Analysis*, observing: "This day I am beginning my Ld. Hales History of the Common Law, a Book borrowed of Mr. Otis, and read once already, Analysis and all, with great Satisfaction. I wish I had Mr. Blackstone's Analysis that I might compare, and see what Improvements he has made upon Hale's." Adams, *Diary*, vol. 1, p. 169.

47. Adams, *Diary*, *supra*, vol. 1, pp. 54–55 (October 5, 1758). See also p. 32, *infra*, and accompanying note.

48. *Id.*, p. 55. See also pp. 31–33, *infra*.

49. See Warren, pp. 175–76.

method.[50] "No gain without pain" was the informal creed of Langdell and his disciple, James Barr Ames, who rejected the predigested pedagogy of the lecture and the Continental treatise. Commonplacing was an antecedent of the agonies of the case method, and it had similar virtues.

These virtues were appreciated by those that suffered through the commonplacing process, even as they developed easier, if not better, methods. Take Joseph Story as an example. Story's "text-and-recitation" system, coupled with his own treatises, certainly rescued the Harvard Law School from near disaster in 1829.[51] His vision of a university professional school has now become the model of modern legal education.[52] But he certainly appreciated the value of what Quincy was doing in the *Law Commonplace*. According to Story:

> The early professors of the common law were compelled to resort to commonplace books, and personal reports of cases, falling under their own observation. Many manuscripts of this description are still extant, exhibiting a patient industry, care, and accuracy, worthy of all praise. The labor, indeed, of these venerable jurists almost transcends the belief of students of the present day. They noted every case, in all its points and principles. They abstracted from records, and general treatises, and private manuscripts, often obscure and crabbed, everything, that could be found to aid them in study, or in practice. They gathered voluminous collections of special pleadings, and unusual writs and judgments, to suit the exigencies of their possible avocations; and thought no labor too great, which brought any solid addition to their knowledge, or any increased facilities to their clients.[53]

This appreciation reflected Story's own training. Story's pupil master was

50. Langdell's pioneering casebook on contracts contains not one word of explanatory text. To Langdell, the essence of study was to "select, classify and arrange all cases which had contributed to the growth, development, or establishment of any of its [contracts] essential doctrines." C. C. Langdell, *A Selection of Cases on the Law of Contracts* (Boston, 1871), p. VII. In a sense, Langdell assisted with one aspect of commonplacing, the arrangement and sequence of cases, but continued to leave the student with the task of analysis and application. As Langdell noted: "Law, considered as a science, consists of certain principles or doctrines. To have such a mastery of these as to be able to apply them with constant facility and certainty to the ever-tangled skein of human affairs, is what constitutes a true lawyer; and hence to acquire that mastery should be the business of every earnest student of law." *Id.*, p. VI.

51. See Sutherland, pp. 92–139; Warren, *History of Harvard Law School* (New York, 1908), vol. 1, pp. 413–506.

52. See Coquillette, *Joseph Story*, *supra*, pp. 24–26. See also note 10, *supra*.

53. *The Miscellaneous Writings of Joseph Story* (ed. W. W. Story, Boston, 1852), pp. 380–81.

Samuel Sewall. Sewall rejected the "catch as catch can" apprenticeship, "mechanically obtained," in favor of examining "the theory and General doctrines and the origins of the Municipal Law [i.e., national law], and descending from generals to particulars, to discover afterwards the partial applications and limits of the system."[54] For structure, Sewall could offer Story something Quincy never had, *Blackstone's Commentaries.* As R. Kent Newmyer has observed, Blackstone was "the primer," and Story found it easy and "most elegant."[55] But Sewall soon directed Story to harder stuff: *Coke on Littleton* and the other classic English treatises. In Story's words, these were filled with "dry and technical principles, the dark and mysterious elements of the feudal system, the subtle refinements and intricacies of the middle ages of the common law . . ."[56]

In addition, Sewall required Story to go beyond the treatises, and to read the American reports (there were but a few, and none published for Massachusetts in 1801) as well as many of the same English reports that Quincy digested, including the 13 volumes of *Coke's Reports* (published in installments between 1600 and 1659), *Plowden's Commentaries or Reports* (published in Law French in 1571 and translated in 1761) and *Saunder's Reports* (published in Law French in 1686 and translated in 1722). By his own account, Story plunged into these reports and many others, reading them in conjunction with treatises like Hawkins's *Pleas of the Crown* (1716–1721), all at Sewall's direction.[57] As Story's biographer, Newmyer, has acutely observed, this was a process of integration of knowledge into a structure. Blackstone helped. "[I]t would give Story, as it gave others, the tools of legal language, a compendium of guiding principles, an introduction to English legal history, and a vision of law as a science—that

54. Newmyer, p. 40.

55. *Id.*, p. 40.

56. *Id.*, p. 40.

57. *Id.*, pp. 41–42. For an account of the sparse early American law reporting, see Erwin C. Surrency, "Law Reports in the United States," 25 *Am. J. Legal Hist.* 58 (1981); Alan V. Briceland, "Ephraim Kirby: Pioneer of American Law Reporting," 16 *Am. J. Legal Hist.* (1972). There is an excellent book about early Supreme Court reports, Morris L. Cohen & Sharon Hamby O'Connor, *A Guide to the Early Reports of the United States* (1995). See also W. Hamilton Bryson, "Virginia Manuscript Law Reports," 82 *Law Libr. Jour.* 305–11 (1990) and my case for Josiah Quincy's claim as the first true American law reporter, Daniel R. Coquillette, "First Flower—The Earliest American Law Reports and the Extraordinary Josiah Quincy, Jr. (1744–1775)," 30 *Suffolk Univ. L. Rev.* 1 (1976), pp. 1–15 (hereafter, "Coquillette, *Law Reports*").

is to say, as a system of interrelated principles and rules."[58] But it was just the beginning. The law reports, current American practices, and the technicalities of common law pleading had to be mastered too.

The vehicle Story used for the integration was commonplacing. As Newmyer observed, "The working lawyer's key to survival, if not success was his form or commonplace book. . . . wherein practicing lawyers mobilized English precedent under the main header of law with a running count of leading American cases . . ."[59] Story's commonplace was prepared at Sewall's direction but, it appears, despite Sewall's promises to "assist you in arranging your learning," it was Story's own work. Story saw this effort and struggle as essential to mastering law. "I felt that I breathed a purer air . . . and that I had acquired a new power."[60]

Story's law training was the training of a future Justice of the United States Supreme Court and the savior of Harvard Law School. Note how close it was to that of Quincy! Although Story's apprenticeship ended in 1801, more than thirty-five years after Quincy's *Law Commonplace*, the basic ingredients were the same. Of course, Story had *Blackstone*. Initially, lacking *Blackstone*, Quincy had to turn to Matthew Hale's *Introduction to Rolle's Abridgment* (1668), Thomas Wood's *An Institute of the Laws of England* (1720), and Charles Viner's *General Abridgment of the Law and Equity* (23 vols., 1741–1753) for structured categories. In addition, by 1801 Story had a few American reports to integrate with the English reporters. Quincy had to create his own. But the process, and the struggle, was the same. At its best, it was a pedagogy that created good, even great, lawyers. As Newmyer observed:

> If a good education is one that equips its recipient to do what has to be done, Story's law-office education was an excellent one. He learned the theory and was at home in the practical application of it. He was ready to do business. But he learned more, too. The three years of apprenticeship had left him with a deep love of the law and a lasting admiration of legal science.[61]

The same was true of Quincy. How many of our law students could say the same today?

58. Newmyer, p. 41.
59. Newmyer, p. 42.
60. Newmyer, p. 41.
61. *Id.*, p. 44.

There remains one final pedagogical aspect of the *Law Commonplace*. To modern legal educators it seems particularly alien and strange: learning by maxims. Quincy sprinkled Latin maxims throughout the *Law Commonplace*. Many were extracted from *Coke on Littleton* or from *Justinian's Institutes* and the *Digest*. In addition, in both "Vol. 3" and "Vol. 4" of his notebooks, he set out a collection of two hundred and twelve Latin maxims grouped together, at ("Vol. 3") P 347, Reel 4, QP57, pp. 161–63, 171–83, and ("Vol. 4") P347, Reel 4, QP58, pp. 151–56. Forty-four of these are almost entirely from Roman law sources, particularly the *Digest*, Title Fifty, Section XVII, *De Diversis Regulis Juris Antiqui*. The rest are from common law authorities, particularly Coke's *Reports* and *Institutes*. Thanks to the tireless work of two of my former research assistants, Susannah B. Tobin, Harvard Law School, Class of 2004, who continued her efforts long after graduation, and Elizabeth Papp Kamali, Harvard Law School, Class of 2007, these collected maxims have been brilliantly transcribed and translated as Appendix I, Quincy's *Latin Maxims*, at the end of the *Law Commonplace*.

Perhaps Quincy's extensive study of Latin maxims should not be surprising. He and his peers were fluent in Latin. Both John Adams and Joseph Story integrated the study of civil and Roman law into their original legal studies.[62] Adams had served an apprenticeship with John Putnam of Worcester between 1756 and 1758, which did not always go smoothly. When he arrived in Boston in 1758, he sought the support of Jeremiah Gridley, then the informal dean of the Boston bar. Adams recounted the meeting:

> Then Mr. Gridley inquired what Method of Study I had pursued, what Latin Books I read, what Greek, what French. What I had read upon Rhetorick. Then he took his Common Place Book and gave me Ld. Hales Advice to a Student of the Common Law, and when I had read that, he gave me Ld. [Chief] [Justice] Reeves Advice [to] his Nephew, in the Study of Common Law. Then He gave me a Letter from Dr. Dickins, Regius Professor of Law at the University of Cambridge, to him, pointing out a Method of Studying the civil Law. Then he turned to a Letter He wrote himself to judge Light-

62. See *Id.*, p. 41; Coquillette, *Adams*, pp. 360–76. As M. H. Hoeflich has observed: "During the period from the Revolution to the Civil War. . . . American lawyers were far less parochial than they were in the succeeding century. Many had a lively interest in Roman law and its descendent, the modern civil law. At the same time, this interest rarely became expertise." M. H. Hoeflich, "An Aborted Attempt to Translate Justinian's Digest in Antebellum America," *Zeitschrift der Savigny-Stiftung für Rechtgeschichte*, 122 Band, p. 198 (Vienna, 2005).

> foot, Judge of the Admiralty in Rhode Island, directing to a Method of Studying the Admiralty Law. Then Mr. Gridley run a Comparison between the Business and studies of a Lawyer or Gentleman of the Bar, in England, and that of one here. A Lawyer in this Country must study common Law and civil Law, and natural Law, and Admiralty Law, and must do the duty of a Counsellor, a Lawyer, an Attorney, a solicitor, and even of a scrivener, so that the Difficulties of the Profession are much great here than in England. The Difficulties that attend the study may discourage some, but they never discouraged me.[63]

Adams took the advice on Roman and civil law study seriously. "I have read no small Number of Volumes, upon the Law, the last 2 Years [1758–1760]. Justinian Institutes I have read, thro, in Latin with Vinnius's perpetual Notes, Van Muydens Tractatio Institutionum Justiniani, I read thro, and translated, mostly into English, from the same Language. Woods Institute of Civil Law, I read thro. These on the civil Law . . ."[64]

As we have seen, five years later, Quincy set out on an almost identical path. Copied into the same volume as Quincy's *Law Commonplace* are the two suggested courses of study Gridley gave to Adams, Matthew Hale's *Advice to a Student* (1668) and Lord Chief Justice Reeve's *Advice to His Nephew in the Study of the Common Law* (1736?). See ("Vol. 1") P347, Reel 4, QP56, Quincy, pp. 122–41 and unnumbered Quincy pages at commencement, pp. [7]–[10], respectively. But there is something even more remarkable. Dr. Dickins's *Method of Studying the Civil Law*, as recommended to Adams, was also copied into "Vol. 4" of Quincy's notebooks, although not in Quincy's hand. See ("Vol. 4") P347, Reel 4, QP58, pp. 148–50. This is the same volume that contains some of Quincy's *Latin Maxims*.[65]

63. Adams, *Diary*, *supra*, vol. 1, pp. 54–55 (October 25, 1758). Francis Dickins was the 16th Regius Professor of Civil Law at Cambridge, serving from 1714 to 1755, nearly 41 years!

64. *Id.*, vol. 1, pp. 173–74. See also vol. 1, p. 199. By "Vinnius," Adams was referring to Arnoldus Vinnius (1586–1657), whose popular commentary on Justinian's *Institute*, *In Quattuor libros institutionum imperialium commentarius academicus* was to be found in many eighteenth-century editions, such as the Venice edition of 1736. These were usually edited by Johann Gottlieb Heineccius (1681–1741). Johannes Van Muyden, a civilian scholar, lived from 1652 to 1729. His *Compendiosa institutionum Justiniana tractatiae* was eventually acquired by Adams from Gridley's library and remains today in the Boston Public Library. See Adams, *Diary*, *supra*, vol. 1, p. 57, n. 2. See also p. 27, *supra*, and accompanying notes.

65. These extraordinary similarities were first noticed by my talented research assistant, Kevin Cox, Harvard Law School 2006. Dickins's program was not too strenuous! According to

Of course, studying maxims was not necessarily about Roman and civil law. Throughout the sixteenth, seventeenth and eighteenth centuries, Latin maxims were seen as a major aid to both memory and legal analysis of the English common law. The leading influence was Francis Bacon's *A Collection of Some Principal Rules and Maxims of the Common Lawes* written between 1596 and 1597 and first published posthumously in 1631, but there were many more common law "maxim" books, designed for students and practitioners alike.[66] Of particular importance was John Dodderidge's (1555–1628) *The Lawyer's Light*, which was also published posthumously in 1629 from a manuscript entitled

---

the letter copied into Quincy's notebook, "If a general knowledge only of the Civil Law is desired in the most short and compendious Method, the most advisable way is to read Wood's Institutes [Thomas Wood, *A New Institute of the Imperial or Civil Law* (London, 1704), with subsequent editions in 1712, 1721, and 1730] in its natural order, translated into English by W. Strahan: [Jean Domat, *Civil Law in its Natural Order* (trans. William Strahan, London, 1722), with subsequent printings in 1737 and 1772]. [T]hese two authors will furnish a careful reader with the main principals [sic] of the Civil Law in all its several branches." "Vol. 4" P347, Reel 4, QP58, p. 148. Only if "the intent be to become as compleat a master as may be of the Civil Law" was it "necessary to begin with the first Element and to read Justinian's Institutions . . ." *Id.*, p. 148. In short, no need for a gentleman to actually read law from the original sources to have "a general knowledge of the civil law"! This rather cavalier approach was reflected in other "quick and easy" civil law guides of the period, some of which were cross-cited to Blackstone's *Commentaries*. See, for example, the short book by one of Dickins's successors as Regius Professor, Samuel Hallifax, who served from 1770 to 1782. Hallifax's *An Analysis of the Roman Civil Law* (Cambridge, 1774) was extensively cross-referenced to Blackstone, and was certainly not "heavy lifting," even by the standards of modern student "outlines"! Certainly no Latin was required. Quincy's laborious collection of Latin maxims was not a Roman Law course, but it involved much more effort and familiarity with original Latin sources than the "courses" of civil law Dickins and Hallifax prepared for the "gentleman scholar" of Cambridge in the eighteenth century!

66. "There was a continuing tradition in England of small books purporting to assist law students by isolating the 'principal grounds and maxims' of the law. This tradition went back to Abraham Fraunce's (1557?–1633) *The Lawyiers Logick* (1588), a book designed to introduce Fraunce's fellows at Gray's Inn, London, which included Bacon, to the Ramis dialectic. Indeed, the tradition could be said to include St. German's *Doctor and Student*, as early as 1523, where the 'Student of the Common Law' invoked 'dyvers pryncyples that be called *by those learned* in the lawe maxymes . . . for every one of those maxymes is suffycyent auctorytie to hym selfe to such an extent that it is fruitless to argue with those who deny them.' The maxims in St. German's book were apparently the basis of the first English collection of maxims, *Principia sive Maxima Legum Anglie* (London, 1546) located and described in a most scholarly study by John C. Hogan and Mortimer D. Schwartz. There followed books like William Fulbeck's (1560–1603) *A Direction or Preparative to the Study of the Lawe* (1600) (Fulbeck being another Gray's Inn lawyer), Sir Henry Finch's (1558–1625) *Nomotechnia* (1613), and William Noy's

Methodus Studendi. Dodderidge divided his book between "primary principles," which he called "maxims," and "secondary principles," which he called "rules." "'Rules' differed from 'maxims' in that they are 'not so well known by the light of nature . . . and are peculiarly known for the most part, to such only as profess the study and the speculation of the law.'"[67] Bacon also distinguished between "*legum leges*," "law of laws," and "ordinary and vulgar" maxims.

> And therefore, whereas these rules are some of them ordinary and vulgar, that now serve but for grounds and plain songs to the more shallow and impertinent sort of arguments; other of them are gathered and extracted out of the harmony and congruity of cases, and are such as the wisest and deepest sort of lawyer have in judgment and use, though they be not able many times to express and set them down: for the former sort, (which a man that should write rather to raise a high opinion of himself than to instruct others would have omitted, as trite and within every man's compass,) yet nevertheless I have not affected to neglect them; but having chosen out of them such as I thought good, I have reduced them to a true application, limiting and defining their bounds, that they may not be run upon at large, but restrained to point of difference.[68]

Thus, the collection and the study of maxims can be used to structure legal principles, as well as to aid memory.

Bacon saw this use of maxims as a way to improve commonplacing. "For as, both in the law and other sciences, the handling of questions by commonplace, without aim or application, is the weakest so yet nevertheless many common principles and generalities are not to be contemned, if they be well derived and deduced into particulars, and their limits and exclusions duly assigned."[69] In addition, whether the source of a maxim be from the Roman law or the common law, the inherent reason of the maxim was seen by Bacon

---

(1577–1634) *A Treatise of the Principall Grounds and Maximes of the Lawes of this Kingdome* (1641). The latter was a treatise written originally in Law French and published in English long after the author's death. It remains difficult to show when any of these little treatises was first written and circulated at the Inns of Court. It is therefore hard to prove the exact sequence of ideas between them, and from them to Bacon." Daniel R. Coquillette, *Francis Bacon* (Stanford, 1992), p. 37 (hereafter, "Coquillette, *Bacon*").

67. *Id.*, pp. 37–38.

68. *Id.*, p. 39.

as a source of authority in legal argument, quite apart from case precedent. Thus, while Bacon claimed his maxims were all derived from legal authorities, and "in mine own copy I had them quoted," he deliberately omitted the citations and let the maxims stand on their own!

> [T]he reason is, because I judged it a matter undue and preposterous to prove rules and maxims. . . . Well will it appear to those that are learned in the laws, that many of the cases are judged cases, either within the books or of fresh report, and most of them fortified by judged cases and similitude of reason; though, in some few cases, I did intend expressly to weigh down the authorities by evidence of reason, and therein rather to correct the law, than either to soothe a received error, or by unprofitable subtlety, which corrupteth the sense of the law, to reconcile contrarities.[70]

This view of the inherent "authority" of maxims was not limited to Bacon or the seventeenth century. In a number of important cases in Quincy's *Reports*, leading advocates such as Gridley or James Otis Jr. used "naked" maxims in the abstract as part of their argument. For example, in his historic appearance before the Governor and Council in 1765, in the *Memorial of Boston*, Jeremiah Gridley argued that the Stamp Act contravened basic human reason. There could be no legal proceedings without the stamps, but the stamps "were not to be obtained." "That the Law never requires Impossibilities Is a Maxim of the Law."[71] No other authority was given!

Where Roman maxims also supported a common law principle, the "antiquity" and "universality" made it particularly compelling. Thus, in the same historic *Memorial of Boston* in 1765, John Adams argued "That the Subject is not bound by Acts, when he is not represented, is a sound Maxim of the Law, and not peculiar to the British Constitution, but a Maxim of the antient Roman Law: 'What concerns All shall be judged of by All.'"[72] This special authority of concurrent Roman and common law maxims was also argued by Bacon.

> [W]hereas some of these rules have a concurrence with the civil Roman law, and some others a diversity, and many times an opposition; such grounds as are common to our law and theirs I have not affected to disguise into other words than the civilians use, to the end they might seem invented by me, and

69. *Id.*, p. 39.
70. *Id.*, p. 40.
71. *Reports*, p. 209.
72. *Reports*, p. 201.

> not borrowed or translated from them: no, but I took hold of it as matter of great authority and majesty, to see and consider the concordance between the laws penned and as it were dictated *verbatim* by the same reason.[73]

Thus, Quincy's list of 44 Latin maxims from the *Digest's De Diversis Regulis Juris Antiqui* (Title 50, Section 17), and other civil law sources, was not just an antiquarian exercise. Rather, it served three important functions: as a way to classify and learn legal principles, a form of comparative law study, and an independent source of authority.[74] This was a legal system lacking all native law reports and facing a high rate of change. Appeal to the universal principles represented by maxims was not just tempting, it was necessary. James Otis, following John Adams in the Memorial of Boston–Stamp Act appearances, gave what all contemporary witnesses agreed was a great legal argument.[75] At its core was an appeal to a "naked" or "self-evident" legal maxim. "It was once a fundamental Maxim, that every subject had the same Right to his Life, Liberty, Property and the Law, that the King had to his Crown . . ."[76] Whether as an aid to memory, a structure for commonplacing, or as a source of authority in itself, the study of maxims, "aphoristic pedagogy," was important to Quincy and his legal world.

73. Coquillette, *Bacon*, p. 39, citing Bacon's *Maximes* (1631), *Works of Francis Bacon* (ed. J. Spedding, R. L. Ellis, D. D. Heath, London, 1857–74), vol. VII, p. 321. (Hereafter, "*Works of Francis Bacon*.")

74. As to "the comparison of legal systems to discover universal rules when they existed" and its importance to Joseph Story and other American lawyers of the early Republic, see M. H. Hoeflich, "Comparative Law in Antebellum America," 4 *Washington University Global Studies Review* 535, 537–44 (2005). Bacon compared maxims to a 'magnetic needle' that "points at the law, but does not settle it." *Works of Francis Bacon*, vol. XIII, p. 67. "The magnetic needle was useful because it accurately reflected the natural phenomenon of the earth's polarity. Likewise, useful jurisprudence began with the empirical facts of the law that existed in the courts and the statute books, and then moved, step by step, to generalities that were genuinely *useful*, because they were a product of induction from reality. But it was also already plain that Bacon's maxims were intended to do more than simply describe and restate existing law. By accurately identifying the rational, consistent and systematic 'middle axioms' of the system, the development of the law could be directed toward more harmony and more reason." Coquillette, *Bacon*, p. 46.

75. "Mr. Otis reasoned with great learning and zeal . . ." Adams, *Diary*, vol. 1, p. 267 (Dec. 20, 1768).

76. *Reports*, p. 203.

III. THE DOCTRINES AND THE SOCIETY

Quincy's *Law Commonplace* can teach us a lot about colonial legal education, but it is also a treasure house of information about what the law was, and how people lived. In a commonplace book, the last two really are inseparable. Books like Wood's *An Institute of the Laws of England* (1720) or Blackstone's *Commentaries* (1765–1769) could, and often did, exist in a theoretical test tube, far removed from what Langdell called "the ever-tangled skein of human affairs."[77] But the purpose of commonplacing was to apply doctrine to that "ever-tangled skein," in actual practice. Again, as discussed in Section A, *supra*, Quincy's *Law Commonplace* was not a defined, closed, formal, system of learning, but was designed to be constantly updated through the *Legis Miscellanea* sections, as Quincy gained experience.[78]

Both the initial "index" of Quincy's *Law Commonplace* and the retroactive index of the *Legis Miscellanea* indicate what was considered important in practice. But this is particularly true of the *Legis Miscellanea* index, because it shows what was "added" on as Quincy studied and observed his pupil master and court cases. The former index is like the "suggested curriculum" of today's law schools. The *Legis Miscellanea* is more like the little notebook I kept when I first practiced law. It did not reflect what my law teachers thought was important, but rather what I learned in the "school of hard knocks," day by day, at my Boston law firm. A lot of my notebook was about my clients and their needs, rather than just legal rules and doctrines, and that is certainly true of Quincy's *Law Commonplace*. This is where society meets doctrine.

Here is an example from the "Case Note Section" of the *Law Commonplace*, also cross-referenced to Quincy's "Law file C."

77. C. C. Langdell, *A Selection of Cases on the Law of Contracts* (Boston, 1871), p. vi.

78. Matthew Hale talked of a seven-year period, or longer, for the commonplacing process. "Touching the Method of the study of the Common Law, I must in general say thus much to the Student thereof; It is necessary for him to observe a Method in his Reading and Study; for let him assure himself, though his memory never be so good, he shall never be able to carry on a distinct serviceable Memory of all, or the greatest part he reads, the end of seven years, nor a much shorter time, without the helps of Use or Method; yea what he hath Read seven years since, will, without the help of Method, or reiterated use, be as new to him as if he had scarce ever read it: A Method therefore is necessary, but various, according to every Man's particular Fancy . . ." Matthew Hale, "Preface Directed to the Young Students of the Common Law," in Henry Rolle, *Un Abridgment Des Plusieurs Cases . . . del Common Ley . . .* (London, 1668), n.p.

> W[h]ether, a negro woman being with child complains to a Just Pacis [Justice of the Peace] of a free White Man being the father, can the Justice upon such Complt [Complaint] issue his Warrant ag[t] the Man + recognize him to appear before the Sessions as provided by the Prov. Law p. 10. 11 in Case of a White Woman gotten with Child. This Question answer'd in the Negative. + the reasons Why. vid. Law-file C.
>
> *Law Commonplace*, p. 106 [91].

Colonial welfare law depended on taking responsibility for your children, and justices of the peace had a general power to issue warrants to question witnesses. See *Province Laws* (Geo. II anno. 17, 1744) Chap. 222, *The Charters and General Laws of the Colony . . . of Massachusetts Bay* (Boston, 1814), pp. 551–52 (hereafter, "*General Laws*"). See also *Colony Laws* (1642, 1665) Sections 1–3, and the discussion at page [92], note 6. See also Douglas Lamar Jones, "The Transformation of the Law of Poverty in Eighteenth-Century Massachusetts," *Law in Colonial Massachusetts* (D. R. Coquillette, R. J. Brink, C. S. Menard, eds., Boston, 1984), pp. 153–90. (Hereafter, "Jones, Law of Poverty.") At almost exactly the time Quincy made this notation, there was a well-documented case in 1765 of an Amos Jewett Jr. being found liable for five shillings per week to support two bastard children, twin boys, by one Sarah Moor of Rowley. *Id.*, p. 162, see Rowley Sarah Moor, File Papers, 1767, Essex Sessions. In 1767, Jewett was sent to debtors' prison because he could not keep up the payments. This was a serious concern to the selectmen of Rowley, who would otherwise have to "absorb the costs of raising Sarah's children." *Id.*, p. 163.

So the usual legal doctrine was one of responsibility, backed by a powerful social policy of enforcement, to keep the cost from falling on the relevant town or city. Justices of the peace had statutory power to hear such complaints and subpoena witnesses. Why not here?

Quite obviously, Quincy's notation tells us as much about race and gender politics in 1763 as it tells us about a rule of law. We would like to see "the reason why" in Quincy's last "Law file C," but it is quite clear that accusations by a black woman against a white man would not be allowed, despite strong policy reasons to establish paternity. Perhaps the relevant town could bring the complaint instead, but this case is more than a legal doctrine, it is a window into colonial racial politics.

There are many such windows in the *Law Commonplace*. Here are just a few examples, taken from three of Quincy's most "active" alphabetical categories,

"Baron + Feme" (husband and wife), "Apprentices and Servants," and "Jury." Each of these categories contains a number of legal rules and doctrines, but also graphically illustrates the "real world" of colonial society in which these laws existed and operated.

In Quincy's Massachusetts social reality and legal doctrine were closely linked. This was because of the state of the legal system and public attitudes toward legal authority. These attitudes can be particularly well understood by studying the *Law Commonplace* together with Quincy's manuscript *Law Reports*, against which the *Law Commonplace* was cross-referenced. Most colonial judges were laymen, who rarely gave reasons for their decisions. In addition, these decisions, as in England, were usually given orally from the bench. Quincy's *Reports*, therefore, consist mainly of reciting the facts of the case, the arguments of counsel, and the base vote of the judges at the end—although the judges often asked questions and made remarks that reveal the reasons for their vote.[79] Many of these cases demonstrated a strong social pragmatism, in both the rationales of the arguments and the judicial comments.

This pragmatism was supported by ambiguity as to the source of law and legal authority. Massachusetts was subject to what my colleague Mary Sarah Bilder calls "the transatlantic constitution."[80] Under the charter of 1691, the colony could make laws "not repugnant or contrary to the laws of this our realm of England."[81] There was also a strictly limited appeal to the Privy Council in London in civil actions "wherein the matter in difference doth exceed the value of three hundred pounds."[82] This was a large sum of money, and, in practice, leave to appeal was granted with great reluctance.[83]

79. See Coquillette, *Law Reports*, pp. 1–15.

80. See Mary Sarah Bilder, *The Transatlantic Constitution: Colonial Legal Culture and the Empire* (Cambridge, Mass., 2004), pp. 1–11. (Hereafter, "Bilder.")

81. *The Charters and General Laws of the Colony and Province of Massachusetts Bay* (Boston, 1814), The Charter of the Province . . . (1691), pp. 31–33. (Hereafter, "*Charters and General Laws.*") It is interesting to note that oaths had to be "not repugnant to the laws *and statutes* of this our realm of England." *Id.*, p. 33 (emphasis added). Was the omission of "and statutes" from the general power to make law significant? Could colonial statutes conflict with individual English statutes, but not with the common law itself?

82. *Id.*, p. 32.

83. See, for example, the discussion and the refusal to grant an appeal in *Scollay* v. *Dunn*, Case 30 (1763), *Reports*, pp. 80–83.

There were no published colonial law reports. Colonial statutes often did not pertain to key areas of legal dispute and, even then, could be ambiguous and badly drafted. Thus, the courts had quite a bit of discretion. The real issue was how closely they were required to follow English common law doctrines, as set out in the English texts and reports available in the colony. After Coke's famous decision in *Calvin's Case* (1608), it was clear that English law "was not automatically received in conquered territories" and, thus, arguably not in the American colonies.[84] In addition, English authorities were often not cited in oral argument, particularly in less lucrative cases. In these "lesser" cases, the lawyers often took little time to prepare their legal authorities, sometimes to the annoyance of the judges—and Quincy.[85] When English precedents were relied on, as in the major inheritance cases, they were often invoked by both sides, with a cavalier disregard for what the cases actually said, again to Quincy's expressed irritation.[86] Even in major cases, the final decision could depart markedly from English legal doctrine. The justification given was sometimes local customs, or practical necessity, or social policy, or all three. As we will see in the *Introduction to Quincy's Reports*, *Quincy Papers*, Volume 4, sometimes the judges gave no reasons at all, even for important departures. The inherent assumption, infrequently voiced explicitly, was that such departures did not violate the "repugnance" provision of the Charter, an easy argument to make if the English Common law was uncertain or, as was often the case, poorly researched. Appeals to the privy council were extremely scarce in Quincy's *Reports*, and were clearly looked on with disfavor.[87] Practical, social

84. See Morton J. Horwitz, *The Transformation of American Law, 1780–1860* (Cambridge, Mass.), p. 17 (hereafter, "Horwitz"). See also Bilder, pp. 35–40.

85. See, for example, *Hanlon* v. *Thayer* Case 37 (1764), *Reports*, pp. 99–103, where Chief Justice Hutchinson remarked, "I should have been extremely glad if this case had been argued a little more largely by the Gentlemen of the Bar, and more Authorities cited, in Matter of so great Consequence." *Id.*, p. 102.

86. See, for example, the discussion in the important case of *Banister* v. *Henderson* (Case 42, 1765) at pp. 122–45. At one point, Quincy questioned Gridley's argument, noting, "*Sed quaere*, and see Dr. Sullivan's Lect. On the Laws of England 182, 3 [published as F. S. Sullivan, *Lectures on the Constitution and Laws of England etc.* (London, 1770)], and *Qu.* If ye Act of Parliament extends, or is binding here." *Id.*, p. 145. (Quincy's note must have been added after the case report.) In the same case, Chief Justice Hutchinson again admonished the bar, "Have you no Authorities, Gentlemen?" to have Gridley reply, "There is no Authority that the Sun shines." *Id.*, p. 122.

87. Appeals "to his Majesty in Council" were not allowed in major cases such as *Dudley* v.

policy arguments, made in argument by counsel, were sometimes reinforced by *ad hoc* judicial comments, picked up by Quincy, and often seen to explain the decision itself.[88]

Scholars like Morton Horwitz have argued that "[t]he generation of Americans who made the American Revolution had little difficulty in conceiving of the common law as a known and determinate body of legal doctrine," quoting Chief Justice Hutchinson's remark, recorded by Quincy in 1767, that "laws should be established, else Judges and Juries must go according to their Reason, that is, their Will." *Reports*, pp. 234–35, "Charge to the Grand Jury," 1767.[89] Quincy himself, in his *Southern Journal*, criticizes the South Carolina bar for ignorance of the law, pointing out that it meant that the courts were free to do whatever they wanted.[90] But the remarks of Hutchinson and Quincy cut both ways. Hutchinson was increasingly frustrated that juries, particularly the grand juries he charged, simply ignored what he regarded as "the law," and Quincy pointed out the indifference of practicing lawyers and judges, in both the North and South, to common law doctrine, and the total ignorance in South Carolina of the common law forms of action.[91] In this void, both lay judges, jurors and practitioners could be pragmatic and policy oriented. Indeed, they had little choice. Blackstone's conception of a rigid judicial adherence to precedent and a clear distinction between legislation and judicial decisions required not only a "knowable" and determinate body of common law, but lawyers and judges that knew it.

As both his *Law Commonplace* and *Reports* demonstrated, Quincy wanted to know the law, and he knew a lot of it. The start of the *Law Commonplace* in

---

Dudley Case 9 (1762), apparently because the Charter of 1691 allowed appeals in "personal" actions only and not land cases. See *Reports*, p. 25, *Charters and General Laws*, *supra*, p. 32. Cases that directly presented conflicts between English and colonial law, such as *Bromfield* v. *Little* Case 40 (1764), *Reports*, p. 108, although of "much Importance to the Community," were not appealed, possibly because the monetary requirement of the Charter was not met. See also the discussion in *Scollay* v. *Dunn* Case No. 30 (1763), where leave to appeal was denied. *Reports*, pp. 80–83.

88. See, for example, *Baker* v. *Frobisher* Case 2 (1761) on "unmerchantable soap" where the justices distinguished between ordinary retail sales and bulk sales sold "by sample." *Reports*, p. 4.

89. Horwitz, *supra*, p. 4.

90. See *Southern Journal* (1773), p. 61, and accompanying notes, and its introduction, "An Odyssey of America on the Brink of Revolution," *Quincy Papers*, vol. 3, pp. 52–58.

91. *Id.*, p. 61, and accompanying notes.

1763 predated the appearance of Blackstone's first volume of his *Commentaries* in 1765. There is but one citation to *Blackstone's Commentaries,* to the 1765 first volume, and only an occasional reference to Blackstone's *Analysis of the Law* (1756).[92] Quincy's conception of the role of common law decisions, the jury, and statutes can neither be blamed on ignorance of the law nor on Blackstone. Thus Quincy makes a particularly interesting test case for our theories about colonial jurisprudence.

It is Horwitz's famous thesis that between "[t]he generations of Americans who made the American Revolution" and the world of the new Republic of 1820, a major change occurred, a "transformation of American law."[93]

> By 1820 the legal landscape in America bore only the faintest resemblance to what existed forty years earlier. While the words were often the same, the structure of thought had dramatically changed and with it the theory of law. Law was no longer conceived of as an eternal set of principles expressed in custom and derived from natural law. Nor was it regarded primarily as a body of rules designed to achieve justice only in the individual case. Instead, judges came to think of the common law as equally responsible with legislation for governing society and promoting socially desirable conduct.[94]

This "transformation," in Horwitz's view, was symbolized by a shift from a "Blackstonian" conception of the law, with a strict adherence to common law precedent by judges and a clear distinction between the role of a statute and a judicial decision, to something altogether different, where instrumental judicial legislation was candidly recognized.[95]

The *Law Commonplace* can hardly be an adequate test of this major theory.

92. See the references to the *Analysis* at the beginning of the *Law Commonplace*, p. n.p., [6], p. n.p., [10], and at "Of Statutes or Acts," *id.*, p. 89 [77]. The sole reference to Blackstone's *Commentaries* is at p. 94 [82], and may be a later addition. See notes 37, 46, *supra.*

93. Horwitz, *supra*, p. 4.

94. *Id.*, p. 30.

95. Horwitz quotes the 1817 lectures of Tapping Reeve and James Gould at the Litchfield Law School: "Theoretical[ly] courts make no law, but in point of fact they are legislators." *Horwitz*, p. 23. Horwitz regarded Blackstone's "dichotomy between the nature of the two forms of law" as "a fairly recent creation," noting that Coke in deciding *Calvin's Case* in 1608 did not make the distinction. "[T]here was no suggestion of a distinction between statute and common law, for statutes were still largely conceived of as an expression of customs." *Id.*, p. 17. But, Horwitz argued, in the period "[b]efore the American Revolution common law and statute law were conceived of as two separate bodies of law, and the authority of judges and legislators was justified in terms of the special category of law that they administered." *Id.*, pp. 16–17.

Quincy was just one colonial lawyer, and an atypical one at that—particularly bright, rich, and well-educated. But he was very interested in the things that constitute the core of Horwitz's theory, such as the nature and source of common law precedent, the role of jury in "achieving justice . . . in the individual case" and the function of statutes. The resulting record describes a legal world which, while mindful of doctrine, was remarkably pragmatic and sensitive to understanding economic and social needs. Let us look at some examples from the *Law Commonplace*.

A. Doctrines of Gender

As my distinguished colleague, Mary Sarah Bilder, observed: "The laws of England preferred inheritance practices that were gendered (favoring the eldest son), lineal (favoring keeping land within bloodlines), and ancestral (favoring inherited land)."[96] Thus the "pigeon holes" for gender in Quincy's *Law Commonplace* include "Estates, and Lands, Tenements and Hereditaments"[97] as well as the more obvious "Baron + Feme"[98] [husband and wife] and "Marriage."[99] Also included should be "Powers,"[100] which include the critical issues of what a married woman can do legally, and "Base Possession,"[101] which include issues of whether a wife's mere possession of goods or property is imputed to the husband.

Massachusetts had early rejected the English doctrine of "primogeniture," that intestate land descends solely to the eldest son.[102] The "repugnancy" to English law clause of the 1689 Charter was carefully circumvented.[103] "Partibility" [i.e., equal division to each child] or "coparcenage," the usual English doctrine when a testator had only daughters, was imposed by statute.[104] The

96. Bilder, *supra*, p. 91.
97. See *Law Commonplace*, pp. 25 [30], 47 [45], 49 [47].
98. See *Id.*, pp. 22 [27], 176 [119].
99. See *Id.*, p. 179 [122].
100. See *Id.*, p. 181 [124].
101. See *Id.*, p. 176 [119].
102. Quincy's *Law Commonplace* made no mention of the Massachusetts provincial statute William & Mary 4 (1692) "An Act for the Settlement and Distribution of the Estate of Intestate," *Charters and General Laws* (Boston, 1814), Chapter 8, pp. 230–32, which established partibility in the colony, rather than primogeniture! See, in contrast, *Dudley* v. *Dudley* Case 9 (1761), p. 12; *Elwell* v. *Pierson* Case 20 (1762), p. 42; *Baker* v. *Mattocks* Case 29 (1763), p. 69; and *Banister* v. *Henderson* Case 42 (1765), p. 119.
103. See *Law Commonplace*, pp. 47 [45]–49 [47].
104. See William & Mary 4 (1692), *Charters and General Laws*, *supra*, pp. 230–32.

major issues arose when the "partibility" doctrine was circumvented by will, usually by attempting an "entail male," i.e., descent by male blood heir only, or reversion to testator's direct heirs.[105] The Superior Court of Judicature felt constrained to accept such gendered restrictions, but only if the will was legally correct. Ambiguities were resolved for partibility, a distinct difference from English law.[106]

Quincy's *Law Commonplace* emphasized two important distinctions. Land brought into a marriage by the wife may be in control of the husband during the wife's life, but on her death is certainly treated differently from lands brought to the marriage by the husband. "But where lands do descend from the part of the mother, the Heirs on the part of the father never inherit so on the contrary. Observe then the difference where the son purchaseth lands in Fee-s[imple] + where he comes by them by descent, on the part of the mother, or of the father."[107] In addition, bias against female gender was trumped by the bias toward blood lines. "A sister of the whole blood shall be preferred before the younger of Brother of the Half Blood."[108] Absent, however, from the *Law Commonplace* were the struggles over male entail so carefully chronicled in Quincy's *Reports*.[109]

More prominent in the *Law Commonplace* was the legal subordination of a married woman. In fact, "Baron & Feme" ("Husband and Wife") constitutes the largest section of the "core" commonplace, not counting related sections, like "Marriage" in the *Legis Miscellanea*.[110] Quincy's world was one of social, racial and gender hierarchies, and it is not surprising that a law student would

105. See cases cited at note 102, *supra*.

106. Unlike his *Reports*, Quincy's *Law Commonplace* simply copied in the traditional English law under the "Of Lands, Tenements + Hereditaments" caption, taking it mostly from Thomas Wood's *An Institute of the Laws of England* (1st ed., London, 1720), book 2, chap. 3, pp. 228–30. See *Law Commonplace*, page [7], note 3, *infra*. Thus he writes: "In short, Lands + Tenements in Fee-s: Descend, 1st to the eldest son or Heir + to his issue: The sons first in order of birth + for want of sons to all the Daughters equally," although that was not the law in Massachusetts. The section "Of Estates" in the *Legis Miscellanea* also simply reproduces English common law, but focuses instead on the more difficult *Coke on Littleton* (London, 1628) and William Hawkins, *Abridgment of Coke on Littleton* (London, 1711). See vol. 4, pp. 5–10, *infra*, and accompanying notes, and pp. [24], n. 9, [68], n. 6.

107. *Law Commonplace*, p. 48 [46].

108. *Id.*, p. 48 [46].

109. See note 102, *supra*.

110. *Law Commonplace*, Index "Legis Miscellanea," p. 179 [122].

organize the law in this way. Indeed, modern critical jurists and legal realists would see such a structure as more "honest" or natural than the doctrinal formalism of Langdell and the "categories" of legal education that have persisted to this day.[111]

In theory, the marital subordination of women "cut both ways"; married women had clear privileges and rights based on their status, as did married men. Sometimes the disabilities were mutual. Evidentiary privilege is one example of a mutual disability, duly noted by Quincy. "Baron + feme cannot be witnesses for or ag.^{t} each other," with the exception of high treason and "3 H.7 Chap.2"[112] The latter statutory exception was also carefully noted by Quincy, "where the wife may be evidence against her husband forcibly taking her away and marrying her," tracking the 1488 statute of Henry VII which established penalties for "carrying a woman against her will, that hath lands or goods."[113] Thus while evidentiary disabilities were, in theory, mutual, the "force" exception shows that in practice they might particularly harm women. In any event, if so much depended legally on marriage, a forced marriage was reprehensible.

Again, in theory, the feme "covert," the married woman, could not contract, could not appear in court, and could not have "seisin" of land except through her husband. "The wife is so much under the power of her husband, that she is disabled to contract with any person without his consent . . ."[114] But Quincy added some key, underscored words, "without his consent, <u>precedent</u> or <u>subsequent</u>, <u>express</u> or <u>pre-sum'd</u>."[115] Here we have another window into the reality of the colonial world. Despite his English sources, Quincy observed:

> She [the married woman] cannot bind her H [husband] in Strictness for <u>Necessaries</u> by any contract, unless a precedent or Subsequent assent is proved or presumed; But usually her Contracts are allowed, if She buys goods for herself,

111. See, for example, Duncan Kennedy's "How the Law School Fails," 1 *Yale Rev. of Law and Social Action* 71 (1970), Mark Tushnet, "Critical Legal Studies: A Political History" 100 *Yale L.J.* 1515 (1991), and the discussion in Laura Kalman, "The Dark Ages," in *History of the Yale Law School* (A. T. Kronman, ed., New Haven, 2004), pp. 203–06.

112. *Law Commonplace*, p. 20 [25].

113. See *Law Commonplace*, p. 20 [25], n. 4. See also Ferdinand Pulton, *A Collection of Sundrie Statutes* (London, 1632), p. 401.

114. *Law Commonplace*, p. 20 [25].

115. *Id.*, p. 20 [25].

> Children, or family, as Bread etc. or for her own necessary Apparel. The H is bound to maintain his W [wife] in Necessaries, + therefore if Goods come to H's Use it is Evid. to prove his Assent, but not binding Evid; for it may be contradicted by Other Proof as that He gave his Wife ready money; Admitting then that the H sh.^{d} be charged in strictness for necessaries; tho' he knows nothing of them; [yet if][1] he forbids particular Persons to trust his W, he shall not [be] charged after such Prohibition.[116]

So, as a practical matter, a colonial wife could engage in normal shopping, and trades-people could enter into normal supply contracts with her, unless they had actual notice that there was no normally "pre-sum'd" consent from the husband. Even general notice was not enough, according to Quincy. "A prohibition in general not to trust a wife, as by putting her in the gazette, etc. cannot amount to legal notice."[117]

The problem came when the wife engaged in a trade or business outside of household "necessities." There is evidence in both Quincy's *Reports* and the *Law Commonplace* that this certainly occurred. Such activities ranged from criminal activity, such as acting as a "fence" for stolen goods or running a "bawdy house," to the practice of medicine.[118]

> A man shall not be charged by the contract of his W, (except as above for necessaries) if he hath no notice of it, tho' the things do come to his use. Neither, shall a H be bound by his W's receipt of his money.[119]

But actual practice was more complex. In his *Legis Miscellanea*, Quincy emphasized an English case in which a woman was practicing medicine, *Brashford* v. *Buckingham and his wife* (1601), 2 *Croke's Reports* (London, 1657), p. 77.[120]

> • Action brôt by Baron and Feme on a promise made to ye Feme in consideration, she w^{d} cure such a wound and alleges she did cure. Adjudg'd good upon Writ of Error, in Exchequer Chamber because the Action is grounded upon a promise made to ye feme + upon a matter arising upon her Skill + a performance to be made by her Person + such an Action w^{d} survive to the feme.

116. *Id.*, pp. 20 [25]–21 [26].
117. *Id.*, p. 21 [26].
118. See *Id.*, p. 152 [95] (medicine). See also *Reports*, *Dom. Rex* v. *Doaks* Case 34 (1763), p. 90 (bawdy house); *Dom. Rex* v. *Pourkdorff* Case 38 (1764), p. 104 (theft).
119. *Law Commonplace*, p. 21 [26].
120. *Id.*, p. 152 [95], n. 8, see also p. 16 [21].

> Cro. James 77 This case is [discussed?] at Barnardiston 75.+ [And] debt upon judgment in Trespass for 10/ Damages + 40/ Cost, + the Statute pleaded. Vide. 2. Vent. 36.[121]

Quincy also emphasized another English case where a woman was "carrying a trade in her own name as a widow," and then sought to use "coverture" to escape her obligations.

> A woman whose husband has left her about 12 years before had carried on trade in her own name as widow + given receipts in her own name, being sued for debt contracted in the course of her trade gave coverture in evidence + that her H. had been lately in Ireland+ Holt directed the Jury to find for Defn + so they did. 1. Bac. 308. On N. A. Deft proved she had a H. alive in France Jury found for plf. On motion for a new trial as a verdict against evidence it was denied for a divorce shall be intended. 1. Salk. 117.[122]

Thus if a woman's husband was dead, or if a divorce "shall be intended," she would have the power to enter binding contracts, even entered into while married, as long as the people dealing with her believed they were doing business with the woman on her own account, a doctrine similar to the "sole trading" cases "according to the custom of the . . . City of London."[123]

Quincy added a final English case relating to "separation by consent."

> If B. + Feme separate by consent + she has a separate allowance tis unreasonable she should have it in her power to charge him + it is not to be presumed but tradesmen trust her on her own credit + not the credit of her H. + a personal notice is not necessary it is sufficient that it be public + generally known. Holt ruled a H. was liable to his wifes contracts, because they cohabitated. 1. Salk. 113—Everyman is obliged to maintain his wife + an action may be maintained against him for necessities provided suitable to her rank in life[124]

While the selective mixture of English precedents in Quincy's *Law Commonplace* can be no more than a suggestion as to the colonial law, the picture that emerges is fairly practical, given the overall gender bias of the law. In theory a

121. *Id.*, p. 152 [95].

122. *Id.*, p. 27 [32]. "N.A." is for "non-assumpsit," "she did not promise." This was the standard plea by way of traverse denying the existence of an express promise "or of matter of fact from which the promise alleged would be implied by law, and thus raised to general issue." Earl Jowitt, *The Dictionary of English Law* (ed. C. Walsh, London, 1959), p. 1231. (Hereafter, "Jowitt.")

123. *Id.*, p. 27 [32], n. 5.

124. *Id.*, p. 27 [32].

married woman had no legal personality, except to protect herself from being forced into marriage itself and, in Quincy's words, "If the husband threaten his wife to beat or to kill her, she may make him find security for the peace."[125] But in practice, the legal obligation of the husband to provide "necessaries," including "necessities provided suitable to her rank in life," provided implied consent to most domestic transactions, absent actual notice.[126] Where the woman was doing business on her own, she could use her husband's legal personality, where appropriate, to appear in court or enforce deals. Where death or separation made this impossible, Quincy's precedents were sympathetic to enforcing the contracts as to the woman, so long as the other parties believed they were dealing with the woman in her own capacity or on her own credit.

The system gave the married woman three sources of security, besides simply not being beaten. We have mentioned the husband's duty to provide "necessities . . . suitable to her rank in life." The other two, which attach on the husband's death, receive much attention in Quincy. These are the right of the woman to "dower," a one-third life interest in her deceased husband's estate, and, equally important, the return to her legal ownership of the real property she brought to the marriage.[127] Of course, if the husband survived the wife, he had his own security in her property, "Curtesy of England," which, assuming a child of the marriage had been born alive capable of inheriting the wife's lands, gave the husband an estate in all of those lands for life.[128] Dower was particularly important to women if efforts had been made to place lands in a male entail to the prejudice of a woman's inheritance, a growing source of litigation in the colonies.[129]

Quincy's notes also emphasized the effect of marriage on previously held debt.

> **DEBTS** of the **WIFE** dum sola. [i.e., "contracted while single"] If the W before M [marriage] was in Debt, the H + W must be sued for this Debt, living the W. But if the W dies, the H shall not be charged for the debt of his W after her Death, if the Creditors of the W do not get Judgm[t] during the Cover-

125. *Id.*, p. 21 [26].
126. *Id.*, p. 27 [32].
127. *Id.*, p. 22 [27]. Where the property taken is in the form of personal chattel or "choses in action" (monetary legal claims), the result can be complicated! See *id.*, p. 22 [27].
128. See David M. Walker, *The Oxford Companion to Law* (Oxford, 1980), p. 327.
129. See Bilder, *supra*, pp. 96–97.

> ture. The H, as such is not chargeable in a C^{t} of Equity, anymore than at Law, with the Debts of the W after her Decease; not even tho' he had a large Fortune with Her; as on the Other Hand he is, during the Coverture liable to all her Debts, altho' he did not get a shilling with her.[130]
>
> Citing Thomas Wood's *An Institute of the Laws of England* (London, 1700), vol. 1, c. 6, pp. 61–63, "effects and consequences of marriage." (notes deleted).

While the husband would be fully chargeable with the wife's debts while she was alive, he was not responsible on her death. But the biggest trap was the other way around. If a woman with "a large fortune" married an insolvent husband, all her property could be seized by his debtors, without her consent.

This appears to have been the subject of one of Quincy's most interesting reported cases, *Hanlon* v. *Thayer*, Case 37, (1764), *Reports*, p. 99 (the so-called "naked wife" case).[131] Mrs. Mary Hanlon brought suit in trover[132] through her husband, Mark, to recover "Apparell" attached by her husband's creditors, altogether twenty-one entries of clothing and household goods.[133] Mary Hanlon was a widow of a fairly wealthy merchant, John Salmon, and Mark was her second husband, "a mariner and a Yoeman."[134] The first issue in the case was whether it made any difference whether the clothes were brought into the marriage by Mary. On this, the court had little trouble. Justices John Cushing and Peter Oliver observed that, although "the Case was very hard upon the Wife, who brought all these Cloaths at Marriage, yet 'as they are personal Property, they become the Husband's on Marriage, and therefore liable.'"[135] The more interesting issue was whether there was an exception for "necessary" clothes. There were two separate grounds for this exception: (1) the "necessities . . . suitable to her rank in life" exception to the ban on contractual pow-

130. *Law Commonplace*, p. 23 [28].

131. See the full discussion in Coquillette, *Law Reports*, *supra*, pp. 23–25.

132. Chief Justice Hutchinson observed that it would "have been better to have brought Detinne." *Reports*, p. 103. He was right. "Trover" was the correct action for wrongful deprivation of goods, where the remedy was "damages merely," i.e., money. Jowitt, *supra*, p. 1785. "Detinue" was the correct action for "a plaintiff who seeks to recover goods *in specie* [i.e., the actual thing], or on failure thereof the value . . ." *Id.*, p. 623. Assuming the plaintiff wanted her actual clothes back, she should have sued in detinue.

133. See the excellent paper by Sally Ann Carter, Harvard Law School Class of 1997, "An Exploration of *Hanlon* v. *Thayer*," pp. 21–22, on file with the author.

134. *Id.*

135. *Reports*, p. 102.

ers and (2) the "necessary bedding utensils and implement of the household necessary for the upholding of life, to the use of the wife and family of the deceased" exception to the assets of an insolvent estate established by the 1710 Provincial Statute.[136] See *Charters and General Laws*, *supra*, Chap. 100 (Ann. 9, 1710), Sect. 2, p. 390.

Chief Justice Hutchinson observed that this was a "Matter of great Consequence," and scolded the bar for failing to argue "more largely" with "more Authorities cited."[137] He continued:

> I always took it to have been the Custom in such Cases as this, for the Wife to have her Cloaths; in Cases that have come before me as Judge of Probate I never knew it denied to the Wife where the Estate was insolvent. In the Case cited [by Mr. Gridley] I suppose the Woman was a Party, and the Debt contracted by her; this alters the Case much, but yet I apprehend (here *Ch. Just.* Makes an Apology for what follows) that this may be one of those Cases where the Justice says a Thing *obiter*, or suddenly; for one Gown can never be supposed sufficient—must she go naked when that is washing? Upon the Whole I think it would be very hard upon the Wife, should such a Precedent as this take Place, that her *Cloaths* which she *brought* in *Marriage* must go to discharge the Husband's Debts. I should think it safer to verge towards Conveniency than to strain the Word *Necessary*.[138]

It remains unclear from the report if the other justices agreed, but Quincy noted that "the Jury found for the Defendant Costs."[139]

Despite the hazards of marriage to a woman's legal powers, it could be more dangerous to be unmarried. In at least two Quincy cases women desperately sought to prove their marriages. In the first, the defendant's life depended on it, as she was charged with the murder of a bastard child. Quincy began the report of *Dom. Rex* v. *Mangent* with the caption "Life and Death."[140] Under a 1696 Provincial Statute, the unmarried mother of a stillborn child without a witness was presumed a murderer.[141] Fortunately, it was decided that her marriage certificate from a minister "in another Government . . . without any

136. *Id.*, p. 102, n. 6.

137. *Id.*, p. 102.

138. *Id.*, pp. 102–03 (note omitted).

139. *Id.*, p. 103.

140. *Id.*, p. 163.

141. *Id.*, pp. 162–63. See "An Act to Prevent the Destroying and Murdering of Bastard Children," Gul. III, 8 (1696), Chap. 38, *Charters and General Laws*, *supra*, p. 293.

authentication from any Magistrate" was acceptable.[142] In the leading entail case of *Banister* v. *Henderson*, also reported by Quincy, the widow's children were hard pressed to prove marriage in the absence of a certificate of marriage, despite the fact that their mother and father had lived together for many years as a married couple "both in Old and New England."[143] Once again the Chief Justice scolded the bar "for Want of Authorities,"[144] and found for himself a passage in Thomas Wood's *A New Institute of the . . . Civil Law* (first published, London, 1704) that "half Proof, ought to be extended in Favour of Marriage, rather than contrary to it."[145]

Quincy's *Law Commonplace* contained many more examples of "baron and feme" legal power issues, particularly in his "add on" Section, "Legis Miscellanea Cursim," indicating that these were common issues observed in practice and in his assigned legal reading.[146] Strangely lacking from the *Law Commonplace*, however, is any extensive discussion of the most pressing gender issue outside of marriage, male entails. As emphasized before, a string of important cases in Quincy's *Reports* show that the colonial bench and bar were deeply divided as to whether to encourage a construction of ambiguous or poorly drafted wills to lock land up in an eldest male only line, or to encourage "partiblility" among male and female heirs equally.[147] Except for a cursory mention of testator intent in the *Legis Miscellanea*, however, these issues were simply not dealt with by the *Law Commonplace*, emphasizing the importance of the later *Reports* as a valuable, and often more sophisticated, complement to the earlier *Commonplace*.[148]

B. Doctrines of Servitude

In addition to married women, Quincy's *Law Commonplace* contains many other sections describing the legal rights of different types of people. Some such categories are still familiar to us today, and Quincy's notations in the *Legis Miscellanea* index covering "Infants, Ideots, + Madmen, etc." seem

142. *Reports*, p. 163.
143. *Id.*, p. 121.
144. *Id.*, p. 123.
145. *Id.*, p. 124.
146. *Law Commonplace*, pp. 156 [99], 174 [117].
147. See discussion at note 102, *supra*.
148. See *Law Commonplace*, "*Legis Miscellanea*," p. 161 [104].

familiar.[149] Slavery was omitted from the *Law Commonplace* altogether. Quincy's *Reports* contain cases that make it clear that slaves had no legal personality in Quincy's Massachusetts, and were regarded as chattel.[150] They were not just people with diminished legal rights—they were simply not considered people at all. As discussed before, Quincy did note the different treatment of whites and free blacks, whose civil rights were curtailed by numerous provincial statutes.[151] Also, "in the middle" were indentured "apprentices and servants."

The importance of the "apprentice and servant" class to Quincy's legal world was emphasized by long sections in the "core" *Commonplace* and by an important 1763 case in the *Reports*, *Dunten* v. *Richards*.[152] Like marriage, apprenticeship was a two-way street, based on a legal undertaking whose terms were often implied by law. Thus "[i]t is a reasonable cause of Departure from service if the servant is not allowed sufficient meat, Drink, etc. or if the master's wife beats him."[153] Also like marriage, the apprentice lost much of his or her legal personality. As Quincy noted, summarizing two English cases:

> A waterman's widow took an Apprentice, who went to sea (being pressed into ye Queen's service) + earned 2 tickets [entitlements to accrued pay], wch came to ye dft's hands [probably a money lender]. She bro't trover for ye tickets, + had judgment; for what ever an apprentice gains belongs to his master, She may action for it. 1 Salk 68. Barber v. Dennis.[4] And if he be an appren[tice] only de facto it is sufficient. 6 Mod. 64. cited 3 Vin: 23. notes q: v.[5] [154]

But, like the wife, the apprentice had rights to "necessities" and could not sim-

149. See *Law Commonplace*, p. 179 [122]. See also *id.*, at pp. 155 [98], 159 [102], 165 [108], 171 [114], 172 [115].

150. See, for example, *Reports*, *Allison* v. *Cockran*, Case 36 (1764), p. 94 ("trover for a negro") and *Oliver* v. *Sale* (Case 13, 1761), p. 29 (suite for selling "two free Mulattos for Slaves").

151. *Id.*, p. 106 [91]. See, for example, "An Act to Prevent Disorders in the Night" which prohibited an "Indian, negro or mulatto servant or slave" from being "abroad in the night time after nine o'clock unless it be upon some errand for their respective masters or owners" (October, 1703). *Charters and General Laws*, *supra*, pp. 746–49. "Fornication" between the races was prohibited and if "any negro or mulatto shall presume to smite or strike any person of the English, or other Christian nation, such negro or mulatto shall be severely whipped . . ." (October, 1705), *id.*, pp. 747–48.

152. Case No. 28 (1763), *Reports*, p. 67.

153. *Law Commonplace*, p. 15 [20].

154. *Id.*, p. 15 [20].

ply be "dumped." This was true of long term "servants" as well. "If a servant retain'd for a year falls sick, etc. the Master cannot put away his servant, or abate his wages."[155] And, to some extent, the master took over the servant's legal personality as well, particularly when that servant was acting on the master's business. "If any servant is cozen'd of any money. I may have an action against the Person that cozen'd him."[156]

When doctrines of servitude and doctrines of marriage collided, it could get complex. For example, if an apprentice married without the master's consent, "the master cannot turn him away for that reason," but the master could sue in covenant if the marriage violated the explicit apprenticeship agreement.[157] What if a woman servant married and became a *feme covert*, can her husband break her servitude? Or, suppose she becomes pregnant, in or out of marriage? Quincy noted the following answers:

> If a Woman that is a Servant doth marry, yet she must serve out her Time, + her Husband cannot take Her out of her Master's service. And if a Woman, being with Child of a Bastard, procures Herself to be retain'd with a Master, who knoweth nothing therof, or if She begotten with Child during her Service, this is a reasonable Cause why the Justices sh[d]. dicharge her from her Service, for She hath made herself incapable to serve any longer.[158]

Apprenticeship was a special type of servitude because it was always based on a writing, and had to be terminated by a writing and a magistrate. Quincy paraphrased the section of Dalton's *Countrey Justice* (London, 1618, many editions before 1746).

> An apprentice cannot be sent out of England, unless the Nature of his Service does require it. As an apprentice cannot be made without Writing, so He cannot be discharg'd by his Master without Writing under his Hand, + with the Allowance of One Justice.[159]

In addition, an apprenticeship did not terminate on a master's death, but became part of the assets of the estate, just like a slave.

155. *Id.*, p. 15 [20].
156. *Id.*, p. 16 [21].
157. *Id.*, p. 14 [19].
158. *Id.*, p. 15 [20].
159. *Id.*, p. 15 [20].

> If any Master dies, the apprentice goes to the Ex^{tt}or or adm^{tt}nor, to be maintained, if their be assets. But the Ex^{tt}or he may bind Him over to Another Master for the remaining Part of his Time. Wood. B.1.c6. p 52.[160]
>
> [Thomas Wood, *An Institute of the Laws of England* (London, 1700), vol. 1, c.c., p. 52.]

Henry Sumner Maine famously described the progress of modern law as from "status" (i.e., "where old law fixed a man's social position irreversibly at his birth") to "contract" (i.e., where "modern law allows him to create it for himself").[161] What Quincy would have thought of Maine's ideas remains uncertain. Despite obvious unfairness and adhesion, he would probably have regarded the apprenticeships and servitudes of his day as free contracts with mutual advantage—unlike slavery, which Quincy detested.[162] His *Law Commonplace* looked to English law on all these things, and the sections selected emphasized this contractual nature. But, like the law of marriage, this law gave little real protection to those in servitude, only a minimal security from beating and starvation. These "status" relationships represented a view of civil and legal rights that we, today, would find intolerable. But within these severe constraints, Quincy's *Law Commonplace* demonstrated an effort to find pragmatic and humane solutions to social problems.

C. Doctrines of Legal Authority and Power

Quincy's organization of the *Law Commonplace* was inspired by others, but the captions and subdivisions were uniquely his own. This was especially the case for the *Legis Miscellanea* retroactive index, which was literally created by his experience. Thus, this structure tells us a good deal about Quincy's legal world. We have already seen how colonial hierarchies were reflected in this structure—particularly the relative legal powers of wives, apprentices, children, and servants.

A second important set of subdivisions related to sources of legal authority: in particular, doctrines relating to the division of authority between British legislation, colonial legislation, the colonial judiciary, and the jury. These topics, gathered under the captions "Jury," "Of Laws" and "Statute + Acts" took

160. *Id.*, p. 15 [20].

161. Henry Sumner Maine, *Ancient Law* (1st American from 2d English ed., New York, 1864), pp. 295–96. (Maine used the male pronoun, ironically appropriate for 1864.)

162. See the *Southern Journal* (1773), *infra*, pp. 91–95, 109–10, 113–14.

up a great deal of space in the "core" *Law Commonplace*, 24 pages of the 71 page total! Three Quincy pages, 44 to 46, transcript [42] to [44], were originally assigned to "Jury," but the subject spilled over to page 50 to 52, [48]–[50], following "Lands, Tenements + Hereditaments," and then again to pages 58 to 63, [55]–[59], following "Legacy," a clear example of Quincy underestimating a subject!

I. OF JUDGES AND JURIES

Under "Jury," Quincy tackled two central issues: 1) What was the proper division of authority between judge and jury and 2) How should the jury go about finding the facts? This was done in the context of Quincy's obvious belief in the jury's importance. Quincy emphasized the power of the jury, invoking Hume. "Hume calls, the Institutions of Juries, admirable in itself + the best calculated for the Preservation of Liberty + ye administration of Justice, that ever was devised by the wit of man."[163] "Nothing contributes more, than the institution of tryals by Jury, to the support of that equity + Liberty, for which the English Laws are justly celebrated."[164]

But jurors are "lay gents," and, according to Quincy, therefore cannot be presumed to know the law. Quincy's *Commonplace* walked a fine line here. The chosen excerpts emphasized, on one hand, that "[M]atter of law shall never be put in the mouth of lay gents"[165] and that "Tis ye property of ye Court, jus dicere [to speak the law]."[166] Even as to matters of pure fact, the court had some power. "[I]f ye Court do believe that ye Jury have given their verdict agt evid: they may order a new Trial," wrote Quincy, relying on Lilly's *Practical Register*; or *General Abridgment of the Law* (London, 1719), vol. 2, p. 605.[167] "[Y]e Court may direct ye Jury to find according to ye evidence."[168] "Matter in LAW *shall not be given in Evid: to ye Jury*, but ye other may demur upon it, for Lay Gents can not discuss matter in Law as it seems there, but it is not expressly adjudged there . . ."[169]

163. *Law Commonplace*, p. 44 [42].

164. *Id.*, p. 44 [42]. Quincy was using "equity" in the sense of "fairness." Juries were not used in "equity" cases, in the legal sense, such as "equity" cases in Chancery. See Jowitt, *supra*, pp. 724–26.

165. *Law Commonplace*, p. 58 [55].

166. *Id.*, p. 58 [55].

167. *Id.*, p. 50 [48].

168. *Id.*, p. 51 [49] (Lilly again).

169. *Id.*, p. 52 [50].

While Quincy dutifully selected and copied out the above passages, it quickly became clear that the issues, in practice, were much more problematic. Jurors had an obligation to go beyond "the naked fact only,"[170] "plain Truth + fact + common sense, + not political convenience far-fetch'd inference, or ingenious innuendo, being the proper object . . ."[171] Quincy goes on to quote one of his favorite books, Catharine Macaulay's (1731–1791) *The History of England from the Accession of James I to The Elevation of the House of Hanover* (1st ed., 1763–1765, London).[172] (Hereafter, "Macaulay's *History*.") "A privilege of the constitution of England . . . the jury [are] . . . judges of Law as well as fact . . . *The Court cannot refuse a General Verdict if the Jury will take the Law upon themselves*."[173] "The Jury may take the Law upon them if they will."[174]

Quincy attempted to resolve this tension as best he could. First, the jury, in the terms later invented by Wesley Newcomb Hohfeld, might have the power, but not the right, to go beyond the evidence. "[T]ho' ye evidence given be conclusive, yet ye Jury may find against it, + hazard ye attaint if *they please*."[175] Quincy also noted a case of Sir John Strange. "[T]he question . . . being merely a Point of Law, the ch: Justice told the Jury, they must find for the Debt. which they were very unwilling to do + therefore to prevent this going contrary to his opinion . . . suffer'd a Nonsuit."[176] The threat of attaint and the remedy of new trial left the jury's power intact, but, at least in theory, provided some check, although, as will be discussed later, attaint was obsolete by Quincy's time.

Further, certain issues were clearly reserved for the judges. "It is Province of the Justices to determine what the meaning of any word or sentence in an act of Parliament is."[177] In addition, "The Judges shall judge what is a reasonable Time . . ."[178] More problematic was the question of erasure, or forgery, in a document.

170. *Id.*, p. 46 [44] (emphasis in original).

171. *Id.*, p. 45 [43].

172. See *id.*, p. 51 [49], n. 6. A copy of Catharine Macaulay's *History* was in Quincy's estate at his death. See *Reports*, *Quincy Papers*, Volume 5, Appendix 9, item 230.

173. *Id.*, p. 51 [49] (emphasis in the original).

174. *Id.*, p. 44 [42].

175. *Id.*, p. 52 [50]. See also p. 44 [42] as to attaint, already an archaic remedy in Quincy's day. See William Blackstone, *Commentaries on the Laws of England* (Oxford, 1768), vol. 3, p. 404, pp. 389–93. Attaint at English law was abolished by the Juries Act, 1825, S. 60. See Jowitt, *supra*, p. 114.

176. *Law Commonplace*, p. 44 [42].

177. *Id.*, p. 44 [42].

178. *Id.*, p. 44 [42].

> Of ancient Time if a Deed appear'd to be erased or interlined in Places material, the Judges adjudged upon their view; the Deed to be void: But of latter Times, the Judges have left that to the Jurors to try wether [*sic*] the rasing or interlining were before the Delivery.[179]

In tackling these serious problems, Quincy turned to authorities that demonstrated that he was still updating his *Law Commonplace* on important subjects as late as 1772. Quincy notes, "See the question—whether juries are Judges of Law as well as fact treated in a masterly manner by the authors of 'Considerations on Criminal Law' (p. 128 of that work) Reviewed in the Monthly Review May 1772 page 471, 472 etc." [H. Dagge, *Considerations on Criminal Law* (London, 1772) 3 vols.]. Then follows an extensive quotation from Sir John Maynard's (1602–1690) argument in *Skinner's Case*, as recorded by Anchitell Grey's *Debates of the House of Commons* (1667–1694) (London, 1769) see page [56], note 3, *infra*. This argument is copied in the *Commonplace* in a noticeably different script, but probably still Quincy's.

Maynard's argument challenged any judicial review of a jury judgment, except on matters of law, narrowly construed:

> Every judgment is established on two things of which the judge must have a care, vizt the Verity of the fact & what the law is upon such fact; ex facto jus oritur ["the law becomes operative after the fact"] now by the constitutions of the Law of England, the trial of the fact is in one hand, & the determination of the Law by judges sworn. The judge may not try the fact, nor the juror the Law, but at their extreme peril: for by the Common-Law, the jurors, if they give a false verdict, under went the villanous judgment vizt to have their houses raised, lands wasted, meadows plowed, woods felled, body imprisoned, & infamy perpetual never to be credited more.[180]

Maynard eloquently argued that this delicate balance be unreviewable on appeal, except in the most blatant circumstances:

> But by this way of proceeding before your Lordships, all these advantages are lost; for the trial of fact & of Law, the office of the judge & juror, are confounded. There is no challenge or exception that can be taken to any of the Lords tho' one or more of them be enemies, or friends or allies to either party, or engaged by opinion or solicitation, or interest in the cause, of all these together, or any other; for tho' a juror may be challenged, a Judge cannot.[181]

179. *Id.*, p. 45 [43].
180. *Id.*, p. 60 [57] (emphasis in original).
181. *Id.*, p. 61 [58] (emphasis in original).

Quincy's *Law Commonplace*, of course, is just a collection of legal statements copied from largely English authorities. While the selections were carefully made, they tell us more about colonial legal education than the actual state of the law—something that would be true of law student notes today! Further, like my old notebook from my Boston legal practice, the *Law Commonplace* was designed to provide Quincy with convincing arguments on both sides of potential issues—the selection to depend on the client's interests. My distinguished colleague, Adriaan Lanni, has emphasized to me that most surviving sources of ancient Athenian law consist of "court speeches," arguing one side or the other. This leaves the actual "Rule" of law to be determined.[182] Thus with Quincy's *Law Commonplace*. But, for reasons every practicing lawyer can appreciate, these sources define the orbit of the arguable law. Further, Quincy's *Reports* are evidence of the actual law of the colony, and show how Quincy, quite sensibly, combined "book learning" with direct observation. The *Reports* frequently verified the impression left by the *Law Commonplace*. The resulting picture was of a pragmatic, not a dogmatic, world.

This was certainly true with the controversies over jury trial. No less than six cases in Quincy's *Reports* involve jury trials. Four focus on the power of the jury, and two on conditions of jury service.

One of the issues emphasized in the *Law Commonplace* was whether alteration of a document was a question of law for the judge, or a question of fact for a jury. In *Norwood* v. *Fairservice*, Case 47 (1765), *Reports*, pp. 189–93, the plaintiff produced an indenture for £13.68 *per* quarter rent, and the defendant produced the other half of the indenture for £13.68 *per* year, a big difference! It was argued by Gridley and Samuel Fitch for the plaintiff that "it had always been the Custom of this Court" to determine the legal effect "in such Cases." Robert Auchmuty replied for the defense:

> *Mr. Auchmuty*. I take it, the Gentleman is too early in his Objection; for Fraud or no Fraud shall be try'd by the Jury, and not by the Court. It is a plain Matter of Fact, of which the Jury are the sole Judges. Besides, of what Advantage will it be for the Court to determine this Matter? The Jury, after all, will determine whether this Variance was made before, or since the Execution of this Deed; and will give what Credit they please to it: so that for this Court to pass

182. See Adriaan Lanni, "Verdict Most Just: The Modes of Classical Athenian Justice," 16 *Yale Journal of Law & the Humanities* 227 (2004).

> their Judgment will avail Nothing. Neither do I think the Court have any Right to determine this Matter; for 'twill be abridging the Priviledges of the Subject, to settle a Point which wholly lies with the Jury to determine.[183]

As the *Commonplace* indicated, it was a close question. The justices split on the issue.

> *Just. Oliver* This properly belongs to the Jury. I am for admitting it to go in.
> *Just. Cushing* The Jury is sole Judge of this; they must give what Credit they please.
> *Just. Lynde* As the Practice of this Court has always been otherwise, I am for viewing it.
> *Ch. Justice* I know the Custom has been otherwise, but, for my Part, I think 'tis Time it was altered—am for admitting it.[184]

The counterpart of the Indenture ultimately went to the jury.[185]

An even tougher issue was presented by a case where the word "or" had been omitted on a note. The note obliged the promisor "to pay Plaintiff *Order*" instead of "to pay Plaintiff *or* Order." Was this promissory note negotiable? And was that a factual or legal issue? Auchmuty argued that this was a question for the jury.

> *Mr. Auchmuty*. The Note is, to pay Plaintiff *Order*: The *or* is left out. Where a Note is nonsensical we are not obliged to follow it. There can be no Doubt but whether this is Evidence to a Jury or not. In Favour of Justice doubtless it is.[186]

The Court permitted the case to go to the jury, but on a different issue.

> *The Court ruled*, that the Note should go in as Evidence, on another Point.* That, as the Note *had not been indorsed*, the Omission of *Order* was immaterial—*otherwise* had it been indorsed.
>
> *Ch. Juft*. did not give his Opinion.[187]

The Chief Justice's abstention was meaningful. In *Russell* v. *Oakes*, Case 21 (1763), *Reports*, p. 49 it had been held, over his dissent, that there was no difference between a negotiable and non-negotiable note until it was endorsed.[188]

183. *Reports*, pp. 189–90.
184. *Id.*, p. 191.
185. *Id.*, p. 193.
186. *Id.*, p. 118.
187. *Id.*, p. 118.
188. *Id.*, p. 50.

An even more fundamental issue, emphasized several times in the *Law Commonplace*, was whether a jury had the power to "give a verdict against the Evidence," or whether the judge may grant a new trial to avoid injustice. In *Angier* v. *Jackson*, Case 31 (1763) *Reports*, p. 84, Auchmuty argued that there was no right to a new trial in that case because there was evidence to support the jury verdict, and observed that:

> The Court is not to be Judge of the Law and Fact too absolutely; if it should be, it takes away all Verdicts but such as are agreeable to the Mind of the Court. It would be opening a Door to great Inconveniences to the Subject, even if Attaints did not lie; but here Attaint lies.[189]

The Court was split again as to the scope of review, but decided against a new trial in this case.

> *Ch. Justice.* Are you not agreed that, were it evidently against Law and Evidence, there the Court may grant a new Trial, but not where there is Evidence on both Sides.
>
> *Trowbridge.* It can never be supposed that a Verdict will be given against direct Evidence, without Shadow of Evidence to support it. This differs from the Case of *Fuller & Clark* at Cambridge—there was plainly Evidence against Evidence. I hold, this Court always have Right to grant new Trials when they think Injustice like to be done.
>
> *Justices Oliver, Cushing, Russell & Lynde* against a new Trial, because the Court were not clear in the former Trial.[190]

Thus, the ambiguity in the *Law Commonplace*, which sets out arguments for and against a wide scope for jury power, accurately reflected the law of the colony. By 1763, the only effective control over a jury was a new trial. Despite Auchmuty's argument, the deterrence of attaint had become obsolete by 1763. See Samuel M. Quincy's note 3, *Reports*, p. 85, and William Blackstone, *Commentaries on the Laws of England*, vol. 3 (1st ed., Oxford, 1768), pp. 389–93. "[A]ttaint is now as obsolete as the trial by battle which it succeeded: and we shall probably see the revival of the one as soon as the revival of the other." *Id.*, p. 389. Under these conditions, tensions over the power of the jury were inevitable, and important.

189. *Id.*, p. 85. But attaint was an archaic remedy by this time. See n. 175, *supra*, and text below, *infra*.

190. *Id.*, p. 85.

The power of the jury was certainly a centerpiece of both the *Law Commonplace* and the *Reports*, and *Angier* v. *Jackson* continues to be relevant to major modern constitutional cases about the scope of the Seventh Amendment right to jury trial and the "Reexamination Clause" of the Seventh Amendment.[191] ("[N]o fact tried by a jury, shall be otherwise re-examined in any Court of the United States, than according to the rules of the common law.") The "rules of the common law," of course, must refer to those in effect in 1791, the date of the Seventh Amendment, and there are few American sources on this important issue as authoritative as Quincy.[192]

The *Law Commonplace* also focused on *how* the jury found facts. To begin, unlike a modern jury, the jury of Quincy's day could rely on their own sources and knowledge. This, of course, increased their power even more, because even if no evidence was presented in court, they could still bring in a verdict supported by evidence, their *own* knowledge. Quincy noted, citing *Plowden's Commentaries* (London, 1522), "The Jury may give their verdict without testimony, or against testimony, when they themselves have cognisance of ye fact."[193]

But this could clearly lead to abuses. First, Quincy noted that "If a Jury give a verdict on their own knowledge, they ought to tell ye Court so . . ."[194] Why? So that the lawyers on both sides would have a chance to examine such knowledge "openly in Court."[195]

> If any one of ye Jury, that is sworn to try ye issue, be desired to give his testimony concerning some matter of fact, that lies in his own knowledge, + con-

191. The issue was recently revisited by the Supreme Court of the United States in *Gasperini* v. *Center for Humanities, Inc.*, 518, U.S. 415 (1996). This author, together with a group of legal scholars including Akhil Reed Amar, Erwin Chemerinsky, Arthur F. McEvoy, and Arthur R. Miller, filed an amicus brief supporting the power of the jury at common law. The majority of the court were unconvinced, but a powerful dissent by Justice Scalia, joined by Chief Justice Rehnquist and Justice Thomas, observed that "the court frankly abandons any pretense at faithfulness to the common law, suggesting that 'the meaning' of the Reexamination Clause was not 'fixed at 1791,' contrary to the view of all our prior discussions . . ." 518 U.S. 415, at 461 (citation omitted). See Coquillette, "*Law Reports*," Quincy, *Works*, vol. 4.

192. See *id.*, at pp. 12–15. See also David L. Shapiro & Daniel R. Coquillette, "The Fetish of Jury Trial in Civil Cases: A Comment on *Rachal* v. *Hill*," 85 *Harv. L. Rev.* 442, pp. 228–55 (1971), cited with approval in *Parklane Hosiery Co.* v. *Shore*, 439 U.S. 322, 333, arguing 1791 as the appropriate date for assessing common law jury rights for Seventh Amendment purposes.

193. *Law Commonplace*, p. 51 [49]. See *id.*, p. 51 [49], n. 8 on *Plowden's Commentaries.*

194. *Law Commonplace*, p. 50 [48].

195. *Id.*, p. 50 [48].

> cerns the matter in Q:on [Question], as evid: to his fellow-jurors, ye Court will have him examined openly in Court upon his oath, touching his knowledge therein, + he is not to deliver his testimony in private to his fellow-jurors; for ye Court + Council on both parts are to hear the evidence given on either side as well as ye Jury, that it may be answered by ye other party, if need require, + that ye Court may direct ye Jury to find according to ye evidence.[196]

Quincy's *Reports* do not shed further light on the practical functioning of a jury, except for two cases indicating that jury service could be a hardship. In *Reed's Case*, Case 67 (1772), *Reports*, pp. 331–32, a member of the standing Grand Jury for a county was exempted from service as a trial juror. In *The Petition of the Jurors in the Truth of Captain Preston and the British Soldiers*, Case 71 (1771), *Reports*, pp. 382–86, a "reasonable Allowance" for jurors who served in the Boston Massacre Cases, "said Preston's Trial holding six Days, and said Soldiers nine Days, said Jurys being kept together every Night by two or more Officers" was unanimously denied for lack of statutory authority.[197]

2. OF JUDGES AND LEGISLATURES

Second only to Quincy's focus on juries (10 pages) was his concern with the construction of legislation (9 pages).[198] Of course, both could be constraints on judicial power, and both were highly controversial in Quincy's world (as they still are in our world). In addition to the inherent "turf" issues of division of power, there were also troubling questions of whether Parliamentary statutes should be given full effect in the colonies, and how to resolve apparent conflicts between colonial legislation and established English common law, particularly given the "repugnancy" clause of the Charter.[199]

To make matters even more subtle, Quincy linked his section "Of Statutes or Acts" to another 5-page section, "Of Laws." The latter section, relying extensively on Montesquieu's *L'Esprit des Lois* (1748), looks at the "different orders of laws" in which domestic civil law is only one. Montesquieu (1689–1755), based on his study of Locke and other English sources, developed an early theory of separation of powers, with separate roles for the legislature and the judiciary. His "orders of laws" superficially resemble Roman law cat-

196. *Id.*, p. 51 [49], Relying on *Lilly's Abridgment* (London, 1719). See *id.*, p. 50 [48], n. 3.
197. See *Reports, supra*, pp. 382–83, 385.
198. See "Of Statutes or Acts," *Law Commonplace*, pp. 89 [77]–97 [85].
199. See Bilder, *supra*, pp. 2–7, 40–46, 55, 104–07.

egories, but are more subtle and complex. For example, for the Romans, "natural law," *jus naturale*, was really a law of nature, like the rules of physics. Montesquieu's natural law, on the other hand, combined the laws of natural science with "the law of God" of the neo-Thomists and the law of reason of the Enlightenment. Quincy carefully extracted and copied these passages.

> The Laws of Nature derive y^{r} force entirely from our frame + being, + therefore so call'd.
>
> The law wch by imprinting on our minds ye idea of a creator inclines us to Him, is ye first in importance, tho' not in order, of natural Laws.
>
> Peace is ye first Law of Nature. Another Law of Nature prompts to seek Nourishment. The attraction arising from ye Difference of Sexes, + ye natural inclination they have for each other, form a third Law.
>
> A fourth Law of Nature arises from the Desire of living in Society. Ib. ch: 2.[200]

Quincy also copied in excerpts from Jean Jacques Burlamaqui (1694–1748), professor of natural law at Geneva and another Enlightenment jurist. His views of "natural law" were even more rationalist than Montesquieu.

> By natural Law we understand, a law that God imposes on all men, + wch they are able to discover + know by the sole light of Reason, + by attentively considering their state + Nature.
>
> Natural Law is likewise taken for the system, assemblage, or Body of the Laws of Nature.
>
> Burlamaqui's Poin: Nat^{l} Law. p. 126.[201]

Theories of statutory construction and natural law were hardly "academic" in Quincy's world. The Stamp Act of 1765 brought all these issues to the fore, only two years after Quincy began the *Law Commonplace*.[202] Quincy's *Reports* contain the challenges to the Stamp Act in the *Memorial of Boston* of December 18, 1765, in which Enlightenment "natural law" arguments featured prominently. As John Adams began:

> There are certain Principles fixed unalterably in Nature. Convention and Compact are the Requisites to make any Law obligatory. That the Subject is

200. *Law Commonplace*, p. 64 [60]. Montesquieu also was extracted in Quincy's *Political Commonplace*. See *Quincy Papers*, vol. 1, p. 109.

201. *Id.*, p. 65 [61].

202. See John C. Miller, *Origins of the American Revolution* (Stanford, rev. printing, 1959), pp. 109–46.

> not bound by Acts, when he is not represented, is a found Maxim of the Law, and not peculiar to the British Constitution, but a Maxim of the antient Roman Law: "What concerns All shall be judged by All."[203]

James Otis Jr., further argued:

> "The Laws which forbid a Man to pursue his Right one way, ought to be understood with this equitable Restriction, *that one finds Judges to whom he may apply*. When there are no Courts of Law to appeal to, it is then we must have Recourse to the Law of Nature," &c. Hugo Grotius, *de Jure B. & P.* Lib. 1, C. 3 §2. Lib. 2, C. 4 §9. C. 7 §2, n. 2. C. 20 §2, p. 4 & 5, with Mr. Barbeyrac's Notes. Code, Lib. 1, Tit. 9, *De Jud. & Cal.*[204]

Montesquieu added at least two more "orders" of law to which colonists could appeal against the Stamp Act. These were carefully recorded by Quincy in the *Law Commonplace*. The first "order" was based on the old Roman *jus gentium*, the "Law of Nations." As Quincy noted, citing to Thomas Hobbes's (1588–1679) *De Cive* (1642).

> The Law of Nations, properly so called, + consider'd as a law proceeding from a superior, is nothing else, but the Law of Nature itself, not applied to men consider'd simply as such; but to Nations or States. Ibid. p. 195. Says Hobbes very justly, is divided into the natural Law of Man, + the natural Law of States; + the latter is what we call the Law of Nations.
>
> De Civi. Cap. 14 p. 4.[205]

The second "order" was unknown to Roman law. Montesquieu divided the Roman "Law of Nations," the "*ius civile*," into two parts. First there was the "Politic law," the "Laws relative to ye Govenors + ye governed; + this we call *Politic Law*."[206] Then there was "another set of laws relating to the mutual communication of citizens; by which is understood ye *Civil Law*."[207]

Both "the Law of Nations" and the "Politic Law" were invoked in the Stamp Act arguments of the *Memorial of Boston*. James Otis, who Quincy reported "opened with Tears," appealed both to the "Law of Nations" and the fundamental "Politic Law" of the realm.

203. *Reports*, p. 201.
204. *Id.*, p. 204.
205. *Law Commonplace*, p. 65 [61].
206. *Id.*, p. 64 [60].
207. *Id.*, p. 65 [61].

My Brother Adams has entered so largely into the Validity of the Act, that I shall not enlarge on that Head. Indeed, what has been observed is sufficient to convince the most illiterate Savage that the Parliament of England had no Regard to the very first Principles of their own Liberties.

Only the Preamble of that oppressive Act is enough to rouse the Blood of every generous Briton—"We your Majesty's Subjects, the Commons of Great Britain, &c., do Give and Grant"—What? Their own Property? No! The Treasure, the Heart's Blood of all your Majesty's dutiful and affectionate British-American Subjects.

But the Time is far spent—I will not tire your Patience. It was once a fundamental Maxim, that every Subject had the same Right to his Life, Liberty, Property and the *Law*, that the King had to his Crown; and 'tis yet, I venture to say, as much as a Crown is worth, to deny the Subject his *Law*, which is his Birth-right. 'Tis a first Principle, "that Majesty should not only shine in Arms, but be armed with the Laws." The *Administration* of Justice is necessary to the very Existence of Governments. Nothing can warrant the stopping the Courte of Justice, but the impossibility of holding Courts, by Reason of War, Invasion, Rebellion or Insurrections.* 1 Inft. 249, a & b. This was Law at a Time when the whole Island of Great Britain was divided into an infinite Number of petty Baronies and Principalities; as Germany is, at this Day. Insurrections then, and even Invasions, put the whole Nation into such Confusion, that Justice could not have her equal Course; especially as the Kings in antient Times frequently sat as Judges. But War has now become so much of a Science, and give so little Disturbance to a Nation engaged, that no War, foreign or domestic, is a sufficient Reason for shutting up the Courts. But, if it were, we are not in such a State, but far otherwise; the whole People being willing and demanding the full Administration of Government. Vid. Bracton, 240.[208]

Otis concluded with an appeal to the *Magna Carta* (1215), the core of English "Politics Law."

The King is always presumed to be present in his Courts, holding out the Law to his Subjects; and when he shuts his Courts, he unkings himself in the most essential Point. 18 E. 3, ch. 1. 1 H. 4 20 E. 3, ch. 2 4 H 4. ch. 1. Vattel, p. 20. And Magna Charta, and the other Statutes are full, "That they will not defer, delay or deny to any Man Justice or Right." "That is shall not be commanded *Charta*, it is said we deny no Man Justice, we delay no Man Justice. 2 Inft. ch. 29, p. 56 (1).[209]

208. *Reports*, pp. 203–04. Otis's "first principle" was a translation of the opening of Justinian's *Institutes*, also quoted at the outset of the great English treatise, *Bracton*.

209. *Id.*, pp. 205–06.

All of this was present in Quincy's *Law Commonplace*, section "Of Laws." This cannot help but impress us today. Just look at the breadth of the selections, starting with Montesquieu, but extending to Burlamaqui, Vattel, Hobbes, Beccaria, and Bacon, giants of the Renaissance and the Enlightenment. These were companions on Quincy's bookcase![210]

But Quincy's familiarity with the technical side of statutory interpretation was also impressive. This, too, was featured in both the *Law Commonplace* and his *Reports*. The section in the *Law Commonplace*, "Of Statutes or Acts," was cross-referenced to "Of Laws," as well as to Quincy's Preface to the *Law Commonplace* and to excerpts to Richard Burn's *Ecclesiastical Law* (London, 1760), set out in Quincy's Notebook 4, at page 101 (P347, Reel 4, QP58). There was a heavy emphasis on the "four factors" enunciated by Edward Coke in *Heydon's Case* (1584), 3 *Coke's Reports*, p. 7a, at 7b.

> For the sure + true interpretation of all statutes in general (be they penal or beneficial, restrictive or enlarging of the Com. Law,) four things are to be discern'd + consider'd. 1. What was the Common Law before the making of the Act. 2. What was the mischief + defect for which the Common Law did not provide. 3. What remedy the Parliament hath resolved + appointed to cure the decease of the CommonWealth. And 4. the true reason + remedy. 3 Rep. 7. b.[211]

At least in his early career, Coke took a "contextualist" view of statutes and this, of course, gave common law judges a very decisive role to play, particularly as to the "true reason and remedy."[212]

In addition, there was the common law doctrine of "Equity of the Statute." Here Quincy uncharacteristically relied on Blackstone's *Analysis of the Laws of England* (Oxford, 1756).[213]

> To interpret a Law, we must inquire after the will of the Maker: which may be collected either from the words, the context, the subject-matter, the effects + consequences, or the spirit + reason of the Law.

210. See *Law Commonplace*, p. 63 [59], n. 2, (Montesquieu); p. 65 [61], n. 2, (Burlamaqui); p. 65 [61], n. 4, (Hobbes); p. 65 [61], n. 5, (Vattel); p. 67 [63], n. 2, (Bacon) and (Beccaria); p. 67 [63], n. 3.

211. *Id.*, p. 89 [77].

212. *Id.*, p. 89 [77].

213. See discussion at notes 37 and 46, *supra*.

> From the latter method of interpretation arises EQUITY, or the correction of that wherein the Law (by reason of its universality) is deficient.
>
> Blackstone's Anal. B. 1. ch 2. p 3.[214]

"Equity of the Statute" asks what the legislators would have done if confronted with a situation unanticipated by the drafting or the policy of the statute.

> The preamble of a statute is like a key to open the intent of the makers of the Act; and as it is deem'd true, good Arguments may be drawn from it. But the best way to explain a statute is to consider what answer the Lawgivers wou'd probably have given to the question made, if propos'd to them.[215]

Again, relying heavily on Coke, Quincy noted that words of a statute should be construed to promote consistency within the statute, and "must be taken in a law full + rightful sense."[216] "That construction must be made of a statute in suppression of the mischief, and in advancement of the remedy."[217]

While nothing in Quincy's *Law Commonplace* suggested the judicial review of Marshall's *Marbury* v. *Madison* (1803),[218] or even the *dicta* of *Dr. Bonham's Case* (1610),[219] the doctrines of contextual interpretation and "Equity of the Statute" could, in practice, give the judiciary a powerful role, as Coke intended. Quincy also seemed aware of the dangers of too much "equity of intendment."[220] In theory, "Equity of the Statute" was not a substitution of the views of the judge for the legislator, but solely the perfection of the legislator's will by remedying oversights. Where statutes are penal, or "made in *any* right of the subject," they should be "strictly construed" to prevent unanticipated harm.[221] Quincy also copied a section from *Bedell* v. *Constable*, *Vaughan's Reports* (London, 1677) that "[w]hen an acts alters the Common Law, the

214. *Law Commonplace*, p. 89 [77].
215. *Id.*, p. 91 [79].
216. *Id.*, p. 91 [79].
217. *Id.*, p. 91 [79].
218. 5 U.S. (1 branch) 137 (1803) (Marshall, C. J.)
219. 8 *Coke's Reports* (London, 1611), p. 114a. Coke suggested "that in many cases, the Common Law will control Acts of Parliament, and sometimes adjudge them to be utterly void. . . ." *Id.*, p. 118a. See Daniel R. Coquillette, *The Anglo-American Legal Heritage* (2d ed., Durham, N.C.), pp. 318–19, 342. See also S. E. Thorne, "Dr. Bonham's Case," 54 *L.Q. Rev.* 543–52 (1938); C. M. Gray, "Barnham's Case Revisited," (1972) 116 *Proc. American Philosophical Society*, pp. 35–58 and T. F. T. Plucknett, "Bonham's Case and Judicial Review," *Studies in English Legal History* (London, 1985), pp. 33–70.
220. *Law Commonplace*, p. 93 [81].
221. *Id.*, p. 93 [81].

meaning shall not be strain'd beyond words, except in cases of publick utility, when the end of the act appears to be larger than the words themselves."[222]

Some of Quincy's excerpts seem directly contradictory, such as the section from *Hobart's Reports* (1641), "Judges have liberty + authority over statutes to mould them to the truest + best use, according to reason + best use, according to reason + best convenience,"[223] and the immediately following selection from Beccaria, especially emphasized by Quincy, with a special caption, "The Danger of Considering ye Spirit of Laws":

> There is nothing more dangerous, than the common axioms: <u>the spirit of the laws is to be considered</u>. To adopt it is to give way to the torrent of opinion. This may seem a paradox to vulgar minds, which are more strongly affected by the smallest disorder before their eyes, than by the most pernicious, tho' remote, consequences produced by one false principle adopted by a nation. Marquis Beccaria's Essay on Crimes + punishments. p. 15, 6. quod vide.[224]

Beccaria, coming from a civilian tradition, might be expected to have more deference to the letter of the code or statute, but the excerpt was followed by another from *Entick* v. *Carrington* (1765), *Wilson's Reports*, p. 290, where the issue was whether a statute should be expansively read to permit a search warrant by the Secretary of State, rather than a constable.

> When ye code of laws is once fixed, it should be observed in ye literal sense, + nothing more is left to ye judge, than to determine, whether an action be, or be not conformable to the written Law. When the rule of right which ought to direct the actions of the philosopher, as well as the ignorant, is a matter of controversy, not a fact, the people are slaves to the magistrates. Ibid. 16. 17. The best way to construe <u>modern</u> statutes is to follow ye words thereof. Per Cur: Wilson's Rep: 290. Entick v. Carrington[225]

Quincy's choice of extracts was not random. He seemed keenly aware both of how a too rigid application of statutes can cause unnecessary injustice, and how a too expansive interpretation can cause surprise and can prejudice preexisting rights. In addition, as noted before, the *Law Commonplace* was designed to give Quincy authority to argue either side of a contentious case,

222. *Id.*, p. 93 [81] (almost an exact quote).
223. *Id.*, p. 95 [83].
224. *Id.*, p. 95 [83] (emphasis in original).
225. *Id.*, p. 96 [84] (emphasis in original).

depending on the client. In addition, at the close of the "Statutes or Acts" section, he also exhibited some critical judgment. Quincy challenges Sir George Treby's argument in *Horton* v. *Ruerby* that he knew "the intention of the Parliament" because "he was present at ye making ye statute . . ."[226]

> [Quincy] How ye intention of Parliament can be rightly discovered in this way: unless ye informant knew absolutely <u>what determined the concurrence</u> of <u>Each</u> branch of ye Legislature:—qu: w[hether] y^{e} is possible to be known: —and qu: of ye Consequences of their mode of determin:g + judging of ye intent of Law-makers, and Qu: etc.[227]

In this Quincy anticipated the jurisprudence of Lon Fuller, and others, who regarded the "legislative intent" argument for judicial construction as a transparent fiction.[228]

Quincy's *Law Commonplace* certainly reflected the actual local arguments in court on statutory construction. *Derumple* v. *Clark,* Case 17 (1763), *Reports*, p. 38, contemporary with the start of the *Law Commonplace*, was a classic example. The "Province Law called the Tax Act," the annual tax act passed each year in Massachusetts, had for years contained the following language, "where no Contract is, the Landlord shall reimburse the Tenant half the Taxes."[229] Here there was no contract, the tenant had paid the tax, and sued the landlord for half. Quincy's pupil master, Oxenbridge Thacher, argued for the defendant landlord.

> *Mr. Thacher, for Defendant.* It has been the uninterrupted Custom of this Town for the Tenant to pay the whole Taxes, and though this Law is of very antient Date, (3) we find no Action on it till 1752; so that it always supposed that such a Contract is made. The Words of the Law are not—where no express—no written—no verbal—but "where *no Contract is.*" And I think the continual paying Rent for several Years without any Demand of Deduction, and several Receipts having been given by the Plaintiff to the Defendant in full of all Accounts, are full Evidence that such was the Intention and Meaning of the Parties, which is a sufficient Contract. To have this Point called in Question would be big with the greatest Inconveniences. If Landlords who from

226. *Id.*, p. 97 [85].
227. *Id.*, p. 97 [85] (emphasis in original).
228. See Fuller's classical parable of statutory construction and application, "The Case of the Speluncean Explorers," 62 *Harv. L. Rev.* 616 (1949).
229. *Reports*, p. 38.

> Year to Year have received their whole Rents, and given Discharges for them, are to be called to account for many Years' Taxes, it would be productive of an ample Harvest of Suits, of which perhaps our Brotherhood might reap the Gleanings.[230]

Auchmuty, for the plaintiff tenant, replied:

> *Mr. Auchmuty.* As to the Custom of the Town; if there had been no Law, that might have been an Argument of some Weight; but the Law is express, and shall any pretended Custom control it? As for the Consequences they must not be considered—if it is Law, it is Law, &c.[231]

Despite the plain words of the statute, the court held for the defendant. Justice Benjamin Lynde Jr. observed:

> *Justice Lynde.* I always thought that the Intention of this Law was not to affect the Taxes in such Towns as this, but merely where Farms are let to the Halves, where the Benefit of the Estate being divided, 'tis but just the Charges should be divided too. I think the Custom of the Town is a great Thing, and that the Parties are to be supposed to intend according to the Custom. I think the Evidence sufficient to prove a Contract within the Intendment of the Law.[232]

Perhaps even more striking, Chief Justice Hutchinson appealed to "Equity." Here there was no evidence in the *Reports* of legislative intention, i.e., "Equity of the Statute." This was pure "judicial" equity, i.e., judicial "discretion"!

> *Ch. Just.* You are to go according to Law and Evidence Where the Law is in any Case doubtfull and the Equity of it plain, you should verge towards Equity. Custom shall not be placed in Opposition to Law, but it may be a Circumstance going to interpret the Intention of the Parties.[233]

An even more important case was *Bishop* v. *Brig Freemason*, Case 78 (1763), *Reports*, p. 387, an Admiralty case before Admiralty Judge Chambers Russell. Here the question focused on the word "importation" as used in the Act of 15 Car. 2, c. 7, §6, which stated:

> No Commodity of the Growth, Production or Manufacture of Europe shall be imported into any Land, Island, Plantation, Colony, Territory, or Place to His Majesty belonging in *Asia, Africa, or America,* (*Tangier* only excepted) but

230. *Id.*, pp. 38–39.
231. *Id.*, p. 39.
232. *Id.*, p. 40.
233. *Id.*, pp. 40–41.

what all be *bona fide* and "without Fraud laden and shipped in *England*, *Wales* or the Town of *Berwick* upon *Tweed*, and in *English* built Shipping.[234]

The *Freemason* had been seized, loaded with French wine, entering Boston harbor. The wine had not been unloaded, and the Master claimed that the ship "came from Bourdeaux being bound to St. Eustatia," with no intent to land the wine. Was there "importation"? Auchmuty argued for the validity of the seizure.

> Whether she [the Brig *Freemason*] is within the Meaning of this Act, which is for the Encouragement of Trade: What the Trade is that is to be encouraged, Sec. 5 shews: It is to render Great Britain the Staple. The only sensible Meaning of Importation is *Bringing in*, exclusive of Landing. 13&14 Car. 2, ch. 13 shews this ought to be the Construction. In the same Sense 'tis taken in 13 & 14 Car. 2, ch. 19, and in 13 & 14, Car. 2, ch. 11, §§22, 23, and in 22 & 23 Car. 2, ch. 26. From these Acts, I think it was evident that *Bringing in* is all they meant by Importation, as all these Acts use the Words. The Statute 6 Geo. 2, ch. 13, §§2 & 3, makes a Distinction between Landing and Importing: They designed to make a Distinction between Goods that are customable, and not forfeited till Landing, and those which, begin prohibited, are forfeited by bare Importation. If these Laws should be otherwise construed, they would be completely evaded.—For, if they have not a fair Opportunity of *Running*, they will *Report*. The Consequences of this Act to any particular Plantation cannot now be considered. There is a great Difference between Goods that may be imported and pay a Duty, and those which are absolutely prohibited.[235]

Oxenbridge Thacher, Quincy's pupil master, argued for the Brig *Freemason*:

> Let us consider whether it comes within the Letter of this Act. If any Vessell approaches or comes into a Port, without any Intent to unload, shall her Cargo said to be imported? Can a Thing be said to be imported, because the Vessell that holds it comes into Port? What Mischief do they mean to suppress? 'Tis lawfull for us to be Carriers from one French Port to another. Shall then an English Vessell, Carrier for other Nations, leaking and wanting Provisions, with Liberty from the Owner to touch at an English Port for a few Days to procure Store, not be permitted to touch at such English Port? I challenge an Instance of a Seizure on this Act, till Landing or Bulk broken. Can it be said

234. *Id.*, pp. 387–88, n. 2. Auchmuty was suggesting that the *Freemason* was looking for an opportunity to smuggle the wine ashore, i.e., "running" as in "rum runner."
235. *Id.*, pp. 388–89.

> that this Stopping is the Mischief? 'Tis supplying the Colonies that is intended to be prevented. This will be still plainer from several Acts the Advocate has cited. 13 & 14 Car. 2, ch. 13 §2. The Meaning must still be the same.[236]

Not surprisingly, the Vice-Admiralty judge, "having heard Council for two whole days, gave his opinion that landing was not necessary to make an importation contrary to that Act," arguing that "effectually the Act would be defeated" if the contrary were true.[237] Whether Quincy assembled the section of his *Law Commonplace* on "Statutes or Acts" while assisting Thacher in this case cannot be known, but the *Brig Freemason* certainly illustrated why a colonist might favor a "strict construction" of statutory language! Even more impressive, ample authority for both sides of the argument was assembled in Quincy's *Law Commonplace*.

There were several more important statutory construction cases, not the least being the historic argument over the authority given by "Acts of 15 Car. 2 ch. 22 and 7 28 of Wm & Mary" in *Paxton's Case of the Writs of Assistance* Case 22 (1761) *Reports*, p. 51, and the question of whether the Statute of Frauds (1677) 29 Charles II, c. 3, was adopted in Massachusetts before the colony "made a like law here," Prov. St. 4 W. & M. (1692). These cases, and more, are discussed at length in the annotations to the *Reports*. But it is appropriate to close this discussion with a revealing sidelight of the Boston Massacre Cases of 1771, *The Petition of the Jurors in the Trials of Captain Preston and the British Soldiers* Case 77 (1771), *Reports*, p. 382. The issue was simple: did the "Act of 4 of W. & M. c. 12, (3)" provide authority for reimbursing the severely oppressed jurors for a six-day trial for Preston and a nine-day trial for the soldiers, "said Jurys being kept together every Night by two or more Officers"?[238]

The text of the Act reads as follows:

> The Act is intitled "An Act for the Settlement of the Bounds and defraying the PUBLICK and NECESSARY CHARGES *arising within each respective County* in this Province." "And for the due and equal *raising of Monies for defraying of the Charges arising within each respective County*, for the necessary Repairs and Amendments of Bridges, Prisons, the Maintenance of poor Pris-

236. *Id.*, pp. 390–91.
237. *Id.*, p. 393.
238. *Id.*, pp. 382–83.

oners, and ALL PROPER COUNTY CHARGES, It is enacted, that, when and so often as there shall be NEED OF RAISING MONEY FOR THE ENDS AFORESAID in any County, the Justices in Quarter Sessions for such County receiving Information thereof from the County Treasurer, shall agree and determine the whole Sum to be raised, &c., and issue their Order, &c., to assess the same upon the Inhabitants," &c.[239]

After "Debates at the Bar [that] took up the Day," the Justices (only Mr. Justice Dunbar doubting) were unanimously of Opinion that the Prayer of the Petition of the jurors should not be granted."[240] It can be justly doubted if this was a popular decision. Here Quincy interjected his own comments, printed in the *Boston Gazette*, Monday, May 20, 1771, confirming the impression given by his *Law Commonplace* that he distrusted what today we would call "judicial activism."

> It gives a most sensible Pleasure *in these Times* to find a Court of Justice deciding a *Point of Law* against an Extension of *their* Power: *especially*, as that Power would affect *the Purse of the Subject*—This Decision is of no small Moment; its Importance will appear more conspicuous upon a close Examen and Reflection. However, it is yet a Matter of deep Concern with some that the Superiour Court seem to entertain a different Opinion on the Point in Question. *They ordered a Recommendation of the Allowance to be made.* They are presumed to know the Law, and we are willing to suppose they would not *influence*, and *much less recommend* to a subordinate Court the Exertion of an illegal Power; a Power derogatory to the natural and primary Right of the Subject over his Property; and of the highest Consequence to the Community, considered in a separate or collective View.[241]

All in all, the sections "Of Laws" and "Of Statutes or Acts" in the *Law Commonplace* remain of great importance. When read, as intended, with Quincy's accompanying *Reports*, they testify eloquently to Quincy's legal ability, and the sophistication of his study.

239. *Id.*, p. 385.
240. *Id.*, p. 385.
241. *Id.*, p. 386 (emphasis in original). "Printed in the *Boston Gazette* (Edes & Gill) Monday, May 20, 1771."

IV. CONCLUSION

The topics just discussed only scratch the surface of what there is to learn from the *Law Commonplace*. For the economic historian, there are the extensive sections on "Insurance,"[242] "Notes,"[243] "Bills of Exchange,"[244] and "Arbitrament, Arbitrators & Award,"[245] which give an excellent sense of how business was actually done. For the proceduralist, a member of an esoteric tribe to which this editor belongs, there is a mass of information under captions from "Action,"[246] "Arrest,"[247] and "Attachment"[248] to "Tryal"[249] and "Variance."[250] What modern lawyers would call "Real Property" was represented by "Estates,"[251] "Freehold,"[252] "Joint Tenants,"[253] "Of Lands, Tenements or Hereditaments,"[254] "Lease, Lessor + Lessee,"[255] "Of Releases,"[256] and other captions. "Torts" was represented by "Account,"[257] "Battery,"[258] "Trespass,"[259] "Words Actionable or Not,"[260] and "Contract" by "Accord"[261] "Assumpsit"[262] "Obligation + Deed,"[263] and "Usury."[264] The entire modern law school curriculum, as envisioned by Joseph Story and structured by Christopher Columbus Langdell, can find its eighteenth-century counterpart in these

242. *Law Commonplace*, p. 42 [40].
243. *Id.*, p. 72 [64], *Legis Miscellanea*, p. 150 [93], p. 154 [97].
244. *Id.*, *Legis Miscellanea*, p. 154 [97].
245. *Id.*, p. 18 [23], p. 29 [33].
246. *Id.*, *Legis Miscellanea*, p. 153 [96], pp. 162 [105]–164 [107].
247. *Id.*, *Legis Miscellanea*, p. 153 [96].
248. *Id.*, p. 11 [16].
249. *Id.*, *Legis Miscellanea*, p. 158 [101].
250. *Id.*, *Legis Miscellanea*, pp. 152 [95]–158 [101].
251. *Id.*, p. 25 [30]. See also "Notebook 4," p. 5.
252. *Id.*, *Legis Miscellanea*, p. 170 [113].
253. *Id.*, *Legis Miscellanea*, p. 154 [97].
254. *Id.*, p. 47 [45].
255. *Id.*, p. 53 [51], *Legis Miscellanea*, p. 153 [96], p. 163 [106].
256. *Id.*, p. 81 [71].
257. *Id.*, *Legis Miscellanea*, p. 162 [105].
258. *Id.*, *Legis Miscellanea*, p. 167 [110].
259. *Id.*, p. 98 [86], *Legis Miscellanea*, pp. 166 [109]–167 [110].
260. *Id.*, p. 151 [94], p. 153 [96].
261. *Id.*, p. 12 [17].
262. *Id.*, *Legis Miscellanea*, pp. 158 [101], 167 [110], 170 [113].
263. *Id.*, *Legis Miscellanea*, pp. 150 [93]–151 [94], 153 [96]–154 [97], 157 [100], 159 [102], 161 [104], 163 [106], 166 [109].
264. *Id.*, *Legis Miscellanea*, p. 150 [93].

pages. Perhaps more to the point, today's practicing lawyer will find this a remarkably familiar world, and the *Law Commonplace* easily accessible.

At one level, Quincy's *Law Commonplace* was just a notebook full of extracts, largely from English sources, copied out by a still very young man. Quincy was just over nineteen when he began. But this was no ordinary young man, and these were not ordinary times. Many surviving "commonplace books" were truly "commonplace," but not this one. Quincy had a subtle and brilliant mind, and he created a powerful and unmistakable picture by this quilt of authorities and precedents. The *Law Commonplace* will never be as accessible to the layperson as Quincy's *Political Commonplace* or the *Southern Journal*, but it can tell us a great deal about the origins of American legal education and American law. It also tells us a great deal about the social and economic culture in which Quincy lived. Read together with Quincy's remarkable *Reports*, which will occupy the forthcoming volumes 4 and 5 of the *Quincy Papers*,[265] the *Law Commonplace* paints a surprisingly complete and nuanced picture of the legal world at the birth of our nation.

265. Volume 5, Appendix, will also contain the "Catalogue of Books Belonging to the Estate of Josiah Quincy Jun: Esq: Deceas'd" (1775), an exceptionally valuable reference given Quincy's sudden death in mid-career.

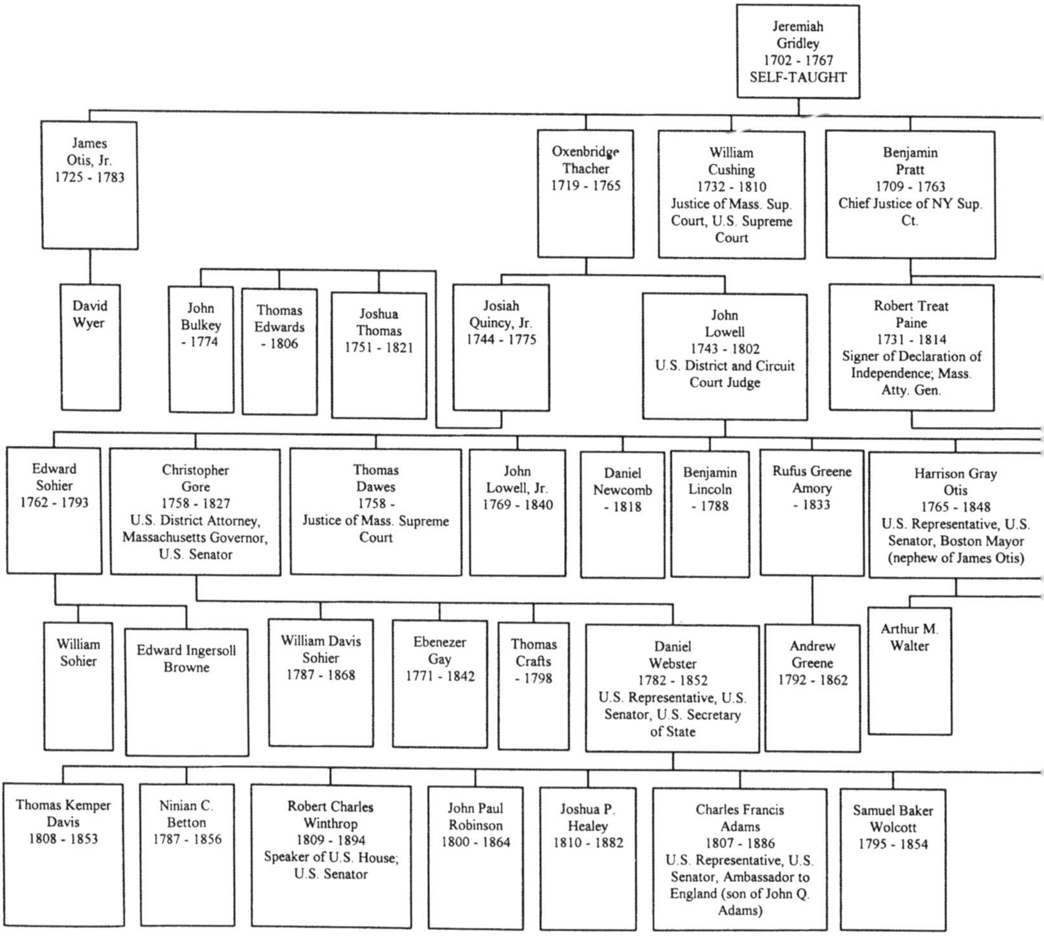

TABLE I. The accompanying chart was prepared by my brilliant research assistant, Kevin Willoughby Cox, using biographical resources including the *Professional and Industrial History of Suffolk County, Massachusetts*, Vol. 1, *History of the Bench and Bar*, by W. T. Davis (Boston, 1894), and later volumes of *Sibley's Harvard Graduates*, variously compiled by Clifford K. Shipton, Conrad Edick Wright and Edward W. Hanson (Cambridge, 1933–). Focusing on the first "Dean" of the Boston bar, Jeremiah

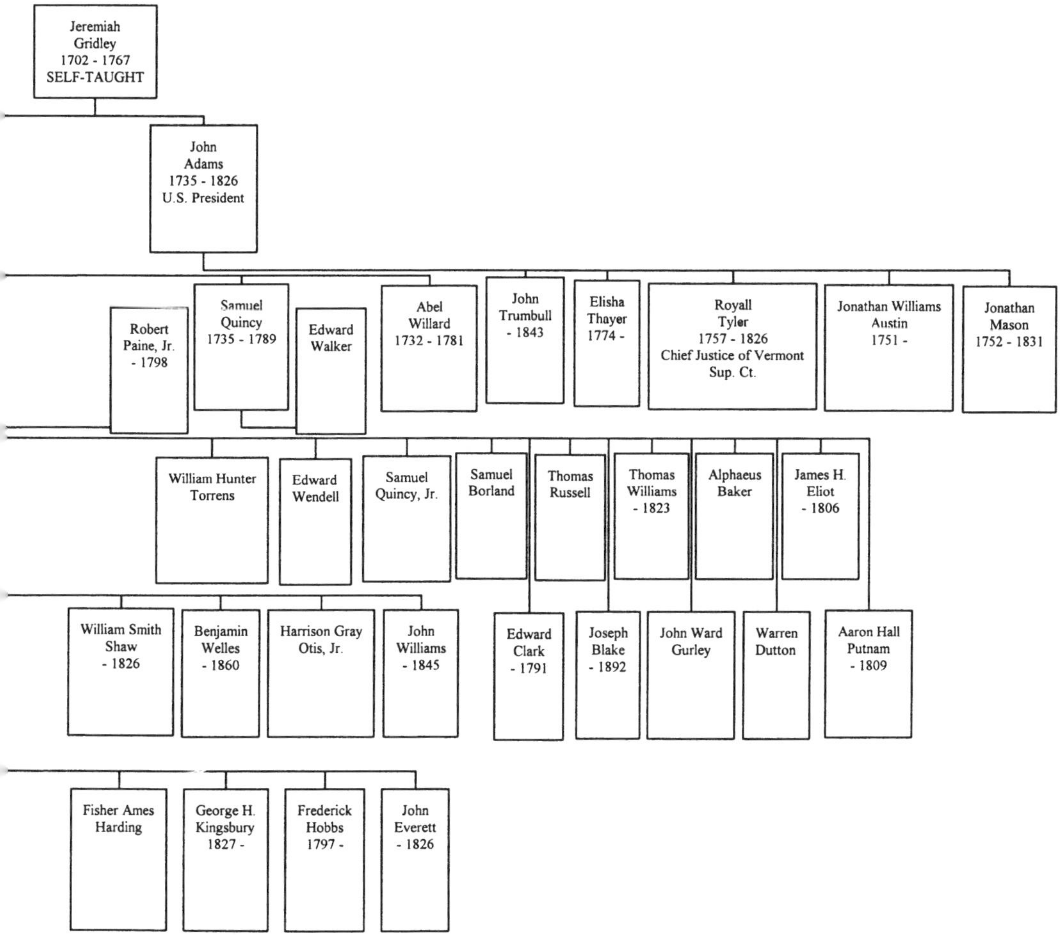

Gridley (1702–1767), it illustrates the "genealogy" of apprenticeships among the elite practitioners. Note, particularly, the position of Oxenbridge Thacher (1719–1765), Quincy's pupil master, and Quincy himself. Through Thacher, Quincy was part of a tradition that links men like Governor Christopher Gore (1758–1827), Daniel Webster (1782–1852), and Charles Francis Adams (1807–1886).

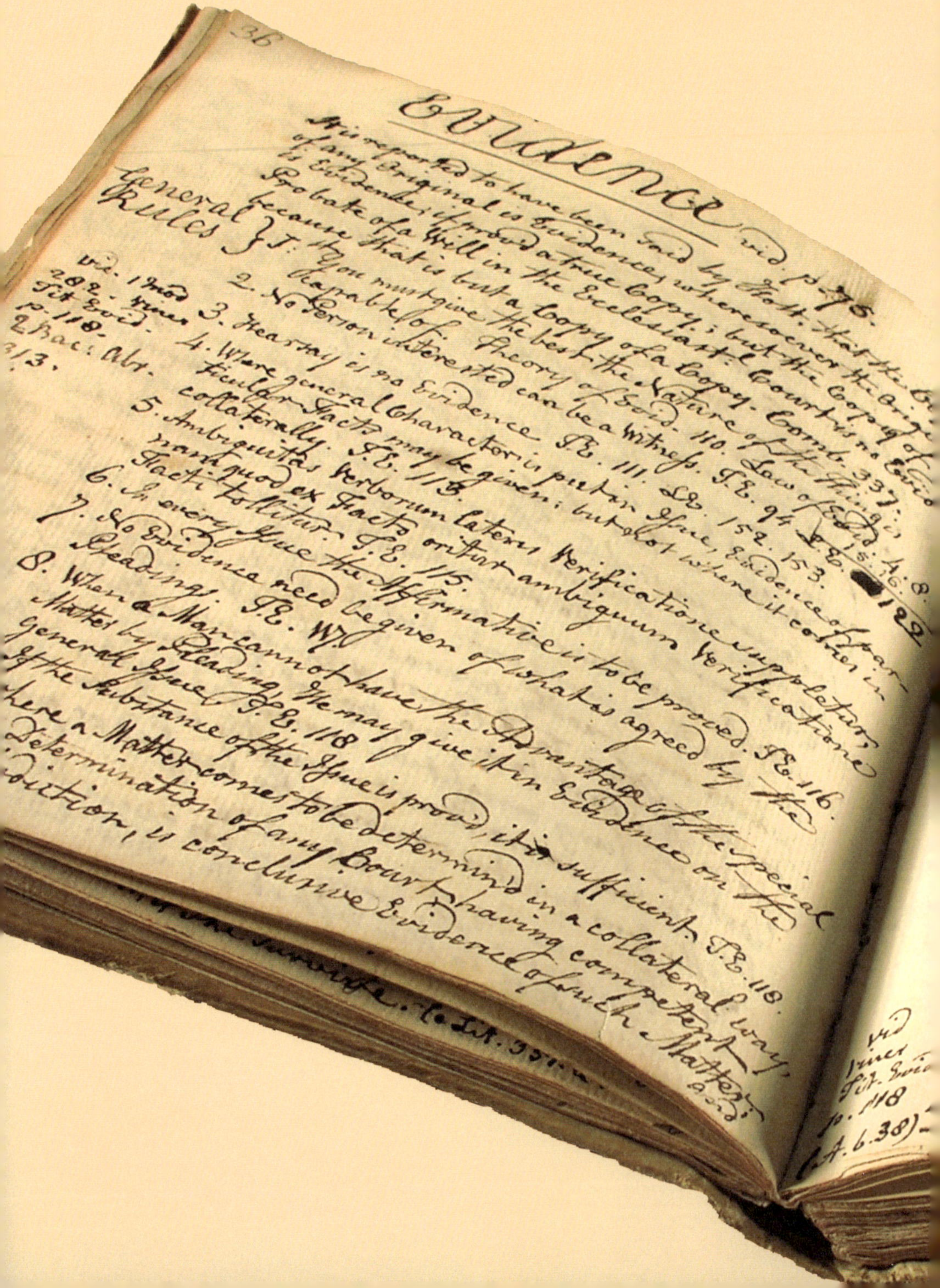

36

Evidence vid. p. 75.

It is reported to have been said by Holt. that the Copy of any Original is Evidence, if prov'd a true Copy, wheresoever the Original is; but the Copy of a Copy is no Evidence. Probate of a Will in the Ecclesiast. Court is no Evidence, because that is but a Copy of a Copy. Comb. 337.

General Rules } 1. You must give the best the Nature of the Thing is capable of. Theory of Evid. 110. Law of Evid. 15. 4. 8. T. E. 94. 122

2. No Person interested can be a Witness. T. E. 94

3. Hearsay is no Evidence. T. E. 111. L. E. 152. 153.

vid. 1 Mod. 282. Tit. Evid. p. 118. 2 Bac: Abr. 313.

4. Where general Character is put in Issue, Evidence of particular Facts may be given; but not where it comes in collaterally. T. E. 113.

5. Ambiguitas verborum latens, verificatione suppletur; nam quod ex Facto oritur ambiguum, verificatione Facti tollitur. T. E. 115.

6. In every Issue the Affirmative is to be proved. T. E. 116.

7. No Evidence need be given of what is agreed by the Pleadings. T. E. 117.

8. When a Man cannot have the Advantage of the special Matter by Pleading, he may give it in Evidence on the general Issue. T. E. 118

If the Substance of the Issue is prov'd, it is sufficient. T. E. 118

Where a Matter comes to be determin'd in a collateral way, the Determination of any Court, having competent Jurisdiction, is conclusive Evidence of such Matter; and

vid. Viner Tit. Evid. p. 118

(A. 6. 38)

... Co. Lit. 331.

THE LAW COMMONPLACE

COMMENCED, 1763

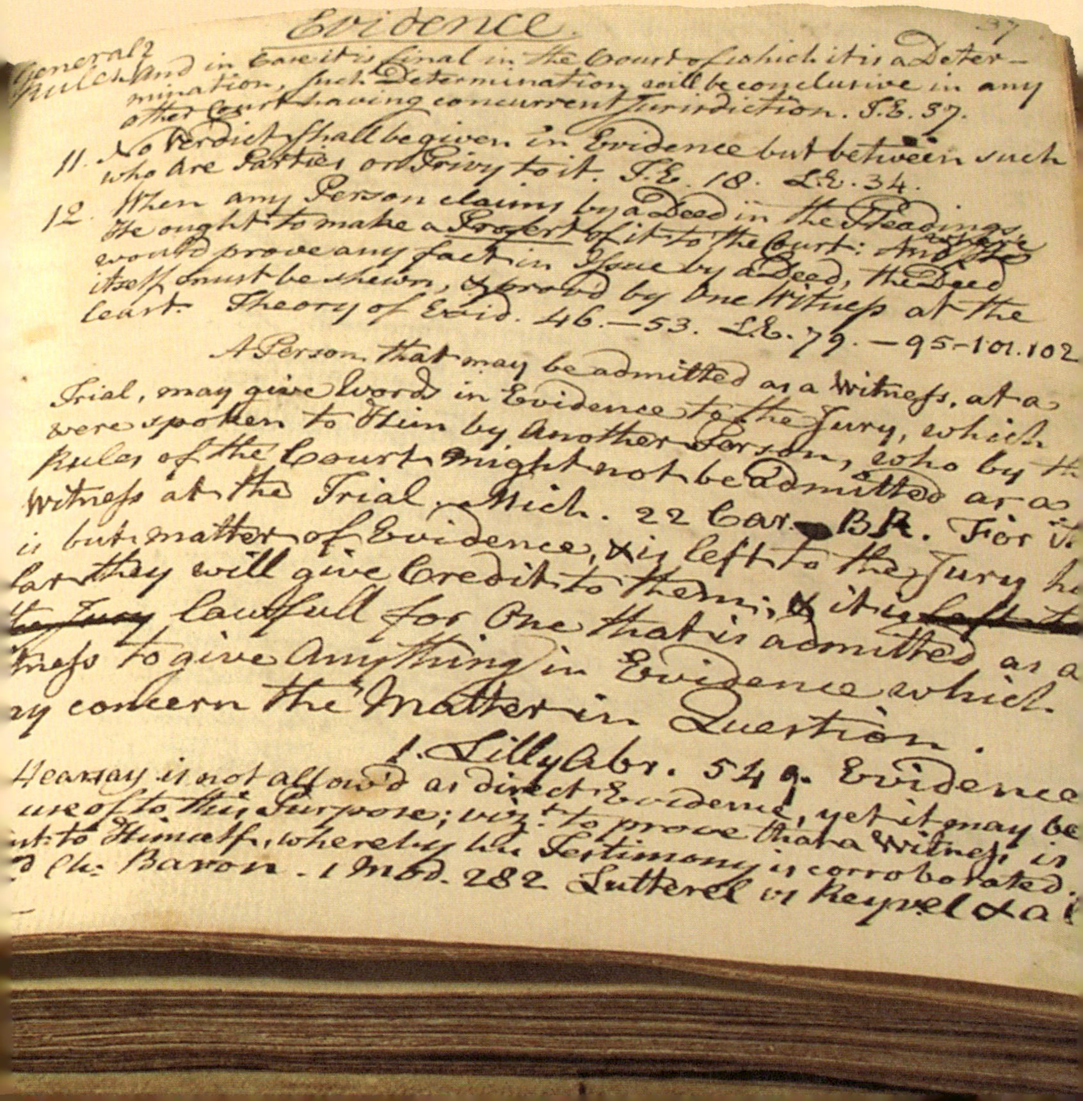

Evidence. 37

General Rules And in Case it is final in the Court of which it is a Deter-
mination, such Determination will be conclusive in any
other Court having concurrent Jurisdiction. S.E. 37.

11. No Verdict shall be given in Evidence but between such
who are Parties or Privy to it. S.E. 18. L.E. 34.

12. When any Person claims by a Deed in the Pleadings
He ought to make a Profert of it to the Court: And if he
would prove any fact in Issue by a Deed, the Deed
itself must be shewn, & proved by One Witness at the
least. Theory of Evid. 46.—53. L.E. 79.—95-101.102

A Person that may be admitted as a Witness, at a
Trial, may give Words in Evidence to the Jury, which
were spoken to Him by Another Person, who by th
Rules of the Court might not be admitted as a
Witness at the Trial. Mich. 22 Car. B.R. For th
is but matter of Evidence, & is left to the Jury h
far they will give Credit to them; & it is
lawfull for One that is admitted as a
tness to give Anything in Evidence which
y concern the Matter in Question.
1. Lilly Abr. 549. Evidence

Hearsay is not allowed as direct Evidence, yet it may be
use of to this Purpose; viz.t to prove that a Witness is
nt to Himself, whereby his Testimony is corroborated.
d Ch: Baron. 1 Mod. 282. Lutterel vs Keynel & ai

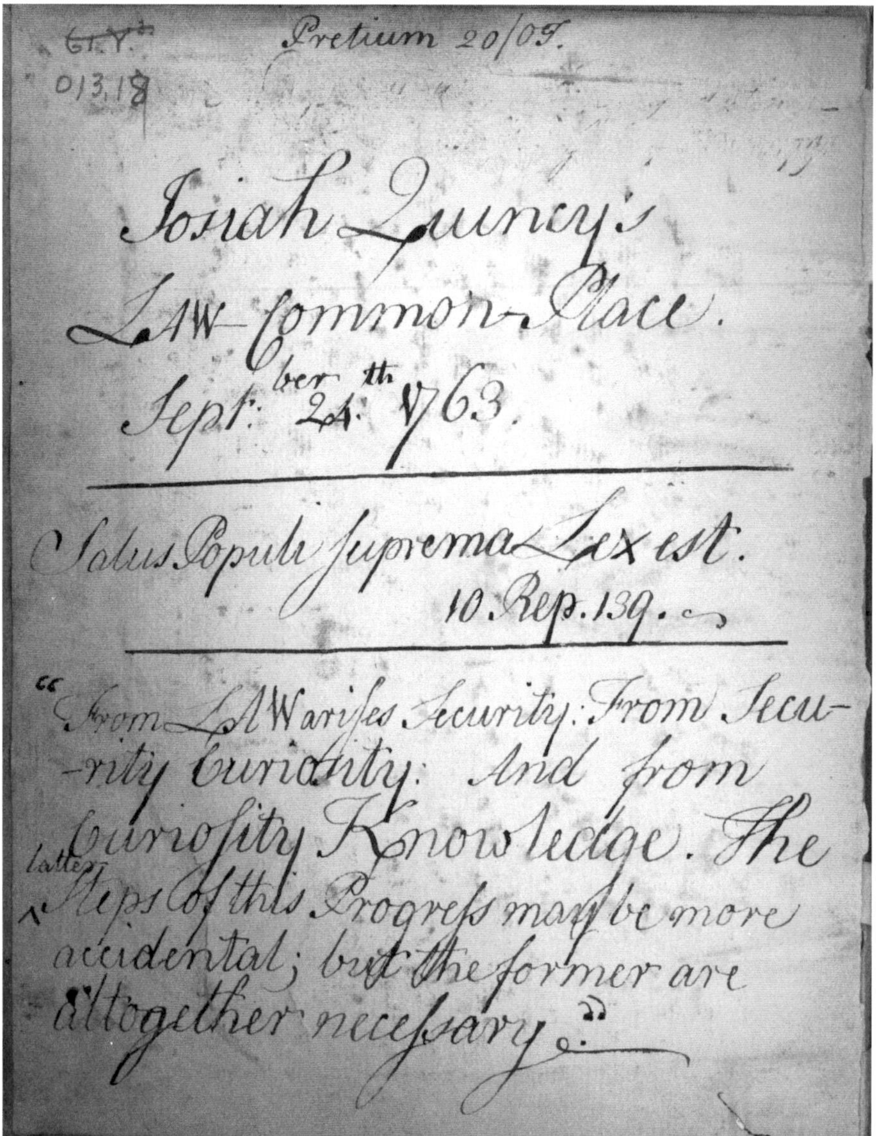

Pretium 20/0S.

Josiah Quincy's
Law-Common-Place.
Sept:ber 24th 1763.

Salus Populi suprema Lex est.
10. Rep. 139.

"From LAW arises Security: From Secu-
-rity Curiosity: And from
Curiosity Knowledge. The
latter Steps of this Progress may be more
accidental; but the former are
altogether necessary."

ILLUSTRATION 1. The first page of Quincy's *Law Commonplace*, featuring quotations from Sir Edward Coke and David Hume. Quincy was only nineteen years old when he wrote this page, which gives a good example of his early, less mature handwriting. Image courtesy of the Massachusetts Historical Society. My thanks to Kevin Cox.

Pretium 20/09[1]

Josiah Quincy's Law Common-Place

Sept:ber 24.th 1763.

Salus Populi Suprema Lex est.
10. Rep. 139.[2]

"From LAW arises Security: From Secu-
-rity Curiosity: And from
Curiosity Knowledge. The
latter Steps of this Progress may be more
accidental; but the former are
altogether necessary."[3]

Page [1]

1. "pretium" = "price" (Latin). Did Quincy pay "20 shillings, nine pence" for this notebook, or for a set of four leather-bound notebooks? See the discussion at "Introduction: The Legal Education of a Patriot: Josiah Quincy Jr.'s *Law Commonplace* (1763), Section 1, The Manuscript," *supra*, p. 12. See also *Illustration 1.*

2. Quotation is loosely from *Coke's Reports*, vol. 10 (covering 1572–1616), p. 139b. "*Salus Populi est Suprema Lex.*" Translation of Quincy's text: "The welfare of the people, or of the public, is supreme law." (E. H. Jackson, *Latin for Lawyers*, London, 1915, p. 241.) The first edition of Sir Edward Coke's *Reports*, in English, was published in London in 1658. The first volume of *Coke's Reports* in French had been published in 1600. Subsequent English editions were produced in 1680, 1727, 1738, 1793, 1797, and 1826. See Sweet and Maxwell's *Legal Bibliography*, vol. 1, pp. 295–97 (2nd ed., London, 1955; hereafter, Sweet & Maxwell).

3. The quote, "From law arises security, from security curiosity. And from curiosity knowledge. The latter steps of this progress may be more accidental; but the former are altogether necessary," is nearly identical to a passage of David Hume's essay, "Of the Rise and Progress of the Arts and Sciences," which appeared in 1742 in Volume 2 of *Hume's Essays, Moral and Political.* The version online, at http://rit.minsk.by/cgi-bin/showtext.pl/Philosophy/1700-1799/hume-of-737.txt-ps50-pn1, was based on the 1875 Green and Grose edition of the essays. The only differences between the quote above and Hume's passage are some minor punctuation differences. Many thanks to my excellent research assistant, Brian Sheppard, Boston College Law School, 2001.

[2]

I hold this for an undoubted Verity, that there
is no Knowledge, + Case, or Point in Law, seem it
of never so little Account; but will stand our stu-
-dent in stead at one Time or other, + therefore
in reading, Nothing to be pretermitted.
+ vid. Proem to 4th Inst. Coke Litt: Page 9. a.[1]

I would have our Student follow the Advice given
in these antient Verses, for the good spending of the
Day.
Sex Horas Somno, totidem des Legibus aequis.
Quatuor orabis, des Epulisq: duas.
Quod superest ultro sacris, largire Camenis.
Ibid. 64. b.[2]

There be two Things to be avoided by our Student
as Enemies to Learning praepostera Lectio &
praepropera Praxis. Ibid. 70. b. top.[3]

No sort of study contributes more to the Knowledge of the
Law, than that which traces it thro its different Periods and
Changes. Hist:^{e} Law—Tracts. p. 366.[4]

Page [2]

1. Loose copy of Edward Coke, *The First Part of the Institutes of the Lawes of England* (hereafter by its common name, "*Coke on Littleton*"), p. 9a.

2. Loose copy of *Coke on Littleton*, p. 64b. Translation of Latin: "Six hours in sleep and you should give just as much equally to the laws, you will pray for four hours, and give two to letters. What is left over you should bestow upon the singing of sacred songs."

3. Loose copy of *Coke on Littleton* (1st ed., London, 1628), p. 70b. Quincy's note, "top," is correct for early editions. Translation of Latin: "The unreasonable reading and the hasty reaction."

4. Copied from Lord H. H. Kames's two-volume *Historical Law Tracts* (1st ed., Edinburgh, 1758), vol. 2, p. 128. See Sweet & Maxwell, vol. 1, p. 34.

[3]

Our Student shall observe that the Knowledge of the Law is like a deep Well, out of which each Man draweth according to the Strength of his Understanding. He that reacheth deepest, He seeth the amiable and admirable Secrets of the Law. And as the Bucket in the Depth is easily drawn to the uppermost Part of the Water, (for Nullum Elementum in suo proprio Loco est grave)[1] but take it from the Water, it cannot be drawn up but with great Difficulty. So albeit Be- -ginning of this Study seem difficult, yet where the Professor of the Law can dive into the Depth it is delightfull, Easy, and without any heavy Burthen, so long as He keep Himself in his own proper Element. COKE Lit. 71.a.bot.[2]

Reading, Hearing, Conference, Meditation, and Recordation, are necessary to the Knowledge of the common Law, because it consisteth upon so many, and almost infinite Particulars. But an orderly Observation in Writing is most requisite of them all; for Reading without Hearing is dark and irksome, and Hearing without Reading is slippery and uncertain, neither of them truly yield seasonable Fruit without Conference, nor both of them with Conference without Meditation and Recordation, nor all of them together without due and orderly Observation; "Scribe Sapientiam tempore Vacuitatis tuae," saith Solomon. And yet He that at length by these Means shall attain to be learn'd,

Page [3]

1. Translation of Latin: For "no element in its own place is heavy."

2. Loose copy, with some omissions, of *Coke on Littleton* (1st ed., London, 1628), p. 71a. Quincy's note, "bot." or "bottom," is accurate for early editions.

[4]

when He shall leave off quite for his Gain, or his Ease, soon shall He (I warrant Him) lose a great Part of his Learning; Therefore as I allow not to the Student any discontinuance at all (for He shall Lose more in a Month than he shall recover in many:) So do I commend Perseverance to all, as to each of these Means an inseparable Incident. ___ Pref. to the Reports of L^{d} E Coke[1]

Page [4]

1. Loose copy of *Coke's Reports*, vol. 1, "The Preface to the Reader," n.p. (1st ed., London, 1600). The exact text from Coke reads:

> For reading without hearing is darke & yrckesome, and hearing without reading is flippery and vncertaine, neither of them truly yeeld seasonable fruit without conference, without meditation & recordation, nor all of them together without due and orderly observation, *scribe sapientiam tempore vacuitatis tuæ*, faith *Salomon*. And yet he that at length by these meanes shall attaine to be learned, when he shal leaue them off quite for his gaine, or his ease, soone shal he (I warrant him) loose a great part of his learning, Therefore as I allow not to the Student any discontinuance at all (for he shal loose more in a moneth then he shal recover in many:) So do I commend perseverance to all, as to each of these means an inseperable incident.

The Latin phrase is adapted from the *Vulgate*, specifically the Biblical Book of Sirach, or Ecclesiasticus, Chapter 38, verse 25: "Write wisdom in the time of your leisure."

[5]

The Proofs + Arguments of Littleton, (saith my L:[d] Coke)[1] may be generally divided into two Parts, viz. from the common Law + from Statutes, of both which, + of their several Branches I shall give the studious Reader some few Examples, + leave the rest to his diligent Observation.

From the common Law his Proofs + Arguments are drawn from twenty several fountains or Places.
First, from the Maxims, Principles, Rules, Intendment + Reason of the common Law, which indeed is the Rule of the Law.
Secondly, from the Books, Records, + other Authorities of Law cited by him, ab Authoritate + Pronunciatis.
Thirdly, from original writs in the Register, a rescriptis valet Argumentum.
Fourthly, from the form of good Pleading.
Fifthly, from the right Entry of Judgments.
Sixthly, a Praecedentibus approbatis + Usu.[2]
Seventhly, a non Usu[3]
Eighthly, ab artificialibus Argumentis, Consequentibus + Conclusionibus.[4]
Ninthly, a communi Opinione Jurisprudentum.[5]
Tenthly, ab inconvenienti.[6]
Eleventhly, a divisione, vel ab Enumeratione Partium.[7]
Twelfthly, a Maiore ad Minus, + vice versa, a simili, + a pari.[8]
Thirteenthly, ab Impossibili.[9]

14.

Page [5]

1. This is a loose copy, with some omissions, of *Coke on Littleton*, pp. 11a–11b. Quincy does not follow the punctuation of Coke's 1st edition, although he may be copying from a later edition. He also omits Coke's translations of Latin terms in some places. See notes 2 and 3, below.

2. Coke translated this "from approved Precedents and Use," *Id.*, p. 11a. Quincy omits this translation, and those following in notes 3–9, below.

3. Coke translated this "from not use." *Id.*, p. 11a.

4. Coke translated this "artificial arguments consequents and conclusions." *Id.*, p. 11a.

4. Coke translated this "from the common opinion of the sages of the law." *Id.*, p. 11a.

6. Coke translated this "from that which is inconvenient." *Id.*, p. 11a.

7. Coke translated *a divisione*, "from a division," and *vel ab enumeratione partium*, "from the enumeration of the parts." *Id.*, p. 11a.

8. Coke translated this *a maiore ad minus*, "from the greater to the lesser" or "from the lesser to the greater." *Id.*, p. 11a. Coke does not translate *a simili, a pari*: "from the similar, from the equal" (i.e., reasoning by analogy).

9. Coke translated this "from that which is impossible." *Id.*, p. 11a.

[6]

14. A fine[1]
15. Ab utili vel inutili[2]
16. Ex absurdo, for that whereupon shall follow an Absurdity, quasi a surdo prolatum, because it is repugnant to Understanding + Reason.[3]
17. A Naturâ + Ordine Naturae.[4]
18. Ab ordine Religionis.[5]
19. A communi Pr[a]esumptione.[6]
20. A Lectionibus Jurisprudentium.[7]

From Statutes his (Lit's) Arguments and Proofs are drawn.[8]

1:st From the Rehearsal or Preamble of the Statute.
2.dly By the Body of the Law diversly interpreted. Sometimes by other Parts of the same Statute, which is benedicta Expositio, + ex Visceribus Causae.[9]

Vid, p. 89.[10]

Vid. p.89.[11] 1 Inst. Page. 11.a.b.[12]

+ To Interpret a Law, we must inquire after the Will of the Maker: which may be collected either from the words, the Context, the Subject-Matter, the Effects and Consequence, or the Spirit + Reason of the Law, From the latter Method of Interpretation arises EQUITY, or the Correction of that wherein the Law (by Reason of its Universality) is deficient. Blackstone anal. B1. 62. p3.[13]

Page [6]

1. Coke translated this "from the end." *Coke on Littleton*, p. 11a. Quincy omits this translation, and those following in notes.

2. Coke translated this "from that which is profitable or unprofitable." *Id.*, p. 11a.

3. Here Quincy copies Coke's translation at *Id.*, p. 11a. Perhaps he felt Coke's words added more substance to the straight Latin translation for "*quasi a surdo prolatum.*"

4. Coke translated this "from nature or the course of nature." *Id.*, p. 11a.

5. Coke translated this "from the order of Religion." *Id.*, p. 11b.

6. Coke translated this "from a common presumption." *Id.*, p. 11b.

7. Coke translated this "from the readings of learned men of Law."

8. This continues to loosely copy *Coke on Littleton*, *supra*, at p. 11b. "Lit's" is Quincy's addition to clarify Coke's "his" as referring to Littleton.

9. Translation of Latin: which is "blessed explanation and comes from the depths of reason."

10. This is an internal cross-reference to Quincy's *Law Commonplace*, p. 89 [77], "Of Statutes or Acts."

11. Same cross-reference as note 10.

12. This is Quincy's correct citation to the "star pages" (i.e., the pagination of the first edition) of *Coke on Littleton* (London, 1628), for the above twenty "factors." "Star" pagination does not mean Quincy was actually copying from a first edition, as most later editions follow the original "star" pagination of the first—a convention adopted by lawyers for consistent citations of legal classics such as Coke's writings. There had been twelve editions of *Coke on Littleton* before Francis Hargrave's classic 1775 edition, all published in England. Quincy could have been using any edition before Hargrave's. See Sweet & Maxwell, *supra*, vol. 1, pp. 449–50.

13. This was loosely copied from William Blackstone's *Analysis of the Laws of England*, p. 3, first published while Blackstone was lecturing at Oxford in 1756. Blackstone's *Analysis* was superseded by his far better *Commentaries*. Volume 1 of the four-volume *Commentaries* was published in Oxford in 1765, with volume 2 in 1766, volume 3 in 1768 and volume 4 in 1769. The first American edition was published in installments in Philadelphia in 1771–1772. See Sweet & Maxwell, *supra*, vol. 1, pp. 27–29. (Like the Dublin edition, it was unauthorized.) Quincy clearly had no access to this famous learning aid in September 1763, when he began his *Law Commonplace*, but he did have Blackstone's *Analysis*. There is one citation to the *Commentaries* in the *Law Commonplace*. It is late in the book, and the citation is to *Commentaries* volume 1, the volume first published in 1765. See *Law Commonplace*, p. 94 [82]. It seems to be a later addition, but in Quincy's hand. See Introduction, *supra*, pp. 19–20, n. 37, pp. 26–27, n. 46.

[7]

L:d Chief Justice Reeve to his Nephew. Directions for beginning the Study of the Law.[1] Vid Law A-file[2]

Read Woods Institutes[3] in a cursory manner with an intent only to understand the several Divisions of the Law, + obtain the precise Ideas used in it. For such Terms as Wood does not explain, as he goes along Les Termes de La Loy shd.[4] Be consulted + for more full + modern Explanations of the same, Jacob's Dictionary:[5] But the Authority of the latter shd not be too implicitly relied on. The only Reason why I mention Wood for the present Purpose is because, the Terms will be much better understood by observing with what Latitude or Restriction they are used in the Course of his Work, than by Consulting any Dictionary whatever. And in order to understand his Chapter of Conveyances, it will be necessary to call in the Aid of some old Practitioner who is your friend; if this Advantage can't be acquir'd, you must be contented with such Light as you can strike out of the modern Books of Practice, as Bohun's Institutio legalis,[6] Jacob's practicing Attorney's Companion,[7] (last Edit.on) of all these I can give no other Character than Martial does of Books in general, sunt bona, sunt quodam[8] +c; nor any other other Directions concerning the using them; than that you must by the help of Indexes take what is to your present Purpose. This done read Littletons Tenures, without Notes,[9] consider it well + abridge such parts as the other Books inform you[10] at this Day: Thus arm'd venture upon Coke's Institute or Commentary upon Lit's Tenures,[11] which being well understood the whole is conquer'd + without which a sound Common Lawyer can never be made. To this

Page [7]

1. Sir Thomas Reeve (?–1737). Judge of the Common Pleas in 1733 and Chief Justice in 1736. John Adams notes in his diary from October 25, 1758, that his pupil master, Jeremiah Gridley,

ILLUSTRATION 2. Sir Thomas Reeve (?–1737) was a justice of the Court of Common Pleas in England, serving as its Lord Chief Justice in 1736 as the image indicates. Josiah Quincy incorporates a letter from Reeve to his nephew on pages [7] to [9] of the *Law Commonplace*. The letter provides advice on how to study law, including a list of important sources. John Adams also records that a senior lawyer gave him a copy of the same letter at the outset of his career, and it seems to have formed part of the standard curriculum for the Boston bar at that time. See page 7, note 1, and "Introduction," *supra*, section on "Pedagogy," pp. 26–27. The artist was Amiconi, and the engraver B. Baron. Courtesy of Harvard Law School Library. My thanks to Kevin Cox and David Warrington.

"gave [him] Lord C. J. Reeve's advice to his nephew, in the study of the common law." It seems to have been a common introductory source. See page 8, note 9. This letter was printed in Francis Hargrave's two-volume *Collectanea Juridica*, consisting of *Tracts relative to the Law and Constitution of England* (London), vol. 1, pp. 79–81, which was not published until 1791–1792. (See Sweet & Maxwell, *supra*, vol. 1, p. 32.) Josiah Quincy Jr. refers to Reeve's letter in an address at the dedication of the new law school building in 1832 at Harvard University, of which he was president. See *Illustration 2*.

2. Quincy must have a copy of this manuscript in his filing system "Law A-file."

3. Thomas Wood, *An Institute of the Laws of England* (London, 1720). This relatively primitive precursor to Blackstone's *Commentaries* was republished in 1722, 1724, 1728, 1734, 1738, 1745, 1754, and 1763. A final edition was published in 1772. See Sweet & Maxwell, vol. 1, p. 38.

4. William Rastell, *Les Termes de la Ley* was first published, with parallel columns in Law French and English, in London in 1624. It was greatly enlarged over many editions, including enlarged editions in 1685, 1708, 1721, and 1742.

5. Giles Jacob, *New Law Dictionary* (London, 1729). A big folio, *Jacob's Law Dictionary* was republished in 1732, 1746, 1739, 1744, 1750, 1756, and 1762. (Only editions relevant to Quincy's *Law Commonplace* are given.) See Percy H. Winfield, *The Chief Sources of English Legal History* (Cambridge, Mass., 1925) (hereafter, "Winfield"), p. 18; Sweet & Maxwell, vol. 1, p. 9; William Holdsworth, *A History of English Law*, vol. XII (London, 1938, 1966 reprint) (hereafter, "Holdsworth"), p. 176. Jacob's *Dictionary* was "a new departure because it attempted, with a considerable measure of success, to combine in one work a dictionary and an Abridgment." *Id.*, p. 176.

6. William Bohun, *Institutio Legalis*, or *Introduction to the Study and Practice of the Laws of England* (London, 1708–1709). It was republished in 1713, 1724 and 1732.

7. This probably is a reference to Giles Jacob's *Student's Companion* (London, 1725), republished in 1734 and 1743. Jacob also published a *Complete Attorney* (London, 1737), a *Court-Keeper's Companion* (London, 1717), and a *Every-Man his own Lawyer* (London, 1736). See Sweet & Maxwell, vol. 1, pp. 34, 272, 401, 433, respectively.

8. From the Epigrams (l. 16) of the Roman poet Martial, published in the late 1st century: "Sunt bona, sunt quaedam mediocria, sunt mala plura" ["Some are good, some are mediocre, the majority are bad"]. This same quote is used by Francis Dickins, Regius Professor of Law at Cambridge, in a letter to Jeremiah Gridley on how to study law, which is copied into the fourth volume of Quincy's notebooks. See "Introduction: The Legal Education of a Patriot: Josiah Quincy's *Law Commonplace* (1763)," section B, "Pedagogy," *supra*.

9. English editions of *Littleton's Tenures* without Coke's famous additions were readily available, with dozens of 16th- and 17th-century editions. Sweet & Maxwell, vol. 1, pp. 456–57. Curiously, there were no English editions after 1661 until 1825, such being the importance of *Coke on Littleton* in the eighteenth century. *Id.*, vol. 1, p. 457.

10. The version of this letter recorded in Francis Hargrave's *Collectanea Juridica* reads, "such parts as the books inform you is law at this day." See note 1, *supra*.

11. There were editions of *Coke on Littleton* in 1628, 1629, 1630, 1639, 1656, 1664, 1670, 1684, 1703, 1719, and 1738. The famous 1775 Francis Hargrave edition would come out just too late for Quincy. See page [2], note 1.

[8]

This all the Faculties of the Soul must be applied I
with hearty Attention, it will not be found very difficult
with the Preparation already prescrib'd:—After the
first reading is thro' (for it will require many more
than one) either abridge it thro' or Common place it,
or compare it with some authoritative Abrigment;
Sentence by Sentence, + by Addition and Corrections
make it your own. For this purpose, I recommend
Sergeant Hawkins's Abrigment,[1] which will afford
much Light to L^{d}. Coke. This finish'd I w.^{d} recommend
a Second Review of Wood, with an Intent to digest the
Several Heads of the Law for Use + Memory. And now
it will be proper to read the more usefull Statutes
at large, in the order in which He places them, + to ex-
-amine the several Books of Reports as they are cited for
the Proof of his Opinion, which alone is not Authority
tho' he generally quotes fair: And remember if you read
any Addition [edition] of Wood wherein Salk Rep^{t}.[2] are not cited
to consult them under their proper Titles which may
easily be done, he having put them in a form of a
common-Place.

During the second Stage of study, many Books
may be brot in for variety, which will be very usefull +
not interrupt the main Scheme, as Doctor + Student,[3]
Noye's Maxims,[4] Curson's Office of Executors,[5] Hale's History
of the common Law,[6] Hawkins's Pleas of the Crown[7] but
principally Finch's Law,[8] + Roll's Abrigment.[9] + [10]. In
which last you will find, in the Preface, the best Scheme
for studying the Law of any yet extant. It will about,
the Time this done, + not much sooner, be proper to
give diligent Attendance on the Courts at West-
-minister + to begin orderly to read + common-

Page [8]

1. This must be William Hawkins (1673–1740), who became Sergeant-at-Law in 1723, whose *Abridgment of the First Part of Coke's Institutes* ("*Coke on Littleton*") was published in 1711, and republished in 1714, 1718, 1719, 1725, 1736, 1742 and 1751. Sweet & Maxwell, vol. 1, p. 452; Holdsworth, vol. 12, p. 361.

2. The first two volumes of *Salkeld's Reports* were published in 1717 and republished in 1721, 1731, 1742–1743 and in 1771. There was a third volume, consisting principally of notes. It covered the period from 1689 to 1712 (1 William III to 11 Anne). See John W. Wallace, *The Reporters* (Boston, 1882), pp. 399–400. (Hereafter, "Wallace.") Its alphabetical format lent itself to commonplacing. My thanks to my colleague Mary Bilder.

3. Christopher St. German's (?1460–1540) *Doctor and Student* (1st Latin edition, 1523, 1st English edition, 1530, London). See the extensive discussion of this extraordinary little book at page [10], note 1, where Quincy copies an excerpt from it.

4. William Noy's (1577–1634) *Treatise of the Principall Grounds and Maximes of the Lawes of this Kingdom* (London, 1641). There were convenient printings for Quincy, including 3rd ed., 1663; 4th ed., 1677; and the 5th ed., 1757.

5. Henry Curson's *A Supplement to the Office and Duty of Executors* (London, 1728). Sweet & Maxwell, vol. 1, p. 475. It supplemented Thomas Wentworth's *The Office and Duty of Executors* (London, 1641). Sweet & Maxwell, vol. 1, p. 494.

6. The great Matthew Hale's (1609–1670) *History of the Common Law* (London, 1713). This classic was reprinted in a second edition in 1716, a 3rd edition in 1739, and a 4th edition just after Quincy's time, in 1779. Sweet & Maxwell, vol. 1, p. 239.

7. A major treatise on criminal law, William Hawkins, *Pleas of the Crown* (London, 1716–1721) went through a 2nd edition in 1724–1726, a 3rd edition in 1739, a 4th edition in 1762, and a 5th edition in 1771. See Winfield, pp. 325–26.

8. Heveage Finch, *Law: or, Discourse thereof* (London, 1613). Until Blackstone's *Commentaries* appeared, it "was regarded as the best elementary book to be placed in the hands of the law students. It is one of the few attempts that have been made to reduce the common law into a system. . . ." Sweet & Maxwell, vol. 1, p. 238. It was republished conveniently for Quincy in 1730 and 1739.

9. Henry Rolle (?1589–1656), *Abridgment des Plusieurs Cases et Resolutions del Common Ley* (2 vols. London, 1668). There was a famous preface by Chief Justice Matthew Hale (1609–1670), and an important "Publisher's Preface Directed to the Young Students of the Common Law." Included in the preface were detailed instructions and encouragement regarding the method and benefits of commonplacing. It was apparently a common introductory source for Quincy's contemporaries of the Boston bar as well. In John Adams's diary entry of Oct. 25, 1758, he notes of an early visit to his legal mentor Jeremiah Gridley, "[t]hen he took his commonplace book and gave me Lord Hale's advice to a student of the common law." *Rolle's Abridgment* was, however, a rare book, printed only once in 1668. See John D. Cowley, *A Bibliography of Abridgments, Digests, Dictionaries and Indexes of the English Law to the Year 1800* (London, 1932), pp. 77–78. (Hereafter, "Cowley.") This may explain why Quincy apparently didn't have access to it, but made "a copy of a copy" of a key section. See page [9], note 2.

10. This marker references Quincy's final note on the following page.

[9]

2 placed in such a Manner, as by the Experience you will by this Time have of the Nature of the Study be able to advise yourself. ____ My whole Scheme without naming Books, is no more than this.— 1.st Obtain precise ideas of the Terms + general meaning of the Law. 2.dly Learn the general Reasons whereon the Law is founded. 3.dly Find some authentic System, collect the great leading Points of the Laws, in their natural Order, as the first Heads + Divisions of your future Enquiry; 4.thly Collect the several Particular Points + range them under their Generals, as they occur + as you find you can best digest them.

And whereas Law must be consider'd in a two--fold Respect. 1.st As a Rule of Action. 2.dly As the Art of procuring Redress when this Rule is violated; the Study in each of them may be regulated by the foregoing Method. And the Books so recommended will so carry on your Joint Work, that with this Course so finish'd, the Student may pursue each Branch of either, to its uttermost Extent, or re--turn to his Center of Knowledge without Confusion, which is the only way of rendering Things easy to the Memory.~

A Copy of a Copy.

+ Method of Studying the Common Law

from Roll's Abr.g Preface.[1] Vid Law A-file[2]

Page [9]

1. The famous "Preface" from Henry Rolle's (?1589–1656) *Abridgment des Plusieurs Cases et Resolutions del Common Ley*, edited by Matthew Hale (London, 1668). See page [8], note 9.

2. Another reference to Quincy's law "file" system. See page [7], note 2. It appears that Ld. Chief Justice Reeve's "Advice to his Nephew" and the excerpt from Rolle's *Abridgment* were copied from manuscripts in this file, i.e., "A Copy of a Copy," as Quincy says.

[10]

the six Grounds of the Law of England.~ 3

The Law of Engl:[d] is grounded, first on the Law of Reason, 2.[dly], On the Law of GOD. 3.[dly], On divers general Customs of the Realm. Fourthly, On divers Principles that be call'd Maxims. 5:[thly] On divers par--ticular Customs. 6:[thly], On divers Statutes made in Parliaments by the King, + by common Counsel, of the Realm. Doct.[r]+Stud.[t] Ch. 4.th p. 14.~[1]

Of the COUNTRIES subject to the LAWS of ENGLAND.

The Laws of England are not rec.[d] in their full extent in any other Territories, besides the Kingdom of England, + the Dominion of Wales; which have, in most Respects, an entire Community of Laws.

Scotland, notwithstanding the Union, retains it's own muni--cipal Laws; tho' subject to Regulations by the British Parliament,

Berwick is subject to the Scots Laws, but bound by all Acts of Parliament.

Ireland is a distinct subordinate Kingdom, governd by the common Law of England; but not bound by modern Acts of the British Parliament, unless particularly nam'd.

The Isle of Man, the Norman Isles, (as Guernsey, etc.) + our Plantations abroad, are govern'd by their own Laws; but are bound by Acts of the British Parliament, if specially nam'd therein.

The Territory of England is divided, Ecclesiastically, into Provinces, Dioceses, Archdeaconries, rural Deanries, + Parishes.

The Civil Division is, first, into Counties, of which some are palatine; then sometimes, into Rapes, Lathes, or Frithings;[2] next into Hundreds, or Wapentakes;[3] and lastly, into Towns, Vills, or Tithings. Blackstone's Anal: B1. Chap 3.[4]

Page [10]

1. This is an excerpt from Christopher St. German's (?1460–1540) *Doctor and Student.* This little book was first published in Latin in 1523 and in English in 1530. It is a dialogue between a

"doctor" of divinity and a "student" of the common laws of England that explores, for one of the first times in English history, the theoretical underpinnings of the law. In particular, it helped to establish a secular basis for equity courts, which had previously been closely tied to the Catholic Church, but, following Henry VIII's repudiation of Catholicism, had to find a new basis in secular morality. "Equity" was seen as supplementing the rigidity of the common law by providing discretion to give special relief to those to whom mechanical application of the law would be cruel or unfair. See W. S. Holdsworth, *Sources and Literature of English Law* (Oxford, 1923), pp. 185–88. Although *Doctor and Student* was an ancient book in Quincy's day, it was very much in print, with recent editions in 1709, 1721, 1746, 1751, and 1761. See Sweet & Maxwell, vol. 1, p. 25. The citation is to chapter IV of *Dialoge I*, and page 14 is correct for the Nutt and Gossing printing in London of 1721.

2. A "rape" is a subdivision of the County of Sussex. The Kent equivalent is a "lathe." Earl Jowitt, *The Dictionary of English Law* (London, 1959), p. 1474. (Hereafter, "Jowitt.") A "frith" is a tract of communal land. *Id.*, p. 844.

3. A "hundred" is a district forming part of a county. It has been debated whether it consists of a hundred hides (of about 80 acres) or a hundred free families. A "wapentake" is a Yorkshire district that is roughly equivalent to a hundred. See Jowitt, *supra*, pp. 928, 1850. See also page [21], note 7.

4. This description came from William Blackstone's *Analysis of the Laws of England* (Oxford, 1756). See page [6], note 13.

[11]

4 Index

To y[e] following Little Abridgment for private Use.~

A

Page [11]

1. "Arbitrament" is from the Norman French "arbitrement" meaning "the award or decision of arbitraments." Jowitt, *supra*, p. 144.

[12]

[13]

6 Index etc page

L

[14]

Index etc 7

page,

N

P

[15]

[16]

11

Attachment

Attachment was prayed for a contempt, but ye C:^{S} (BR)[1] denied it, tho' some cases were cited in which it had been lately done; for they said it was a new practice to imprison men thus without being heard; [illegible] Sid. 452 22 Car. 2. BR. Tremenhere v. Tresilian. Cited 3 Vin : 131.[2]

Page [16]

1. "Ye C:^{S} (BR)" refers to "Carlos II Rex: Banco Regis," i.e., the King's Bench of Charles II, which in 1682 decided *Tremenhere* v. *Tresilian*, described below at note 2.

2. The double underscore is added by Quincy in the original, doubtless indicating his view that this could be an important precedent in Massachusetts. The passage is copied closely from Charles Viner, *A General Abridgment of Law and Equity*, vol. 3, p. 131 (London, 1741–1753). (Hereafter, "*Viner's Abridgment.*") See *Tremenhere* v. *Tresilian, Sid.* 452. pl. 20 Pasch. 22 Car.2. B.R., i.e., King's Bench, 1682. The case supports the proposition Quincy is discussing. Quincy relied heavily on *Viner's Abridgment*, which was first published between 1741–1753 in London by Charles Viner (1678–1756). The completed work includes 23 volumes, with topics arranged alphabetically. It was an enormous success. Viner eventually left the residue of his estate—including unsold copies of the *Abridgment*—to Oxford University. The proceeds established the famous Vinerian Chair, the first to be dedicated to teaching common law within a university. Its first occupant was Sir William Blackstone (1723–1780), whose *Analysis of the Laws of England* (1754) was used by Quincy and whose subsequent four-volume *Commentaries on the Laws of England* (1765–1770) would be of the utmost importance in conveying the common law heritage to the American colonies. See Daniel R. Coquillette, *The Anglo-American Legal Heritage* (Durham, N.C., 2nd ed., 2004), pp. 437–39. It is interesting to note the physical size of this huge 23-volume folio set. Quincy's access to such a collection was no small privilege. The 1790 Catalogue of Harvard College shows that the 23 volumes were there by that date. See *The Printed Catalogues of the Harvard College Library 1723–1790* (eds. W. H. Bond & Hugh Amory, Boston, 1996), p. 251. Did Jeremiah Gridley's (1701–1767) famous law library in Boston also contain a copy available to the likes of Quincy and John Adams, who were among the young lawyers encouraged to use it? See *Law in Colonial Massachusetts* (eds. D. R. Coquillette, Robert J. Brink, Catherine S. Menand, Boston, 1984), pp. 363–76.

[17]

12 **Accord.** Vid. arbitram:t [etc.][1] p. 18.
vid. <u>Accord.</u> in the <u>Index.</u>

---

a Terms of	*a* Accord (Concordia) is an agreem.t betwixt 2 at least,
the Law[2]	to give + accept something in Recompense for a
verb. accord	Trespass, + done by One to Another. If this agreem.t
	is executed, it is a good Bar in Law, in some Cases
b 4 Rep. 1.	of the personal Injuries, to any action for the same
6 Rep. 44	Trespass or Injury. Accord with <u>Satisfaction</u>
9 Rep. 78.	is a good Plea in <u>personal</u> actions, where Damages
79. 80[3]	only are to be recover'd; not in <u>Real</u> Actions.—
	Therefore Right or Tithe to Freehold Land cannot
x vid	be barred, by Acceptance of any collateral Satis-
p 81.[4]	-faction or Recompence. It must be by x<u>Release</u>
	confirmation etc But because the Action of
	<u>Ejectione Firmae</u> + Trespass are so woven together,
	that they cannot be parted, or an Accord is a good
	Plea in Trespass, it must be so in Ejectment.
c 9 Rep.78	*c* If one is bound in an Obligation, to deliver Goods,
1 Inst	or to do any collateral Thing, The Obligee cannot, by
212. b.[5]	Accord betwixt them, give Money in Satisfaction
	thereof; for the Contract being made by writing, to do
	such a Collateral Act, it cannot be alter'd without
	writing. But when One is bound to pay Money, He
	may give Money [or any other valuable thing][6] in Satisfaction [because]
	All Things are estimated + valued by
	Money, + not Money by Things. If a Contract <u>with</u>
	-<u>out Deed</u> is to deliver Goods, or to do any other

Page [17]

1. Quincy here cites ahead to his page 18 [our 23], where he discusses arbitration, arbitrament, arbitrators, and arbitration awards, doubtless because "Where an Accord with Satisfaction may be pleaded, an Award may be pleaded + *vice versa*." Quincy, p. 19 [24].

2. Here Quincy begins to write authorities in the margin, sometimes indicating by use of

small case letters where the authority belongs "in text." Citation "a" is to William Rastell's dictionary. See the discussion at page 7, note 4. But the definition in the text is very differently worded from Rastell, although roughly consistent, at least if one is looking at the 1721 edition [William Rastell], *Les Termes de la Ley* (London, 1721), p. 14.

3. The "b" citations are to *Vernon's Case*, 4 *Coke's Reports*, p. 1a (1572), *Higgins Case*, 6 *Coke's Reports*, p. 44b (1606), and *Henry Peytoes Case*, 9 *Coke's Reports*, p. 77b (1611), all cases on accord and satisfaction supporting Quincy's notes. There is no "b" in text.

4. Citation to page 81 [71] of the *Law Commonplace*, beginning the section "of Releases."

5. These "c" citations are to *Henry Peytoes Case*, see note 3 above, and to *Coke on Littleton*, at page 212b, referring to Littleton's Section 344. Coke's annotation to that section observed: "But if the condition be, that a stranger shall pay to the Obligee or feoffee a sum of money, there the Obligee or feoffee may receive a horse, etc. in satisfaction." *Id.*, p. 212b.

6. "Or any other valuable thing" was inserted by Quincy in the text.

[18]

Accord 13

collateral Thing, there Money may be paid by Accord, in Satisfaction of such a Contract. For as a Contract upon Consideration may commence by words, so by an Agreem.[t] by words for any valuable Consideration, the Contract may be dissolved.

(vid of the Condition of an Obli[tt]gon, Wood. B2. C3[1] Of Obligations.)

[a]6 Rep. 44
9 Rep. 80[2] Note, that the best + safest way to plead an Accord, is to plead it by way of a Satisfaction, + not by way of Accord only. For if it be pleaded by way of Accord, a precise Execution thereof in every Part must be pleaded etc. You need not say any more but that you paid the Plt a Bottle of Wine, etc. in full Satisfaction of the Accord, w[ch] the Plt rec[d.] In all cases where Arbitram[t]. is a good Plea, acc[d.] with Satisfaction is a good Plea. Wood B4 ch 3 p 553[3]

Page [18]

1. Thomas Wood's *An Institute of the Laws of England* (London, 1720). See page [7], note 3. The citation is to book 2, chapter 3, which covers pages 210–88 in the 1772 edition. What Quincy has in mind must be the section on obligation and conditions for an obligation, at pages 278–80.

2. These are citations to *Blake's Case* (1606), *Coke's Reports*, vol. 6, pp. 43b at 44a, wrongly cited as "6 Rep. 44" by Quincy, and, again, to *Henry Peytoes Case*. See page [17], note 3. There is no "a" in the text.

3. This is another citation to Wood's *Institute of the Laws of England*, Book 4, chapter 3, page 553. See note 1, above. The book and chapter citation are correct, but Quincy's point appears on page 527 of the 1772 edition, which states: "where an Accord with satisfaction may be pleaded, an Award may be pleaded," also citing *Blake's Case* as "6 Rep. 44," with the same error as Quincy. See note 2, above. This implies Quincy may have copied the authority from Wood, but his statement of the legal principles, although largely consistent with Wood, is not copied.

[19]

14. Of Apprentices & Servants.

If an apprentice in London marries w[th]out his master's consent, the master cannot turn him away for that reason, but he must sue his covenant. 2 Vern. 293.[1] The end of ye case of Stephenson v. Holditch cited 3 Vin. 20.[2]

Covenant lies not ag[t]: an apprentice being an infant. 7 Mod 15. Lilly's case. cited 3 Vin: 23.[3]

A waterman's widow took an Apprentice, who went to sea (being pressed into y[e] Queen's service) + earned 2 tickets, w[ch] came to y[e] dft's hands. She bro't trover for y[e] tickets, + had judgment; for what ever an Apprentice gains belongs to his master, She may action for it. 1 Salk 68. Barber v. Dennis.[4] And if he be an appren only de facto it is sufficient. 6 Mod. 69. cited 3 Vin: 23. notes q: v.[5]

Page [19]

1. This is almost a verbatim copy from *Viner's Abridgment*, vol. 3, p. 20 (1742–1753), but Quincy adds the underscoring. The citation is to *Vernon's Reports* (1681–1720). See Wallace, pp. 493–94. The case is *Stephenson* v. *Holditch*, see note 2, below.

2. *Stephenson* v. *Holditch* (pl. 443 Hill. 1704), *Vernon's Reports* (1681–1720), vol. 2, p. 293. The case is consistent with Quincy's notes.

3. This is almost a verbatim copy from *Viner's Abridgment*, vol. 3, p. 23 (1742–53), citing to *Lilly's Case*, 7 Modern Reports (1 Ann. B.R.) (i.e., 1702, Queen's Bench).

4. This is almost a verbatim copy from *Viner's Abridgment*, vol. 3, p. 23 (1742–53), with the underscoring in the original. Viner cites to *Barber* v. *Dennis*, 1 Salkeld 68, pl.8 Trin. 2 Ann. B.R. (i.e., 1703, Queen's Bench). *Salkeld's Reports* covered 1689–1712. It was republished in six editions, including a printing in Philadelphia in 1822. See Wallace, p. 399.

5. Seamen's "tickets" were official acknowledgements of back wages due and were negotiable, usually at a steep discount. This paraphrases a note in *Viner's Abridgment*, vol. 3, p. 23 (1742–1753), citing "6 Modern 69," which, as Quincy indicates, is in the marginal notes on the right of the page. The cited case is *Barber* v. *Dennis*, 6 *Modern Reports* 69 (1703). The case supports the proposition in Quincy's notes.

[20]

Of Apprentices & Servants.[1]

15

1 Hob 134[2] *1*An apprentice cannot be sent out of England, unless the Nature of his Service does require it.

*2*As an apprentice cannot be made without Writing,
2 Dalt. ch 58 so He cannot be discharg'd by his Master without Writing
p 121[3] under his Hand, + with the Allowance of One Justice.

If any Master dies, the apprentice goes to the Exc^{tt}or or adm^{tt}nor, to be maintained, if their [*sic*] be assets. But the Exc^{tt}or he may bind Him over to Another Master for the remaining Part of his Time. Wood. B.1.c6. p 52.[4]

If a servant retain'd for a year falls sick, etc. the Master cannot put away his Servant, or abate his Wages.

If a servant shall refuse to do his Service, this is a Departure in Law, altho' he continue with his Master.

It is a reasonable Cause of Departure from Service if the Servant is not allowed sufficient Meat, Drink, etc. or if the Master's Wife beats Him.

If a Woman that is a servant doth Marry, yet She must serve out her Time, + her Husband cannot take Her out of her Master's Service. And if a Woman, being with Child of a Bastard, procures Herself to be retain'd with a Master, who knoweth nothing therof, or if She begotten with Child during her Service, this is a reasonable Cause why the Justices sh^{d}. dicharge her from her Service, for She hath made herself incapable to serve any longer. If He retains
3 a Servant for ten pounds per annum, + he departs within
Noy's the year; *3*He can have no Wages: And if Wages are to be paid
max. 90[5] Half-yearly, + the Master dies after the first Half

Page [20]

1. Apprentices and indentured servants formed an important "underclass" in Boston in the 1760s. See, for example, the case of *Dusten* v. *Richards* (1763), on page 67 of *Reports of Cases Argued and Adjudged in the Superior Court of Judicature of the Province of Massachusetts Bay*

Between 1761 and 1772. Samuel M. Quincy, ed. (New York, 1865). See generally Holdsworth, vol. 2, pp. 493–99, and vol. 8, pp. 59–62.

2. The citation is to *Coventry* v. *Woodhall, Hobart's Reports*, vol. 1, p. 135 (1650), and supports the proposition in Quincy's notes. *Hobart's Reports* covered the King's Bench, 1603 to 1625. See Wallace, p. 220. The bold "1" is Quincy's note, as are the bold numbers following.

3. The reference must be to one of the many editions of Michael Dalton's *The Countrey Justice* (1st ed., London, 1618). Likely editions appeared in 1666, 1677, 1682, 1690, 1697, 1705, 1727, 1742, and 1746. The 1666 edition at chapter 36, page 98 stated: "The Master may discharge his servant by word, but an apprentice cannot be discharged by his Master, except it be by writing, for that an apprentice cannot be but by writing."

4. The citation is to Wood's *Institute*, see page [7], note 3, and is accurate for the London, 1772 edition, book 1, chap. 6, p. 51, which stated a different rule: "If any Master dies, the Apprentice may go to the Executor or Administrator, to be maintained, if there be Assets. But the Executor cannot bind him over to another Master for the remaining part of his time, unless by special Custom, or with the concurrence of the Apprentice; neither is the Apprentice bound to serve the Executor or Administrator of the Master." *Id.*, p. 51. Perhaps Boston had a "special custom," such as London, permitting such "binding over."

5. This is a citation to William Noy's *Treatise of the Principall Grounds and Maximes of the Lawes of this Kingdome*, p. 90. (Hereafter, "Noy's *Maximes*.") There was a London edition in 1757. See page [8], note 4, *supra*.

[21]

16 Of Apprentices & Servants

Qu. If The Serv:t wd. not recover upon a Quan: meruit.

Half-Year, the Servant shall have Wages only for the first half year. Wood. B 1. Ch. 6. p54 + onward.[1]
Vid. Viners Tit Apportionment. Worth v. Diner. p 8.[2]

1 5 Rep 14.[3]
2 Latch 127[4]
2 Roll abr 686[5].
1 Cro 142[6]
3 Cro 37 336.[7]
3 1 Roll abr 98.[8]
2 Cro. 223.[9]
4 FNB.[10] 167. 168
2 Lev. 63.[11]

1 If a Servant damages any goods by his negligence, an Action of the Case lieth against Him.

2 If a Servant is robbed on the highway, of the Master's money, the Master being absent, the Master or the Servant may bring the action Against the Hundred; + the Master may be a Witness to prove the Delivery of the Money to the Serv:t before the Robbery, tho' he brings the Action in his own name.

3 If any Servant is cozen'd of My Money, I may have an action agt. the Person that cozen'd Him.

The Master may have an+ Action agt. one that entices away his Servant; or *4* hires Him, knowing Him to be his Servant.

Trover lies agt. the Master for goods ddtt [delivered to] the apprentice Strange 505.[12] And the Master is liable for the Fraud of the Apprentice Ibid 653.[13]

How the Servant is to justify an Assault in Defense of his Master. 2 Strange 953.[14]
In an Action agt. the Master for his Servant's Default, the Servant having a Release from the Master, admitted a witness for Him. Ibid. 1083.[15]
+ Vid. Vol. 2. p 268. Under Case in the Index.[16]

Page [21]

1. Another citation to Wood's *Institute*. See page [20], note 4, and page [7], note 3. Quincy's question in the margin is an intelligent one, i.e., "Question, if the servant would not recover upon a *quantum meruit*?" *Quantum meruit* is a common law action that lies where an unjust enrichment has been conferred, but there is no contractual price. It is limited to restitution of

the fair market value of the benefit received. The Latin literally means "as much as he has deserved." See *Holdsworth*, vol. 8, pp. 75–76, vol. 13, pp. 551–52.

2. *Worth* v. *Diner*, cited at *Viner's Abridgment*, vol. 3, p. 8 under the title "apportionment," was the occasion of a controversy between Sir John Strange, counsel for the plaintiff and author of *Strange's Reports* cited by Quincy below, and the author of the *Abridgment*, Charles Viner, who challenged Strange to produce "some cases, or One single case at least . . . wherein it has been adjudged that a contract for wages is apportionable." Strange, according to Viner, could not produce such a case, took unjustified offense, and behaved with "little Decency." See *Viner's Abridgment*, vol. 3, p. 9 (1741–1753). Quincy reproduces Strange's view, citing *Worth* v. *Diner* and Wood's *Institutes of the Common Law* (1722) at p. 54.

3. This is a citation to the *Countess of Shrewburies Case* (1605), 5 *Coke's Reports*, pp. 13b–14a (1605). This case is an action on the case for negligence, that states that "if my shepherd, which I trust with my sheep, and by his negligence they be drowned . . . Action upon the Case lieth." *Id.*, p. 14a.

4. This is a citation to *Drope* v. *Thaire*, *Latch's Reports* (covering 1625–1628), p. 127. See Wallace, pp. 262–65.

5. This is a citation to *Rolle's Abridgment* (1668), vol. 2, p. 686, enter *Benet et le Hundred de Hertford in comitat Hertford*, [Benet vs. the Hundred Hertford in the Hertford court], (Mich. 1650).

6. This is a citation to *Green's Case* (1661), *Croke's Reports*, vol. 1, p. 142 (where servant was robbed, Master should not be sworn, but the servant, who had actual knowledge, should be sworn on Master's behalf). *Croke's Reports* were published between 1657–1661, and were republished in 1669, 1680, 1683, and 1790–92. See Sweet & Maxwell, *supra*, vol. 1, p. 298.

7. A "hundred" was "a district forming part of a county." Jowitt, *supra*, p. 988. It could be sued for failure to maintain safe highways. The first citation to *Reymond* v. *Hundred de Okins* (1657), *Croke's Reports*, vol. 3, p. 37 (action against the Hundred by servant for robbery on the highway . . . Master to bring action, and servant—who was robbed, should be his witness). The second is to *Against the Inhabitants of the Hundred* (1657), *Croke's Reports*, p. 336 (same holding). See note 6, above. See also page [10], note 3.

8. This is a citation to Pasch. 8 Jac. In camera Scacarii, Paul Tracies case per curiam 1 *Rolle's Abridgment* 98 (1668). See page [9], note 1.

9. This is a citation to *Tracy v. Veal* (1609), of *Croke's Reports* (Croke Jac), vol. 2, p. 223 ("cozen'd servant" case). See note 6, above. The case is consistent with Quincy's notes.

10. This is a citation to Anthony Fitzherbert's *The New Natura Brevium* ("FNB") (London, 1534). First published in English in 1652, and repeatedly republished, with likely Quincy editions, "star paged," in 1704, 1718, 1730 and 1755. See Sweet & Maxwell, *supra*, p. 269. The citation is to the "star paged" sections 167 and 168, which concern, among other things, writs against one who entices away a servant and writs to require a servant to serve.

11. This is a citation to *Fawcet v. Beavres* (1702), *Levinz's Reports*, vol. 2, p. 63 and supports the proposition in the text. *Levinz's Reports* covers the King's Bench and Common Pleas, 1660–1697. See Wallace, pp. 304–05.

12. This is a citation to *Mead* v. *Hamond* (1755), *Strange's Reports*, vol. 1, p. 505 (trover against Master based on delivery to servant). These reports cover 1716–1749 in all of the royal courts, including chancery, and were republished in 1782 and 1795.

13. This is a citation to *Grammer* et al. v. *Nixon* (1755), *Strange's Reports*, vol. 1, p. 653 (servant forges essay mark on ingot of gold and silver. Master answerable. See note 12, above).

14. This is a citation to *Barfoot* v. *Reynolds* et al. (1755), *Strange's Reports*, vol. 2, pp. 953–54

(servant can claim, in defense of assault claim, that he acted in defense of Master **only** if in order to prevent an injury to Master. Just the fact plaintiff assaulted Master in not good defense "for the assault on the master must be over").

15. This is a citation to *Jarvis* v. *Hayes* (1755), *Strange's Reports*, vol. 2, p. 1083. ("On showing a release from the master to the servant, the Chief Justice allowed the master to examine the servant; though it was urged, that if the plaintiff fails against the master, he may sue the servant, which is a bias upon the servant.")

16. A citation to Volume 2 of Quincy's personal notebooks. Volume 2 was apparently lost in a fire or otherwise. This reference to a high page number suggests the potentially great quantity of its contents. If the subsequent reference to "under Case in the Index" is integrated with the "vol. 2" citation (and there is no entry for case in the index of the current volume), then this suggests that Quincy's Volume 2 was not only long, as are his notebooks of law reports, but also indexed and perhaps another form of commonplace. See discussion at "Introduction: The Legal Education of a Patriot," Part 1: "The Manuscript," *supra*.

[22]

Bailment vid the same Tit in the last 17
Index.

Bailiff to 2. 1 pties [parties?]: Action lies for the Survivor, + not for Him + Ex^tt^cor of the Dec'^d^ jointly. Comb. 474.[1]
If goods be bail'd to a Feme, or if Goods come to her as Exc^tt^ix to a Bailiff, this bare Possession is not given to the Husband, but the Action of Detinue must be brôt
xvid ag^t^: the Husband + Wife. Co: Lit: 351. b.[2] In like
p. 156.[3] manner^x^ Trover may be brot vs. H+W but Conversion must be laid only in the Husband. 1 Bac. abr: 307.[4]

Action of Account is maintainable ag^t^: a servant, but not ag^t^ an Apprentice. 3 Vin: 23. bot, 22 top.[5]
Sim: points.[6]

Page [22]

1. This is a citation to *Comberbach's Reports* (1685–1699, King's Bench), p. 474. See Wallace, pp. 396–97. The case is *Martin* v. *Crump* (1698), and supports the proposition.

2. A loose translation of *Coke on Littleton*, p. 351b. See page [2], note 1, and page [7], note 9.

3. A citation to a related point on page 156 [99] of this volume. Essentially the same idea is also commonplaced on page 174 [117]. See page [117], note 8.

4. This is a citation to Matthew Bacon, *New Abridgment of the Law*, a five-volume set published between 1736–1766, and then reprinted from 1768–1770. It was updated in further editions until 1832. See Sweet & Maxwell, *supra*, p. 16. The citation, page 307, is to the correct page of the 1768 edition, which explains that the reason why conversion is only brought against the husband is that the wife is legally incapable of converting "Goods to her own Use," while both may be involved in the "Trespass of taking them [the goods]."

5. A citation to *Viner's Abridgment* (1742–1753), vol. 3, pp. 22–23. See page [16], note 2.

6. Illegible. Referring to "similar points" in *Viner's Abridgment* (1742–1753) at the bottom of vol. 3, p. 23 and the top of vol. 3, p. 22?

[23]

18 **Arbitram.+, Arbitr[tt]ors, & Award** vid Accord. p 12. and Accord in the Index at y[e] End[1]

text 29.

The Matter of Controversy, which may be committed To arbitram[t]., is either of Fact, or of a Right in Things + Actions Personal + Uncertain: but so as no[t] Freehold, tho' the submission is by Deed, nor Lease for Years of Land (Qu.) [Quare] may be ajudged from One to Another. Thus Debts due on Record or upon bill, or on certain Contracts, Matters concerning Matrimony, or Criminal Offenses, cannot be made matters of Arbitram[t]. But if men enter into Bond with Condition (as is usual) to stand to the Abritrament or Award, the Bond may be forfeited for Non-performance of the Condition. Wood. B4. ch 3. p. 553[5] [sic 523?] Quare, if the Award ajudged a Freehold from One to Another vid the case Rogers vs. Kemick Red. Rep. 52[6].

[1] West Symb 2 part p 164 s. 33[2] 1 Roll Abr 242. 244. 246. 265. 266.[3] 9 Rep 78.[4] 1 Cro. 233. 422.[7] Noy's max 108[8] 1 Danv Abr. 513.[9]

[2]Submission may be either General or, special: it may be by Word or Writing, Absolute or Conditional. If the Parties give a Bond to Each other, it must be Word for Word alike on both sides, only changing the Names etc.

2. West Symb. 2 Part p. 163. s.2. 3. 4. p 165. s 34. p. 166. s. 38[10]. 8 Rep. 98,[11]

Wood B4. ch 3.p 553.[12]

Page [23]

1. This is Quincy's cross-referencing system. As most arbitrations result in an "accord" you would need to look at that section on his numbered page 12 [17], which is duly cross-referenced to this page. He also had a front "index," his pages 4 [11] to 8 [15]—a sort of table of contents giving each section heading—and an "index at ye end," his pages 175 [148] to 182 [155], which contained extensive cross-references, primarily to notes between pages 150 [93] and 174 [117]—such as a cross-reference under "accord" to a "New Bond Pleaded by Way of Accord-Bad Idea" citing to his page 166 [109], which lays out the dangers involved, i.e., the new bond "is not any discharge."

2. This is a citation to William West's *Symboleography*, printed in two volumes, "part one" appeared in 1590 and "part two" in 1594. (Hereafter, "West's *Symboleography*.") See Sweet & Maxwell, *supra*, p. 487. It is one of the earliest known collections of sample legal forms, including bills of exchange, wills, and fines and concords. The citation refers to Part 2, page 164 (an outline for "Compromise and Arbitrement") and particularly "section 33," which describes "What things are arbitrable, and what are not."

3. These are a series of citations to *Rolle's Abridgment*, vol. 1 (1668). See page [9], note 1.

4. This is a citation to *Henry Peytoes Case* (1613), *Croke's Reports*, vol. 9, p. 77b, deciding that "accord and satisfaction by one should discharge all the Executors and Trespassors." *Id.*, p. 79b. See page [17], note 3, and page [8], note 2, for other references to Henry Peytoe's case.

5. This is a citation to Wood's *Institute* (1745 edit.), Book 4, Chapter 3. See page [7], note 3. Quincy closely copies from Wood.

6. A citation to a case, *Rogers* v. *Kenwrick* (1763), in Quincy's own first book of *Law Reports*, which he called the *Red Reports*. See page [90], note 3. The 1865 edition of *Quincy's Reports*, repaginated from the original contains the case on page 62. Note that Quincy twice questions the accuracy of the point cited by "Quare!"

7. The first citation is to *Brunkhornes Case* (1661), *Croke's Reports*, vol. 1, p. 233 (obligation with a condition). See page [21], note 6. The second is to *Sower* v. *Bradfield* (1661), *Croke's Reports*, vol. 1, p. 422 (debt upon an arbitrement).

8. A citation to Noy's *Maximes*, Maxime 108. See page [8], note 4.

9. A citation to Knightly D'Anvers, *A General Abridgment* (London, 1705–1727)? See John D. Cowley, *A Bibliography of Abridgements, etc* (London, 1932), p. 97. (Hereafter, "Cowley.")

10. A citation to West's *Symboleography* (London, 1618 ed.). See note 2, above. The section cited on pages 163, 165, 166 constitute an outline of how "a compromise is defined" (page 163, sections 2, 3, 4), and requirements, such as that "every compromise be made in writing" (page 165, section 34) and methods for "binding the parties to perform the award" (page 166, section 38). Note, early editions of West have many errors in pageation, i.e., page "163" is given "136" in the 1618 edition.

11. This is a citation to *Baspole's Case* (1611), 8 *Coke's Reports* vol. 8, p. 98, specifically pp. 97b–98a, which describes different types of submission to arbitration.

12. This is another citation to Wood's *Institute* (1720), book 4, chapter 3, p. 553. See note 5, above.

[24]

Arbitrament etc 19

a Note, That [a] Submission to an Award by
8 Rep Bond may be countermanded by Deed. Such
82[1] Authorities in their own Nature are Revo-
-cable as a Letter of Attorney etc tho' made
irrevocable by Express Words. But then the
Bond is forfeited. If it had been without
b Obligation, etc. one might revoke and
forfeit Nothing.

6 Rep. 44[2] [b] Where an Accord with Satisfaction may be pleaded, an Award may be pleaded+ vice versa, vid Accord. p. 18.[3]

Where one of the Parties to an Award made on a Submission in Court pursuant to the act of 9+10 W. 3. ch 15.,[4] dies before the money p[d]. [paid] no Sci. fac. [scire facias], can issue ag[t]. his Heir or Exc[tt]or, to enforce Paym[t]: for the award tho' established by Court, is not in the Nature of a Judgm[t] or Degree to be prosecuted but in the Nature of a Contempt, which dies with the Person. By all the Judges St. [sitting?] in Chan. 22.3.[5]

If there be an award to pay a Sum of Money, a Tender + Refusal has been formerly held no Per-
-formance, as in the Case of Hunt + Craven.[6] But it has be ajudged otherwise since. 2 L[d]. Raym. 964.965.[7] Wood B. 4. ch. 3 p. 555.[8]

How differently a Submission + a Release of All Actions operate and the Reason of this operation. Haw. Abr. 381[9] vid p. 84[10].

Page [24]

1. Citation to *Vynior's Case* (1611), *Coke's Reports,* vol. 8, p. 82b (revocation submission to an award).

2. Citation to *Blake's Case* (1607), *Coke's Reports,* vol. 6, pp. 43b–44a. ("[N]either Arbitrament, or Accord with satisfaction is a Plea, when the Action is grounded upon a Deed." *Id.*, p. 43b.) "That this Action of Covenant was founded upon the Deed, and could not be discharged but by matter of as high nature, and not by any accord. . . ." *Id.*, p. 43b.

3. Cross-citation to Quincy's entry on "Accord," at his page 18 [23].

4. The Statute 9 & 10 William the Third, Chapter 15 (1699). This Statute provides that parties may agree that their submission to arbitration by made a rule "of any of His Majesty's Courts of Record." It is set out in full in Wood's *Institute* (1722) at p. 527.

5. This citation has not been identified. It could have been to one of the many chancery reports published before 1763. See Sweet & Maxwell, vol. 1, pp. 344–49. It was not unknown for chancery judges to consult with the other royal judges in a process not unlike the "informal" Exchequer Chamber proceedings. My thanks to my learned colleague Charles Donahue Jr.

6. "*Hunt + Craven*" refer to a citation in *Squire* v. *Grevett* in *Lord Raymond's Reports* (1703), pp. 964–65. See note 7, below. "*Craven*" appears to refer to *London* v. *Craven* (1655), which can be found in *Style's Reports*, pages 481–82: "for if he should sue the plaintiff may plead his tender and refusal against him, and that will be judged as payment."

7. This citation to *Squire* v. *Grevett* 2 *Lord Raymond's Reports* (1703), pp. 964–65, is directly from Wood's *Institute* (1772 ed.), Book 4, ch. 3, at p. 527. "If there be an Award to pay a Sum of Money, a Tender and Refusal has been formerly held no Performance, without actual Payment: But it has been adjudged otherwise since." *Id.*, p. 527. But it appears here that Quincy worked directly from *Lord Raymond's Reports*, for the language of *Squire* v. *Grevett*, which also mentions Hunt and Craven, more closely matches Quincy's text. *Lord Raymond's Reports*, vol. 2, p. 964, records "A tender and refusal has been formerly held no performance without actual payment, as in the case of Hunt and Craven. But it has been adjudged otherwise since."

8. Wood's *Institute* (first folio edition, 1722) citation to the above passage in note 7 (book 4, chapter 3).

9. Citation to *Hawkins's Abridgment*, p. 381. See page [8], note 1. Quincy does not directly copy these words, but rather comments on the distinction that Hawkins presents.

10. Reference to Quincy's page 84 [74], where he more fully discusses releases of all actions relative to submissions to arbitrament.

[25]

20 Baron & Feme.[1]

vid Baron + Feme in the Index at the End of this Book. vid Vol. 4. p. 6. Tit Curtesy.[2]

Husband cannot grant Lands etc to his Wife, during the Coverture, nor any Estate or Interest to her, nor enter into Covenant with her. But he may covenant with others for her Use etc. Wood. B 1. ch 6. p 61.[3]

A Feme cannot devise to her Husband.

Baron + Feme cannot be Witnesses for or ag^{t} Each other, except they may be Witn^{s} ag^{t} Each other in Case of high Treason for the sake of Govern^{t}:, or upon the statute of 3 H7. chap. 2.[4] Where the Wife may be Evid. ag^{t}. her Husband for forcibly taking her away + marrying her. The Wife is so much under the Power of her H, that She is disabled to contract with Any Person without his Consent, precedent or subsequent, express or pre-sum'd. If the W plays + loses[5] her H's money, the H may recover it. She cannot bind her H in Strictness for Necessaries by any contract, unless a precedent or Subsequent assent is proved or presumed: But usually her Contracts are allowed, if She buys goods for herself, Children, or family, as Bread etc or for her own necessary Apparel. The H is bound to maintain his W in Necessaries, + therefore if Goods come to H's Use it is Evid. to prove his Assent, but not binding Evid; for it may be contradicted by Other Proof as that He gave his Wife ready money; Admitting

Page [25]

1. "Baron and Feme" is from the Law French for "husband and wife." "A wife being under the protection and influences of her *baron*, lord, or husband, is styled a *feme-covert* . . ." Jowitt, p. 214. Due to the constricted legal personalities of wives in Quincy's time, this is an important section.

2. Another reference to Quincy's excellent cross-referencing system at the end of the book,

and to his six-page compilation of "Legis Miscellanea . . . of Estates" which he placed in his volume 4, and which has been reproduced as pages [126] to [131] in this volume. The second page of that compilation is page 6 [127] of volume 4, and begins a discussion of "curtesy," i.e., the husband's right in the wife's lands at her death.

3. A citation to Wood's *Institute* (1720) on "the effects and consequences of marriage," Book 1, ch. 6, p. 61. See page 7, note 3.

4. A citation to the statute of the 3rd year of Henry VII, chap. 2 (1488), which established penalties for "carrying a woman away against her will, that hath lands or goods." See Ferdinand Pulton, *A Collection of Sundrie Statutes*, London (1632), p. 401. Obviously, this would be a situation where a woman must be able to testify against her husband.

5. "[P]lays and loses," as in gambling.

[26]

Baron & Feme 21

Admitting then that the H sh.[d] be charged in strict
-ness for necessaries; tho' he knows nothing of
them; [yet if] he forbids particular Persons to
trust his W, he shall not [be] charged after such Pro-
-hibition. A Prohibition in general not to
trust a W, as by putting her in the Gazzettte etc.
cannot amount to a Legal Notice. A Man
shall not be charged by the Contract of his W, (ex-
-cept as above for Necessaries) if he hath no
Notice of it, tho' the Things do come to his Use.
Neither, shall a H be bound by his W's receipt
of his money.

If the H threaten his W to beat
or to kill her, She may make him find security
for the Peace.

1. Sed vid. 1 L.[d] Raym[d]. p 515 Cage vs. Acton[2]

It is generally true, that the Agree-
-ments between H + W*1* before Marriage are
extinguished by the Marriage. Wherefore it is
usual for the H to covenant with Others for the
Use of his Wife, as for her jointure, etc.[1] When there is no
Agreem[ts]: or Settlem[ts] before Marriage, *x* the H gaineth by the

*x*Co: Lit. 351. a.[3] y[rs]

Mar.[ge] a Freehold in Right of his W, if he taketh a Woman
to W that is seised in Fee⊕. And He may make a Lease of 21

⊕yet the estate gain'd by the H is uncertain. vid. ibid.351.a.[4] + vid vol. 4. p. 6+7.[5]

or three Lives of her Estate, + it shall be good + effectual in
Law ag.[t] the W, if it be made according to the Statute of
the 32 H8 chap 28 (vid of Leases, Wood B 2 chap 3 p 281.)[6]

Page [26]

1. "Jointure" normally refers to a provision made by the husband for his wife for her support after his death. It could be both beneficial to the wife, or it could be a device to attempt to bar her common law entitlement to dower (income on one-third of her husband's lands at his death), or to force the wife to choose between the jointure and the dower. See Jowitt, p. 1018. Quincy's point is that any valid promise of jointure for the wife's "use," or equitable benefit, had better be with third parties, as an agreement with the wife herself would be "extinguished" by the marriage.

2. "*Sed vid*," or "but see," *Cage* v. *Acton, Lord Raymond's Reports* (London, 1743), vol. 1, p. 515, which notes the opposite of Quincy's point, "the marriage of obligor and obligee will not extinguish a bond . . ." These two-volume reports covered the period 1694–1732, and are heavily relied on by Quincy. A likely edition for Quincy's use was published in 1765. See Sweet & Maxwell, pp. 307–08.

3. A citation to *Coke on Littleton*, p. 351a ("what things are given to the husband by marriage . . ."). See page [7], note 9; page [2], note 1.

4. Another citation to *Coke on Littleton*, p. 351a ("[I]f a man taketh to wife a woman seised in free, he getteth an estate for freehold in her right . . .").

5. A citation to Quincy's "Legis Miscellanea . . . of Estates" in his fourth volume of notebooks. Pages 6 [127] and 7 [128] discuss curtesy and also cite to *Coke on Littleton*, p. 351a.

6. Citation to the statute 32 Henry VIII, chap. 28 (1541) "Leases made by tenants in Fee or Fee-taile, in the right of their wives . . . which be good, which void," and a citation to Wood's *Institute* (1720), book 2, chap. 3, p. 281. See page [7], note 3. Correct citation seems to be page 282.

[27]

22 **Baron & Feme**

The H also gaineth a Chattel real, as a Term for Years etc. to dispose of, if He pleases, by Grant or Lease in her Life time, or by surviving her. Otherwise it remains with the W *x*; for the H cannot charge it⊗ with a Rent, etc + can make no Disposition thereof by his last will, if He doth not survive his W. If he grants away only Part of the Term, the W shall have the Reversion; but if he grants the whole term of his W upon Condtton, etc + the Condtton is broken, the W is barred; for the whole Interest is passed away. Where He may dispose of the W's Term He may forfeit it upon Exctton for the H's Debt; the shff may sell the Term during the Life of the W. Where the Wife is out of Possession during the Coverture, or hath only a possibility, or is possessed of a Chattel Real as Exttrix, the H cannot have it, tho' he survives her. Lastly, the H by the M [marriage] hath an absolute Gift of all Chattels personal in Possession of the W in her own Right; wether the H survives the W or no. But if these chattels personal are Choses in Action (ie. Things to be demanded by Action) as Debts by Obligtton, Contract, +c the Husband shall not have them, unless He + his W recover them. A Chose in Action tho' not assignable at Law, yet is so in Equity; +the H may assign it alone, as he may any other part of his W's Estate personal: so he may a contingent Interest which

x And if H be outlaw'd or attainted, it is a gift in Law. Co: Lit 351.a.[1] But if he make no disposition or forfeiture of it in his Life, yet it is a Gift in Law unto Him if He do survive his Wife but if He make no Disposition + die before his W, she shall have it again. Ibid 351.a.[2]

⊗ So as to bind the W, if she survive. Co Lit. 351.a.[3]

Page [27]

1. A citation to *Coke on Littleton*, p. 351a. ("Also if the husband bee attained of felony, the king gaineth no freehold but a pernancie [i.e., "pernancy" . . . to take profits of the land] of the profits during the Coverture [i.e., marriage] and the freehold remaineth in the wife.") This could be an important point in times of civil unrest, when people might be accused of treason. See page [2], note 1; page [7], note 9.

2. Almost a direct quotation from *Coke on Littleton*, p. 351a.

3. The statement in the text marked by Quincy with ⊗ is inaccurate, unless modified by the statement below, directly from *Coke on Littleton*, page 351a. The husband can change such land with a rent, the rent just will not survive his death as an obligation of the wife. In Coke's words, "But if the husband change the chattell reall of his wife, it shall not bind the wife if she survive him." *Id.*, p. 351a.

[28]

Baron & Feme 23

[continues from page 22 [27]]

He has in Right of her, or a Possibility, wch tho' not strictly good by way of Assignm[t]; yet will operate as an Agreem[t], when there is a valuable Consider- -ation. All the foregoing from Wood B 1 C6 p61–63.[1]

DEBTS of the WIFE dum sola.[2] If the W before M [marriage] was in Debt, the H + W must be sued for this Debt, living the W. But if the W dies, the H shall not be charged for the debt of his W after her Death, if the Creditors of the W do not get Judgm[t] during the Coverture. The H, as such is not chargeable in a C[t] of Equity, any more than at Law, with the Debts of the W after her Decease; not even tho' he had a large Fortune with Her; as on the Other Hand he is, during the Coverture liable to all her Debts, altho' he did not get a shilling with her. Ibid. 63–64.[3]

COVENANTS

USE to the + with the Wife.

A Husband may covenant with Others to stand seis'd to the Use of his Wife, or He may make a Feofment to her Use; but if He make a Covenant with his wife to stand seis'd to her Use, it is VOID.

Hawk Abr. 168[4]

Chattels reals, as Leases for Years, Wardships, + the like, are not given to the husband absolutely, (as all Chat- -tels personal are) by the Intermarriage, but conditio- -nally if the Husband happen to survive Her, + He hath Power to alien them at Pleasure but in the mean time, the Husband is possess'd of the Chattels reals in Right of his Wife. Co. Lit. 299.b. 300. a.[5]

If a Feme sole be possess'd of a Chattel real, + be

thereof

Page [28]

1. A citation to Wood's *Institute* (1720), book 1, chapter 6, pp. 61–63 ("effects and consequences of marriage"). See page [7], note 3.

2. Debts "*dum sola*" are contracted while the wife is single, i.e., unmarried.

3. Continued citation to Wood's *Institute* (1720), book 1, chapter 6, pp. 63–64.

4. Citation to *Hawkins's Abridgment*, page 168. See page [8], note 1. The "use," or "trust" is void because a person cannot covenant with themselves, and a husband and wife have one legal personality. Quincy very closely copies this text from Hawkins.

5. *Coke on Littleton* at pp. 299b to 300a. Almost an exact copy of Coke's annotations. See page [2], note 1; page [7], note 9.

[29]

24 J. p. 27[1] <u>Baron & Feme</u>

+ The Reason of this. vid. sup. 22.[2]

thereof <u>dispossess'd</u>, ++ then taketh H, + the W dieth, if ye H surviveth, this Right is not given to the H by the Intermar:ge, but Excttors or Adminttors of the Wife shall have it, so it is if the W had but a Possibility. Co Lit. 351.a[3] In the same manner it is if W be possess'd of the Chats: reals in <u>auter Droit</u>,[4] as exittx or adminix, etc + she marrieth, the Law maketh no Gift of them to the H, altho' He surviveth her. In the same manner if a Woman grant a Term to Her own Use, taketh H + dieth, the H surviving shall not have this Trust but the Excttors or Adminttors of the W, for it consists in Privity. <u>Chattels reals</u> consisting <u>merely in Action</u> the H shall not have by the Marriage, unless he recovereth them in the Life of the W, as a Writ of Right of Ward, <u>a valore maritagii</u>,[5] a Forfeiture of marriage, + the like, whereunto the W was intituled before Marriage. But <u>Chattels reals</u> being of a mixt Nature, vizt, partly in Possession, + partly in Action, which happen during the Coverture, the H shall have by ye Marge if he survive ye W, albeit he reduceth them not into Possession in her Lifetime: but if W survive Him, She shall have them: as if H be seis'd of a Rent Servi. Char:or Seck,[6] in right of his W the Rent become due during the Coverture, the W dieth, the H shall have ye Arrearages, but if W surviveth the H, She shall have them, + not ye Excttors of the H. <u>Et sic de similibus</u>.[7] But if the arrearages had become due before the Marriage, there they were merely an Action before the Marriage and [CONTINUES IN LEFT MARGIN]

And therefore the H shall not have them by the Comn: Law, altho' He survive Her. And so it is of Releases, <u>mutat: mutand</u>: But now by Stat: 32.H.8. cap. 37 if H survive W He shall have ye arrearages, as well incurr'd before the Mar:e as after. Co Lit: 351.b[8]

Page [29]

1. Quincy runs out of space on this page, which is densely written and is written down the left margin. He indicates here that he continues "Baron & Feme" on his page 27 [32]. That page may contain additions by a later hand. See notes, page [32], *infra*. His page 28 is blank, and he continues "Arbitram^{t} + Award" from his page 18 [23] to his page 29 [33]. Obviously, he entered topics like "Estates" in alphabetical order in his notebook, but did not estimate correctly how much space was needed for "Baron & Feme." This suggests how important husband and wife "law" and arbitration "law" was in Quincy's Massachusetts.

2. A reference back "*vid. sup[ra]*" to Quincy prior discussion at his page 22 [27].

3. *Coke on Littleton*, p. 351a ("what things are given to the husband by marriage").

4. "*Auter droit*," i.e., "in the right of another." For example, when the wife holds possession as an executor, rather than in her personal rights, she holds for others, i.e., the person entitled in the estate. See P. G. Osborn, *A Concise Law Dictionary* (London, 1964), p. 39.

5. *A valore maritagii*, "on account of marriage."

6. "Rent Servi. Char:or Seck." Quincy has abbreviated Coke's words at *Coke on Littleton*, p. 351a. Written out, they are "rent service, charge or seck." "Seck" refers to a "dry" rent service, i.e., one where no tenure is created and thus there are "no incidents such as the right of distress and escheat." Osborn, *A Concise Law Dictionary*, p. 289. The Landlord and Tenant Act of 1730, s.5 gave the owner of every rent seck a right of distress for it. This act, passed long after the *Coke on Littleton* text, is not noted by Quincy. *Id.*, p. 275. Instead, he copies the seventeenth-century law.

7. "*Et sic de similibus*," i.e., "and thus regarding similar cases," "same for the husband as for the wife."

8. *Coke on Littleton*, p. 351b ("what things are given to the husband by marriage"). This is almost an exact copy. *Mutatis mutandis*: "with the necessary changes made."

[30]

vid. Vol 4 p.5 + onward[1]

Estates. vid Lands, Tenements + Hereditaments. p. 47[2] 25

Estates by (course of) the Common Law are divided into, 1st: Estates of Inheritances. 2 Estates less than Inheritance. Estates of Inheritance are, 1st Fee--simple. 2. Fee-tail. Hale's Analy. Sect 29.[3]

Sect 31. Estates at Common Law less than Inhe--ritance are, 1st: Estates of Freehold. 2dly: Estates less than Freehold. Estates of Freehold are divided into, 1st: Such as arise by Act of Law. 2 Such as arise by Act of the Party. Freehold Estates arising by Act of Law are, 1st: Tenant by the *x* Curtesy of England. 2. Tenant in Dower. *x* *x* vid Vol. 4. p 6+7.[4]
Freehold Estates arising by Act of Party are,
1:st Tennant for his own Lifet: which is either,
1:st Simply so; Or 2. With a priviledge annex'd;
as Tenant after Possibility.
2. Tenant pur auter Vie *t*. *t* vid Vol. 4. p.9.[5]
2. Estates less than Freehold are of two Kinds:
1:st Certain. 2. Incertain. Estates less than Freehold certain are, Leases for Years.*ø* *ø* vid Vol.4. p.10.[6]
2. Incertain Estates less than Freehold are, Estates at Will.

The Incidents to all these particular Estates, except Tenancy at Will, are these, viz. They are transferable from One to Another, unless particularly restrain'd, By Condition; or By Limitation. They are forfeitable. Ibid.s31[7]

Page [30]

1. Reference to Quincy's volume 4, where he places a six-page "Legis Miscellanea cursim, libris exscprita [sic] of Estates" at his page 5 [126].

2. Quincy's cross reference to his following notes on "Lands, Tenements + Hereditaments" at his page 47 [45].

3. Citation to Matthew Hale's *Analysis of the Law by a Learned* (London, 1713), republished in a 2nd edition, 1716, Sect. 29.

4. The above passage comes from *Id.*, Sect. 31, with a citation to Quincy's volume 4, page 9 [130], part of his Legis Miscellanea of Estates. See note 1, above.

5. "Pur auter vie," a life tenancy defined by the life of someone other than the person in possession. Citation is to Quincy's volume 4, page 9 [130], part of his Legis Miscellanea of Estates. Page 9 [130] is dedicated to "Tenant for Life" and references back to this page of the *Law Commonplace.*

6. *Id.*, vol. 4, p. 10 [131].

7. This "Ibid" reference appears not to refer back to the Vol. 4 citations but to the earlier citation to Hale's *Analysis* (see note 3 above), section 31. This sequence suggests that the two Hale's *Analysis* citations were noted by Quincy before he later inserted internal cross-references to other notes in this and other of his volumes.

[31]

26 Estates

All Estates may be reduced to Inheritance, Freehold or Chattels. Wood B. II.. ch 1 p 119.[1]

An Interest, in legal Understanding, extendeth to Estates, Rights, + Titles that a man hath of, in, to, or out of Lands; so that by Grant of his whole Interest is such Lands, Reversions as well as Possessions in fee simple shall pass. Ibid. 120[2] .

Page [31]

1. Wood's *Institute*, book 2, chapter 1, p. 119. The correct page in the 1772 edition is p. 113. An almost direct quote.

2. *Id.*, book 2, chapter 1, p. 120. An almost direct quote. Underscoring in original.

[32]

Baron & Feme 27

A feme covert has no power to make a contract without her H.[1] + therefore such Contract is absolutely void. 1 Com. Dig 567[2]
FemeCov: by herself alone cannot plead. Cro: Jac. 239-288-445[3]
F.C. [feme covert][4] was not liable to an Exec^tt^ion as Com.Law.3Bur. 1785-[5]
A woman whose husband had left her about 12 years before had carried on trade in her own name as widow + given re ceipts in her own name, being sued for debt contracted in the course of her trade gave coverture in evidence + that her H. had been lately in Ireland+ Holt directed the Jury to find for Defn + so they did. 1. Bac. 308.[6]
On N. A. Deft proved she had a H. alive in France Jury found for plf. On motion for a new trial as a verdict against evidence it was denied for a divorce shall be in- tended. 1. Salk. 117.[7]
If B. + Feme separate by consent + she has a separate al- lowance tis unreasonable she should have it in her power to charge him + it is not to be presumed but tradesmen trust her on her own credit + not on the credit of her H. + a personal notice is not necessary it is suf-
Ray: 444[9] ficient that it be public + generally known. H.
Holt ruled a H. was liable to his wifes contracts, because they cohabited. 1. Salk. 113-[8]Everyman is obliged to maintain his wife + an action may be maintained against him for necessities provided suitable to her rank in life

4.Bur.2178[10]

[QUINCY'S PAGE 28 IS BLANK.]

Page [32]

1. "H" stands for "husband." This page purports to be a continuation of Quincy's section on Baron & Feme at his page 24 [29], but it appears to be in a different hand. Even more significantly, it contains citations to vols. 3 and 4 of *James Burrow's Reports* (covering 1756–1772), which were not published until 1771 and 1776, respectively. See Wallace, pp. 446–52; Sweet & Maxwell, *supra*, vol. 1, p. 294. That puts the citation to volume 4 after Quincy's death on April 26, 1775.

2. Citation to John Comyns, *Digest of the Laws of England* (London, 1762–1767), vol. 1, p. 567. See Sweet & Maxwell, *supra*, vol. 1, p. 17; Cowley, p. 135.

3. Citation to *Croke's Reports* (covering 1582–1641), vol. 2 [James], p. 239, *Watson* v. *Thorpe and his Wife* (1611) ("The *feme* by her self cannot plead"); p. 288, *Tampion* v. *Newson and Bridget his Wife* (1612) (accord); p. 445, *Anonymous* (1618) ("for the *feme* without the *Baron* cannot be sued").

4 "F.C." and "Feme Cov" refer to "feme covert," i.e., a married woman with a living husband.

5. A citation to *Burrow's Reports* (covering 1756–1772; London, 1771), vol. 3, p. 1785. The case is *Lavie and Another, Assignees of Jane Cox, A Bankrupt,* v. *Phillips and Others, Assignees of John Cox, A Bankrupt* (King's Bench, 1765), *Id.*, p. 1776. (Wife was a "sole trader," carrying on a separate trade from her husband "according to the Custom of the . . . City of London." Held that "this custom subjected the Wife to an Execution [of creditors to her 'effects in trade']: to which She was not liable at *Common Law.*" *Id.*, p. 1785 (Wilmot J.). In other words, only the special London custom of "sole-trading" for women enables a creditor to reach the married woman's effects without regard to the husband. At common law she could not be sued directly, i.e., the holding of the case in note 6, below.

6. Citation to *Bacon's Abridgment* (1736), vol. 1, p. 308. See page [37], note 5. ("Where a Wife shall be considered as a feme sole.") The case cited is *Anonymous* (1701), *Modern Reports*, vol. 12 (covering 1690–1702; London, 1738), p. 603.

7. "N. A." is for "non-assumpsit," she "did not promise." This was the standard plea by way of traverse denying the existence of an express promise "or of matter of fact from which the promise alleged would be implied by law and thus raised the general issue." Jowitt, *supra,* p. 1231. The citation is to *Salkeld's Reports* (covering 1689–1712; London, vol. 1 and 2, 1717), vol. 1, p. 117. See Sweet & Maxwell, p. 308; Wallace, p. 399. *Dearly* v. *Duchess of Nazarene* supports the proposition that Quincy is discussing.

8. *Id.*, vol. 1, p. 113. The case cited is *Langfort* v. *Tiler* and supports the proposition cited.

9. *Lord Raymond's Reports* (covering 1694–1734; London, 1743), vol. 1, p. 444. See page [26], note 2. The case is *Langfort* v. *Tiler*, for which he cites to *Salkeld's Reports* as well. See note 8, above.

10. A citation to *Burrow's Reports* (covering 1756–1772), vol. 4, p. 2178. See note 5, above. Volume 4 was first published in London in 1776, so this notation, at least, cannot be Quincy's. The case is *Thompson* v. *Hervey* (1768). The action was by a landlord, who had provided lodging in Bristol for the wife of the second son of the late Earl of Bristol, Thomas Hervey. He refused to pay. Held for the plaintiff, as the wife "had no maintenance from her Husband, no admittance to his House. She was obliged to procure Lodging and Maintenance somewhere else. Every Man is obliged to maintain his Wife" and provide "necessary Subsistence Suitable to her Degree and Rank of Life." *Id.*, vol. 4, p. 2178.

[33]

Arbitram[t] & Award 29

See before p. 18.

Neither natural or legal disabiities do hinder any one from being an arbitrator. If they are incompetent judges, y[e] fault is in those who chuse them. _______ If they observe their commission + keep within their jurisdiction, their sentences are definitive, from which there lies no appeal RSL. 1 Vol. 103. cites Wood 921 cited 3 Vin. 41.[1]

[QUINCY'S PAGES 30, 31, 32 ARE BLANK.]

Page [33]

1. This citation is an exact copy of a citation in 3 *Viner's Abridgment* (1742–1753), p. 41: "R.S.L. 1 Vol. 103. cites Wood, 921." See page 16, note 2. Quincy clearly took the citation from Viner directly. R.S.L. refers to *Readings on Statute Law*, an alphabetical digest by a "gentleman of the Middle Temple" (London, 1723–1725). See Sweet & Maxwell, vol. 1, p. 547. The second part of the citation refers to Wood's *Institute*, *supra*, p. 921. Notice the extrordinary emphasis is in the original.

[34]

Of Estoppels

vid. Estoppel in the Index to this Book. p.178.[1] 33

a Lit: 58
1 Inst: 45.a.
47 b. 352.a.+b[2]
4 Rep. 53.
s4.[3]

In Deeds indented all Parties are *a* Estopped to say against any Thing contained in it. It stops a Lessee, to plead that the Lessor had nothing in the Land. But where an Interest passes from the Party, there can be no Estoppel against him.

b Lit 58.
1 Inst. 47.b[4]

In Deeds-poll a Lessee is *b* not estopped to plead, That the Lessor had nothing at the Time of the lease made. For the Lessor only puts His Seal to it, + delivers it only as His Act.

Page [34]

1. Cross-reference to Quincy's detailed index at the end of the book, with a further citation under Estoppel at his page 178 [121].

2. Citation to *Coke on Littleton*, p. 45a, commenting on Littleton's Section 58, *Id.*, at pp. 43b–44a, on issue of estoppel against leasee. Also to *Id.*, p. 47b (accord) and pp. 352a & b (definition of "estoppel").

3. Citation to *Rawlyns Case* (1588), *Coke's Reports*, vol. 4, pp. 52a at 53a, sec. 4, for proposition cited after "b" in text.

4. Citation to *Coke on Littleton*, p. 47b, commenting on Littleton's Chapter 58, *Id.*, at pp. 43b–44a. "If the lease be made by deed indented then are both parties concluded, but if it be by deed pool the Lessee is not estoppel. . . ." *Id.*, p. 47b [as only the lessor has sealed the deed, thus it is only the lessor's act].

[35]

34 Evidence. vid. P: 75[1]

If there be an express Promise of marriage by the man + it appears the woman embrac'd it + by her actions at that time behav'd herself so as if she agreed to the matters tho there be no actual Promise, yet that shall be sufficient Evidence of a Promise on her Side. 6 Mod: 72.[2]

Indeb: Assum:[3] For money rec[d] to the Plf's Use, + produc'd his Debtor who paid it as a Witness. Rejected by Holt, because if He be nonsuited the matter is at large again + He may sue the Debtor, + therefore the debtor swears to the Discharge of Himself + by Consequence is no Witness. Ibid. 151[4]

Of the Party's Confession. vid 2 Haw: pl. 429 etc[5]

It is an obvious principle, that a witness who perjures himself in one circumstance, is credible in none: 2 Hume's Hist.y of y B [Britain] 288 Edit 1757.[6]

Page [35]

1. Cross-citation to Quincy's "Of Pleading" entry on his page 75 [66].

2. Citation to *Modern Reports or Select Cases adjudged in the Courts of K.B., Chancery, G.P. and Exchequer* (consisting of 12 parts, covering 1669–1732), vol. 6, p. 172. London, 1682, 1698, 1698, 1703, 1711, 1713, 1716, 1730, 1730, 1736, 1737, 1738. See Sweet & Maxwell, pp. 304–05; Wallace, pp. 347–90.

3. "*Indeb: Assum*" for "*indebitatus assumpsit*," the famous legal fiction that permitted an action on the case in trespass to permit a recovery of money, in place of the old writ of debt. See J. H. Baker, *Introduction to English Legal History* (4th ed., 2002), pp. 346–48.

4. Citation to *Clark* v. *Dealy* (1704), *Modern Reports*, vol. 6 (covering 1669–1732), p. 151. The correct citation to volume 6 is important to note here, since Quincy regularly cites to volume 6 as volume 7, incorrectly, elsewhere in the *Law Commonplace*. See, e.g., page [97], note 1. See note 2, *supra*. The debtor is obviously an interested witness, as he could be sued himself on the debt, if the plaintiff is "nonsuited," as Holt observed. Holt is named throughout Quincy's note, clearly a favorite.

5. Citation to William Hawkins, *Pleas of the Crown* (London, 1716–1721), vol. 1, p. 429. This was a leading treatise on criminal law. See Sweet & Maxwell, vol. 1, p. 362.

6. Citation to David Hume's *History of Great Britain* (London, 1754–1762), vol. 2, p. 288, as printed in 1757. Hume (1711–1770) was a great British philosopher, mathematician, economist and ethicist. It is interesting that Quincy knows Hume's *History*, and cites it as legal authority.

[36]

Evidence. vid. p. 75. 35

The constant Rule of Law has been, to reject all parole Proof brôt to supply the words of a will, or to explain the Intent of the Testator, + that nothing dehors[1] should be averred, is the express Resolution in Lord Cheyney's case[x]: And this Rule has since been thôt necessary to be adhered to, not only on Account of the Statute of Frauds + Perjuries,[3] which was made to prevent Perjury, Contrariety of Evidence, + Uncertainty; but because little regard ought to be had to the Expressions of the Testator, either before or after making his Will; because possibly those expressions might be used by Him, on Purpose to controul or disguise what He was doing, or to keep his family quiet; or for other secret motives + Inducements, which cannot after his Death be found out; but this Rule has rec[d] a Distinction which has greatly prevail'd of late, viz[t] between Evidence offer'd to a Court, + Evidence offer'd to a Jury; for in this last Case, no parol Evidence is to be admitted, lest the Jury might be inveighed by it, but in the first Case it can do no Hurt, being to inform the Conscience of the Court; who cannot be biassed or prejudiced by it. Cases in Equity abr. 230[4]

[x] 5 Coke 68,[2]

A witness must give the very words even before a Judge, + not say, they were to this Effect etc. Ibid. 231 s.3.[5] It

Page [36]

1. "*Dehors*," i.e., "outside" the document.

2. Citation to *The Lord Cheyneys Case* (1592), *Coke's Reports*, vol. 5 (covering 1572–1616), p. 68a, holding that "construction of wills ought to be collected out of the words of the will in writing." *Id.*, p. 68b. See page 1, note 2.

3. A reference to the famous Statute of Frauds (1677) 29 Car. 2 c.3., which required that conveyance of land interests, wills of real estate, declaration and assignment of trusts, and certain

types of contract be in writing. See J. H. Baker, *An Introduction to English Legal History* (4th ed., 2002), pp. 349–50, 368.

4. A citation to *Cases in Equity* (covering 1730–1737; London, 1741), p. 230. See Sweet & Maxwell, vol. 1, p. 345.

5. *Id.*, at p. 231, sec. 3.

[37]

36 Evidence vid. p. 75.[1]

It is reported to have been said by Holt, that the Copy of any Original is Evidence, wheresoever the Original is Evidence, if prov'd a true Copy; but the Copy of a Probate of a Will in the Ecclesiastl: Court is no Evidence because that is but a Copy of a Copy. Comb. 337.[2]

General Rules

1:st You must give the best the Nature of the Thing is capable of. Theory of Evid. 110.[6] Law of Evid. 4. 8. 15. 16.[7]

2. No Person interested can be a witness. T.E. 94 T. E. 122[8]

vid. 1 Mod 282.[3] Viner Tit. Evid. p.118.[4] 2 Bac: abr. 313.[5]

3. Hearsay is no Evidence T.E. 111. T.E. 152. 153.[9]

4. Where general character is put in Issue, Evidence of particular Facts may be given; but not where it comes in collaterally. T.E. 113.[10]

5. Ambiguitas Verborum latens Verificatione suppletur nam quod ex Facto oritur ambiguum Verificatione Facti tollitur. T.E. 115.[11]

6. In every issue the Affirmative is to be proved. T.E. 116.

7. No Evidence need be given of what is agreed by the Pleadings. T.E. 117.[12]

8. When a Man cannot have the Advantage of the special Matter by Pleading, He may give it in Evidence on the general Issue. T.E. 118[13]

9. If the Substance of the Issue if prov'd, it is sufficient. T.E. 118[14]

10. Where a Matter comes to be determin'd in a collateral way, the Determination of any Court having competent Jurisdiction, is conclusive Evidence of such Matter: and

Page [37]

1. Quincy's cross-citation to his section "Of Pleading" at his page 75 [66], which also cites back to this page.

2. "Ecclesiastical Court." Citation is to *Comberbach's Reports* (covering 1685–1699), p. 337, *Rex* v. *Hains* and supports the proposition in the text. See Wallace, p. 396. These reports were published in 1724, and covered King's Bench cases. See Sweet & Maxwell, vol. 1, p. 298.

3. Citation to *Lutterel* v. *Reynell* (1670), *Modern Reports* (1669–1732), vol. 1, p. 282. See page [35], note 2. This case offers the proposition of evidence for which it is cited on the following page, 37 [38]. See page [38], note 6.

4. *Viner's Abridgment* (1742–1753), vol. II title "Evidence" at p. 118. See page 16, note 2.

5. Citation to Matthew Bacon, *A New Abridgment of the Law*, 5 vols., vol. 2, p. 313 (London, vols. 1–2, 1736, vol. 3, 1740, vol. 4, 1759, vol. 5, 1766). See Sweet & Maxwell, vol. 1, p. 16; See Cowley, p. 121. The relevant section in the 1768 section starts on page 312, "Where the Law requires the highest proof the Nature of the Thing is capable of," and continues to page 313 to discuss "Of hearsay Evidence" etc.

6. This is a citation to [Bathurst (H.)] *Theory of Evidence* (Dublin, 1701), p. 110 (hereafter, "*Theory of Evidence*"). This book was later incorporated into Buller (Sir F.), *Introduction to the Law relative to Trials at Nisi Prius* (Dublin, 1773). See Sweet & Maxwell, vol. 1, pp. 378, 335. Quincy is here making heavy use of a new book published in Ireland.

7. This is a citation to [Nelson (W.)] *Law of Evidence* (London, 1717), pp. 4, 8, 15–16, republished in 1739 and 1744. See Sweet & Maxwell, vol. 1, p. 379.

8. *Theory of Evidence*, *supra*, pp. 94, 122.

9. *Id.*, pp. 11, 152–53.

10. *Id.*, p. 113.

11. *Id.*, p. 115. "Latent ambiguity of words may be supplied by evidence; for ambiguity arising upon the deed is removed by proof of the deed." See E. Hilton Jackson, *Latin for Lawyers* (1915), p. 124.

12. *Id.*, p. 117.

13. *Id.*, p. 118.

14. *Id.*, p. 118.

[38]

General Rules

Evidence. 37

And in case it is final in the Court of which it is a Determination, such Determination will be conclusive in any other Court having concurrent Jurisdiction. T.E. 37.[1]

11. No Verdict shall be given in Evidence but between such who are Parties or Privy to it. T.E. 18. T.E. 34.[2]

12. When any Person claims by a Deed in the Pleadings, he ought to make a Profer of it to the Court: And where he would prove any fact in Issue by a Deed, the Deed itself must be shewn, + prov'd by one witness at the least. Theory of Evid. 46.-53. T.E. 79.-95.-101.102.[3]

A Person that may be admitted as a Witness, at a Trial, may give words in Evidence to the Jury, which were spoken to him by Another Person, who by the Rules of the Court might not be admitted as a Witness at the Trial. Mich. 22 Car. BR.[4] For it is but a matter of Evidence, + is left to the Jury how far they will give Credit to them; + it is lawfull for One that is admitted as a witness to give anything in Evidence which may concern the Matter in Question.

1. Lilly abr. 549. Evidence.[5]

(vid. Viner Tit. Evid. 118 A. b. 38).[7]

Tho' Hearsay is not allow'd as direct Evidence, yet it may be made use of to this Purpose; vizt to prove that a Witness is constant: to Himself, whereby his Testimony is corroborated. By L^{d} Ch: Baron. 1 Mod. 282 Lutterel vs Reyvel + al.[6]

Page [38]

1. *Theory of Evidence*, *supra*, p. 37. See page [37], note 6.
2. *Id.*, pp. 18, 34.
3. *Id.*, pp. 46–53, 79–95, 101–02.
4. Reference to a case that occurred in the 22nd year of Charles I (1647) and was decided in

the "BANCO REGIS," or King's Bench. *Croke's Reports*, vol. 3, referred to by Quincy, covers only the first 16 years. See page 21, note 6.

5. A citation to John Lilly, *Practical Register; or, General Abridgment of the Law*, 2 vols. (London, 1719), vol. 1, p. 549. Republished in 1735 and 1745. See Sweet & Maxwell, vol. 1, p. 273; Cowley, p. 105.

6. *Lutterel* v. *Reyvel*, *Modern Reports*, vol. 1, p. 282 (1670). See page [35], note 2. This case is also cited on the preceding page, see page [37], note 3.

7. A citation to *Viner's Abridgment* (1742–1753), vol. II, title "Evidence," p. 118. "A. b. 38" is the title of the section on hearsay on page 118 to which this citation is directed.

[39]

38 Exec^{tt}ors & Co-Exec^{tt}ors. vid. Tit. Pleading etc. in the index at the End. vid. Admin^{tt}or etc. in the index at the End.[1]

15. H. 6 Fitz Exor. 12[2]

Debt ag^{t} one as <u>Exec^{tt}or</u>, + ag^{t} the other as <u>Exec^{tt}or of an Exec^{tt}or</u>; it was objected, That the Action ought to be brôt ag^{t} the Survivor alone; but adjuged, That it lies ag^{t} both; for the Exec^{tt}or who was <u>dead</u>, might have the Possession of the Goods whilst <u>living</u>, + if the Action should be brôt ag:^{t} the Survivor <u>alone</u>, he might plead <u>Plene administravit</u>,[3] wch w^{d} be a good Plea.

Fitz Exor. 29[4]

But about 24 years afterwards, the contrary Judgm^{t}: was given in a like Case; + the Reason was, because the Plf might have brôt his Action whilst the other was living + that it was either his Folly or Negligence to omit it, + therefore the action wd. [would] not lie ag:^{t} the Exec^{tt}or of the dead Exec^{tt}or. <u>quod nota</u>.[5]

4 Leon. 193 vid Guillam vs. Gill. 1 Leon. 164[7]

The like Judgm^{t} was given many years afterwards: SC.[6] The Testator made two Exec^{tt}ors, who prov'd the Will, + one of them <u>died</u>, + then an action was brôt ag^{t} the <u>Survivor</u> + the Exec^{tt}or of the other, + for that Cause it was abated, + adjudg'd. That it ought to be brôt ag:^{t} the <u>Survivor Alone</u>.

Nelson's Lex Testa: p.164. 165.[8]

Page [39]

1. Cross-reference by Quincy to his useful index at the end. See "Pleading" and "Administrator," Quincy's pages 180 [123] and 175 [118], respectively.

2. "15 H. 6" refers to the 15th regnal year of Henry VI, or 1437. The citation appears to be to Anthony Fitzherbert's *La Graunde Abridgment* (London, 1516), republished in 1565. See Sweet & Maxwell, p. 18. The citation appears to be to the abridgment entry "Executor," passage 12, the earlier one probably being a year book case of 1437, hence the date. It is highly impressive that Quincy could have had access to such a rare and valuable book. See Joseph H. Beale, *A Bibliography of Early English Law Books* (Cambridge, 1926), p. 105. The book's "Beale No." is R463.

3. "Plene administravit" or "fully administered." This is the defense raised by an executor when sued on a testator's debt after he "has fully administered the deceased's estate and . . . has no assets to satisfy the claims." Osborn, *A Concise Law Dictionary*, p. 243.

4. Fitzherbert's *La Graunde Abridgment* (London, 1516) at "Executor," p. 29.

5. "*Quod nota*," i.e., "note this."

6. Illegible. "SS." Or perhaps "SC.," Latin *scilicet*, "namely."

7. Citation to an anonymous case of an executor's action in *Leonard's Reports* (covering 1540–1615), vol. 4, p. 193. These reports were published in four parts between 1658 and 1675, with a 2nd ed. in 1687. See Sweet & Maxwell, p. 303, Wallace, pp. 142–43. The second citation is to *Levinz's Reports* (covering 1660–1697), vol. 1, p. 164. The case is *Guillan* v. *Gill* (1665).

8. The citation is to William Nelson's *Lex Testamentaria* (London, 1728), pp. 164–65. There was a second edition in 1724, republished in 1728 and 1733. See Sweet & Maxwell, p. 493.

[40]

42 Insurance

Barratry in a Policy is the same as fraud. 1 Strange 581.[1]

Where Salvage fall short of the freight, it is a total Loss. 2 Strange 1065.[2]

Where the Master deviates for the Benefit of his Owners, it is not Barratry, tho' it may be a Breach of Contract. Ibid. 1173.[3]

Concealing an Information of Danger avoids a Policy, tho' the Loss does not happen by such Danger. Ibid. 1183[4]

A ship never heard of is presumed to be founder'd at Sea. 2 Strange 1199.[5]

Goods lost after the Owner had taken them from the ship, Insurer is discharg'd. Ibid. 1236.[6]

Insurer is liable where a ship goes back to perform Quarentine. Ibid. 1243.[7]

Policy on any ship the Plf shd: sail in from V [Virginia] to L [London], not transfer'd to another ship that the Plf goes on Board of in the voyage. Ibid 1248.[8]

An intention [to] deviate does not discharge the Underwriters. Ibid. 1249.[9]

On a Policy, Interest or no Interest, a Recapture after being in an Enemy's Port, will not avail the Insurer. Ibid. 1250.[10] Insurance

Page [40]

1. *Strange's Reports* (covering 1716–1749), vol. 1, p. 581. See page 21, note 12. The case is *Knight* v. *Cambridge* (1724) (defining "Barratry of master and mariners"), *Id.*, p. 581. "Barratry" refers here to its maritime significance, i.e., a "wrongful act wilfully committed by the master or crew of a ship to the prejudice of the owner or charter," such as "stealing the cargo." See Osborn, *A Concise Law Dictionary*, p. 45. See p. [42], n. 2, *infra*.

2. *Strange's Report's*, *supra*, vol. 2, at p. 1065. The case is *Boyfield* v. *Brown* (1737), holding as stated. *Id.*, p. 1065.

3. *Id.*, vol. 2, at p. 1173. The case is *Stamma* v. *Brown* (1743), which holds that such a deviation is not insurable barratry when the master is "acting all the while for the benefit of his owners. . . ." *Id.*, vol. 2, p. 1174.

4. *Id.*, vol. 2, at p. 1183. The case is *Seaman* v. *Fonereau* (1744) (The ship was leaky. This should have been disclosed to insurers, although loss was due to capture by Spaniards). *Id.*, p. 1183.

5. *Id.*, vol. 2, at p. 1199. The case is *Green* v. *Brown* (1744), holding as stated.

6. *Id.*, vol. 2, at p. 1236. The case is *Spanaw* v. *Caruthers* (1745), holding as stated.

7. *Id.*, vol. 2, at p. 1243. The case is *Wapler* v. *Eames* (1740), holding as stated.

8. *Id.*, vol. 2, at p. 1248. The case is *Dick* v. *Barsell* (1746) (The plaintiff embarked on one ship from Virginia to London. He insured any ship he "should come in on." The first ship sprang a leak. He then went aboard a second ship, which arrived safely. The first ship was captured. Held, the insurance was due on the first ship, and would not have been due if the second ship had been lost).

9. *Id.*, vol. 2, at p. 1249. The case is *Foster* v. *Wilmer* (1740) (The captain intended to deviate from the agreed voyage, but the ship was captured before it left the agreed route. Held, the insurer must pay).

10. *Id.*, vol. 2, at p. 1250. The case is *Dean* v. *Dicker* (1740) (Insured ship captured, and then rescued from Spanish port after 8 days. Held, the insurer must pay, even though the owner lost only the cargo, the ship being returned after paying salvage). *Id.*, p. 1250.

[41]

Insurance 43

Insurance of ships + freight comprises only the freight of Goods actually shipped. 2 Strange 1251[1]

The mariners force the master to return; that is no Deviation nor Barratry. Ibid. 1264.[2]

A ship warranted to depart with Convoy, She may go to the Place of general Rendezvous,[3] at the Hazard of the Underwriters. Ibid 1265.[4]

Page [41]

1. A citation to *Strange's Reports* (covering 1716–1749), vol. 2, p. 1251. See page [21], note 2. The case is *Tonge* v. *Watts* (1746) (Ship is wrecked by tempest while being "careened," before voyage begins and cargo loaded. Owner cannot recover for loss of voyage profits "as the goods were not actually on board." *Id.*, p. 1251).

2. *Id.*, at 1264. The case is *Elton* v. *Brogden* (1747). "Deviation" is intentional departing from the agreed "due course" of the voyage. "Barratry" in maritime law is when a master or crew of a ship commits a wrongful act against the owner, without the owner's "conivance." See p. [40], n. 1, *supra*. It is generally covered by insurance. Here, the master did not intentionally deviate, but was forced to return by the crew. The return voyage was found to be covered by the insurance. The plaintiff did not recover on the grounds of "barratry," but because there was no "deviation." *Id.*, pp. 1264–1265. See page [40], note 1.

3. *Id.*, at p. 1265. The case is *Gordon* v. *Morley*, joined with *Campbell* v. *Bordieis* (1747). The ship *Ranger* was trying to make the convoy rendezvous when taken. The policy read "warranted to depart with convoy." It was held that the loss was covered by the policy. *Id.*, p. 1265.

4. Quincy's method in all of these cases was to go through *Strange's Reports* in strictly chronological order, excerpting interesting insurance holdings, largely relating to ships.

[42]

44 **Jury** See same Title p.50.[1]

The Jury may take the Law upon them if they will. 1 Stran. 105 cites Litt. § 368.[2]

The Question, in the Case of ___________[3] being merely a Point of Law, the Ch: Justice told the Jury, they must find for the Dft which they were very unwilling to do, + therefore to prevent their going contrary to his Opinion, I suffer'd a Nonsuit 2 Stran. 1221.[4]

Where the Evidence of a Witness is false in an immaterial Part, the Jury need not give him Credit in any other Part. 1 Cro. 310.[5] But if They find upon Evidence that does not prove the Allegata, there it is easy to subject them to an Attaint, because it is manifest that what is found is on Evidence not corresponding to their Issue; + hence it is necessary that ye matters in Issue should be set forth with all convenient Certainty, that it may be seen how far + when the Jury are mistaken; as in Trespass etc.; + so on special Contracts they must be set forth so precisely, that if Evidence be given of another Contract, + not that in the Allegations, + yet the Jury find for the Plf, They may be subject to an Attaint. 3 Bac: Abr: 278.[6]

It is Province of the Justices to determine what the meaning of any word or sentence in an Act of Parliam^t^. is. 5 Bac: Abr: 218[7]

The Judges shall judge what is a reasonable Time Ibid.

Hume calls, the Institution of Juries, admirable in itself, + the best calculated for the Preservation of Liberty + ye administration of Justice, that ever was devised by the Wit of Man. History of Eng^d^ 65. Edit 1762.[8]

Nothing contributes more, than the institution of tryals by Jury, to the support of that equity + liberty, for which the English laws are justly celebrated. Hume Histry 4v. 704[9]

Page [42]

1. Quincy's system for filing out his book meant that he sometimes underestimated the space that should be alloted to the alphabetical titles. "Jury" proved to be such a highly important category, which is an insight into Quincy's legal world.

2. A direct quote from *Dominus Rex* v. *Bennett* (1718), *Strange's Reports* (covering 1716–1749), vol. 1, p. 105. See page [21], note 12, *supra*. *Strange* in turn cites to *Littleton's Tenures* §368 (1st ed., circa 1481). See *Coke on Littleton*, fol. 228, where Coke comments on Littleton that "Although the Jurie, if they will take upon them (as Littleton here saith) the knowledge of the Law . . . yet it is dangerous for them so to do, for if they doe mistake the Law, they runne into the danger of an Attaint. . . ." See page [7], note 9, *supra*.

3. Left blank in text. Quincy is referring to *Lekeux* v. *Nash* (1745), *Strange's Reports* (covering 1716–1749), vol. 2, p. 1221.

4. This is almost a direct quote from *Lekeux* v. *Nash*, *supra*, note 3. "I" must refer to the plaintiff, who suffered a nonsuit.

5. A rough summary of the holding in *The Queen* v. *Ingersall*, *Croke's Reports* (covering 1582–1641), vol. 1, pp. 309–10. See page [21], note 6.

6. Almost a direct quote from *Bacon's Abridgment* (1736), vol. 3, p. 278. ("Juries" "Where punishible by Attaint.") This is the same point made by Coke. See note 2, *supra*. Attaint had become an anachronism by Quincy's day. See Introduction, *supra*, pp. 60–61.

7. Almost a direct quote. *Id.*, vol. 5, p. 218. (Page 217 in the 1770 edition.)

8. This is a citation to David Hume's (1711–1776) famous *History of Great Britain*, which was published in four volumes, in 1754, 1757, 1759 and 1762, respectively. Quincy's political *Commonplace Book*, set out in full in this series at *Quincy Papers*, vol. 1, pp. 100–93, extracts large sections of Hume. See *Id.*, pp. 101, 123–27, 139–40, 165. Hume was highly trained in the law and was appointed Advocates' Librarian in Edinburgh in 1752. Hume's work has been seen as in the school of John Locke, seeing a need to balance the conflicting roles of reason and experience and "instinct or sentiment." See *The Oxford Companion to English Literature* (Margaret Drabble, ed., 5th ed., 1985), p. 995; *The Dictionary of Philosophy* (Dagobert D. Runer, ed., 4th ed., 1942), p. 132. This would have appealed to Quincy's own political inclination as a moderate. See Neal L. York, "Quincy's Literary Arsenal," *Quincy Papers*, vol. 1, pp. 56–57.

9. *Id.* A citation to Hume's fourth volume of 1762, p. 704. This remains a most eloquent testimonial to jury trial.

[43]

JURY. See Same Title. p. 50. 45

A Jury shall try whether there is a particular Custom or no, + not the Judges; except the Custom in Debate is of Record in the same Courts Wood. p.6.[1]

X Of ancient Time if a Deed appear'd to be rased or interlined in Places material, the Judges adjudged upon their view; the Deed to be void: But of latter Time, the Judges have left that to the Jurors to try wether the rasing or interlining were before the Delivery. Co: Lit: 225. b.[2] vid. 3 vol. p. 85. 121.[3] Theory of Evid. 72. L.E. 106. 107.[6]

vid. 10 Rep 92.[4] g. Law of Evid. 106. 107.[5]

Were I therefore a Juror; (says the author of the L^r^[?], on Libels, etc: p. 11.[7]) I should take nothing implicitly or upon Trust, in this Respect. X from any man, but should endeavour to form my own Judgment of the matter as an impartial Juror, + not as a Statesman: plain Truth + fact, + common sense, + not political Convenience, far-fetch'd Inference, or ingenious Innuendo, being the proper Object + Interest of my Oath by the Law of the Land.

X Viner Evid. page 58 pl.3[8]

Mr Hawles, (says the same author. p. 14) in his excellant Treatise upon the Duty of petty Juries, call'd The Englisman's Right,[9] says, "When the "Matter

that is, what affects the Person of a man, his Liberty or Life.[10]

Page [43]

1. Wood's *Institute*, p. 6. See page [7], note 3. A direct quotation.

2. *Coke on Littleton*, p. 225b. See page [2], note 1; page [7], note 9. Almost a direct quote. "Rasing" in the original would be "erasing" today.

3. As with most of Quincy's unidentified "*vid.*" citations, this is to the massive 23 volume *Viner's Abridgment*, to which Quincy clearly had access. See p. 16, note 2.

4. A citation to *Doctor Leyfields Case*, 10 *Coke's Reports* 88a at 92b. "That it be not raised or interlined in material. . . ."

5. This could be a citation to *Viner's Abridgment* (1742–1753), volume on "Evidence" (vol. 11), where pages 106 and 107 discuss writings whose validity is in question. See page [16], note 2.

6. Same citation as note 5, above.

7. "Letter on Libels"? Citation to Sir Roger L'Estrange, *A Word Concerning Libels and Libellers* (London, 1681). See Sweet & Maxwell, *supra*, p. 106.

8. Citation to *Viner's Abridgment* (1742–1753), vol. 11, Section on "Evidence," p. 53, pl. 3. See p. 16, note 2, *supra*. This marginal citation is relevant to both "x" notations in Quincy's text.

9. Citation to Sir John Hawles, *The Englishman's Right; a dialogue between a Barrister-at-Law and a Jury-Man, setting forth the Antiquity, the excellent designed Use, the Office and Priviledges of Juries, by the Law of England* (London, 1680), pp. 22 and 25–26 in the 1732 edition. There were subsequent editions in 1680, 1693, 1732, 1763 and 1764, and four more subsequent to 1770. See Sweet & Maxwell, *supra*, p. 376. See Holdsworth, *supra*, vol. 9, pp. 213, 223, 234, vol. 12, pp. 459–60. Hawles (1645–1716) was solicitor-general (1695–1702) and a "sturdy Whig." *Id.*, vol. 9, p. 459. His books were "popular in America." *Id.*, vol. 9, p. 460.

10. This phrase is found in the bottom left margin of the page. It appears to explicate the word "Matter," which appears in the bottom right corner.

[44]

46 **Jury**[1]

"Matter in Issue, is of such a Nature, as no Action, Indict-
"ment or Information will lie for it singly, but it is work'd
"up by special Aggravation into matter of Damage or Crime,
"as that it was done to scandalize the Government, raise Sedition,
"affront Authority, or the like, or with such or such an evil In-
"tent: if these Aggravations, or some overt Act to manifest
"such ill Design be not made out in Evidence, then ought the
"Jury to find the Party Not Guilty. And if a Jury shall refuse
"to find that such an Act was done falsely, scandalously, ma-
"liciously, with an intent to raise Sedition, defame the Gov^{t},
"or the like, their mouths are not to be stopped, or their Con-
"sciences satisfied, with the Court's telling them you have
"Nothing to do with that, it's only matter of Form on matter of
"Law, you are only to examine the fact, whether He spoke such
"words, writ or sold such a Book or the like: for if they should
"ignorantly take this for an answer, + bring in the Prisoner
"Guilty, tho' they mean of the naked fact only, yet the Clerk
"recording it demands a further Confirmation thus, Then you
"say D. is guilty of the Trespass or misdemeanor in the manner+ form
"as He stands indicted, + so you say All ? And the verdict is drawn
"up, the Jurors do say, upon their Oaths, that D. maliciously, in
"Contempt of the King + Gov^{t}, with an intent to scandalize the
"Administration of Justice, + to bring the same into Contempt, +
"to raise Sedition, tc (as the words were laid) spoke such words,
publish'd such a Book, or did such an Act, ag:^{t} the Peace of our
Lord the King, his Crown + Dignity.[2]

Page [44]

1. Quincy's section of "Jury" continues for three more pages after "Of Lands, Tenements, + Hereditaments" on his pages 50–52 [48–50].

2. Quotation from Sir John Hawles, *The Englishman's Right*, *supra* (emphasis in original). It is actually a combination of two excerpts, first from page 22 (of the 1734 edition), which ends with "Not Guilty," and then, beginning with "And if to a jury" to the end, from pages 25–26 (of the 1734 edition). See page [43], note 9, *supra*. The underlining is added by Quincy. The issue discussed was of the greatest importance in the eighteenth century and featured in major political trials like that of William Penn in England in 1670 and Peter Zenger in America in 1735. See *The Trial of Peter Zenger* (V. Buranelli, ed., 1957).

[45]

Of Lands, Tenements or Hereditaments. 47

Vid Estates. p.25[1]

vid. vol 4. p. 5.[2]

[a] 1 Inst 41. b. 388. a.[3] — How may They be Acquired? 1:st By [a] Occupan--cy, where the Title Accrues by the first Entry. Wood. B2. c3. p 227.[4]

2dly By Descent

[b] Lit. 3[5] — Inheritances may lineally [b] descend but not Ascend. x[7]

3 Rep 40.[6] — So the X Father can never come to the Lands which his Son has purchased in Fee simple by lineal Ascent, tho' He may by collateral Ascent; As when the Son's Lands come to his Uncle (as Lands may Ascend in the collateral Line), They may afterwards come to his Father as Heir to the

[c] 1 Inst. 11.[6] b. — Uncle. [c] The Uncle in this Case is Heir, but not absolute Heir. For if after the Des--cent to the Uncle, the Father hath Issue another Son or D:ter, that Issue shall enter upon

[d] Lit. 8 — the Uncle, + take the Estate from Him, etc.

1 Inst. 11. b. 15, a+b[8] — One must be Heir to Him that was last [d] actually

3 Rep. 41[9] — seised, or that hath actually enter'd on the Lands. For if a Tenant in Fee-s:[10] of Land, Rent, Advowson, Use, etc., hath a Son + a Daughter by one Venter,[11] + a Son by Another, + dies

---

X — This was formerly settled Law here, but has since been ruled otherwise, in the case of Ames + Fisher. And Savage + Glover and Leveret + Clark. These Determinations directly against Law, said to be by some sound common lawyers.[12]

Page [45]

1. Reference back to page 25 [30] of *Law Commonplace*, on "Estates."

2. Reference to Quincy's volume 4, where Quincy begins a six-page compilation of "Legis Miscellanea cursim, Libris exscprita [sic] of Estates" at his page 5 [126].

3. Citation to *Coke on Littleton*, p. 41b, definition "occupant," and p. 388a. "That the heyre of the Lessee shall have the land to prevent an Occupant. . . ."

4. Citation to Wood's *Institute*, Book 2, chap. 3, p. 227. "How Lands, Tenements or Hereditaments may be Aquired (vis.) By Occupancy." Direct quotation.

5. Citation to *Littleton*, Sec. 3 (1481). See *Coke on Littleton* (1628), pp. 10b–11a. See also page [2], note 1; page [7], note 9. Rough quotation of rule against "lineal ascent."

6. Citation to *Ratcliffe's Case* (1592), *Coke's Reports*, vol. 3, p. 37 at p. 40, affirming proposition in *Littleton* about collated inheritance of uncle due to rule against "lineal ascent."

7. "x" refers to Quincy's inclusion below. Thus if a son acquires a land, and then dies, his living father cannot inherit directly. If the uncle is the next nearest kin, the uncle can inherit from his nephew, as the inheritance is collateral, not lineal. If the uncle then dies, the father can inherit the land from his brother, as that is also collateral. The land could conceivably be inherited eventually by the father, who could never inherit directly from the son, as that would be a prohibited "lineal ascent." Even more odd, the old common law held that if the father had additional issue of any sex, they would then be collateral heirs of the dead son, and entitled to take the land, even if they were born after the death of the son and after the uncle had received the land. The uncle was not an "absolute" heir as long as the father might have more children!

Quincy notes that the prohibition against lineal ascent was "formerly settled Law here, but since has been ruled otherwise," presumably by the Massachusetts Superior Court of Judicature, although the cited cases do not appear in Quincy's own *Reports*. See note 12, *infra*.

In addition, in setting out the "canons of descent" on his page 49 [47], Quincy indicates that a father can inherit directly from a child in the absence of any uncles or aunts or their issue, and ahead of any half-blood heirs, although this would appear to be "lineal ascent." The argument may be that the father is inheriting through lack of collateral heirs, i.e., collaterally. But is this true if the father had no siblings?

8. Citation to *Littleton* (1481), Sec. 8 and *Coke on Littleton*, *supra*, at p. 11b, which discusses *Littleton*, *supra*, Sec. 3. See note 5, *supra*. Also citation to *Coke on Littleton*, *supra*, at p. 15 a and b, discussing *Littleton*, *supra*, Sec. 8, for the proposition that actual possession, or seisin, by the deceased is required for an heir to take. For example, if an elder brother is actually seized of an inheritance from his father, and then dies, his next oldest sibling by his mother will inherit collaterally, even if a sister. But if the eldest brother has not actually entered the land, a "half blood" younger brother by another "venter," or mother, will inherit before a "full blood" older sister, because the younger son is "Reine to the father, but not to his brother." See *Coke on Littleton*, *supra*, p. 14b, and *Littleton*, *supra*, Section 8.

9. *Ratcliffe's Case* (1592), *Coke's Reports*, vol. 3, p. 37 at p. 41. See note 6, *supra*. Stands for proposition cited.

10. "Fee-Simple."

11. Quincy uses the Latin "*venter*," or "womb," to mean "mother." "In the old books [*venter*] was equivalent to mother . . . two brothers 'by divers venters', meaning two brothers having different mothers." Jowitt, *supra*, p. 1826. See also *Cassell's Latin Dictionary* (J.R.V. Marchant. J. F. Charles, eds., London), 1946, p. 610.

12. See discussion at note 7, *supra*. This comment shows Quincy to be highly alert to the current state of the law, and no "slave to his books." This is also evidence that he may be receiving guidance from other senior lawyers, or from his peers.

[46]

48 Of Lands, Tenements, + Hereditaments.

[a] Lit. 4.	dies without Issue before actual Seisen, the younger
1 Inst: 12	Brother is Heir to the Father. But if the Elder Bro[r].
a+b[1]	had enter'd, the Sister should have been Heir to Him.
	None can inherit any Lands as Heir, but Only the Blood
⊗ Otherwise	of the [a] first Purchaser. ⊗ As if the Father purchases, the
Hume (v p 47)	blood of the Mother shall never inherit. But if a Son
N.B. The Honbl	purchases, and there is no Heir on the Part of the Father,
Judge Prat	then shall the Lands go to the Heirs on the Part of the
said, "that the	Mother. For they are of the Blood of the Son, the first
Com. Law w[d]	Purchaser. But where Lands do X Descend from the Part
hereafter be	of the Mother, the Heirs of the Part of the Father
again restored."[2]	shall never Inherit. So on the Contrary. Observe then
	the Difference where the Son purchaseth Lands
[b] Lit. 6.7.8.	in Fee-s:[4] + where He cometh to Them by Descent
3 Rep. 41. 42.[3]	on the Part of the Mother, or of the Father.
	None shall have Land of Fee-s:[4] by Descent as Heir to any man,
	unless He is Heir of the [b] Whole Blood ´ As if a man has two
	Sons by Divers Venters,[5] + the Elder purchaseth Lands in
	Fee-s: + dies without Issue, the younger Brother shall not
	Inherit, but the Uncle of the Elder Brother, etc. A Sister
[c] 1 Inst. 10. a	of the Whole Blood shall be preferred before the younger
15. b	Brother of the Half-Blood. But the younger Brother
3 Rep. 41. 42.[6]	may be Heir to his Father or Uncle, for He is of the
	whole Blood to them. [c] Half-Blood is no Impediment
	of Descent as to Fee-s: Lands of the Crown, or to Dignities.[7]
	neither is it respected in Estates in T;[8] because the Issues
	do claim in by Descent per Formam Doni;[9] + the Issue
	in T is ever of the Blood to the Donee.

X Paterna paternis, materna maternis. 1 Inst. 13. a.[10]

Page [46]

1. Citation to *Littleton* (1481), Section 4, as annotated at *Coke on Littleton*, pp. 12a–12b. See

page [2], note 1, page [7], note 9. According to Coke's annotations: "And note, it is an olde, and true Maxime in Law, That none shall inherit any lands as heire, but only the blood of the first purchaser . . ." *Id.*, at p. 12a.

2. Citation to David Hume (1711–1776) *History of Great Britain* (1754–1762), vol. 5, p. 47. Hume was a favorite of Quincy's *Political Commonplace Book.* See *Quincy Papers*, vol. 1, pp. 101, 123–27, 139–40, 165. See also page [42], note 8. Hume was also a trained lawyer, as well as a philosopher and historian, and served as Judge-Advocate to General St. Clair in 1747 and was appointed Advocate's Librarian in Edinburgh in 1752. See *Oxford Companion to English Literature* (M. Dabble, ed., 1985), pp. 482–83. See also page [42], note 8.

The comment to "Judge Prat" is extremely significant. Benjamin Prat (1711–1763) was Chief Justice of New York, following a highly successful practice in Boston. He was one of John Adams's inspirations. See *Law in Colonial Massachusetts*, p. 363. See also pp. 230, 366, 370, 378. Quincy is clearly referring to a pronouncement by Prat in his judicial capacity. That Quincy was aware of Prat's views, in the absence of colonial law reports, is remarkable, and may have been the kind of experience that led Quincy, in 1761, to begin his own *Reports*. See *Quincy Papers,* vol. 3, "Introduction."

3. Citation to *Littleton* (1481), *supra*, Sections 6–8, and *Ratcliffe's Case* (1592), *Coke's Reports* vol. 3, at pp. 41–42, supporting text.

4. "Fee Simple."

5. "Mothers." See page [45], note 11.

6. Citation to *Coke on Littleton*, p. 10a, commenting on *Littleton*, *supra*, Section 2, for the principle of collateral inheritance of the half-blood brother, as full blood to father and father's brother, and *id.*, page 15b, commenting on *Littleton*, *supra*, Section 8, for same principle. In Littleton's words, the younger brother is "of the whole blood to him [his uncle on his father's side], albeit he be but of the halfe blood to his elder borther." *Id.*, p. 15a. There is a citation to *Ratcliffe's Case*, *supra*. See note 3, *supra*.

7. "Dignities" refer to the right to "bear a title of nobility or honour," such as an hereditary knighthoods, baronetcies, or ordinary peerages. Jowitt, *supra*, p. 630.

8. "Estates Entailed," i.e., the inheritance was limited to lineal "heirs of the body." If the grant was "in tail male," only heirs of the body male could inherit. The word "entail" comes from the Norman French "entaille" or "tailler," "to cut," i.e., a "cut down fee." See Jowitt, *supra*, pp. 715–16.

9. The action *per forma doni* ("form of the gift"), through the writ of formedon, enforced the rights of reverter and of remaindermen in an entailed grant. Thus, if there was a failure of issue when land was granted subject to an entail, the heirs of the original grantor could recover the land, i.e., "reverter." If a tenant in tail tried to sell the land as if it were a fee simple, not a limited fee, his own heirs, the remaindermen, had a claim to recover the land according to the form of the gift. In the past, this had created conceptual problems, as their interest in the land was still contingent while the tenant was alive. See J. H. Baker, *An Introduction to English Legal History* (4th ed., 2002), pp. 273–74.

10. From *Coke on Littleton*, *supra*, p. 13a. "That whensoever Lands doe descend from the part of the mother, the heires of the part of the father shall never inherit. And likewise when Lands descend from the part of the father, the heires of the part of the mother shall never inherit. *Et sic paterna paternis & e converso, materna maternis.*" *Id.*, p. 13a. The citation supports the passage marked "X" in the text.

[47]

Of Lands, Tenements +Hereditaments 49

[a]1 Inst: 50. b.[1] [a] Note, That an Heir shall never enter + take as a Purchaser, if He is named only to take by way of Limitation of Estate in Course of Descent.

In short, Lands + Tenements in Fee-s:[2] Descend, 1st To the Eldest Son as Heir, + to his Issue: The Sons first in order of Birth, + for want of Sons to all the Daughters equally. For where there are Females in Equall Degree, they all inherit as one Heir, + as Coparceners.[3] 2:dly If the Eldest Son has no Issue, then to the next eldest Brother of the whole Blood, + his Heirs; + for want of a Brother to a sister, or Sisters of the Whole Blood, + to Her + their Issue. 3:dly For want of a Brother or Sister, to an Uncle + his Issue; or for want of Uncle to a Aunt or Aunts, + her + their Issue, 4.thly Thence to the Father. 5.thly Thence to the half-Blood + their Issue. 6thly for want of Uncle, Father + half-blood + their Issue, to the next of Kin in the Collateral Line.

Wood B2. c3. p. 228. 229. 230.[4]

Page [47]

1. A citation to *Coke on Littleton*, fol. 50b. See page [2], note 1 and page [7], note 9. Quincy must be referring to the annotation by Coke to Littleton's Section 62, which states that where two parties exchange land ". . . if one of them dieth, before the exchange be executed by entrie, the exchange is void; for the heirs cannot enter and take it as a Purchasor, because he was named only to take by way of limitation of estate in course of descent." *Id.*, fol. 50b.

2. "Fee-simple."

3. "Coparcenge" is where females in equal degree divide the land equally. In English common law, the eldest male heir usually took everything, and his younger brother nothing, i.e., "primogeniture," but if there was no male heir, sisters divided the land equally. This was because the feudal system valued the concentration of land in male heirs, but not in females, who usually lost control by marriage, anyway. See Daniel Coquillette, *The Anglo-American Legal Heritage* (1999), pp. 104–05.

4. A citation to Wood's *Institute* (1720), book 2, chap. 3, pp. 228–30. See page [7], note 3, *supra*. This is a rough summary of the canons of descent set out in Wood's section on "How Lands, Tenements or Hereditaments may be Acquired . . . By Descent." Quincy does a good

job of clarifying and summarizing the poorly organized Wood's *Institute.* Note also that Quincy indicates that a Father can inherit if there are no full-blooded collateral heirs, which seems to contradict Wood's statement that "the Father can never come to the Lands which his Son has purchased in Fee-simple by lineal Ascent." See the discussion at page [45], note 7.

[48]

50 **Jury.** See Same Tit: p.44, 5.[1]

If a Jury give a verdict on their own knowledge, they ought to tell ye Court so-etc. 1 Salk 405. anon:[2]

If ye Court do believe that ye Jury have given their verdict ag^{t} evid: they may order a new Trial. 2 Lill: abr: 605.[3]

If ye plt do fail in proving his issue, ye verdict ought to be found for ye dft, except if Jury do know of their own knowledge, that ye dft is guilty. So that ye Jury is not tied up by ye evid: that they must always give their verdict according to it, for a man's own knowledge is ye best proof of things. Ibid. 644.[4]

If any one of ye Jury, that is sworn to try ye issue, be desired to give his testimony concerning some matter of fact, that lies in his own knowledge, + concerns the matter in Q:^{n},[5] as evid: to his fellow-jurors, ye Court will have him examined openly in Court upon his oath, touching his knowledge therein, + he is not to deliver his testimony in private to his fellow-jurors; for ye Court + Council[6] on both parts are to hear the

Page [48]

1. A reference to pages 44 [42] and 45 [43] of Quincy's commonplace, where the entry "Jury" had left off.

2. A citation to *Salkeld's Reports* (1689–1712), *Anon.*, vol. 1, p. 405. See page [32], note 7.

3. A citation to Lilly's *Practical Register; or General Abridgment of the Law*, 2 vols. (London, 1719), vol. 2, p. 605. "*Lilly's Abridgment*" was republished in 1735 and 1745. See Sweet & Maxwell, *supra*, vol. 1, p. 273. See also Cowley, *supra*, at pp. 105–06.

4. *Lilly's Abridgment*, vol. 2, p. 644. See note 3, *supra*. As usual, Quincy abbreviates "plt" for "plaintiff" and "dft" for "defendant." This is an important aspect of colonial jury trial that differs from modern practice, i.e., jurors could decide cases on their own knowledge. See Daniel Coquillette, *The Anglo-American Legal Heritage* (1999), *supra*, pp. 160–62.

5. "Question."

6. “Counsel,” i.e., the lawyers on both sides. This was an important safeguard on a jury’s reliance on its own knowledge, as opposed to what it learns in the courtroom, and indicates a transition to today’s ideal of a “neutral” jury, i.e., a jury with no prior knowledge of the case outside the courtroom.

[49]

Jury Same Tit. ante.[1] 51

S.E. Trials evidence given on either side as well as ye Jury,
Per Pais that it may be answered by ye other party, if need
221. Per. require, + that ye Court may direct ye Jury to find
Cur: Sty: according to ye evidence. 1 Lill: Abr: 512:
233. Bennet Viner Evid: 2 Lill: Abr: 126.[3]
v Hartford.[2] (L.a.3.). pl: 1.[4]

A privilege of the constitution of England——
—the jury——judges of Law as well
as fact. 2 Macaulay's hist:^{y} of Eng:^{d}
135. q.v. Edit. 1769.[5]

The Court cannot refuse a Gen:^{l} Verd:^{t} if the Jury will take the Law upon themselves. Trials per Pais 7th Edit: 1739. p.250.—and 246. 247, 8,9.[6]

The Jury may give their verdict without testimony, or against testimony, when they themselves have cognisance of ye fact. Ibid. 295. cites Plow: Com: 86.[7]

Page [49]

1. Referring to the same title "before," i.e., "Jury" starting on Quincy's page 44 [42].

2. This annotation is a copy of citations appearing in *Viner's Abridgment* (1742–1753), vol. II, title on Evidence (col. 11), p. 47, where Viner adds a marginal note "S E. Tr. Per Pais 221" and follows the adjoining text with the citation "Per Curiam, Sty. 233. Mich. 1670. B. R. Benet v. Hartford (Hundred)." See note 4, below. The first part refers to [George Duncombe's] *Trials per Pais: or Law concerning Juries by* Nisi Prius, *By S.E.* (London, 1665), pp. 221, 233; reprinted in 1666, 1682, 1700, 1702, 1718, 1725, 1739, and 1766. See Sweet & Maxwell, *supra*, vol. 1, p. 375. The second refers to the holding "per curiam" (i.e., by the court) reported in the case of *Bennet* v. *Hundred of Hartford* (1650), *W. Style's Modern Reports* (1646–1655), p. 233. See Sweet & Maxwell, *supra*, vol. 1, p. 210.

3. Two citations to *Lilly's Abridgment*, vol. 1, p. 512, vol. 2, p. 126, supporting the text. See full discussion at page [48], note 3.

4. Citation to *Viner's Abridgment*, title on Evidence, vol. 11, p. 47. See page [16], note 2. Citation supports the text.

5. A reference to the 2nd volume of Catharine Macaulay's (1731–1791) *The History of England from the Accession of James I to the Elevation of the House of Hanover* (3d ed., London, 1769–1772), 5 vols. There were previous multi-volume editions published between 1763–1765 (1st) and 1766–1771 (2nd). Quincy closely paraphrases and condenses from Macaulay's text regarding the case of Lord Balmerino.

6. This is highly controversial, and reflects a previous discussion in Quincy's notes. Obviously, a jury that can disregard an instruction of law from a judge has more power, a significant point in the Boston of Quincy's day. But such a jury also takes a serious risk of attaint, if it errs, a point emphasized by judges like Sir Edward Coke. But by Quincy's day, attaint had become an anachronism. See Introduction, *supra*, pp. 60–61. See the discussion at page [42], notes 6–7. Citation is to *Trials per Pais* (7th ed., 1739), pp. 246–50. See note 2, *supra*.

7. Citation to *Trials per Pais* (7th ed., 1739), p. 295. See note 2, *supra*. It, in turn, cites to Edmund Plowden's *Commentaries*, page 86, an important early set of reports first published in French in London in 1571. In its final editions, it covered the period 1550–1580. It was translated into English in 1761, and republished four times thereafter. See Sweet & Maxwell, *supra*, vol. 1, pp. 306–07; Wallace, *supra*, pp. 143–53.

[50]

52 Jury Same Title antea. + postea 50.[1]

Jury may go upon Evid: of their own personal knowledge, being returned de vicineto. Per Vaughan CJ. Viner Evid: (H) pl: 4. cites Vaugh. 147. Bushel's Case[2]

Evidence is only given for information of ye Consciences, + therefore if no Evid: is given on either part, yet may ye Jury find ye verdict either for ye plt or dft. 3 H. 7. 11. a Frowicke,[3] tho' ye Evid; given be conclusive, yet ye Jury may find ag^t^ it, + hazard ye attaint if they please. Ibid. Evid. (N. a.) pl: 6. cites Raym: 405 Chichester v. Phillips[4] & Jones. 146. SE. but it does not appear.[5]

Matter in LAW shall not be given in Evid: to ye Jury, but ye other may demur upon it; for Lay Gents can not discuss matter in Law as it seems there, but it is not expressly adjudged there. Viner Evid. (Z.a) pl: 1. cites Br: General Issues. pl: 51. wch cites 9. H. 6. 33.[6] It seems it ought to be such a matter y^t^ [that] ye judge may take to be doubtfull. Ibid (U. b: 1) pl: 1 note note cites Heath's max: 95. SE.[7]

In Demr: on Evid: ye consent of both parties is requisite. Ib: pl: 5. cites Heath's Max: 96.[8]———But

See post: 58[9]

Page [50]

1. Quincy is referring back to the "Jury" entries before at his pages 44–46 [42–44] and pages 50–52 [48–50], i.e., "before and after."

2. Being returned "*de vicineto*" refers to "from the vicinity, or neighborhood." The jury, in other words, came from the "vicinage," or nearby, and may therefore have personal knowledge of the case in question. As Coke said, "*Vicini vicinora praesumuntur scire*" ("Persons living in the neighborhood are presumed to know the neighborhood"). See Jowitt, *supra*, pp. 1836–1837. The citations are to *Viner's Abridgment* (1742–1753), *supra*, at title on Evidence. See page [16], note 2, which, in turn, cites *Bushel's Case* in Sir John Vaughan's *Reports and Arguments in the Common Pleas*, page 147 (1665–1674), published in London in 1677 and then, again, in 1706. See Sweet & Maxwell, vol. 1, p. 310. See also Wallace, *supra*, at pp. 334–37.

3. A citation to *Frowicke's Case*, Y.B. 3 Hen. 7, p. 11 (1488). This would have been found in

Sir John Maynard's great edition of the Yearbooks, published in London between 1678–1679. In particular, the 3d year of Henry VII would be in Part 11, published in 1679. See Sweet & Maxwell, *supra*, pp. 312–13. It would be impressive if Quincy had access to such a series, but by no means impossible. For example, the Harvard College Catalogue of 1723 had a "Yearbook" entry, "under K. Henry V. and K. Henry VI, from the 40 to the 50 of Edw. III." See *The Printed Catalogues of the Harvard College Library, 1723–1790* (W. H. Bond, H. Amory eds., Boston, 1996), at p. 40.

4. Another citation to *Viner's Abridgment* (1742–1753), Section on Evidence. See page 16, note 2. This in turn cites *Lord Raymond's Reports* (1694–1734), p. 405, *Chichester* v. *Phillips.*

5. This is a mysterious abbreviated citation. "SE." may refer to "S.E." *Trials Per Pais*, written by George Duncombe and published in 1665, page 146. Quincy cited this book before. See page [49], note 2. "[B]ut it does not appear" may refer to the fact that the cited case does not appear where it should in *Trials Per Pais*. This would indicate that Quincy was doing more than copying references, but was also looking them up!

6. Once again Quincy is citing to *Viner's Abridgment* (1742–1753). See page [16], note 2. *Viner's* in turn is citing Sir Robert Brooke's *La Graunde Abridgment* (London, 1573), reprinted in 1576 and 1586. See Sweet & Maxwell, *supra*. The section on "General Issue & Special Evidence" begins on fol. 14b of vol. 2 of the 1576 edition, and entry 51 is on fol. 16a, which summarizes Y.B. 9 Henry VI, 33 (1431), as indicated by Quincy. Brooke's entry supports Quincy's principle. "Car lay gents re discusses matter in ley . . ." *Id.*, vol. 2, fol. 16a. Quincy's careful notation of yearbook precedent more than three centuries old, as summarized in abridgments two centuries old, is impressive.

7. A further citation to *Viner's Abridgment, supra*, which in turn cites Sir Robert Heath's *Maxims and Rules of Pleading* (London, 1694), at p. 95. For "SE," see n. 5, *supra*, and p. [49], n. 2.

8. "In demurrer on evidence, the consent of both parties is requisite." Quincy cites back to *Viner's Abridgment, supra*, which cites *Heath's Maxims*, note 7, *supra*, p. 96. A "demurrer" was "a pleading by which one of the parties in effect alleged that the facts stated by the opposite party . . . assuming them to be true, did not sustain the contention based on them." Jowitt, *supra*, p. 609. If the demurrer is based on a question of evidence, it requires the consent of both parties.

9. Citation to Quincy's page 58 [55], which continues the obviously important topic of the "Jury."

[51]

Lease, Lessor, + Lessee. vid. same Titles in the Index at the End[1] 53

If a lease be made at Will, after a Quarter of a Year is commenc'd, the Lessee may determine it, but then He is oblig'd to pay that Quarter's rent; + in Case the Lessor determine his Will, after the commencement of a Quarter, He shall lose the Rent for that Quarter: But here a Lease is made from year to year so long as both Parties please, there after a year is commenc'd, neither the Lessor nor Lessee can determine their Wills for that year, they having for so long certainly Will'd the Estate. Holt. 415. 416.[2]

X or Will. vid Lit Sect 72.[4]

Lessor may distrain or bring debt for Rent arrear ag[t] Lessee for years, [x] but then it behoveth that the Lessor was seis'd of the Tenements at the Time of the Lease made, for nil habuit etc. is a good Plea for the Lessee unless the Lease be made by Deed indented. Lit. Sect. 58. (Co: Lit: 44.a) Co: Lit 47.b.[3]

[QUINCY'S PAGE 54 IS BLANK]

Page [51]

1. Quincy had a relatively sophisticated cross-referencing system at the end of his *Law Commonplace*. See Quincy's page 179 [122].

2. A citation to Sir John Holt's *Report of Cases determined by Holt [King's Bench] 1688–1710*, pp. 415–16 (published in London in 1738). See Sweet & Maxwell, vol. 1, p. 301.

3. A citation to *Littleton* (1481), *supra*, Section 58 "Tenant for tearme of yeares" as annotated in *Coke on Littleton*, *supra*, at p. 44a, with the specific point of the defense of *nihil habuit* described p. 47b, i.e., "If the lease be made by deed indented then are both parties concluded . . . but if it be by deed poll the Lessee is not estopped to say that the lessor had nothing [*nihil*] at the time the lease was made." *Id.*, at p. 47b.

The plea *nihil habuit in tenementis* (he had no interest in the tenements) denies the lessor's title. It is successful only for lessee "for years, or at will, without occupation by the lessee, for if the lessee had become tenant he would have been estopped from denying his landlord's title." Jowitt, *supra*, at p. 1226.

4. A citation to *Littleton*, *supra* (1481), at Section 72, i.e., "[I]f the lessor upon a lease at will, reserve to him a yearly rent, he may distreine for the rest behinde, or have for this an action of debt at his own election." See *Coke on Littleton*, at p. 57a. See also page [2], note 1; page [7], note 9.

[52]

LEGACY. 55

1 Wood p 345.[1] *1* Legacy is a particular Bequest or Gift of Goods + Chattels to one or more by Testament.

2 p 344.[2] *2* If there is a specifick legacy, or any particular Thing given in Specie, as a Lease, a Horse, a Silver Crop, etc. This must be deliver'd accordingly before any Other Legacy, if there are Assets.

3. p 345[3] *3* There is a Difference where the Property of a Thing is given, + when the Use of it only is given. For a Man may give the Use of his Plate, etc to One for Life, Remainder to Another. But if the Plate was given for Life, or for an Hour, a Remainder to Another would be void, + the Legatee may dispose of it. But if He does not dispose of it, He in Remainder shall have it. (A Bequest of a Chattel personal for Life, etc is now con--strued to mean the same Thing as a Bequest of the Use of it. 1 Vern 35.)[5]

4 2 Salk 415. vid Cases in Eq: abr: 294 295[4] *4* A, devises £100 a peice to two Children of IS at the End of ten years after his (the Testator's) Decease: The Children died within the ten years. This is a lapsed legacy + shall not go to the Exc^{tt}ors of the Children; for the Diversity is where the Bequest is to take Effect at a future Time, + where the Payment is to be made at a future Time. Whenever the Time is annex'd to the Legacy itself + not to the Payment of it, if the Legatee dies before the Time of Payment; in that Case it is a lapsed Legacy. If a Legacy be devised generally, + no Time ascertained for the Payment, + the Legatee be an infant, He shall be paid Interest from Expiration of the first year after the Testator's Death: But if the Legatee be of full Age, He shall only have Interest from the Time of his Demand, Otherwise it is in the Case of an Infant because

Page [52]

1. Citation to Wood's *Institute*, p. 345. See page [7], note 3.
2. *Id.*, p. 344.

3. *Id.*, p. 345.

4. *Salkeld's Reports* (1689–1712), vol. 2, p. 415. Also a citation to *Anonymous, General Abridgment of Cases in Equity*, vol. 1, pp. 294–95 (*Smell* v. *Dee*), which supports the proposition Quincy discusses. Vol. 1 was published in 1732 and vol. 2 published in 1756. There were several later editions, and continuing controversy as to the author or authors of both volumes. See Sweet & Maxwell, vol. 1, *supra*, p. 286. See also Wallace, *supra*, pp. 490–91.

5. A citation to T. Vernon, *Cases argued and adjudged in the High Court of Chancery, 1746–55, in the time of Lord Chancellor Hardwicke*, vol. 1, p. 35 (2 vols., London, 1726–1728). There were several subsequent editions. See Sweet & Maxwell, *supra*, vol. 1, p. 349. See also Wallace, *supra*, pp. 493–97.

[53]

56 LEGACY.

no Laches[1] are imparted to Him. But where a certain Le-
-gacy is left payable at a Day certain, it must be paid with Interest from that Day. 2 Salk. 415.[2]

1 1 And 33.[3] *1* A father bequeth'd Goods to his Son, when He sh[d] be of the Age of twenty one years, + if He die before that Time, then his Daughter sh.[d] have them; Afterwards the Father died, + then the Son died before He was of Age; Adjudged, that the Daughter sh.[d] have the Goods given in Legacy immediately, + not stay till her Brother w.[d] have been of Age, if He had lived.

2 1 Leon 278.[4] *2* A Legacy was devis'd to an Infant, to be paid when He sh.[d] come of Age, + he died before that time; Ruled that his Admn[tt]or sh.[d] have it presently, + not stay untill the Infant w.[d] have been of Age, had He lived.

Devise of a Legacy of £100 charg'd on Lands, + to be paid on the 29[th] Day of September, 1668; the Legatee died Intestate before that Day, + her Admini[tt]ix exhibited a Bill for the Money, w[ch] the Dft w.[d] have avoided, because the Intestate had it upon Condition, (viz.) if She had lived till the 29[th] of Sept:[ber] w[ch] Condition is now dispensed with by the Act of GOD, (viz) by the Death of the Legatee before the Time this Condition was to be perform'd, and w[ch] now is impossible to be perform'd; but the Court held, that an Interest was vested in the Legatee, + by Consequence it shall go to her Admini[tt]ix. Chan. Cases 112. Innocent + Ux v. Taylor.[5]——

And this agrees with the Civil Law, by which the Right of the Legatee is consider'd in two Capacities; One which makes him Master of the Legacy immediately so that He may

Page [53]

1. "Laches" refer to "unreasonable delay" in enforcing or pusuing a legal remedy "whereby the party forfeits the benefit." Jowitt, p. 1050.

2. A citation to *Salkeld's Reports* (1689–1712), vol. 2, p. 415. The case is *Smell* v. *Dee.* See p. 32, n. 7; p. 52, n. 4.

3. A citation to *Anderson's Reports*, vol. 1, p. 33. (*Les Reports des mults principals Cases, cibien en le Common Bank*) (1534–1604), 2 parts. The case is *Lee* v. *Mayer*, and begins on page 31. It was first published in London in 1664–65. See Sweet & Maxwell, *supra*, vol. 1, p. 292 and Wallace, *supra*, pp. 136–42.

4. A citation to *Leonard's Reports*, vol. 1, p. 278. (*Reports and Cases of Law in the Courts at Westminster*) (1540–1615). See page [39], note 7. Published in London in four parts between 1658–1675. There was a second publication in 1687. See Sweet & Maxwell, *supra*, vol. 1, p. 303. See also Wallace, *supra*, pp. 142–43. The case is *Lady Lodge's Case* (1584), which begins on page 277.

5. A citation to *Cases in Chancery* (1660–1688), p. 112, *Innocent and "Ux."* ["*uxor*" or "wife"] v. *Taylor*. *Cases in Chancery* were published in three parts: part 1 was published in 1697, and again in 1707 and 1730; part 2 was published in 1701, and again in 1702; part 3 was published in 1702, and again in 1715 and 1730, all in London. There was an undated fourth edition. See Sweet & Maxwell, *supra*, vol. 1, p. 345. See also Wallace, *supra*, pp. 480–86. A copy of *Cases . . . in . . . Chancery* (London, 1697) was in the possession of James Otis of Boston (1702–1778), and is now in the editor's library.

6. "Civil Law," (emphasis in original) i.e., the Roman law-based system of the continent, as opposed to the "common law" of the English Court of King's Bench and Court of Common Pleas. The differences included procedural and substantive contrast, such as the lack of jury trial in "civilian" courts. Some English courts followed "civil" law, including the Admiralty courts and the Court of Requests. See a full discussion in Daniel R. Coquillette, *The Civilian Writers of Doctors' Commons, London* (Berlin, 1988) pp. 15–46; Coquillette, *The Anglo-American Legal Heritage*, pp. 1–11, 205–13. For a discussion of the importance of civil law in the Vice Admiralty Courts of the colonies during Quincy's time, see Daniel R. Coquillette, "Justinian in Braintree," *Law in Colonial Massachusetts* (Boston, 1984), pp. 359–418. Many legacies, including legacies involving chattel, were subject to the special expertise of the English civilian jurists of Doctors' Commons in London. See Daniel R. Coquillette, *The Civilian Writers of Doctors' Commons, London*, *supra*, pp. 29–32.

[54]

Legacy 57

demand the Delivery of it; the Other is a Right wch puts him in a Condition to demand it, tho' not immediatly; now in the first Case, the Time is come in wch the Right is vested in the Legatee, + the Legacy is then due; + in such case if the Legatee dies before he hath rec.^{d} the Legacy, 'tis transmitted to his Admin^{tt}or, for in that moment of Time when the Testator died, the Right is vested in the Legatee; + tho' there is a certain Time appointed for the Payment of the Legacy, yet since the Legatee hath acquir'd a Right by surviving the Testator, he transmits that Right to his Admin^{tt}or, tho' He die before that Time. 2 Dom. 180. 181.[1]

By the Civil Law there is no Survivorship amongst Legatees; for if Goods are devised to Two jointly, + afterwards One of them dies, the Exc^{tt}or of the dead Legatee shall have his Share, but where the Testator devised goods to Two jointly, + the Exc^{tt}or assented to the Legacy, + then one of them died; ajudged that by this Assent an Interest is vested, + 'tis become a Chattel, and governable by the Rules of Common Law. 2 Lev. 209 Bustard v. Stakely.[2]

Page [54]

1. A citation to William Strahan's translation of Jean Domat's *The Civil Law in the Natural Order: Together with the Publick Law* (London, 1722), 2 vols., vol. 2, pp. 180–81. The translation from the French was published in new editions in 1737 and 1777. See Sweet & Maxwell, *supra*, vol. 1, p. 611. For a full discussion, see Daniel R. Coquillette, *The Civilian Writers*, *supra*, at pp. 203–09. In the 1737 2nd edition, the section referred to by Quincy is Book IV, Title 2, Section 7, in vol. 2, p. 173. Quincy very roughly paraphrases, but does not copy, this section.

2. A citation to *Bastard* v. *Stukely*, *Levinz's Reports* (1660–1697), vol. 2, p. 209. It supports the text. See Wallace, *supra*, 304–315; Sweet & Maxwell, vol. 1, *supra*, p. 81. *Levinz's Reports* were published in London in 1702 and published in a second edition in 1722, and in subsequent editions. See *Id.*, vol. 1, p. 303.

[55]

58 Jury See Same Title Ant: 44 + 50.[1]

If a plt. in evid: shows any matter in writing, or of record, or any sentence in ye Ecclesiastical C.^{t} + ye Dft offers to demur thereto, ye plt may not refuse to join in Dem:^{r},[2] but he must do it, or wave his evid:. So if ye plt produce wit:^{s} to prove any matter in fact upon which a Q:^{n} in law arises, if ye dft admits there [for "their"] testimony to be true, he may demur upon it, for matter of law shall never be put in the mouth of Lay gents;[3] so may ye plt demur upon evid: of dft, Mu tatis mutandis.[4] Vin: Evid (U: b: 1.) pl 8. cites 5 Rep: 104. a. Baker's Case. Cro: E. 751. pl. 9. Midleton v Baker S C & S P per tot: Cur: accordingly.[5] But in this latter case of Evid: by wit:^{s}, ye other unless he pleaseth shall not be compelled to join, because ye testimony is to be examined by ye jury, + ye Evid: is certain, + may be enforced more or less.[6]

'Tis ye property of ye Court, jus dicere.

Tri: per Pais. 1. Edit: 7.1739.[7]

Page [55]

1. Quincy is referring back to his original "Jury" page, at his page 44 [42], and his following "Jury" section, at his page 50 [48]. "Jury" was clearly a topic that outstripped the anticipated space.

2. "Dem:^{R}" for "demurrer." For a discussion of the "demurrer" see page [50], note 8. Since the defendant offering the demurrer assumes the plaintiff's evidence to be true, it is obviously fair to require the plaintiff to consent, or to waive the evidence. Demurrers were, at least in theory, efficient, as they permitted rulings on key points of law. See page [50], note 8.

3. This maxim, "for matter of law shall never be put in the mouth of Lay gents," repeats Quincy's notation at page 52 [50]. The source of the quotation is Y.B. 9 Henry VI, 33 (1431), summarized in Sir Robert Brooke's *La Graunde Abridgment* (London, 1573), vol. 2, fol. 16a. See page [50], note 6.

4. "*Mutatis mutandis*" for "the necessary changes being made."

5. A further citation to *Viner's Abridgment* (1742–1753) on "Evidence" (U:b:1) pl. 8. See page [16], note 2. *Viner* cites in turn to *Baker's Case*, *Coke's Reports* vol. 5, p. 104a, decided in 1597, in which the court held that "the Plaintiff cannot refuse to joyn in demurrer, but he ought to joyn in the demurrer, or waive his evidence . . . The Defendent may demurre in Law upon it, but then he ought to admit the evidence given by the Plaintiff to be true; and the reason thereof is, That matter in Law shall not be put to Laymen. So may the Plaintiff demurre upon the Defendants evidence, *mutatis mutandis* . . ." *Id.*, p. 104a. *Viner* also cites to *Middleton* v. *Baker*, *Croke's Reports* (covering 1582–1641) vol. 1, p. 751, dated 1600: "the Plaintiffs ought to joyn in the demurrer, or waive the evidence, because the Defendant shall not be compelled to put a matter of difficulty to Lay gents . . ." *Id.*, at p. 752.

6. This is an accurate summary of the secondary holding of *Middleton* v. *Baker*, *supra*. "[T]he other, unless he pleaseth, shall not be compelled to joyn, because the credit of the testimony is to be examined by the Jury, and the evidence is certain, and may be enforced more or less . . ." *Id.*, at *Croke's Reports*, vol. 1, *supra*, p. 752.

7. "Tis ye property of ye court, *jus dicere* [to interpret the law]." This is cited to "S.E." [G. Duncombe], *Trial Per Pais* (1665), *supra*, page 1 of the 1739 edition. See page [49], note 2, and page [50], note 5. This quotation was made famous by Francis Bacon's essay, "Of Judicature," which begins "Judges ought to remember that their office is *Ius dicere*, and not *ius dare*; To interpret Law, and not to Make Law, or Give Law." Francis Bacon, *The Essayes* (London, 1629), p. 316. Quincy's *Political Commonplace Book* contains substantial Bacon excerpts. See *Quincy Papers*, vol. 1, pp. 100, 103–04, 148, 187–93, *infra*. See also Neil L. York, "Ideas, Ideals and Interpretations," *Id.*, p. 88. The first publication of the expanded *Essays* including "Of Judicature" was published in London in 1612. See Daniel R. Coquillette, *Francis Bacon* (Edinburgh, 1992), Appendix III (Chronology of Publications Up to 1631), p. 333.

[56]

Jury 59

See the question—whether juries are judges of law as well as fact ?—treated of in a masterly manner by the Author of "Considerations on Criminal Law." (p. 128 of that work) Reviewed in the Monthly Review May 1772 page 471 472 etc.[1]

Upon the same Q:n see Barrington's Observations on the more ancient statutes. p. 86. 120.[2]

By this way of proceeding, (in Skinner's Case)[3] the Subject loses that legal and indifferent Way of Trial, which the Law hath provided for him, by Jurors for his own Condition, which is as much his right, yea Birthright & Inheritance, as his Lands are, & without which he is not sure to keep them, or any thing else.[3] This Way of trial is his fence of Protection against all Storms of Power, & against all frauds & Surprises, if the Institution thereof were duly observed, as it ought to be; therefor the Commons are careful (even) to jealousy, that this their Liberty & Buckler be not taken from them; for if we look into the Institution of it, nothing can be established with more caution & care for Indifferency, & for finding out the truth, & we think that we much owe these liberties which we enjoy beyond our Neighbors (of whom some once had it, but have lost it) to this Way of Trial. True it is that herein sometimes Miscarriages happen; but the fault is not constituting the Law, but in the Execution. Jurors are Men, & therefore may, & sometimes will err, but they err not the more because they are sworn, & other Men err as much as they,

Page [56]

1. A reference to H. Dagge, *Considerations on Criminal Law* (London, 1772), 3 vols. The book was republished in 1774 in Dublin. See Sweet & Maxwell, *supra*, vol. 1, p. 361. This is a crucial reference, because it establishes that Quincy was still adding to his *Law Commonplace* after May of 1772, and was reading the *Monthly Review*.

2. A citation to Daines Barrington, *Observations upon the Statutes, chiefly the more ancient from* Magna Carta *to 21st James the First* [1624] (1st ed., London, 1766), p. 86. The small font represents a smaller hand probably added at a later date after the *Monthly Review* citation in 1772, but it could still be Quincy. See n. 3, *infra*.

3. The text here, and continuing, is taken from Sir John Maynard's (1602–1690) argument on *Skinner's Case* as recorded by Anchitell Grey's *Debates of the House of Commons* (1667–1694) (London, 1763). See page [57], note 2 and page [58], note 1. The handwriting is smaller and finer, commencing with "Upon the same Q:^{n}" through the citation to Grey's *Debates*, *supra*, on page 58 [61]. The word "Jury" at the top of page 60 and 61 [57 and 58] is clearly in Quincy's hand, and the later addition is written later and across the words "Jury" on both pages. It is difficult to tell if this is an addition by Quincy, or another hand altogether, but it is the opinion of my learned co-editor Neil York, who has worked closely with Quincy's hand in the *Political Commonplace*, Quincy *Works*, vol. 1, and myself that this is still Quincy.

[57]

60 Jury

and possibly it would be much better, if the Ministers of Justice according to their Duty, did return sufficient Persons, & that such Persons were more willing to serve on Juries. Every Judgment is established on two things of which the Judge must have a Care, vizt the Verity of the fact & what the Law is upon such fact; ex facto Jus oritur.[1] Now by the Constitutions of the Law of England, the Trial of the fact is in one hand, & the determination of the Law by Judges sworn. The Judge may not try the fact, nor the Juror the Law, but at their extreme peril: for by the Common-Law, the Jurors, if they give a false Verdict, under went the villanous Judgment vizt to have their houses raised, lands wasted, meadows plowed, woods felled, body imprisoned, & Infamy perpetual never to be credited more.—

(The) Law hath singular Care for the Indifferency, secondly & for the sufficiency, a neutrâ parte suspecti.[2] The Shff[3] is bound by Oath to return such; next, if he fail, each party hath his Chal lenges (to wit) that such or such Juror is of kin, interested, engaged by opinion while unsworn, tenant tc. If this Challenge be denied, the Truth of the Challenge must be tried by Persons sworn, & the Jury serve on their Oath, & proven [?] of their Souls to the Truth.

And after the Jury sworn, if any matter of Law arise on the Evidence, it is ordinarily specially found, & if the Judge deny a special Verdict, & will overrule the matter, whoever therein is greived may require the Judge or Judges, to seal him a bill of Ex ception,[4] which he or they cannot refuse to do, or if he do, the party grieved hath remedy against him—

Then after Verdict the Judges who give Judgment, do it on their Oaths according to their best Skill; & when they have done if any party think himself greived, he hath his remedy by Writ of Error,[5] before other Judges who act on their Oaths likewise.

Again; the Persons who try the fact, are persons of the same rank with the suitors, not too mean for they may be open to unhandsome temptations; nor too high for great Lords serve not on Juries, not only in regard of their Privileges

Page [57]

1. "*Ex facto jus oritur*," i.e., "The law becomes operative after the fact." See Sir Edward Coke's *Second Institutes* (London, 1641), p. 49 and E. Hilton Jackson, *Latin for Lawyers* (London, 1915), p. 154.

2. "*A neutro parte suspecti*," i.e., "whose neutrality is suspect for the reasons following." The important emergence in the eighteenth century of jury neutrality is evidence by Sir John Maynard's (1602–1690) argument set out here. See page [58], note 1.

3. "Sheriff."

4. A "bill of exception" was a document containing objections by an aggrieved party to the trial judge's direction to the jury on a point of law, or an objection to the trial judge's decision to permit evidence to go to the jury, or to preclude the jury from considering evidence. It had to be sealed by the trial judge before the verdict. The bill was then argued before the appropriate court of error. See Jowitt, p. 238.

5. A "writ of error" was directed to the appropriate court of error on the face of the record. See the discussion at Baker, pp. 137–38; Coquillette, *The Anglo-American Legal Heritage*, p. 244. It was a very narrow form of appeal, compared to today's forms of appellate review.

[58]

Jury 61

but their Grandeur & Power, whereby other may be overawed. The Institution is cautious & bound together & carried on, from the beginning to the End, by the most sacred bonds, to find out truth, that can possibly be imposed by Men.—

But by this Way of proceeding before your Lordships, all these Advantages are lost; for the trial of fact & of Law, the office of the Judge & Juror, are confounded. There is no Challenge or Exception that can be taken to any of the Lords tho' one or more of them be Enemies, or friends or allies to either party, or engaged by Opinion or solicitation, or Interest in the cause, of all these together, or any other; for tho' a Juror may be challenged, a Judge cannot. Again, as the Subject is deprived of his Trial in point of Difference, viz.[t] by Persons of his own Quality, touching whom he may provide by Challenge, that the partial or suspected be removed, so he is hereby put to vast Charge, & Attendance, & Trouble. Serg[t] Maynard's Argument in the House of Commons at a Conference with the Lords in 1671.——Grey's Debates in Parliam[t]:

1 vol. 449, 8,9[1]

[QUINCY'S PAGE 62 IS BLANK]

Page [58]

1. (Emphasis in original). A citation to Anchitell Grey's (?–1702) *Debates of the House of Commons* (1667–1694), vol. 1, p. 449, first published in London in 1769, from which were copied the text on this page and the preceding two pages. (Quincy, pp. 59–61 [56–58].) Grey's record of the parliamentary debates was "the first continuous record of debates to be published." See *The Oxford Companion to Law* (1980), *supra*, p. 540.

[59]

Of Laws. vid of Statutes or Acts. p. 89. 63

vid. 4 vol. p. 101.[1]

The Advantages resulting from Laws lie often closely conceal'd while ye little Inconveniences y^{t} [that] attend them are most sensibly felt. Spirit of Laws. B 27. ch: 1.[2]

Men are govern'd by several kinds of laws; by ye Law of Nature; by ye devine Law, wch is y^{t} [that] of[3] Religion; by ecclesiastical, otherwise call'd canon Law, wch is y^{t} [that] of religious Polity; by ye Law of Nations, wch may be consider'd as ye civil Law of the Universe, in wch Sense every Nation is a Citizen; by the general political Law, whose Object is y^{t} [that] human wisdom which has been the foundation of All Societies; by ye particular political Law, wch relates to each Society; by ye Law of Conquest founded on this, y^{t} [that] One Nation has been willing + able, or has had a Right to offer Violence to Another; by ye civil Law of every Society by wch a Citizen may defend his Possessions + his Life, against ye Attacks of any other Citizen; in fine, by domestic Law, wch proceeds from a Society's being divided into several families, all wch have need of a particular Government.

There are therefore different Orders of Laws, + the Sublimitly of human Reason consists in perfectly knowing to wch of these Orders ye Things y^{t} [that] are to be determin'd ought to have a principal Relation, + not to throw into Confusion those Principles wch sh.^{d} govern Mankind. Ib. B 26. c: 1[4]

Page [59]

1. A cross-citation to the Section "Of Statutes or Acts," Quincy's *Law Commonplace*, p. 89 [77]. Also a citation to Quincy's volume 4 of his notebooks, wherein page 101 begins an 8-page copy of the introduction to *The Ecclesiastical Law*, by Richard Burn (1709–1785).

2. Citation to the English translation of Charles-Louis de Secondat, Baron de la Brede et de Montesquieu (1689–1755), *De l'esprit des lois* (1st edition, 1748), book 27, chapter 1. The book "analyzes a variety of political constitutions, and advocates a liberal constitutional monarchy or the true English model." Drabble, *The Oxford Companion to English Literature*, *supra*, p. 663. "It may be regarded as the first work on Comparative or sociological jurisprudence. It is also note-

worthy as having enunciated, on the basis of his observations of English government, the doctrine of separation of powers . . ." Walker, *The Oxford Companion to Law*, *supra*, p. 854. The first English translation, *The Spirit of Laws*, was published in Edinburgh in 1750, to be followed by Dublin editions in 1751, 1752, 1756, 1758, and 1766, and another Edinburgh edition in 1768. See Sweet & Maxwell, *supra*, vol. 1, p. 104. Quincy also included Montesquieu in his *Political Commonplace Book*. See *Quincy Papers*, vol. 1, pp. 56, 210–11. Book 27, ch. 1, addresses the ancient Roman law of Successions, and Quincy closely quoted this text.

3. The "y^{t}" marks in the manuscript mean "that."

4. Montesquieu, *Spirit of the Laws*, *supra*, at book 26, chapter 1. See note 2, *supra*. This long excerpt forms the whole of chapter 1, a summary of book 26, "Of Laws in Relation to the Order of Things Which They Determine."

[60]

64 **Of Laws**

Laws in their most general Signification, are ye necessary Relations resulting from the Nature of Things. In this Sense All Beings have their Laws, the Deity has his Laws, ye material World its Laws, ye Intelligences superior Man have y^{r} [their] Laws, ye Beasts y^{r} [their] Laws, Man his Laws. Sp: Laws B1. c:[2]

Laws of[1] Nature — The Laws of Nature derive y^{r} [their] force entirely from our Frame + Being, + therefore so call'd.

The Law wch by imprinting on our Minds ye Idea of a Creator inclines us to Him, is ye first in Importance, tho' not in Order, of natural Laws.

Peace is ye first Law of Nature.

Another Law of Nature prompts to seek Nourishment. The attraction arising from ye Difference of Sexes, + ye natural Inclination they have for Each Other, form a third Law.

A fourth Law of Nature arises from the Defire of living in Society. Ib. ch: 2.[3]

Laws of Nations — Men consider'd as Inhabitants of so great a Planet which necessarily implies a Variety of Nations, they have Laws relative to their mutual Intercourse, wch is what we call ye Law of Nations. Consider'd as Members of a Society that

Politic Law — must be properly supported, they have Laws relative to ye Governors + ye governed; + this we call Politic Law.

Page [60]

1. On this page, and on the next (Quincy 65 [61]), Quincy sets out the Roman classifications in the margin, i.e., *Laws of Nature* (*ius naturale*); Law of Nations (*ius gentium*); Civil Law or "Politic" Law (*ius civile*). See *Justinian's Institutes*, Lib.1, Tit. 11, pr-4; *Digest*, Lib.1, tit. 1, 1; Lib. 1, tit, 4, 5. See *Illustration 3*.

2. A reference to Montesquieu's *The Spirit of the Laws* (1750 translation), book 1, chapter 1. See page [59], note 2. These are the first words of book 1.

3. *Ibid.*, chapter 2.

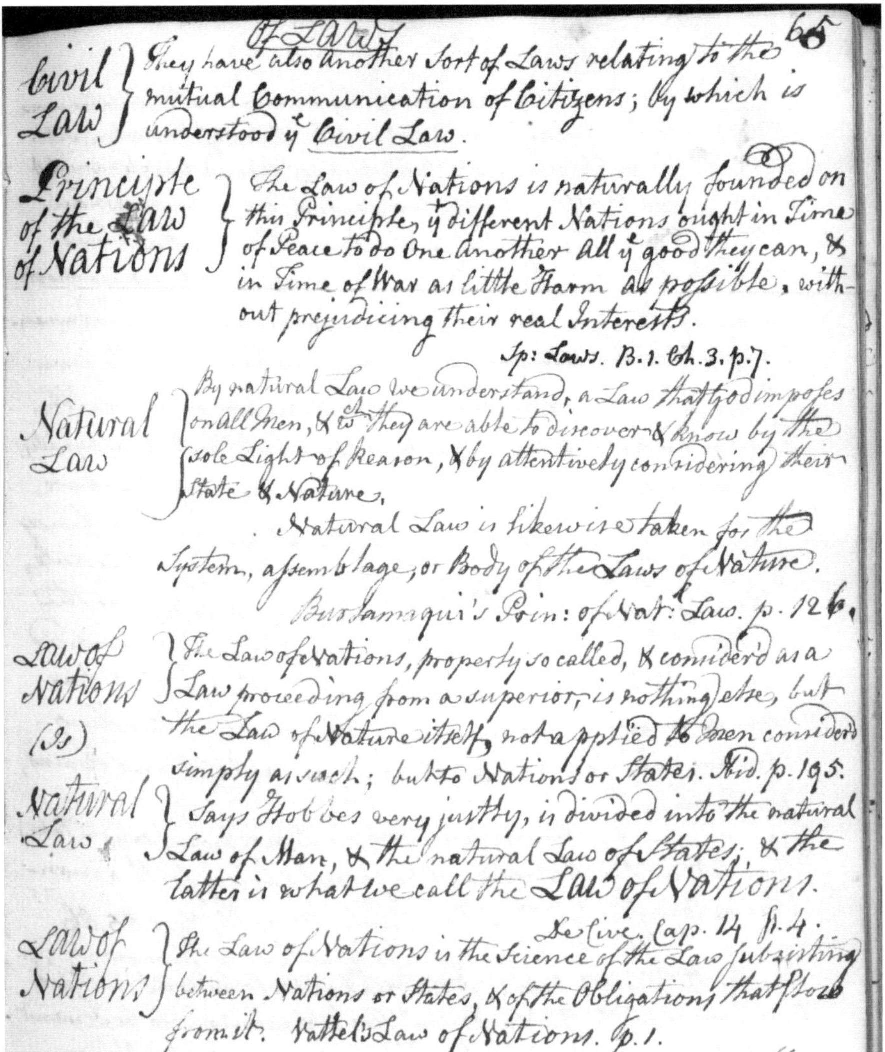

ILLUSTRATION 3. Page 65 [61] of the *Law Commonplace*. Image courtesy of the Massachusetts Historical Society. My thanks again to Kevin Cox.

[61]

Of Laws 65

Civil Law	They have also another Sort of Laws relating to the mutual Communication of Citizens; by which is understood ye Civil Law.
Principle of the Law of Nations	The Law of Nations is naturally founded on this Principle, y^t^ [that] different Nations ought in time of Peace to do One Another All ye good they can, + in Time of War as little Harm as possible, without prejudicing their real Interests. Sp: Laws. B. 1. ch. 3. p. 7.[1]
Natural Law	By natural Law we understand, a Law that God imposes on All Men, + wch they are able to discover + know by the sole Light of Reason, + by attentively considering their State + Nature. Natural Law is likewise taken for the System, assemblage, or Body of the Laws of Nature. Burlamaqui's Poin: of Nat:^l^ Law. p. 126.[2]
Law of Nations (&)	The Law of Nations, properly so called, + consider'd as a law proceeding from a superior, is nothing else, but the Law of Nature itself, not applied to Men consider'd simply as such; but to Nations or States. Ibid. p. 195.[3]
Natural Law	Says Hobbes very justly, is divided into the natural Law of Man, + the natural Law of States; + the latter is what we call the Law of Nations. De Civi. Cap. 14 p. 4.[4]
Law of Nations	The Law of Nations is the Science of the Law subsisting between Nations or States, + of the Obligations that flow from it. Vattel's Law of Nations. p. 1.[5]

Page [61]

1. A reference to Montesquieu's *The Spirit of the Laws* (1750 translation), book 1, ch. 3, p. 7. See page [59], note 2.

2. A reference to the Swiss jurist, Jean Jacques Burlamaqui's (1694–1748) *Principes du droit naturel* (1st ed. 1747). Burlamaqui, along with the German Samuel von Pufendorf (1632–1694)

and his fellow Swiss, Emmerich de Vattel (1714–1767), was the leading authority on public international law in his time. *Principes* was translated by Nugent as *Burlamaqui on Natural Law* and first published in London in 1748. There were many subsequent eighteenth-century editions. See Sweet & Maxwell, *supra*, vol. 1, p. 592.

3. *Ibid.*, at p. 195.

4. A citation to Thomas Hobbes's (1588–1679) *De Civi*, chapter 14, p. 4, first published in 1642 while Hobbes was in exile (1640–1660). Hobbes's jurisprudence and political theory was highly controversial, then and now, and was essentially authoritarian. He was cordially hated by Whigs and Tories alike, and anticipated modern legal positivism. Hobbes himself was strongly influenced by Francis Bacon, whom Hobbes served as a private secretary. See Coquillette, *Francis Bacon*, pp. 237–43, 295.

5. A citation to Emmerich de Vattel's (1714–1767) *Le Droit des Gens ou Principes de la Loi Naturelle* (1758), translated into English from the French in 1760 as *Law of Nations*. See Sweet & Maxwell, *supra*, vol. 1, p. 598.

[62]

66 Of Laws

"In our Law, the Judges are bound, by a sacred Oath, to determine according to the known Laws + antient customs of the Realm, set down in judicial Decisions + Resolutions of learned, wise, + upright Judges, upon variety of particular facts + Cases, which, when they have been thus in use + practised Time out of mind, are Part of the Common Law of the Kingdom. And it is a most dangerous thing to shake or alter any of the Rules or fundamental Points of the Common Law, which in Truth; are the main Pillars + Supporters of the Fabrick of the Commonwealth. To have no Rule to decide Controversies but the Rule of Equity, is to begin the World again, + to make Choice of that Rule, which out of mere Necessity was made Use of in the Infancy of the State + Indigency of Laws. And to set up this Rule, after Laws are establish'd to relieve hard Cases + leave the Matter at large, is it not rather unravelling, by unperceiv'd Degrees, the fine + close Texture of the Law, which has been so many years making The Laws of this Kingdom are not, now-a-days, to be spun out of mens' Brains, pro Re nata."[1]

"To allow any man's Discretion (says Ld Coke) that sits in the Seat of Justice, would bring forth a monstrous Confusion." L^r^: on Libels, Warrants tc p. 85. 86.[2]

Old Sir Edward Coke said, with some Humour, in Charles the First's Reign, at the Head of the Commons in their Conference with the Lords—"For a Freeman to be Tenant at will of his Liberty! I will never agree to it: it is a

Page [62]

1. "*pro re nata*," i.e., "to meet the emergency, as the occasion arises." Jowitt, *supra*, p. 1414.

2. This is a citation to [John Almon], *Letters concerning Libels, Warrants, the Seizure of Papers, and Sureties for the Peace or Behaviour, with a view to some late proceedings and the defence of them by the majority* (2d ed., 1764), first published as *Enquiry into the Doctrine concerning Libels, War-*

rants, and the Seizure of Papers . . . in a letter to Mr. Almon from the Father of Candor (London, 1764). See Sweet & Maxwell, *supra*, vol. 1, p. 245. John Almon (1737–1805) was a friend of John Wilkes and a distinguished contemporary historian and political writer. He compiled the *Parliamentary Register* from 1774 to 1781, and summarized debates in Parliament from 1742 to 1774. See David M. Walker, *The Oxford Companion to Law*, *supra*, p. 50. Quincy's references to Almon show that this part of the *Law Commonplace* must date after 1764.

[63]

Of Laws 67

Tenure not to be found in all Littleton. "It is (as He says, in one of his Treatises) a great Deal better for the State, that a particular Offender should go unpunished, on the one hand, or that a private Person, or public minister, should be damnified on the other by the Rigour of the Law, than that a general Rule of Law should be broken to the general Trouble + Prejudice of many." L^{r}: on Libels, Warrants, etc.,[1] p.92.

Laws are the instruments + sinews of all blessings.——A law ought to give warning before it strickes: and it is a good rule,—That is the best Law which gives least liberty to the arbitrage of the Judge,—which is that, the CERTAINTY thereof affecteth. Ld Bacon's Adv: of Learning p. 293–294. Edit: 1674. Lib.8.[2]

Laws are the Conditions, under which men, naturally equal, united themselves in society. Beccaria on Crim: + Pun: p 5. c:1.[3]

Laws are the Anchors of the Republick. Ld Bac: Adv^{t}: of Learning 307.[4]

[QUINCY'S PAGES 68 THROUGH 71 ARE BLANK]

Page [63]

1. A citation to [John Almon] *Letter Concerning Libels, Warrants* etc. (2nd ed., 1764), p. 92. See discussion at page [62], note 2, *supra.*

2. A citation to Francis Bacon (1561–1626), *The Advancement of Learning* (London, 1674), pp. 293–94 (book 8), a later publication of the original *The Twoo Bookes of Francis Bacon Of the proficience and Advancement of Learning, divine and humane* first published in London in 1605. See R. W. Gibson, *Francis Bacon: A Bibliography of his Works and of Baconiana to the Year 1750* (Oxford, 1950), p. 124, which gives this edition Gibson No. 142. Quincy also referred frequently to Bacon in his *Political Commonplace Book.* See *Quincy Papers,* vol. 1, pp. 100, 103–04, 148, 187–93. See also Neil L. York's "Ideas, Ideals, and Interpretations," *Id.*, p. 86. For a full discussion of Bacon's jurisprudence, which tends to favor prospective legislation to retroactive judicial lawmaking, see Coquillette, *Francis Bacon*, with a specific discussion of the *Advancement of Learning* at pp. 77–90.

3. A citation to Cesare Bonesana, Marchese de Beccaria (1738–1794), *Dei Delitti e delle Pene* (1764, 1st ed.), which was translated by J. A. Farrer into English from the French as *Essay on Crimes and Punishments* (London, 1767). This book was highly popular in America, and was republished in Philadelphia by R. Bell in 1778. Again, Quincy seems to be reading the latest in English and Continental sources, and this part of the *Law Commonplace* cannot predate 1767. Beccaria's book "represented a great advance in criminological thought; it advocated prevention of crime rather than punishment and condemned capital punishment and torture." See David M. Walker, *The Oxford Companion to Law*, *supra*, p. 121.

4. A further citation to Bacon's *Advancement of Learning* (1674 ed.), p. 307. See note 2, *supra*.

[64]

72 Notes. vid Bills etc. in the Index
at the End of this Book[1]

Note to pay two Months after the Ship is paid off is good, + negotiable. 1 Strange 24.[2]
Note payable so many Days after Marriage, not negotiable. 2 Ibid. 1151.[3]
Note payable so many Days after Death Drawer's father is good + negotiable. 2 Strange 1217.[4]
Note to be accountable for money is within the
Qu. Statute + negotiable. 1 Strange 629.[5]
Note to deliver Horses, tc + pay Money, not within the Statute 2 Strange 1271.[6]
A Note to pay for the Debt of Another; is negotiable. 1 Strange 264.[7]
Consideration of a promissory Note may be inquir'd into. Ibid 674.[8]
Ch Justice said there was no standing Rule, for the Time in which a Note must be demanded, but must be left to the Jury. 2 Strange 910.[9]
x Vid. 1 Burr. 375
x That Indeb. assum.[10] will lie on a Note of Hand; vid 2 Strange 725.[11] And of the Alteration made by Statute of Ann. vid the whole Case of Story vs Atkins. Str. 719.[12]

Page [64]

1. Again, Quincy refers to his excellent index under "Bills of Exchange + Notes," Quincy 177 [120].

2. A citation to *Andrews* v. *Franklin* (1717), *Strange's Reports*, *supra*, vol. 1, p. 24. See page [21], note 12. The issue was whether the bill was void, because it was "a contingency which may never happen." *Id.*, p. 24. Held, the "paying off the ship is a thing of a publick nature, and this is negotiable as a promissory note." *Id.*, p. 24.

3. A citation to *Beardesley* v. *Baldwin* (1741), *Strange's Reports*, *supra*, vol. 2, p. 1151. Presumably, the event was both contingent and "not of a publick nature." Cf. *Andrews* v. *Franklin*, note 2, *supra*.

4. A citation to *Cooke* v. *Colehan* (1745), *Strange's Reports*, *supra*, vol. 2, p. 1217. This involved a note payable six weeks after the death of the defendant's father. Held to be negotiable "for there is no contingency, whereby it may never become payable, but it is only uncertain as to the time." *Id.* This was not an easy case, however, as it "held three arguments" in the Common Pleas and then was upheld on writ of error to the King's Bench.

5. A citation to *Morris* v. *Lee* (1725), *Strange's Reports*, *supra*, vol. 1, p. 629. The defendant had argued that there was a distinction between the words "accountable to the plaintiff on order for 100£" and a promise to pay the money "absolutely," which is needed to make a note negotiable under the statute 3 & 4 Ann. ch. 9 (1704). (That statute, adopted in 1704, made inland promissory notes negotiable as if they were international bills of exchange, long recognized as negotiable under the law merchant.) Held "[t]here is no precise words requisite to make a promissory note: it is enough if it may be brought within the intention of the act." *Id.* Quincy marks this case "Qu" for "Query," perhaps because of the argument that an "accountable" defendant "might discharge himself by payment of the plaintiff's debts or otherwise." *Id.*, p. 629. This would have been different from "payment of money absolutely" and could cause negotiability problems. The King's Bench heard this argument, and rejected it, but it is still a good point.

6. A citation to *Martin* v. *Chauntry* (1748), *Strange's Reports*, *supra*, vol. 2, p. 1271. The note was to "deliver up horses and a wharf, and pay money at a particular day." This was clearly not negotiable under the statute 3 & 4 Ann. ch. 9 (1704) as it was not just a promise to pay cash.

7. A citation to *Poplewell* v. *Wilson* (1720) *Strange's Reports*, *supra*, vol. 1, p. 264. The argument was that this was not necessarily for "value received" as required by 3 & 4 Ann. ch. 9 (1704) to be negotiable. It was held that "it is to be within the statute, being an absolute promise, and every way as negotiable as if it had been generally for value received." *Id.*

8. A citation to *Jefferies* v. *Austin* (1726), *Strange's Reports*, *supra*, vol. 1, p. 674. This is a very interesting case, as it could defeat negotiability of a note good on its face. But here the action was not brought by a third-party holder without notice, but rather by the original payee. The defendant was allowed to show that the payee held the note "in the nature of an escrow, *viz.* as a remand, in case be procured the defendant to be restored to an office . . ." which the payee/plaintiff "did not effect." Thus the defendant prevails.

9. A citation to *Hoar* v. *Dacosta* (1732), *Strange's Reports*, *supra*, vol. 2, p. 910. Plaintiff took defendant's note to a bank, which demanded payment on a goldsmith the next day with other notes, all refused. If plaintiff had demanded payment that day directly, the note would have been paid. The jury, quite reasonably, found that the plaintiff's demand, through the bank, was timely, and found against the defendant for the value of the note. This is an interesting use of jury discretion within commercial law, which can prefer "bright line" legal rules.

10. "[I]ndeb. Assum." for the cause of action "*indebitatus assumpsit*," the general cause of action for contractual actions other than those that involve formal covenants under seal signed by the party to be charged. To distinguish it from the old cause of action for debt, a legal fiction was adopted that the defendant "being indebted did promise" (again) to pay, with the second promise being the source of the general action on the case, hence the "*indebitatus assumpsit*" language of the writ. If we believe Coke, in *Slade's Case* (1602), *Coke's Reports*, vol. 4, p. 92b, it was held that "every contract executory imparts in itself an *Assumpsit*," and the fiction was fully adopted. See Coquillette, *The Anglo-American Legal Heritage*, pp. 250–52, 261–63. See the full discussion on Baker, *An Introduction to English Legal History* (4th ed., 2002), pp. 341–45.

11. A citation to the famous case of *Story* v. *Atkins* (1727), *Strange's Reports*, vol. 2, p. 719 at 725. The issue was whether the statute 3 & 4 Ann. c.9 (1704) that made inland promissory notes negotiable removed the preexisting general common law cause of action for informal contracts, i.e., action on the case *indebitatus assumpsit*. See note 10, *supra*. Held by Lord Raymond, C.J. that "the statute 3 & 4 Ann. only gives an additional remedy upon promissory notes, but does not take away the old one."

12. This is just a citation to the entire case of *Story* v. *Atkins* (1727), which began at *Strange's Reports*, vol. 2, at p. 719.

[65]

Notes 73

Sed vid Cunningham from p 62. to 74[2]

There must be a Demand on the Drawer of the Note, before the Indorsor can be charged. 1 Strange 649. 1087.[1] Contra in Bills of Exchange. 1 Strange 441. 515.[3] But if Indorser pays Part of the Note, demand on the Drawer is unneccessary. Strange 1246.[4]

Notes may be indors'd by an Administrator. Strange 1260.[5]

Innocent Indorsee of a gaming Note can maintain no Action against the Drawer. 2 Strange 1155.[6]

Where Part of a Note is rec.[d] of the Drawer, the Indorsor is not to be resorted to for the rest. Ibid. 745.[7]

Notice of the Indorsement of a negotiable Note is not necessary. Comyns. 563. Skip vs. Hook.[8]

Page [65]

1. A citation to *Syderbottom* v. *Smith* (1726), *Strange's Reports*, *supra*, vol. 1, p. 649. See page 21, n. 12. Here the jury was directed by the Chief Justice, Common Pleas, to find for the defendant "because the plaintiff had not proved diligence to get the money for the drawer: being of the old opinion, that the indorsor only warrants upon the default of the drawer." *Id.* Also cited is *Collins* v. *Butler* (1738), *Strange's Reports*, *supra*, vol. 2, p. 1087, to the same effect, noting this rule was established in the Easter term of the Common Pleas in 1731 "on great debate." *Id.*

2. "*Sed vid*" ("but see"). By a Gentleman of the Middle Temple [T. Cunningham], *The Law of Bills of Exchange, Promissory Notes, etc.* (London, 1760), pp. 62–74. (There were also editions in 1761, 1766 and 1778. See Sweet & Maxwell, *supra*, vol. 1, p. 521.) Cunningham summarized the cases set out in note 3, *infra*, observing that "Now to require a Demand upon the Drawer will be laying a clog upon these Bills, as will deter every Body from taking them." *Id.*, p. 63. While this related to a foreign bill of exchange, not an inland promissory note, the argument that such a requirement obstructs "the Convenience of Commerce, that they might pass from Hand to Hand in the way of Trade, in the same Manner as if they were *Specie*" seems the same. *Id.*, p. 63.

3. A citation to *Bromley* v. *Frazier* (1721), *Strange's Reports*, *supra*, vol. 1, p. 441, holding that "in the case of a foreign bill of exchange, a demand upon the drawer is not necessary to make a charge upon the indorsor, but the indorsee has his liberty to resat to either for the money." *Id.*, at 442. There is also a citation to *Lawrence* v. *Jacob* (1722), *Strange's Reports*, *supra*, vol. 1, p. 515, for an identical holding for "a bill of exchange."

4. A citation to *Vaughan* v. *Fuller* (1746), *Strange's Reports*, *supra*, vol. 2, p. 1246, to that effect.

5. A citation to *Robinson* v. *Stone* (1747), *Strange's Reports*, *supra*, vol. 2, p. 1260. The objection for the defendant was that "an administratix was not within the custom of merchants in the case of bills of exchange. And the statute 3 & 4 *Ann. c.9* makes notes assignable only in the same manner as bills of exchange are." *Id.*, p. 1260. But the court held, *per curiam*, that "It should have been pleaded, or found, not to be within the custom: and it is every day's practice, to have indorsements made by executors." *Id.*, p. 1260.

6. A citation to *Bowyer* v. *Bampton* (1741), *Strange's Reports*, *supra*, vol. 2, p. 1155, which so held. The statute 9 *Ann. c.14 s.1* provided that notes where any part of the consideration is "money knowingly lent for gaming, shall be void to all intents and purposes whatsoever." *Id.*, p. 1155. This outcome is not as harsh as it might be, as the innocent indorsee can sue the indorser who lent the money for the gaming "on his indorsement." *Id.*, p. 1155.

7. A citation to *Kellock* v. *Robinson* (1727), *Strange's Reports*, *supra*, vol. 2, p. 745, which held that, when "it appeared the plaintiff had after the indorsement received part of the drawer of the note . . . ," the result was "a taking upon himself to give the whole credit to the drawer of the note, and absolutely discharged the indorsor." *Id.*, p. 745.

8. A citation to *Comyn's Reports* (covering 1695–1741; London, 1744), p. 563. See p. 32, n. 1. The case is *Skip* v. *Hook* (1737), and it supports Quincy's discussion.

[66]

Of Pleading 75

Vid. Pleading + Evidence in the Index at the End of this Book.
and also, Under Abatement. Vol. 2. p. 129. vid. p.36.[1]

Pleas that go to the Right or Merit of the Complaint, are of
two Sorts: 1st pleas to the Action, which denies the Substance
of the Complaint: And commonly make either, 1:st A
general Issue; As, In Trespass, not Guilty. In Debt
upon a contract, Nil Debet. In Assumpsit, Non
Assumpsit. In assize, Nul Tort, Nul Disseisin. In
Dower, Nunque dei Seize de Dower. In a Writ of Right,
that the Tenant has more Right to hold, than the Demandant
has to demand. 2. Or a common Issue; as In Debt
on a Bond, or Action of Covenant, Non est factum.[2]
In an Assize of Mort D'ancestor, Aile, Besaile etc, That
the Ancestor was never seised.[3] 2 Pleas in Bar: These
are very various + different; according to the several
Kinds of the Ten't's or Dft's Case. Bars are either such
as are, 1:st proper. 2. Common. Pleas in Bar are con-
siderable, 1:st In their (Nature or) Matter. 2. In their
Qualities or Manner of Pleading. 1:st Bars, according to the
nature of the Action, + Case of the Parties, are very various
+ different, yet Somewhat concerning them follows: 1:st Proper
Bars are, 1:st such as are applicable only to real or mix'd Actions
as, Fine; Feoffment; Release of Right; Warranty, etc Of the
Plt; or his Ancestor. 2. Such as are proper to personal
actions only; as Accord with Satisfaction. Arbitrament;
Performance, 1st of the Condition. 2. of the Bond.

Page [66]

1. Cross references to Quincy's book-ending Index and to volume 2 of his legal notebooks, which is apparently lost. This note suggests something of the length and content of the lost book. See Introduction, *supra*, Sect. 1, "The Manuscript," p. 17, n. 34. Page [36] of the *Law Commonplace* treats evidence.

2. The only defense to a Writ of Covenant, which requires a document under seal signed by the party to be charged, is "*non est factum*," i.e., "it is not his [the defendant's] deed." In other words, the hand and seal on the deed is not the defendant's.

3. The Writ of Mort D'ancestor, a "Possessory Assize," is to remedy the relatively common situation in medieval England of land being disseized from a rightful heir after the "death of his ancestor" (hence, "*mort d'ancestor*"). The remedy was to restore "seisen" (i.e., "possession"). See Baker, *An Introduction to English Legal History* (4th ed., 2002), *supra*, p. 234. Mort d'ancestor was restricted to children, siblings, and nephews and nieces of the deceased, so it was early supplemented by writs available to grandsons (*aiel*) and great-grandsons (*besaiel*) and other blood relations (*cosinage*). *Id.*, p. 268, n. 43. See *Coke on Littleton*, *supra*, p. 159a. Quincy uses "aile" and "besaile," variant spellings derived from the law French "*aieul*" and "*besaieul*." See Jowitt, *supra*, pp. 91, 231.

[67]

76 Of Pleading

2. Such Bars as are common to both, yet diversify'd oftentimes with such Diversifications As are applicable to the Nature of the Action; As, 1:st Release of Action. 2 Limitation of Time by Act of Parliament. 3. Estoppels. The several kinds of Estoppels: 1st By Matter of Record. 2. By Matter in Pais; as Deeds Indented or Poll.[1] NB[2] Estoppels are not only Matter of Bars, but of Replications, Rejoinders, + all other Pleadings.

2. Concerning Bars as to their Qualities or Manner of Pleading the same common Rules of Pleading, for the most Part concerns all Kinds of Pleading. And therefore they are here inserted once for all, viz. 1:st That the Plea be single, + not double. 2. That it have convenient Certainty of Time, Place, + Persons. 3. That it answer to Demand--ant's or Plf's count or Plaint. 4. That it be so pleaded, that it may be try'd.

Replications must be, 1:st Certain. 2. Single. 3. Answering the Bar, etc. A Replication either, 1:st denies or traverses the Bar or Plea of the Dft; 2. Or confesses + avoids.

Rejoinders must maintain the Bar + not depart from the Plea. Hale's Anal: 49.[3] vid Co: Lit: 125. a+b[4]
Haw. Abr. 188–9.[5]

Page [67]

1. "Matters in pais" refer to "conveyance between two or more persons 'in the country' [Law French "pais"], i.e., upon the land to be transferred." Jowitt, *supra*, p. 1287. This could be done by deeds in the form of indentures (made between two or more parties and cut in angles so that each party's copy "fits" the other's) or by deed poll, a single deed declaring "to all the world of the grantor's act and intention." The top edge of a deed poll was "polled" or shaved even, unlike the cut edge of an indenture. *Id.*, p. 596.

2. "N.B." for "*nota bene*" (i.e., "mark well").

3. A citation to Sir Mathew Hale, *Analysis of the Law by a Learned Hand* (London, 1713), p. 49. Further editions in 1716 and 1779. See Sweet & Maxwell, *supra*, vol. 1, p. 239.

4. A citation to *Coke on Littleton*, *supra*, pp. 125a and b. See p. [2], n. 1, p. [7], n. 7. This includes Coke's famous summary of the purpose of trial, i.e., "to finde out by due examination

ILLUSTRATION 4. Sir Edward Coke (1552–1634). Coke, one of England's greatest lawyers, was Chief Justice of the Common Pleas (1606–1613) and of the King's Bench (1613–1616). Most significantly for Quincy, Coke's writings formed an important basis for the study of the common law and left an unmistakable influence on lawyers of England and America for many generations. See Stephen D. White, *Sir Edward Coke and "The Grievances of the Commonwealth 1621–1628"* (Chapel Hill, N.C., 1979); Coquillette, *The Anglo-American Legal Heritage*. Coke's *Institutes* (see page [2], note 1) and *Reports* (see page [1], note 2) are repeatedly cited throughout Quincy's *Law Commonplace*. Image courtesy of Harvard Law School Library. My thanks to Kevin Cox and to David R. Warrington, the ever helpful Librarian for Special Collections, Harvard Law School.

the truth of the point in issue or Question betweene the parties, whereupon judgement may be given." *Id.*, pp. 124b, 125a. See *Illustration 4.* Pleading is to determine the point in issue.

5. A citation to *Hawkins's Abridgment*, pp. 188–89, which generally discusses this issue. See page [8], note 1 and page [68], note 6.

[68]

Of Pleading 77

a In Pleading, Estates in fee simple may be
*a*1 Inst 303. b[1] generally alleged; but the Commencement of Estates T[2] + other particular Estates regularly must shewed. Wood B 2. c 1. p 123[3]

b 1 Inst 282.b 283. a. 5 Rep 119.[4] In *b* TRESPASS, if one plead not guilty, He ⊗ cannot give the special +[5] matter in Evidence.[6]

Qu. vid. p. 158[7]

In DETINUE, the Dft on Non Detinet, pleaded cannot give in Evidence, that the Goods were pawned to Him.

⊗ vid. Hawk abr: 379. etc.[6] In WASTE, on Nul Waste pleaded, one may give in Evidence, Lightning, Enemies, etc for this will prove it to be no Waste. But He cannot give in Evidence justifiable Waste, or that He cut down Trees to Repair the House, or any other special Matter. In all these Cases, + the like, one must plead specially. Wood. b. 4. Ch. 4. p. 610.[8]

*d*1 Roll. abr 328. 329 330 1 Inst. 283. a[9] Whenever one cannot have the advantage of the special Matter, *d*[9] He shall take Advantage of it in Evidence. Ibid. 611.[8]

+ But see, The two cautions laid down by Coke. Co: Lit. 283. + that whole Page read Carefully.[5]

Page [68]

1. A citation to *Coke on Littleton* (Coke's *First Institutes*), p. 303b. See p. [2], n. 1 and page [7], n. 9, *supra*. Quincy's note is almost a direct quote, except he substitutes "+" for "estates taile" in the original.

2. "T" is used as an abbreviation for "estates tail," i.e., a "cut down" estate [L. *tailliatum*], which can only be inherited by an heir of the body, or a male heir of the body, i.e., "entail male." See Coquillette, *Anglo-American Legal Heritage*, *supra*, pp. 101–02; J. H. Baker, *An Introduction to English Legal History*, *supra*, pp. 272–73. See also page [46], note 8, *supra*.

3. A citation to Wood, *Institute*, Book 2, chap. 1, p. 123. See page [7], note 3, *supra*. This section contains an extensive discussion of estates, including entailed estates.

4. A citation to *Coke on Littleton*, pp. 282b–283a. See page [2], note 1 and page [7], note 9. Thus "[I]f one doth waste, and before the action brought the Lessee repaireth it, and after the lessor bringeth an action of waste, and the Lessee plead *Quod non fecit vastum*, hee cannot give in evidence the special matter." *Id.*, at p. 283a. For example, you cannot deny you did something, and expect to give evidence that you did do it, but repaired the harm. There is also a citation to *Whelpdale's Case* (1605), *Coke's Reports*, *supra*, vol. 5, at p. 119a. In that case it was held that you could not plead that an obligation was "not [your] deed," i.e., not your signature, and also prove a special matter, i.e., that the terms of the obligation were usury, prohibited by statute.

5. Quincy notes "+" in the text, which refers to the "two cautions" set out by Coke in *Coke on Littleton*, p. 283a, at the page given. Quincy notes that the "whole page" be "read carefully." Coke's "two cautions" are: "first that whensoever a man cannot have advantage of the speciall matter by way of pleading, there he shall take advantage of it in the evidence." *Id.*, p. 283a; and "[s]econdly, that in any action upon the case . . . against any Justice of reale [or other local government officers] . . . they may plead the general issue, and give the special matter for theire excuse or justications." *Id.*, p. 283a.

6. Here Quincy "cites over" to Hawkins, *Abridgment*, p. 379. See Sweet & Maxwell, vol. 1, p. 452:10. Hawkins' *Abridgment* was a compact (12 mo) and handy summary of Coke's long and complex commentary on *Littleton*. It was first published in 1711, with subsequent editions in 1714, 1718, 1718, 1719, 1725, 1736, 1742, and 1751. Quincy's citations match the 1725 edition, among others. Hawkins observes, "In trespass if the Fact were not committed, the Defendant ought to plead not guilty, but if the Fact were committed, and he have Cause of Justification and Excuse, he must confess the Fact, and plead the special Matter." *Id.*, p. 379. The reason was sensible enough: "[T]he End of the Law in requiring such Exactness in Pleadings . . . is that the Matter which is truly in Question between the Parties, should only be put in Issue," for fairness and to avoid "unnecessary Charge." *Id.*, p. 379.

7. A cross citation to Quincy's *Law Commonplace*, page 158 [101], where Quincy observes in an action against a Justice of the Peace etc. "they may plead ye general Issue & give the special matter for their Excuse or Justification in Evidence." Page 158 [101] cites back to this page.

8. A citation to Wood's *Institute*, *supra*, book 4, chapter 4, pp. 610, 611 (page 581, 1772 edition). Almost a direct quotation.

9. Citations to *Rolle's Abridgment* (1688), pp. 328–30. See page [9], note 1. There is also a citation to *Coke on Littleton* (1628), *supra*, p. 283a. Coke states that "whensoever a man cannot have advantage of the speciall matter by way of pleading, there he shall take advantage of it in the evidence." *Id.*, p. 283a.

[69]

78 Of Pleading

Demurrer. vid. the opposite Page

He that demurreth in Law confesseth all such matters of Fact as are well + sufficiently pleaded. If there be a Demurrer for part + an Issue for Part, the more orderly Course is to give Judgment upon the Demur^{r}; first, but yet it is in the Discretion of the Court to try the Issue first if they will. After Demurrer join'd in any Court of Record, the Judges shall give Judgm^{t}. according as the very Right of the Cause + Matter in Law shall appear, without Regarding any Want of Form in any Writ, Return, Plaint, Declaration or other Pleading, Process or Course of Proceeding; except those only which the Party demurring shall specially + particularly set-down + express in his Demurrer. Now what is Substance + what is Form you shall read in 3 Rep. 57. Linc: Col:'s Case, 5 Rep. 74 Wymeck's Case, 10 Rep. 88 usque 98 Dr. Leyfield's Case.[1] Co: Lit. 72. a.[2]

If one pleads a Lease, Gift or Feoffment of Ten'ments which lie in Livery, or a Grant of Things which lie in Grants; he shall conclude Virtute cujus fuit inde seisitus;[3] but He that pleads a Lease of Lands, shall say, Virtute Cujus intravit, & fuit inde Possessionatus,[4] for a Man is not possess'd by force of such Lease before Entry. Haw. abr. 284[5]

Page [69]

1. A citation to a series of cases in *Coke's Reports* (covering 1582–1641). The first is to the *Lincoln College Case* (1595), which appears at page 53a of the first edition, not page 57, as Quincy has it. The second is *Wymark's Case*, *Coke's Reports*, *supra*, vol. 5, p. 74a, and the third is *Doctor Leyfield's Case*, *Coke's Reports*, *supra*, vol. 10, p. 88a. That case concludes on page 95b, however, not 98, as Quincy indicates. These citations are exactly the same, however, as the marginal citation in *Coke on Littleton*, *supra*, p. 72a. In the latter case, *Doctor Leyfield's Case*, the Exchequer Chamber overturned, on Writ of Error, a King's Bench judgment that the defendant's plea in bar was insufficient because he did not show to the Court certain letters patent. According to *Coke's Reports*, the Exchequer Chamber observed that "the same is but matter of form, and not of substance . . ." *Id.*, p. 88a.

2. A citation to *Coke on Littleton*, *supra*, p. 72a. See p. [2], n. 1, and p. [7], n. 9. The entire preceding passage, starting with "He that demurreth . . ." was copied verbatim from *Coke on Littleton* by Quincy, including the citations from the margin. The fact that two of them were inaccurate leads one to think Quincy did not actually look them up. The underscoring is Quincy's, and he uses "plaint" instead of Coke's "pleint."

3. "*Virtute cujus*" is "a clause in a pleading justifying an entry upon land, by which the party alleged that it was in virtue of an order from one entitled that he entered." Jowitt, *supra*, p. 1840. "*Virtute cujus fuit inde seisitus*" is pleaded when the defendant is entitled to "seisin," i.e., legal possession of a fee. See Coquillette, *Anglo-American Legal Heritage*, *supra*, p. 102 on "seisin" and "fee."

4. A lease of lands was not originally regarded as a legal "fee" in land, therefore it could not be "seised." Thus the defendant would plead "*virtute cujus*," that he was entitled to "enter and possess" the land, rather than have "seisen." See note 3, *supra*.

5. A citation to Hawkins, *Abridgment*, p. 284. See page [68], note 6. Quincy closely copied this text from Hawkins.

[70]

Of Pleading 79

Regularly whensoever a Man doth Anything by Force of a Warrant or Authority, He must plead it. Co: Lit. 283. a.[1]

DEMURRER confesses only Matter of Fact, + that only when it is well pleaded, but it never confesses Matter of Law. L[d] Raym[d]. p. 18.[2]

Vid. The Title——Of Special Pleas on Debt. 2 Mod. Ent. 302.[3] Of Pleading Estates. Ibid. 327.[4]

[QUINCY'S PAGE 80 IS BLANK]

Page [70]

1. A citation to *Coke on Littleton*, *supra*, p. 283[a]. See p. [2], n. 1; p. [7], n. 9. Coke precedes this statement by observing "Of this learning you shall reade plentifully in our bookes, and in my Reports." *Id.*

2. A citation to Sir Robert (Lord) Raymond's *Entries* (London, 1765), p. 18 (Transl. G. Wilson). This was vol. 3 of *Raymond's Reports*, added in 1765 to the first two volumes of 1743. See Sweet & Maxwell, vol. 1, *supra*, pp. 277, 307–08. See p. [26], n. 2.

3. A citation to *Modern Entries in English, etc., By a Gentleman of the Inner Temple* [J. Mallory] (London, 1734–1735), 2 vols., 1741, vol. 2, p. 302. See Sweet & Maxwell, vol. 1, *supra*, p. 273.

4. *Id.*, vol. 2, p. 327.

[71]

Of Releases vid Release in the Index 81

at the End of this Book. vid vol. 2. p. 224. vid vol. 4. p. 5.[1]

1 Ter. of law release N's Max. 74[2]

2 Lit 445. 1 Inst. 264. b 2 Roll Abr. 409[3]

3 1 Inst. 264 a[5]

4 Lit 305. etc 465. 1 Inst 193.b 273.b 275.a 279.b. 280.a[7]

A*1*[2] Release is a Deed or Instrum[t], whereby a Man doth give or discharge the Right or Action, which He hath or claimeth ag.[t] another out of or in Lands etc. *2*[3]It is usually made by the words, Have remised, Released, + for ever Quit (Quiet) Claims, or by other words to the same Purpose. Wood B2. c. 3. p 289[4] Releases are either *3*[5]Express or implied. Express re: is by Deed. An Implied R is that which the Law makes, + is sometimes by writing, + sometimes without Writing. A Release in Law is more favorable expounded than a R in Deed Ibid.[6]

4[7]Releases either ensure 1:[st] By way of Enlarging an Estate; being made by a Reversioner to a Lessee in Privity with Enlarging Words. 2. By Way of Mitter le Estate,[8] or transferring it; As if One Jointenant or Parcener Release to Another. For this must be between Privies. 3. By Way of Mitter le Droit,[9] which transfers the Right of Rsor to the Rsee;[10] as when Disseisee releases to Dissor,[11] + makes his Estate Rightfull which was wrongfull. Here a release of a bare Right for an [Hour] etc. is as good as if it where made to the Other + his Heirs + It is not requisite that there sh[d] be any Privity between the Parties to such a Release. By way of Ex- -tinguishment only against all Persons, when the Releasee cannot have the Thing released. As when the L.[d] releases his Territory to his Ten't[12] of the Land, or when the Grantee of a Rent-Charge, or of a Common, releases to the Ten't of the Land the Rent-Charge or Common. For One

Page [71]

1. Cross-reference to *Law Commonplace*, page 181 [124] (an excellent index entry). The subsequent citations are to Quincy's other volumes. Volume 4, page 5 [126] begins the *Legis Mis-*

cellanea of Estates, reproduced in this volume as pages [126] to [131], and cross-references back to this page. Quincy's vol. 2 is unidentified and presumably lost.

2. Quincy "note 1." A citation to the legal dictionary, J. Rastell, *Termes of the Lawes*, word "Release," (1st English ed., 1563), Sweet & Maxwell, vol. 1, *supra*, pp. 10–11, and to Noy, *Maximes*, *supra*, p. 74. See p. [8], n. 4. The marginal note is hard to read.

3. Quincy "note 2." A citation to Littleton's *Tenures* (*circa* 1481), Chap. 445, "Of Releases," annotated in *Coke on Littleton*, *supra*, pp. 264a–264b. Although Littleton and Coke support Quincy's text, it is not a paraphrase.

4. A citation to Wood, *Institute*, *supra*, book 2, chapter 3, p. 289. See page [7], note 3. (In the 1772 ed., the "Release" section begins on p. 265.) Wood says that a release "is usually made by the words, *Remire, release,* and for ever *quit claim*, or by other words to the same purpose." *Id.*, p. 265. Quincy's account adds "quiet" and is an intelligent, if not exact, paraphrase.

5. Quincy "note 3." Another citation to *Coke on Littleton*, *supra*, p. 264a where Coke describes the law of releases. Quincy's text, however, follows Wood, not Coke.

6. Quincy's text is a close paraphrase of Wood's *Institute*, *supra*, book 2, chapter 3, p. 289. "R" is just an abbreviation for "release."

7. Quincy "note 4." A citation to *Littleton's Tenures* (c. 1481), *supra*, as annotated in *Coke on Littleton*, *supra*. *Littleton* chapter 305 on deeds of release, is annotated by Coke at *Coke on Littleton*, *supra*, at p. 193b; and Chapter 465, on use of releases to enlarge estates, is annotated by Coke at *Coke on Littleton*, pp. 273a–273b. Here Quincy identifies *Coke on Littleton* as "1 Inst 193.b," i.e., Coke's *First Institutes* (or *Coke on Littleton*), at p. 193b. See p. [2], n. 1, p. [7], n. 9. Quincy then cites to subsequent Coke annotations on releases at *Coke on Littleton* (1628), *supra*, pp. 275a, 279b, and 280b. Some of Quincy's text is a paraphrase of *Id.*, p. 275a, but this is not slavish copying, but an intelligent summary, including a structure not in Coke.

8. "Mitter le Estate" is law French for "to pass an estate." See Jowitt, *supra*, p. 1182. In the context of a release, it means to pass "an estate to one or more already in possession," thus expanding their estate. *Id.*, p. 1509.

9. "Mitter le Droit" is law French for "to pass a right." Jowitt, *supra*, p. 1182. In the context of a release, it means transferring right that extinguishes forever a right to a disseisor, heir or grantee. *Id.*, p. 1509.

10. "Rsor" and "Rsee" for "Releasor" (the maker of a release) and "Releasee" (the person to whom a release is made).

11. "Dissor" for "disseisor" (a person "who unlawfully puts another out of his land" by wrongfull seising a fee). Such a person would require a release from the rightful owner to have full seisin. See Jowitt, *supra*, p. 643.

[72]

82 **Of Releases**

1 1 Inst. 298. b[1] man cannot be Lord + Ten't, He cannot have Land & Rent, nor Land + Common of Pasture out of the same Land.

1 A R[1] is of more force in Law than a Confirmation. But Note that if a Charge or Duty grows by Record, the Release must be upon Record. If By Deed, the R must be by Deed. p. 289.[2]

Who may make or take Releases?

2 5 Rep 27[3] As a man may release any Debt or Duty due to Himself, so a Man may release any Thing or any Wrong due to His Wife before or after Marriage. And if the Wife is *2* Exi^tt^x[4] to Another, The H may release any Debt or Duty due to the Testator, but the Femme Exi^tt^x cannot to the Prejudice of her H. Regularly the R of an Infant is void. An Infant Exc^tt^or may release a Debt duly paid to Him as Exc^tt^or. But if He releases that which He doth not receive, the R is void. An Exc^tt^or before *3*[5] Probate of ye Will, may release a Debt or Duty due to the Testator, because he Hath an absolute Interest of the Debt in Him. And tho' He cannot have an Action before Probate, yet He may release an Action.

3 5 Rep. 27 9 Rep. 39 1 Inst 292 b[5]

4 2 Roll abr.404409.444 cont^rd^ Show Rep. 153. 155.[5] If one Releaseth, + then taketh Admin^tt^on, This R shall not bar Him: for He had no Right of Action at the Time of the R. + If one releases an Exc^tt^or, this shall release*4*[6] all Actions, which He had also in his own Right. (Qu.)[7]

5 1 Inst. 200. b.[8] One Tenant in *5*[8] Common cannot release to the other, because the Freehold is several.

\+ Qu.[7] If this is not wrongly expressed. Vid Showers as cited in the margin.[9]

It

Page [72]

1. Quincy "note 1." A citation to *Coke on Littleton*, *supra*, p. 298b. See page [2], note 1; page [7], note 9, *supra*. "R" is for "release." The passage in Quincy does not follow Coke, however, past the first sentence.

2. A citation to Wood, *Institutes*, *supra*, book 2, chapter 3, p. 289. See page [7], note 3. This is the page "289" cited on Quincy's preceding page, 81 [71], and corresponds to page 265 in the 1772 edition. It is an almost exact copy of Wood.

3. Quincy "note 2" a citation to *Russel's Case* (1584), *Coke's Reports*, *supra*, vol. 5, p. 27a. This case decided that the release of an underaged infant was void and indicated that the same would be true of a "feme covert Executrix" because "she can doe nothing to the prejudice of her husband. But without question in such Case the release of the Husband is good." *Id.*, p. 27b. The point, as Quincy indicated, is the full legal power of the husband over the wife, which extends to releases.

4. "Exi^{tt}x" for "executrix."

5. Quincy "note 3." Another citation to *Russel's Case* (1584), *Coke's Reports*, *supra*, vol. 5, p. 27a. See note 3, *supra*. Quincy also cited to *Hensloe's Case* (1600), *Coke's Reports*, *supra*, vol. 9, 36b, at p. 39a. Both cases support Quincy's observation that an executor ("exc^{tt}or") usually has the absolute interest of a debt owed to the estate in him, and thus can make a valid release. Quincy also cites to *Coke on Littleton*, *supra*, p. 292b, which supports Quincy's statement that an executor cannot have an action before probate, but "an Executor before probate [may] release an Action." *Id.*, p. 292b.

6. Quincy "note 4." Here Quincy cited to *Rolle's Abridgment*, *supra*, pp. 404, 409, 444. See page [9], note 1. He also cited to *Knight* v. *Cole* (1691), *Shower's Reports* (covering 1678–1694), London (pt. 1) 1708, (pt. 2) 1720, pp. 150 at 153, 155. See Sweet & Maxwell, *supra*, vol. 1, p. 309 (119). See also J. W. Wallace, *The Reporter*, *supra*, pp. 392–94. The opinion in *Knight* v. *Cole*, at page 152, refers to the case of *Morris* v. *Wise* in *Rolle's Abridgment*, p. 409. On page 155 of *Knight* v. *Cole* is recorded Chief Justice Holt's view that, "I think the case in Rolls no law."

7. Quincy queries "Qu" the preceding statement, which as written makes no sense. At the bottom of the page he notes the reason for the queries after "+Qu," "if this is not wrongly expressed. *vid* Showers [*Shower's Reports*] as cited in the margin." See n. 6, *supra*. The statement probably should read "if one releases an executor, this shall [also] release all actions which that person has against the executor personally, "in his own right," as well as releasing the estate." Even this statement really makes no policy sense. Quincy clearly did not just copy, but questioned statements that looked wrong to him, or were inconsistent with other cited authority.

8. Quincy "note 5" cites again to *Coke on Littleton*, *supra*, p. 200b. Coke states that "[O]ne Tenant in common may enfeoffe his companion, but release, because the freehold is reversed." *Id.*, p. 200b.

9. See discussion at n. 7, *supra*.

[73]

Of Releases 83

*I*Lit. 446	It is to be observed, that no *I* Right passeth by a R,
447. 450.	but the Right which for the Res^{tt}or[1] had at the Time of the
499.	R made. If He has no Right the R is void.
1 Inst.	If he <u>to whom</u> an R is made, hath nothing
265.a.+b.	in the Lands, that R is void also.
266. a. 267 a.[1]	*x*[2] It behoveth Him to whom the R is made,
	that He hath a Freehold in the Land in Deed or
*x*Lit p.	in Law, or a Reversion or Rem^{tt}der[4] in Fees: Fee T
447.[2]	or for Life at the Time of the R made, or else He
	<u>cannot take</u> the R.
*2*1 Inst. 264.	What Things may, or may not, be released?
a + b. 265.a.270. a+b	Supposing a Right in the R^{e}sor, + that the R^{e}see hath
Lit 450	Something in the Lands, tc. *2*[3] <u>Lands, Ten^{tt}ments</u> +
460. etc.[3]	<u>Hereditaments</u> may be given + transferred by
	way of R + all <u>Rights</u> to Lands + may be give +
	Discharged by it. A R by a L'sor to his L'see for
	<u>years</u> or at <u>Will</u>, having enter'd by force of such Lease,
3.	is good in Respect of the Privity betwixt Them; Therefore
1 Rep.	not to a Tenant at <u>Sufferance</u>. A R to a Lessee for years
112. 2 Rep	<u>in Futuro</u>, or before Entry, (tho' it may extinguish the rent reserved)
51. 5 Rep.	yet it cannot inlarge it for want of Possession. If a next Avoidance
71. 10 Rep.	is granted to two, one may release to the Other, before the Church
48. 49	is void, not afterwards, because it is (as it were) but a Chose in Action
1 Inst.	Rights, Titles to <u>Goods</u> + <u>Chattels</u>, <u>Actions</u>, real, personal &
237. a.	mixt, may be released. *3*[4]Also <u>Conditions</u> annexed to Estates,
265. b.	<u>Powers</u> of <u>Revocations</u> of Uses, <u>Warranties</u>, <u>Covenants</u>,
274. b.[4]	(even before they are broke by a R of all <u>covenants</u>).

Services

Page [73]

1. Quincy "note 1." A citation to *Littleton's Tenures* (c. 1481), *supra*, chapters 446, 447, 449 and 450, all concerning "releases." See p. [2], n. 1; p. [7], n. 9. These chapters are annotated by Coke in *Coke on Littleton*, *supra*, at 265a + b (chapter 446), at 266a (chapter 447), and 267a (chapters 449 and 450). These citations illustrate by many examples Quincy's basic statement "Right pas-

seth by a R [Release], but the Right [only] which for the Res^{tt}or [Releasor] had at the time of the R [Release] made."

2. Quincy "note ^{x}." A citation to *Littleton's Tenures*, *supra*, chap. 447. See note 1, *supra*. The chap. 447 illustrates Quincy's statement.

3. Quincy "note 2." Further citations to *Littleton's Tenures*, *supra*, chapters 450 and 460 and to *Coke on Littleton*, *supra*, pp. 264a, b, 265a and 270a, b. *Coke on Littleton* at pp. 270a and b, annotates *Littleton's Tenures*, chapter 460. Quincy here continues his use of "tt" to indicate abbreviation of words, such as "L^{tt}or" for "lessor," "L^{tt}see" for "lessee," etc. Both Littleton's chapters and the Coke annotations provide illustrations of Quincy's summary of the law.

4. Quincy "note 3." This note cites to a string of four cases in *Coke's Reports* (covering 1572–1616; London, English trans., 1658). See page [11], note 2, *supra*. The first is *Buckler's Case* (1597), *Coke's Reports*, *supra*, vol. 1, p. 112. This decided that "an estate of freehold cannot begin in *futuro*," among other points. Also cited was *Sir Hugh Cholmley's Case* (1597), *Coke's Reports*, *supra*, vol. 2, p. 49b, at p. 51b (release of a remainder in tail to tenant for life); *Hoe's Case* (1592), *Coke's Reports*, *supra*, vol. 5, p. 70b, at p. 71a (in a "release of all Actions" a "covenant before the breach of it [the Covenant] is not released," because there was no cause of action or any "certain duty before the breach"); *Lampet's Case* (1613), *Coke's Reports*, vol. 10, p. 46a, at pp. 48b–49a (five methods set out to release "a right or title to a freehold or inheritance." "[A]ll rights, titles and actions may by the wisdom and policy of the Law be released to the terre tenant [tenant seised of the land], for the same reason of his repose and quiet, and for the avoiding of contentions and suits, and that everyone may live in his vocation in peace and plenty." *Id.*, p. 48a).

[74]

84 Of Releases

Services, Rents, Commons + other Profits to be taken out of Lands may be discharged Extinguished + De--termined by a R[1] to the Ten't of the Land. etc. A Condition cannot be released upon Condition; but

a3 the R will be good, + the Condition void. Wood p. 290.[2]

10 Rep. 51 Mere Possibilities cannot be released-yet see what Possibilities may be released. Ibid._

Debts, a Legacies by a R of a Legacy, + other

b1 Roll abr 412 490. 439.[4] Duties, may be Released before or after they become due. A man cannot release a b4Personal Thing as an Obligation upon Condition Sub--sequent, because a Personal Thing once Suspended is Extinguished forever.

The Construction of Releases. Sed vid.[5]

Wood. B2. Ch 3. 291.\ More at large

Where there are two Exec^tt^ors, a R of one, before judgment bars of the other, not after judgment.

†Co Lit: 285.a.[6] †In a R of All Actions, Causes of Actions are released. But within a Submission of All Actions to Arbitram†ø Causes of Action are not contained.ø[7]

He that hath Right of Entry may enter tho' He hath released all actions, and if one takes my goods, I may take them out of his Possession, tho' I have released all Actions.

øBecause nothing shall be intended to be referred to Arbitration, but matters then in Controversy, between them. Haw Abr: 381.[7]

A

Page [74]

1. "R" for "Release," here and below. Thomas Wood, cited by Quincy below at note 2, defined a "Release" as "a Deed or Instrument, whereby a Man doth give or discharge the Right or Action, which he hath or claimeth against another out of or in his Land." *An Institute of the Laws of England* (10th ed., London, 1772), p. 265.

2. Two citations to Wood, Ch. 3, p. 290. See page [7], note 3 [10th ed., 1772, p. 266]. "A Condition cannot be released upon Condition, but the Release will be good, and the Condition void." *Id.*, p. 266.

3. Quincy's note "a" referred to "a" in the margin, a citation to *Lampert's Case* (1613), *Coke's Reports,* vol. 10, at p. 51a. But the cited case does not appear to be directly on point, being a catalogue of circumstances in which releases are not valid. *Id.*, pp. 51a–51b.

4. Citations to *Rolle's Abridgment*, vol. 1, pp. 412, 439, 490. See page [9], note 1, *supra.* Quincy marked the relevant spot in his text with a "b," and then gave the citation at "b" in the margin.

5. "Sed vid.," or "but see," with a reference to Thomas Wood, *An Institute of the Laws of England*, *supra* note 2 at Ch. 3, p. 291. [10th ed., London, 1772 at pp. 266–67]. Under "of the Construction of Releases," Wood contains an exhaustive catalogue of types of release, i.e., "More at large."

6. A citation to *Coke on Littleton*, p. 285a. See page [2], note 1, and page [7], note 9, *supra.* This is Coke's Chapter 8, "Of Releases," beginning on page 264a. A direct quote follows Quincy's "t" in the text, with the citation accompanying the "t" in the margin. According to Coke, "And by the release of all Actions, causes of action be released, but within a submission of all action to arbitrement, causes of action are not contained." *Id.*, p. 285a. Note Quincy abbreviates "arbitrement" as "Arbitram t."

7. A citation to Hawkins, *Abridgment*, p. 381. See page [68], note 6, *supra.*

[75]

Of Releases 85

[a]Lit 504 507. 8 Rep. 152. 153. 154. 1 Inst 289a, 291a[1]	A R of all Actions will not discharge [a][1] Executions or bar one to take out Excon. But a Discharge of All Suits will be A bar to n Excon.[2]
[b]Lit 512, 513. 1 Inst 292. b 8 Rep. 153[3]	A R of All Actions will not Discharge Any Thing, for which the Releasor had [b][3]No Cause of Action at the Time of the R made. But money on Bond to be paid at Michaelmas[4] may be released by the Obligee; because the Right of Action was in Him before. Yet Rent payable at that Time cannot be discharged by a R of all actions; nor an Annuity.[5] But one may Release the Rent etc. before the Day, by Special Words. It will Release the Arrears due before the Making the R.
[c]1 Inst 191.a. 8 Rep 153 2 Roll. 484.[6]	A R of all [c][6]Dues (Debita) will release Personal Actions + Executions; but it will not bar an Account. For there is nothing certainly due before Account made.[7] But a R of all Actions will be a good Bar in Account. A R in full of All Accounts, shall be extended only to an Account.
[d] 1 Vent 29.[8]	One cannot release a Debt or Duty by his [d][7]Will.
[e]1 Roll Abr. 123. 2 Roll Abr 404 8 Rep. 151. 152.[9]	A R of all [e][9]Rights in any Lands or Tenements does release + discharge all Manner of Rights of Action + Entry; but not a Possibility of a Right, that He hath at the Time of the R; or a Right that shall Descend to Him afterward.

A

Page [75]

1. Quincy marked "a" in the text and in the margin. The marginal note contains citations to *Littleton's Tenures*, sections 504 and 507. This is one of the oldest printed law books, first pub-

lished c. 1481, and then republished with Coke's annotations in *Coke on Littleton* (London). See page [2], note 1, and page [7], note 9. Section 504 stated that an execution, which follows judgment, is not discharged by an "all manner of Actions" release, "[f]or Execution upon such a Writ cannot bee said an Action." *Coke on Littleton*, *supra*, p. 289a. Section 507 stated that for a release to cover executions, "it behoueth that the plaintiff make a release to him of all manner of executions." *Id.*, p. 291a. Coke added, "As if a man release all suites the Execution is gone..." *Id.*, p. 291a. Quincy then added the citations to *Coke on Littleton* where Littleton's Sections 504 and 507 are found, annotated by Coke, i.e., *Coke on Littleton*, *supra*, pp. 289a and 291a. He also added a citation to *Edward Altham's Case* (1611), 8 *Coke's Reports* p. 150b at p. 152a to p. 153a. That case supports Quincy's notes that a "release of all actions" is not a release of executions, but only by "a release of all suits" are executions barred. *Id.*, pp. 152a, 153b.

2. Quincy abbreviated "Execution" as "Excon." The proposition noted is supported by *Edward Altham's Case*, *supra*, note 1.

3. Quincy again made a note in the text, "b," and added more citations, after another "b" in the margin, to *Littleton's Tenures*, *supra*, note 1, sections 512 and 513, to the relevant page in *Coke on Littleton*, *supra,* note 1, p. 292b; and to *Edward Altham's Case*, *supra*, note 1, p. 153. Littleton compared two situations. In the first, a man "bee bound to another in a certaine sumne of money, to pay at the Feast of Saint Michael next ensuing," a release of "all actions" would bar "the duty forever and yet he could not have an Action at the time of the Release made." *Id.*, p. 292b. Coke explains that this is "because the right of the Action is in him" at the time of the release. *Id.*, p. 292b. On the other hand, a lease "to another for a yeare, to yield to him at the Feast of St. Mich. Next insuing 40s" would not be barred by a release before that date. *Id.*, p. 292b. Coke explained that the obligation to pay the lease was "neither debitum nor soluendum at the time of the release," i.e., there was no specific debt or payment made at the time of the release that would vest the action "in" the obligee. See *id.*, p. 292b.

4. "Michaelmas" here refers to the "Feast of Saint Michael next ensuing," i.e., the next September 29. See Jowitt, *supra*, p. 1170. It is a customary quarter day. See *id.* Quincy is referring to the first example discussed by Littleton, as described in note 3, *supra.*

5. Coke added, "If a man hath an Annuity . . . and he before it be behind doth release all Actions, this shall not release the Annuity, for it is not meerely in Action, because it may be granted over." *Coke on Littleton*, *supra*, note 1, p. 513b.

6. This entire section of Quincy's notes closely followed Wood, *Institute*. See page [7], note 3 and page [74], note 2. This included Quincy copying Wood's margin notes, with some discrepancies. Quincy again inserted a marker, "c," in the text, and then a marginal citation was again to *Coke on Littleton*, *supra*, note 1, at p. 191a [almost certainly erroneous, correct citation would be page 291a], to *Edward Altham's Case*, *supra*, note 1, page 153a, and to *Rolle's Abridgment* (London, 1668), vol. 2, p. 484. See page [9], note 1, *supra.* Assuming Quincy meant page 291a in *Coke on Littleton*, the proposition in his notebook is supported by Coke. "If A be accountable to B, and B releaseth him all his duties, this is no barre in an Action of account, for Duties extend to things certaine, and what shall fall out upon the account is incertaine." *Id.*, p. 291a. An action of "account" lay against a receiver or bailiff, or a fellow merchant, in respect of financial dealings between them, as "for not rendering a proper account of profits." Jowitt, *supra*, p. 27. The citation to *Edward Altham's Case*, *supra* note 1, referred to *Coke's Reports,* vol. 8, p. 153. On page 153a Coke stated that "a debt or duty shall be barred by a release of all actions." *Id.*, p. 153a. See also *id.*, p. 152a, where Coke discussed the effect of the words "*quod alicui debetur*" in a release (i.e., "which is due to any").

7. As the action of "account" was essentially to examine the financial dealings between the plaintiff and someone like a bailiff or a receiver or a business partner, it only arrived at sums cer-

tain after examination of balance sheets, etc. See note 6, *supra*. Quincy's discussion here came almost verbatim from the section in Wood, *Institute*. See note 6, *supra*, and Wood, *Institute* (10th ed., 1772), p. 268. He also copied some, but not all, of Wood's marginal notes.

8. A citation to *Ventris' Reports*, "Part I. K.B." (London, 1690) covering King's Bench cases from 1668 to 1684. See page [89], note 7.

9. Again Quincy inserted a marker in his text, "e," and added a marginal note, once again citing to *Rolle's Abridgment*, vol. 1, p. 123, vol. 2, p. 404. See note 6, *supra*. He also cited again to *Edward Altham's Case*, *supra*, note 1, at "pages 151–152." The relevant discussions by Coke in that case is at pages 152a to 153a, and generally supports Quincy's notes, subject to the discussions and limitations described in notes 3, 5 and 6, above.

[76]

86 Of Releases

a	A R of One's *a*[1]Title to Lands + Ten^tt^ments is
Lit 509	A R of All One's Rights.
8 Rep	A R of All *b*[2]Demands (a Word
153. 154.	of Art) or Claims in the best R of All,
1 Inst. 192.a[1]	is the most effectual words to bar etc. Vid
	Wood B2. C3. p. 292[3]
*b*Lit 508.	(vid p. 26 of this Book)[4]
1 Inst 291.b.	A R of a Right to One that hath
5 Rep. 71	but a bare Right regularly is void; for He
8 Rep. 153	to whome a R is made of a bare Right in Lands
154.	+ tenements must have Either a Freehold
1 Lev. 99	in Deed, or in Law in Possession, or a
3 Lev. 274[2]	State in Remainder or Reversion in F
	or T, or for Life. Co: Lit. 267.a.bot.[5]

If a Lease for Years be made to two, albeit the Lessor before they enter cannot release to them to enlarge their Estate, yet One of them may Before Entry Release to the Other. Ibid. 270. b.[6]

A Freehold in Law may be enlarg'd by R before Entry. Ibid.[7]

[QUINCY PAGES 87–88 ARE BLANK.]

Page [76]

1. Quincy inserted "a" into the text, and added a marginal note labeled "a." These were citations to *Littleton's Tenures*, section 508 (release bars title of entry to lands or tenements), see page [2], note 1 and page [75], note 1, and the corresponding sections of *Coke on Littleton*, which is at pages 291b and 292a. (Quincy's manuscript does say "192a," which is erroneous. See also page [75], note 6.) The case citation is, once again, to *Edward Altham's Case*, *Coke's Reports*, vol. 8, p. 150b at "153.154." By this, Quincy must have been referring to the foliated pages 153a to 154a, where proper words for a release are discussed. (Does lack of foliated numbering indicate that

Quincy was unfamiliar with the original, and/or just copying the citation?) Coke stated there that "And as a release of suits is larger and more beneficial than a release of quarrels, or of actions; so a release of demands is more large and beneficial than any of them, for thereby is released all that is by the others released, and more . . ." *Id.*, p. 154a.

2. Quincy inserted "b" into the text, and added marginal notes labeled "b." The citations were to *Littleton's Tenures*, *supra*, note 1, section 508, in which Littleton stated that "[i]f a man release to another all manner of demands, this is the best release to him where the Release is made . . ." *Coke on Littleton*, *supra*, note 1, p. 291b. Quincy then added the relevant citation to Coke's annotations of Littleton's section 508 at *id.*, p. 291b. In addition to another citation to *Edward Altham's Case*, *supra*, note 1, he also referred to *Hoe's Case* (1592) *Coke's Reports* (London, 1605), vol. 5, p. 70b at p. 71a. "[B]y a release of all actions, suits, and quarrels a covenant before the breach of it is not released, because there is not any cause of action, nor any certain duty before the breach of it . . ." *Id.*, at p. 71a. Also included are two citations to *Sir Charles Levinz's Reports* (London, 1702), covering King's Bench and Common Pleas cases from 1660–1696. The first citation is to the case of *Henn* v. *Hanson* (1663), which appears on page 99 of the first volume of *Levinz's Reports* (first edition published in 1702). The second citation is to the case of *Knight* v. *Cole* (1690), which appears in the third volume of *Levinz's Reports*, and begins on page 273. Although Sweet & Maxwell, *supra*, vol. 1, p. 303:81, indicates that the 1702 edition of *Levinz Reports* had only one volume and that a three-volume edition was not produced until 1790, a review of *Levinz Reports* themselves demonstrates that the 1702 edition was indeed in three volumes, as Quincy cited. Many thanks to my colleague David Warrington and research assistant Kevin Cox for helping solve this mystery.

3. Again Quincy returned to Wood, *Institute*, which he closely copied through at this discussion "Of Releases." See page [7], note 3, page [74], note 2. The section in Wood, *Institute* reads "A Release of all <u>Demands</u> or Claims is the best Release of all, and the most effectual word to bar Actions, Appeals, Rights of Entry . . ." *Id.* (10th ed., 1772, p. 268). In such a confusing area, Quincy focused on "words of art," as any law student would, looking for the magic term, "the most effectual Word."

4. This was apparently a reference to this notebook, not Wood's *Institute*. On Quincy page 26 [31], Quincy discussed the nature of a legal "interest" in all its different forms, and it would not be irrational to link the nature of a legal interest to the effectiveness of words to release such interests.

5. This is almost a direct quotation of *Coke on Littleton*, *supra*, note 1, at p. 267a. Quincy uses "F" as an abbreviation for "fee" and "T," for "fee taile."

6. This sentence was <u>not</u> derived directly from the cited page in *Coke on Littleton*, *supra*, note 1. Coke spoke of "an Advowson to two." There "the one of them may before the Church become voide release to the other, for although the Grantor cannot release to them to encrease their estate, because their interest is future, and not in possession, yet one of them to extinguish his interest may release to the other in respect of the privity." *Id.*, p. 270b. On page 270a Coke further stated that "if before the lessee doth enter the lessor releaseth all the might that hee hath in land, albeit this release cannot in large his estate, yet it shall in respect of the privitie extinguish the rent." Thus it is clear that Quincy's statement is correct, but the principle was not quoted directly. An "advowson" was "the right of presentation [of a pastor] church or benefie." This was "in the nature of a temporal property and a spirited trust." Jowitt, *supra*, p. 74. Usually the bishop had to agree with the patron of the advowson as to the appointment, but it was regarded as a valuable property right, and a right to present *in perpetuum* was considered to be real property right than a lease, which was seen as a personal contract. *Id.*, pp. 76–77.

7. An apparent citation to *Coke on Littleton*, *supra*, notes 1 and 6, Coke stated there that "if a man make a Lease for life, the Remainder for life, and the first Lease dieth, a Release to him in the remainder and to his heires in good before he doth enter to enlarge his estate, for that he hath an estate of a Freehold in Law in him, which may be enlarged by Release before entrie." *Coke on Littleton*, p. 270b.

[77]

Of Statutes or Acts. †[1] 89

Vid. The two Pages preceeding L.d Reeves Directions to his Nephew: (in this Book at the Beginning.)[1] vid. Of Laws p.63. 4 vol. 101.[2]

Vide 4. Bac: Abr: 644 645.[3]

For the sure + true interpretation of all Statutes in general (be they penal or beneficial, restrictive or enlarging of the Com. Law,) four things are to be discern'd + consider'd. 1. What was the Common Law before the making of the Act. 2. What was the Mischief + Defect for which the Common Law did not provide. 3. What Remedy the Parliament hath resolved + appointed to Cure the Decease of the CommonWealth. And 4. the true Reason + Remedy. 3 Rep. 7. b.[4]

To Interpret a Law, we must inquire after the Will of the Maker: which may be collected either from the words, the Context, the Subject-matter, the Effects + Consequences, or the Spirit + Reason of the Law.

From the Latter Method of Interpretation arises EQUITY, or the Correction of that wherein the Law (by Reason of its Universality) is deficient.
Blackstone's Anal. B. 1. Ch 2. p 3.[5]

The Obscurity & Uncertainty of the Law now under our Consideration, proceeds from a

---

† For the COUNTRIES subject to the Laws of ENGLAND; vid. page 3 of this Book.[1]

Page [77]

1. The "†" refers to the note at the bottom of the page which is an internal citation to Quincy's *Law Commonplace*, *supra*, p. 3 [10]. The following list is derived from Blackstone's *Analysis*, *supra*. See page [10], note 4.

2. See page [7], note 2, *supra*. Quincy makes a cross-citation to *Law Commonplace*, p. 63 [59] and to unnumbered pages in Quincy's introduction, numbered [5] and [6] in this edition, which cross-reference forward to this page. The second citation is to Volume 4 of Quincy's notebooks,

where page 101 begins an 8-page copy of the introduction to Richard Burn's (1709–1785) *The Ecclesiastical Law*. See also page [59], note 1.

3. A citation to *Bacon's Abridgment*, vol. 4, pp. 644–45, "Rules to be Observed in the Construction of a Statute." The text of Quincy's notebook, however, comes from *Heydon's Case* (1584), *Coke's Reports*, vol. 3, p. 7a. See note 4, *infra*.

4. The four principles of statutory construction are taken directly from *Heydon's Case* (1584), *Coke's Reports*, (1572–1616), vol. 3, p. 7a, at p. 7b. See page [11], note 2. Coke continued "[T]he Office of all the Judges is always to make such constructions as shall repress the mischief, and advance the remedy, and to suppress subtil inventions and evasions for continuance of the mischief . . ." *Id.*, p. 7b.

5. A citation to *Blackstone's Analysis*, book 1, chapter 2, p. 3. See n.p. [6], note 13, *supra*. For an introduction to "equity" and "equity of the statute," see Coquillette, *The Anglo-American Legal Heritage*, *supra*, pp. 183–204; Baker, *An Introduction to English Legal History*, *supra*, pp. 209–10.

[78]

90 very a very[1] natural Cause, a Cause which renders all Laws obscure, that are intended by the Promoter to incroach upon the Rights, Liberties + Priviledges of the People. . . . .

When we talk of the Meaning + Intention of (such) Laws, we ought to distinguish between the Meaning + Intention of those that were the cheif Promoters of them, + the Meaning + Intention of those who only gave their Consent to the passing Them. As to the former, I make no Question, but it was their Intention to oblige etc. . . . . tho' they durst not declare their Meaning + Intention in express words, because
it w.^{d} either have thrown out their Bill, or have occasion'd the inserting some express words against what they intended: They therefore chose to draw up their Bill in a dubious Sort of Expression, that after they had got it pass'd into a Law, they might make the most of it in the Execution.

Cn. Octavius. L-M Jany 1742[2]

The Exposition of Statutes or Acts
shews the extension of the words of the Law to Cases unexpress'd, yet having the same Reason: So that where one Thing is enacted, All other Things of the like Nature are included. Thus the Statute of Gloucester[3] gives an Action of Waste against Him that holds Land for Life, or Years: For which Reason, a Person shall have an Action

Page [78]

1. The words repeat in the original.

2. January 8, 1742? A citation to Lord Justice Reeve's "Directions for Beginning the Study of the Law to his nephew?" See page [7], note 1. That was in Quincy's "Law A-file." See page [7], note 2. Are the letters "L–M" another file reference? "Cn. Octavius" seems to reference Gnaeus

(Latin abbreviated Cn.) Octavius, the most famous of that name being a Roman consul killed during Civil war in 87 B.C.E. See *Oxford Classical Dictionary* (1999), p. 1059. Was Cn. Octavius the pseudonym of someone who published in January 1742?

3. The Statute of Gloucester was 6 Edw. (1278) c1 ff. The section on waste was chapter 5. See Baker, *An Introduction to English Legal History*, *supra*, pp. 264–65.

[79]

of Waste against Tenant for One Year or 91
half a Year, though without the Words of the Act;
because within the Meaning of it. The a[1]Preamble
of a Statute is like a Key to open the Intent of
the Makers of the Act; And as it is deem'd true,
good Arguments may be drawn from it. But the
best b[2] way to explain a Statute is to consider what Answer the Lawgivers wou'd probably have given to the Question made,
if propos'd to them. Introd. Know. Laws + Con.
of Eng. p. 117. vid. 4 Bac: Abr: 649.[3]

a 1st Inst. 11.[1]

b Plowd 465 3 Nels. abr. 265.[2]

Acts of Parliam.t are to be construed,
as no Man that is innocent or free from Injury or Wrong,
be by a litteral Construction punish'd or indamag'd: †[4]
therefore in this Case x albeit the Letter of the Statute
is generally to give Damages agt Him that is found
Tenant, yet in this Case x, the Tenant shall not be charg'd
with Damages. x 1 Inst. 360. a.[5] x A Case put by Littleton.[6]

† For the rule is Nemo punitur etc. and actus legis etc. (vid. 3 vol.183) 2 Inst. 287.[4]

Three things are worthy of Observation concerning the
Construction of Statutes. 1:st That it is the most natural and
genuine Exposition of a Statute to Construe one Part of the Statute
by another Part of the same Statute, for that best expresseth the
Meaning of the Makers. 2:dly The words of an Act of Parliament
must be taken in a lawfull + rightfull Sense. And the general Rule
is, quod non praestat impedimentum quod de Jure non sortitur
Effectum.[7] 3:dly That Construction must be made of a Statute in
Suppression of the Mischief, + in Advancement of the Remedy.
Et Qui haeret in Literâ, haeret etc. Co: Lit. 381. a. + b.[8]

Page [79]

1. A citation to *Coke on Littleton*, *supra*, p. 11b. See page [2], note 1; page [7], note 9, where Coke observed that one of the "severall fountaines or places" to derive legal arguments was "from the rehearsal or preamble of the statute." *Id.*, p. 11b.

2. A citation to *Plowden's Commentaries*, *supra*, p. 465. See page [49], note 7. The citation matches the edition of London, 1761. (The editor's copy was in Boston not long thereafter, in the library of Levi Lincoln, to become Governor of Massachusetts.) On that page, Plowden annotates the case of *Eyston* v. *Studd* (1574), Plowden 459, with an extensive discussion of statutory construction, observing "that it is not the Words of the Law but the internal Sense of it that makes the Law . . ." *Id.*, p. 465. The Plowden citation is followed by one to William Nelson's *Abridgment of the Common Law*, 3 vols. (London, 1725–1726), p. 265. See Sweet & Maxwell, *supra*, vol. 1, p. 19. See Cowley, pp. 110–11.

3. The "Intro. Know. Laws + Con. of Eng. p.117" (or perhaps "7") may be a cross-reference to the unnumbered 7th page of the *Law Commonplace*, which contains a discussion of this subject. See *Law Commonplace*, p. [7]. The preceding two pages contain an extensive paraphrase of the section of *Coke on Littleton* cited by Quincy on this page as "a." See note 1, *supra*. The other citation is to *Bacon's Abridgment*, vol. 4, p. 649.

4. The "*vid.* 3 vol. 183" is to *Viner's Abridgment* (1742–1753), vol. 3, p. 183. See page [16], note 2. The second citation to Sir Edward Coke, *Second Part of the Institutes of the Lawes of England, containing the exposition of many ancient and other Statutes* (London, 1642), p. 287. See Sweet & Maxwell, *supra*, vol. 1, p. 546:4. Coke here set out the maximes "*nemo punitur sine injuria*" ("no one is punished unless for some injury") and "*actus legis nemini est damnosur*" ("an act in law shall prejudice no man"). See E. Hilton Jackson, *Latin for Lawyers*, pp. 118, 200. He was discussing the correct construction of the Statute of Gloucester, 6 Edward (1278) c.1 ff. See page [78], note 3.

5. Quincy's "x" notes a citation to *Coke on Littleton*, *supra*, p. 360a. See page [2], note 1; page [7], note 9. It is a close paraphrase from "Acts" to "found tenant," with the rest Quincy's words.

6. Littleton was also discussing the Statute of Gloucester's proper construction. *Coke on Littleton*, *supra*, Sect. 685, pp. 359b–360a. See 6 Edw. (1278) c.1 ff., and page [78], note 3.

7. Roughly "where there is no real harm, the law is not strictly enforced."

8. A citation to *Coke on Littleton*, *supra*, pp. 381a and b. Coke here sets out both the "*quod non praestat*" and the "*et qui haeret in litera, haeret in cortice*" maxims. *Id.*, p. 381b. The latter is usually translated as "He who sticks to the letter sticks to the bark" meaning "he who considers the letter merely, of an instrument [or statute], cannot comprehend its meaning," i.e., "he does not get at the substance or meaning." See Jackson, *Latin for Lawyers*, *supra*, p. 227; Osborn, *A Concise Law Dictionary*, *supra*, p. 263.

[80]

92 Littleton in Sect:^{n} 108, speaking of the Statute of Merton, says, "That no action can be brought upon this Statute, insomuch as it was never seen or heard, that any Action was brought upon that Statute: And if any action might have been brôt, it shall be intended that at some time it would have been put in Use."[1] Hereby it appeareth, saith my L:^{d} Coke, how safe it is to be guided by judicial Presidents. The rule being good, Periculosum existimo quod bonorum Virorum non comprobatur Exemplo.[2] And as Usage is a good Interpreter of Laws, so non Usage where there is no Example is a great Intendment, that the Law will not bear it; for saith Littleton, if any Action etc.[3] Not that an Act of Parliament by non Use can be antiquated or lose its/his force, but that it may be expounded or declar'd how the Act is to be understood. Co: Lit. 81. a + b. Sed vid Vaugh. 169 170.[4]

The best expositor of All Statutes are our Books + Use or Experience. 2 Inst. 25.[5]

A statute (<u>albeit it be penal</u>) shall not be so
vid. literally expounded, as it will have no Effect, for Verba
2. Lilly intelligi debent cum Effectu. Ibid. 84.[6]
527.

1 Plowd. 86.b. Partridge v. Strange[7]

Statutes must be so construed, as no collateral Prejudice grow thereby. Ibid. 112.[8]

It is a good Exposition of a Statute, when the Reason of the Common Law is pursued. Ibid. 148.[9]

A

Page [80]

1. A citation to *Littleton's Tenures*, section 108. See page [2], note 1; page [7], note 9. The quotation excerpts Littleton's text with rough accuracy, but does not note a deleted passage.

2. This is an almost direct quote from Coke's annotation to Littleton's text in *Coke on Littleton* (1628), p. 81b. See page [2], note 1; page [7], note 9. Translation: "I consider dangerous that which is not confirmed by the example of good men."

3. *Id.*, p. 81b. Left out at the "etc." is "might have been grounded upon such matter, it shall be intended that sometime it should have been put in use."

4. *Id.* A citation to *Coke on Littleton*, *supra*, pp. 81a and b. The passage is a rough quotation of a passage at 81b. Quincy has corrected an error in Coke which gave "his" instead of "Hs" in reference to the statute. There is a "but see" ["*sed vid*"] citation to *Sheppard* v. *Gosnold* (1672), *Vaughan's Reports* (covering 1685–1674), p. 159 at pp. 169–70. See page [50], note 2. The report here includes the statement that "if usage hath been against the obvious meaning of an Act of Parliament, by the vulgar and common acceptation of the words, then it is rather an oppression of those concerned, than an exposition of the Act, especially as the usage may be circumstanc'd."

5. A citation to Edward Coke, *The Second Part of the Institutes of the Lawes of England* (London, 1642), p. 25. See Sweet & Maxwell, *supra*, vol. 1, p. 546:4. Coke stated, "Hereby it appeareth (that I may observe it once for all) that the best expositions of this and all other Statutes are our bookes and use or experience." *Id.*, p. 25.

6. *Id.*, p. 84. Quincy changes Coke's statement, substituting "have no effect" for "cannot be tried *per primos Juratores*," a simplification of Coke's point. Translation: "Words ought to be understood with effect."

7. A citation to *Lilly's Reports*, vol. 2, p. 527 (1719), covering 1688–1693 (see page 38, note 5), and to *Partridge* v. *Strange & Croker* (1571), *Plowden's Commentaries*, vol. 1, p. 77b at p. 86b, holding that statutes should not be readily extended by "equity of the statute," i.e., a common sense extention of the literal meaning of the words. See page [49], note 7. Quincy was probably using an English translation of Plowden, which originally appeared in 1571 in Law French. There was such a translation in 1761. See Sweet & Maxwell, *supra*, vol. 1, at pp. 306–307:97.

8. A citation to *Coke's Second Institutes*, *supra*, p. 112, where the passage appears exactly as quoted.

9. A citation to Coke's *Second Institutes*, *supra*, p. 148, where the passage appears exactly as quoted.

[81]

93

A Statute of Explanation shall be constru'd only according to the Words, + not with any Equity of Intendment: For there cannot be an Explanation upon an Explanat:n, as it is held in Butler + Baker's Case in L:d Coke's 3:d Rep.t[1] and Jones said it was so resolv'd in the Court of Wards by the Opinion of the Cheif Justice in Anno. 43. Eliza. Cro Car. 23.[2]

All Statutes whatsoever, which are made in abridgment of any Right of the Subject ought to be strictly construed.
Haw: P.C. B2. ch23. s. 42.[3]

Where a mischief is to be remedied by a Statute, the Remedy in the Exposition of the Statute is to be applied according as the Mischief doth require.
2 Leon. Case. 114.[4]

When an Act alters the Common Law, the Meaning shall not be strain'd beyond the Words, except in Cases of publick Utility, when the End of the Act appears to be larger than the Words themselves. Vaugh. 179.[5]

When the words of a statute extend not to an Inconvenience rarely happening, but doth to those which often happen, it is a good Reason not to strain the Words farther than they will reach, by saying, that it is **Casus omissus**, and that the Law intended quae frequentius accedunt.
Vaugh. 373.[6]

Page [81]

1. A citation to *Butler and Baker's Case* (1591), *Coke's Reports*, vol. 3, p. 25a. See page [1], note 2, *supra*. As Chief Justice Wray observed, "[F]or if any exposition shall be made against the direct letter of the exposition made by Parliament, there shall never be an end of expounding." *Id.*, at p. 31a.

2. A citation to the *Third Part of the Reports of Sir George Croke*, covering the reign of Charles I, hence "Cro. Car. [Latin *Carolus*] 23." See page [21], note 6. Quincy mistakenly cites to page 23 when he is clearly copying from *Case out of Court of Wards* (1626), *Croke Car.* p. 33 at p. 34. Here one finds the text that Quincy accurately copied, including the citation to *Butler and Baker's Case*, to form this entire notation.

3. A citation to William Hawkins, *Pleas of the Crown* (London, 1716–21), Book 2, chap. 23, sec. 42, with many subsequent editions. See Sweet & Maxwell, vol. 1, pp. 362–64:37. Hawkins

was arguing that *Magna Carta* c.35 be strictly construed. "[A]ll statutes whatsoever which are made in abridgment of any rights of the subject, ought to be strictly construed." *Id.*

4. A citation to *Leonard's Reports* (London, 1658–1675), vol. 2, case number 114, which appears on pages 91–92. These reports covered 1540–1615. See page [39], note 7, page [53], note 4. The citation is to *Foskew's Case* (1587), from which this excerpt is quoted nearly verbatim.

5. A citation to *Vaughan's Reports* (London, 1677; covering 1665–1674), p. 179. See page 50, note 2, *supra*. The case is *Bedell* v. *Constable* (1664), which begins on *Vaughan's Reports*, p. 177, and is almost exactly quoted by Quincy.

6. A citation to *Vaughan's Reports*, p. 373. See page [50], note 2, *supra*. The case is *Bole* v. *Horton* (1673), which begins on page 360 and is almost exactly copied. Addition of the word "will" is Quincy's only modification.

[82]

94 'Tis a known rule in Interpretation of Statutes, that such a Sense is to be made upon the Whole, as that no Clause, Sentence or Word shall prove superfluous, void or insignificant, if by any other Construction, that may All be made usefull and pertinent. 1 Show. 108.[1]

The fairest + most rational method to interpret the will of the legislator, is by exploring his intentions at the time when the law was made; by signs the most natural + probable. And these signs are either the words, the context, the subject matter, the effects + consequence, or the spirit + reason of the law. 1 Black: Comment: Introd. s. 2. p.59 q.v.[2]

The true key for construing a statute is to consider the subject matter of it, and the ends and purposes for which it was made.__ But perhaps this may be better done from the history + circumstances of the times, than ex visceribus of the statute. Wilson's Rep. 192. b.[3]

The words of the statutes are not only to be considered, but rather the intent of the makers is to be weighed; for the intent is the principal thing to be considered. Ibid. 193[4]

<u>And sometimes statutes are to be expounded against the letter</u>, to preserve the intent. Ibid.[5]

Page [82]

1. A citation to Sir Bartholomew Shower's *Reports* (London, 1708) covering King's Bench 1678–1694. See Sweet & Maxwell, *supra*, vol. 1, p. 309:119, Wallace, *supra*, pp. 392–94. The case is *Rex* v. *Berchet* (1690), which begins on page 106. Quincy copies this line from it nearly exactly.

2. A citation to Blackstone, *Commentaries*, vol. 1, sec. 2, p. 59. See Sweet & Maxwell, *supra*, vol. 1, p. 27:8. Volume 1 was first published in 1765. The second volume followed in 1766; the third in 1768; and the fourth, in 1769. This is an accurate, direct quote, except for Quincy's abbreviation. The handwriting in the paragraph beginning with "the fairest" is different, but may be a later addition by Quincy. This is the only citation to Blackstone's *Commentaries* in the *Law Commonplace*. See discussion in Introduction, Section II, "The Pedagogy," pp. 19–20, n. 37. This is a most significant citation, because Blackstone, *Commentaries* was the first treatise to

cover the common law as an entity that was clear and easy to follow structurally. As such, it had a huge following in the American colonies. See Lawrence M. Friedman, *A History of American Law*, 2d ed., 1985, p. 112. It is important that it was available to Quincy, although apparently well after he began work on the *Law Commonplace* on Sept. 24, 1763. John Adams said that Blackstone "smoothed the path" of the American law student. See Coquillette, "Justinian in Braintree," p. 373. The character of the handwriting here also suggests it was from a later period of Quincy's writing, although it may be authentic. It is most significant that there was no other citation to Blackstone's *Commentaries* in the *Law Commonplace*.

3. A citation to *George Wilson's Reports* (London, 1770–1775) covering King's Bench [1742–1753] and Common Pleas [1753–1774]. See Sweet & Maxwell, *supra*, vol. 1, p. 310:131. The case is *Wolferstan* v. *Bishop of Lincoln* (1763), which begins on page 174 of Wilson's second volume. Quincy's copy is exact. Like the reference to Blackstone, note 2 *supra*, this reflects Quincy's use of a contemporary source that was published after he began his *Law Commonplace* in 1763. "Ex visceribus": "from the depths," "from the bowels."

4. *Wilson's Reports*, *supra*, vol. 2 at p. 193. Also an exact copy.

5. *Wilson's Reports*, *supra*, vol. 2 at p. 193. Another exact copy. In the opinion, this line also immediately follows the preceding one copied by Quincy.

[83]

What L:d Hobart fo: 157, says, is very strong to the same purpose, "It is, says he, the office of judges to advance laws made for religion, according to their end:_ 95

And again, L:d Hobart says, 346, "Judges have liberty + authority over statutes to mould them to the truest + best use, according to reason + best convenience. Wilson's Rep. 193: b.[1]

The Danger Of Considering ye Spirit of Laws

There is nothing more dangerous, than the common axioms: <u>the spirit of the laws is to be considered</u>. To adopt it is to give way to the torrent of opinion. This may seem a paradox to vulgar minds, which are more strongly affected by the smallest disorder before their eyes, than by the most pernicious, tho' remote, consequences produced by one false principle adopted by a nation. Marquis Beccaria's Essay on Crimes + punishments. p. 15, 6. quod vide.[2]

The disorders that may arise from a vigorous observance of the <u>letter</u> of penal laws, not to be compared with those produced by ye

Page [83]

1. These first two statements are both directly quoted from the second volume of *Wilson's Reports*, the case of *Wolferstan* v. *Bishop of Lincoln* (1763), which Quincy's preceding page cited three times. See page [82], notes 3–5. The "Hobart" to which the opinion refers is *Sir Henry Hobart's Reports* (London, 1641) covering 1603–1625. See Sweet & Maxwell, *supra*, vol. 1, p. 301:63, Wallace, *supra*, pp. 220–29. The case there cited is *Colt and Glover* v. *Bishop of Coventry and Lichfield* (1612), which begins on page 140. There is nothing to suggest that Quincy actually looked at this source rather than copying from *Wilson's Reports* alone.

2. A citation to Beccaria's *Crimes and Punishments*, pp. 15–16, and following. This influential book was first translated from the French in 1767. See Sweet & Maxwell, *supra*, vol. 1, p. 358:5. Beccaria (1738–94) was an Austrian official, and this book was "the first systematic study of the principle of punishment, which had immediate success and enormous influence." D. M. Walker, *supra*, at p. 121. There was an American edition published in Philadelphia in 1778. Bec-

caria observed, at the pages cited, that it was necessary to defend the long-term common good "from the usurpation of each individual, who will always endeavor to take away from the mass, not only his own portion, but to encroach on that of others." *Id.*, at p. 16. The passage copied by Quincy appears in the American edition at pages 24–25. It is an accurate, but rough, copy.

[84]

96 interpretation of them. The first are temporary inconveniences which will oblige ye legislator to correct ye letter of ye law, the want of preciseness, + uncertainty of which has occasioned these disorders; and this will put a stop to the fatal liberty of explaining; the source of arbitrary + venal declarations. When ye code of laws is once fixed, it should be observed in ye literal sense, + nothing more is left to ye judge, than to determine, whether an action be, or be not conformable to the written Law. When the rule of right which ought to direct the actions of the philosopher, as well as the ignorant, is a matter of controversy, not a fact, the people are slaves to the magistrates. Ibid. 16. 17.[1]

The Best Way to construe Modern Statutes is to follow ye words thereof. Per Cur: Wilson's Rep: 290. Entick v. Carrington + ors—'Gen.^{le} War:^{T}[2]

Page [84]

1. A citation to Beccaria's *Crimes and Punishments*, pp. 16–17. See page [83], note 2. The passage is a rough, but accurate, copy of the translation appearing at pages 26–27 of the first American edition. Beccaria, of course, was a continental jurist in the Roman civilian tradition. His views of the judicial function would seem narrow to most common lawyers from the Anglo-American tradition.

2. A citation to *Entick* v. *Carrington* (1765), *Wilson's Reports*, covering 1742–1774, vol. 2, p. 290. The case begins on page 275 of the second volume of *Wilson's Reports*. See page [82], note 2. Quincy's language is a direct quote from the report. The final words of Quincy's script are difficult to construe, but likely relate to the case, one part of which focused on statutory interpretation to determine the legality of a Secretary of State's, rather than a Constable's, use of a warrant to search Entick's property. The final notation, difficult to translate, might be a reference to a "general warrant."

[85]

In a case upon ye Stat. of Frauds, Sir Geo. 97
Treby, as Amicus Curiae, informed ye court
y^t he was present at ye making ye Statute
+ what was ye intention of the
parliament. 2 Vin: 476. pl. 12.[1]
cites Comb: 33. Horton v. Ruesby[2]

Qu: How ye Intention of Parliament can
be rightly discovered in this way:
unless ye Informant knew absolute-
ly what determined the concurrence
of Each Branch of ye Legislature:—qu:
w[hether] y^e is possible to be known:—and qu:
of ye Consequences of their mode of
determin:g + judging of ye Intent of
Law-makers, and Qu: etc.[3]

Page [85]

1. In the original, Quincy writes in huge letters, "what was ye Intention of the Parliament." The citation is to *Viner's Abridgment*, vol. 2, p. 476, paragraph 12. See page [16], note 2.

2. Citation to *Horton* v. *Ruesby* (1686), *Comberbach's Reports* (1724), p. 33, covering 1685–1698. See page [37], note 2.

3. These *Queries* are remarkable, in that this is another place where Quincy was openly critical of the reasoning of the English authorities.

[86]

98 Trespass

Lies for an accidental Hurt. 1 Strange 596.[1]
Where the Act is lawfull, as the fixing a Spout, & the Consequence injurious, the Remedy is by Case, & not Trespass. Ibid. 634.[2]
Laying hold of a Horse, no Trespass without particular Damage:__ And the Dft, on Not Guilty, may justify in Evidence. 2 Ibid 872.[3]
Lies for setting the End of a Bridge, on the Plt's Soil, tho' a Highway. 2 Str. 1004.[4]
Officers of the Customs liable in Trespass for wrong Seisure, notwithstanding probable Cause.__ One Partner brings Trespass without his Companion, it must be pleaded in Abatement.——Aliter in Assumpsit. 2 Strange 820.[5]
Amends not pleadable to Trespass for the taking goods. 1 Strange 549.[6]

[QUINCY'S PAGES 99–102 ARE BLANK]

Page [86]

1. A citation to *Underwood* v. *Hewson* (1724), *Strange's Reports* (1755), vol. 1, p. 596. The reports covered 1716–1749. See page [21], note 12. According to the report, "The defendant was uncocking a gun, and the plaintiff was standing to see it, it went off and wounded him: and at the trial it was held that the plaintiff might maintain trespass." *Id.*, p. 596.

2. A citation to *Reynolds* v. *Clarke* (1722), *Strange's Reports* (1755), *supra*, vol. 1, p. 634. This involved repair of a drain spout so that "the water came into the yard and rotted the walk of the plaintiff's house." *Id.*, p. 634. The act lacked the violence of the gun accident in *Underwood* v. *Hewson*. The requirements of an act "*vi et armis*" ("force of arms") *contra pacem nostram* ("against our [the king's] peace") that characterized the old trespass writ thus lived on. See Baker, *An Introduction to English Legal History*, *supra*, pp. 61–64.

3. A citation to *Slater* v. *Swann* (1718), *Strange's Reports*, *supra*, vol. 2, p. 872. According to this case, "assault on a horse" is unlike assault on a man, which would be "trespass *vi et armis* (i.e., "force of arms")." The horse had been left in front of the defendant's door, preventing a cart from picking up the defendant's goods. It was left to the jury "whether defendant did any more than was necessary to remove the horse and cart from the door, or beat the horse immoderately." *Id.*, p. 872. The jury found for the defendant.

4. A citation to *Sir John Lade* v. *Shepherd* (1722), *Strange's Reports*, *supra*, vol. 2, p. 1004. It was held that the placing of the bridge on the plaintiff's soil was trespass, even if the plaintiff permitted right of passage over the land, as that "never was understood to be a transfer of absolute property in the soil." *Id.*, p. 1004.

5. A citation to *Leglise* v. *Champante* (1716), *Strange's Reports*, *supra*, vol. 2, p. 820. In this case a custom officer seized wine with probable cause (that it was contraband). Held that "the officer seizes at his peril, and that probable cause is no defense." *Id.*, p. 820. Further, the fact that the joint owner of the wine was not a party to the case must be pleaded in abatement, and not "taken advantage of at the trial." *Id.*, p. 820. Otherwise ["aliter"] in contract ["assumpsit"]. *Id.*, p. 820.

6. A citation to *Bailee* v. *Vivash* (1723), *Strange's Reports*, *supra*, vol. 1, p. 549, which held that a defendant's offer of amends only can be pleaded for "involuntary trespass with a disclaimer," not "taking away goods." *Id.*, p. 549.

[87]

A Copy of Mr. Prat's Minutes.[1] Vid. vol. 3 p. 12 103
Banister vs. Cunningham. + p. 24. + p. 64.[2]

25 Jany 1708	T Banister devises all his Lands + personal Estate after Payment of Debts + to his 3 sons Thomas, Samuel, + John to be equally divided among them in equal shares, or Proportions + if Either his 3 Sons die without Heirs lawfully begotten in wedlock, their share or Proportion to the surviving Son or Sons + their Heirs forever. And died leaving such 3 Sons + one Daughter.
28th March 1713 date ackn by a witness 15 July 1714	Saml + John gave Thos, the Son a Power of At- -torney to sell etc execute any Deeds for con- -veying + assuring the Same. Recorded 11 Sep.^{t} 1714
14 July 1714	Thos for himself + as Attorney to Saml + John sells to Dyer with Warranty. Deed ackn. + recorded immediately.
15 July 1714.	Dyer reconveys to Thomas. John died without Issue June 30th 1714.
10 Dec.^{ber} 1714.	Thomas for himself + as Attorney to Saml (re- citing that John was dead) sells with Warranty to Dyer a moiety of the demanded Premises inter alia, duly ackn. + recorded.—
21 June 1714 .	Dyer reciting the afores.^{d} Deeds tc reconveys all in them convey'd to him (excepting etc) to Samuel and his Heirs.—

12

Page [87]

1. This page marks a new approach for Quincy. From pages 4 [11] to 98 [86], Quincy makes what he calls "A Little Abridgment for Private Use." See page 4 [11], *supra*. It is structured alphabetically from "Arbitram: Arbitrors + award" to "Trespass." As such, it is a typical "Commonplace Book" of a law student in the eighteenth century. Then he leaves four blank pages between 98 [86] and page 103 [87], and starts some very different approaches. This page con-

tains "A copy of Mr. Prat's Minutes" concerning the case of *Banister* v. *Cunningham*. Mr. Prat is Benjamin Prat[t] (1711–1763) of Boston, who served as a law tutor to the likes of John Adams, Quincy's brother, Samuel, and perhaps to Quincy himself, who primarily read law with Oxenbridge Thacher. See *Law in Colonial Massachusetts*, *supra*, pp. 350–51, 377–78. In November 1761, Prat left Boston to become Chief Justice of New York. See *Id.*, p. 377, and John Adams, *Legal Papers* (eds. L. K. Wroth, H. B. Zobel, 1965) vol. 1, p. cvi. "Vid. vol. 3, p. 12" is a citation to the third volume of Quincy's notebooks, and leads the reader to Quincy's report of *Banister* v. *Henderson*, a 1765 case involving a dispute over the same will involved in *Banister* v. *Cunningham*. See *Quincy Reports*, p. 119. In the 1865 publication of the reports, Quincy's great-grandson Samuel M. Quincy includes a note to *Banister* v. *Henderson* on page 156 which cites the case of *Banister* v. *Cunningham* (1754). In the note, he excerpts a record from the law papers of John Adams, which he describes as a copy of John Read's opinion. That record is substantially similar to "Prat's minutes" in content, and Samuel M. Quincy notes a comment at the end of the record, "N.B. This last was, I think, in Mr. Pratt's handwriting." Pratt and Read argued for the partibility of entailed estates tail in the case. The absence of any reference in the *Quincy's Reports* to Josiah Quincy's own record of *Banister* v. *Cunningham* suggests that Samuel Quincy was unaware of its presence in the *Law Commonplace*.

[88]

104[1]

12 Sept.ber 1716 Thomas died leaving Issue the Plts.

28 Dec.m 1733 Saml. conveys the Warranty to the Dft's father.

Saml. dies without Issue 1744.

Upon the whole it seems the Intent of the Testator was to convey to the 3 Sons an equal Tenancy in common in Fee determinable upon either of them dying without Issue in the Life of some other Son, + then an executory Devise over of such Deceased's Share to the Survivor of the Survivors. And the Intent is well enough consistent with Law.

But 'tis enough for our Purpose to say + prove.

1 Tis no intail. vid. Kanchet's Case 3 Mod. 104 per cur. 107.[2] 3 Cro. 57.[3] Vid. also Miller's Case Barn Chan. 7[4]

(1) There is no express words to make an Inheritance; if there is any created, 'tis but Implication: And Implication from paying is as strong for a Fee, as any Thing is for an In--tail. 2 Vern. 687.[5]

(2) Double Implication.

2 If an Intail. Rem.rs[6] were executed.

(1) Not executory Devises for if dying etc means failure of Issue generally at any Time, it could not be follow'd by an executory Devise. vid. 2 Bacon 72 top.[7]

Page [88]

1. Quincy numbered two consecutive pages "104," [88] and [89]. This page is a continuation of Quincy's notes on *Banister* v. *Cunningham*. See the discussion of the case at *Quincy's Reports*, pp. 156–57.

2. A citation to *Kanchet's Case* (1698), *Modern Reports* (covers 1667–1732), vol. 3, p. 104, at p. 107 ("per curiam" or by the unanimous court without a particular judge indicated as delivering the opinion).

3. A citation to *Hearn* v. *Allen* (1627), *Croke's Reports* (1657) (the three volumes cover 1582–1641), vol. 3, p. 57. See page [21], note 6. This case backs up the principle that land does not

pass by the words "*cum pertinentiis*," but "only such things which properly may be pertaining." *Id.*, 57. "Otherwise it is, if it had been '*cum terris pertinentibus*', then that which was used to it (here two acres of meadow) would have passed; but by the bare words '*cum pertinentiis*'; without other circumstances to declare his [the testator's] intent, they shall never pass . . ." *Id.*, pp. 57–58.

4. A citation to *Miller's Case*, *Barnardiston's Reports* (London, 1742), 7, covering the Chancery Court, 1740–41. See Sweet & Maxwell, *supra*, vol. 1, p. 345:5. The case is *Miller* v. *Moor* (1740).

5. A citation to *Vernon Reports* (*Cases argued and adjudged in the High Court of Chancery*) (1726–1728; covering 1681–1720), vol. 2. See Sweet & Maxwell, vol. 1, p. 349:42, and p. 52, n. 5. Page 687 does not match Quincy's point, and there is no case 687. The closest relevant case in *Vernon Reports* is *Bampfield* v. *Popham* (1703), which appears on page 449 of volume 2. It has some similar language to Quincy's entry but is not the source of an exact quote.

6. "Rem.^{rs}" for "Remainders." When land is entailed, i.e., descends only to the lineal heirs of the blood (not ascendant or collateral heirs) or such male heirs (if an entail male), the donor's heirs hold a "remainder," i.e., if issue of the donee fails ("failure of issue"), the fee reverts to the heirs of the donor. That interest in land is called a "remainder" and those that hold it "remainder men." See Baker, *Introduction to English Legal History*, *supra*, pp. 284–85.

7. A citation to *Bacon's Abridgment* (1736), vol. 2, p. 72 "at top." "An Executory Devise Is defined as a future Interest, which cannot vest at the Death of a Testator, but depends upon some Contingency which must happen before it can vest." *Id.*, p. 71. Thus, there cannot be an executory devise if the testator's death cuts off the underlying estate before the contingency occurs.

[89]

E converso. (2) No contingent Remainders 105

3 The Rem^rs^ or Devises over are fees i.e. on John's Death to Thos + Saml. + their heirs + the Survivors of them. vid. Mo. 864.

Ergo |N1190.[1]

4 No cross Rem^rs^ i.e. on Saml.'s death, no going back to the heirs of Thos——No Survivor. Vid. 2 Cro. 655.[2]

Ergo.

On the Death of John, Thomas + Saml. were Joint-tenants in fee of his undisposed of Part, + what was undisposed of by Thomas went on his death to Saml. as Survivor.

---

vid. 2 vol. 149. 150[3]

Gridley's Minutes

Allen vs. Allen. Uncle + Nephew

vid. Law-file C[4]

Nephews do not take by Representation, are therefore a Degree further off——take by Polls, not by Stocks.

Vinnius 555.[5]

Successions vary in different Countries.

The only Question about the Degree, the Law must be follow'd, without Regard to Lines. 1 Ld Raymond, 574,[6]

According to the civil Law our Law in one path + the statute in another. vid. Ventris 316. 2. Modern 205. Jones 93. 2 Lev 173 Raymond's Rep.^ts^ 497. Novel 118.[7] Minutes

Page [89]

1. "*E converso*," from the Latin *converto*, to "turn around," i.e., "on the other side." See *Cassell's Latin Dictionary* (1959), 151. The rest are mysterious citations. "Mo." could be to *Modern Reports* (1667–1732), vol. 1, p. 864. See page [35], note 2. Or it could be to *Modern Entries* (1734–1735). See page [90], note 11. "Ergo," i.e. "therefore," may refer to the same volume, p. 1190, or could be an internal reference to Quincy's law files or his lost second volume. See note 3 and 4, *infra*. *Modern Entries* was in Quincy's library (Catalogue No. 29), but none of the suggested citations check out.

2. A citation to *Gilbert* v. *Witty* (1623), *Croke's Reports* (1582–1641), vol. 2, pp. 655–56. See page [21], note 6, finding no cross remainder.

3. This appears to be a citation to Gridley's own notes, but vol. 2, pp. 149–50 refers to the lost second volume of Quincy's four notebook set.

4. A case contained in Quincy's Law File "C." It is not in *Quincy's Reports*.

5. A citation to Arnoldus Vinnius (1588–1657), a major Dutch jurist, probably to an edition *In IV libros Institutionum commentarius* (1642), such as that loaned by Jeremiah Gridley to John Adams in 1758 and bought by Adams from Gridley's estate in 1767. See Coquillette, "Justinian in Braintree," *supra*, p. 365. "Take by Polls, not by Stocks" refers to the fact that nephews do not take *per stirpes*, i.e., "by stock or branches," as do children, with any deceased child's heirs taking equally that child's share, i.e., take by "representation." See page [91], note 5.

6. A citation to *Lord Raymond's Reports* (1694–1734), vol. 1, p. 574. See page [26], note 2, *supra*. The citation is to *Rex* v. *Raines* (1700), which begins on page 571. Quincy's synopsis does not borrow from the text, but loosely captures its holding.

7. A citation to Ventris's *Reports* (1668–1684), editions appearing in 1696, 1701, 1716, and 1726. See Sweet & Maxwell, *supra*, vol. 1, p. 310:127; Wallace, *supra*, pp. 345–46 (1667–1684); Sweet & Maxwell, vol. 1, p. 301:66. Further citations to *Modern Reports* (covering 1667–1732), vol. 2, p. 205, also *Smith* v. *Tracy*, see page [35], note 2; *Jone's Reports* (1620–1640), p. 93, see page [81], note 2; and *Levinz's Reports* (covering 1660–1696), vol. 2, p. 173, first published in London in 1702 with 1 volume, with a 2nd edition of two volumes following in 1722. See page [76], note 2, *supra*.

[90]

105[1] Minutes from Strange[2]

restating New Tryals

vid. p. 158.[3] vid. Red Rep. 70. Angier vs. Jackson.[4]

vid Law file A[5]

Strange. 691. Price vs. Brown.[6]

No new Tryal where the Party might have had Evidence before.

692.[7] Not a second Time for excessive Damages:

1105[8] Not to be granted where the Evidence is doubtfull.

1142. Ashley vs. Ashley.[9] No new Tryal were Evidence on both Sides, the Jury judges which Scale preponderates.

1151.[10] New Tryal comes in the Room of Attaint.

vid. Tit. New trial. 2. Mod Ent. 354. b.[11]

Minutes relative to Wills. vid Lfile C.[12]

The Law requires a certain Integrity of Mind to ye making a Testament: And it is not Sufficient y^t^ ye Testator can answer to common Questions

Swinburn 69. 70. 74. Swinburn 68.[13]

6 Rep.^t^ 23. a. Mary Winchester's Case[14]

Legatee may be a Witness ag^t^ a Will. 2^d^ Salk^d^ 692.[15]

Minutes for the

Argument upon P's Will. The Points are curious. Many Auth:^s^ cited. vid. Law-file C.[16]

Minutes relative to Wills, Sanity etc. Ibid

Page [90]

1. Quincy numbered two consecutive pages, our [89] and [90], "105."

2. Reference to *Strange's Reports* (1716–1749). See page [21], note 12. It is unclear which trials Quincy refers to, although there are many appropriate "new trial" cases in *Strange*. See *Id.*, pp. 101, 113, 584, 691, 692; vol. 2 at pp. 814, 899, 968, 995, 1051, 1105, 1142, 1238.

3. Citation to page 158 [101] of Quincy's *Law Commonplace*, where the first entry refers to a prohibition against new trial and cites back to page 105 [90].

4. A citation to the "Red Reports," 70 *Angier* v. *Jackson*, and Quincy's "Law File A." The "Red Reports" was Quincy's term for his own first volume of law reports, because of their red

cover. See Samuel Quincy's description in the preface page iii of the 1865 edition of *Quincy's Reports*. *Angier* v. *Jackson* was reported by Quincy in his *Reports* at p. 84, his page 70. It was a Superior Court of Judicature 3 Geo. 3 (1703) where a motion was made for a new trial after the jury "gave a Verdict in Damages in Favour of . . . [the Plaintiff] contrary to the Mind of the Court." The court decided against a new trial. The Chief Justice (Thomas Hutchinson) observed "Are you not agreed, that, were it evidently against Law and Evidence, then the Court may grant a new Trial, but not where there is Evidence on both sides." *Id.*, at p. 85. Trowbridge dissented. See the discussion in the notes at *Id.*, at pp. 84–85.

5. Another reference to Quincy's "Law Files," this time "A." See page [91], notes 1, 2, 7; page [92], note 1.

6. A citation to *Price* v. *Brown* (12 Geo. 1 Hil., 1726) in *Strange's Reports* (1716–1749), vol. 1, p. 691, *supra*, note 2, holding that there should be no new trial due to new evidence where a party might have had the evidence admitted at the first trial, because it would be "of dangerous consequence, to suffer people to be setting up new evidence, after they knew what was sworn before." *Id.*, p. 691.

7. See note 5, *supra*. The citation to page 692 is incorrect. It should be page 691.

8. A citation to *Smith* v. *Parkhurst* (1739), *Strange's Reports* (1716–1749), vol. 2, p. 1105, *supra*, note 2. This case did not turn on excessive damages, but rather "the evidence was doubtful, and in such a case a verdict at bar ought to stand." *Id.*, at p. 1106.

9. A citation to *Ashley* v. *Ashley* (1741), *Strange's Reports* (1716–1749), vol. 2, p. 1142, *supra*, note 2. The court did not grant a new trial, observing "As there was evidence on the part of the defendant, the jury are the proper judges which scale preponderates. It cannot be said to be a verdict against evidence . . ." *Id.*, p. 1142.

10. Quincy must mean to cite to *Strange's Reports,* vol. 2, p. 1142, cited in note 8, above, rather than *Strange's Reports*, vol. 2, p. 1151, where there is nothing relevant.

11. A citation to the title "New Trial" in [J. Mallory] *Modern Entries in English* (1734–1735), vol. 2, p. 354b. See Sweet & Maxwell, *supra*, vol. 1, p. 273:100.

12. Another citation to Quincy's "Law File C." See note 5, *supra*; page [91], notes 1, 2, 7, and 8; page [92], n. 1.

13. Citations to H. Swinburne, *Brief Treatise of Testaments and Lost Willes*, pp. 68–69, 70, 74 (1590–1591), with many appropriate editions, including folios in 1728 and 1743. Quincy had a copy of "Swinburne of Wills" in his library. (Estate Catalogue, p. 30.)

14. A citation to *Pawlet Marquis of Winchester's Case* (1599), *Coke's Reports* (1572–1616), vol. 6, p. 23a. See page [1], note 2. In this case prohibition from the King's Bench to the Ecclesiastical courts, on the grounds that the late Marquis's sanity affected both the will of land and goods. "For if he were of sane memory at the time of the Testament of the Goods [ecclesiastical jurisdiction], he cannot be not of sane memory at the time of the making of the Will of the Land [common law jurisdiction], both being made at one instant; and the Common Law ought to determine whall be said perfect memory at the time . . ." *Id.*, p. 23b. The case states, as well, that "it is not sufficient that the Testator be of memory, but he ought to have a disposing memory, so that he is able to make a disposition of his Lands with understanding and reason . . ." *Id.*, p. 23a.

15. A citation to *Salkeld's Reports* (1689–1712), vol. 2, p. 692. See page [32], note 7. The case is *Rex* v. *Ford* and begins on page 690. The quoted text appears on page 691, instead of page 692 as cited. Oddly, this is the second time on this single page that Quincy mistakenly recorded 692 for 691, citing to different reporters. See *supra*, note 7.

16. Another citation to Quincy's "Law file C." See page [91], notes 1, 2, 7, 8; and page [92], note 1.

[91]

Minutes concerning Church Wardens 106
vid Law-file C.[1]

Minutes in a Cobbiseconte Cause.
vid. Ibid. vid below in this page.[2]

Messrs Read + Auchmuty's arguments in favor of the Partibility of Estates-tail.
at Ply. Sup. Court. Anno 1720 Vid. Ibid,[3]
Vid Red Rep^ts^ p. 57 Baker vs. Mattocks[4]

Minutes in the Question, whether Nephews take by Representation or per Capita.
Vid. Ibid. and G's minutes supra.[5]

W[h]ether, a negro woman being with Child complains to a Just Pacis[6] of a free White Man being the father, can the Justice upon such Complt issue his Warrant ag^t^ the Man + recognize him to appear before the Sessions as provided by the Prov. Law p. 10. 11 in Case of a White Woman gotten with Child. This Question answer'd in the Negative. + the reasons Why. vid. Law-file C.[7]

Minutes relative to Kennebeck Lands
Law-file C. vid above, in this Page.[8]

Page [91]

1. Reference to Quincy's "Law File C."
2. Reference to Quincy's "Law File C." The case does not appear in *Quincy's Reports.*
3. Reference to arguments of John Read (1680–1749) and Robert Auchmuty, Senior, in the

Plymouth Superior Court in 1720, contained in Quincy's "Law File C." See *Law in Colonial Massachusetts*, *supra*, pp. 195–241, 339–40, 351.

4. The reference is to *Baker* v. *Mattocks* in the "Red Reports, p. 57." The *Red Reports* are Quincy's first collection of law reports. *Baker* v. *Mattocks* begins on page 57 of his original manuscript, and on page 69 of *Quincy's Reports* (1865 edition).

5. Another citation to Quincy's law file and presumably Jeremiah Gridley's minutes. See page [89], note 3. See also discussion of a nephew's inability to take "representation" at page [89], note 5. "*Per capita*" means "individually." "Distribution of the property of an intestate is *per capita* if it is divided amongst all entitled to it in equal shares." Osborn, *A Concise Law Dictionary*, p. 238. Children of an intestate, as opposed to nephews, take "*per stirpes*," or "by stock or branches." "Distribution of the property of an intestate is *per stirpes* if it is divided amongst those entitled to it according to the number of stocks of descent; that is, if it is divided equally amongst the surviving children of an intestate individually, and the descendants of deceased children collectively, so that the descendants of a deceased child take that child's share between them." *Id.*, at p. 239. That such descendents stand in the child's place, as if he or she had lived, is called "the rule of representation." *Id.*, at p. 277.

6. For a full discussion of this important note, see Introduction, *supra*, pp. 37–38. "Just Pacis" for "Justice of the Peace." "Prov. Law" could refer to the Acts against Fornication, Section 3 (1665). See *Charters and General Laws of the Colony and Province of Massachusetts Bay* (Boston, 1814), p. 116. That "colony law" read as follows:

> Sect 3. Whereas there is a law provided by this court for punishing of fornicators, but nothing as yet for the easing of towns, where bastards are born, in regard of the poverty of the parent or parents of such children sometimes appearing, nor any rule held forth touching the reputed father of a bastard for legal conviction:
>
> It is therefore ordered, and by this court declared, that where any man is legally convicted to be the father of a bastard child, he shall be at the care and charge to maintain and bring up the same, by such assistance of the mother as nature requireth, and as the court from time to time (according to circumstances) shall see meet to order: and in case the father of a bastard, by confession or other manifest proof, upon trial of the case, do [sic] not appear to the court's satisfaction, then the man charged by the woman to be the father, she holding constant in it, (especially being put upon the real discovery of the truth of it in the time of her travail) shall be the reputed father, and accordingly be liable to the charge of maintenance as aforesaid (though not to other punishment) notwithstanding his denial, unless the circumstances of the case and pleas be such, on the behalf of the man charged, as that the court that hath the cognizance thereof shall see reason to acquit him, and otherwise dispose of the child and education thereof: Provided always, in case there be no person accused in the time of her travail, it shall not be available to abate the conviction of a reputed father; any law, custom or usage to the contrary notwithstanding.

7. Another citation to Quincy's "Law File C." "Negative" in the manuscript appears to be written over another word, suggesting he initially wrote "positive," and it was revised.

8. "Kennebeck Lands" refers to the territory of Maine, then part of Massachusetts. Again, a citation to Quincy's "Law File C."

[92]

107 The 10 Queries in the Salt-Case answer'd.
Ship, cargo, + all the Salt she brôt, seis'd for bringing Salt three Weeks after it was stored in a warehouse etc. vid. Law-file C.[1] Many Points worthy notice in this Case.

Kellock Admin^{tt}ix vs. Kellock.[2] April 1756. Kellock Dft + one Haven had Admin^{tt}or granted, but the Judge, upon finding Kellock Dft indebted to the Intestate, revok'd s.^{d} Admin^{tt}on + granted adminon to Kellock Plt, who brings this Suit for the Recovery of the Debt afores^{d}.

Minutes in this Case in favor of the Dft.

(1) Admin^{tt}on duely granted cannot be revoked
3 Salk. 21. bot.[3]
1 Ld Raymond. 685. bot.[4] 1 Lill. 38.[5]

(2) If revocable it cannot be revoked without a Citation
1 Ld Raym. 685.[6]

(3) If both Points against Us,[7] this action will not lie. For Admin^{tt}on being, while it continued, good, the Debt is Assetts in the Hand of the Admin^{tt}or + therefore the Admin^{tt}on Bond being sued Judgm^{t} w^{d} be against Us for so much as we rec^{d}, and the Debt would be as so much Money received.

[QUINCY'S FOLLOWING PAGES 108 TO 113 ARE CUT OUT OF THE BOOK.[8]]

Page [92]

1. A citation to Quincy's "Law File C." The "Salt-case" appears to be seizure for "landing goods before entry," i.e., goods "disappear" between point of arrival and inspection by royal officers. For a famous case of "landing goods before entry" involving Madeira and John Hancock's "good sloop *Liberty*," see *Sewall* v. *Hancock* (1768–1769), Case No. 46, *Legal Papers of John Adams*, L. K. Wroth, H. B. Zobel, eds., (Cambridge, Mass., 1965), II, pp. 173–210. See also Coquillette, "Justinian in Braintree," *supra*, *Law in Colonial Massachusetts*, *supra*, pp. 386–90.

2. The case is not in *Quincy's Reports*, which start in 1762.

3. A citation to *Salkeld's Reports* (covering 1689–1712), vol. 3, p. 21. See page [32], note 7. The case is *Earl of Banbury* v. *Wood*, which begins on page 20 and holds the proposition cited.

4. A citation to *Lord Raymond's Reports* (covering 1694–1734), vol. 1, p. 685. See page [26], note 2. The case is *Blackborough* v. *Davies* (1701), which begins on page 684 and supports the cited proposition.

5. A citation to *Lilly's Reports* (covering 1688–1693), vol. 1, p. 38. This cites to a section entitled "the Assise for offices" and gives an example of a grant to an incapable grantee being properly revoked.

6. A citation to the same case as n. 4, *supra*.

7. "Against us." Was Quincy's assisting with this case? He would have been only 12 in 1756. "Us" must have referred to the Minutes of the Defendant's counsel.

8. Quincy's book resumes at his page 114, with six pages. But what is contained on Quincy's page 114 to 143 is not his hand. On Quincy's page 122 is a note that "From page 122 to page 143. The extracts were not made by J. Quincy Jr. but by his son, in an early period of his legal studies, Josiah Quincy." But Quincy pages 114 to 121 are also not his hand. After Quincy's page 143, pages 144 to 149 are blank. Quincy's writing resumes on his page 150. See the Introduction, "The Legal Education of a Patriot: Josiah Quincy's *Law Commonplace* (1763)," section 1, "The Manuscript," pp. 11–17.

[93]

Legis Miscellanea cursim, Libris |exscripta[1] 150

vid. Vol.4.p.5.[2]

• "Subscribing the Name is not essential + the Name in the Bond is only material. Holt

Comberb. 477 Cromwell vs. Grimsdale[3]

• If I covenant to pay £100 a year hence, + if I do not pay it, to pay £20 it is not Usury but only in Nature of Nomine Poene.[4]

Comberb. 133[5]

Vid. 2 Mod. Ent. 320 pl. 8.9.[6] 2 Roll: Abr. 801. 802[7] 2 Lev. 7[8]

• Holt said obiter y^t^ [that] no Information w.^d^ be quash'd Ibid. 142[9]

vid Haw: P.C. B. 2. ch 25. ss. 151[10]

• Debt on Bond condoned to perform an Award; Submission was of all Matters to ye Time of the Award; awarded y^t^ one of ye Parties sh.^d^ release all Actions in December following: Yet good unless it be shewn [that] new Matter arose. Ibid 100 Short vs. Maynard[11]

• Dft had given a Note to pay E.G. or Order a certain Sum of Money + E.G. by Indorsement order'd Part of this Money to be p.^d^ ye Plt, Action brôt upon it + Special Custom alleg'd. On Demurrer adjudg'd this is a void Custom, because the Dft in this Way w.^d^ be subject to as many Actions as the Plt pleases.

Carthew 466 Hawkins vs. Farr[12]

(Salk. 65. vid Wegersloffe v. Keen in 1 Strange[13]

• H having a Note of £100 on a Goldsmith goes to receive[14] it, while in the Shop D. brings Money in to pay Gold--smith; the Goldsmith orders H to receive D's Money

Page [93]

1. "Miscellaneous Laws Cursorily Copied Out of Books." The preceding pages, Quincy's 144–149, were blank. See the full discussion in the "Introduction," *supra*, pp. 11–17.

2. A citation to Volume 4 of Quincy's notebooks, reproduced as pages [126]–[131] in this volume. Page 5 [126] begins a six-page section entitled "Legis Miscellanea cursim, Libris exscprita [for exscripta] of Estates."

3. A citation to *Cromwell* v. *Grimsdale* (1698), *Comberbach's Reports* (covering 1685–1698), p. 477. See page [37], note 2.

4. "*Nomine Poenae*," "under the description of a penalty," a penalty due for nonperformance of an agreement. See Jowitt, *supra*, p. 1230. In other words, the £20 was not a usurous rate of interest, but a penalty for nonperformance, a dubious distinction retained in modern credit card "late fees." See Daniel R. Coquillette, "The Mystery of the New Fashioned Goldsmiths: From Usury to the Bank of England (1622–1694)," *The Growth of the Bank as Institution and the Development of Money Business Law* (ed. V. Piergiovanni, 1993), pp. 91–118.

5. Another citation to *Comberbach's Reports* (covering 1685–1698), p. 133. See page [37], note 2. Quincy exactly quotes text from *Garret* v. *Foot* (1689).

6. A citation to [Mallory (J.)] *Modern Entries in English* (covering 1734–1735), vol. 2, 320 pl. 8.9. See page [90], note 11.

7. A citation to *Rolle's Abridgment* (1668), pp. 801, 802. See page [9], note 1.

8. A citation to [Sir C.] *Levinz's Reports* (covering 1660–1696), vol. 2, p. 7. See page [76], note 2, *supra*. This is clearly a cite to the second edition. See Sweet & Maxwell, *supra*, vol. 1, p. 303:81; *Wallace*, *supra*, pp. 304–15. The case is *Rex* v. *Drury* (1671).

9. "Ibid.," another citation to a Holt opinion in *Comberbach's Reports* (covering 1685–1698), p. 142. See note 2, *supra*. The case is *Rex* v. *Abraham* (1689), beginning on page 141. Here the Attorney-General had brought information against several persons. The question is whether the informations must be answered, or if they are too inherently oppressive. Quincy indicated that Holt's opinion was "obiter," i.e., *obiter dictum* ("a saying by the way"), in other words, it was an aside remark, not part of the binding precedent of the decided case. See Osborn, *A Concise Law Dictionary*, p. 227.

10. A citation to Hawkins, *Pleas of the Crown* (covering 1716–1721), book 2, ch. 25, sec. 151. See page [81], note 2. This citation appears to correspond to book 2, ch. 25, sec. 149 of the 1795 7th edition, vol. 4, p. 84 (Thomas Leach), which states that "the Court never quasheth an information exhibited by a common person, but will quash an information exhibited by the attorney-general, or by the master of the crown office, upon motion, if there be cause: But this was denied in one Nixon's Case [*Rex* v. *Nixon*, Trin. 3 Geo. 1 *Strange's Report* 185 (1717)] wherein the Court seemed to be agreed, that they never have, or will Quash any information whatsoever." *Id.*, p. 84.

11. A citation to *Short* v. *Maynard* (1689), *Comberbach's Reports* (covering 1685–1698), which appears on page 150. See note 2, *supra*. Quincy loosely copies this short opinion nearly in its entirety.

12. A citation to *Hawkins* v. *Cordy* (1698), *Carthew's Reports* (covering 1687–1700), p. 466, first published in London, 1728, and republished in 1741 and 1743. See Sweet & Maxwell, *supra*, vol. 1, p. 294:22; Wallace, *supra*, pp. 397–98. Carthew was known by some as "bad authority," and defended by others as a "very faithful reporter." *Id.*, at p. 398.

13. A citation to *Salkeld's Reports* (1689–1712), vol. 1, p. 65, where *Hawkins* v. *Cardy*, referenced in the previous note, is also reported. See page [32], note 7. Quincy worked from Comberbach's version. Next is a citation to *Wegersloffe* v. *Keene*, *Strange's Reports* (1716–1749),

vol. 1, pp. 214–25. See page [21], note 12. This was an action brought "upon the custom of merchants" by the payee of a foreign bill of exchange against the acceptor. The issue was whether "partial acceptance be good or not within the custom of merchants." *Id.*, p. 215. It was held "that the drawer is bound to pay all, the drawing being an actual promise, but the acceptor is bound to pay but one, and no action can be maintained but upon the very note which he accepts . . . In Molloy and the other books there is a whole paragraph about the partial acceptance of a bill of exchange, and they allow it to be good." (Fontescue J.) Judgment was then given for the plaintiff. Quincy's case is different because the defendant is the drawer (E.G. was the acceptor) and no "special custom" (i.e., of merchants) was found, perhaps because this was not a foreign bill of exchange. See generally James S. Rogers, *The Early History of the Law of Bills and Notes* (1995), pp. 194–222.

14. On goldsmiths as bankers, see Coquillette, "The Mystery of the New Fashioned Goldsmiths," *supra*, pp. 91–118.

[94]

151 • H receives 50£ Part of ye 100 ^{of} D, pulls a bag out of his Pocket, puts the Money into the Bag + lays it down on the Counter + while tolling the rest the first Bag is stole. Adjudged y^{t} H had appropriated the Money by putting it into his Bag + must be the Loser.

2 Salkeld 507. Carter vs. Shepard.
Same 398.5 Mod.[1]

• You are a Cheat + I will prove you a Cheat for many years. Adjudged not actionable. 5 Mod. 398. quod nota

Savage vs. Robury[2]

• Debt brôt on agreement by Deed. Oyer demanded the Parties Names not inserted in the Agreement, nor any mention of their Names, but sign'd by the Parties, demurrer Adjudg'd good

1 Ld Raymond 28. N vs. Frampton[3]

• Where a Deed bears Date, at a Place, certain it is local + must be pleaded there. 1 Ld Raymond. 184.[4]

• If the Shff[5] takes insufficient Bail he is liable to an Action as well as Amercements.

vid. vol. 4. 161. 162.[6] 1 L^{d} $Raym^{d}$ 425.[7]

• If the Shff dies + before another is made, one who is in Excon[8] breaks the Prison + ~~escapes~~ goes at Liberty, it is no Escape; for when the Shff dies all the Prisoners are in the Custody of the Law, till a new Shff be made.

3 Rep. 71; b. Westby's Case.[9]

Page [94]

1. A citation to *Carter* v. *Sheppard*, *Salkeld's Reports* (covering 1689–1712), vol. 2, p. 507. See page [32], note 1. Also to *Modern Reports* (covering 1669–1732), vol. 5, p. 398, where it appears as *Carter* v. *Shephard* (1698). See page [35], note 7.

2. "*Quod nota*" ["but note"] *Savage* v. *Robury* (1698), *Modern Reports* (covering 1669–1732), vol. 5, p. 398. See page [35], note 2. This concerned whether the words were slander or libel on their face. This case has nothing to do with the prior entry other than that it was reported on the same page of *Modern Reports*, and displays the freer commonplace structure that Quincy used here.

3. Citation to *Lord Raymond's Reports* (covering 1694–1734), vol. 1, p. 28. See page [26], note 2. The case is *Nurse* v. *Frampton* (1694), which involved an interesting wager over whether a grey nag could run twenty-five miles in two hours.

4. Citation to *Lord Raymond's Reports* (covering 1694–1732), vol. 1, p. 184. See page [26], note 2. The case is *Errington* v. *Thompson* (1697), and begins on page 183.

5. "Shff" for "sheriff."

6. Citation to Volume 4 of Quincy's notebooks, where page 161 begins a 24-page section of untitled and generally unstructured commonplace notes on a variety of legal topics, perhaps from a very early stage of Quincy's study. An entry on 161 records "In taking bail, the sheriff acts at his own peril. Arguendo. 1 Burr: 29." On the following page Quincy writes in a note "But no action lies vs. Shff for taking insuff:[t] bail . . . 2 L.[d] Raym:[d] 941. But 1 L.[d] Raym:[d] is contra." The second citation is captured here, i.e., that the Sheriff is liable, and illustrates the critical approach with which Quincy studied and commonplaced his sources.

7. A citation to *Lord Raymond's Reports* (covering 1694–1732), vol. 1, p. 425. See page [26], note 2. The case, whose opinion consists of this one-line holding, is *Ethericke* v. *Cooper* (1698).

8. "Excon" for "execution." The prisoner was being held "in execution" of his debts to the plaintiff by the sheriff defendants. See note 9, below.

9. A citation to *Westby's Case* (1598), *Coke's Reports* (covering 1572–1616), vol. 3, p. 71b. See page [1], note 2. The prisoner was being held "in execution" of his debts to the plaintiff. He "broke prison" during the transition in sheriffs. No notice of the plaintiff's execution on the prisoner had been given to the new sheriff. Held: "[N]o escape can be in prejudice of the plaintiff, but when some person may be charged for it; and the Law deceives no man." *Id.*, p. 72b.

[95]

• Assumpsit Plt declares y^t [that] in Consideration the Dft sh^d enjoy such Goods etc he w^d pay the Party £25. the jury upon non assumpsit find that he promis'd to pay if he enjoy'd such Goods, + it was adjudged for the Dft because the Plt declar'd of an absolute promise + the Jury found a conditional one. Cro. Eliz. 149 Mustard vs. Hopper[1] 152

• If two Men be bound jointly + severally to One + Obligee release to one of them, both are discharg'd. 1 Inst. 232.a.[2]

• Like Law of a Trespass done by two or three + ye party release to one of them but all these Cases the deed must be shown. Ibid.[3]

• If a man wounded, die not within a Year and Day it is no felony. Hawkins Abr. 343. 1 Inst. 254.[4]

• Action brôt by Baron + Feme[5] on a promise made to ye Feme in Consideration, She w^d cure such a wound + alleges she did cure. Adjudg'd good upon Writ of Error,[6] in Exchequer's Chamber[7] because the Action is grounded upon a promise made to ye Feme + upon a matter arising upon her Skill + a performance to be made by her Person + such an Action w^d survive to the feme. Cro. James 77[8] This case is denied at Barnardiston 75.[9]

X Debt upon Judgment in Trespass for 10/ Damages + 40/ Cost, + the Statute pleaded. Vide. 2. Vent. 36.[10]

Page [95]

1. "Assumpsit" was the general contract remedy for an agreement not under seal. See page [96], note 9, *infra*. A citation to *Mustard* v. *Hoppey* (1590), *Croke's Reports* (1582–1641), vol. 1, p. 149. See page [21], note 6. The case is copied in full, almost exactly.

2. Citation to *Coke on Littleton*, p. 232a. See page [2], note 1; page [7], note 9. Coke, in his commentary, states "... [I]f he release to one of them, all are discharged, because his own Deed shall be taken most strongly against himself ..." *Id.*, p. 232a.

3. Identical citation. Deed must be shown. *Id.*, p. 232a.

4. A citation to Hawkins, *Abridgment*, p. 343. See page [68], note 6, and also *Coke on Littleton*, p. 254. Coke states the rule slightly differently: "if a man be wounded or poysoned etc. and dieth thereof within the yeare and the day, it is felony." *Id.*, p. 422b. Quincy exactly copies Hawkins's text, except for Quincy's insertion of a comma.

5. "Baron and Feme": i.e., husband and wife.

6. Writ of Error lay from the Exchequer Chamber to the King's Bench for error on the face of the record. See Baker, *An Introduction to English Legal History*, pp. 157–58; Coquillette, *The Anglo-American Legal Heritage*, pp. 243–44.

7. The statutory Exchequer Chamber, consisting of all royal judges except King's Bench judges, heard writs of error for the King's Bench. It is not to be confused with the "nonstatutory" Exchequer Chamber, which consisted of every royal judge, or the Council Chamber, which heard writs of error from the Exchequer, or the later 1830 Court of Exchequer Chamber. See Baker, *supra*, note 6, p. 158; Coquillette, pp. 243–44.

8. A citation to *Brashford* v. *Buckingham and his wife* (1601), *Croke's Reports* (covering 1582–1641), vol. 2, p. 77. See page [21], note 6. The case is accurately stated. It is an important precedent on the rights of women.

9. A citation to *Barnardiston's King's Bench Reports* (covering 1740–1741), p. 75. See page [88], note 4. The case is *Homes* v. *Wood* (1728), and reports with reference to *Brashford* v. *Buckingham* (see note 8, *supra*) that the court's holding had since been overruled. These contrasting entries demonstrate Quincy's critical reading of his sources.

10. A citation to *Ventris Reports* (1668–1684), vol. 2, p. 36. See page [89], note 7. The case is *Page* v. *Kirke* (1681). Cases marked with an "X" in the margin by Quincy were not included in his index. See discussion at page [125], note 15.

[96]

153 • If a Parish be indicted for not repairing of a Way within their Precinct, they cannot plead not guilty + give in Evidence that Another by Prescription or Tenure ought to repair it, for they are chargeable De communi Jure. 1 Ventris 256.[1]

• In Action of Debt ag^{t} a Lessee he may plead nil debet,[2] + give ye Expulsion in Evidence. 1 Ventris 258[3]

• A Confession of a person guilty of perjury voluntarily made (without any Indictment or Information) recorded, + he punished as in Case of Perjury.

Mod. Cases in Law + Equity p:179
King vs. Thorowgood.[4]

• When a Debtor pays Money indefinitely ye Creditor may apply it to any Debt he pleases. Ibid. 236. Anonymous.[5]

• Two jointly bound in a Bond, Action brôt ag^{t} one Verdict for Obligee mov'd in Arrest of Judgment y^{t} [that] ye Plt by his own showing had no Cause of Action ag^{t} One + overruled because it did not appear on ye Record y^{t} [that] ye other sign'd, sealed + deliver'd it.: Cloud vs Nicholson. Ibid. p.242.[6]

• A Rascal, Villain + Liar spoken of Justice of the peace + a Colloquium[7] laid of his Office Adjudged actionable.

Ashton vs Blagrove. Ibid. 271.[8]

• Indebitatus assumpsit[9] for several Things due to the Plt, Dft pleads in Barre y^{t} he gave a Note of hand of £20 to the Plt in full satisfaction of ye Debt. On Demurrer[10] Judg^{t} + for ye Plt because a Note thus given is no Discharge of a Debt or Duty.
1 Brown. 47. vid 1 Strange 426. Springett vs. Chadwick. Ibid. 290 vid Hob. 68
3 Lev 55 Salk 124. 442 2 Vent. 184. 3 Cro. 85. 86. Mod. Rep.221.225. 2 Cro 650.[11]

• Debt on ye Penalty of a Covenant, Dft pleads Nil debet plt demurs + Judg^{t} for him, for that is no good Plea to such an Action. Ibid. Warren vs Consett p. 323. 382.[12]

Page [96]

1. A citation to *Ventris' Reports* (1668–1684), vol. 1, p. 256. See page [89], note 7. This is a nearly exact copy of an anonymous 1674 case on page 256.

2. "*Nil debet* (he owes nothing), the plea of general issue in actions of debt not founded on specialty [such as a deed under seal]." Jowitt, *supra*, p. 1227. A lessee expelled from the premises can give the expulsion in evidence that he does not owe the lessor.

3. A citation to *Ventris' Reports* (1668–1684), vol. 1, p. 258. This text is closely copied from an anonymous 1674 case on page 258, and different than the one in note 1, *supra*.

4. A citation to *Rex* v. *Thorogood* (1723) in *Modern Reports,* vol. 8–9 (1712–1726), p. 179, sometimes referred to as "Modern Cases in Law and Equity." The two parts were published together. See Sweet & Maxwell, *supra*, vol. 1, p. 305:88, and page [35], note 2. This case involved a defendant who confessed to making a false affidavit, for which perjury he was set to the pillory.

5. A citation to *Anonymous* (1724), *Modern Reports,* vol. 8–9 (1712–1726), p. 236. See note 4, *supra*. The text is loosely copied from one line of the case.

6. A citation to *Cloud* v. *Nicholson* (1724), *Modern Reports,* vol. 8–9 (covering 1712–1726), p. 242. See note 4, *supra*. Quincy nicely summarizes the case.

7. "Colloquium," "a talking together," is here used in the legal sense as "an old term in pleading applied to the statement in declarations of libel or slander that the libellous or slanderous imputation had reference to the plaintiff." Jowitt, *supra*, p. 406.

8. A citation to *Ashton* v. *Blagrove* (1724), *Modern Reports,* vol. 8–9 (covering 1712–1726), p. 271. See note 4, *supra*. The case supports Quincy's note.

9. "*Indebitatus assumpsit*" (being indebted he undertook). This was the standard contractual action, being originally based on a fiction of subsequent undertaking, or "assumpsit," to escape the more narrow action of debt. See the full discussion at Baker, *An Introduction to English Legal History*, *supra*, pp. 347–48; Coquillette, *The Anglo-American Legal Heritage*, *supra*, p. 157.

10. "Demurrer," "A pleading by which one of the parties alleged that the preceding pleading of the other party showed no good cause of action or defence." Osborn, *A Concise Law Dictionary*, *supra*, p. 107.

11. String citations. The first two, before the cite to *Springett* v. *Chadwick*, appear to have been added later. The first is to *Bearbrook* v. *Read* (or *Bead*), in 1 *(R.) Brownlow and (J.) Goldesborough Reports* (covering 1569–1624), which had two parts (pt. 1, 1651 and pt. 2, 1652) and was published again in 1654 and 1675. See Sweet & Maxwell, *supra*, vol. 1, p. 294:18 and Wallace, *supra*, p. 158. The second cite is to *Cumber* v. *Wane* (1721), *Strange's Reports* (covering 1716–1749), vol. 1, p. 426, at pp. 426–27. In that case the court held that £5 could not be reasonable satisfaction of a £15 debt, despite the defendant's alleged agreement. The cause of action "can only be extinguished by a satisfaction he [the defendant] agrees to accept; and it is not his agreement alone that is sufficient, but it must appear to the courts to be a reasonable satisfaction; or at least the contrary must not appear, as it does in this case." *Id.*, pp. 426–27. The next citation is to *Springett* v. *Chadwick* (1724), with an "*Ibid* 290" citation, which refers back to *Modern Reports,* vol. 8–9. See note 4, *supra*. Quincy clearly copied this entry from *Springett* v. *Chadwick.* The next citations are to *Lovelace* v. *Cocket*, *Hobart's Reports* (1603–1625), p. 68, see page [83], note 1;

Lobly v. *Gildart* (1682), *Levinz's Reports* (1660–1696), vol. 3, p. 55, see page [76], note 2, *supra*; *Salkeld's Reports* (1689–1712), p. 124 (*Clark* v. *Mundal*), p. 442 (*Ward* v. *Evans*, in vol. 2 of *Salkeld's Reports*), see page [32], note 7; and *Ventris' Reports* (1668–1684), vol. 2, p. 184. The next citation is to *Lovelace* v. *Crockett*, *Croke's Reports* (1582–1641), vol. 3, pp. 85, 85–86, see page [21], note 6. In this case the defendant pleaded acceptance of one bond in discharge of another bond. Held, "no good plea." *Id.*, p. 86. The next citation is to two reported cases of *Blythe* v. *Hill* (1676), in volume 1 of *Modern Reports*, page 221, at page 225. See page [35], note 2. The final citation is to *Noyes* v. *Hopgood* (1622), *Croke's Reports* (1582–1641), vol. 2, pp. 649–50, see page [21], note 6. This was an action in debt upon an obligation for £80, "conditioned for the performance of divers covenant." Defendant pleaded that the bond was discharged in exchange for an annuity. Held: no good plea, for the agreement was "but a Concord and verbal agreement which can never be in discharge of a Specialty (i.e., a contract under seal)." *Id.*, p. 650.

12. A citation to two cases of *Warren* v. *Consett* (1724), *Modern Reports*, vol. 8–9 (1712–1726), pp. 323, 382, sometimes referred to as "Modern Cases in Law and Equity." See note 4, *supra*. Quincy loosely copies a line from the first case. The second case affirms the judgment of the first.

[97]

• A Man may claim a Way by Necessity + Where. 154

7 Mod. 3. 2 Cro. 170[1]

• If a Master send his Servant to receive Money on a Goldsmith's Bill[2] or any other, + he takes another Bill upon another person for payment, this shall not bind the Master without some subsequent Act of Consent. 7 Mod. 37.[3]

• Two joint-tenants in fee any of them levies a fine of ye whole this is no ouster of his companion, yet is a Severance of ye Jointure. Ibid. 45[4]

• If you set out ye Title of an Act of Parliament, which it is not necessary to do, you must at your own Peril set it forth right. 7 Mod. 623. vid Co: Lit 98.b.[5]

• A Writ may be executed on the Day of its Return.

7 Mod. 81[6]

• If a person be in Execution for a fine it is a Contempt for any to charge him with a civil action without Leave of the Court. Ibid p 88.[7]

• Where a Date of a Bond is impossible or mistaken, this shall not hurt upon <u>non est factum</u>[8] pleaded. 2 Rep. 5 Goddard's Case[9]

• Always ye Manner of the tender of ye payment shall be directed by him who made the tender or payment + not by him who accepts it. 5 Co. 117.[10]

• A Bond is delivered to another for Obligee who disagrees to it the Bond has lost its force. Obligee can never after agree it + Obligor may plead no est factum. 5 Rep. 119.b[11]
vid 3 Mod. 298. pl. 9.[12]

Page [97]

1. A citation to *Staple* v. *Heydon* (1703), *Modern Reports* (1669–1732), vol. 6, 3, see page [35],

note 2. Curiously, Quincy mislabels the volume as 7, and continues to do so for the rest of this page. *Staple* v. *Heydon* is a case of trespass against Heydon, who damaged some obstructing rails to reach the adjoining property. The next citation is to *Clark* v. *Cogge* (1607), *Croke's Reports* (1582–1641), vol. 2, p. 170, see page [21], note 6. There the purchaser of land had no way to his land except over the plaintiff's land. Held: "it is a thing of necessity; for otherwise he could not have any profit of his land." *Id.*, p. 170.

2. Goldsmiths essentially acted as banks, issuing receipts or bills for bullion deposited in their strong rooms. These receipts often circulated as a safe alternative for cash. See Coquillette, "The Mystery of the New Fashioned Goldsmiths," *supra*, pp. 101–13.

3. A citation to *Ward* v. *Evans* (1703), *Modern Reports* (1669–1732), vol. 6, which begins on p. 36. See page [35], note 2. Quincy nearly exactly copies this line from the holding.

4. A citation to *Ford* v. *Lord Grey* (1703), *Modern Reports* (1669–1732), vol. 6, which begins on p. 44. See note 3, *supra*. Quincy loosely copies this part of the holding from page 45.

5. A citation to *Mills* v. *Wilkins* (1703), *Modern Reports* (1669–1732), vol. 6, p. 62. See note 3, *supra*. It is unclear why Quincy cites to page 623, when the language that he loosely copies appears on page 62. Also a citation to *Coke on Littleton*, p. 98b. See page [2], note 1, and page [7], note 9. Coke makes a slightly different point. "[H]e that citeth a Statute is not bound to recite the very words thereof so long as he misseth not of the substance and necessary consequence thereupon, and yet the safer way is to vouch the words of a Law as they be." *Id.*, p. 98b.

6. A citation to *Brough* v. *Perkins* (1703), *Modern Reports* (1669–1732), vol. 6, which begins on p. 80, though Quincy quotes from 81. See note 3, *supra*.

7. A citation to *Anonymous* (1703), *Modern Reports* (1669–1732), vol. 6, p. 88. See note 3, *supra*. Quincy nearly exactly copies this line.

8. "*Non est factum*," "it is not his deed," is the only effective defense in an action in covenant on a specialty, i.e., the defendant's deed with its required seal. The deed could never be challenged as a legal matter. The defense was that the deed was never executed by the defendant "in point of fact." See Jowitt, *supra*, p. 1232.

9. A citation to *Goddard's Case* (1584), *Coke's Reports* (covering 1572–1616), vol. 2, p. 4b at p. 5a. Here the deed was dated after the death of the plaintiff, but the jury held that it was the defendant's deed, and the date was an error. Coke observed, "And the date if the deed is not of the substance of the deed; for if it want date, or if it have a false or impossible date, as the thirtieth day of February, yet the deed is good; for there are but three things of the essence and substance of a deed, that is to say, writing . . . reading and delivery. . . ." *Id.*, p. 5a.

10. A citation to *Pinnel's Case* (1602), *Coke's Reports* (1572–1616), vol. 5, p. 117a. See note 9, *supra*. Quincy's note is almost an exact quote.

11. A citation to *Whelpdale's Case* (1604), *Coke's Reports* (1572–1616), vol. 5, p. 119a. See note 9, *supra*. Coke states that "[I]f an Obligation be delivered to another, to the use of the obligee, and the same is tendered to him, and he refuseth it, then the delivery hath lost his force, and the obligee can never after agree to it, and therefore the obligee may say that it is not his deed . . ." *Id.*, p. 119b.

12. A citation to *Modern Reports* (1669–1732), vol. 3, p. 298. The "3" is partially illegible, but the case appearing there, *Thompson* v. *Leach* (1690), beginning on page 296, discusses the circumstances under which agreement is necessary for devises and conveyances. The notation "pl. 9" is less clear. "Pl" often refers to pleadings, but it is uncertain to what Quincy was referring here.

[98]

155 • Debt upon a Bond dated 1:[st] May condon'd to pay £140 y[e] 15 Day of May next ensuing. Adjudged it sh.[d] refer to the same May. 2 Cro 646 Prescot's Case[1]

Ibid 677. Sed vid. Lilly. Abr. 392.[2]

• Six Months in a quare impedit shall be accounted according to the Calendar viz half a year, in other Cases shall be reckoned 28 Days to a Month: 6 Rep 62.

Cateby's Case[3]

• Infants + Madmen may sue + the Suit must be in their Names tho' it shall be follow'd by Others. Co. Lit. 135. b.[4]

• Defences not necessary in a Plea in Abate:[nt]

Nelson's Lutwyche p 3.[5]

X Misnomer sh.[d] not be pleaded by an Attorney, for a Warrant of Attorney sh.[d] agree with the pleadings.

Ibid. p 5.[6]

Quare of this, it is not law.[7]

• A man grants to Another 20 of the best Trees in a certain wood to be taken at Grantee's Election within 11 years. Adjudged the Grantor cannot cut himself without Leave from y[e] Grantee before y[e] y:[rs] are finish'd, unless the grantee have cut y[e] whole before. 2 Lev 142. Mottram vs. Jolly[8]

• By y[e] Grant of a Reversion Land in possession will not pass. Cro. Charles 290[9]

• Where Matter in Abate[nt] is pleaded in Bar + concluded in bar, Judg.[t] final ought to be given.

7 Mod. (edit 1713) p 102. Crosse vs. Billson.[10]

• A Writ returnable on a Sunday shall abate. Ibid 148

Harvey vs. Broad.[11]

Page [98]

1. "Condon'd" for "conditioned." The citation is to *Prescot's Case* (1623), *Croke's Reports* (1582–1641), vol. 2 (Croke Jac), p. 646. See page [21], note 6. Quincy's note is almost a direct quotation at page 647.

2. "Ibid 677" should be "678," the case of *Buckley* v. *Guildbank* (1623), which presented another question of which month of May would be construed. See note 1, *supra*. The *Sed vid.* ("But see") is to *Lilly's Abridgment*, p. 392. See page [48], note 3.

3. A citation to *Catesby's Case*, *Coke's Reports* (1572–1616), vol. 3, p. 61b, at p. 62b. Quincy misspells the case name and omits the folio citation "b." A *quare impedit* ("wherefore he hindered") is a possessory action to recover the right to appoint clergy, i.e., a "presentation" or "advowsman," which used to be a valuable right subject to private ownership, with the concurrence of the bishop. See Jowitt, *supra*, p. 1454. In *Catesby's Case* the six-month period within which the power of appointment had to be exercised to avoid its loss was calculated "by the kalendar," i.e., six full months, rather than at 28 days per month (4 weeks). *Id.*, p. 63a. As Coke observed, "[T]here is a great difference in our ordinary speech, between the singular number, as a twelve month, doth include all the year, according to the kalendar, but twelve month shall be reckoned according to 28 days to the Month." *Id.*, p. 62a.

4. A citation to *Coke on Littleton*, p. 135b. See page [2], note 1, and page [7], note 9. Quincy's note is a close paraphrase.

5. "Nelson's Lutwyche." A citation to Lutwyche's *Livre des Entries* (1683–1704), p. 3. This was first published in French and Latin in 1704 in 2 volumes and then, in 1718, translated by W. Nelson, omitting the entries, but including the common pleas reports. See Sweet & Maxwell, *supra*, vol. 1, p. 304:85 and Wallace, pp. 395–96.

6. A citation to *Lutwyche's Livre des Entries* (Nelson translation), p. 5. See note 5, *supra*. Cases marked with an "X" by Quincy were not included in his index. See discussion at page [125], note 15.

7. Quincy is questioning the above statement. He did not automatically accept what he read, but was a critical student. "Misnomer" was an effective defense plea in both civil and criminal cases, but today a mistake as to name can be easily corrected. See Jowitt, *supra*, p. 1180. "Attorney" for the purpose of this note is a "private attorney" acting on another's behalf. The point, apparently, is that the power of attorney and the pleadings should be identical, so that a private attorney only has the power to plead misnomer at the cost of challenging his own power of appointment. This seems ridiculously technical. Quincy also seems to know of contrary "law." An American case? See the discussion in the "Introduction," *supra*. Coke believed that "a mistake in the name does not matter when there is no mistake in the body or person." *Id.*, p. 1180. See *Dr. Ayray's Case*, *Coke's Reports*, vol. 11, p. 18b, at p. 21a.

8. A citation to *Mottram* v. *Jolly* (1675), *Levinz's Reports* (1660–1696), vol. 2, p. 142. See page [76], note 2, *supra*. Quincy nicely paraphrases the case.

9. A citation to *Bland* v. *Inman* (1633), *Croke's Reports* (1582–1641), vol. 3, p. 290. See page [21], note 6. This case held that a particular "reservation shall continue only 'during the life of the husband and wife,' and not during 'the term [of a lease];' and if the wife has omitted to execute the deed, the reservation as to her is void, and will continue no longer than the life of the husband." Divorced from its facts, the value of this note is hard to extract.

10. A citation to *Crosse* v. *Bilson* (1704), *Modern Reports*, vol. 6, p. 102. See page [35], note 2.

11. A citation to *Harvey* v. *Broad* (1704), *Modern Reports*, vol. 6, p. 148. Here, the writ was returnable on a day which happened to be a Sunday, and "though the return be kept on the next day, [the writ] cannot be executed on the next day."

[99]

156

• Action brot ag[t] a femme sole,[1] she marries, + Judg[t] is ag[t] her + then Execution; + the Shff takes her by that Name, She shall be estopped to say the contrary. Salkeld 311.[2]

• A Power to four Jointly + Severally three cannot execute. 5 Co. 91[3]

• Disseisee levies a fine to a Stranger, Dissor[4] shall re tain the land forever, for a Dissee ag[t] his own fine can't Claim + Connusee[5] cannot enter, for the Right which Conusor[6] had, can't be transferr'd, but by y[e] fine, y[t] Right is extinct, whereof the Dissor shall take Advantage. 2 Co. 56. a[7]

• Femme covert submits herself to the Award of J.N.[8] + takes husband + after an Award is given, this shall not bind her for ye Submission by Marriage is revoked. 1 Bacon's Abrig[nt] p 291. Cites 1 Roll's Abrig.[nt] 332.[9] Quare Wether debt on a Bond condition'd to submit to such Award can y.[t] [that] be brôt ag.[t] Husband + Wife?[10]

• If a wife alone or with her husband bargain + sell her Land by Deed indented or inroll'd it shall not bind her. 1 Bacon's Abrig[nt] 302 Cites 2 Inst 673. Hob:[s] 223.[11]

• If goods come to a feme covert by trover[P];[12] the Action may be brot ag.[t] Husband + Wife, but the conversion must be laid only in the Husband. 1 Bacon's abrig.[t] p. 307[13]

[P] Detinue brot vid p 174[12]

Page [99]

1. "Femme sole," i.e., an unmarried woman, "whether a spinster, a widow, or a divorced woman." Jowitt, *supra*, pp. 793–94.

2. A citation to *Rock* v. *Leighton*, *Salkeld's Reports* (1689–1712), which begins on page 310. See page [32], note 7. The closely quoted text, which appears not on page 311 but on page 310, does not pertain directly to the facts, but is rather an illustration by analogy.

3. A citation to *Hoe's Case* (1600), *Coke's Reports* (1572–1616), vol. 5, p. 91a. See page [1], note 2. In the case Coke explains the consequences of having a power "jointly, or severally," i.e., "each person is liable severally and all are liable jointly." "Several liability" is for an ascertained part of the whole, while joint liability is for "an undivided share." See Jowitt, *supra*, pp. 1014, 1627–28.

4. "Dissor" for "disseisor," "a person who unlawfully puts another out of his land." Jowitt, *supra*, p. 643. "Dissee" for "disseissee," "a person turned out of possession." *Id.*, p. 643.

5. "Conusor," "cognisor," or "he who passed or acknowledged a fine of lands or tenements to another." Jowitt, *supra*, p. 400. "Connusee" is for "cognisee," "he to whom the fine was acknowledge." *Id.*, p. 400.

6. See notc 5, *supra.*

7. A citation to *Buckler's Case* (1598), *Coke's Reports* (1572–1616), vol. 2, p. 55a at p. 56a. Quincy loosely, but accurately, paraphrases Coke.

8. "Femme covert," i.e., a married woman. The initials "J.N." were from the passage in *Bacon's Abridgment*, see note 9, *infra*, and simply were the initials of a hypothetical arbitrator. See note 9, *infra.*

9. A citation to *Bacon's Abridgment* (1736), vol. 1, at p. 291. See page [37], note 5. The *Abridgment* was more thorough than Quincy's paraphrase. "If A on the one Part, and B and C (a Feme Sole) on the other Part, submit themselves to the Award of J.N. and after C takes J.S. to Husband, and after the Arbitrator, before any Notice of this Marriage makes an Award that B and C shall pay £30 to A, yet this shall not bind J.S. and C. his wife, nor B, for the submission of the Marriage of C is revoked as to B also . . ." *Id.*, p. 291. *Rolle's Abridgment* (1668), *supra*, p. 332 is cited by *Bacon's Abridgment*, as Quincy notes. See page [9], note 1.

10. Quincy asks if a creditor can protect himself or herself against revocation by remarriage of a debt secured by a bond of making the bond conditional on submission to an award of an arbitrator like "J.N.." This would be important to a single woman seeking credit, as to a lender afraid the woman would evade the debt by marriage. It is a good question.

11. A citation to *Bacon's Abridgment* (1736), vol. 1 at p. 302. "But if a Wife alone, or with her Husband, bargain and sell her Lands by Deed indented and inrolled, yet it shall not bind her; for a Wife cannot be examined by any Court without Writ, and there is no Writ allowed in this Case." *Id.*, at p. 302, citing *Coke's Second Institute* (1642), p. 643, see page 80, note 5, and *Hobart's Reports* (1603–1625), p. 225, see page 83, note 1, as Quincy indicates. The case in *Hobart's Reports* is *Needler* v. *Bishop of Winchester* (1615), which begins on page 220.

12. "Trover" is a cause of action ("trover and conversion") "maintained by any person who had a right to possession of goods, for recovering the value of such goods against another who . . . wrongfully converted them to his own use," withholding them from the plaintiff. Jowitt, *supra*, p. 1785. It was originally based on the fiction that the goods were lost and then "found" (trover) by the defendant. It differed from detinue, which was for return of the goods themselves, not just the value. *Id.*, p. 1785. The "p" mark by Quincy refers to a "detinue" citation in the margin, showing he made this connection. It is a citation to page 174 [117], later in the *Law Commonplace*, which discusses a situation in which detinue must be brought against husband and wife.

13. A citation to *Bacon's Abridgment,* vol. 1, p. 307. See note 11, *supra*. "[F]or the Possession of the Wife is the Possession of her Husband, and so is the Property; so that the Conversion cannot be to the Damage of the Wife, but of the Husband only." *Id.*, p. 307.

[100]

157 • A Woman makes her Will + devises Lands + afterwards marries, y^t [that] Marriage is a Countermand.

4 Rep. Forse + Hembling's Case[1]

• If a Deed of Gift of Goods + Chattels be deliver'd to the Use of ye Donee; the Goods and Chattels are in ye Donee presently, before Notice or Agree.^t;[2] but ye Donee may make refusal in pais[3] + by y^t [that] ye property + Interest shall be devested + such Disagreement need not be in a Court of Record.

3 Rep. 26. b. bott^m +27. a. top.[4]

• If A makes an Obligon[5] to B + delivers it to C to ye use[5] of B y^t [that] is the deed of A presently, but if C offers it to B there B may refuse it in pais,[6] + thereby ye obligon will lose its force; But perhaps in such Case A in an action brôt on this Obligon cannot plead non est factum,[7] because it was once his Deed.

3 Rep. 26. b.[8]

• One cannot release a Debt or Duty by his Will.

Wood cites (p 346) 1 Ventr. 39[9]

• Where a Statute says a Thing <u>may</u> be done it is always understood <u>must</u> be done. Carthew. 294.[10]

vid. Salk 609. Vern. 154[11]

• Tenants in common may either join or sever at Election in an Action of Debt for Rent reserv'd. Ibid. 289 M v L[12]

• It is a certain Rule y^t [that] a Will shall never operate by way of executory Devise, if it may take Effect by Way of Remainder. Ibid. 310[13]

Page [100]

1. A citation to *Forse and Hembling's Case* (1588) *Coke's Reports* (1572–1616), vol. 4, p. 60b. See page [1], note 2. "And in this Case it was agreed . . . The taking of husband, and coverture [marriage] at the time of her death, the Will was countermanded, and that for two causes . . . 1. [I]t shall be against the nature of a Will to be so absolute, that he Who maketh the same being of good and perfect memory cannot countermand it; and therefore this taking of husband being in the Case at Barre her proper act shall amount to a countermand in Law . . . 2. It shall be mis-

chievous to women that after their intermarriage they could not for no cause countermand their wills." *Id.*, p. 61b. It is interesting that Quincy did not note the obvious policy reasons for the decision.

2. "Agree't" for "agreement."

3. "In pais" means "without legal proceedings" or, in reference to estoppel to enforce deeds, "without writing." "'[M]atters *in pais*' are opposed not only to 'matters of record' but also to 'matters in writing' that is, deeds, as where estoppel by deed is distinguished from estoppel by matters *in pais.*" Jowitt, *supra*, p. 949.

4. A citation to *Butler and Baker's Case* (1591) *Coke's Reports*, vol. 1, *supra*, note 1, p. 25a. Quincy accurately paraphrases Coke's statement at pages 26b, 27a, as indicated by Quincy.

5. "Obligon" for "obligation."

6. "In pais." See note 3, *supra*.

7. "Non est factum," i.e., "it is not his deed." See the discussion of this plea at page [97], note 8.

8. Another citation to *Butler and Baker's Case* (1591), *Coke's Reports*, vol. 3, p. 25a. See note 4, *supra*. As Coke stated, "[B]ut perhaps in such Case A. in an Action brought upon this obligation cannot plead that it was not his deed, because it was once his deed." *Id.*, p. 26b.

9. A citation to Wood, *Institute*, p. 346. See page [7], note 3. Wood in turn cites *Ventris Reports* (covering 1668–1684), p. 39. See page [89], note 7. The case in *Ventris Reports* is *Wingate* v. *Stanton* (1779), which begins on page 38.

10. A citation to *Rex* v. *Barlow and Jeans* (1693), *Carthew's Reports* (covering 1686–1701), p. 293. It was published in London in 1728, 1741 and 1743. See Sweet & Maxwell, vol. 1, p. 294:22; Wallace, *supra*, pp. 377–98. The loosely quoted text appears on page 294.

11. Futher "vid." ("see") citations to *Salkeld's Reports* (1689–1712), vol. 2, p. 609, see page [32], note 7; *Vernon's Reports* (1681–1720), p. 154, see page [52], note 5. The *Salkeld* citation is to *Rex* v. *Barlow*, as in note 10, *supra*. It is unclear to what the *Vernon* citation is directed. The case on page 154 is not on point, though case number 154, *Duke of Norfolk* v. *Howard* (1683), which begins on page 163, includes the proposition that though it was a hard case, "the rule of law must be observed."

12. A citation to *Midgley and Gilbert* v. *Lovelace* (1693), *Carthew's Reports* (covering 1686–1701), p. 289. See note 10, *supra*.

13. A citation to *Reev* v. *Long* (1694), *Carthew's Reports* (covering 1686–1701), p. 310. See note 10, *supra*.

[101]

• After a Tryal at Bar no new trial shall be 158
granted in any Case unless for Corruption or Misdemea-
-nor in the Jury. Carthew 507 vid. p 105 of this book[1]

• Plt having declar'd on a Note of a special Date
cannot give in Evidence a Note of a different
Date. Fitz Gibbons 131. Baynham v. Matthews[2]

• Baron of a full Age + feme under Age, he may make
Attorney for her. 1 Showers 13.[3]

• Administrator is chargeable as Assignee, for y^{e}
Time he is in possession + enjoys the Land.
Ibid. 348[4]

• If A assures B to pay money to C, C may
have an action on y^{t} [that] promise. Said by Holt. 1. Ld Ray^{d} 369[5]

• In any Action on ye Case Trespass, Battery, false
Imprisonm.^{t} ag^{t} [that] any Justice of ye Peace-Constable con
-cerning any thing done by reason of any of their Officers
+ all other in their Aid + Assistance or by their Command-
-ment, they may plead ye general Issue + give the
special Matter for their Excuse or Justification in
Evidence. Quare 1 Inst. 283.a. Stat. 7 Ja: 1.5
vid. p. 77 of this Book[6]

• Information ag^{t} the Dft for a Cheat on Tryal the Case
appear'd y^{t} he had got a promise, from his Mother, for a
note of hand for £ 1 by Slight got her hand to a
note of £ 100. Ld Holt ch. Just the Mother cannot
be a witness being concern'd in ye Consequence of
ye Suit. Salkeild 283.[7]

Page [101]

1. A citation to *Argent* v. *Darrel* (1699), *Carthew's Reports* (1686–1701), p. 507. See page [100], note 10. Quincy also cited to his page 105 [90] of the *Law Commonplace*, which discusses when a new trial should be granted, i.e., "No new Tryal where the Party might have had Evidence before . . . etc.." See *supra*, page [90].

2. A citation to *Baynham* v. *Matthews*, *Fitz-Gibbons' Reports* (1727–1732), p. 131, published in London in 1732. See Sweet & Maxwell, vol. 1, p. 300:55; Wallace, *supra*, pp. 427–30.

3. A citation to *Humfreys* v. *Vaughan* (1689), *Shower's Reports* (covering 1678–1694), vol. 1, p. 13. See page [82], note 1. "Baron" is for "husband," "femme" is for "wife." Quincy actually substitutes the terms "Baron" and "femme" for "husband" and "wife" as they appeared in the report.

4. A citation to *Buck* v. *Barnard* (1692), *Shower's Reports* (covering 1678–1694), vol. 1, p. 348. See page [82], note 1.

5. A citation to Chief Justice Holt in *Lord Raymond's Reports* (covering 1694–1732), vol. 1, p. 369. See page [26], note 2. The case is *Cook* v. *Harris* (1698), which begins on page 367.

6. A citation to *Coke on Littleton*, p. 283a. See page [2], note 1 and page [7], note 9. Quincy's notations accurately summarized Coke, although Coke was more detailed in defining the offices in question. *Id.*, p. 283a. Coke also cited the statute of 7 James I, 5 (1668). Quincy also cited to his own *Law Commonplace*, at page 77 [68], which lists authorities on special pleading. See page 77 [68], *supra*. This was an alert, intelligent cross-reference.

7. A citation to *Rex* v. *Whiting*, *Salkeld's Reports* (1689–1712), vol. 1, p. 283. See page [32], note 1. Quincy closely paraphrased these facts and their legal result.

[102]

• An heir apparent may be a Witness concerning ye Title of Land—but where there is Tenant in tail, remainder in tail, Remainder men[1] cannot be Witnesses. Salkeid 283.[2] 159

• In Strictness no funeral Expenses are allowable ag.^{t} a Creditor except for the Coffin, ringing the Bell, parson, Clerk + bearer fees, but not for Pall or Ornaments. Salkeid 296. vid. Comb. 342. 4 Burr. 252[3]

• Case of Administration Bond. Ibid 315.[4]

• An Infant admitted by Guardian to sue accompt[5] ag.^{t} his Guardian in Socage for the profits rec.^{d} after ye Infant had accomplish'd his Age of 14 years + the Action was brôt ag.^{t} him as [against] his Bailiff, + so it ought to be as the Justices held. Cro. Jam. 219[6]

• Case of a Master's hypothecating[7] a Vessell Bridgman's Case. Hobart 11.[8]

• After Demurrer there shall be no Repleader. 3 Rep. 52 b. Qu. vid. 3 Lev. 440[9]

• A Remainder is limited to the right Heirs of J.S. he dies having a Daughter she shall have it as a purchaser + shall keep the Land ag.^{t} the Son born after. 3 Rep. 61. b.[10]

• Where two are bound jointly + severally + the Obligee gets judgm^{t} ag^{t} one + takes him in Excon,[11] yet he may proceed ag.^{t} the Other, because the Debt is not paid

Page [102]

1. A tenant "in tail" holds a "cut down" fee (from the Law French "tailler," to cut). See Jowitt, *supra*, p. 715. Unlike a fee simple, the fee is only inheritable by the heirs of the tenants blood, i.e., legitimate biological sons or daughters, or, as in the common "entail male," legitimate biological sons only. In the event of failure of issue, the fee reverts to the heirs of the original

grantor who established the entail, often the father of the bride who was happy to see his son-in-law control the land only as long as there were legitimate grandchildren. Such heirs of the tenant in tail were called "remainder men" and their interest in the entailed land was called a "remainder." They had an interest in the entail as, in theory at least, the tenant "in tail" could never alienate more than a life estate. See Coquillette, *The Anglo-American Legal Heritage*, *supra*, pp. 110–51, Baker, *An Introduction to English Legal History*, *supra*, pp. 271–76.

2. A citation to *Smith* v. *Blackham*, *Salkeld's Reports* (1689–1712), p. 283. See page [32], note 7. Quincy often refers to these reports, erroneously, as *Salkeid's Reports*. This case immediately follows *Rex* v. *Whiting*, cited on the prior page in *Salkeld's Reports*. See page [101], note 7.

3. A citation to *Shelly's Case*, *Salkeld's Reports* (covering 1689–1712), p. 296. See note 2, *supra*. "Vid" (see) citations to *East India Company* v. *Skinner* (1695), *Comberbach's Reports* (1685–1698), p. 342. See page [37], note 2, *supra*. A further citation to *Burrow's Reports* (1756–1772), vol. 4, p. 252 makes no sense, as volume 4 starts with page 1925. *Burrow's Reports*, famous for containing the decisions of Lord Mansfield, was first published in vols. 1 and 2 in 1766, with vol. 3 in 1771, vol. 4 in 1776, and vol. 5 in 1780, with all but the first three volumes too late for Quincy. See Sweet & Maxwell, *supra*, vol. 1, p. 294:20.

4. A citation to *Archbishop of Canterbury* v. *Wills*, *Salkeld's Reports* (1689–1712), p. 315. See page [32], note 7.

5. To sue "accompt" refers to an action of "account," the proper action to bring against a fiduciary. See Jowitt, *supra*, p. 27.

6. A citation to *Anonymous* (1609), *Croke's Reports* (1582–1641), vol. 2, p. 219. See page [21], note 6. Accurate, except Quincy omits "against" before "his Bailiff." Under age heirs were watched over by their feudal lords as "guardians," but the guardian's powers were limited by the doctrine of "waste" and other fiduciary duties. See Baker, *An Introduction to English Legal History*, *supra*, note 1, at pp. 240–41 ("wardship").

7. "Hypothecation," also known as "bottomry," was the power of a ship's master to bind the ship as security for needed repairs, etc., even without the master's knowledge. This doctrine was obviously essential if the ship needed urgent repairs in foreign ports, and was traditionally enforced by the Admiralty Courts against the master, despite lack of privity. See Jowitt, *supra*, p. 932.

8. A citation to *Bridgeman's Case*, *Hobart's Reports* (covering 1603–1625), p. 11. See page [83], note 1.

9. A citation to *Rigeway's Case* (1594), *Coke's Reports* (covering 1572–1616), vol. 3, p. 52a. Coke observed "That after demurrer there shall be no repleader, for the parties have by their mutual assent put themselves upon the Judgement of the Court . . ." *Id.*, p. 58[a]. There is also a "Qu. vid." [but see] citation to *Stephens* v. *Cooper* (1696), *Levinz's Reports* (covering 1660–1696), vol. 3, p. 440. See page [76], note 2, *supra*. This case also discusses the permissibility of repleader after demurrer.

10. A citation to the *Lincoln College Case* (1596) *Coke's Reports* (covering 1572–1616), vol. 3, p. 58b at p. 61b. Quincy accurately paraphrases the holding.

11. "Excon" for "execution" ("to carry into effect"). See Jowitt, *supra*, pp. 755–56.

[103]

or satisfied. 3 Salkld 6 cites 1 Cro. 75, Yelv. 67[1] 160

• Always the manner of ye tender + ye payment shall be directed by him who made the tender, or payment + not by him who accepts it. 5 Co. 117. Penant's Case.[2]

X Debt upon an Obligon ye Condon was y^t^ [that] ye Dft sh^d^ pay to ye Plt £11 which was for Rent Dft alledges y^t^ [that] ye plt had enter'd upon the Land + so suspended ye Rent. Plt demurs + Judgm^t^ for him, for that being but a Recital, y^t^ [that] it was for Rent, bindeth not. Hob. 130[3]

• A Man marrieth the Daughter of the Sister of his first Wife + was drawn in Question to ye ecclesiastical Court for it, + it was resolv'd by the Court of Common Pleas y^t^ [that] ye Marriage could not be Impeach'd for the same was good according to the Statute not being prohibited by the Levitical Degrees. 1 Inst. 235. a.
Vid. Lev. 364[4]

• He y^t^ [that] dieth seised in Law only may be said, he died seis'd in his Demesne as of fee. 1 Inst. 239 b. top.[5]

• Debt ag.^t^ an Excor who pleads y^t^ [that] J.S. is an Excor not nam'd in ye Writ, but who does not say y^t^ [that] he has administer'd ajudg'd ill upon a Demurrer. 1 Lev. 161.[6]

X Case of Deceit + false Affirmation, Danvers 200.18[7]

Page [103]

1. A citation to *Parker* v. *Webb*, *Salkeld's Reports* (1689–1712), vol. 3, p. 6. See page [32], note 7. This in turn is said to cite to *Croke's Reports* (1582–1641), vol. 1, p. 75. See page [21], note 6.

This citation, however, appears to be wrong. Salkeld's report of *Parker* v. *Webb* does not offer these specific cites. This citation could be to *Brown* v. *Wootton* (1605), *Croke's Reports,* vol. 1 (Croke Jac), p. 73, which is also reported (as *Broome* v. *Wooten*) in the adjoining citation to *Yelverton's Reports* 67. Finally there is a citation to *Yelverton's Reports* (covering 1602–1613) 67, where the case *Broome* v. *Wooten* (1605) is somewhat on point. These reports were first published, translated from law French into English, in 1735, and republished in 1742. See Sweet & Maxwell, *supra*, vol. 1, p. 311:134 and Wallace, *supra*, pp. 211–20.

2. A citation to *Pinnel's Case* (1602), *Coke's Reports* (1572–1616), vol. 5, p. 117a. See page [4], note 1. See also page [97], note 10 for another citation to this case.

3. A citation to *St. John* v. *Diggs* (1613), *Hobart's Reports* (1603–1625), p. 130. See page [83], note 1. Quincy is using his usual abbreviations here, i.e., "oligon" for "obligation," "condon" for "condition," "dft" for "defendant," "plt" for "plaintiff," etc. Cases marked with an "X" by Quincy were not included in his index. See discussion at page [125], note 15.

4. A citation to *Coke on Littleton*, p. 235a. See page [2], note 1; page [7], note 9. Quincy paraphrases Coke accurately and adds the citation to *Levinz's Reports* (1660–1696), p. 364. See page [76], note 2, *supra*. The "Levitical Degrees" are the degrees of affinity set forth in the *Bible* at *Leviticus*, c.18, and incorporated in 1540 in the Statute 32 Hen. 8, c.38, s.2. See Jowitt, *supra*, p. 1081.

5. Another citation to *Coke on Littleton* (1628), *supra*, note 4, at p. 239b. Quincy paraphrases Coke accurately. For the concepts of "seisin," "demesne" and "fee," the essence of legal possession of land in English common law, see Baker, *An Introduction to Common Law*, *supra*, pp. 226, 232–34, 262–63.

6. A citation to *Swallow* v. *Emberson* (1665), *Levinz's Reports* (covering 1660–1690), vol. 1, p. 161. See page [76], note 2, *supra*. "Excor" for "executor," "agt" for "against" etc. This is a standard pleading issue. Simply saying "J.S." is an executor not named in the writ is not a good pleading defense ("demurrer") unless you add that "J.S." has administered the estate.

7. A citation to D'Anvers (Knightley), *General Abridgment of the Common Law*, p. 200.18. This work was first published in 3 vols., with vol. 1 in 1705, vols. 1 and 2 in 2d ed. in 1722–1725, and vol. 3 in 1737. See Sweet & Maxwell, *supra*, vol. 1, p. 17.7. This page citation matches the 2nd edition of 1722–1725. (Special thanks to Mark Sullivan, reference librarian extradordinaire!) Cases marked with an "X" by Quincy were not included in his index. See note 3, *supra*, and discussion at page [125], note 15, *infra*.

[104]

161 • The Value upon Appraisement of Goods is not bind-
-ing, nor much respected at common Law. If it be too
high it shall not prejudice the Excor, if too low it
shall not Advantage him: but ye Value found by the
Jury upon plene administravit[1] is binding.
Office of an Excor. p. 327. cites Ray.^{d} 470.471.[2]

• A man hath Issue a Son + Land is devised to ye father
habendum sibi + haeredibus de corpore suo
Legitime procreandis,[3] + after the Devisee hath
Issue another Son, ye 2.^{d} Son shall have the Land.
Swinburn 136. cites Dyer-Sect. 18.[4]

• No Estate shall pass by Implication of Law ag.^{t}
ye Express Limitation of the Party, altho' his
Limitation be void. 2 Rep. 55. b. top. Cro. Eliza 254
H. v. Crosse[5]

• If an Action is brôt ag.^{t} two Excors + they plead
severally by several Attorneys plene Administravit[6]
+ the Jury find [that] one hath assets + ye other none
Judgment shall be ag.^{t} him alone, that hath Assets.
Nelson's Lex testam p. 835 cites Roll Abr. 929.[7]

• If a Man devise Land for ye payment of his Debts +
make his Executor + leave personal Estate, no part
of the personal Estate shall go to ye payment of his
Debts. 1 Lev. 203 Feltham v. Excors.[8]

• A Mortgagor or Obligor must on ye Day of payment
seek ye Mortgagee or Obligee + tender ye Money, if the
Mortgagee or Obligee be in the Realm of England, but
if he be out of ye Realm of Eng. he is not bound to

Page [104]

1. "*Plene administravit*" ("he has fully administered") is a "defense by an executor or administrator that he has fully administered all the assets which have come to his hands." Jowitt, *supra*, p. 1354.

2. A citation to *Office of an Executor*, p. 327. This is Henry Curson's 1728 *A Supplement to the Office and Duty of Executors* (supplementary Thomas Wentworth's *The Office and Duty of Executors*), listed in Quincy's Estate Catalogue as No. 102 "Cu[ ]on's Office of an Executor." See page [8], note 5. There is a derivative citation to *Raymond's Reports* (1694–1732), pp. 470–71. See page [26], note 2.

3. "Habendum," i.e., "to hold," "sibi + haeredibus de corpore suo legitime procreandis," i.e., "it must be possessed by him and by the heirs legitimately begotten from his own body."

4. Citation to H. Swinburne, *Briefe Treatise of Testaments and Last Willes*, p. 136. This book was first published in 1590–1591 with many subsequent republications, including republication in 1677, 1728, and 1743. See Sweet & Maxwell, *supra*, vol. 1, p. 494:34. The book was in Quincy's Estate Catalogue as "Swinburne of Wills," Item 30. The 1728 edition was the source of an extract on the history of Roman and Civil law that Quincy copied into pages 108–11 of his volume 4 of legal notebooks. There is a further citation to *Dyer's Reports* (1513–1582), sect. 18. These very old reports, originally published in Law French, were republished many times, with a new edition edited by Chief Justice Treby in 1688. It was translated into English in 1794. See Sweet & Maxwell, *supra*, vol. 1, p. 299:47; Wallace, *supra*, pp. 126–32.

5. Citation to *Buckler's Case* (1597), *Coke's Reports* (covering 1572–1616), vol. 2, p. 55a. See page [1], note 2. The point is accurately paraphrased from Coke at *Id.*, p. 55b. There is also a citation to *Hogg* v. *Cross, Hill* (1592) *Croke's Reports* (1582–1641), vol. 1, p. 254, to the same effect. See page [21], note 6.

6. See note 1, *supra*.

7. A citation to W. Nelson, *Lex Testamentaria* (1714), p. 835. There were subsequent editions in London in 1724 and 1733. See Sweet & Maxwell, *supra*, vol. 1, p. 493:26. This in turn cites *Rolle's Abridgment* (1668), p. 929. See page [9], note 1. Neither volume of *Rolle's Abridgment* has up to 929 pages, so Nelson's citation is uncertain.

8. A citation to *Feltham* v. *Executors Harlston* (1667), *Levinz's Reports* (1660–1696), vol. 1, p. 203. See page [76], note 2, *supra*. Quincy closely copied the line.

[105]

seek him, but shall have ye same Benefit as if he 162
had made a tender. Hawkins Abr. 297. 1 Inst. 210. b. bot.[1]
Qu. If such Mortgagor may plead y^{t} [that] ye Mortgagee
was out of ye Realm of Eng. without pleading y^{t} [that] he was
ready at ye Day.

• Nil habuit in Tenementis may be given in Evidance
on nil debet pleaded. 4 Mod. 254. C v. Talbot.[2]

• Case brot, The Dft had rc^{d} sundry Goods of ye Plt to trade withall
+ to render his Acc.^{t} had promis'd but had had not done it;
Plea in Abate.^{nt} y^{t} ye action was not well brôt + sh.^{d}
be Acc.^{t} and overruled. 1 Shower 71.[3]

• If A sues B for mere vexation in some Case upon parti-
-cular damages B may have an Action: And If a
Stranger who is not concern'd excites A to sue an
Action ag.^{t} B, B may have an Action ag.^{t} ye stranger.
1 Ld Raym.^{d} 380 for ye Institute FNB 89. m.
3 Cro 378. + 2 Inst. 444. FNB 648.m.[4]

• The Action commences from the Teste of ye writ
1 Ld Raym.^{d} 383.[5]

• Divers indicted of a Riot, only two found guilty,
no Judgm.^{t} can be entered for ye King because there
must be three to a Riot. 1 Ld Raym^{d} 484. Sudbury[6]

• Trover for 72 Ounces of Cloves, Mace and
Nutmegs + does not show how much of each
motion in arrest of Judgm.^{t} for Default + held
good. 1 Ld Raym^{d} 588.[7]

Page [105]

1. A citation to Hawkins, *Abridgment*, p. 297. See page [68], note 6. Also a citation to *Coke on Littleton* (1628), p. 210b. See page [2], note 1, page [7], note 9. Coke noted that if an obligee "be out of the Realme of England, hee [obligor] is not bound to seeke him or to goe out of the Realme unto him." *Id.*, p. 210b.

2. "*Nil habuit in Tenementis,*" i.e., ("he had no interest in the tenements") "a plea to be pleaded only in an action of debt which was brought by a lessor against a lessee . . . it put the plaintiff to strict proof of his title." Jowitt, *supra*, p. 1227. "*Nil debet*" ("he owes nothing"), the "plea of general issue in action of debt." See *Id.*, p. 1227. There is a citation to *Coombs* v. *Talbott* (1694), *Modern Reports* (1669–1732), vol. 4, p. 254. See page [35], note 2.

3. A citation to *Wilkins* v. *Wilkins* (1689), *Shower's Reports* (1678–1694), vol. 1, p. 71. See page [82], note 1.

4. Citations begin with a reference to *Savile* v. *Roberts* (1698), *Lord Raymond's Reports* (1694–1732), vol. 1, p. 374. The text from which Quincy copies is on page 380, as he cites, and also contains the citations he notes to "FNB." "FNB" refers to *Fitzherbert's Natura Brevium* at *89.m. See page [21], note 10. The correct citation to Fitzherbert is *98n. See 91 English Reports (1909), p. 151. (The second citation appears to be incorrect. Quincy was apparently not using *Fitzherbert* directly!) The next citation is to *Robodham* v. *Venleck* (1635), *Croke's Reports* (1582–1641), vol. 2, p. 378. See page [21], note 6. There is also a citation here to *Coke's Second Institutes* (1642), p. 444.

5. A citation to *Anonymous* (1698), *Lord Raymond's Reports* (covering 1694–1732), vol. 1, p. 383. See page [26], note 2. "Teste" refers the "witness myself" words ("*teste meipso*") at the conclusion of the writ. "Writs are 'tested' (that is, the *teste* runs) in the name of the Lord Chancellor." Thus an action starts when the writ is witnessed. See Jowitt, *supra*, p. 1743.

6. A citation to *Rex* v. *Sudbury* (1699), *Lord Raymond's Reports* (1694–1732), vol. 1, p. 484.

7. "Trover" was the action on the case brought "by any person who had a right to possession of goods, for recovering the value of such goods against another . . ." Jowitt, *supra*, p. 1785. "Arrest of judgment" was a motion urging the trial judge not to enter judgment until reporting the matter for consideration by his judicial colleagues in London. It served the function of an appeal, although technically no judgement had been entered. *Id.*, pp. 153–54. There is a citation to *Hartford* v. *Jones* (1700), 1 *Lord Raymond's Reports* (1694–1732), p. 588.

[106]

163 • Debt upon a Judgment Dft pleads that he was taken by the Marshall upon a Capias[1] + paid the Money to him. On Demurrer adjudged no Plea for the Marshall upon a Capias hath no Right to receive Money, but only to detain the person. Otherwise upon a fieri Facias.[2] 2 Lev. 203 T. v. B.[3]

• Obligation joint + several A B + C the Seal of B torn off, the Obligon is thereby destroy'd as to all. 2 Lev. 220–2.[4]

X Case of the half Blood + Whole. 2 Lev. 173[5]

• A man cannot sue an Excor + another in one Action, for the Excor shall be charg'd de Bonis Testatoris + the other de Bonis propriis. 2 Lev. 228[6]

• Lessee assigns the Moiety of the Land for the Whole Term: Lessor may bring Debt for the Moiety of the Rent ag^{t} Assignee. 2 Lev. 231.[7]

• A Man can't bind himself to 3 or 2 jointly + severally[8] so as to make ye Obligons joint + several at the will of the Obligees. 5 Co. 14.a.[9]

• Negative pregnant when good. 1 Lev. 83[10]

• Bond for performance of an Award, Arbitrators award a Sum to be paid, which is tender'd by the party to pay it, + refused by the party to receive it. It is lost forever. 3 Lev. 24[11]

Page [106]

1. "Capias" ("that you take") "the generic name of several writs directing the sheriff to arrest the person therein named." Jowitt, *supra*, p. 307.

2. "Fieri facias" ("that you cause to be done"). See page [125], note 1.

3. A citation to "T v. B," *Taylor* v. *Bekon* (1677), *Levinz's Reports* (1683–1704), vol. 2, p. 203. See page [76], note 2, *supra*. Quincy clearly had these three-volume reports in front of him here, as this is the first of seven citations.

4. Another citation to *Seaton* v. *Henson* (1678), *Levinz's Reports* (1683–1704), vol. 2, p. 220. See note 3, *supra*. The citation clearly refers to a case limited to page 220, so it is unclear why he extends his reference to "-2."

5. Another citation to *Tracy* v. *Smith* (1673), *Levinz's Reports* (1683–1704), vol. 2, p. 173. It is curious that Quincy does not describe this case in his notes, and specially marks it with an "X"! The question was whether a distribution following one's death should go equally to his full and half-brothers. An equal distribution was decided. Quincy did not list cases marked with an "X" in his index. See discussion at page [125], note 15, *infra*.

6. "*De bonis testatoris*" (i.e., "of a testator's goods") and "*de bonis propriis*" (i.e., "of a person's own goods"). An executor, if sued, as executor, is liable for the testator's goods in his control. A person sued as a private party is liable for his own goods. See Jowitt, *supra*, p. 570. There is an additional citation to *Hall* v. *Huffman* (1678), *Levinz's Reports* (covering 1683–1704), vol. 2, p. 228. See note 3, *supra*.

7. "Moiety" usually means "half," although occasionally it means another fractional part. See Jowitt, *supra*, p. 1184. There is another citation to *Gamon* v. *Vernon* (1678), *Levinz's Reports* (covering 1683–1704), vol. 2, p. 231. See note 3, *supra*.

8. "Jointly and severally" (i.e., "two or more people are each liable individually or together as a group"). "[A] creditor . . . may sue one or more severally, or all jointly, at his option." See Osborn, *A Concise Law Dictionary*, *supra*, p. 175.

9. This text is clearly taken from *Slingsby's Case* (1587), *Coke's Reports* (1572–1616), vol. 5, p. 18b. See page [1], note 2. Quincy's citation to 14a appears to be an error.

10. "Negative pregnant" "in pleading is where a person gives an evasive answer to an allegation . . . by answering it literally, without answering the substance of it." Jowitt, *supra*, p. 1215. For example, it is alleged that "A gave B 3 horses," and B answers "that he did not receive 3 horses." The substance of the allegation is that B received horses from A. B should either deny having received any horses, "or state how much he received." See *Id.*, p. 1215. There is another citation to *Pullin* v. *Nicholas* (1662), *Levinz's Reports* (covering 1683–1704), vol. 1, p. 83. See note 3, *supra*.

11. Another citation to *Genne* v. *Tinker* (1681), *Levinz's Reports* (covering 1683–1704), vol. 3, p. 24. See note 3, *supra*.

[107]

• Trover[1] for an Horse in an Inn-keeper's Hands 164
Denial to deliver no Evidence of Conversion
unless the Money was tender'd for the Horse's keeping.
2 Show. 161[2]

• If Money be deliver'd to one to keep generally without any Consideration or Reward for so doing, if the person be robbed he is discharged + the Owner shall bear the Loss. Contrary to Co. in 1 Inst. 89.a.
Ibid 172.[3]

• Trees in a Box in a Garden shall not pass by ye grant of ye Garden + all the Trees in it. 7 Mod. (edit 1713) p. 171. Oliviere v. Vernon[4]

• No Arrest without Touch. Ibid. p. 173. 1 Lill abr. 96.[5]

• When any thing is prohibited by Statute, ye party griev'd shall have an Action upon the Statute, tho' no Action by expressly given by it. 10 Rep. 75. b.
1 Mod. 233. 1 Inst. 159. a.[6]

• There is a Diversity between a Warrant of Record, + a Warrant or Authority in law, for if a Capias[7] be awarded to the Shff to arrest a Man for felony, albeit the party be innocent, yet cannot he make rescous.[8] But if a Shff will by Authority which the Law giveth him, ar- -rest any Man for felony who is not guilty, he may rescue himself. Co. :Litt. 161.a.[9]

• If 2 are bound jointly in a Bond + one of 'em only is sued he cannot plead non est factum,[10] if judgm^t shall be ag^t him + if both are sued + one appears + the other makes default + by process of law is outlawed he who appears shall be charged

Page [107]

1. For a discussion of "trover," see page [105], note 7.

2. A citation to *Anonymous* (1681), *Shower's Reports* (1678–1694), vol. 2, p. 161. See page [82], note 1.

3. A citation to *Coke on Littleton*, p. 89a, with a citation over to *Rex* v. *Viscount Hertford* (1681), *Shower's Reports* (1678–1694), vol. 2, p. 172. See page [2], note 1; page [7], note 9. See also note 2, *supra*. Coke's statement of the law was, as Quincy observed, to the contrary. "So it is if goods be delivered to a man to be safely kept, and after those goods are stolen from him, this shall not excuse him, because by the acceptance he undertooke to keepe them safely, and therefore he must keepe them at his perill." *Coke on Littleton*, *supra*, p. 89a. Coke's other examples, however, involve people who were paid for keeping goods safe, and he observed: "Note, Reader it is necessary for any one that receiveth goods to be kept . . . to be kept as his owne, or keepe them at the perill of the owner." *Id.*, p. 89b. Apparently, Coke believed you could "opt out" of the implied agreement to safeguard goods by explicitly agreeing to keep them "at the perill of the owner."

4. A citation to *Oliver* v. *Vernor*, *Modern Reports*, vol. 6, p. 170 at p. 171. See page [35], note 2. This is one of the few times Quincy identified the edition of a legal source book. Quincy usually cites to volume 6 of *Modern Reports* as volume 7. See page [97], notes 1, 3, 4, 5, 6, and 7.

5. A further citation to *Modern Reports*, vol. 6, p. 173. The case is *Genner* v. *Sparks* (1704). See note 4, *supra*. Also cited is *Lilly's Abridgment* (1719), vol. 1, p. 96. See page [48], note 3.

6. A series of citations, the first being to *The Case of the Marshalsea* (1613), *Coke's Reports* (1572–1616), vol. 10, p. 75b. Coke observed "[T]he party grieved shall have an action upon the statute . . . although the words of the Statute do not give any action to the party, but the same is a consequent, and a thing implied in everything forbidden by any statute." *Id.*, p. 75b. There is a further citation to *Lord Townsend* v. *Hughes* (1677), *Modern Reports*, vol. 1, p. 232 at p. 233. See note 4, *supra*. Finally there is a citation to *Coke on Littleton*, *supra*, p. 159a. The latter discusses statutory remedies where "no speciall writ is given by the statute." *Id.*, p. 159a.

7. For "*capias*," see page [106], note 1.

8. "Rescous" is from the Old French "rescosse" and means "release." See Jowitt, *supra*, p. 1535.

9. A further citation to *Coke on Littleton* (*First Institutes*) (1628), p. 161a. See note 3, *supra*. Quincy gives an almost exact paraphrase.

10. In other words, "it was not his deed." For "*non est factum*," see page [97], note 8.

[108]

165 with the whole Debt. But in the Case at Bar he might have pleaded in Abatement of the Writ.

5 Rep. 119. a.[1]

• Administration durante minore aetate[2] of an infant Exor ceases as soon as the Infant arrives at 17 years.

5 Rep. 29. Piggot's case[3]

• Yet an Adminon during the Minority of a residuary Legatee shall continue during his Legal Minority; ie, till full Age 21. Woods Inst. 350 cites

1 Ld Raym^{d} 668.[4]

• And if an infant Executrix before 17 taketh husband of full Age, the Adminon presently ceaseth. If an Infant is entitled to an Adminon of the Goods of an Intestate, Adminon shall be granted durante etc,[5] till he is full age, ie. 21. Wood's Inst. 350.[6]

• A husband shall be charg'd as Adminor to his Wife, by Reason of such part only of her Estate, as he did not reduce into possession during the Coverture.[7]

Ibid. p. 353 cites Ca. in Eq. temp. Ld Talbot 173[8] During the Coverture he is answerable for her Debts, tho' he has Nothing with her; + e contra, if he has rec^{d} a personal Estate with her, + happen not to be sued during the Coverture, he will be liable afterwards. Woods Inst. p 353 cites 1 W:^{ms} 469.[9]

• If a Lunatick hurt a Man he shall be answerable in Trespass. Hobart Rep. 134. W vs. Ward[10]

Page [108]

1. A citation to *Whelpdale's Case* (1604), *Coke's Reports* (1572–1616), vol. 5, p. 119a. Coke observed that "when two men are jointly bounden in an Obligation, although none of them be bound by himself, yet none can say, That the Obligation is not his deed, for he hath put his Seal to it and delivered it, and each of them is bounded in the whole." *Id.*, p. 119a. "But in the Case

at Barre, he might have pleaded in abatement of the Writ, but cannot plead, It is not his deed." *Id.*, p. 119a. In other words, as John Farquer Fraser notes in his annotations to the case, "If one only be sued he must plead the matter in abatement, and cannot take advantage of it afterwards upon any other plea. . . ." *Coke's Reports*, vol. 5, p. 119 (c), 243, note (A) (Thomas, Fraser, eds. London, 1826). My thanks to my learned colleague Charles Donahue Jr. For another citation to *Whelpdale's Case*, see page [97], note 11.

2. "*Durante minore aetate*," i.e., "during the minority." See Jowitt, *supra*, pp. 685, 876. "Exor" for "executor."

3. A citation to *Piggot's Case* (1598), *Coke's Reports* (1572–1616), vol. 5, p. 29a. See note 1, *supra.* Quincy accurately paraphrases the rule.

4. A citation to Wood's *Institute* (1754 edition), where this closely copied text appears on page 351 instead of 350. See page [7], note 3. A further citation to *Freke* v. *Thomas* (1701), *Lord Raymond's Reports* (1694–1732), vol. 1, p. 667 at p. 668. See page [26], note 2.

5. "Adminon" for "administration." "*Durante* tc." for "*durante minore aetate,*" as it appears in Wood's original. See note 2, *supra.*

6. A citation to Wood's *Institute* (1754 edition), p. 350. Quincy closely quotes this text from Wood. See note 4, *supra.*

7. "Coverture" (i.e., "the condition of a woman during marriage, or the fact of her being married"). See Jowitt, *supra*, p. 533. "Covert" comes from the Law French "feme covert," a woman "under protection" [of her husband]. *Id.*, p. 533.

8. A citation to Wood's *Institute* (1754 edition), p. 353. See note 4, *supra.* The cross-cite is to "Ca. Eq. temp Ld. Talbot. 173.," i.e., *Cases in Equity during the time of Chancellor Talbot* (1730–1737), p. 173, first published in London in 1741, with a second edition in 1753. See Sweet & Maxwell, *supra*, vol. 1, p. 345:11; Wallace, *supra*, pp. 506–09.

9. A citation to Wood's *Institute* (1720), p. 353. See note 4, *supra.* Quincy closely quotes this text from Wood. A citation over to W. Williams, *Jus Appellandi ad Regum ipsum a Cancellaria* (1683–1684), part 1, p. 469. See Sweet & Maxwell, vol. 1, p. 342.

10. A citation to *Weaver* v. *Ward* (1616), *Hobart's Reports* (covering 1603–1625), p. 134. See page [83], note 1. This proposition is compared to the rule that there is no felony "if a lunatick kill a man," because there was no felonious intent. The actual question of the case is whether a soldier is liable for assault and battery after an accidental discharge of his musket injures a fellow soldier, conjuring questions of negligence.

[109]

• If there be tennant in tail, the Remainder to his right heirs, he may grant his remainder over or devise it. 166

2 Rep. 61. a. Wiscot's case[1]

• A femme covert[2] y^{t} [that] hath power to sell Lands by Will, may sell the same to her Husband. Co Lit. 187. b. bot.[3]

X Question of Precedency between LD's Wife + the Wife of a Justice of peace argued. 2 Lev. 133.[4]

• If a Bond of 20 y.^{rs} standing, + no Demand proved thereon or good Cause of so long forebearance shewn, I shall intend it paid, a fortiori, upon a Note, if it be any con--siderable Value. L:^{d} Holt Ch. Just. 7 Mod. (Edit. 1713) vid Strange 826 Searle v. Ld B. (p. 22. Hothershell v. Bows Trials per Pais. 311.7 Edit. See 4 vol 182, cites 1 Vin. 373.[5]

X Care of public Bridges. Ibid 307.[6] In the same Case it was determin'd one of the County a good witness, tho' not a good juror.

• Case of Bail upon a joint + several Recognizance 1 Lev. 225.[7]

• Debt upon an Obligon. Dft. pleads an Accord with the plt + new Bond given plt demurs + Judg.^{nt} for him; for an Obligon given in Satisfaction of ano-ther Obligon is not any Discharge; even tho' an Excor gives the Obligon for the Debt of his Testa--tor. 3 Lev. 55. Lobly v. Gildart.[8]

• Trespass—the Dft. justifies by Virute of a Re--plevin[9] out of the Shff's C.^{t} + a precept thereupon to J.S. an Officer, + Dft came in Aid of the Officer. Plt replies that before the taking away of the Goods, he claim'd pro--perty in them, + gave Notice thereof to the Dft. Adjudg'd per tot. Cour. a trespasser ab initio.[10] 7 Mod. (E 1713) p 139. L v. S[11]

Page [109]

1. A citation to *Wiscot's Case* (1599), *Coke's Reports* (1572–1616), vol. 2, p. 61a. See page [1], note 2. This is an exact paraphrase of Coke.

2. "Femme covert," i.e., a married woman. See page [108], note 7.

3. An accurate citation to *Coke on Littleton*, p. 187b. See page [2], note 1; page [7], note 9. While a husband and wife are usually "one person in Law," and therefore unable to "give any estate or interest to the other," here, as Coke points out "they are but Instruments for others, and the estate passeth from the feoffee or devisee." *Id.*, p. 187b.

4. A citation to *Ashton* v. *Jennings* (1675), *Levinz's Reports* (1660–1696), vol. 2, p. 133. See page [76], note 2, *supra*. Cases marked with an "X" were not listed by Quincy in his index. See discussion at page [125], note 15.

5. This is a complex string citation. For Chief Justice Holt, see Quincy's extensive references to this particular judge at page [93], note 9; page [110], note 4 and note 7; page [111], note 3; and page [117], note 4. The citation is apparently to *Anonymous* (1703), *Modern Reports* (1669–1732; 1713 ed.), vol. 6, p. 22. See page [35], note 2. Quincy generally cites volume 6 as volume 7 of *Modern Reports*. See page [97], note 1. The citation to *Hothershell* v. *Bows* (1703), which appears in *Modern Reports*, vol. 6, p. 21, continuing to page 22, is clearly in error. It has nothing to do with the note other than being near the *Anonymous* case from which Quincy extracts the proposition. The following "*vid*" ("see") citation is to *Searle* v. *Lord Barrington* (1729), *Strange's Reports* (1716–1749), vol. 2, p. 826. See page [21], note 12. (This case involved an action upon a bond dated 1697, more than 20 years old.) The next citation is to *Trials Per Pais* (1665), (the 7th edition being 1725), p. 311. See page [49], note 2; page [50], note 5. The next citation appears to be to the fourth volume of Quincy's notebooks, page 182, the last entry of which reads "A contract shall be taken out of hand, or else it vanishes into nothing. 1 Vin: 373 cites as Holden 108.4.6." See page [94], note 6 for more about this section. Finally there is a citation here to *Viner's Abridgment*, vol. 1, p. 373. See page [16], note 2.

6. A citation to *Regina* v. *Inhabitants of the County of Wilts* (1704), *Modern Reports* (1669–1732), vol. 6, p. 307. See note 5, *supra*. Cases marked with an "X" were not listed by Quincy in his index. See discussion at page [125], note 15.

7. A citation to *Gee* v. *Fane* (1667), *Levinz's Reports* (1660–1696), vol. 1, p. 225. See page [76], note 2, *supra*.

8. A citation to *Lobly* v. *Gildart* (1682), *Levinz's Reports* (1660–1696), vol. 3, p. 55. See note 7, *supra*. See page [117], note 1 for another citation to this case.

9. "Replevin," "the remedy for a person whose chattels are unlawfully taken from him." "The replevisor [the person whose goods are taken] . . . obtains a replevy of the the goods by procuring . . . a warrant directing the high bailiff to cause the goods to be delivered to him . . . ," Osborn, *A Concise Law Dictionary*, *supra*, p. 276.

10. For "trespasser *ab initio*," see page [110], note 4.

11. A citation to "L.v.S.," *Leonard* v. *Stacy* (1704), *Modern Reports* (1669–1732; 1713 ed.), vol. 7, p. 139. See page [35], note 2.

[110]

167 order

• If a Man takes a Note, + after its [it is] payable makes no Demand, + that he might be paid if he had been diligent enough, there if the party, on whom the Note is, fails, it is at his peril who took the Note. 7 Mod. (E 1713) 147. + 8 Popley v.[1]

• Spitting in the face, a Battery. Ibid. 172.[2]

• Case upon mutual Promises of Marriage + Breach in the Man, the Dft. No Evidence of express promise on the Woman's Side. Adjudg'd good. Hutton v. Mansell. Ibid.[3]

• Landlord distrains Goods for Rent + among other things certain Barrels of Beer, + it appearing y^{t} [that] the ~~Dft~~ He drew Beer out of one of em, by Holt Ch. Jus. he is a Trespasser ab Initio as to that Barrel only.
Ibid 215 + 216 Dod v. Monger.[4]

• Bond may be gived to save harmless ag.^{t} past Escapes, but not ag.^{t} future, + to save harmess ag^{t} a penalty already incur'd by Law. Ibid. 225. Fox v. Tilly.[5]

• If there be 2 partners in trade + one of them buy goods for both + the other dieth, the Survivor may be charg'd generally in indeb. Ass.[6] without taking, Notice of the partnership + survivor. Said by Holt.[7] Cumberb 383.[8]

• If a Conveyance be made by fraud + afterwards the Land is conveyd over upon a valuable Consideration the fraud is purged. Ibid. 222. Porter v. Clinton[9]

• Trover ag.^{t} 2 [two] one pleads non cul.[10] t'other a release of Actions the first Issue found for the Plt, the other for the Dft + Judm^{t} quod querens nil capiat per Billam. Ibid 310.[11]

Page [110]

1. A citation to *Popley* v. *Ashley* (1704), *Modern Reports* (1669–1732; 1713 ed.), vol. 6, pp. 147–48. See page [35], note 2. This is the first of five citations to what Quincy cites as 7 *Modern Reports*, though they are actually found in *Modern Reports*, vol. 6. He routinely makes this substitution, for an unknown reason. See page [97], note 1. Following these citations to *Modern Reports* are three citations to *Comberbach's Reports*. Quincy seems to be reading through these reports, and noting interesting cases. Quincy added the word "order" above "Note," probably to indicate that the same rule would apply for a bill (order to pay) as a promissory note. My thanks to my learned colleague James Rogers.

2. A citation to *Regina* v. *Cotesworth* (1704), *Modern Reports* (1669–1732; 1713 ed.), vol. 6, p. 172. See note 1, *supra*.

3. A citation to *Hutton* v. *Mansell* (1704), *Modern Reports* (1669–1732; 1713 ed.), vol. 6, p. 172, immediately following *Regina* v. *Cotesworth*. See notes 1 and 2, *supra*.

4. For Chief Justice Holt, see page 117, note 4. Quincy mentions Holt more than any other judge. See the discussion in the "Introduction," *supra*. The citation is to *Dod* v. *Monger*, *Modern Reports* (1669–1732; 1713 ed.), vol. 6, p. 215 at p. 216. "Trespass ab initio" (i.e., "from the beginning") is a term of art. "If a person authorized by law to enter upon the land [or beer barrels!] of another, after entry Commits a positive act of misfeasance which amounts to a trespass, he becomes a trespass *ab initio*, that is to say, from the beginning, and everything done by him in purported exercise of such authority become wrongful . . ." Jowitt, *supra*, pp. 2–3.

5. A citation to *Fox* v. *Tilly*, *Modern Reports* (1669–1732; 1713 ed.), vol. 6, p. 225. See note 1, *supra*.

6. "Indeb. ass." for "*indebitatus assumpsit*." See page [96], note 9.

7. For Chief Justice Holt, see note 4, *supra*. See also page [93], note 9, and page [117], note 4.

8. A citation to *Hyat* v. *Hare* (1696), *Comberbach's Reports* (1685–1698), p. 383. See page [37], note 2.

9. A citation to *Porter* v. *Clinton* (1693), *Comberbach's Reports* (1685–1698), p. 222. See note 8, *supra*. "Consideration" is another legal term of art meaning "an act or promise by which some right, interest, profit or benefit accrues to one part, or by which some forebearance, detriment . . . is given, suffered, or undertaken by the other . . ." Jowitt, *supra*, pp. 456–57. It is most commonly encountered as a requirement for enforceability of a contract not under seal, the person seeking to enforce the contract having given "consideration" for it.

10. "Non cul." is for "*non culpabilis*," i.e., "not guilty," usually a criminal plea. "Issue was joined on the plea by the abbreviation *prit.*, i.e., *paratus*, ready to prove . . . eventually the officer of the court began to apply the abbreviations to the accused, 'culprit, how wilt thou be tried?'." Jowitt, *supra*, p. 1232.

11. "Judmt Quod Querens nil capiat per Billam" for "judgment *quod querens nil capiat per billam*," i.e., judgment for the defendant because the plaintiff ("querens") could not succeed by the writ ("*per billam*"). Citation is to *Kiffin's Case* (1695), *Comberbach's Reports* (covering 1685–1698), p. 310. See note 8, *supra*.

[111]

• Debt upon Bond for performance of an Award. Ob- 168
-jected that one of the parties to the Submission was an Infant, so no Submission + therefore no Award. But the C.^{t} held that ye Guardian of an Infant may submit for him + bind himself to perform the award. Ibid. 318. Roberts v. N[1]

• The Attorney gen. cannot ex Officiis[2] enter a non pros:[3] without a warrant for that purpose from the Crown. Ibid. 325.[4]

• Holt[5] said upon fieri facias[6] ye shff may take any thing but wearing apparel, nay if the party hath two Gowns he may take one of 'em. Ibid 356.[7]

• If a Man names himself Excor or Adminor + it appears y^{t} [that] ye Cause of Action is in his own Name; it is well enough + he calling himself Excor is but Surplusage. 1 Ventris 119.[8]

• Where a Covenant is broken by an Excor, yet the Judgm^{t} must be ag.^{t} him de Bonis Testatoris.[9]
2 Lill ab. 116. cites 2 Saund. 118.[10]

• Excon may be sued out after the Death of the Dft.
Comyns 117.118[11]

• Dft indicted by the Name of Eliza Newman alias Judith Hancock + quash'd because a Woman cannot have two Christian Names.
1 Ld Raym.^{d} 562.[12]

Page [111]

1. A citation to *Roberts* v. *Newbold* (1695), *Comberbach's Reports* (1685–1698), p. 318. See page [37], note 2. This is the fourth of six consecutive citations to *Comberbach's Reports*, beginning at

page [110]. See page [110], note 8. The subjects are completely diverse, suggesting that Quincy is reading through the reports and making notes, as he apparently did with *Modern Reports*, vol. 6, which he recorded as *Modern Reports*, vol. 7. See page [110], note 1. The pages in *Comberbach* are usually successive, so Quincy was usually reading from beginning to end, but there are exceptions. See page [110], note 8. Most of the opinions in *Comberbach* are brief and succinctly stated, making it easier for Quincy to record quick notes of their facts and holdings.

2. "*Ex officiis*," by "virtue of his office." See P. G. Osborn, *A Concise Law Dictionary*, *supra*, p. 128.

3. "*Non pros*" for "*non prosequitur*," i.e., "He does not follow up." "Judgment *non pros* was [generally] available for the defendant in an action when the plaintiff failed to take the proper steps within the prescribed time." *Id.*, p. 223.

4. A citation to *Lampton* v. *Collingwood* (1695), *Comberbach's Reports* (1685–1698), p. 325. See note 1, *supra*. It is also another holding by Chief Justice Holt.

5. For Chief Justice Holt, an apparent favorite authority for Quincy, see page [93], note 8; page [110], note 4 and note 7; and page [117], note 4.

6. For "*fieri facias*," see page [125], note 1.

7. A citation to *Hardistey* v. *Barney* (1696), *Comberbach's Reports* (1685–1698), p. 356. See note 1, *supra*. Curiously, Quincy substitutes "apparel" for "clothes." For a relevant Massachusetts case reported by Quincy, see *Hanlon* v. *Thayer* (1764), *Reports*, p. 99.

8. A citation to *Hornsey* v. *Dimocke* (1671), *Ventris' Reports* (1668–1684), vol. 1, p. 119. See page [89], note 7. "Excor" is for "executor" and "adminor" for "administrator," usual Quincy abbreviations. See page [103], note 3.

9. "*De Bonis Testatoris*" (i.e., "of a testator's goods"). The testator's goods would be liable if an executor broke a covenant.

10. A citation to *Lilly's Abridgment*, vol. 2, p. 116. See page [48], note 3. There was a further citation which appears to be to Sir E. Saunders, *Les Reports des Divers Pleadings et Cases en le Court del Bank le Roy* . . . (covering 1660–1685). These were first published in London in 1686 in 2 volumes. A second edition, translated into English, followed in 1722. See Sweet & Maxwell, *supra*, vol. 1, p. 308:112; Wallace, *supra*, pp. 338–43. This citation appears to be to *Saunder's Reports* (1660–1685; 2nd ed. 1722), vol. 2, p. 118, but the case reported there, *Chandler* v. *Vilett* (1670), does not seem to be on point.

11. A citation to *Parsons* v. *Gill* (1701), *Comyn's Reports* (covering 1695–1741) at pp. 117–18. See page [32], note 1.

12. "Quash" (i.e., "to discharge or set aside"), Osborn, *A Concise Law Dictionary*, *supra*, p. 262. The citation is to *Rex* v. *Newman* (1700), *Lord Raymond's Reports* (1694–1732), vol. 1, p. 562. See page 26, note 2. Quincy substituted "Eliza" for "Elizabeth." The indictment was for "keeping a bawdy house."

[112]

169 • A Writ of Error cannot be amended being for a Reversal of Judgm^{t}: Ld Raym^{d} 564 + 5[1]

• Original writs are [a]mendable. Ibid. cites 8 Co. 156.[2]

• Where a man does such an Act, as cannot be good by any other Means but by Virtue of his Authority, it shall be intended to be an Excon of his Authority; but where a Man has an Interest and Authority, + does an Act without reciting his Authority, it shall be be intended to be done by Virtue of his Interest.
1 Ld Raym:^{d} 660 cites 6 Co. 17.[3]

• When any has Authority, as Attorney, to do any Act, he ought to do it in his Name who gives the Authority; for he appoints the Attorney to be so in his place, + to represent his person; + therefore the Att:^{y} can't do it in his own Name, nor as his Act, but in the Name, + as the Act of him who gives the Authority. 9 Rep. 76. b. bottom.[4]

• It was s.^{d} by Hale + not denied y^{t} [that] if A die having Goods in several Provinces of York + Canterbury several Admnons must be com--mitted: So it is of Goods in Eng.^{d} + Ireland. 2 Lev. 86 Shaw vs. S.[5]

• Rent may be reserv'd by the Ancestor to ye Heir, without reserving it to himself, y^{o} [though] a Warrantry or Obligon can--not bind the Heir, which does not first bind ye Ancestor, but then in such reservation, it must be reserv'd to him by the Name of heir.
Hobart 130. Oates + Frith[6]

Page [112]

1. A "writ of error" was the general appellate remedy for error of the face of the record. See Baker, *An Introduction to English Legal History* (4th ed.), *supra*, pp. 136–38. The citation is to

Tomkin v. *Croker* (1700), *Lord Raymond's Reports* (1694–1732), vol. 1, pp. 564–65. See page [26], note 2.

2. This is a further citation to *Tomkin* v. *Croker* (1700), *Lord Raymond's Reports* (1694–1732), vol. 1, pp. 564–65. See note 1, *supra*. The cross-cite is to *Blackamore's Case* (1610), *Coke's Reports* (1572–1616), vol. 8, p. 156a, which supports the proposition. See page [1], note 2.

3. "Excon" for "execution." A further citation to *Parker* v. *Kett* (1701), *Lord Raymond's Reports* (1694–1732), p. 658 at p. 660, from which Quincy closely copies this text, with an apparent cross-cite to *Clere's Case* (1599), 6 *Coke's Reports* (1572–1616), p. 17b, *supra*, note 2.

4. A citation to *Combes's Case* (1612), *Coke's Reports* (1572–1616), vol. 9, p. 75a at p. 76b. Quincy paraphrases Coke exactly. The cross-citation to Coke in notes 2 and 3 above may never have been examined by Quincy, as he was relying on *Lord Raymond's Reports*. Quincy rarely omitted foliation citations to *Coke's Reports* when they were his primary authority.

5. A citation to *Shaw* v. *Stoughton* (1673), *Levinz's Reports* (1668–1684), vol. 2, p. 86. See page [76], note 2, *supra*. Quincy frequently cited Chief Justice Holt by name. See pages [109], note 5; [110], note 4 and note 7; [111], note 5; and [117], note 4. Here he cited by name to another great common lawyer, Sir Matthew Hale (1609–1676), who was Chief Justice of the King's Bench from 1671–1676. Hale's great *History of the Common Law* was published in 1713, and his *Pleas of the Crown* (1682), republished in 1685, 1694, 1716, and 1759, was in Quincy's library. See Estate Catalogue, No. 116. See Sweet & Maxwell, *supra*, vol. 1, p. 239:17 and p. 362:35, 36.

6. A citation to *Oates* v. *Frith* (1614), *Hobart's Reports* (covering 1603–1625), p. 130. See page [83], note 1.

[113]

Hawkins' Abr. 301. contra[1] 170

vide etiam 5 Rep. 111.[2]

• A Gift in Tail may be made upon Condon, That Tenant in tail may alien for the Profit of his Issues, + y^t [that] hath been holden to be good_It must be for the profit of the Issues. 1 Inst. 224. b. Perk. 728[3]

• Tho' upon Evidence another Time or place may be given in Evidence, yet upon the face of y^e Declaration the plt ought to make himself a good Title to the Action 1 Ld Raym^d 576 G. v. J.[4]

• A Claim within View reduces a freehold in Law to an actual Possession. Hawkins Abr. 342. 1 Inst. 254. b.[5]

•Same Judge sits on the same Cause at 2 different Courts 2 Lev. 244[6]

• Indeb. assum.[7] vs. A + B. Judgm^t v. A by Default, B pleaded payment + Issue thereupon. And so Holt[8] no finding upon ye Issue can discharge A, for he has confess'd ye whole. 1 Salk 23.d[8]

• Deliver'd as an Escrow may given in Evid. on <u>non est factum</u>[9] vid 2 Mod. Ent. 298. pl. 9. 7 Mod. (Edit 1713) 218 B. v. P.[10]

• Its s^d by Coke, a Rent service[11] cannot be suspended in part by ye Act of ye party, + in esse for other part. 1 Inst. 148. b top.[12] Twisden says, this is s.^d without any Reason or Authority. H vs. T. 2 Lev. 143.[13]

• A Man may submit for another's Debt, but y^n[14] it must be specially mentioned in ye Submission. 2 Showers. 61[15]

Page [113]

1. A "*contra*" (opposing) citation to Hawkins, *Abridgment*, 301. See page [68], note 6. Here Quincy noted a conflict in authority, further evidence that he was reading critically.

2. A "*vide etiam*" ("see also") citation to *Mallory's Case* (1601), *Coke's Reports* (1572–1616), vol. 5, p. 111a. See page [1], note 2. The citation is on point.

3. A citation to *Coke on Littleton*, p. 224b. See page [2], note 1; page [7], note 9. Quincy extracted Coke's observation accurately, leaving out the references to the Statute 46 Edward 3, 4 (1373). See *Id.*, p. 224b. There is a further citation to John Perkins, *A Profitable Book* (1528), p. 728, translated from Law French to English in 1555 and reprinted many times from 1555 to 1757. See Sweet & Maxwell, *supra*, vol. 1, pp. 485:56–58. The citation is to *Perkins's* section 728, which is on page 275 of the 1657 edition, and is on point.

4. A citation to "*G* v. *J.*," *Garret* v. *Johnson* (1700), *Lord Raymond's Reports* (1694–1732), vol. 1, p. 576. See page [26], note 2. Quincy exactly quotes one of the case's final lines.

5. A citation to Hawkins, *Abridgment* (1711), p. 342. See note 1, *supra*. A further citation is *Coke on Littleton*, p. 254b. See note 3, *supra*. Coke observed "[B]ut where the claime is not to Devest any estate, but to bring him who maketh it into actual possession, there a claime within the view sufficeth . . ." *Id.*, p. 254b. "Claim within view" refers to the old writ of view, "which provided that all things which used to be done upon the writ could be done upon a rule or order to view." Jowitt, *supra*, p. 1838.

6. A citation to *Strode* v. *Berager* (1679), *Levinz's Reports* (1668–1684), vol. 2, pp. 243–44. See page [93], note 7. Quincy comments on an interesting, though not central, aspect of this case, focusing on its language: "Scroggs, Chief Justice, continued his former opinion, saying, he was never satisfied with the first judgment [in the Communi Banco, where he dissented], and that the judgment ought to be reversed." It eventually was reversed. The English procedure of "arrest of judgement" permitted the judge below to participate in the review of the decision, in theory because judgement had not been officially entered. See Baker, *supra*, pp. 138–40.

7. For "*indebitatus assumpsit*," see page [96], note 9.

8. For Quincy's many references by name to Chief Justice Holt, a clear favorite, see page 93, note 8; page [109], note 5; page [110], note 4, and note 7; page [111], note 5; and page [117], note 4.

9. "Escrow," "a writing sealed and delievered . . . [to a nonparty] to be held by him until certain conditions to be performed . . ." Osborn, *A Concise Law Dictionary*, *supra*, p. 125. For "*non est factum*," see page [97], note 8. "Vid." ("see") citation is to [J. Mallory] *Modern Entries* (1734–1735), vol. 2, p. 298 pl. 9. See page [70], note 3.

10. A citation to "*B.* v. *P.*," *Bushell* v. *Pasmore* (1704), *Modern Reports*, vol. 6, p. 217 at p. 218. See page [35], note 2; page [96], note 4. Quincy regularly cited to volume 6 of *Modern Reports* as volume 7. This quote is yet another from Chief Justice Holt.

11. "Rent service" is a rent incident to tenure. "[I]t is that which is due when one man holds land of another by fealty (or any other service) and rent . . . or where an owner of land leases it to another for 99 years at a yearly rent." Jowitt, *supra*, p. 1522.

12. A citation is to *Coke on Littleton*, p. 148b. See note 3, *supra*. The statement by Coke, at the top of the page 148b as Quincy indicates, is accurately paraphrased. (The "top" and "bottom" marks certainly indicate that Quincy actually looked up these citations!) "In esse" (i.e., "existing"), as distinguished from *in posse* ("that which is not, but may be"). "A child before birth is *in posse*; after birth, *in esse*." Jowitt, *supra*, p. 947.

13. A citation to "*H.* v. *T.*," *Hodgson* v. *Thornborough* (1675), *Levinz's Reports* (1660–1696), vol. 2, p. 143. See note 6, *supra*. "S.^{d}" is for "suspended." Here, again, Quincy showed a critical approach to the law, identifying conflicting precedents.

14. "y^{n}" for "then."

15. A citation to *Adams* v. *Staley* (1679), *Shower's Reports* (1678–1694), vol. 2, p. 61. See page [82], note 1. Quincy copies this line almost exactly.

[114]

171 An arrest by Night, as well as Day, lawfull. 9 Rep. 66.[1]
If 3 joint Tenants be disseised,[2] + they arraign an Assise[3] and one of them release to the Disseisor[4] all Actions personal, this shall bar Him, but it shall not bar the other Plts, for having regard to them the Realty shall be prefer'd, + Omne maius trahit ad se Minus. 1 Inst. 285.a.[5]

It is regularly true, that when [one] does less than He commanded or authorised, there the act is void; because the Command or Authority was not pursued. But where One doth that which he is Authorised to do, + more, it is good for that which was warranted, + void for the rest. Wood B1. 66. p 58 cites 1 Inst. 258. a and 8 Rep. 85.[6] Agreeable to that Maxim, Quando plus fit etc Vid. Vol 3. p. 172.[7]

Note that when an Ideot doth Sue or Defend,
vid He shall not appear by Guardian, Prochein amy,[8] or
Haw Attorney, but He must be ever in Person, but An
abr Infant or Minor shall sue by Prochein Amy +
208[9] Defend by Guardian. 1 Inst. 135. b.[10]

Generally, whatsoever an Infant[11] is bound to do by Law, this same shall bind Him, albeit He doth it without Suit of Law. Ibid. 172. a.[12]

An infant may bind himself in a single

Page [114]

1. A citation to *Mackalley's Case, In Killing of the Serjeant of London* (1612), *Coke's Reports* (1572–1616), vol. 9, pp. 65b, 66a. See page [1], note 2. Quincy stated the holding accurately.

2. For "*disseisin*," see page [99], note 4.

3. "Arraign an assise," i.e., to call "to account" before an assise court—the courts held by the justice of assise in their regular visits to each country. See Jowitt, *supra*, p. 167.

4. "Disseisor," one who "disseises" (i.e., "dispossess, deprives"). See page [99], note 4. See also Jowitt, *supra*, p. 643.

5. "*Omne maius trahit ad se minus*" (i.e., "The greater whole drags the lesser to itself . . ." See Jowitt, *supra*, p. 1266). A citation to *Coke on Littleton*, p. 285a. See page [2], note 1; page [7], note 9. Quincy accurately paraphrased Coke, but left the "*dignum*" out of the Latin quotation. *Id.*, p. 285a.

6. A citation to Wood's *Institute* (1754 edition), Book 1, where this closely copied text appears on page 59 instead of 66. See page 7, note 3. This cited further to *Coke on Littleton*, p. 258a. See note 5, *supra*. Quincy's note was an accurate paraphrase of Coke, but omitted Coke's warning that "both these rules have divers exceptions and limitations." *Id.*, p. 258a. There was also a citation to *Sir Richard Pexhall's Case* (1610), *Coke's Reports* (1572–1616), vol. 8, p. 83b. See page 1, note 2. "Then in the case at barr . . . Sir Richard had not power to charge but 2 parts; yet when he chargeth the Whole, he chargeth 2 parts and more, and therefore it shall be good, for so much as the Statute doth enable him, and void for the residue, *Quia Quando plus Fit Quam fieri debet, videtur etiam ipsum fieri Quid faciendum est* . . ." *Id.*, p. 85a. See note 7, *infra.*

7. "*Quando plus Fit* etc" referring to "*Quando plus Fit Quam fieri debet, videtur etiam illud fieri Quid faciendum est*" ("when more is done than ought to be done, then that is considered to have been done which ought to have been done.") Jowitt, *supra*, p. 1452. See *Sir Richard Pexhall's Case*, *Coke's Reports*, vol. 8, at p. 85b, note 6, *supra*. See also *Wade's Case* (1601), *Coke's Reports*, vol. 5, note 6, *supra*, at p. 115a. Volume 3 of Quincy's notebooks, referenced here, features a list of Latin maxims on pages 161 to 163 and 171 to 183, included as Appendix III in this volume.

8. "Prochein amy," Law French for the "next friend or next of kin to a child in his nonage, who in that respect was allowed to deal for the infant in the management of his affairs." Jowitt, *supra*, p. 1418. A "guardian" is appointed by the court to take care of an infant, or anyone "incapable of acting for his own interest." Guardians are always appointed when such a person is sued. *Id.*, pp. 883–84.

9. A "vid" ("see") citation to Hawkins, *Abridgment*, p. 208, where Hawkins comments on page 135b of Coke. See page [8], note 1.

10. A citation to *Coke on Littleton*, p. 135b. See note 5, *supra*. Coke observed that: "[A]n Infant or a Minor shall sue by Procheine Amy, and defend by Gardeine . . ." *Id.*, p. 135b. See note 8, *supra*.

11. "Infant," i.e., "a person under twenty-one years of age." See Jowitt, *supra*, p. 964.

12. A citation to *Coke on Littleton*, p. 172a. See note 5, *supra*. Coke observed "[G]enerally whatsoever an Infant is bound to doe by Law, the same shall bind him, albeit he doth it without suit of Law. But of this common learning this little [taste] shall suffice." *Id.*, p. 172a. Thus an infant who was an executor must issue an acquittance for a debt owed to the testator if the debt is actually paid, because the executor is bound to do so by law—even if the minor could not be sued directly, but only through a guardian. On the other hand, an infant executor cannot exercise discretion to release a debt to the estate, and any release issued by the minor is void. The infant cannot be bound because the release was not required by law. This was Coke's example. See *Id.*, p. 172a.

[115]

Bill to pay for Necessaries, but a Bond with a Penalty, for the payment of such Debt is not good. Haw Abr. 258.[1] 172

There is a Diversity when the condition is for Paym[t] of Money; and when for Delivery of a Horse, Robe etc. For where it is for Paym[t] of Money, there if the Feoffee or, Obligee accept an Horse etc. in Satisfaction, This is Good—But if the Condition were for the Delivery of a Horse, Robe etc., there albeit the Obligee or Feoffee accept money or any other thing for the Horse etc., it is NO Performance of the Condition. The like law is, if the Condition be to acknowledge a Recognizance of £20. etc. If the Obligee or Feoffee accepts 20£ in Satisfaction of the Condition it is Not Sufficient in LAW, but not-withstanding such Acceptance, the Condition is broken. And so it is of all other Conditions collateral, tho' the Obligee or Feoffee himself accept it.

Secondly, in the Case when the Cond[tt]on is for Paym[t] of Money, there is a Diversity, when the Money is to be paid to the Party + when to an Estranger[2] for, when it is to be to an Estranger, there if the Estranger accept an Horse or any col-lateral Thing, it is NO Performance of

Page [115]

1. A citation to Hawkins's, *Abridgment*, p. 258. See page [8], note 1. Quincy closely paraphrases Hawkins' text.

2. "Estranger" for "stranger."

[116]

173 the Condttion, because the Condttion in that Case is strictly to be perform'd. But if the Condttion be, that a Stranger shall pay to the Obligor or Feoffor a Sum of Money, there the Obligee or Feoffee may receive a Horse in Satisfaction.

Thirdly, where the Condon[1] is for Paym.t of 20£, the Obligor or Feoffor cannot at the Day appointed pay a lesser Sum in Satisfaction of the whole, because it is apparent that a lesser Sum of Money cannot be a Satisfaction of a greater. But if the Obligee or Feoffee do at the Day receive part, + thereof make an Acquitance under his Seal in full Satisfaction of the Whole, it is Sufficient, by Reason the Deed amount'd to a Acquittance of the Whole. If the Obligor or Lessor pay a lesser Sum before the Day, or at another Place, than is limit'd by the Condttion + the Obligee or of Feoffee re--ceiveth it, This is a Good Satisfaction.

Fourthly, Not only Things in Possession may be given in Satisfaction, but also if the Feoffee or Obligee accept a Statute or a Bond in Satisfaction of the Money, it is a Good Satisfaction. (Qu. vid Mod. Cases in Law

Page [116]

1. "Condon" for "condition."

[117]

+ Equity. p 290. 2 Strang 426. 3 Lev 55)[1] 174

If the Obligor or Feoffor be bound by Condttion to pay 100£ at a certain Day + at the Day the Parties do Account together, + for that the Feoffee or Obligee did owe 20£ to the Obligor or Feoffor that Sum is allow'd + the Residue of the 100£ paid, this is a Good Satisfaction, + yet the 20£ was a Chose in Action[2] + no paymt was made thereof, but by Way of Retainer or Discharge. Co Lit. 212. b. 213. a.

vid Haw. Abr. 299. 300.[3]

Holt[4] If a Bailiff find an outward Door open, He may break all the inner to come at the Party, whom He hath a Warrant to arrest. 12 Mod. Rep. 73.[5]

xvid. p. 156 Trover brot.[6] Where Wife has but a bare Possession, as if She find Goods, or they be bail'd to Her, or She be Exttix to a Bailee, + marry, Detinuex must be brôt ag.t H + Wife. Haw. Abr. 448.[7] For this bare possession is not given to the Husband: And this is a Diversity, worthy of Observation, between a Property in personal Goods + a bare Possession. Co. Lit. 351. b.[8]

Page [117]

1. A citation to *Modern Cases in Law and Equity*, p. 290, otherwise known as 8 and 9 *Modern Reports* (covering 1669–1732), the 1712–1726 period. See page [35], note 2 and page [96], note 4. The case is *Springett* v. *Chadwick* (1729). A further citation to *Cumber* v. *Wane* (1721), *Strange's Reports* (1716–1749), vol. 1, p. 426. (Wrongly cited by Quincy as "2 Strange.") This case held that a promissory note for £5 could not extinguish a debt of £15. "Even the actual payment of £5 would not do, because it is a less sum . . . Much less shall a note payable at a future day." *Id.*, p. 426. A further citation is given to *Lobly* v. *Gildart* (1682), *Levinz's Reports* (covering 1660–1696), vol. 3, p. 55. See page [93], note 7. Also see page [109], note 8 for an earlier citation to this case. This is another example of Quincy's careful, and critical, analysis of the legal rules he recorded.

2. "Chose in Action" (i.e., "a right of proceeding in a court of law to procure the payment of a sum of money . . . or to recover pecuniary damages . . ."). See Jowitt, *supra*, p. 367.

3. A citation to *Coke on Littleton*, pp. 212b–213a. Quincy has the example in Coke wrong. In Coke the debt owed is "an hundred Markes" and the account is for "twentie pound," different

currencies. *Id.*, pp. 212b–213a. This could distinguish the resolution from simply accepting a lesser sum for a greater sum of the same currency. A further citation is given to Hawkins's *Abridgment*, pp. 299–300. See page [8], note 1.

4. A reference to Sir John Holt (1642–1710), Chief Justice of the King's Bench from 1689–1710. There is a change in the script here, but it appears to be still Quincy, perhaps with a new pen nib. Holt issued the judgment for the case noted in the adjoining text. See, *supra*, note 5.

5. A citation to *Anonymous* (1695), *Modern Reports* (1667–1732), vol. 12, p. 73. See page [35], note 2. Excluding notes, the line that Quincy copied is essentially the entire case.

6. A cross-reference to Quincy's page 156 [99], which discusses when detinue should be brought against a husband and wife. Quincy's page 156 also cross-referenced this page.

7. A citation to Hawkins's *Abridgment*, p. 448. See note 2, *supra*.

8. A citation to *Coke on Littleton*, p. 351b. See note 3, *supra*. Quincy's note is a complete reformulation of the passage in Coke, but it parapahrases Coke's conclusions accurately. Quincy also cites to *Coke on Littleton*, p. 351b for essentially the same point on page 17 [22] under Bailment.

[118]

175 A. Page

Account
Case brôt y^{t} [that] ye Dft promis'd to render Acc:^{t} + had not. Abate:^{nt} 162.

Accord.—New Bond pleaded by Way of Accord—Bad Plea. 166.

Action.—B may have an Action ag^{t} One, who excites A to sue B. 162

• commences from ye Teste[1] of ye Writ 162
• cannot be vs. Execors + al. 163
• shall be, for one griev'd by any thing prohibited by Statute, tho' Action not expressly given. 164
• brôt vs. one only—Motion in ar- -rest of Judgm.^{t} y^{t} [that] 2 were bound—overul'd. 153.

Admnor. Admnix Excors[2] etc. vid p. 38
• chargeable as Assignee, for the Time. Land is in Posson+enjoy'd. 158.

• Bona notabilia in 2 Provinces[3] admon in both. 169
• What funeral Expenses Admnor shall be allow'd vs. Creditor 159.
• Value on Appraisement shall not prejudice or advantage an Excor or Admnor+when it shall. 161.
• 2 Excor sued, plead severally pl. ad.[4] Different Verdicts found; how the Judg.^{t} was given. 161.

A Page

same continued
• Land devis'd for paym:^{nt} of Debts, personal estate left shall not pay. 161
• Admnon durante minore aetate[5] of an Excor + residuary Legatee when they respectively cease. 165.
• Infant Exex[6] taketh Husband of full Age, Admon presently ceaseth. Also an Infant institut'd to Admnon, how it shall be granted. 165.
• Husband Admnor on Wife's Estate what he shall be charg'd with. 165.
• Case of an Adminon Bond. 149.
covenant broken by an Excor,[7] Judgm.^{t} must be ag.^{t} him de bonis Testatoris.[8] 168.

Appraisement.—Value on appraisem.^{t} not material. Value found by a Jury on pl. ad.[9] binding 161

Arrest
• cannot be without Touch. 164.

• Motion in arrest of Judg:^{mt} an Obligon[10] seal'd by 2 jointly action brôt vs. One only overul'd. 153.
• for felony, party being guilty or not guilty. The Difference 164
In the Night, lawfull 171

Assignor+Assignee.
chargeable while in Posson.[11] 158

[All pages cited in Quincy's index are to Quincy's own page numbers, the large bold-faced numbers at the top of each page.]

Page [118]

1. "Teste," i.e., "the concluding part of a writ, giving the date and place of its issue. It is so called because it begins with the words 'witness myself' (*teste meipso*) . . ." Jowitt, *supra*, p. 1743. Before the Judicature Acts of 1873–1875, most writs were "tested in the name of the Lord Chancellor, if issuing from the Court of Chancery, or of the Lord Chief Justice, if issuing from the Queen's Bench . . ." *Id.*, p. 1743.

2. "Admnor. Admnix. Excor.," i.e., "administrator, administratrix, executor."

3. "Bona notabilia in 2 Provinces." Before 1857 wills were proved in England "before the bishop of the diocese in which the property of the deceased was located." Jowitt, *supra*, p. 260. "[I]f the deceased had *bona notabilia*, or chattels to the value of £5 in two or more distinct dioceses, then the will was proved before the metropolitan of the province comprising the dioceses, or, if the dioceses were comprised partly in one province and partly in the other, then before the metropolitan of each province." *Id.*, p. 260. In Quincy's words, "admon." or "administrator" "in both." "*Bona notabilia*" itself refers to "goods situated in another diocese to that in which a deceased had died." Osborn, *A Concise Law Dictionary*, *supra*, p. 53.

4. "pl. ad." for "*plene administratvit.*" See page [104], note 1.

5. "Admon *durante minore estate*," i.e., "administration *durante minore aetate.*" See page [108], note 2.

6. "Infant exex," i.e., an executor under twenty-one years old. See page [114], notes 11, 12.

7. "Exor" for "executor." See note 2, *supra.*

8. "*De bonis Testatoris.*" See page [111], note 9.

9. "Pl. ad." for "*plene administratvit.*" See note 4, *supra*, and page [104], note 1.

10. "Obligon" for "obligation."

11. "Posson" for "possession."

[119]

176

A.B.	Page
Same continued	
Lessee assigns the Moiety[1] of ye Land, for ye whole Term—Lessor may have an Action vs. the assignee for a Moiety of ye Rent.	163
Assumpsit[2] vid Partners etc.	
• A assumes to B to pay money to C. C may an Action.	158.
• Promise of Marriage made by ye man, not by feme—[3]yet good	167
• Assum vs 2. 1 defaulted. Issue found for ye other.	170
Authority—Diversity between that of record + yt [that] in Law.	164
Award.—good to release all Actions to a Time after Submission—Unless etc.	150

B.	Page
Bailment, Bailor + Bailee. Bailee robb'd, Bailor shall bear the Loss, in Case—	164
Case of Bail upon a joint + sev Recognizance	166
Bailiff finds the outward Door open, may break ye inner.	174

B.	Page
Baron + Feme[4] vid p. 20[5]	
• Promise to a feme covert, in conson she[6] wd cure a wound, wd survive to her.	152
• Feme covert[7] finds Goods etc. Action may be brot vs. H + W, but Conversion alledg'd in him ye Husband	156
• A feme sole marrying revokes a submisnon enter'd into while sole.—With a Quare.[8]	156
• Bargain + sale of a feme covert not good.	156
• Baron of full age may make an Attorney for feme under age.	158
• Marriage a revocation of a will made dum Sola[9]	157
• Feme indicted by the name of EN alias JH. quash'd.[10]	168
• Assupsit vs. 2. 1 defaulted, Issue for ye other.	170
• Husband liable for Debts of ye Wife after her Death.	165
Bare Possession of W not given to ye H. & Detinue[11] brot vs. H & W.	174
Battery. Spitting in the face is Battery.	167

B.

Page [119]

1. "Moiety" (i.e., "half"). "The word is, however, occasionally used to signify any fractional part, such as a third, fourth, etc.." Jowitt, *supra*, p. 1184.
2. "Assumpsit" or Quincy's abbreviation "assum," etc. See page [96], note 9.
3. "Feme," i.e., "wife." See Jowitt, *supra*, pp. 793–94.

4. "Baron + Feme," i.e., "husband and wife." *Id.*, at p. 214. See page [108], note 7.

5. A citation to the "Baron & Feme" section beginning on page 20 earlier in the *Law Commonplace*. That page cross-cites to this index entry.

6. "Feme covert," see page [108], note 7. "Conson" for "consideration." See page [110], note 9.

7. "Feme covert," see page [108], note 7.

8. "Submisnon," i.e., "submission," "entere'd into whole sale," i.e., while woman was single. With a "*quare*," i.e., "wherefore," "whether a debt on a bond condition'd to such award can yt [that] be brot agt husband and wife?," see page [99], note 10.

9. "*Dum sola*," i.e., "while she remains single or unmarried." Jowitt, *supra*, p. 684.

10. "Quash'd," i.e., "to discharge or set aside an order of an inferior court." *Id.*, p. 1456, see page [111], note 12.

11. "Detinue," the standard cause of action to recover things, i.e., chattels. See Baker, *An Introduction to English Legal History* (4th ed.), *supra*, pp. 384–85, 391–94.

[120]

177 B.C Page

Bills of Exchange + Notes.
- can't be indorsed for pmt.[1] 150
- Drawee failing, Endorsee shall lose, if he has neglected to call in Season.[2] 167
- A servant's taking not binding on the master, without Subseq. Consent. 154

C.

Computations
- Months how to be computed. 155

Conditions.- Many Diversities in, + concerning the Performance of Them. 172. 173.174

Condition. – Of Estate tail y^{t} [that] tenant in tail may for ye profit of his Issue [when] good. 170
- to submit to an Award, money tender'd + refus'd is lost. 163

C. Page

Same continued.
- to save harmless ag^{t} future Things- void, ag.^{t} past-good.[3] 167

Contempt. to charge a person, imprison'd for a fine, with a civil action without Leave of the Court. 154

Constructions of Words.
- 16th of May next ensuing the 1st, Adjudg'd Same May. 155.
- 20 of the best Trees in a Wood. 155.
- May be done in a Statute, means must be done. 157
- Seis'd in his Demesne[4] as of fee, true of a Seisin in Law only. 160

Page [120]

1. "Pmt" for "payment."

2. "[C]all in Season," i.e., endorsee of a note fails to demand payment in a diligent way after note becomes payable. "[H]e might be paid if he had been diligent enough." See page [110], note 1.

3. "[A]gt past-good," i.e., it is a valid condition to hold a party harmless against past occurrences, but not future, and inherently unknowable, occurrences. See page [110], note 5.

4. "Seis'd," i.e., "seised," in possession of a fee. See Jowitt, *supra*, p. 1608. "Seised in demesne as of fee" meant that "the immediate freehold in severality was vested in him for an estate in fee simple, as opposed to one who held land for a term of years or for life only, or in common with others . . ." *Id.*, pp. 606–07. See page [103], note 5.

[121]

178

C.D	Page
same continued	
• A Grant of a Garden + all the Trees in it, Trees in a Box pass not.	164
Covenant. [no citation]	
Conveyance made by fraud, + after--wards the Land is convey[1] upon a valuable consideration ye fraud is purg'd.	167
D	
Declaration. must be con--sistent with itself even in Things not material or tra--versable.	170
Devise. A will shall not operate by Way of executory Devise, where it may take Effect by way of Remainder.	157
• to A + haeredibus de corpore pro-creandis[2] how it shall operate.	161

D.E.F	Page
same continued	
• Estate shall not pass ag^{t} express Limitation of testator, tho' Limitation be void.	161
• Land devis'd for paymt of Debts personal Estate shall not pay.	161
E	
Estoppell Feme sole[3] sued, she marries. –Estopp'd.	156
Execution. may be sued out after Death of Dft.	168
Extinguishment. Disseisee[4] levies a fine, his Right extinguish'd.	156
Evidence. vid. Pleading	
F	
Fraud. how purged.	167
Felony. A man wounded dies not within a Year + Day- not felony.	152

Page [121]

1. "Convey," i.e., "conveyed."
2. "*Haeredibus de corpore procreandis*," i.e., "heirs begotten from the body." See page [104], note 3.
3. "Feme sole," i.e., "an unmarried woman." See Osborn, *A Concise Law Dictionary*, *supra*, p. 135. See also page [119], note 3.
4. "Disseisee," i.e., one who has been "disseised." See page [99], note 4.

[122]

179

Page [122]

1. "Hypothecation." "A pledge in which the pledges retain possession of the thing pledged." Jowitt, *supra*, p. 932. Usually this was a vessel, pledged for repairs, but still in possession of the captain so that the voyage can be completed. See also "bottomry," a common form of agreement that "binds or hypothecates the ship and freight, or the cargo, for the performance of a contract . . ." *Id.*, p. 269. See page [102], note 7.

2. "Sue his guardian [in socage] by guardian." See page [102], note 5.

3. "Prochein amy," i.e., "next friend." See page [114], note 8.

4. "Fine," i.e., a fictitious judicial proceeding used to convey interests in property. See Jowitt,

supra, p. 803. See also Baker, *An Introduction to English Legal History* (4th ed.), *supra*, pp. 282–83. See also page [97], note 4.

5. "[*N*]*il debet.*" See page [105], note 2.

6. "Negative preg" for "negative pregnant." See page [106], note 10. "[I]n pleading . . . where a person gives an evasive answer to an allegation . . . by answering it literally . . . Thus if it is alleged that A received a certain sum of money, and he denies that particular amount, this is a negative pregnant, because the substance of the allegation is the receipt of some money." Jowitt, *supra*, p. 1213.

[123]

180

N.O.	Page
Nolo prosequi[1] Attorn^{y} gen.^{l} can't enter without a Warrant.	168

O

Obligation + Deed.	
• Subscribing the name not essential, name in the bond only material.	150.
• Partics' names not inserted in ye body of the deed, but subscrib'd + seal'd. Adjudg'd good.	151
• Oblon[2] dated at a place is local.	151
• Date impossible or absurd shall not hurt upon non est factum[3] pleaded.	154
• Deliver'd to ye use of obligee absent who disagrees after, has lost its force:	154. 157
• Deed of Gift of Goods dd [delivered][4] to ye Use of donee absent, property in him before Notice	157
• Oblon j+s put in a Suit ag.^{t} one obligor, he taken in Excon, yet the other may be sued.[5]	159
• Obligor must seek Obgee at ye Day of paym^{t} if in the realm,	161
• Oblon by 3 j+s ye seal of one torn off, destroy'd as to all.	163
• can't be to 3 j + severally.[6]	163
• 20 y:^{rs} standing + no good Cause of forebearance, intended to be p.^{d}	166
• Oblon[7] seal'd by 2 jointly. Action brot vs. 1. Motion in arrest of Judg.^{nt} overul'd.	153

P	Page
Partners in Trade.	
Assumpsit[8] lies ag.^{t} ye Survivor generally without setting forth ye partnership + survivor.	167
Payment. made indefinitely creditor may apply to any Debt he pleases.	153
• The manner + tender to be directed by him who makes it.	154. 160
Pleading + Evidence	
Expulsion may be given in Evid. On nil debet[9]	153
• Note of hand given in discharge of a debt on simple Contract no barr.	153
• Nil debet[10] to debt on penalty for breach of Covenant-bad plea.	153
• Title of an act of Parlmnt must be set out right, if at all.	154
• Defence not necessary in a plea in Abatement	155
• Matter in Abatem^{t}[11] pleaded in Bar + concluded in bar. Judg.^{t} final.	155
• Assumpsit[12] vs. 2. 1 defaulted. Issue found for the Other.	170
• Note of hand of a different Date cannot be given in Evidence.	158
• In trespass etc. gen. Issue may be pleaded + sp. matter given in Evid.	158

Page 123

1. "*Nolo prosequi*" (i.e., *nolle prosequi*, "to be unwilling to prosecute"), "a proceeding in the nature of an undertaking by the plaintiff when he had misconceived the nature of the action . . . to forbear to proceed in a suit altogehter, or as to some point of it, or as to some of the defendants." Jowitt, *supra*, p. 1229. The reference to Quincy page 168 [111] is actually to a "*non pros*," or "*non prosequitus*." See page [111], note 3. These are not identical, and this was a rare error by Quincy. "It [*nolo prosequi*] differed from a *non pros.*, which put a plaintiff out of court with respect to all the defendants." *Id.*, p. 1229. "[A] *nolle prosequi* to stay proceedings may be entered

by leave of the Attorney-General [in criminal proceedings] at any time before judgment: it is not equivalent to an acquittal and is no way to a new indictment for the same offense." *Id.*, p. 1229.

2. "Oblon" for "obligation."

3. "*Non est factum*," see page [97], note 8.

4. "Dd" for "delivered." See page [100], note 4.

5. "Oblon j+s," i.e., "obligation joint and several." "An obligation entered into by two or more persons is joint and several when each is liable severally and all are liable jointly." Jowitt, *supra*, p. 1014. See page [102], note 11. "Excon.," see page [102], note 11.

6. "J+s," i.e., "joint and several." See note 5, *supra*.

7. "Oblon," i.e., "obligation." See note 2, *supra*.

8. "Assumpsit," the general contractual cause of action. See page [96], note 9. See also Baker, *An Introduction to English Legal History* (4th ed.), *supra*, pp. 330–45.

9. "*Nil debet*," see page [105], note 2.

10. See note 9, *supra*.

11. "Abatemt" for "abatement." A plea "which, without either admitting or denying the existence of the cause of action, alleged some fact (such as the non-joinder of a necessary party . . .) which would preclude the plaintiff from recovering on the writ as then framed." Jowitt, *supra*, p. 5.

12. "Assumpsit," see note 8, *supra*.

[124]

181

P Page

Pleading + Evidence

Excor pleas another Excor, does not say he admn'd.—ill.[1] 160.

• Nil hab. in Ten.[2] may be given in Evid on nil debet.[3] 162.

• Oblor only sued on a joint Bond, can't plead non est factum.[4] If both etc.[5] 164.

• Deliver'd as an Escrow may be given in Evid. on non est factum.[6] 170.

How Execttors must plead when etc.[7] 38.

Powers. to 4 j +s.[8]3 can't execute 156.

• to a feme cov.[9] to sell, she may sell to her husband. 166.

• Attorny must do ye Act in ye name of ye principal + not in his own name. 169.

• An act done, yt [that] can't be done, but by ye power, shall be intended to be done by ye power. And where there is an Interest + a power etc. 169

Less done Void More done than commanded--good as far as the Authority went.[10] 171

Property. were it was adjudg'd chang'd 150.151

• Is in Donee absent, on Excon[11] of ye Deed. 157

Purchases. Remainder to right heirs of JS. Daughter shall take as a purchaser, ag.t the Son born after 159

R, Page

Record. made of a voluntary Con--fession in C.t pun. as in Case of Perjury. viz sitting in ye pillory[12] 153.

Release. to 1 of 2 bound j+ severally,[13] both are discharged. 152.

• Like Law of a joint Trespass 152.

• Debt or Duty can't be releas'd by Will

• 3 j tennants disseis'd, 1 releases 157. to Dissor.[14] this bars him, but not the other 2. 171.

Remainder. to the right Heirs of a Ten. in Tail,[15] he may grant it. 166.

• to right heirs of JS. Daughter shall take ag.t a Son born after. 159.

Rent. Wether rent Issue may be suspended in part + in Esse in part by Act of ye party. 170.

• Debt for it, Ten. in com.[16] may either join or sever. 157.

• may be reserv'd by the An.[17] to ye heir with.t reserving it to himself. 169.

Repleader. Shall not be after Demurrer. Qu.[18] 159.

Riots. there must be 3 to it. 162

Shff. taking insufficient Bail liable to an action. 151.

finds ye outward Door open may break the inner. 174

Page [124]

1. "Exor," i.e., "executor," "pleas another executor," i.e., "pleads that there is another executor not named in writ," but does not say he has administered the estate, "adjudged ill upon a demurrer." See page [103], note 6.

2. "*Ni hab.*," i.e., "*nil habuit in tenementis.*" See page [105], note 2.

3. "*Nil debet*," see page [96], note 12; page [105], note 2.

4. "*Non est factum*," see page [97], note 8.

5. "If both etc.," i.e., if both are sued and one appears and the other defaults . . . "he who appears shall be charged with the whole debt. But in the Case at Bar he might have pleaded in Abatement of the Writ." See page [108], note 1.

6. "Escrow," see page [113], note 9.

7. "[W]hen etc.," i.e., when sued in debt etc. See page [39], note 3.

8. "[J]+S," i.e., "joint and several." See page [123], note 5.

9. "[F]eme cov.," i.e., "feme covert," a married woman. See page [108], note 7.

10. Quincy's placement of "void" moved from beneath "Less done" to following it, to keep the correct sense of the notation. See page [114], note 6.

11. "Excon" for "execution." See page [102], note 11.

12. Record of a voluntary confession of perjury in court, "without . . . indictment or information . . . punished as in case of perjury." Here Quincy added, "[V]iz sitting in ye pillory." Here Quincy's index contained more information than the original note, where the nature of the punishment was not set out. See page [96], note 4.

13. "J + severally," i.e., "jointly and severally." See page [123], note 5.

14. "Dissor," i.e., "disseisor." See page [99], note 4.

15. "Ten. in tail," i.e., "tenant in tail," the owner of an estate tail. Estate tails descended solely to heirs of the grantee's body, "general entail," or to the heirs of the grantee's body by a particular spouse, "special entail." Otherwise the estate, in theory, reverted back to the heirs of the grantor, "possibility of reverter." See Baker, *An Introduction to English Legal History* (4d ed.), *supra*, pp. 272–76.

16. "Debt for it," i.e., action of debt to recover rent. "Ten in com.," i.e., "tenancy in common." "Where two or more persons are entitled to land in such a manner that they have an undivided possession but several freeholds: that is, no one of them is entitled to the exclusive possession of any part of the land, each being entitled to occupy the whole in common with the others." Osborn, *A Concise Law Dictionary*, *supra*, p. 309.

17. "An." for "ancestors." See page [112], note 6.

18. "Qu." for "*quaerere*," i.e., "ask, inquire." Quincy indicated questionable propositions by the notation "Qu" or "Qu. vid.," followed by the inconsistent authority. This is further evidence of his critical attitude. He was not simply copying. See page [102], note 9.

[125]

182

Those thus X mark'd are omitt'd in this Index.[15]

X Page. 152
155
160
160
163
166
166.

Page [125]

1. "*Fieri facias*" ("that you cause to be made"), "a writ of execution to levy a judgement debt." Jowitt, *supra*, p. 800. "It commands the sheriff or other officer to whom it is directed to cause a levy to be made on the goods and chattels of the debtor . . ." *Id.*, p. 800. See also page [106], note 2; page [111], note 6.

2. "[M]ay 1 gown if he has 2," i.e., the sheriff can take 1 gown, but only if the defendant has another. See page [111], note 7. This issue arose in a case Quincy reported, the so-called "naked wife" case, *Hanlon* v. *Thayer* (1764). See *Quincy's Reports*, *supra*, p. 99.

3. "Capias," see page [106], note 1. "[F]ieri F." for "*fieri facias*." See note 1, *supra*. See also page [106], note 2; page [111], note 6.

4. "Submission," i.e., "a man may submit for another's debt," usually in connection with a written submission, as an arbitration submission. See page [113], note 15.

5. "Surplusage," i.e., an unnecessary allegation in pleading. See Osborn, *A Concise Law Dictionary*, *supra*, p. 307.

6. "[T]ryal at bar, *Nisi*." Common law trials were originally held before a full court at Westminster Hall, usually consisting of several royal judges. This was called a "tryal at bar." *Id.*, p. 221. Trials *nisi prius* were usually before a single judge and a jury sitting in the assize courts during the country assizes outside of London, or in specially designated courts within London and Middlesex, the most famous being the "Old Bailey," the central London criminal court. The order to the sheriff, since the statute 13 Edward I, would direct him to bring jurors from the relevant county to Westminster Hall "unless before" (*nisi prius*) "the justices of assize came into the county." *Id.*, p. 221. The Massachusetts Superior Court of Judicature was a stationary trial and appellate court by Quincy's day, but the Inferior Court of Common Pleas (1692–1859) roughly followed English practice of "riding circuit." See *Law in Colonial Massachusetts*, *supra*, pp. 541–49.

Here again Quincy added something to the index not found in the body of the notes, which referred solely to "trials at bar." See page [101], note 1. He probably meant that the same rule should apply to both trials at bar and trials *nisi prius*.

7. Trespass . . . *ab initio*, see page [110], note 4.

8. Trover, see page [105], note 7.

9. "Denial to deliver no Evid. [Evidence] of Conversion, unless—." Action was for recovery in trover of an "Horse in an Inn-Keeper's Hands." See note 8, *supra*. "[N]o Evidence of Conversion unless the Money was tender'd for the Horse's keeping." See page [107], note 2.

10. "Non cul," see page [110], note 10. "Trover agt 2 one pleads non ent. T' other a release of actions. [T]he first issue found for plt, the other for the deft + Judm't . . ."

11. "V + judgt," i.e., "verdict and judgment."

12. "Oblon," i.e., "obligation." See page [112], note 6.

13. "Remainder men," i.e., those entitled to the estate if the "heirs of the body" die, and it is an estate in tail. See page [102], notes 1 and 2.

14. "Quod Nota," i.e., "note that" or "take notice." See page [94], note 2.

15. This is a mystery. Each of these pages does have a case marked with the "X" and, indeed, the marked cases are omitted from the index. But why? See pages [95], [98], [103], [106], [109]. The notation on the case omitted from page [98] warned "Quare of this, it is not law." See page [98], note 7. The case omitted from page [106] was cryptic, "case of the half blood + whole," and may have been a controversial slavery case. But the other cases appear to have been good authority. Why did Quincy omit them?

[126] 5
[From Quincy's "Volume 4," QP58]

Legis Miscellanea

cursim, Libris exscprita.[1] vid. Vol. 1. p. 150

Of Estates vid. Vol. 1 p. 25. 47,

FEE.

+no Deed shall be void, wch by any construction can be made good.
Hawk: abr. 11.[6]

+A Deed, without Premises, Habend., Tenend., Reddend.,[4]
Clause of Warranty, the Clause of In Cuius Rei Testimonium
the Date, & the Clause of Hiis Testibus, is Good. Co:Lit:7.a.[5]

ϕ If A devise 20 acres to B, & that He shall pay to his Exc^tt^ors for the same ten pounds, hereby the Devisee
hath a Fee Simple, without the words his Heirs, albeit it
be not to the Value of the Land. Ibid. 9. b.[7]

ϕ So a Devise to A, to give or sell, or forever, or in Fee simple, or to Him + his assigns forever,
or to Him & Sang. suo. give
a ffee. Ibid 14.[8]

[PAGE CONTINUES]

[5 cont.]

⊕ vid.
Vol. 1:st
p. 81.
Tit.
Releases.[10]

If there be 3 Coparceners or Jointenants, +one of
them ⊕ releases to the other two, or to one of them
generally
without this word (Heirs.) a Fee passes. Ibid.[9]

Where the Lord releases to the Tenant, or
the Grantee
of a Rent, etc such Release to the Ten't of the Land
generally
of all his Right, etc, hereby the Seignory, Rent etc
are ex- [‡]
tinguish'd forever, without this word (Heirs.)
Ibid[11]

‡ omit
this word
forever
+ it w.d be
only an
Estate for Life
Haw. abr. 14[13]

When a bare Right is released, as when the
Disseisee release to the Disseisor all his Right, He
need not speak of his Heirs. Ibid[12]

If a Feoffment or Grant by Deed to a
mayor + communality, or any other Corporation
aggregate of many Persons capable, they have a ffee without the
word (Successors) because in Judgment of Law they never
die. Ibid[14]

In Grants sometimes an Inheritance shall pass
without this word (Heirs), as if Partition be made between
coparceners of Lands in Fee simple, + for Owelty

Page [126]

1. "*Exscprita*" should be "*exscripta.*" The whole phrase: "Miscellaneous Laws Cursorily Copied Out Of Books." Compare page 150 [93] of the *Law Commonplace*, which bears the same title without limitation to estates. The following five pages continue Quincy's *Legis Miscellanea* and are found on pages 5–10 of Vol. 4, together with 71 pages of *Law Reports*. See the Cox Chart, Appendix II, pp. 432–33, and MHS p. 347, Reel 4, QP58. See also Introduction, *supra*, pp. 21–22.

2. Volume 1 refers to Quincy's *Law Commonplace*, where at page 150 [93] he begins a twenty-five-page collection of briefly stately legal precepts on a variety of topics. Page 150 [93] also references back "vid. Vol. 4. p. 5."

3. Volume 1 refers to Quincy's *Law Commonplace*, which at page 25 [30] begins a two-page treatment of estates. It cross-references "vid Vol. 4 p.5 & onward." Page 47 [45] begins a three-page section on the subject "Of Lands, Tenements or Hereditaments."

4. Clauses of "*habendum*" (to have), "*tenendum*" (to hold), and "*reddendum*" (to give back).

5. Citation to *Coke on Littleton*, p. 7a ("for if such a deed be without *premissis*, *habendum*, *tendendum*, *reddendum*, Clause of Warranty, the Clause of *In cuius rei testimonium*, the Date, and the Clause of *hiis testibus*, yet the deed is good"). See page [2], note 1.

6. Quincy copies this text from William Hawkins, *Abridgment*, p. 11. See page [1], note 1, *supra.*

7. Citation to *Coke on Littleton*, page 9b (". . . an Estate of inheritance may pass without these words [his Heirs]. As if a man devise twenty Acres to another, and that he shall pay to his Executors for the same ten Pounds; hereby the Devisee hath a fee-simple by the Intent of the Devisor, albeit be not to the value of the Land").

8. A close copy from Hawkins's, *Abridgment*, p. 14. See page 8, note 1, *supra.* "Sang. suo" is short for "sanguini suo" (to his own blood). "ffee" is Quincy's shorthand for "fee simple."

9. A citation to *Coke on Littleton*, p. 9b ("as if there be three Coparceners or Jointenants, and one of them release to the other two, or one of them generally without this word [Heirs] by *Littleton's* own Opinion they have a fee-simple").

10. A reference to Quincy's *Law Commonplace*, where he cites forward to this page. Pages 81 [71] through 86 [76] of the *Law Commonplace* treat the topic of Releases generally.

11. An almost exact copy from *Coke on Littleton*, p. 9b.

12. *Id.* ("When a bare Right is released, as when the Disseisee releases to the Disseisor all his Right, he need not (saith our Author in another Place) speak of his Heirs").

13. Citation to Hawkins, *Abridgment*, p. 14. See page [8], note 1, *supra.* Quincy restates the implication of the cited text in his own words.

14 Another close copy from *Coke on Littleton*, p. 9b.

[127]

6

Legis Miscellanea &c < Of Estates >

NB. Gen: words, as Honour, isle, Castle, will pass things compound, as Honour or Castle will pass divers manors, or things simple of different Natures, as Farm will pass. Houses, Lands & Tenements Haw. abr 7.[2] +vid Co. Lit 31.a[4]

of Partition, the one grant a Rent to the other generally the Grantee shall have a Fee Simple, without this word (Heirs). because the Grantor has a Fee Simple, in consideration whereof He granted the Rent; Ipsae etenim Leges cupiunt ut iure regantur. Co:Lit: 9.b.10.a[1]

Of Lands of the Nature of the Gavelkind be given to B + his Heirs, having issue divers sons, all his sons · after his Dicease shall inherit: but if a Lease for Life · be made be made the Remainder to the Right Heirs of B, & B dieth, his Eldest Son only shall inherit, for He only to take by Purchase is Right Heir by the Common Law: So Note a[X] Diversity between a Purchase & a Descent. Ibid. 10. a[3]

[PAGE CONTINUES]

[6 cont.]

CURTESY.[x]
[x] vid. Vol. 1. p. 25. & vid. Vol. 1. p. 22[5]
Lands to A & her Heirs male— Issue female—

Lands come to the wife after Issue dec'd In these cases— How Co: Lit 29. b [9]

A Seisin in Deed is necessary (if it may be attain'd unto) to make a man Tenant by the Curtesy: A man (nor tenant in Dower. Hawk. abr. 42)[6] shall not be Tenant by the Curtesy _ of a bare Right, Tithe, Use, or of a Reversion or Remainder expectant upon any Estate of Freehold, unless the particular Estate be determin'd or ended during the Coverture. Ibid 29.a.[7] And Memorandum (says Lit: S.52)[8] that in every case where a man taketh a wife seis'd of such an Estate of Tenements &c as the Issue which He hath by his wife may by possibility inherit the same Ten'ments of such an Estate as the wife hath, as Heir to the wife, in such case, after the Decease of the wife, the Husband shall have the same Tenements by the Curtesy of

Page [127]

1. A nearly exact copy from *Coke on Littleton*, pp. 9b–10a. The translation of the concluding phrase is "for truly the laws themselves desire that they be governed by justice." My thanks to Elizabeth Kamali. "Owelty" means "equality." "[C]ompensation is said to be given for owelty or equality of exchange," Jowitt, *supra*, p. 1283. My thanks to my colleague Charles Donahue, ever a friend in need! See page [2], note 1.

2. Citation to Hawkins, *Abridgment*, p. 7. See page [8], note 1, *supra*.

3. An almost exact copy from *Coke on Littleton*, p. 10a.

4. Citation to *Coke on Littleton*, p. 31a, where follows a discussion of seisin in deed and rights of dower the words, "And here *Note* a Diversity between a Descent and a Purchase."

5. Volume 1 refers to Quincy's *Law Commonplace*. Page 25 [30] is the first page of a section on "Estates" and is also referenced on the preceding page. The page briefly mentions curtesy. Page 22 [27] is the third page of his section on "Baron & Feme," and does not specifically mention curtesy.

6. "Curtesy" refers to "an estate which arose by act of law, and was that interest which a husband had for his life in his wife's fee simple or fee tail estates . . . after her death." Jowitt, *supra*, p. 553. Citation to Hawkins's, *Abridgment*, p. 42. See page [8], note 1, *supra*. The passage corresponds to page 29a of *Coke on Littleton*.

7. Citation to *Coke on Littleton*, p. 29a ("And here *Littleton* intendeth a seisin in Deed, if it may be attained unto . . . . But a Man ſhall not be Tenant by the Curtesy of a bare Right, Title, Use, or of a Reason or Remainder expectant upon Estate of Freehold, unless the particular Estate be determined or ended during the Coverture").

8. *Id.*, p. 40a, where the English translation of *Littleton*'s Section 52 states, "And *memorandum* [i.e., it must be remembered], that in every case where a Man taketh a Wife seised of such and Estate of Tenements, &c. as the Issue which he hath by his Wife, may by Possibility inherit the same Tenements of such and Estate as the Wife hath, as Heir to the Wife: In this cafe after the Deceafe of the Wife, he shall have the fame Tenements by the Curtesy of England, but otherwise not".

9. *Id.*, p. 29b, addresses both of these situations posed in the margin. As to the first matter, where lands are granted to a woman and her male heirs, but she only has female issue, *Coke on Littleton* states "he shall not be Tenant by the Curtesy." As to the second, where the land descends to a woman after her issue have died, *Coke on Littleton* states that even though the "Issue had died in the Life-time of her Father before any descent of the Land, yet shall He be Tenant by the Curtesy." *Id.*, p. 296.

[128] 7

< Of Estates >

Legis Miscellanea &c

England, but otherwise not.— Coke's Com Lang.—If a man taketh a wife seis'd of Land or Tenements in ffee, & hath Issue, & after the wife is attainted[x] of Felony so as the Issue cannot inherit to her, yet He shall be Tenant by Curt.y, in Respect of the Issue which He had before the Felony, & wch by Possibility might then have inherit'd. But if the wife had been attainted of Felony before the Issue, albeit He hath Issue afterward, He shall not be Ten't by the Curtesy. "As Heirs to the wife" Lit: This (says Coke) doth imply a Secret of Law, for except the wife be actually seis'd, the Heir shall not make Himself Heir to the wife: and this is the Reason, that a man shall not be Ten't by Curt:y of a seisin in Law. Co. Lit: 40.a [2]

x If ye H is attainted ye King gaineth &c. vid Co Lit: 351 · a[1]

DOWER.+

+ vid Vol. 1. p 25.[3]

A man must be seis'd Either in Deed or in Law, during the Coverture to intitle his wife to Dower. For a woman shall be endow'd of a Seisin in Law, for it lieth not in the Power of the wife to bring it to be an actual Seisin, as the Husband may of the wife's Land, when He is Ten't by Curtesy, wch is worthy observation. Yet of every Seisin in Law or in Deed, the wife shall not be endow'd. For Example &c Co: Lit.31.a[4]— Also the Husband may be Seised in his Demesne, as of Fee absolutely, yet the woman shall not be endowed both of the Land given in Exchange, & of the Land taken in Exchange, & yet the Husband was Seised of Both, but She may have her Election to be endowed of which She will Co: Lit: 31.b.[5]

Page [128]

1. Citation to *Coke on Littleton*, p. 351a. ("Also if the Husband be attainted of Felony, the King gaineth no freehold, but on Pernancy [taking] of the Profits during the Coverture, and the freehold remaineth in the Wife".) Quincy makes a similar notation in the same location on page 22 [27] of the *Law Commonplace*, also citing to p. 351a of *Coke on Littleton.*

2. *Id.*, p. 40a ("If a Man taketh a Wife seised of Lands or Tenements in Fee, and hath Issue, and after the wife is attainted of Felony, so as the Issue cannot inherit to her, yet he shall be Tenant by the Curtesy, in respect of the Issue which he had before the Felony, and which by Possibility might then have inherited. But if the Wife had been attainted of Felony before the Issue; albeit he hath Issue afterward, he shall not be Tenant by the Curtesy. *Come heire al feme* [quote from Littleton's text on the same page, translated as "as heir to the wife"]. This doth imply a secret of Law, for except the Wife be actually seised, the Heir shall not (as hath been said) make himself heir to the Wife: And this is the reason that a Man shall not be Tenant by the Curtesy of a Seisin in Law").

3. In beginning the topic of dower, Quincy again cross-references to his *Law Commonplace*, where page 25 [30] begins treatment of the topic of Estates. Page 25 [30] of the *Law Commonplace* specifically mentions dower and provides a cross-reference to this page and the preceding one.

4. Citation to *Coke on Littleton*, p. 31a ("Here this word [seised] extendeth it self as well to a Seisin in Law, or a civil seisin, as a Seisin in Deed, which is a natural Seisin: But seised he must be either the one way or the other, during the Coverture. For a Woman shall be endowed of a Seisin in Law. . . . for it lieth not in the power of the Wife to bring it to be an actual Seisin, as the Husband may do of his Wife's Land, when he is to be Tenant by Curtesie, which is worthy of the Observation. And yet of every Seisin in Law . . . a Woman shall not be endowed. For example . . .").

5. *Id.*, p. 31b. Another almost exact copy.

[129]

8

Legis Miscellanea &c

Of Estates.

DOWER.

cont.

x also if He had died without making a F'ment She w.d not have been endow'd, but the wife of Ten't in Common shall be endow'd: vid Co. Lit. 37. b.[5]

If two jointenants be in Fee, & the x one maketh a Feoffment in fee, his wife shall not be endowed. Co: Lit: 31.b[1] The wife shall have Dower according to the improv'd value, & not according to the value as it was in her Husband's Time, for her Title is the Quantity of the Land, viz one third Part. Ibid. 32.a[2] And the like Law it is if the Heir improve the Value of the Land by Building: and on the other side, if the value be impair'd in the Time of the Heir, She shall be endowed according to the value at the Time of the assignment. Ibid.[3] (vid Co: Lit 171.a & b concerning Partition among Parceners)[4]

A devise by will cannot be averred to be in Satisfaction of Dower, unless it be so express'd in the will. Ibid. 36.b.[6]

Page [129]

1. Citation to *Coke on Littleton*, p. 31b ("Likewise if two Joint-tenants be in Fee, and the one maketh a Feoffment in Fee, his Wife shall not be endowed.") See page [2], note 1.

2. *Id.*, p. 31a. Another close copy.

3. *Id.*, p. 31a. Another close copy. Quincy omits Coke's concluding phrase, "and not according to the Value as it was in the Time of her Husband."

4. *Id.*, pp. 171a and 171b contains discussions of partitions between husbands and wives (by Coke's correction) in Section 257 and partition between coparceners, the youngest of whom is below the age of twenty-one, in Section 258.

5. *Id.*, p. 37b, where the English of Littleton's original text in Section 45 states "And it is to be understood that the wife shall not be endowed of Lands or Tenements which her Husband holdeth jointly with another at the Time of his Death: But where he holdeth in common, otherwise it is, as in the cafe next abovesaid." Coke's commentary explains, "The reason for this Diversity is, for that the Jointenant which surviveth, claimeth the Land by the Feoffment and by Survivorship, which is above the Title of Dower, and may plead the feoffment made to himself without naming his companion that died . . . ; But Tenants in Common have several Freeholds and Inheritances, and their moieties shall descend to their Several Heirs; and therefore their Wives shall be indowed." *Id.* p. 37b.

6. *Id.*, p. 36b. Another nearly exact copy.

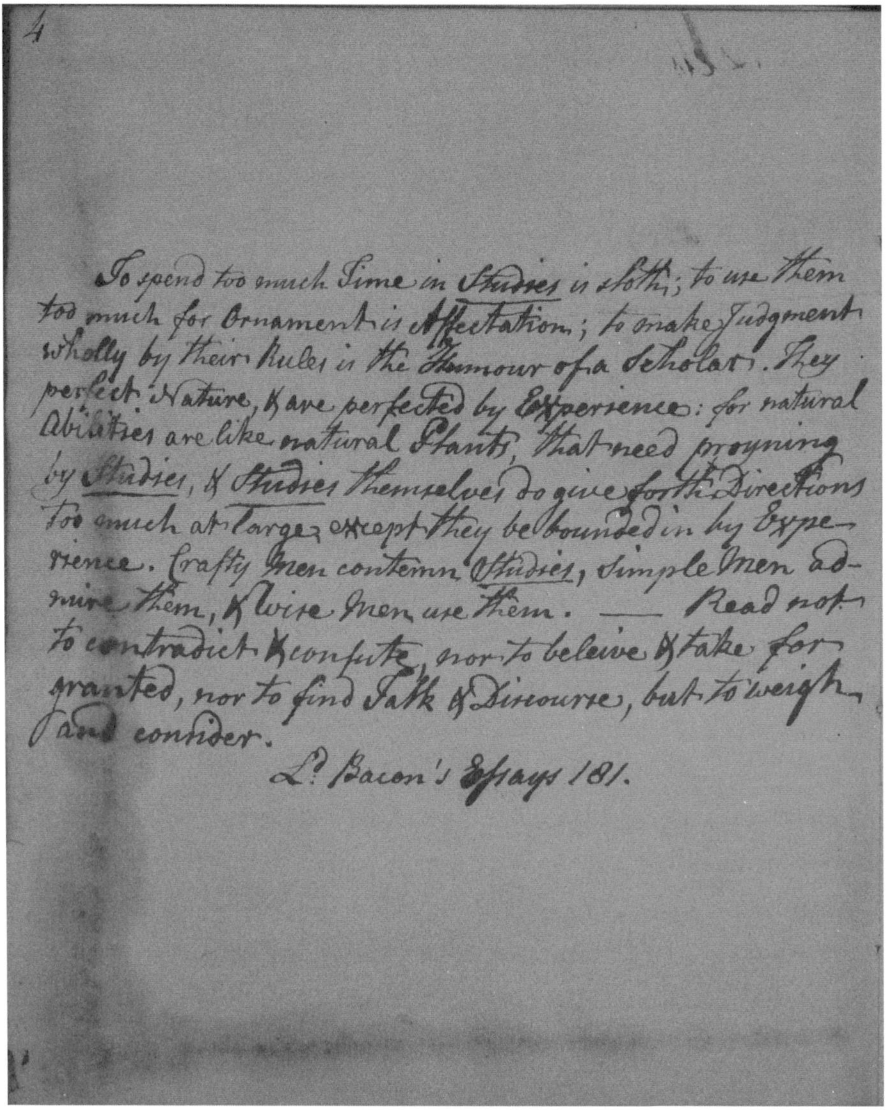

4

To spend too much Time in Studies is Sloth; to use them too much for Ornament is Affectation; to make Judgment wholly by their Rules is the Humour of a Scholar. They perfect Nature, & are perfected by Experience: for natural Abilities are like natural Plants, that need proyning by Studies, & Studies themselves do give forth Directions too much at Large, except they be bounded in by Experience. Crafty Men contemn Studies, simple Men admire them, & wise Men use them. — Read not to contradict & confute, nor to beleive & take for granted, nor to find Talk & Discourse, but to weigh and consider.

Ld Bacon's Essays 181.

ILLUSTRATION 5. Quincy preceded the last section of his *Legis Miscellanea* in Quincy "Volume 4" QP58, starting at page [126], *supra*, with this exhortation to study from Francis Bacon, *The Essays or Counsels Civill and Morall* (M. Kiernan, ed., 1985), pp. 152–53. There were many 17th- and 18th-century editions. See R. W. Gilson, *Francis Bacon: A Bibliography of His Works* . . . (1950), pp. 3–58. See also "Introduction," *supra*, p. 33. Courtesy, Massachusetts Historical Society.

[130] 9

Legis Miscellanea &c
Of Estates.

Tenant for LIFE[x]

[x] vid Vol. 1 p. 25.[1]

A, Ten't in ffee simple, makes a Lease of Lands to B to have & to hold for Term of Life, without mentioning for whose Life, it shall be. it shall be deem'd of the Life of the Leasee, for it shall be taken most strongly against the Lessor, & an Estate for a man's own Life is higher than for Life of Another. But if Ten't in T make such a Lease, without expressing for whose Life, this shall be taken for the Life of the Lessor, for two Reasons. 1:st when the Construction of any Act is left to the Law, the Law wch abhoreth Injury of wrong will never so construe it, as it shall work a wrong: And in this case, if by the construction it sh:d be for Life of the Lessee, then sh.d the Estate T be discontinued; and a new Reversion gain'd by wrong. But if it be construed for the Life of Ten't in T, then no wrong is brought. And it is a General Rule, that whensoever the words of a Deed, or of the Parties, without Deed, may have a double Intendm:t & the one standeth with Law & Right, & the other is wrongfull & ag:t Law, the Intendment that standeth with Law shall be taken. 2:dly The Law more respecteth a Lesser Estate by Law, than a larger Estate by wrong. Co: Lit: 42. a & b.[2]

Page [130]

1. Quincy cites to his own *Law Commonplace*, where page 25 [30] begins a discussion and specifically mentions "Tenant pur auter vie" (i.e., for the life of another) with a cross-reference to this page of his Legis Miscellenea of Estates in his Volume 4.

2. Citation to *Coke on Littleton*, p. 42a. Quincy closely copies the entire passage intact.

[131]

10
Tenant
for
YEARS⊕

⊕ vid
Vol. 1. p. 25.[1]

x vid Co: Rep.
22. a.[3]
Hawk abr:
77. 389[4]

Legis Miscellanea &c
Of Estates.

If Ten't in Fee take wife, & make a Lease for Years, & dieth, the wife is endow'd, She shall avoid the Lease, & after her Decease, the Lease shall be in force again. Co: Lit 46. a.[2]

x Note the Diversity between a Rent reserv'd upon a Lease for Years, reserving a yearly Rent: The Lessor may have several actions of Debt for every years Rent. But upon a Bond or Contract for Payment of several sums, no action of Debt lieth till the last Day be past. Co: Lit 47. b.[5] 292. b[6] vid Massachusetts perpetual Laws. 8 & 9. Geo. 2. ch. 2.[7]

Page [131]

1. Citation to Quincy's *Law Commonplace*, where page 25 [30] begins a discussion of "Estates." Page 25 [30] specifically mentions "leases for years" with a citation back to this page.
2. An almost exact copy from *Coke on Littleton*, p. 42a. See page [2], note 1.
3. Citation to *Coke Reports* (covering 1572–1616), vol. 3, p. 22a, which reports *Walker's Case* (1587) and states the principle that "if a man makes an obligation or other contract to pay several sums at several days, he shall not have an action of debt till all the days are past." The reporter cites to Co. Lit. pp. 47b and 292b. See Notes 5 and 6 *infra*.
4. Citation to Hawkins's, *Abridgment*. See page [8], note 1, *supra*. Pages 77 and 389 correspond to *Coke on Littleton*, p. 47b and p. 292b respectively.
5. An almost exact copy from *Coke on Littleton*, p. 47b.
6. *Id.* at p. 292b ("But if a Man be bound in a Bond or by Contract to another to pay an hundred Pounds at five several Days, he shall not have an Action of Debt before the Laft Day be past").
7. Quincy adeptly cites to a relevant provincial law of 1735–36, whereby "when any action shall be brought . . . on any bond . . . with penaltys for the payment of sums of money, performance . . . or things to be done at several times, and the plt recover the forfeiture of such penalty, the court shall enter up judgment for the whole of such forfeiture, and award execution only for so much of the debt or damage as is sustained at that time: so always that the said judgment shall stand as a security to the plt. . . ." See *The Acts and Resolves Public and Private of the Province of the Massachusetts Bay, Vol. II* (Boston, 1874), p. 755.

APPENDICES

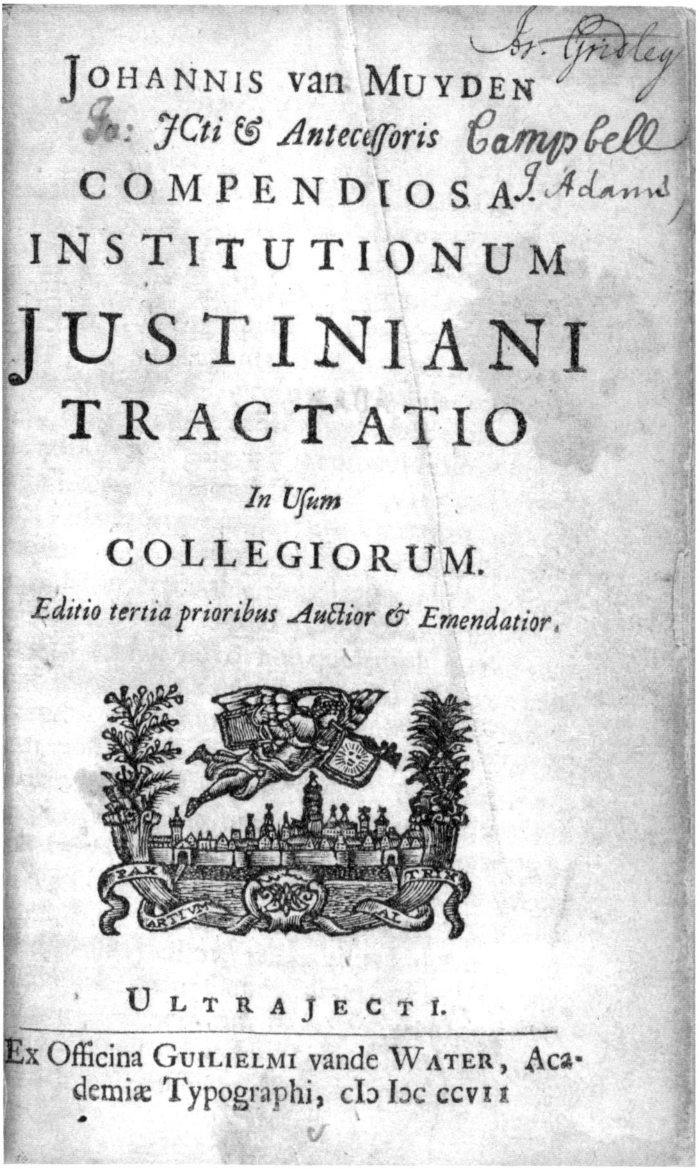
JOHANNIS van MUYDEN

JCti & Antecessoris

COMPENDIOSA

INSTITUTIONUM

JUSTINIANI

TRACTATIO

In Usum

COLLEGIORUM.

Editio tertia prioribus Auctior & Emendatior.

ULTRAJECTI.

Ex Officina GUILIELMI vande WATER, Academiæ Typographi, cIↃ IↃc ccvii

The Gridley-Adams copy of Johannis Van Muyden's *Compendiosa Institutionum Justiniani Tractatio* (Utrecht, 1707). This book was loaned by Jeremiah Gridley to Quincy's first cousin, John Adams, in 1758, and bought by Adams from Gridley's estate after 1767. Image courtesy of The John Adams Library at the Boston Public Library, Copley Square, Rare Books & Manuscripts Department. Adams was proud of his learning in Roman law. See "Introduction," *supra*, pp. 31–32.

Appendix I

QUINCY'S *LATIN MAXIMS*

EDITOR'S NOTE

Daniel R. Coquillette

THE DISCOVERY AND ANALYSIS of this important document is a tribute to skilled research assistance. First discovered and partially transcribed by Michael H. Hayden, Esq., Boston College Law School, Class of 2004, Quincy's *Latin Maxims* were initially translated with great skill by Susannah B. Tobin, Harvard Law School, Class of 2004, and then were put, with amazing persistence and intelligence, into this final translated and annotated form by Elizabeth Papp Kamali, Harvard Law School, Class of 2007. I have already expressed my deep appreciation to all three of these talented scholar professionals, but I should say again what a privilege it has been to have them as students and colleagues.

The lost art of learning and persuading by maxims has already been described in the Introduction, "The Legal Education of a Patriot: Josiah Quincy Jr.'s *Law Commonplace* (1763)," set out above at Section II "The Pedagogy," pp. 31–36. Two masterful works, Francis Bacon's *Maxims of the Common Lawes* (written 1596–1597, 1st ed., London, 1631) and Frances A. Yates's *The Art of Memory* (Chicago, 1966) are separated by more than three centuries, but they both remind us what a powerful legal and intellectual tool the maxim was, and still can be. Thanks to the intelligent alertness of my three young colleagues, and to the exceptional translation and annotations by Elizabeth Papp Kamali, we can revisit, again, this extraordinary form of learning.

In this section of his *Law Commonplace*, Quincy thankfully numbers his pages accurately, neither skipping nor repeating page numbers. Thus all Quincy page references use his original numbering.

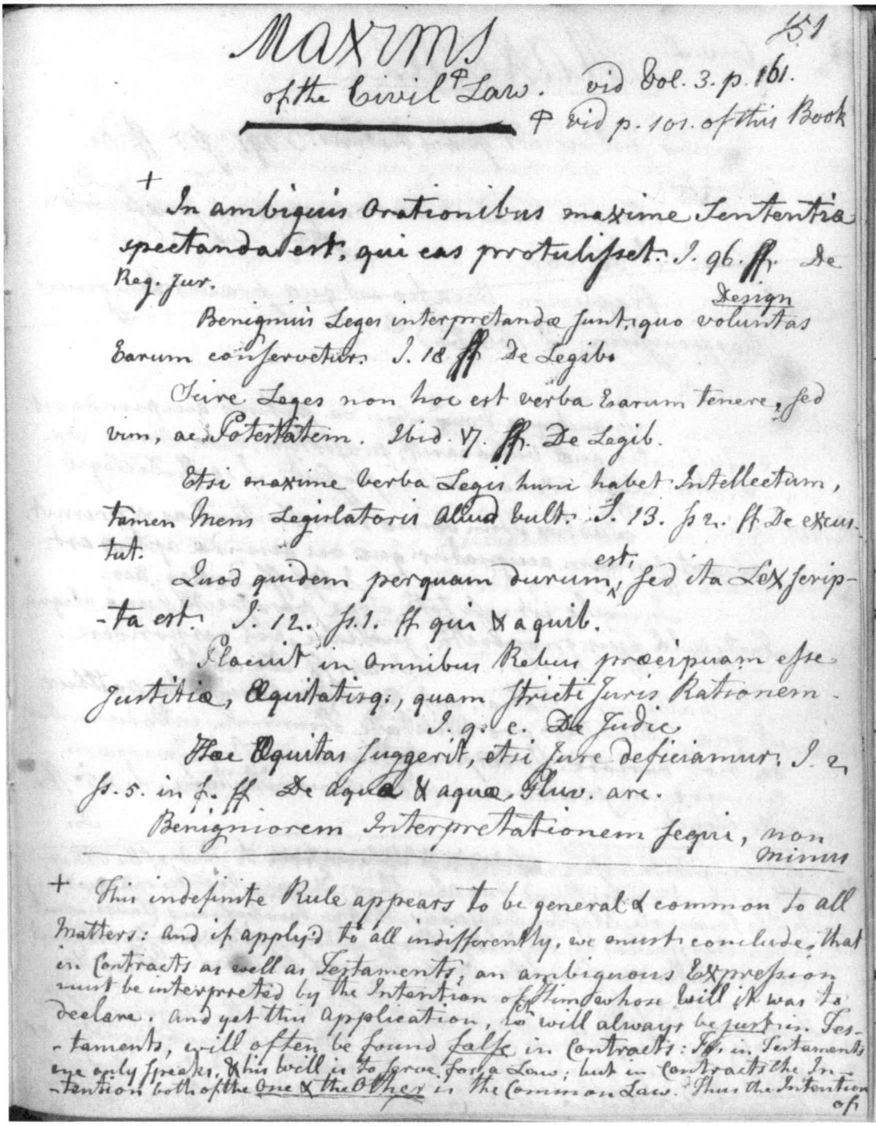

The first page (p. 151) of Quincy's maxim collection in volume four of the *Law Reports*, P347, Reel 4, QP 58. See Cox Chart, Appendix II, *infra*. The page is entitled "Maxims of the Civil Law" and offers a careful, neatly compiled list of Roman law maxims in a fairly even hand. Following the title, Quincy cross-references another collection of maxims in volume three of his *Law Reports*, as well as another section within volume four discussing ecclesiastical and civil law. The first maxim is the focus of a footnote at the bottom, set off from the main text by a line scored across the page. The note, an excerpt from Wood's *Civil Law*, continues on the following page. My thanks to Elizabeth Papp Kamali. Reproduced courtesy of Massachusetts Historical Society.

QUINCY'S LATIN LEGAL MAXIMS

Translator's Note and Introduction

*Elizabeth Papp Kamali**

> *Ch. Just.* Have you no Authorities, Gentlemen?
> *Mr. Gridley.* There is no Authority that the Sun shines.
> *Mr. Auchmuty.* But there is Evidence.[1]

BY THE EARLY TWENTIETH CENTURY, a scholar could assert, without controversy, that the "principal service performed by the average maxim is . . . to bolster or support a legal viewpoint rather than to decide a case."[2] In Quincy's time, however, reception of English law was an ongoing process, domestic precedents were not systematically recorded, and American lawyers were taking tentative steps toward defining the weight of various authorities in the colonial courtroom. The exchange quoted above, excerpted from a case recorded by Quincy in his *Law Reports*, was followed shortly by quotation of a maxim, although the ensuing conversation touched upon a variety of authorities.[3] A maxim could carry considerable weight when, for example, the English common law provided a contradictory or unsatisfactory answer. Representing principles that transcend time and space, maxims offered the colonial American lawyer a fresh outlook on perplexing legal questions and a broad framework within which to weigh the merits of either side of an action.

*Harvard Law School, 2007, Harvard College, 1997

1. An exchange between the Chief Justice and attorneys Jeremy Gridley and Robert Auchmuty, representing the opposing parties in *Banister* v. *Henderson* (1765). Josiah Quincy Jr., *Reports of Cases Argued and Adjudged in the Superior Court of Judicature of the Province of Massachusetts Bay, between 1761 and 1772* (Boston: Little, Brown, 1865), p. 122 (hereafter, "Quincy, *Reports*").

2. Ward E. Lattin, "Legal Maxims, and their Use in Statutory Interpretations," *The Georgetown Law Journal*, vol. 26, no. 1 (November 1937): p. 10 (hereafter, "Lattin").

3. See Quincy, *Reports*, pp. 122–27.

Regretfully, Quincy's early death, which brought his legal career to an abrupt close, precludes a study of his maxim collection in action. Undoubtedly, with his meticulously cross-referenced arsenal of maxims, Josiah Quincy Jr. would have been a dynamo in the courtroom.

Josiah Quincy Jr.'s collection of Latin legal maxims comprises twenty-two pages within two volumes of his *Law Reports*.[4] In volume four, six pages of maxims, entitled "Maxims of the Civil Law" (referred to here as *Maxim I*), are followed by four blank pages and twenty-four pages of miscellaneous notes on evidence and other legal topics.[5] The first of two sets of maxims in volume three is entitled "Maxims & Rules of the Law" (*Maxim II*).[6] Oddly, seven blank pages precede the next set of maxim pages (*Maxim III*), entitled "Maxims, etc." Quincy evidently conceived of these as three distinct maxim collections. In both volumes, Quincy's placement of the maxims toward the end of the book suggests that they may have been viewed as an appendix to the law reports; alternatively, the blank pages available after the *Law Reports* may have simply been a convenient locale for situating the maxims. Regardless, Quincy's use of distinct titles for the three separate groupings of maxim pages, while possibly inconsequential, is likely indicative of some schematic vision, perhaps divisible into Roman law (*Maxim I*), broad principles of law (*Maxim II*), and

4. The maxims are located on pages 151–56 of Quincy's fourth volume of *Law Reports*, comprising the years 1765–1769, and pages 161–63 and 171–83 of volume three (1764–1767). P347, Reel 4, QP 57; P347, Reel 4, QP 58. See Cox Chart, Appendix II, *infra*, pp. 429–37.

5. See Quincy's pages 151–56. Pages 157–60 are blank, and pages 161–84 contain miscellaneous notes on the law.

6. See Quincy's page 161, where an internal cross-reference to volume four of the *Law Reports* follows the title. One might inquire why the maxims in volume four are presented in this appendix ahead of the maxims in volume three. This originated in an erroneous assumption on my part, but has been retained upon further reflection. The transcription I was working from listed the maxims in this order, as this is the order of the page numbers on which the maxims appeared in the two volumes (i.e., the maxims in volume four occur on pages 151–56, while those in volume three appear on pages 161–63 and 171–83 of that volume). Only upon examining the detailed manuscript roadmap compiled by Kevin Cox did I discover that the maxims appeared in two separate volumes. It is impossible to determine the order in which these three sets of maxims were compiled, although intuitively one would expect Quincy to complete volume three before four. There is an argument to be made that Quincy's maxims in volume four were his initial project. But, given the increasing complexity of his citation format in volume three, the more simple Roman law maxim pages may have been compiled earlier. Ultimately, I have retained the order of *Maxim I, II, and III* here despite the fact that this places the volume four maxims ahead of those in volume three.

maxims dealing with particular substantive legal topics (*Maxim III*).[7] Unfortunately, Quincy's heavy reliance on Edward Coke in compiling both *Maxim II* and *Maxim III* stymie any conclusive effort to differentiate between these two sets of maxims.

All three groupings of maxim pages are written in the same hand, with a large underscored title at the top of each page. Structurally, however, the three sets of maxims differ somewhat. For example, neat organization characterizes the Roman law section in *Maxim I*, with indentations for each maxim and a separate footnote section at the bottom of some pages.[8] *Maxim III* evokes chaos by contrast, with maxims penned in script ranging from miniscule to large, most likely due to the addition of maxims at later points.[9] Furthermore, Quincy employs marginal footnotes to add extensive citation references in *Maxim III*, sometimes combining alphabetical footnotes with symbols when incorporating a combination of internal and external references or, perhaps, when adding further citations at a later time, thereby disrupting the original alphabetical scheme.[10] On one page, Quincy started with the letter *b* for his first footnote and proceeded next to *d*, apparently leaving out letters *a* and *c* in the anticipation of adding more footnotes later on.[11] Quincy's listing of citations was a work in progress, a reference to which he added further sources over time. He also added maxims at later points, as demonstrated by the fact that some maxims are sandwiched in, penned in a smaller hand, between two other maxims.[12] Unfortunately, it is impossible to determine whether the three sets of maxims were compiled simultaneously or at different times, which might explain some of these differences in format.

A few clues hint at Quincy's method in assembling the maxims and footnotes. Quincy's references are almost entirely impeccable. When I have run

7. The topical organization of Quincy's maxims is much looser than that employed in his commonplace book, which was organized with topical headings.

8. For an example of this careful organization and footnoting, see the original manuscript at P347, Reel 4, QP 58, page 151. Just as in a modern print edition, Quincy sometimes allowed his footnotes to extend into the lower part of a subsequent page when space ran short. See, e.g., *Id.*, pp. 151–52.

9. For an example of this variation in script size, see the original manuscript at P347, Reel 4, QP 57, page 171.

10. See, e.g., Quincy's pages 171–72.

11. See Quincy's page 181.

12. See, e.g., maxims [2] and [9] on Quincy's page 171.

into difficulty tracking down a source, the problem has almost always revolved around my failure to access a particular edition or to recognize at first that Quincy was not citing to an explicit quotation of a maxim, but instead to a more generalized discussion of a related topic. On one occasion where Quincy did provide an erroneous page number, however, I discovered that Coke's index of maxims (located toward the end of his volume of *Reports*) provided the same incorrect page number. In this instance, Quincy may have copied the page number, and perhaps the maxim itself, from Coke's maxim index, rather than accessing the maxim within the body of Coke's text.[13] At the same time, it is possible that Quincy employed a secondary source of maxims and citations, such as a fellow law scholar's commonplace book, and that this source, in turn, repeated the erroneous page number from Coke's list. Similarly, one of Quincy's Roman law maxims has a closer analogue in Coke's *Institutes* than in the *Digest* citation provided by Quincy, suggesting that Quincy was not referencing a copy of Justinian directly but was instead getting his maxims from another source.[14] Thus, Quincy may not have been simply paging through Coke's *Institutes*, Justinian's *Digest*, and other cited texts in search of maxim material, but may have relied instead, at least in part, on other sources.

Quincy's maxims are largely a study of Coke, and his reliance on Coke may have extended to questions of format as well. Some editions of Coke's *Reports* display a similarly heavy use of marginal citation notes, employing essentially the same format as that used by Quincy.[15] What was the purpose behind these extensive references to Coke and various reporters? Quincy's careful work in compiling his commonplace book and multiple volumes of law reports seems to rule out an idiosyncratic obsession with compiling lists of citations. The sheer number of marginal citations suggests also that these maxim lists were not merely a memory aid or study guide, in which case a single citation, or perhaps none at all, would have sufficed. Rather, Quincy likely intended to employ these maxim lists actively in devising legal arguments. Perhaps a

13. For the erroneous page citation, see Quincy's page 171, maxim [6], which references Coke, *Institutes*, part 2, page 309 rather than page 306. See also the index of maxims, provided toward the end of Coke's volume, which references the same incorrect page number.

14. See Quincy's page 153, maxim [3] and its footnote for further discussion.

15. See, e.g., Sir Edward Coke, *Reports*, part 1 (London, 1727), page 100.b (displaying alphabetical footnotes in the lefthand margins, with references to various reporters using standard abbreviations).

maxim with several citations carried greater legal weight in his estimation than one which appeared only once in Coke's *Reports*. Or perhaps the citations were a means to accessing more extensive supporting material to illuminate the possible application of a particular maxim.[16]

Several examples illustrate Quincy's plan for using the maxims. Quincy glossed one maxim with a footnote indicating that exceptions to the maxim's rule were possible in cases where otherwise "an inconvenience should follow."[17] In another instance, Quincy qualified a maxim describing custom as the best interpreter of laws with the comment that custom may sometimes prevail against a statute.[18] He traced this maxim to two sources: one regarding a slander action, and the other discussing the interpretation of charters. Perhaps Quincy viewed the maxims as general propositions of law that could be applied to a variety of causes of action, and his references were an aid to help him track down relevant material to cite in court. In another instance, Quincy referenced a source stating a proposition contrary to that communicated by the maxim itself.[19] After recording the familiar maxim that a personal action dies with the person, Quincy cited to Nelson's *Lex Testamentaria* with a note-to-self indicating that the referenced text describes how the maxim is "extended & limited."[20] This sophisticated gloss suggests that Quincy likely intended his maxims to serve as a reference to be used in practice, perhaps both for constructing legal arguments and for anticipating potential contrary arguments. This was not a rudimentary index of maxims, but a complex study of legal principles and their limitations.

While Quincy did separate his maxims into three distinct groupings,[21] he did not use the same precision in categorizing them as he did, for example, in dividing his commonplace book into distinct topical headings. Broadly speaking, *Maxim I* cited propositions from Roman law sources. *Maxim II* dealt in

16. Quincy's extensive use of internal cross-references, primarily to other pages within his collection of maxims, would have provided him with information on an extensive range of topics.

17. See maxim [10] on Quincy's page 173 and the corresponding footnote, which cites to Coke, *Institutes*, part 1, page 152.b.

18. See maxim [7] on Quincy's page 171 and the corresponding footnote.

19. See maxim [7] on Quincy's page 172 and the corresponding footnote.

20. See maxim [4] on Quincy's page 162 and the corresponding footnote.

21. For a rough breakdown of themes in Quincy's maxims, see the table of *Themes and Sources in Quincy's Maxims*, *infra*, pp. 336–38.

matters pertaining to lawsuits and the administration of justice. This section may have been compiled by Quincy with an eye toward use in the courtroom, where persuasive rhetoric might have employed general statements about law and justice. *Maxim III*, by contrast, dealt more with the nuts and bolts of what we would today categorize as property law, contracts, testaments, and evidence. Clearly this overlaps with the concept of *Maxim II*, but the goal here may have been to dig deeper into specific questions of law, rather than speaking of law in its more abstract and general sense.

My translation of Josiah Quincy Jr.'s collection of Latin legal maxims involved close work with the manuscript[22] but was aided tremendously by the earlier work undertaken by two other research assistants: Michael H. Hayden, who prepared an initial transcription, and Susannah B. Tobin, who commenced a translation of the maxims and took time out of her busy clerkship schedule to acquaint me with the project. In addition to Tobin's work, I relied on the Perseus on-line Latin reference,[23] my dog-eared copy of Lewis & Short,[24] and the various sources cited by Quincy, which often helped clarify the meaning of an otherwise ambiguous maxim.[25] When a maxim could lend itself to a more literal or classical translation, as opposed to a "legalistic" paraphrasing, I have erred in favor of the former. In some instances, I have footnoted alternative translations from *Latin for Lawyers*[26] or some other maxim reference book. My final task was to decipher the multitude of textual citations provided by Quincy and to track down his sources,[27] with the hope of deter-

22. I primarily relied on a photocopy of the manuscript, but also visited the Massachusetts Historical Society in November 2005 to clarify remaining ambiguities and to undertake a final review of the transcription. I am thankful to the Stephen T. Riley Librarian Peter Drummey and Reference Librarian Kimberly Nusco for their assistance in providing access to the manuscripts.

23. Gregory R. Crane, ed., *The Perseus Project*, http://www.perseus.tufts.edu. Last accessed 12/1/05.

24. Charlton T. Lewis, *An Elementary Latin Dictionary* (Oxford University Press, 1981).

25. For example, a maxim translated as, "The more liberal meaning should be preferred for general, or doubtful, statements" might appear to discuss witness testimony or interpretation of charters. However, Quincy's source for the maxim is a section of Coke's *Reports* dealing specifically with actions for slander. See maxim [7] on Quincy's page 179 and Coke, *Reports*, part 4, page 15.b.

26. E. Hilton Jackson, *Latin for Lawyers* (NY: The Lawbook Exchange, 1992) (reprint of 1915 Sweet & Maxwell edition).

27. Deciphering Quincy's abbreviated references required assistance from Professors Daniel Coquillette and Charles Donahue, the latter of whom explained the older method of citing the *Digest*, as employed by Quincy in the early pages of *Maxim I*. For instance, the *ff* notation used

mining why Quincy ever undertook this maxim collection in the first place. I hope the ensuing pages of translated maxims will provide some conclusions.

I should add a note on using the facing pages of Latin and English translation to follow. Generally, footnotes on the left-hand Latin page highlight oddities in the manuscript or, in some cases, alternative phrasings of the maxims as provided in Quincy's referenced sources. The footnotes on the right-hand page, on the other hand, primarily set out Quincy's citations in full detail, rendering "3 Rep. 40.a.", for instance, into "Sir Edward Coke, *Reports*, part 3 (1st French edition, 1602; 1st English edition, 1658), 40.a (Ratcliff's Case)." As in the above example, references have been fleshed out, wherever practicable, to include chapter headings or other identifying section titles. Where a citation is provided with no additional parenthetical explanation beyond a section title, as above, the reader may assume that the maxim quoted by Quincy was quoted directly in the source. However, where parentheticals are provided and do not expressly indicate that the maxim was quoted, the reader should assume that the maxim was not directly quoted in the source. In many cases, particularly in his marginal footnotes, Quincy referenced texts not for their direct quotation of a maxim but for their discussion of a related legal topic.

In compiling his maxim collection, Josiah Quincy Jr. recognized what Chancellor Kent would declare nearly a century later: "There are scarcely any maxims in the English law but what were derived from the Romans."[28] Perhaps this explains why, on the pages immediately following the curriculum recommended by Professor Francis Dickins at Cambridge, Quincy commenced a collection of excerpts almost exclusively derived from Justinian's *Digest*. Aside from footnoting related discourses from Wood's *Civil Law* to gloss three of the maxims, Quincy presented his "Maxims of the Civil Law," as he titled the collection, with only a single citation per maxim. It would appear that these maxims, as suggested by Lord Coke, were propositions "to be of all men confessed and granted without proofe, argument, or discourse."[29] Quincy may have viewed these Roman law maxims as propositions which

---

in early *Digest* citations has its origins in an erroneous reading of what was actually a fanciful uppercase letter D.

28. Lattin, 1, quoting 2 *Kent's Commentaries* (1858) sect. 553.

29. Lattin, 2, quoting Co. Litt. (1853) sect. 11.a. As to Professor Dickens's curriculum, see Daniel R. Coquillette, "Introduction," *supra*, pp. 32–33.

could stand on their own and, to quote Bacon, which could be "delivered to more several purposes and applications" accordingly.[30] Yet Quincy did not entirely adopt Bacon's approach toward maxims; whereas Bacon favored the delivery "of knowledge in distinct and disjoined aphorisms," so as to "leave the wit of man more free to turn and toss,"[31] Quincy appears to have grouped his civil law maxims into distinct legal categories, to which the modern reader might apply the titles interpretation of law,[32] the use of precedent,[33] wills and testaments,[34] contracts,[35] and criminal law.[36] This suggests that Quincy pinned the Roman law maxims to a specific substantive context beyond which they should not be too broadly construed.

In another volume of *Law Reports*,[37] Quincy compiled a separate list of maxims entitled "Maxims & Rules of the Law," comprising a mere three pages.[38] This collection has a loose thematic scheme that revolves largely around the general topic of law, lawsuits, and justice.[39] For this selection of maxims, Quincy relied heavily on Coke's *Institutes*, while also drawing aphorisms from a range of other sources, including Fitzherbert's *Natura Brevium*, Salkeld's and Coke's *Reports*, Plowden's *Commentaries*, and the *Abridgements* of both Lilly and Bacon. In contrast to the Roman law maxims, which could sometimes be compartmentalized into substantive categories as specific as contracts or criminal law, these maxims tend to offer broader legal principles. It may be for this reason that Quincy chose the title "Maxims *&* *Rules*," perhaps viewing the two terms as distinct. In this regard, Quincy's thinking would be aligned with that of John Dodderidge, who distinguished between

30. Daniel R. Coquillette, *Francis Bacon* (Edinburgh University Press, 1992), 38 (hereafter, "Coquillette"), quoting James Spedding, Robert Leslie Ellis, and Douglas Denon Hearth, *The Works of Francis Bacon* (London, 1857–1874), VII, p. 321 (hereafter, "Spedding").

31. Coquillette, p. 38, quoting Spedding, VII, p. 321.

32. See Quincy's pages 151–152, plus select maxims on pages 153 and 155.

33. See Quincy's page 153.

34. See Quincy's page 154.

35. See select maxims on Quincy's pages 154–55.

36. See Quincy's page 156 plus select maxims on page 155.

37. Quincy did not begin this separate compilation of maxims for lack of space in his other volume of *Law Reports*. See final page of the "Maxims of the Civil Law," Quincy's page 156, where the lower half of the page remains blank.

38. Note, however, that only the first page, Quincy's page 161, is entitled "Maxims & Rules of the Law," while the subsequent two pages are entitled "Maxims, etc."

39. See Quincy's pages 161–63.

'primary principles', or maxims, and 'secondary principles', or rules.[40] From Dodderidge's perspective, rules are 'not so well known by the light of nature . . . and are peculiarly known for the most part, to such only as profess the study and the speculation of the law.'[41] By contrast, Coke had little patience for distinguishing among maxims, principles, rules, postulates, or axioms, observing that "it were too much curiosity to make nice distinctions between them."[42] While it is possible to read too much into Quincy's choice of heading, I believe that he took a view of maxims and rules more akin to Dodderidge than Coke in this respect; this might help to explain Quincy's decision to compile three separate collections of maxims.

Coke also opined that "it is well said in our books . . . *n'est my a disputer l'ancient principles del ley.*"[43] Quincy was not so deferential. In his third collection of maxims, a collection entitled "Maxims, etc." and separated from "Maxims & Rules" by seven blank pages, Quincy engages the maxims, tests their limits, expands upon their applications, proffers examples, and cites to multiple sources. Lord Esher would observe over a century later that maxims "are almost invariably misleading: they are for the most part so large and general in their language that they always include something which really is not intended to be included in them."[44] Quincy's view was not so extreme, but he did recognize limits upon the appropriate application of certain maxims. For example, he notes that "*Verba accipienda sunt cum Effectu*" is a maxim that "holds good in Statutes."[45] Perhaps the maxim, in his view, should not be applied as readily to interpreting contracts or testaments. Similarly, Quincy cites to Coke's *Institutes* for guidance as to how the maxim, "*Quolibet Concessio fortissime contra Donatorem interpretanda est*" should be understood.[46] In another

40. See Coquillette, p. 37, quoting John Dodderidge, *The English Lawyer* (London, 1631), p. 194 (hereafter, "Dodderidge").

41. Coquillette, pp. 37–38, quoting Dodderidge, p. 194.

42. *Coke on Littleton*, p. 11a.

43. *Coke on Littleton*, p. 11a (punctuation added). First on Coke's famous list of sources of the common law were "Maxims, Principles, Intendment and Reason of the Common Law, which indeed is the Rule of the Law . . ." *Id.*

44. Lattin, 3, quoting *Yarmouth* v. *France*, 19 Q.B.D. 647, 653 (1887).

45. See Quincy's page 174, maxim [9] and corresponding footnote. "Words should be understood in connection with their effect."

46. See Quincy's page 176, maxim [1] and corresponding footnote. "Every grant should be interpreted most strongly against the donor."

instance, he quotes the maxim "*Res inter Alios acta, alteri nocere non debet*" but cites to "an exception to this Max." in Coke's *Institutes*.[47] In glossing the maxims in this manner, Quincy followed Bacon's example. In his *Maximes*, Bacon listed the rule, described it and the policy behind it, offered examples, and then turned to limitations or exceptions.[48] While not tackling each maxim as systematically as Bacon, or limiting his maxims to a more manageable number, Quincy nevertheless had a similar respect for the depth of information a single maxim could contain. At the same time, Quincy recognized that maxims could be applied erroneously, thereby exposing an uncautious lawyer's argument to attack.

This third maxim collection is almost entirely attributable to Coke, both the *Institutes* and the *Reports*, with a few rare exceptions such as Bulstrode and Salkeld's *Reports*, Hawkins's *Abridgment*, and Saint German's *Doctor & Student*. In fact, of a total of 147 maxims in this collection, a mere six have a primary citation other than to Coke.[49] The maxims are loosely arranged by topic, ranging from property law and interpretation of charters,[50] to criminal law[51] and evidence.[52] I believe that this collection of maxims was designed for active use in Quincy's legal practice, and that the multiple citations were a means for the young lawyer to bolster his maxim-based arguments with specific examples and nuanced interpretations.

POSTSCRIPT

How grateful I am to Professor Daniel R. Coquillette for introducing me to the world of Josiah Quincy Jr., a name only vaguely familiar to me previously in connection with his son, former President of Harvard College. As a budding historian, I take careful note of Prof. Coquillette's academic style, and I have been impressed by the sensitivity, lighthearted wit, and profound respect with which he has approached the subject of this series. In Prof. Coquillette's office at Harvard Law School, a copy of Gilbert Stuart's portrait of Josiah

47. See Quincy's page 173, maxim [10] and corresponding footnote. "Deeds performed among others should not cause harm to another."

48. Coquillette, pp. 41–42.

49. See Quincy's pages 171, 175, 177, and 182.

50. See Quincy's pages 174–76 plus select maxims on pages 171, 173, 177, 181, and 182.

51. See select maxims on Quincy's pages 177, 178, 181, and 183.

52. See select maxims on Quincy's page 180.

Quincy Jr. holds a conspicuous place of honor on the wall, an ever-present reminder of the brilliant young man whose legacy Prof. Coquillette has done so much to promote. I am deeply grateful to Prof. Coquillette for including me in the task of illuminating this portrait of a patriot, and for offering generous guidance, patient mentorship, and an admirable example.

THEMES AND SOURCES IN QUINCY'S MAXIMS

Page	*Total # of Maxims*	*Main Themes*[1]	*Main Sources (# maxims); fn = footnote; only first listed source recorded*	*Observations*
		MAXIMS I ("Maxims of the Civil Law")		
151	8	Interpretation of Law (8)	Justinian's *Digest* (7) Justinian's *Code* (1) Wood's *Civil Law* (fn)	Roman law sources. Clear theme throughout.
152	6	Interpretation of Law (6)	Justinian's *Digest* (6) Wood's *Civil Law* (fn)	Roman law source. Clear theme throughout.
153	6	Precedent (4) Interpretation of Law/ Judgment (2)	Justinian's *Digest* (6) Wood's *Civil Law* (fn)	Roman law source.
154	10	Wills & Testaments (5) Contracts (5)	Justinian's *Digest* (9) Justinian's *Code* (1)	Roman law sources.
155	10	Contracts (6) Criminal Law (3) Interpretation of Law/ Judgment (1)	Justinian's *Digest* (9) Justinian's *Code* (1) Wood's *Civil Law* (fn)	Roman law sources.
156	4	Criminal Law (4)	Justinian's *Digest* (4)	Roman law source. Lower half of page blank.
		MAXIMS II ("Maxims & Rules of the Law ")		
161	13	Law, Lawsuits, and Justice (12) Property (1)	Coke, *Institutes* (11) Fitzherbert, *Natura Brevium* (1) Salkeld's *Reports* (1)	
162	7	Law, Lawsuits, and Justice (7)	Coke, *Reports* (2) Coke, *Institutes* (1) Salkeld's *Reports* (1) Nelson (1) Lilly's *Abridgment* (1) Bacon's *Abridgment* (1)	Theme appears to be lawsuits in general, with some reference to principles of law. Greater variety of sources.
163	2	Interpretation of Law (1) Precedent (1)	Plowden, *Commentaries* (1) Justinian's *Digest* (1)	Most of page left blank.

1. These categories overlap considerably (e.g., precedent could be categorized under lawsuits), but represent my best attempt at pinning modern substantive categories on Quincy's collection of maxims. Some maxims could easily fit within multiple categories, but I have assigned them to only one.

THEMES AND SOURCES IN QUINCY'S MAXIMS (cont.)

Page	*Total # of Maxims*	*Main Themes*	*Main Sources (# maxims); fn = footnote; only first listed source recorded*	*Observations*
		MAXIMS III ("Maxims, etc.")		
171	13	Property (4) Interpretation of Law (3) Custom (3) Precedent (2) Natural Law (1)	Coke, *Institutes* (7) Coke, *Reports* (4) Bulstrode (1) Salkeld (1)	Quincy packs in maxims on this page and seems to add some later, writing them interlineally. Also introduces elaborate footnoting system to record additional citations.
172	14	Interpretation of Law (6) Property/Misc. (8)[2]	Coke, *Institutes* (11) Coke, *Reports* (3)	More difficult to discern a theme. Elaborate marginal footnotes.
173	12	Property/Interpretation of Charters (11) Actions of Court Officers (1)	Coke, *Institutes* (8) Coke, *Reports* (4)	Difficult to find a theme at first glance, but the references to Coke are primarily to matters regarding property law. Quincy has packed in the maxims, added some later, and filled the margins with footnoted citations.
174	9	Property/Interpretation of Charters (9)	Coke, *Reports* (5) Coke, *Institutes* (4)	Marginal footnotes.
175	10	Property/Interpretation of Charters (10)	Coke, *Institutes* (5) Coke, *Reports* (4) Saint German, *Doctor & Student* (1)	Marginal footnotes.
176	8	Property/Interpretation of Charters (8)	Coke, *Institutes* (5) Coke, *Reports* (3)	Marginal footnotes.
177	13	Criminal Law/Deceit (10) Property (3)	Coke, *Institutes* (5) Coke, *Reports* (6) Bacon, *Abridgment* (1) Bracton (1)	A fairly clear theme. Marginal footnotes.
178	13	Criminal Law (11) Misc (2)	Coke, *Institutes* (7) Coke, *Reports* (6)	A clear theme! Marginal footnotes.

2. These maxims appear to tackle a variety of themes, but their exposition in Coke places them largely within the substantive area of property law.

THEMES AND SOURCES IN QUINCY'S MAXIMS (cont.)

Page	*Total # of Maxims*	*Main Themes*	*Main Sources (# maxims); fn = footnote; only first listed source recorded*	*Observations*
179	12	Interpretation of Statements & Actions/Slander (12)	Coke, *Reports* (7) Coke, *Institutes* (5)	Marginal footnotes.
180	10	Proof & Evidence (8) Law, Lawsuits, & Justice (2)	Coke, *Institutes* (8) Coke, *Reports* (2)	Clear theme. Marginal footnotes.
181	14	Interpretation of Law (7) Criminal Law (5) Property Law (2)	Coke, *Institutes* (13) Coke, *Reports* (1)	Marginal footnotes.
182	11	Wills & Testaments (2) Interpretation of Statements & Actions/Slander (1) Property/Misc (8)	Coke, *Institutes* (10) Hawkins, *Abridgment* (1)	Very difficult to discern a theme. Marginal footnotes.
183	8	Criminal Law (4) Law, Lawsuits, & Justice (4)	Coke, *Institutes* (8)	Marginal footnotes.

THE LATIN LEGAL MAXIMS OF JOSIAH QUINCY JR.

151

Maxims vid vol. 3 p. 161.[1]
of the Civil Law[2] vid. p. 101 of this Book

[1] +In ambiguis orationibus maxime sententia spectanda est, qui eas protulisset. l. 96. ff. De Reg. Jur.[3]
[2] Benignius Leges interpretendae sunt: quo voluntas[4] Earum conservetur. l. 18 ff De Legib.
[3] Scire Leges non hoc est verba Earum tenere, sed vim, ac Potestatem. Ibid. 17. ff. De Legib.
[4] Etsi maxime verba Legis hunc habet Intellectum, tamen Mens Legislatoris Aliud vult. L. 13. p 2. ff. De excus-tut[5]
[5] Quod quidem perquam durum est:[6] sed ita Lex scripta est. l. 12. p.1. ff qui & a quib.
[6] Placuit in Omnibus Rebus praecipuam esse, Justitiae, Aequitatisq:, quam Stricti Juris Rationem. l. 9. c. De Judic.[7]
[7] Haec Aequitas Suggerit, etsi Jure deficiamur. l. 2 p. 5. in f. ff De Aqua & aquae Pluv. arc.
[8] Benigniorem Interpretationem sequi, non minus[8]

+This indefinite Rule[9] appears to be general & common to all Matters[10]: And if apply'd to all indifferently, we must conclude that in Contracts as well as Testaments, an ambiguous Expression must be interpreted by the Intention of Him whose Will it was to declare. And yet this Application, wch will always be just[11] in Testaments, will often be found false in Contracts: For in Testaments one only speaks, & his will is to serve for a Law; but in Contracts the Intention both of the One & the Other is the Common Law. Thus the Intention of[12]

1. This note cross-references another series of maxims in volume three of Quincy's *Law Reports*.

2. This collection of maxims, comprising Quincy's pages 151–56, is located in volume four of the *Law Reports*.

3. Another version reads ". . . spectanda est *eius*, qui eas protulisset" (emphasis added). Theodor Mommsen, Paul Krueger, eds., Alan Watson, trans., *The Digest of Justinian* (Philadelphia: University of Pennsylvania Press, 1985), vol. 4, p. 962 (hereafter, "Watson"). Quincy employs an older citation format here but switches to a more modern method for citing Justinian's *Digest* on page 153, maxim [2]. Quincy's *l* is shorthand for *lex*, and *ff* is a reference to the *Digest*. *De Reg. Jur.* identifies the chapter heading. This same maxim is quoted in a footnote in

151

Maxims of the Civil Law see vol. 3 p. 161. see p. 101 of this Book

[1] +With regard to ambiguous remarks, the intention of the one who proffered them must be considered above all else.[1]
[2] Laws must be interpreted liberally so that their will is preserved.[2]
[3] To know the laws is not to grasp their words but rather their force and power.[3]
[4] Even though the words of the law (i.e., a literal reading) have always had this meaning, nevertheless the legislator's intent wills a different interpretation.[4]
[5] Indeed it is extremely strict, but thus has the law been written.[5]
[6] It was decided that, in all things, justice and equity are to be foremost, rather than the rule of strict law.[6]
[7] Equity suggests these things, even though we are failed by the law.[7]
[8] To follow the more liberal interpretation is no less just than safe.[8]

+This indefinite rule appears to be general and common to all matters. And if applied to all indifferently, we must conclude that in contracts as well as testaments, an ambiguous expression must be interpreted by the intention of him whose will it was to declare. And yet this application, which will always be justice. Testaments will often be found false in contracts. For in testaments one only speaks, and his will is to serve for a law. But in contracts the intention both of the one and the other is the common law. Thus the intention of

1. Justinian's *Digest* 50.17.96 (hereafter abbreviated as D) (*De diversis regulis iuris antique*). See Watson, vol. 4, p. 962.

2. D.1.3.18 (*De legibus senatusque consultis et longa consuetudine*). See Watson, vol. 1, p. 12. An alternative meaning for *voluntas* is "intention." See, e.g., Watson, vol. 1, p. 12 (defining *voluntas* as "intendment"), and S. S. Peloubet, *A Collection of Legal Maxims in Law and Equity, with English Translations* (Colorado: Fred B. Rothman & Co., 1985), p. 22 (reprint of 1884 edition) (hereafter, "Peloubet").

3. D.1.3.17 (*De legibus senatusque consultis et longa consuetudine*). See Watson, vol. 1, p. 12.

4. D.27.1.13.2 (*De excusationibus*). See Watson, vol. 2, p. 786. Watson translates this, "if a literal reading of the legislation produces this meaning, nevertheless, the legislator intended a different meaning." Watson, vol. 2, p. 786. The maxim essentially captures the divide between legislative intent and a technical reading of the law.

5. D.40.9.12.1 (*Qui et a quibus manumissi liberi non fiunt et ad legem aeliam sentiam*). See Watson, vol. 3, p. 471. Watson translates the latter portion of the maxim, "but it is the express provision of the law." Watson, vol. 3, p. 471.

6. Justinian's *Code* 3.1.8 (hereafter abbreviated as C) (*De iudiciis*). See S. P. Scott, trans., *The Civil Law* (Cincinnati: The Central Trust Company, 1932), vol. 12, p. 258. Scott, conforming to modern usage, translates the closing phrase as "strict rule of law." Scott, vol. 12, p. 259.

7. D.39.3.2.5 (*De aqua et aquae pluviae arcendae*). See Watson, vol. 3, 397. Watson translates the latter part as ". . . even though we may lack a clear legal right." Watson, vol. 3, p. 397.

8. D.50.17.192 (*De diversis regulis iuris antique*). See Watson, vol. 4, p. 968. Quincy erroneously cites to p. 191.

Thomas Wood, *New Institute of the Imperial or Civil Law* (1st edition, 1704), p. 58 (hereafter, "Wood"), which corresponds with the text footnoted by Quincy on this page. Quincy's page number was confirmed by reference to Wood's 1730 London edition. Quincy uses the + sign preceding this maxim to reference the footnoted text. For further bibliographical information on Wood, see W. Harold Maxwell and Leslie F. Maxwell, *Legal Bibliography of the British Commonwealth of Nations*, vol. 1 (London: Sweet & Maxwell, 1955), p. 613 (hereafter, "Maxwell").

4. In the manuscript, the word "Design" appears, underscored, above *voluntas.*

5. Quincy's citation is not entirely legible. An examination of the original manuscript did not clarify this. Also, one might expect a plural verb form in place of "habet."

6. The word *est* is inserted with a caret above *durum.*

7. Quincy abbreviates *Aequitatisque,* and the letter *C* refers to Justinian's *Code.*

8. In the manuscript, *minus* appears directly below *non.* The maxim continues on page 152. A line is scored across the entire page before Quincy inserts a footnote.

9. Quincy leaves out a couple of phrases between "Rule" and "appears". *Cf.* Wood, p. 58.

10. Aside from some minor alterations, Quincy has been almost entirely loyal to Wood's text, even capitalizing most of the same words. *Cf.* Wood, p. 58.

11. Quincy abbreviates "which", and the underscoring is his.

12. The quote continues toward the bottom of page 152.

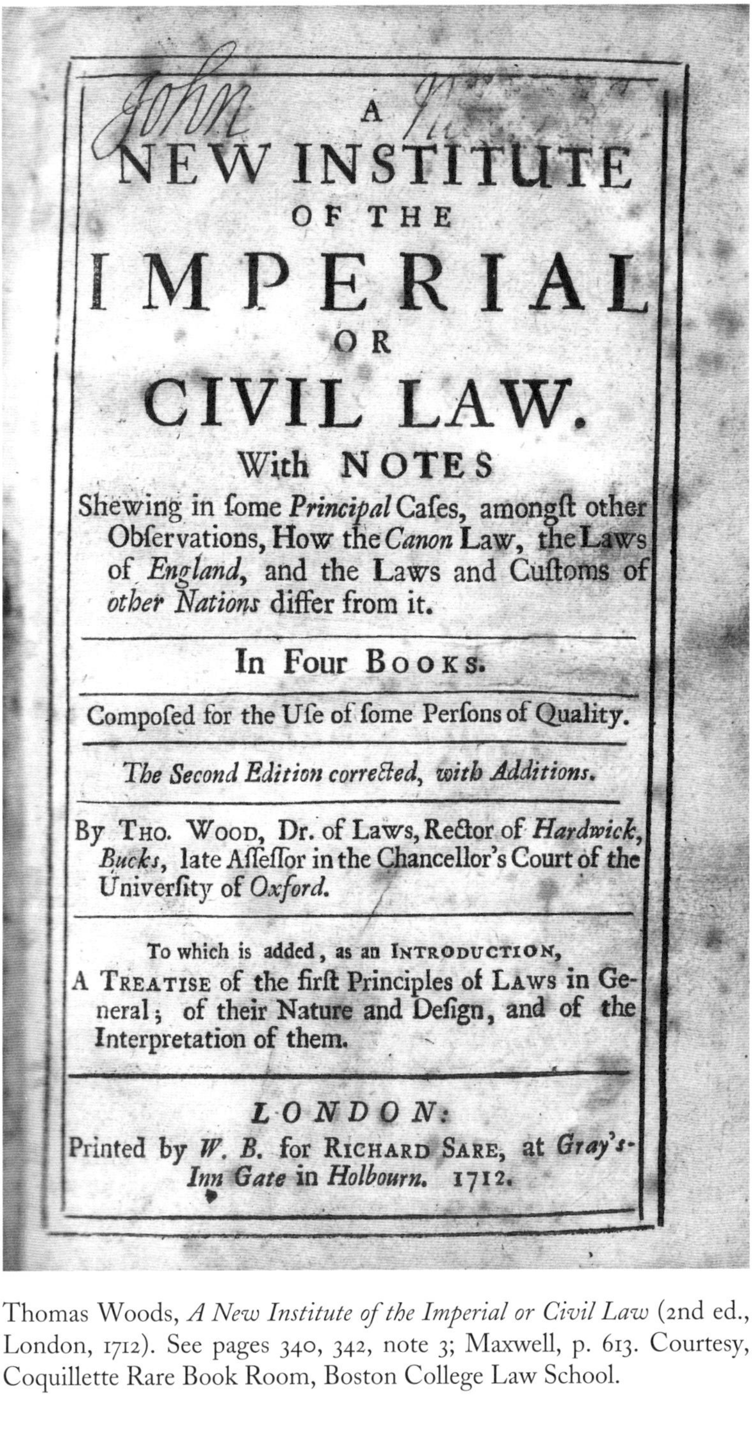

A
NEW INSTITUTE
OF THE
IMPERIAL
OR
CIVIL LAW.

With NOTES
Shewing in ſome *Principal* Caſes, amongſt other Obſervations, How the *Canon* Law, the Laws of *England*, and the Laws and Cuſtoms of *other Nations* differ from it.

In Four Books.

Compoſed for the Uſe of ſome Perſons of Quality.

The Second Edition corrected, with Additions.

By Tho. Wood, Dr. of Laws, Rector of *Hardwick*, *Bucks*, late Aſſeſſor in the Chancellor's Court of the Univerſity of *Oxford*.

To which is added, as an Introduction, A Treatise of the firſt Principles of Laws in General; of their Nature and Deſign, and of the Interpretation of them.

LONDON:
Printed by *W. B.* for Richard Sare, at *Gray's-Inn Gate* in *Holbourn.* 1712.

Thomas Woods, *A New Institute of the Imperial or Civil Law* (2nd ed., London, 1712). See pages 340, 342, note 3; Maxwell, p. 613. Courtesy, Coquillette Rare Book Room, Boston College Law School.

152

Civ. L. Maxims

minus justius est quam tutius. l.191. p.1 ff De
Reg. Jur.
[1] Semper in Dubiis benigniora praeferenda
sunt. l. 56. eod.[1]
[2] Rapienda Occasio est quae praebet benignius
Responsum. l. 168. Eod.[2]⊗

[3] In ambigua voce[3] Legis ea potius accipienda est
Significatio quae vitio caret, praesertim, cum etiam voluntas Legis ex hoc colligi possit: l. 19. ff De Legib.
[4] Quoties[4] Idem Sermo duas Sententias exprimit,
ea potissimum accipiatur[5] quae rei gerendae aptior est.
l. 67. ff De Reg. Jur.
[5] Incivile est nisi totâ Lege perspecta, una aliquâ
Particulâ ejus propositâ, judicare, vel respondere.
l. 24. ff De Legib.
[6] Nulla Juris Ratio, aut Aequitatis Benignitas patitur,
ut quae Salubriter pro Utilitate Hominum introducuntur,
ea nos duriore Interpretatione contra Ipsorum
commodum producamus ad Severitatem. l. 25. ff
De Legib.

---

of One ought to answer[6] to that of the Other,
& they must understand One Another, & agree together, & according
to this Principle it often happens, that an ambiguous Clause is not
to be interpreted by the Intention of him who expresses it, but
rather by the reasonable Intention of the Other. Thus etc.
Wood. Civ. Law. p. 58.[7]
⊗It cannot be fix'd as a general Rule,[8] that the Rigour of the
Law sh^{d}[9] always be follow'd against the Mitigations of Equity, or
that we sh^{d} always recede from the Rigour. Ibid. 72. But we
must judge by the Rigour of the Law, if the Law will not admit of any mitigation,
or by an equitable Mitigation, if the Law will admit of it. Ibid.[10] Although[11]

1. Here and in the maxim below, an abbreviation for *eadem*.
2. Quincy inserted a circled x to reference a footnote below, which is labeled here with a ⊗.
3. Quincy crossed out the final letter and inserted *e* above with a carat.
4. An alternative spelling is *quotiens*. See, e.g., Watson, vol. 4, p. 961.

152
Civ. L. Maxims

[1] The more liberal interpretation should always be preferred in doubtful situations.[1]
[2] The occasion which offers a favorable response must be seized.⊗[2]
[3] In an ambiguous statement of law, that meaning which is without fault should be accepted, especially when the will of the law can also be deduced from this.[3]
[4] As often as the same remark expresses two meanings, that one is to be accepted above all which is more suited to the management of the matter.[4]
[5] Unless the whole law is examined, it is improper to judge or to respond to any part of its propositions.[5]
[6] No reckoning of the law or kindness of equity is allowed when, just as something is introduced advantageously for the benefit of men, we bring forth (a result) contrary to these very advantages, through a harsh interpretation tending toward severity.[6]

---

of one ought to answer to that of the other, and they must understand one another; and agree together, and according to this principle it often happens that an ambiguous clause is not to be interpreted by the intention of him who expresses it, but rather by the reasonable intention of the other. Thus etc.[7]
⊗It cannot be fixed as a general rule that the rigor of the law should always be followed against the mitigations of equity, or that we should always recede from the rigor. Ibid. 72. But we must judge by the rigor of the law if the law will not admit of any mitigation or by an equitable mitigation if the law will admit of it. Ibid. Although[8]

1. D.50.17.56 (*De diversis regulis iuris antique*). See Watson, vol. 4, p. 960.

2. D.50.17.168 (*De diversis regulis iuris antique*). See Watson, vol. 4, p. 967. An alternative translation is "The occasion of offering a mild reply." Watson, vol. 4, p. 967.

3. D.1.3.19 (*De legibus senatusque consultis et longa consuetuedine*). See Watson, vol. 1, p. 13. Alternative translations for "is without fault" include "is consonant with equity" or "avoids an absurdity," and "will of the law" may be translated as "spirit of the law" or "intendment of the act". E. Hilton Jackson, *Latin for Lawyers* (New York: The Lawbook Exchange, 1992) (reprint of 1915 Sweet & Maxwell edition), p. 168 (hereafter, "*Latin for Lawyers*"); Watson, vol. 1, p. 13.

4. D.50.17.67 (*De diversis regulis iuris antique*). See Watson, vol. 4, p. 961. Alternative translations of the closing phrase include "for effecting the proposed end" or "to the conduct of the affair." *Latin for Lawyers*, 235; Watson, vol. 4, p. 961.

5. D.1.3.24 (*De legibus senatusque consultis et longa consuetuedine*). See Watson, vol. 1, p. 13.

6. D.1.3.25 (*De legibus senatusque consultis et longa consuetuedine*). See Watson, vol. 1, p. 13. Watson translates this complex maxim as, "It is not allowable under any principle of law or generous maxim of equity that measures introduced favorably to men's interests should be extended by us through a sterner mode of interpretation on the side of severity and against those very interests." Watson, vol. 1, p. 13.

5. Some versions of the *Digest* read *excipiatur*. See, e.g., Watson, vol. 4, p. 961.
6. Following this word, Quincy has crossed out a phrase.
7. See page 151 for the first half of this quote from Wood's *Civil Law*, p. 58.
8. Quincy has made some minor alterations to Wood's text. *Cf.* Wood, p. 72.
9. Here and in the line below, Quincy's abbreviation for "should."
10. A faithful quote, with the exception of Quincy adding the word "But" to the beginning. *Cf.* Wood, p. 72.
11. See page 153 for remainder of this quote.

7. Wood, p. 58. Wood quotes the same maxim as Quincy (i.e., "In ambiguis orationibus . . ."), noting that "This Rule is found in the *Roman* Law, that in ambiguous Expressions we must chiefly consider the Intention of him that speaks." *Ibid.*

8. Continues toward the bottom of Quincy's page 153.

This is Arnold Vinnius's commentary on *Justinian's Institutes*. See "Introduction," *supra*, pp. 31–32. See also John Adams's diary for Sunday, October 5th, 1758. John Adams, *Diary*, vol. 1 (L. H. Butterfield, ed., 1964), pp. 44–46. Courtesy, Coquillette Rare Book Room, Boston College Law School. See Coquillette, *Anglo-American Legal Heritage*, *supra*, p. 34.

153

Civ. L. Maxims

[1] In levioribus Causis proniores ad Lenitatem, Judices esse debent; in Gravioribus Paenis[1] Severitatem Legum cum aliquo Temperamento Benignitatis subsequi.[2]

[2] Non omnium, quae a majoribus nostris constituta sunt, Ratio reddi potest. D.1.3.20.
[3] Multa in Jure communi contra Rationem disputandi pro Utilitate communi recepta sunt.[3]
D.9.2.51.2.
[4] Quod contra Rationem Juris receptum est non producendum[4] ad Consequentias. D.50.17.141.etc.
[5] Minime sunt mutanda quae Interpretationem certam semper habuerunt. D.1.3.23
[6] Quicquid[5] in Calore Iracundiae vel fit vel dicitur non prius ratum est quam si Perseverantia apparet[6] Judicium Animi fuisse. D.50.17.48.

Although the Rigour of the Law seems to be distinguish'd from Equity, & they appear to be even opposite to one another, yet 'tis always true, that in such Cases wherein this Rigour is to be follow'd, another Consideration of Equity makes it just. And is[7] it can never happen that what is equitable is contrary to Justice, so neither can it happen, that what is just is contrary to Equity. Thus etc. W.civ.Law. 72.

1. An alternative spelling is *poenis*. See, e.g., Watson, vol. 4, p. 849.
2. Quincy leaves a couple of blank lines between this maxim and the following.
3. Quincy records the same maxim, with slight variation, on page 181, maxim [7], but cites there to *Coke on Littleton* instead of the *Digest*.
4. Quincy's word order is unusual. Other versions of the text read "*receptum est, non est producendum*" and "*receptum, non est producendum*". For examples of the former, see Watson, vol. 4, p. 965, and *Latin for Lawyers*, p. 231. For the latter, see Peloubet, p. 253.
5. Another version reads *quidquid*. Watson, vol. 4, p. 960.
6. Quincy appears to have written *apparet*. The expected word is *apparuit*. See, e.g., Watson, vol. 4, p. 960.
7. Quincy clearly wrote "is" here, but presumably he intended "as".

153

Civ. L. Maxims

[1] In less serious cases, judges should be inclined toward leniency; with more serious punishments, the harshness of the laws is to be followed with some measure of kindness.[1]
[2] A reason cannot be given for everything that was established by our ancestors.[2]
[3] Many things contrary to logical argument were received into the common law for the common good.[3]
[4] That which was received against the reason of the law should not be extended to subsequent cases.[4]
[5] Matters that have always had a certain interpretation should be changed as little as possible.[5]
[6] Whatever happens or is said in the heat of anger was not thought out first even if it appeared from perseverance to be a reasoned judgment.[6]

Although the rigor of the law seems to be distinguished from equity, and they appear to be even opposite to one another, yet it is always true that in such cases wherein this rigor is to be followed, another consideration of equity makes it just. And as it can never happen that what is equitable is contrary to justice, so neither can it happen that what is just is contrary to equity. Thus etc.[7]

1. Quincy provides no reference, but this is from D.48.19.11 (*De poenis*). See Watson, vol. 4, p. 849. Watson translates this, ". . . with more serious penalties they should conform to the severity of the statutes, tempered by kindliness." Watson, vol. 4, p. 849.

2. D.1.3.20 (*De legibus senatusque consultis et longa consuetudine*). See Watson, vol. 1, p. 13.

3. Quincy cites to D.9.2.51.2 (*Ad legem aquiliam*), which reads, in relevant part, ". . . *multa autem iure civili contra rationem disputandi pro utilitate communi recepta esse innumerabilibus rebus probari potest . . .*", and which Watson translates "Indeed, it can be proved by innumerable examples that the civil law has accepted things for the general good that do not accord with pure logic." Watson, vol. 1, p. 292. Apparently Quincy was not referencing a copy of Justinian but was instead getting his maxims (and citations to them) from another source. Here, Quincy may have been referencing *Coke on Littleton*, which reads, "*Multa in iure communi contra rationem disputandi pro communi utilitate introducta sunt.*" Sir Edward Coke, *First Part of the Institutes of the Lawes of England: or, Commentarie upon Littleton* (1st edition, London, 1628), p. 70 (hereafter, "Coke, *Institutes*, part 1"). For further bibliographical information on Coke, see Maxwell, p. 449.

4. D.50.17.141 (*De diversis regulis iuris antique*). See Watson, vol. 4, p. 965. An alternative translation of the closing phrase is "advanced to a precedent." *Latin for Lawyers*, p. 231.

5. D.1.3.23 (*De legibus senatusque consultis et longa consuetudine*). See Watson, vol. 1, p. 13.

6. D.50.17.48 (*De diversis regulis iuris antique*). See Watson, vol. 4, p. 960. Watson translates this as, "Anything said or done in the heat of anger is not endorsed unless it appears from perseverance that it was a deliberate intention." Watson, vol. 4, p. 960.

7. Wood, p. 72.

154
Civ. L. Maxims

[1] Ratum non habetur[1] quod non bona fide
gestum est. C.4.44.1.[2]

[2] Quae in Testamento scripta essent, neque
intelligerentur quid significarent,[3] ea perinde sunt
ac si scripta non essent. D.34.8.2.
[3] Voluntas facit quod in Testamento scriptum
valet.[4] D.30.1.12.3.
[4] Cum in Testamento ambigue aut etiam
perperam scriptum est, benigne interpre-
tari & secundum ~~id~~[5] id quod credibile est cogitatum,
credendum est. D.34.5.24.
[5] Non aliter a Significatione Verborum
recedi oportet quam cum manifestum est
aliud sensisse Testatorem. D.30.1.4.
[6] Haeredi magis parcendum est. D.31.1.47.[6]

[7] Uniuscuiusq. Contractus Initium spectandum est,
& Causa.[7] D.17.1.8
[8] Cujusq[8] Rei potissima Pars Principium est.
D.1.2.1.
[9] In Obscuris inspici solere quod verisimilius
est, aut quod plerumque fieri solet. D.50.17.114.
[10] In Conventionibus Contrahentium voluntatem
potius quam verba spectari placuit. D.50.16.219.

1. Another version reads *habebitur*. See Paul Krueger, *Corpus Iuris Civilis* (Berlin, 1959), vol. 2, p. 179 (hereafter, "Krueger").

2. Quincy has left a blank line between this maxim and the next.

3. The second *n* in *significarent* was inserted in superscript with a caret.

4. Although Quincy clearly wrote *valet* here, the expected verb is *valeat*. See, e.g., Watson, vol. 3, p. 3.

5. Quincy apparently wrote *id* twice but crossed out the first.

6. Quincy offers an abridged version of the cited *Digest* text, which Watson quotes, in relevant part, as "*magis heredi* parcendum est" (emphasis added). Watson, vol. 3, p. 48. Peloubet, however, presents the same wording as Quincy. Peloubet, p. 93. It is therefore conceivable

154
Civ. L. Maxims

[1] That which was not done in good faith will not be upheld.[1]
[2] Those things which have been written in a testament, and yet it is not understood what they mean, are just as if they had never been written.[2]
[3] The will makes that which is written in a testament have strength.[3]
[4] When in a testament something was written ambiguously or even incorrectly, it is to be interpreted liberally and according to that which is the likely intent, which must be given credence.[4]
[5] We should not otherwise depart from the meaning of words than when it is clear that the testator intended something else.[5]
[6] One should act sparingly toward an heir to a greater degree.[6]
[7] The beginning of every single contract should be examined, as well as its inducement.[7]
[8] The most important part of everything is the beginning.[8]
[9] In obscure matters, it is customary to consider what is probable, or what is most likely to occur.[9]
[10] In agreements it is resolved that the will, rather than the words, of the contracting parties is to be observed.[10]

1. C.4.44.1 (*De rescindenda venditione*). See Krueger, vol. 2, p. 179 for Latin text. An alternative translation is "the sale will not be valid, because it was not made in good faith." Scott, vol. 13, p. 100.

2. D.34.8.2 (*De his quae pro non scriptis habentur*). See Watson, vol. 3, p. 177.

3. D.30.1.12.3 (*De legatis et fideicommissis*). See Watson, vol. 3, 3. An alternative translation of *voluntas* is "intention," and *testamento* may be translated as "will." Watson, vol. 3, p. 3; *Latin for Lawyers*, p. 255.

4. D.34.5.24 (*De rebus dubiis*). See Watson, vol. 3, p. 175. Watson translates this as, "Where a testamentary provision is either ambiguous or incorrectly drafted, it should be interpreted generously, and any credible intention on the testator's part should be credited." Watson, vol. 3, p. 175.

5. This maxim appears to be from D.32.69 (*De legatis et fideicommissis*), not D.30.1.4 as cited by Quincy. See Watson, vol. 3, p. 92.

6. D.31.47 (*De legatis et fideicommissis*). See Watson, vol. 3, p. 48. "Much is to be overlooked in an heir" and "it is better to deal lightly with the heir" are two alternative translations. Peloubet, p. 93; Watson, vol. 3, p. 48.

7. D.17.1.8 (*Mandati vel contra*). See Watson, vol. 2, p. 481. For *causa*, alternative translations include "cause" and "factors lying behind it." Peloubet, p. 300; Watson, vol. 2, p. 481.

8. D.1.2.1 (*De origine iuris et omnium magistratuum et successione prudentium*). See Watson, vol. 1, p. 3.

that Quincy's source also phrased it this way. In other words, Quincy may not have been abridging the *Digest* directly but instead quoting from an already-abridged source. A blank line appears between this maxim and the following.

7. Quincy abbreviates *uniuscuiusque*. The Watson version of this maxim reads, "uniuscuiusque *enim* contractus initium spectandum *et causam*" (emphasis added), but the Peloubet version matches that of Quincy. Watson, vol. 2, p. 481; Peloubet, p. 300.

8. Abbreviation for *cuiusque*.

9. D.50.17.114 (*De diversis regulis iuris antique*). See Watson, vol. 4, p. 963. Alternative translations of the closing phrase include "what is generally done" and "what usually happens." Peloubet, p. 111; Watson, vol. 4, p. 963.

10. D.50.16.219 (*De verborum significatione*). See Watson, vol. 4, p. 952. An alternative translation for *voluntatem* is "intention." Watson, vol. 4, p. 952.

Justinian, *Corpus Juris Civilis*, Amsterdam, 1681, containing the *Digest*. Courtesy, Coquillette Rare Book Room, Boston College Law School. Continental editions of this type were regularly found in colonial libraries. See, for example, *The Printed Catalogues of the Harvard College Library* (W. H. Bond, H. Amory, eds., Boston, 1996), pp. A9, A10, A19 (1723 Catalogue); p. B15 (1773 Catalogue).

155

Civ. L. Maxims

[1] Non videntur, qui errant, consentire. D.50.17.116.2.
[2] Nemo videtur fraudare eos qui sciunt &
consentiunt. D.50.17.145.
[3] Qui cum alio contrahit vel est, vel essc
debet,[1] non ignarus Conditionis ejus. D.50.17.19.
[4] In pretio Emptionis & venditionis naturaliter
licet[2] contrahentibus se circumvenire. D.4.4.16.4.
[5] Fraudis Interpretatio semper in Jure Civili non
ex Eventu duntaxat, sed ex Consilio[3] quoque Conside-
ratur.[4]
⊗[6] Res tanti valet, quanti vendi potest.[5]
D.36.1.1.16.
[7] Non exemplis sed Legibus judicandum.[6] C.7.45.13
[8] Satius est impunitum[7] relinqui Facinus nocentis, quam
Innocentem damnari. D.48.19.5
[9] In Maleficiis Voluntas spectator non Exitus.
D.48.8.14.
[10] In Maleficiis Ratihabitio mandato aequiparatur.[8]
D.50.17.152.1. Interpretatione

⊗It must not be consider'd, what has been done, or what
is done, but what ought to be done. W.Civ.Law. B.4
Ch. 1. p. 295

1. While the Peloubet version matches that of Quincy, the Watson text reads *vel debet esse.* Peloubet, p. 243; Watson, vol. 4, p. 958.

2. The Watson version reads *licere.* Watson, vol. 1, p. 131.

3. The word "Design" is written interlineally above *Consilio.* For the same insertion, see Quincy page 151, Maxim [2].

4. Quincy may have misquoted his source here, as the expected word is *desideratur.* See, e.g., Peloubet, p. 86, and Watson, vol. 4, p. 961. Also, an alternative spelling of *duntaxat* is *dumtaxat.* See, e.g., Watson, vol. 4, p. 961.

5. This appears to be a summary of the *Digest* text, which reads "*Iulianus autem cavendum non putat, sed aestimandum fundum, quanti valet sine hac cautione, hoc est quanti vendere potest sine cautione . . .*" Watson, vol. 3, p. 227. However, Quincy probably did not abridge this maxim himself, as the sentence appears to have been in common usage. Regarding the relevance of this phrase to medieval commerce, see George O'Brien, *An Essay on Mediaeval Economic Teaching* (Kitchener, Ontario: Batoche, 2001) (first published in London, 1920) (citing Lessius, *De Justitia et Jure*, xxi. 19).

155

Civ. L. Maxims

[1] Those who err are not seen to consent.[1]
[2] No one is perceived to defraud those who understand and consent.[2]
[3] One who contracts with another is not, or should not be, ignorant of his terms.[3]
[4] With regard to the price, in buying and selling, it is naturally permitted to the contracting parties to overreach each other.[4]
[5] In the civil law an explanation of fraud is always examined not only from the outcome but also from the intention.[5]
⊗[6] A thing is worth as much as it is possible to be sold for.[6]
[7] One must judge not from examples but from laws.[7]
[8] It is better that a harmful deed[8] remain unpunished than an innocent person be convicted.[9]
[9] With regard to crimes, the will,[10] not the result, is to be examined.[11]
[10] With regard to crimes, acquiescence is to be equated with a command.[12]

⊗ It must not be considered, what has been done, or what is done, but what ought to be done.[13]

1. D.50.17.116.2 (*De diversis regulis iuris antique*). See Watson, vol. 4, p. 963.
2. D.50.17.145 (*De diversis regulis iuris antique*). See Watson, vol. 4, p. 965.
3. D.50.17.19 (*De diversis regulis iuris antique*). See Watson, vol. 4, p. 958.
4. D.4.4.16.4 (*De minoribus viginti quinque annis*). See Watson, vol. 1, p. 131.
5. Quincy provides no reference, but this appears to be D.50.17.79 (*De diversis regulis iuris antique*). See Watson, vol. 4, p. 961. Watson translates this as, "In the civil law, the interpretation of fraud is sought not only on the basis of the outcome but also on the basis of the intention." Watson, vol. 4, p. 961.
6. D.36.1.1.16 (*Ad senatus consultum trebellianum*). See Watson, vol. 3, p. 227.
7. C.7.45.13 (*De sententiis et interlocutionibus omnium iudicum*). See Krueger, vol. 2, p. 315 for Latin text and Scott, vol. 14, p. 187 for English translation. The Krueger version of this text, unlike that of Quincy, ends with *est*, which combined with the gerundive *judicandum* would result in the passive periphrastic, implying "must" or "should." See Krueger, vol. 2, p. 315.
8. Watson translates this as "crime of a guilty man." Watson, vol. 4, p. 846.
9. D.48.19.5 (*De poenis*). See Watson, vol. 4, p. 846.
10. An alternative translation is "intention." *Latin for Lawyers*, 171; Watson, vol. 4, p. 821.
11. D.48.8.14 (*Ad legem corneliam de sicariis et veneficis*). See Watson, vol. 4, p. 821.
12. D.50.17.152.2 (*De diversis regulis iuris antique*). See Watson, vol. 4, p. 965.
13. Wood, 295. The relevant text reads, "But when he judges, it ought to be according to Law and Custom, not by Precedents or Examples; for he must not consider what is done at *Rome*, but what ought to be done there."

6. This is an abridgement of a longer sentence in Justinian's *Code*. See Krueger, vol. 2, p. 315. A superscript "x" preceding this maxim corresponds with footnoted text, separated from the main body of maxims by a line across the page.

7. The Watson version of this *Digest* quote reads "satius *enim esse* impunitum" (emphasis added). Watson, vol. 4, p. 846.

8. Other versions of this *Digest* excerpt read "In *maleficio* ratihabitio mandato *comparatur*" (emphasis added). Watson, vol. 4, p. 965; R. S. Vasan, ed., *Latin Words & Phrases for Lawyers* (Ontario: D. S. Sodhi for Law and Business Publications, 1980), p. 114 (hereafter, "Vasan").

This is the Frontispiece of Arnoldus Vinnius (1588–1657) *Partitionum Juris Civilis* Libri IV (Rotterdam, 1664). The figure on the left represents the Emperor Justinian. On the right is a modern sovereign, possibly the Holy Roman Emperor. Below is a picture of the modern sovereign with his legal counselors, his judges or jurists. Note this Roman law treatise was published in Holland in 1664. The Dutch still have a civil law system. South Africa, a former Dutch colony, has been remarkably influenced by Roman law. Courtesy, Coquillette Rare Book Room, Boston College Law School. See Coquillette, *Anglo-American Legal Heritage*, *supra*, p. 12.

156

Civ. L. Maxims[1]

[1] Interpretatione Legum Paenae Moliendae sunt, potius quam exasperandae. D.48.19.42.[2]
[2] In paenalibus Causis benignius interpretandum.
D.50.17.155.2.[3]
[3] Nunquam crescit ex post facto praeteriti Delicti Aeftimatio.[4]
[4] Nonnunquam evenit, ut Aliquorum Maleficiorum Supplicia exacerbantur, quoties nimirum,[5] multis Personis grassantibus, exemplo[6] Opus sit. Lib.16. p 10 ff de paenis.

1. The latter half of the page is blank.

2. Quincy appears to have written *Paenae* here, although a more common spelling would be *Poenae.* See also Quincy's spelling of *paenalibus* in the next maxim. The spelling differences are inconsequential, as *paenitere,* or cause to repent, is related to *poena,* or punishment. Also, Quincy writes *moliendae* and *exasperandae,* while Watson's version reads *molliendae* and *asperandae.* Watson, vol. 4, p. 854.

3. Both the Watson and *Latin for Lawyers* versions end with the word *est.* Watson, vol. 4, p. 966; *Latin for Lawyers,* p. 172.

4. Both Quincy and *Latin for Lawyers* write *nunquam,* but Watson uses *numquam. Latin for Lawyers,* p. 211; Watson, vol. 4, p. 965.

5. Watson version reads *quotiens nimium.* Watson, vol. 4, p. 850.

6. A word has been blackened out between *exemplo* and *Opus.*

156
Civ. L. Maxims

[1] In an interpretation of law, punishments are better moderated than toughened.[1]
[2] In penal cases, one should interpret (the law) liberally.[2]
[3] The estimation of a past crime never increases after the fact.[3]
[4] It sometimes comes to pass that as the penalties of some crimes are increased, (this) action truly serves as an example for many people lying in wait.[4]

1. D.48.19.42 (*De poenis*). See Watson, vol. 4, p. 854.
2. D.50.17.155.2 (*De diversis regulis iuris antique*). See Watson, vol. 4, p. 966. Watson translates this as, "In penal cases, the milder interpretation is to be adopted." Watson, vol. 4, p. 966.
3. Quincy provides no reference, but this appears to be D.50.17.138 (*De diversis regulis iuris antique*). See Watson, vol. 4, p. 965. *Latin for Lawyers* translates the latter part of the maxim as "is never increased by a later fact." *Latin for Lawyers*, p. 211.
4. D.48.19.16.10 (*De Poenis*). See Watson, vol. 4, p. 850.

161

Maxims & Rules of the LAW[1] vid Vol. 4. p. 151.

[1] Lex est tutissima Cassis, sub Clypeo Legis Nemo dicipitur.[2] 2 Inst. 56. 526.
[2] Justitia debet esse libera, quia nihil iniquis[3] venali justitia; plena, quia Justitia non debet claudicare; & celeris, quia Dilatio est quaedam Negatio.[4] 2 Inst. 56.
[3] Lex uno Ore Omnes Alloquitur. Ibid 184.
[4] Nihil Aliud potest Rex, etc., quam quod de Jure potest. 2 Inst. 187.
[5] Pendente Lite nihil innovetur. Ibid. 208.
[6] Lex dilatores[5] semper exhorret. 2 Inst. 240.
[7] Potestas regia est facere Justitiam. ibid. 374.
[8] Nemo[6] contra Recordum verificare per Patriam. 2 Inst. 380.
[9] Melior est Conditio Possidentis. Ibid. 391.
[10] Absoluta Sententia Expositore non indiget. Ibid. 533.
[11] Lex beneficialis Rei consimili Remedium praestat. Ibid. 689.
[12] Si Petens deficit in uno cadit in omnibus. Hale's FNB. 452 Note
[13] Ex nudo Pacto non Oritur Actio. 1. Salk. 129 vid. 1 Salk 24 Harrison's Case.

1. This collection of maxims, comprising Quincy's pages 161–163, is located within volume three of the *Law Reports*.

2. The expected spelling is *decipitur*. See, e.g., Sir Edward Coke, *Second Part of the Institutes of the Lawes of England; containing the exposition of many ancient and other Statutes* (1st edition, London, 1642), p. 56 (hereafter, "Coke, *Institutes*, part 2"); *Latin for Lawyers*, p. 183. For further bibliographical information on Coke, see Maxwell, p. 546.

3. Quincy dropped a couple of minims, as the expected word is *iniquius*. Coke, *Institutes*, part 2, p. 56.

4. The original version reads "Justice must have three qualities, it must be *Libera, quia nihil* . . ." Coke, *Institutes*, part 2, p. 56.

5. The expected word is *dilationes*. See, e.g., Coke, *Institutes*, part 2, p. 240; *Latin for Lawyers*, p. 183. The two words are related. *Cf. dilatio*, or "delay", and *dilator*, or "one who delays".

6. Quincy leaves out the word *potest* here. See Coke, *Institutes*, part 2, p. 380.

161

Maxims & Rules of the LAW

see Vol. 4. p. 151.

[1] The law is the safest helmet; under the shield of the law no one is deceived.[1]
[2] Justice should be free, because nothing is as unjust as justice for sale; complete, because justice should not be lacking; and speedy, because delay is a kind of denial.[2]
[3] The law addresses all with one mouth.[3]
[4] The king can do nothing other than what he can do by law.[4]
[5] In a pending lawsuit, nothing is to be altered.[5]
[6] The law always dreads delays.[6]
[7] The power of the king is to do justice.[7]
[8] No one (can) verify against a record by the country (i.e. by a jury).[8]
[9] The condition of the possessor is better.[9]
[10] An absolute proposition does not require an explanation.[10]
[11] A favorable law furnishes a remedy for a similar case.[11]
[12] If the person seeking (i.e. the petitioner) is lacking in one thing he falls in all.[12]
[13] An action does not arise from a bare contract (i.e. a contract without consideration).[13]

1. Coke, *Institutes*, part 2, p. 56 (*Magna Charta*, ch. 29), p. 256 (*Confirmationes chartarum de libertatibus Angliae & Forestae*, ch. 1). The entirety of the maxim, as quoted by Quincy, is found on page 56, while the words "*Lex est tutissima cassis*," but not the remainder of the maxim, may also be found on page 526.

2. Coke, *Institutes*, part 2, p. 56 (*Magna Charta*, ch. 29). An alternative translation for the opening phrase is "Justice ought to be unbought, because nothing is more hateful than venal justice." *Latin for Lawyers*, p. 180.

3. Coke, *Institutes*, part 2, p. 184 (*Statutum de Westminster primer*, ch. 15).

4. Coke, *Institutes*, part 2, p. 187 (*Statutum de Westminster primer*, ch. 15) (quoting Bracton). The same translation is offered in *Latin for Lawyers*, p. 201.

5. Coke, *Institutes*, part 2, p. 208 (*Statutum de Westminster primer*, ch. 25). An alternative translation is, "During a litigation nothing new should be introduced." *Latin for Lawyers*, p. 218.

6. Coke, *Institutes*, part 2, p. 240 (*Statutum de Westminster primer*, ch. 40).

7. Coke, *Institutes*, part 2, p. 374 (*Statutum de Westminster secundo*, ch. 9).

8. Coke, *Institutes*, part 2, p. 380 (*Statutum de Westminster secundo*, ch. 11). In other words, an issue on record may not be put to a jury.

9. Coke, *Institutes*, part 2, p. 391 (*Statutum de Westminster secundo*, ch. 16).

10. Coke, *Institutes*, part 2, p. 533 (*Statutum de Tallagio non concedendo*, ch. 1). An alternative translation is, "Where the language is plain (as in a statute or a deed), no explanation of them is required." Vasan, p. 19.

11. Coke, *Institutes*, part 2, p. 689 (An Exposition upon the Statute of Offices, ch. 1).

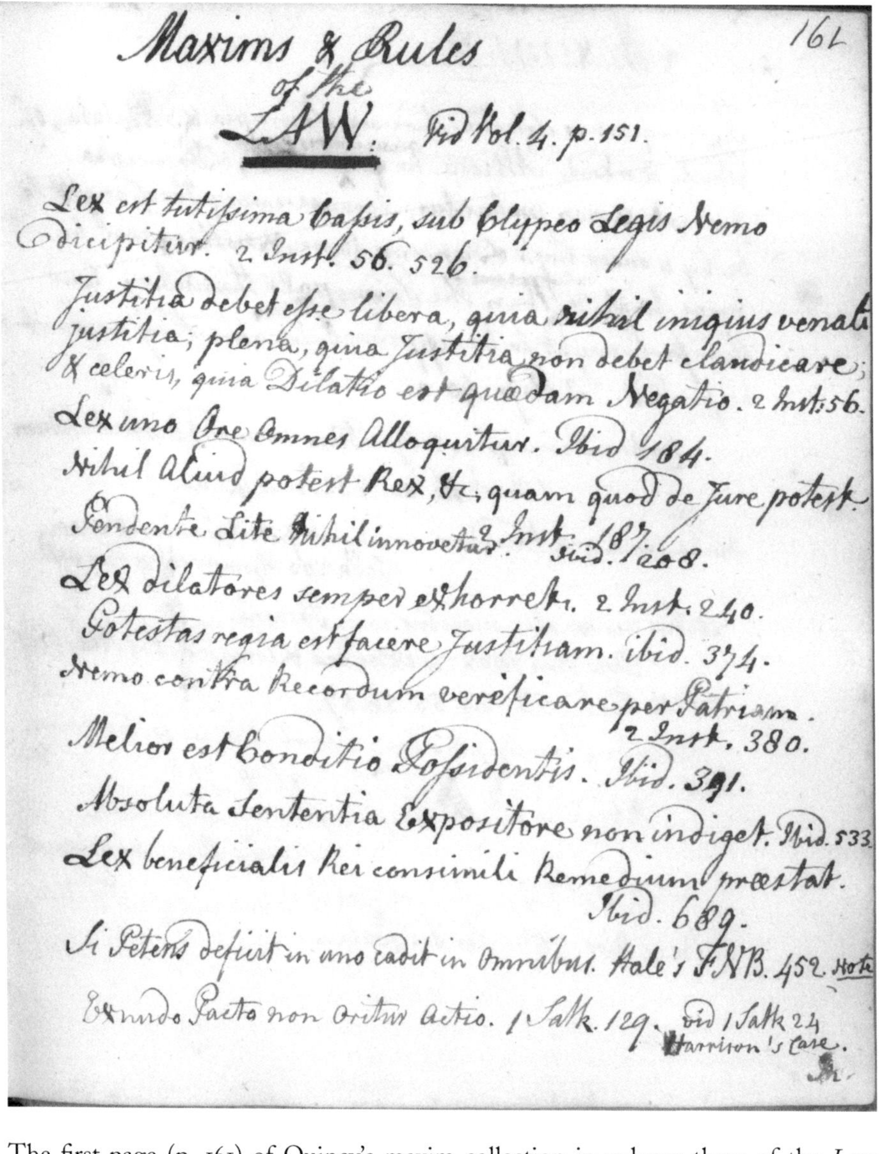

Maxims & Rules of the LAW: Vid Vol. 4. p. 151. 161

Lex est tutissima Cassis, sub Clypeo Legis Nemo decipitur. 2 Inst. 56. 526.

Justitia debet esse libera, quia nihil iniquius venali justitia; plena, quia Justitia non debet claudicare; & celeris, quia Dilatio est quaedam Negatio. 2 Inst. 56.

Lex uno Ore Omnes Alloquitur. Ibid 184.

Nihil Aliud potest Rex, &c, quam quod de Jure potest.

Pendente Lite Nihil innovetur. 2 Inst. 187. ibid. 208.

Lex dilatores semper exhorret. 2 Inst. 240.

Potestas regia est facere Justitiam. ibid. 374.

Nemo contra Recordum verificare per Patriam. 2 Inst. 380.

Melior est Conditio Possidentis. Ibid. 391.

Absoluta Sententia Expositore non indiget. Ibid. 533.

Lex beneficialis Rei consimili Remedium praestat. Ibid. 689.

Si Petens deficit in uno cadit in Omnibus. Hale's FNB. 452. Note

Ex nudo Pacto non Oritur Actio. 1 Salk. 129. vid 1 Salk 24 Harrison's Case.

The first page (p. 161) of Quincy's maxim collection in volume three of the *Law Reports*, P347, Reel 4, QP 57. See Cox Chart, Appendix II, *infra*. The page, which is entitled "Maxims & Rules of the Law," is cross-referenced to Quincy's compilation of Roman law maxims in volume four. As with the Roman law maxims, this collection was written in an even hand and does not present significant evidence of later insertions of additional maxims or citations. My thanks to Elizabeth Papp Kamali.

12. Sir Anthony Fitzherbert, *New Natura Brevium; with a table of the most material things contained therein, composed by William Rastall, [also] the Authorities in Law* (1st French edition, 1534 and 1537; 1st English edition, 1652), p. 452 (hereafter, "Fitzherbert, *New Natura Brevium*"). The page number provided by Quincy was confirmed against Fitzherbert's 7th edition (London, 1730), which includes a commentary by the Lord Chief Justice Hale. The text quoted by Quincy appears in a footnote. For further bibliographical information on Fitzherbert, see Maxwell, p. 269.

13. William Salkeld, *Reports of Cases in the Court of King's Bench, with some special cases in the Courts of Chancery, Common Pleas and Exchequer, alphabetically digested under proper heads, from the 1st of William and Mary to the 10th of Anne [1689–1712]* (1st edition, 1717), vol. 1, p. 129 (*Pottet* v. *Pearson*) (hereafter, "Salkeld"). The page number provided by Quincy was confirmed with reference to Salkeld's 3rd edition (London, 1731–1732). For further bibliographical information on Salkeld, see Maxwell, p. 308. Quincy also references Salkeld, vol. 1, p. 24 (*Harrison's Case*), in which it is stated regarding a promise to marry, if "the Woman's Promise does not bind, the Man's Promise is but *nudum pactum*, and therefore it is not actionable either on both Sides or on neither Side."

162

Maxims etc.

[1] In every Art or Science there are Principia & Postulata, of which it is said, Altiora ne quaesiveris,[1] & Principia probant, & non probantur, because every Proof ought to be by a more high & supreme Cause, & nothing can be more high & supreme[2] than the Principals themselves, and therefore ought to be approved because they cannot be proved. 3 Rep. 40.a.

[2] Contra Principia negantem[3] non est disputandum.
1 Inst.16.a. 232.b. 343.a.

[3] Nulla Curia quae Recordum non habet potest mandare Carceri.
1 Salk 200. Groenvelt vs Burwell

[4] Actio personalis moritur cum Personâ.
How This Max: is extended & limited. Vid Nelson's Lex Test:. 53. 54. 55. 56. 57.[4]

[5] Stabit Presumptio donec probetur in contrarium.
4 Rep. 71.b.

[6] Exceptio in non exceptis firmat Regulam.
1 Lilly Abr. 559 Exceptio

[7] Oportet Politiam obedire Legibus non Leges Politiae.
4 Bac. Abr. 287. Per Twisden.

1. Quincy may have initially misspelled *quaesiveris*, as it is written interlineally above a crossed-out word.

2. Quincy has inserted "supreme" interlineally above "& . . . than" with a caret.

3. Coke writes *negantem principia*. Coke, *Institutes*, part 1, p. 343.a.

4. William Nelson, *Lex Testamentaria; or, System of the Laws of England, as well before the Statute of Henry VIII as since, concerning Last Wills and Testaments* (1st edition, 1714), pp. 53–57 (hereafter, "Nelson"). The page number provided by Quincy was confirmed against Nelson's second edition, published in London in 1724. For further bibliographical information on Nelson, see Maxwell, p. 493. As indicated by Quincy, these pages of Nelson's text offer exceptions to the rule that a personal action dies with the person. For instance, Nelson notes, "most actions which Arise by Contract, as Debt, Covenant, &c. an Executor might maintain at Common Law after the death of his Testator." Nelson, pp. 53–54.

162

Maxims etc.

[1] In every art or science there are principles and postulates, of which it is said, do not seek the higher things, and principles prove, and are not proved, because every proof ought to be by a more high and supreme cause, and nothing can be more high and supreme than the principles themselves, and therefore ought to be approved because they cannot be proved."[1]
[2] Contrary to denying (them), principles should not be disputed.[2]
[3] No court which does not have a record can commit (a person) to prison.[3]
[4] A personal action dies with the person.[4]
[5] A presumption will stand until it is proved to the contrary.[5]
[6] An exception establishes the rule in those things not excepted.[6]
[7] It is necessary that the polity obeys the laws, not that the laws obey the polity.[7]

1. Sir Edward Coke, *Reports*, part 3 (1st French edition, 1602; 1st English edition, 1658), p. 40.a (*Ratcliff's Case*) (hereafter, "Coke, *Reports*, part 3"). For further bibliographical information, see Maxwell, pp. 295–96. This maxim anticipates Kantian categorical imperatives, which are incapable of proof.

2. Coke, *Institutes*, part 1, p. 343.a (ch. XI, Of Discontinuance, Sec. 648). Although the maxim is not quoted therein, Quincy also cites to page 16.a (relevance not apparent) and page 232.b (Ch. 5, Of Estates upon Condition, Sect. 377), discussing the idea of *legitima ratio*, and the simultaneous avoidance of "new inventions" in the law.

3. Salkeld, vol. 1, p. 200 (*Groenvelt* v. *Burwell*).

4. Nelson, pp. 53–57. The same translation is offered in Peloubet, p. 5.

5. Sir Edward Coke, *Reports*, part 4 (1st French edition, 1604; 1st English edition, 1658), p. 71.b (*Hynde's Case*) (hereafter, "Coke, *Reports*, part 4"). For further bibliographical information, see Maxwell, pp. 295–96.

6. John Lilly, *Practical Register; or, General Abridgment of the Law, as practiced in the courts of Chancery, King's Bench, Common Pleas, and Exchequer, with rules of Court,* vol. 1 (1st edition, London, 1719), p. 559. For further bibliographical information, see Maxwell, p. 273. The page number corresponds with the 1719 edition, which defines "exception" as ". . . a Thing taken out of the Deed . . . as if no Mention had been made of it in the Deed." *Id.*

7. Matthew Bacon, *New Abridgement of the Law*, vol. 4 (1st edition, 1759), p. 287 (hereafter, "Bacon, *Abridgment*"). The first edition of Bacon's five-volume abridgement was published in installments between 1736 and 1766. For further bibliographical information, see Maxwell, 16. The quoted text is within the section entitled "Release" and the subsection discussing "Claims and Demands, what are released thereby."

163

Maxims etc.

[1] Mala est expositio[1] quae corrumpit viscera textus. Plowd. Eng: Edit (1761) 288.[2]
[2] Non omnium quae a majoribus constituta sunt ratio reddi potest.

1. A letter has been crossed out at the end of *expositio*.

2. Unlike elsewhere in the manuscript, Quincy has identified the specific edition referenced here.

163

Maxims etc.

[1] Bad is the explanation that destroys the inner parts of the text.[1]
[2] A reckoning cannot be rendered for everything that was laid down by (our) ancestors.[2]

1. Edmund Plowden, *Commentaries or Reports: Divers Cases upon matters of Law, [1550–80]; written in French, now translated, [with his] Quaeries rendered into English* (1st English edition, London, 1761), p. 288 (*Chapman* v. *Dalton*). The commentaries were first published in French in 1579 in two parts, respectively entitled *Les Comentaires, ou les Reportes, de dyuers cases esteantes matters en ley, en les temps des raygnes le Roye Edwarde le size, le Roigne Mary, le Roy and Roigne Phillipp and Mary and le Roigne Elizabeth [1550–1771]* and *Certeyne Cases Reportes, puis le primier imprimier de ses Commentaries, & ore a le seconde imprimier de dites Commentaries, a ces addes [1571–80. With "Un Report del part de vn argument del Plowden."]* in 1579. For further bibliographical information, see Maxwell, pp. 306–07. The Latin maxim is footnoted in the left-hand margin of the 1761 edition, while Plowden explains in the main text, "he is a bad Expositor that destroys the text."

2. Quincy provides no reference, but this is from D.1.3.20 (*De legibus senatusque consultis et longa consuetudine*). See Watson, vol. 1, p. 13. An alternative translation is, "It is not possible to find an underlying reason for everything which was settled by our forebears." Watson, vol. 1, p. 13.

171

Maxims. etc.[1] vid vol. 4. p. 151.
vid. vol. 4. p. 101.[2]

[1] Omnis Innovatio plus Novitate perturbat quam Utilitate prodest.
1 Bul. 138. 1 Salk 20.

[2] Sic utere[3] tuo ut Alienum non laedas. 1 Salk 22.

[3] Qui Rationem in Omnibus quaerunt, Rationem subvertunt. 2 Rep. 75. vid[4] p 181 max. 7

[4] Jura Naturalia sunt immutabilia. 7 Rep. 13. Hob 87.[5]

[5] Lex citius vult tolerare privatum Damnum, quam publicum Malum. 1 Inst. 252.b.[6]

[6] Quando Lex Aliquid Alicui concedit, concedere videtur[7] id sine quo Res ipsa esse non potest. 1 Inst. 56.a. 2 Inst 309.[8] 4 Inst. 111. 3 Rep. 12. 47. 11 Rep. 52.[9]

[7] Optimus Interpres Legum Consuetudo.[10] 2 Inst 18. 228. 282. 4 Inst. 73.[11] Custom has sometimes prevailed ag:^{t} a positive Law.[12]

[8] Malus Usus abolendus est. Lit 212. 1 Inst 141.a. 4 Inst. 274.[13]

[9] Quae in Consuetudinibus non Diuturnitas Temporis, sed soliditas Rationis est considerandae. Co. Lit: 141.a.[14]

[10] Consuetudo licet sit magnae Authoritatis, nunquam tamen praejudicat Manifestae Veritati. 2 Inst. 654. 4 Rep 18.

[11] Et Antecedentibus & Consequentibus sit optima Interpretatio. 2 Inst. 317. 2 Rep. 71.

[12] Relatio sit ad proximum Antecedens, nisi impediatur Sententia.[15] 2 Rep. 71.

[13] Generalis Clausula non porrigitur ad ea quae specialiter sunt comprehensa aut expressa.[16] 8 Rep. 118.[17]

1. This collection of maxims, comprising Quincy's pages 171–83, is located in volume four of the *Law Reports*.

2. Below this text, Quincy has crossed out a maxim.

3. Quincy has drawn an arrow from *utere* to a small box directly below. The *Sic utere* maxim may have been written down at a later time, as Quincy appears to have squeezed it in between two other maxims.

4. Preceding *vid* is a small box, similar to the one below *utere* in maxim [2], attached to an arrow pointing toward *vid.* The boxes and arrows may have served a footnoting function here.

5. This number and the word preceding it are not entirely legible. A superscript *b* preceding this maxim corresponds to a footnote in the left-hand margin reading, "^{b}D^{r}: & S/Diag 1/C1./7 Rep. 12. 13."

171

Maxims. etc. see vol. 4. p. 151.
see vol. 4. p. 101.

[1] All innovation disturbs more by (its) novelty than it benefits by (its) utility.[1]
[2] Use your own in such a manner as not to damage another's property.[2]
[3] They who in all matters seek reason subvert reason.[3]
[4] Natural laws are unchangeable.[4]
[5] The law should sooner tolerate a private harm than a public evil.[5]
[6] When the law grants anything to anyone, it is also seen to grant that without which the thing itself cannot be possessed.[6]
[7] Custom is the best interpreter of laws.[7]
Custom has sometimes prevailed against a positive law.[8]
[8] A bad use should be abolished.[9]
[9] With regard to customs, what should be considered is not the length of time, but the solidity of reason.[10]
[10] Although custom is of great authority, nevertheless it is never prejudicial to manifest truth.[11]
[11] The optimal interpretation is (derived) from that which came before and that which followed.[12]
[12] The preceding is a relation to the next, unless the meaning is impeded.[13]
[13] A general conclusion is not extended to those things that are specifically comprehended or expressed.[14]

1. "1 Bul. 138" likely refers to Edward Bulstrode, *Reports in King's Bench, 1609–26*, vol. 1 (1st edition, 1657–59), p. 138 (hereafter, "Bulstrode, *Reports*, vol. 1), but neither this maxim nor any apparently related text appears on that page in the 1657 or 1688 editions; perhaps Quincy consulted another edition with different pagination. For further bibliographical information on Bulstrode, see Maxwell, 294. Quincy also cites to Salkeld, vol. 1, p. 20 (*Ashby* v. *White*).

2. Salkeld, vol. 1, p. 22 (*Tenant* v. *Golding*). This maxim, often invoked in modern environmental cases, was made famous by Coke in *William Aldred's Case*, *Coke Reports*, vol. 9, p. 57b. See *Id.*, pp. 58b–59a. See also Daniel R. Coquillette, "Mosses from an Old Manse, Another Look at Some Historic Property Cases about the Environment," 64 *Cornell L. Rev.*, 761 (1979), p. 776.

3. Coke, *Reports*, part 2, p. 75 (*Le Seignior Cromwel's Case*).

4. Sir Edward Coke, *Reports*, part 7 (1st French edition, 1608; 1st English edition, 1658), p. 13.b (Calvin's Case) (hereafter, "Coke, *Reports*, part 7"). For further bibliographical information, see Maxwell, p. 296. Quincy also cites to Sir Henry Hobart, *Reports in the reign of James I with some few cases in the reign of Queen Elizabeth, [King's Bench, 1603–25]* (1st edition, 1641). The page number was confirmed by referencing the 1724 London edition. For further bibliographical information on Hobart, see Maxwell, p. 301. In a marginal footnote, Quincy also references Saint German and an additional page in Coke for this proposition. See Christopher Saint German, *Dialogus de Fundamentis Legum Angliae et de Conscientia* (1st Latin edition, 1528, 1st

6. A superscript *c* preceding this maxim corresponds with a footnote referencing "[c]1 Inst 97.b./152 b/258.b."

7. Quincy may have omitted an ampersand here. *Cf.* Coke, *Institutes*, part 1, p. 56.a.

8. Quincy incorrectly cites to page 309. See Coke, *Institutes*, part 2, p. 306, where the maxim reads, "*Quia quando lex aliquid concedit, concedere videtur & id, per quod devenitur ad illud.*"

9. A superscript *d* preceding this maxim corresponds with a footnote referencing, "[d]1 Inst/56.a./2 Inst. 423/424./501."

10. A superscript *e* preceding this maxim corresponds with a footnote reading, "[e]Inst./155.a." Also, a cross mark following the maxim corresponds with a marginal footnote reading "vid/p 175/max.7."

11. Although Quincy cites to page 73, the maxim is actually quoted on page 75. Coke, *Fourth Part of the Institutes of the Laws of England; concerning the Jurisdiction of Courts* (1st edition, 1644), p. 75 (hereafter, "Coke, *Institutes*, part 4"). For further bibliographical information, see Maxwell, p. 258.

12. Below "positive law," Quincy has squeezed in a reference to "Nelson's Lex Test: 10.80."

13. A superscript *f* preceding this maxim corresponds with a footnote in the lefthand margin that appears to read, "[f]1 Inst/62.a./140.a/141.a/2 Inst 664."

14. This maxim was inserted at a later time, as Quincy has squeezed it in interlineally between maxims [8] and [10].

15. Coke's version reads, "*Et ad proximum antecedens fiat relatio nisi impediatur sententia.*" See Sir Edward Coke, *Reports*, part 2 (1st French edition, 1602; 1st English edition, 1658), p. 71 (hereafter, "Coke, *Reports*, part 2"). For further bibliographical information, see Maxwell, pp. 295–96.

16. The phrase *aut expressa* is missing from the original. See, e.g., Sir Edward Coke, *Reports*, part 8 (1st French edition, 1611; 1st English edition, 1658), pp. 118.b, 154.b (hereafter, "Coke, *Reports*, part 8"). For further bibliographical information, see Maxwell, p. 296.

17. In the lefthand margin Quincy has written a reference to "8 Rep 154" followed by the words "and another Rule. Ibid." He has drawn a line separating "and another Rule" from the maxim itself. The other rule referred to by Quincy may be, "*Quando carta continent generalem clausulam, posteaque descendit ad verba specialia, quae clausulae generali sunt consentanea, interpretanda est carta secundum verba specialia.*" Coke, *Reports*, part 8, p. 154.b. Coke translates this roughly, "where a Deed speaks by general Words, and afterwards descends to special Words, if the special Words agree to the general Words, the Deed shall be intended according to the special Words." *Id.*

English edition, 1530) (hereafter, "Saint German, *Doctor and Student*"), pp. 3–5 (The First Dialogue, Chapter 1, Of the Law Eternal) (not quoting the maxim but discussing "the Law Eternal" and the "Law of Nature", which "is never changeable"). The page number was confirmed with reference to the 1721 London edition. For further bibliographical information on Saint German's *Doctor and Student*, see Maxwell, pp. 24–25. For Quincy's final citation, see Coke, *Reports*, part 7, p. 12.b (*Calvin's Case*), which says, "the Law of Nature is immutable."

5. Coke, *Institutes*, part 1, p. 152.b (Ch. 12, Of Rents, Sect. 231). In a marginal footnote, Quincy also cites to Coke, *Institutes*, part 1, p. 97.b (Ch. 6, Of Frankalmoigne, Sect. 138) (discussing how it is better to tolerate "a mischief that is peculiar to one" than "an inconvenience that may prejudice many"), and p. 258.b (Ch. 7, Of Continual Claim, Sect. 434) (containing a related maxim, "*Nihil quod est inconveniens est licitum.*").

6. Coke, *Institutes*, part 1, p. 56.a (Ch. 7, Of Tenant at Will, Sect. 68). Quincy also cites to Coke, *Institutes*, part 2, p. 309, although the maxim (similarly phrased) appears a few pages earlier on page 306 (*Statutum de Glocester*, Ch. 5). This error may provide a clue as to the source of Quincy's citations, as Coke includes an index of maxims toward the end of the volume which incorrectly lists this maxim as on page 309. Quincy may have used this list rather than consulting the actual page containing the maxim. Providing many references for this maxim, Quincy continues with Coke, *Institutes*, part 4, p. 111 (Ch. 11, The Court of Exchequer); Coke, *Reports*, part 3, p. 12 (*Harbert's Case*) (not quoting the maxim, but discussing how, given the fact that only land was subject to execution for debt of a common person at common law, in action of debt against an heir, "if he should not have Execution of the Land against the Heir, he could have no Fruit of his Action"); Sir Edward Coke, *Reports*, part 11 (1st French edition, 1615; 1st English edition, 1658) (hereafter, "Coke, *Reports*, vol. 11"), p. 52.a (*Richard Liford's Case*) (containing similarly phrased maxim). For further bibliographical information on Coke's eleventh volume of *Reports*, see Maxwell, p. 296. Quincy also cites to page 47 of Coke's third edition of reports, but this maxim does not appear to be discussed there. In a marginal footnote, Quincy includes references to Coke, *Institutes*, part 1, p. 56.a (Ch. 8, Of Tenant at Will, Sect. 68) (actually quoting the maxim); Coke, *Institutes*, part 2, pp. 423–24 (*Statutum de Westminster Secundo*, Ch. 30) (discussing *nisi prius*, and indicating that "this branch giving to the justices of *nisi prius* power to give judgment, they have thereby power includedly, as incident, given to award execution"), p. 501 (*Statutum de Westminster 3*, Ch. 1) (discussing *quia emptores* and indicating that the "generall words of this act take not away necessary incidents," and that, although *capitalis dominus* is singular in designation, it connotes "the next immediate lord, and so by degree upwards to every lord paramount"). Additionally, Quincy includes an internal reference to maxim [7] on page 175, which reads, "*Communis error facit jus*".

7. Coke, *Institutes*, part 2, p. 18 (*Magna Charta*, Ch. 7), p. 228 (*Statutum de Westminster Primer*, Ch. 34) (discussing causes of action for slander), p. 282 (*Statutum de Glocester*) (quoting similar maxim, "*Optimus interpres rerum usus*" and indicating that "ancient charters . . . ought to be construed, as the law was taken when the charter was made, and according to ancient allowance."); Coke, *Institutes*, part 4, p. 75 (Ch. 7, The Court of Kings Bench). In a marginal note, Quincy cites to "Inst. 155a", presumably Coke, *Institutes*, part 1, p. 155.a (but relevance of discussion there of *novel disseisin* is not apparent); I consulted the original manuscript to confirm that no volume number was provided.

8. Nelson, 10, p. 80. Nelson, after expounding on the tension between lords and prelates over the distribution of intestate property, discusses a growing Church custom in the 13th century that the Church receive one-third of an intestate's goods. See Nelson, pp. 6–10. On the latter page cited by Quincy, Nelson writes, "To me it seems plain, that Custom hath obtained against

THE
FIRST PART
OF THE INSTITVTES
OF THE LAWES OF
ENGLAND.
OR,
A COMMENTARIE
vpon LITTLETON, not
the name of a Lawyer onely,
but of the Law it selfe.

MARTIAL.
Quid te vana iuuant miseræ ludibria chartæ,
Hoc lege, quod possis dicere iure meum est.

CICERO.
Maior hæreditas venit vnicuiq; nostrum a Iure,
& Legibus, quam a Parentibus.

Hæc ego grandæuus posui tibi candide lector.

Authore EDW. COKE *Milite.*

LONDON,
Printed for the Societie of
Stationers.

Anno 1628.

Edward Coke, *First Part of the Institutes of the Lawes of England* (London, 1628), Maxwell, pp. 449–450. Courtesy, Coquillette Rare Book Room, Boston College Law School. See p. 373, note 9, *infra.*

this positive law, and therefore I shall not enlarge upon it". Nelson, p. 80. This comment refers to the practice of granting Commissions of Review, in contravention of a statute reading, "the sentence of the Delegates shall be definitive, and no farther Appeal shall be had." *Id.* Nelson traces this practice back to the time of papal supremacy, when the Pope "dispensed with human Laws in all Cases which he was pleased to call Spiritual." *Id.*, p. 79.

9. Coke, *Institutes*, part 1, p. 141.a (Ch. 11, Of Villenage, Sect. 212). Quincy's reference to "Lit 212" likely refers to section 212 of this text; such section designations have not been included elsewhere in the maxims. Quincy also cites to Coke, *Institutes*, part 4, p. 274. Furthermore, in a marginal note, Quincy adds citations to Coke, *Institutes*, part 1, p. 62.a (Ch. 10, Of Tenant per le Verge, Sect. 80) (indicating that even a long-held custom, if it goes against reason, "is of no force in law"), p. 140.a (Ch. 11, Of Villenage, Sect. 209) (quoting a related maxim that "all customes and prescriptions that be against reason are voyd."), p. 141.a (Ch. 11, Of Villenage, Sect. 212) (quoting the same maxim as Quincy); Coke, *Institutes*, part 2, p. 664 (Of Tithes, Ch. 13) (discussing how a custom, once reasonable, can be removed by an act of parliament should it become onerous).

10. Coke, *Institutes*, part 1, p. 141.a (Ch. 11, Of Villenage, Sect. 212).

11. Coke, *Institutes*, part 2, p. 654 (Of Tithes, Ch. 13) (quoting the maxim in the lefthand margin); Coke, *Reports*, part 4, p. 18 (Actions for Slander).

12. Coke, *Institutes*, part 2, p. 317 (*Statutum de Glocester*, Ch. 9). Coke, *Reports*, part 2, p. 71 (*Le Seignior Cromwel's Case*).

13. Coke, *Reports*, part 2, p. 71 (*Le Seignior Cromwel's Case*).

14. Coke, *Reports*, part 8, p. 118.b (*Dr. Bonham's Case*). In a footnote, Quincy also cites to Coke, *Reports*, part 8, p. 154.b (*Edward Altham's Case*), which has the same maxim in almost identical phrasing.

172

Maxims etc.

[1] Ubi Lex est specialis & Ratio ejus generalis, generaliter est accipienda. 2 Inst 43. 83. 10 Rep. 101.[1]
[2] Apices Juris non sunt Jura.[2] 4 Rep. 46. 1 Inst 356.a 8 Rep. 56. 1 Inst 283.b[3]
[3] Qui haeret in Litera etc. 283.b. 365.b. 381.b.[4]
[4] Nimia subtilitas in Jure reprobantur. 4 Rep. 7.[5]
[5] Ubi eadem Ratio, idem Jus. 1 Inst 10.a. 191.a.[6] 2 Inst 619.689 7 Rep. 18.
[6] Et cessante Ratione Legis, cessat Lex. 2 Inst. 11.[7]
[7] Nemo contra Factum venire potest. 2. Inst. 66.[8]
[8] Nemo tenetur exponere se Infortuniis & Periculis. 1 Inst 162.a 253.b.[9] 2 Inst. 483.[10]
[9] Talis debet esse Metus, qui cadere potest in Virum Constantem non meticulosum.[11] Ibid.[12]
[10] Qui non cadunt in[13] ~~Virum~~ constantem Virum, vani Timores sunt. 2 Inst 483.[14] 7 Rep. 27.[15]
[11] Qui facit per Alium, facit per se.[16] 1 Inst. 258.a.[17] 4 Inst. 109. 10 Rep. 33. vid p.182. Max 4. p.173 Max 8
[12] Omnis Ratihabitio retrotrahitur, & mandato[18] aequiparatur.[19] 1 Inst. 245.a. 258.a. 9 Rep. 106.
[13] Quando plus fit quam fieri debet, videtur etiam ipsum fieri quod faciendum est.[20] 8 Rep. 85

vid. Vol. 1. p.171.

[14] Modus & Conventio vincunt Legem.[21] 1 Inst 41b.[22] 166.a. 2 Rep. 73. 1 Ld. Raymd. 517

1. The maxim quoted here by Coke is, "*Quando verba Statuti sunt Specialia, ratio autem generalis, generaliter Statutum est intelligendum.*" Sir Edward Coke, *Reports*, part 10 (1st French edition, 1614; 1st English edition, 1658), p. 101.b. (hereafter, "Coke, *Reports*, part 10"). For further bibliographical information, see Maxwell, p. 296.

2. This maxim is preceded by a superscript *a* which references a footnote in the lefthand margin reading "[a]1 Inst/54.b. 468.b/290.b./365.b./2 Inst. 107. 199./649. 3 Rep. 7/11 Rep 34/3 Cro. 71./1 Inst 11.b/42.a. 360.a. 381.b."

3. Here Coke quotes the opposite proposition, "*apices juris sunt jura.*" Coke, *Institutes*, part 1, p. 283.b.

4. *Qui haeret in litera etc.* is written on the same line as the last two references for maxim [2],

172

Maxims etc.

[1] Where the law is specific and its reasoning is general, it should generally be accepted.[1]
[2] Points of law are not the laws (themselves).[2]
[3] He who adheres to the letter (of the law) (adheres to the bark/cork.)[3]
[4] Too much subtlety in the law is rejected.[4]
[5] Where (there is) the same reason, (there is) the same right.[5]
[6] And when the reason for a law ceases, the law (itself) ceases.[6]
[7] No one can go against (i.e. contradict) a deed.[7]
[8] No one is obligated to expose himself to misfortune and peril.[8]
[9] It should be such a fear as could befall a (normally) constant, unfearful man.[9]
[10] Fears that do not befall a constant man are vain.[10]
[11] One who acts through another acts by himself.[11]
[12] Every ratification relates back, and equals a command.[12]
[13] When more is done than should be done, just that which should have been done is regarded as being done.[13]
[14] Moderation and agreement prevail over the law.[14]

1. Coke, *Institutes*, part 2, p. 43 (*Magna Charta*, Ch. 26), p. 83 (*Statutum de Merton*, ch. 3); Coke, *Reports*, part 10, p. 101.b (*Beawfage's Case*) (quoting similar maxim).

2. Coke, *Reports*, part 4, p. 46.b (Cases of Appeals and Indictments); Coke, *Institutes*, part 1, p. 356.a (Ch. 12, Of Remitter, Sect. 675); Coke, *Reports*, part 8, p. 56.b (*Earl of Rutland's Case*); Coke, *Institutes*, part 1, p. 283.b (Ch. 8, Of Releases, Sect. 485) (quoting opposite proposition). In a marginal note, Quincy adds citations to Coke, *Institutes*, part 1, p. 54.b (Ch. 7, Of Tenant for Years, Sect. 67) (quoting related maxim, "*Qui haeret in littera, haeret in cortice*"), p. 290.b (Ch. 8, Of Releases, Sect. 504) (possibly relevant due to its indication that like cases fall within the statutory remedy), p. 365.b (Ch. 13, Of Warrantie, Sect. 697) (quoting same related maxim, "*Qui haeret . . .*"); Coke, *Institutes*, part 2, p. 107 (*Statutum de Marlebridge*, Ch. 4) (possibly relevant due to its indication that "this statute is generall, and extendeth unto all."), p. 199 (*Statutum* de *Westminster primer*, Ch. 20) (stating that "This act extends not to a forest in the hands of a subject, for the law is so penall, as it shall not be taken by equitie."), p. 649 (Of Tithes) (stating that "this act is penall, and shall not be taken by equity"); Coke, *Reports*, part 3, p. 7.b (*Heydon's Case*) (listing four considerations in interpreting statutes: 1) the common law prior to the statute, 2) the "Mischief and Defect" left unaddressed by the common law, 3) the remedy provided for by Parliament, and 4) the "true Reason and Remedy," and providing that judges should aim for a "Construction as shall suppress the Mischief, and advance the Remedy," bearing in mind the intent of the lawgivers); Coke, *Reports*, part 11, p. 34.b (*Alexander Powlter's Case*) (quoting related maxim, "*qui haeret in litera . . .*"); Sir George Croke, *Reports of Cases in King's Bench and Common Bench [1582–1641]*, part 3 (1st edition, 1657) (hereafter, "Croke, *Reports*, part 3"), p. 71 (*The Soldiers Case*) (not quoting the maxim, but debating the appropriate statutory interpretation for a situation where a soldier deserted his Conductor, while the pertinent statute's prohi-

having apparently been inserted at a later time. The three references for this maxim are written one above the other and separated from the rest of the text with a line. The full text of the maxim is *qui haeret in littera haeret in cortice*. See Coke, *Institutes*, part 1, p. 283.b ("*Qui haeret in litera, haeret in cortice; & apices iuris non sunt iura.*"), p. 365.b ("*Sed qui haeret in littera haeret in cortice*"), p. 381.b ("*Et qui haeret in littera, haeret in cortice*").

5. Quincy may have gotten the page number wrong here. See Coke, *Reports*, part 4, p. 5.b.

6. The cited text differs slightly from Quincy's. See Coke, *Institutes*, part 1, p. 10.a ("*ubi eadem ratio, ibi idem jus.*"), p. 191.a ("*Ubi eadem ratio, ibi idem jus*, or *Ubi eadem ratio, ibi idem jus esse debet*, for *Ratio est anima legis.*").

7. This maxim is written on the same line as the final reference to maxim [5], possibly having been inserted at a later date. Coke's version is slightly different: "*Cessante ratione legis cessat ipsa lex.*" Coke, *Institutes*, part 2, p. 11. The latter maxim was cited by the Supreme Court of the United States in the important case of *Zadvydas* v. *Davis*, 353 US 678 (2001) at 699 (Breyer, J.). There it was translated as, "The rationale of a legal rule no longer being applicable, the rule itself no longer applies." *Id.*

8. This maxim is preceded by a superscript letter *b*, which corresponds with a footnote *b* in the left-hand margin. The footnote references "[b]Lit 405./406./1 Inst/247.a./4 Rep. 123/con./FNB 202./Com.45." One version of Coke says "*factum suum proprium.*" Coke, *Institutes*, part 2, p. 66.

9. The word order is slightly different in this Coke reference, which reads, "*Et nemo tenetur se infortuniis & periculis exponere.*" Coke, *Institutes*, part 1, p. 253.b.

10. Quincy's maxim does not appear verbatim in this Coke reference, which quotes Bracton, "*Metus autem est praesentis, vel futuri periculi causa, mentis trepidatio, & praesentem debemus accipere metum, non suspicionem inferendi ejus, vel cujuslibet vani & meticulosi hominis, sed talem qui cadere possit in virum constantem; talis enim debet esse metus, qui in se continet mortis periculum, & corporis cruciatum.*" Coke, *Institutes*, part 2, p. 483.

11. The second *u* in *meticulosum* has been inserted with a carat above a crossed-out letter. This maxim is preceded by an *x* mark, which references a footnote in the left-hand margin stating "[x]vid Co:/Lit/162.a."

12. Coke presents slightly different versions of this maxim. In one instance, he writes, "*Vagus & vanus timor, sed talis quae cadere possit in virum constantem, & non in hominem vanum & meticulosum, talis enim debet esse metus qui in se continet mortis periculum & corporis cruciatum.*" Coke, *Institutes*, part 1, 162.a. In another, he records, "*Talis enim debet esse metus qui cadere potest in virum constantem, & qui in se continet mortis periculum, & corporis cruciatum.*" Coke, *Institutes*, part 1, p. 253.b.

13. This word is followed by a crossed-out word. It appears that Quincy wrote *Virum* too early and crossed it out.

14. Coke's version, quoting Bracton, is slightly different. See *supra*, note 10 (quoting Coke, *Institutes*, part 2, p. 483).

15. Coke, *Reports*, part 7, p. 27.a, ends with "*aestimandi* sunt" (emphasis added).

16. This maxim is preceded by a superscript *c* corresponding to a footnote in the left-hand margin reading "[c]D[r]. &/S. Diag. 2. ch 4."

17. Coke's version reads, "*Qui per alium facit per seipsum facere videtur.*" Coke, *Institutes*, part 1, p. 258.a; Coke, *Reports*, part 10, p. 33.b.

18. The *n* in *mandato* has been inserted with a carat.

19. This maxim is preceded by a superscript *d*, which corresponds to a footnote in the left-hand margin reading "[d]1 Roll/Abr 95./Co: Lit 180.b."

bition applied specifically to desertion of Captains). The page number was confirmed against the 1669 edition. For further bibliographical information on Croke, see Maxwell, p. 298. Quincy's citations continue with Coke, *Institutes*, part 1, p. 11.b (Ch. 1, Of Fee Simple, Sect. 3) (indicating that, "such interpretation must ever be made of all statutes, that the innocent or he in whom there is no default may not be damnified," and also describing the diverse categories of law within England), p. 42.a (Ch. 6, Of Tenant for Life, Sect. 56) (observing that, "when the construction of any act is left to the law, the law which abhorreth injury and wrong will never so construe it, as it shall work a wrong"), p. 360.a (Ch. 12, Of Remitter, Sect. 685) (indicating that "acts of parliament are to be so construed, as no man that is innocent, or free from injurie or wrong, be by a literall construction punished or endamaged"), p. 381.b (Ch. 13, Of Warrantie, Sect. 728) (quoting related maxim, "*qui haeret in litera . . .*," and suggesting that statutes should be interpreted to advance the remedy).

3. I.e., "Adheres superficially." Coke, *Institutes*, part 1, p. 283.b (Ch. 8, Of Releases, Sect. 485), p. 365.b (Ch. 13, Of Warrantie, Sect. 697), p. 381.b (Ch. 13, Of Warrantie, Sect. 729).

4. Coke, *Reports*, part 4, p. 5.b (*Vernon's Case*). Quincy, possibly in error, cited to page 7.

5. Coke, *Institutes*, part 1, p. 10.a (Ch. 1, Of Fee-simple, Sect. 1), p. 191.a (Ch. 4, Of Tenants in Common, Sect. 301); Coke, *Institutes*, part 2, p. 619 (*Articuli Cleri*) (relevance not apparent), p. 689 (Of Offices) (stating that "these interests are within the purview of this act: for that they are not onely within the same mischiefe, being without remedy, but within the expresse reason of this law," and quoting the related maxim, "*ratio legis est anima legis.*"); Coke, *Reports*, part 7, p. 18.b (*Calvin's Case*). *Latin for Lawyers*, quoting a similar maxim, provides the same translation. *Latin for Lawyers*, p. 249.

6. Coke, *Institutes*, part 2, p. 11 (*Magna Charta*, ch. 3).

7. Coke, *Institutes*, part 2, p. 66 (*Magna Charta*, Ch. 32). In the margin, Quincy also includes citations to Coke, *Institutes*, part 1, pp. 247.a–247.b (Ch. 6, Of Descents, Sect. 405–406) (Quincy breaks from his usual citation format in indicating the particular sections of Coke's text he is referencing. These two sections, while not quoting the maxim, discuss inheritance by an individual who is "non compos mentis". Littleton indicates in Sect. 405 that "no man of full age shall be received in any plea by the Law to disable his own person", and Coke recites the common law maxim that "the party shall not disable himelf"); Coke, *Reports*, part 4, p. 123 (*Beverley's Case of Non Compos Mentis*) (indicating that "every Deed . . . which any man *non compos mentis* makes is avoidable, and yet shall not be avoided by himself, because it is a Maxim in Law, that no Man of full Age shall be in any Plea to be pleaded by him receiv'd by the law to stultify himself, and disable his own person.") Also in the margin, Quincy cites a contrary opinion from Fitzherbert's *New Natura Brevium*, which disagrees with the principle that a person *non compos mentis* shall not disable himself or contradict his deed. In Fitzherbert's perspective, this "seemeth to be of little Reason, for this is an Infirmity which cometh by the Act of God". See Fitzherbert, *New Natura Brevium*, p. 202. Quincy's final marginal reference is to Sir John Comyns, *Reports, King's Bench, Common Pleas, and Exchequer, [with] Special Cases in Chancery and before the delegates [1695–1741]* (1st edition, 1744), p. 45 (not quoting the maxim, but discussing the legality of a surrender of land by a person *non compos mentis*). For further bibliographical information on Comyns, see Maxwell, p. 298.

8. Coke, *Institutes*, part 1, p. 162.a (Ch.12, Of Rents, Sect. 240), p. 253.b (Ch. 7, Of Continual Claim, Sect. 419). Coke, *Institutes*, part 2, p. 483 (*Statutum de Westminster secundo*, ch. 48). In a marginal note, Quincy repeats his citation to page 162.a of Coke, *Institutes*, part 1.

9. Coke, *Institutes*, part 1, p. 162.a (Ch. 12, Of Rents, Sect. 240), 253.b (Ch. 7, Of Continual Claim, Sect. 419). Coke is discussing the level of threat that would reasonably prevent a land-

20. This maxim is preceded by a superscript letter *e*, which corresponds with a footnote in the left-hand margin reading "[e]1 Inst./258.a./8 Rep. 85."

21. This maxim is preceded by a superscript letter *d*, written in a more elaborate script than the *d* footnote in maxim [12], and corresponding to a footnote in the left-hand margin reading "[d]1 Inst/51.b."

22. The number 41 has been inserted, with a caret, above what appears to be an inkblot.

lord from distraining for his rent, thus constituting disseisin of a rent. "Littleton here saith it must be for fear of Death, or Mutilation of Members." *Id.*

10. Coke, *Institutes*, part 2, p. 483 (*Statutum de Westminster secundo*, ch. 48). Coke, *Reports*, part 7, p. 27.a (*Calvin's Case*).

11. Coke, *Institutes*, part 1, p. 258.a (Ch. 7, Of Continual Claim, Sect. 433); Coke, *Institutes*, part 4, p. 109.a (Ch. 11, The Court of Exchequer) (quoting similarly phrased maxim); Coke, *Reports*, part 10, p. 33.b (*The Case of Sutton's Hospital*) (quoting similar maxim). Quincy also provides an internal reference to maxim [4] on his own page 182, which indicates that something forbidden directly is also forbidden indirectly, and to maxim [7] on his page 173. Most likely he was referring to maxim [8] on that page, which repeats the same maxim as on page 182. Again, the pagination is likely off due to Quincy's later addition of another maxim to the page. Finally, in a marginal note, Quincy points to Saint German, *Doctor and Student* (Dialogue 2, Ch. 4, The third Question of the Student, of Waste done by a Stranger in the Lands that be in the Hands of particular Tenants, &c), commencing on page 132.

12. Coke, *Institutes*, part 1, p. 245.a (Ch. 6, Of Dissents, Sect. 401), p. 258.a (Ch. 7, Of Continual Claim, Sect. 433) (both pages offering essentially the same wording as Quincy, with minor variation); Sir Edward Coke, *Reports*, part 9 (1st French edition, 1613; 1st English edition, 1658) (hereafter, "Coke, *Reports*, part 9"), p. 106.a (*Margaret Podger's Case*). For further bibliographical information on Coke's ninth volume of *Reports*, see Maxwell, p. 296. In the margin, Quincy also cites to Sir Henry Rolle, *Abridgment des plusieurs Cases et Resolutions del Common Ley* (1st French edition, London, 1668) (hereafter, "Rolle, *Abridgment*"), vol. 1, p. 95 (*Action sur Case*) (not quoting the maxim, but discussing when an action will or will not lie against a master for a sale undertaken by a servant). For further bibliographical information on Rolle, see Maxwell, p. 19. Finally, Quincy also cites to Coke, *Institutes*, part 1, p. 180.b (Ch. 3, Of Joynetenants, Sect. 278) (quoting maxim).

13. Coke, *Reports*, part 8, p. 85.a (*Sir Richard Pexhall's Case*). Quincy also provides an internal reference to his own page 171, which contains maxims similarly offering guidance on interpretation of laws. Additionally, Quincy footnotes a reference to Coke, *Institutes*, part 1, p. 258.a (Ch. 7, Of Continual Claim, Sect. 433) (quoting similar maxim) and a duplicate reference to Coke's eighth volume of reports.

14. Coke, *Institutes*, part 1, p. 41.b (Ch. 6, Of Tenant for Life, Sect. 56), p. 166.a (Ch. 1, Of Parceners, Sect. 244); Coke, *Reports*, part 2, p. 73.b (*Cromwel's Case*); Raymond, *Reports*, vol. 1, p. 517. In a marginal note, Quincy also cites to Coke, *Institutes*, part 1, p. 51.b (Ch. 7, Of Tenant for Years, Sect. 65) (describing the necessary elements for perfecting an exchange).

173

Maxims. etc.

[1] Quicunque Jussu Judicis aliquid fecerit, non videtur ~~alio~~[1] Dolo malo fecisse quia parere necesse est.[2] 10 Rep. 70, 76.

Sed vide. 4 Bac: Abr: 450. bot.[3]

[2] Domus sua Cuiq est tutissimum Refugium.[4] 5 Rep 92. 11 Rep 82. 3 Inst. 162.

[3] Appellatione Fundi omne Aedificium & omnis Ager continetur.[5] 4 Rep. 87. 10 Rep. 33.

[4] Cujus est Solum, ejus est usque ad Caelum.[6] 1 Inst: 4.a. 9 Rep. 54.

[5] Semper expressum facit cessare tacitum.[7] Co Lit. 183.b
210.a

[6] Expressio Eorum quae tacite insunt, nihil operatur.[8] 1 Inst. 191.a. 205.a. 4 Rep 73. 8 Rep 56. 145. 2 Inst. 365.[9] 5 Rep 56. Vid 2^{d} L^{d} $Raym^{d}$. 1154[10]

[7] Quae Dubitationis Causa tollendae inseruntur, communem Legem non laedunt. 1 Inst 205.a.

[8] Quando Aliquid prohibetur fieri ex directo, prohibetur & per obliquum.[11] 1 Inst. 223.b. 3 Inst 158.

[9] Quod necessario (vel tacite) ~~insunt~~ intelligitur,[12] non deest.[13] 4 Rep. 22.[14] 7 Rep 40.[15]

[10] Res inter Alios acta, alteri nocere non debet.[16] 6 Rep. 1.49.51. 2 Inst. 513.

[11] Qui prior est Tempore, potior est in Jure. 4 Rep. 30[17]. 1 Inst. 347.b. 2 Inst. 95.

[12] Utile per inutile non vitiatur.[18] 1 Inst 3.a.

1. This word has been crossed out, and *Dolo* has been inserted above with a carat.

2. A superscript numeral *1* precedes this maxim, corresponding to a footnote in the left-hand margin that also extends interlineally between the two lines of the maxim text. The footnote reads "[1]5 Rep. 64/6 Rep. 54/9 Rep. 168/10 Rep 70/76. 2 Inst. 452. 3 Cro 395. 1 Ventr 273. 2 Saund 193." Quincy's citation to page 168 of Coke's ninth volume of reports is most likely referring to page 68.a.

3. Upon consulting the manuscript, I discovered that this line is written in a significantly lighter ink than the previous and appears therefore to have been a later addition.

4. A superscript numeral *2* precedes this maxim, corresponding to a footnote in the left-hand margin reading "[2]5 Rep 91./92. 6 R 51/4 Inst. 177."

173

Maxims. etc.

[1] Whoever does something on command of a judge does not appear to have acted with evil intent because it was necessary to comply.[1]
[2] To each, one's own house is the safest refuge.[2]
[3] Every building and every field is contained within the name of the estate.[3]
[4] Whose is the soil, owns all the way to the heavens.[4]
[5] That which is expressed always makes that which is unspoken cease.[5]
[6] The expression of those things that are contained in silence has no effect.[6]
[7] Those things which are introduced with the motive of removing doubt do not harm the common law.[7]
[8] When anything is prohibited to be done directly, it is also prohibited indirectly.[8]
[9] What is understood necessarily (or tacitly) does not fail.[9]
[10] Deeds performed among others should not cause harm to another, i.e., a third party.[10]
[11] Whoever is first in time is stronger in the law.[11]
[12] That which is useful is not spoiled by that which is useless.[12]

1. Coke, *Reports*, part 10, p. 70.b (*The Case of the Marshalsea*) (quoting the maxim and concluding that "the Thing which an Officer doth by Warrant or Command of a Court, can't be said [to be] against the Peace."), pp. 76.a–b (also quoting the maxim). A line below this citation to Coke, Quincy includes a "but see" citation to Bacon, *Abridgment*, vol. 4, p. 450 (within a section discussing the duty of sheriffs as judicial officers, and a subsection entitled "2. That he cannot dispute the Authority by which they issue nor any Irregularity in them.") Quincy's reference, which specifies the bottom of the page, is likely to Bacon's statement, "But when the Judge hath no Jurisdiction of the Cause, there the Officer is not obliged to obey, and if he does, it is at his Peril, though he do it by Virtue of a Precept directed to him; a void Authority being the same as none at all." In a footnote, Quincy repeats his citation to Coke's tenth volume of *Reports* and also cites to Sir Edward Coke, *Reports*, part 5 (1st French edition, 1605; 1st English edition, 1658), p. 64 (*Pleadings in Mackalley's Case*) (discussing the death of Serjeant during an arrest attempt) (hereafter, "Coke, *Reports*, part 5"); Sir Edward Coke, *Reports*, part 6 (1st French edition, 1607; 1st English edition, 1658), p. 54.a (*Isabel Countess of Rutland's Case*) (explaining that the sheriff or officer "ought not to dispute the Authority of the Court, but execute the writs directed to them") (hereafter, "Coke, *Reports*, part 6"). For further bibliographical information on Coke's fifth and sixth volumes of *Reports*, see Maxwell, pp. 295–96. Quincy's citations continue with Coke, *Reports*, part 9, p. 68.a (*Mackalley's Case in killing a Serjeant of London*) (indicating that "altho' the Process be apparently erroneous, that yet if the Minister of Justice in the Execution thereof be killed, it is Murder, for the Minister is not bound to dispute the Authority of the Court, which awards the Process, but his Office is to execute the Process". Quincy appears to cite to page 168, but this falls outside the volume.); Coke, *Institutes*, part 2, p. 452 (*Statutum de Westminster secundo*, Ch. 39) (discussing delivery of writs by sheriffs); Croke, *Reports*, part 3, p. 395 (*Nichols* v. *Walker and Carter*) (regarding the jurisdiction of justices of the peace); Sir Peyton Ventris, *Reports in two parts*, part 1 (1st edition, 1696) (hereafter, "Ventris,

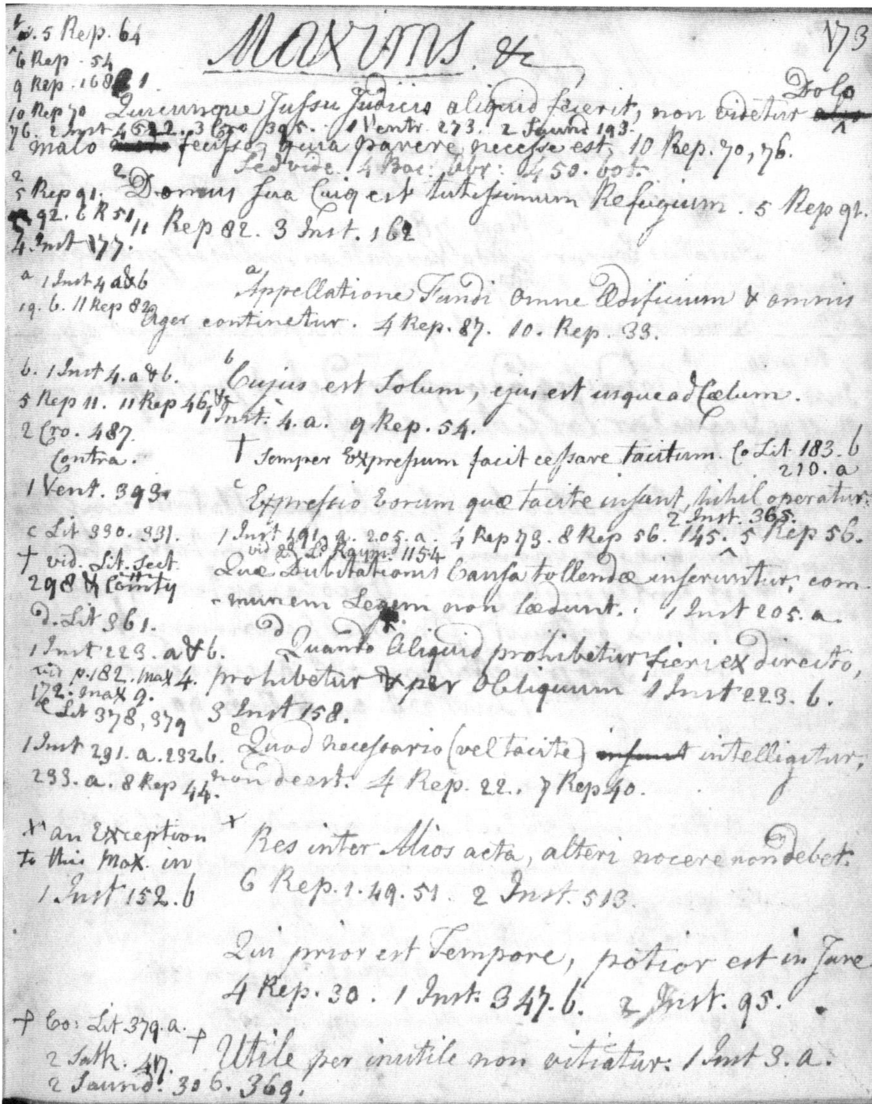
MAXIMS. &c 173

Quecunque Jussu Judicis aliquid fecerit, non videtur Dolo malo fecisse, quia parere necesse est. 10 Rep. 70, 76.

Domus sua Cuique est tutissimum Refugium. 5 Rep. 91.

Appellatione Fundi Omne Aedificium & omnis Ager continetur. 4 Rep. 87. 10. Rep. 33.

Cujus est Solum, ejus est usque ad Caelum. 1 Inst. 4. a. 9 Rep. 54.

Semper Expressum facit cessare tacitum. Co Lit 183. b 210. a

Expressio Eorum quae tacite insunt, nihil operatur.

Quae Dubitationis Causa tollendae inseruntur, communem Legem non laedunt. 1 Inst 205. a.

Quando aliquid prohibetur fieri ex directo, prohibetur per Obliquum 1 Inst 223. b. 3 Inst 158.

Quod necessario (vel tacite) intelligitur, non deest. 4 Rep. 22., 7 Rep. 40.

Res inter Alios acta, alteri nocere non debet. 6 Rep. 1. 49. 51. 2 Inst. 513.

Qui prior est Tempore, potior est in Jure 4 Rep. 30. 1 Inst. 347. b. 2 Inst. 95.

Utile per inutile non vitiatur. 1 Inst 3. a.

The third page (p. 173) of Quincy's maxim collection in volume three of the *Law Reports*, P347, Reel 4, QP 57. See Cox Chart, Appendix II, *infra*, pp. 432–33. The page is entitled "Maxims, etc." and adopts a complicated format, in contrast to the other two maxim compilations. The left-hand margin overflows with multiple source citations, which are tied to the maxim text through an informal footnoting system employing numbers, letters, and symbols alike. Quincy's hand was uneven, and he frequently struck out text. Although he left marginal space for footnotes, Quincy's planning was imperfect. Thus he frequently had to squeeze in additional references interlineally. My thanks to Elizabeth Papp Kamali.

Reports, part 1"), p. 273 (explaining that "the Officer that executes the Process of a Court of Record [is] indemnified, where the proceeding is erroneous."). The page number has been verified against the 1716 London edition. For further bibliographical information on Ventris, see Maxwell, p. 310. Finally, Quincy also cites to Sir Edmund Saunders, *Les reports des Divers Pleadings et Cases en le Court del Bank le Roy en le temp del Reign de le Roy Charles II*, part 2 (1st edition, 1686; 1st English edition, 1722) (hereafter "Saunders, *Reports*, part 2"), p. 193 (*Draper* v. *Blaney*) (discussing the court's jurisdiction in a case involving a viscount). The page number was verified by reference to the 1686 edition. For further bibliographical information on Saunders, see Maxwell, p. 308.

2. Coke, *Reports*, part 5, 92.b (*Cases of Executions*) (not quoting maxim but describing men's homes as "their Castles". The maxim is quoted on page 91.b); Coke, *Reports*, part 11, 82.a (*Lewis Bowles's Case*); Sir Edward Coke, *Third Part of the Institutes of the Laws of England; concerning High Treason and other Pleas of the Crown, and Criminall Causes* (1st edition, 1644) (hereafter "Coke, *Institutes*, part 3"), p. 162 (Ch. 73, Against going or riding armed). For further bibliographical information on Coke's third volume of *Institutes*, see Maxwell, p. 360. In a marginal note, Quincy repeats his citation to Coke's fifth volume of reports and also cites to Coke, *Institutes*, part 4, 177 (Ch. 31, Justices of Peace) (discussing when a suspect's home may be entered). Quincy's marginal citation to what appears to read "6 R 51" is unexplained; it does not appear to be Coke's sixth volume of reports.

3. Coke, *Reports*, part 4, p. 87.b (*Luttrel's Case*); Coke, *Reports*, part 10, 33.b (*The Case of Sutton's Hospital*) (not quoting the maxim but describing how an initial donation of land amounts to a foundation, irrespective of the later building of a hospital on the land.) In a marginal note, Quincy also cites to Coke, *Institutes*, part 1, pp. 4.a–b (Ch. 1, Of Fee Simple, Sect. 1) (not quoting the maxim but discussing, among other things, the fact that *terra* legally includes castles, houses, and other buildings thereupon), p. 19.b (Ch. 2, Of Fee Tail, Sect. 14) (defining *terre* as including ground as well as edifices); Coke, *Reports*, part 11, p. 82.a (*Lewis Bowles's Case*) (discussing the privilege attaching to a man's house, as well as the common law interest of lessees in trees on the leased property).

4. Coke, *Institutes*, part 1, p. 4.a (Ch. 1, Sect. 1 "Of Fee-simple"). In the 1738 London edition, Coke employs the spelling *coelum*, but it is not clear whether Quincy penned *coelum* or *caelum*. Quincy also cites to Coke, *Reports*, part 9, p. 54.b (*Baten's Case*) and includes footnoted references to Coke, *Institutes*, part 1, pp. 4.a–b (quoting the maxim on the first page); Coke, *Reports*, part 5, p. 11.b (*Cases of Leases, Ive's Case*) (not quoting the maxim, but describing how "the Wood remains parcel of the Manor, and by Lease of the Manor shall pass" in ordinary circumstances); Coke, *Reports*, part 11, pp. 46.b–52.b (*Richard Liford's Case*) (discussing property right in trees on leasehold land); Sir George Croke, *Reports of Cases in King's Bench and Common Bench [1582–1641]*, part 2 (1st edition, 1657) (hereafter "Croke, *Reports*, part 2"), p. 487 (*Whilster* v. *Paslow*) (discussing property interest in trees and distinguishing between "Wood and Underwood" on the one hand and "all Timber trees" on the other in determining whether or not the soil passed with the fee when a lessor had reserved an interest in certain trees and an ingress to fell them). The page number was verified against the 1669 edition. For further bibliographical information on Croke's second volume of *Reports*, see Maxwell, p. 298. Finally, distinguishing the citation with a "contra" label, Quincy also references Ventris, *Reports*, part 1, p. 393 (Potter and Sir Henry North) (explaining how, "by a Grant of *Vestura Terrae* by a common Person the Soil will pass," but that a grant of "*prima vestura*" only encompasses "an Interest in the first cutting or taking of the Grass.").

5. Coke, *Institutes*, part 1, p. 183.b (Ch. 7, Of Tenant at Will, Sect. 68), p. 210.a (Ch. 5, Of

5. A superscript *a* precedes this maxim, corresponding to a footnote in the left-hand margin reading "[a]1 Inst 4 a&b/19.b. 11 Rep 82".

6. A superscript *b* precedes this maxim, corresponding to a footnote in the left-hand margin reading "[b]1 Inst 4.a&b./5 Rep 11. 11 Rep 46, &c./2 Cr. 487./Contra./1 Vent. 393."

7. This maxim is preceded by a crossmark for footnote purposes. The varied footnoting systems employed by Quincy on this page suggest that he went back over time and added additional footnotes as he discovered new citations for the maxims he had recorded. The footnote in the left-hand margin reads "vid. Lit. Sect/298 & Comty," referring to Coke's commentary on Littleton's text.

8. A superscript *c* precedes this maxim. The corresponding footnote in the left-hand margin reads "[c]Lit 330. 331."

9. This citation to 2 Inst. 365 was inserted interlineally with a caret.

10. I discovered this line upon consulting the original manuscript; it was written in a very small hand interlineally and had initially escaped transcription.

11. A superscript *d* precedes this maxim. The corresponding footnote in the left-hand margin reads "[d]Lit. 361/1 Inst 223.a&b./vid p. 182. max 4./172. max. 9."

12. This word is preceded by another that has been crossed out.

13. A superscript *e* precedes this maxim, with the corresponding footnote reading "[e]Lit 378, 379/1 Inst 231.a. 232.b./233.a. 8 Rep 44."

14. This version reads, "*Quia quod tacite intelligitur deesse non videtur.*" Coke, *Reports*, part 4, p. 22.a.

15. Coke writes here, "*quaedam tacita habentur pro expressis*" and "*expressum facit cessare tacitum*". Coke, *Reports*, part 7, p. 40.b.

16. This maxim is preceded by an *x* mark, which corresponds to a footnote in the lefthand margin reading "An Exception/to this Max. in/1 Inst 152.b."

17. This maxim is actually found on page 90.a of the cited work. See Coke, *Reports*, part 4, p. 90.a. I consulted the original manuscript to confirm that Quincy cited to page 30, possibly in error.

18. A crossmark precedes this maxim, corresponding with a left-hand footnote reading "Co: Lit 379.a./2 Salk. 417./2 Saund. 306. 369."

Estates upon Condition, Sect. 339) (quoting the maxim, minus the *semper*). In a marginal note, Quincy cites to Coke, *Institutes*, part 1, p. 190.b (Ch. 4, Of Tenants in Common, Sect. 298). Quincy cites to both Littleton's text and the accompanying commentary, which indicates that "an express estate controlls an implied estate."

6. Coke, *Institutes*, part 1, p. 191.a (Ch. 4, Of Tenants in Common, Sect. 301), 205.a (Ch. 5, Of Estates upon Condition, Sect. 331); Coke, *Reports*, part 4, p. 73.b (*Boroughe's Case*); Coke, *Reports*, part 8, p. 56.b (*Earl of Rutland's Case*), p. 145.a (*Davenport's Case*); Coke, *Institutes*, part 2, p. 365 (*Statutum de Westminster secundo*, Ch. 5); Coke, *Reports*, part 5, p. 56.a (*Knight's Case*) (not quoting the maxim, but discussing the "favourable and beneficial Interpretation" accorded to grants made by the king). On the line directly below the maxim, Quincy cites to Robert Raymond, *Reports, King's Bench and Common Pleas [1694–1732]*, vol. 2 (1st edition, 1743) (hereafter, "Raymond, *Reports*"), p. 1154. The page number has been verified against the second edition, printed in London in 1765. For further bibliographical information on Raymond's *Reports*, see Maxwell, p. 307. In a marginal note, Quincy cites to Sections 330–331 of Coke on Littleton, expanding upon his earlier reference to page 205.a.

7. Coke, *Institutes*, part 1, p. 205.a (Ch. 5, Of Estates upon Condition, Sect. 331).

8. Coke, *Institutes*, part 1, p. 223.b (Ch. 5, Of Estates upon Condition, Sect. 361); Coke, *Institutes*, part 3, p. 158 (Of Monomachia) (quoting a related maxim, "*quando aliquid prohibetur, prohibetur et omne, per quod devenitur ad illud*"). In a marginal note, Quincy expands his first reference to include pages 223.a–b while also including internal cross references to his own page 182, maxim [4] (the same maxim) and page 172, maxim [9]. The latter internal reference likely corresponds with maxim [11], which refers to actions undertaken by an agent; as in other cases, Quincy's numbering was likely thrown off by the later addition of further maxims to the page.

9. Coke, *Reports*, part 4, p. 22.a (*Copyhold Cases*); Coke, *Reports*, part 7, p. 40.b (*Bedell's Case*). Neither page in Coke contains the exact same maxim as quoted by Quincy. In a marginal note, Quincy also cites to Coke, *Institutes*, part 1, p. 231.a (Ch. 5, Of Estates upon Condition, Sect. 374–375) (not quoting the maxim, but discussing estates upon condition), pp. 232.b–233.a (Ch. 5, Of Estates upon Condition, Sect. 378) (discussing estates upon condition), p. 234.b (Ch. 5, Of Estates upon Condition, Sect. 379) (discussing grants of office); Coke, *Reports*, part 8, p. 44.b (*Whittingham's Case*) (discussing conditions in fact and in law).

10. Coke, *Reports*, part 6, p. 1.b (*Bruerton's Case*) (quoting similar maxim, "*Res inter alios actae nemini nocere debent, sed prodesse possunt*"), pp. 49a–b (*Boswel's Case*) (discussing the writ of *quare impedit*), 51.b (*Boswel's Case*); Coke, *Institutes*, part 2, p. 513 (*Modus levandi fines*). In a marginal note, Quincy indicates that an exception to the maxim is found in Coke, *Institutes*, part 1, p. 152.b (Ch. 12, Of Rents, Sect. 231), which indicates that an exception to the maxim is permissible if otherwise "an inconvenience should follow."

11. Coke, *Reports*, part 4, p. 90.a (*Drury's Case*); Coke, *Institutes*, part 1, p. 347.b (Ch. 12, Of Remitter, Sect. 659); Coke, *Institutes*, part 2, p. 95 (*Statutum de Merton*, Ch. 8).

12. Coke, *Institutes*, part 1, p. 3.a (Ch. 1, Of Fee Simple, Sect. 1). In a marginal note, Quincy also cites to Coke, *Institutes*, part 1, p. 379.a (Ch. 13, Of Warrantie, Sect. 723); Salkeld, vol. 2, p. 417 (*Dominus Rex* v. *Bear*). The page number corresponds with the third edition (London, 1731–32). Finally, Quincy also cites to Saunders, *Reports*, part 2, p. 306 (*Decanus & Capitulum Windsor* v. *Gover*) (quoting nearly identical maxim), p. 369 (*Sacheverell* v. *Froggatt*).

174

Maxims etc.

[1] Quod alias bonum & justum est, si per Vim vel Fraudem petatur, Malum & Injustum efficitur.
3 Rep. 78.
[2] Fucatus Error nuda Veritate in multis est probabilior.
2 Rep. 72.73
[3] Ex verbo generali Aliquid excipitur.[1] 1 Inst 47.a.
[4] Conditio adimpleri debit priusquam sequatur Effectus.[2] 1 Inst 201.a.

[5] Conditio beneficialis quae Statum construit[3] benigne scundum[4] verborum Intentionem est interpretanda. Odiosa autem quae Statum destruit; stricte secundum Verborum Proprietatem est accipienda.[5]
1 Inst 218.a. 8 Rep. 90.[6]

[6] Benigne faciendae sunt Interpretationes Chartarum, ut Res magis valeat quam pereat.[7] 1 Inst 36.a 183.b.[8]
[7] Verba Intentioni, non econtra, debent inservire.
8 Rep 94.
[8] Verba debent intelligi ut Aliquid operentur.[9]
8 Rep. 94. Bacon. 18
[9] Verba accipienda sunt cum Effectu.[10] 4 Rep 51.

1. A superscript *a* precedes this maxim, corresponding to footnoted text in the left-hand margin that reads "a2 Cro. 296/487."

2. A superscript *b* preceding this maxim corresponds to a left-hand footnote reading "b1 Inst. 217.a/1 Roll Abr/414. 415. 416."

3. The final *t* is inserted above the word with a caret symbol.

4. Quincy likely intended *secundum*.

5. A superscript *c* preceding this maxim corresponds to a left-hand marginal footnote reading "c1 Inst. 219.b./274.b. 205.b/8 Rep. 91/1 Inst/213.a."

6. The maxims above this point in the page are written in a significantly darker ink than the maxims on the lower end of the page, and even the size of the hand differs somewhat. It appears that maxims [1]–[5] were recorded at a different time than maxims [6]–[10].

7. A superscript *d* preceding this maxim corresponds to a left-hand footnote reading "d2 Rep. 23. 6 Rep. 36."

8. Quincy appears to have paraphrased or edited down Coke's version of the maxim. See Coke, *Institutes*, part 1, pp. 36.a, 183.b.

174

Maxims etc.

[1] That which is at other times good and just, if sought through force or fraud, becomes bad and unjust.[1]
[2] A colored error is in many things more acceptable than naked truth.[2]
[3] From a general discourse anything is made an exception.[3]
[4] A condition should be fulfilled before the effect follows.[4]
[5] A beneficial condition which builds an estate should be interpreted liberally according to the intention of the words; however, an odious one, which destroys an estate, should be understood strictly according to the proper signification of the words.[5]
[6] Interpretations of writings/deeds should be made liberally so that the thing is worth more rather than that it come to nothing.[6]
[7] Words should serve intent, not the contrary.[7]
[8] Words should be understood so that they effect something.[8]
[9] Words should be understood in connection with (their) effect.[9]

1. Coke, *Reports*, part 3, p. 78.a (*Fermor's Case*).

2. Coke, *Reports*, part 2, pp. 72.b–73.a (*Cromwel's Case*) (quoting the maxim on the bottom of page 72.b and then continuing its discussion on 73.a).

3. Coke, *Institutes*, part 1, p. 47.a (Ch. 7, Of Tenant for Years, Sect. 58). In a marginal note, Quincy also cites to Croke, part 2, p. 296 (*Bacon* v. *Gyrling*) (not quoting the maxim, but explaining that a lessee for life, being accountable in waste, can validly stipulate an exception for wood, under-wood, and trees when making a lease for years), p. 487 (*Whilster* v. *Paslow*) (also discussing exceptions of wood, under-wood, and trees).

4. Coke, *Institutes*, part 1, p. 201.a (Ch. 5, Of Estates upon Condition, Sect. 325). In a marginal note, Quincy includes citations to Coke, *Institutes*, part 1, p. 217.a (Ch. 5, Of Estates, Sect. 350) (discussing fees upon condition); Rolle, *Abridgment*, vol. 1, pp. 414–16 (Condition) (not quoting the maxim, but discussing conditions precedent and subsequent).

5. Coke, *Institutes*, part 1, p. 218.a (Ch. 5, Of Estates upon Condition, Sect. 350); Coke, *Reports*, part 8, p. 90.b (*Fraunce's Case*). In the margin, Quincy also cites to Coke, *Institutes*, part 1, p. 219.b (Ch. 5, Of Estates, Sect. 352) (not quoting the maxim but describing the same concept, namely that "a condition that is to create an estate, is to be performed by construction of Law, as near the condition as may be, and according to the intent and meaning of the condition, albeit the letter and words of the condition cannot be performed: but otherwise it is of a condition that destroyeth an estate, for that is to be taken strictly"), p. 274.b (Ch. 8, Of Releases, Sect. 467) (distinguishing between conditions "favoured in Law" and those "odious in Law"), p. 205.b (Ch. 1, Of Estates, Sect. 334) ("Albeit conditions be not favoured, yet they are not always taken literally . . ."), p. 213.a (Ch. 5, Of Estates, Sect. 345) (discussing how in some cases "words in a Condition shall be taken out of their proper sense, *Ut res magis valeat quam pereat*"); Coke, *Reports*, part 8, p. 91.a (*Fraunce's Case*) (describing how "Conditions or Provisoes which will destroy former Estates, shall be taken strictly").

9. Although Quincy appears to have written *operentur*, an alternative spelling is *operantur*.

10. A superscript *x* mark corresponds with a left-hand footnote reading "ˣThis holds/good in/Statutes./vid. vol. 1. p. 92."

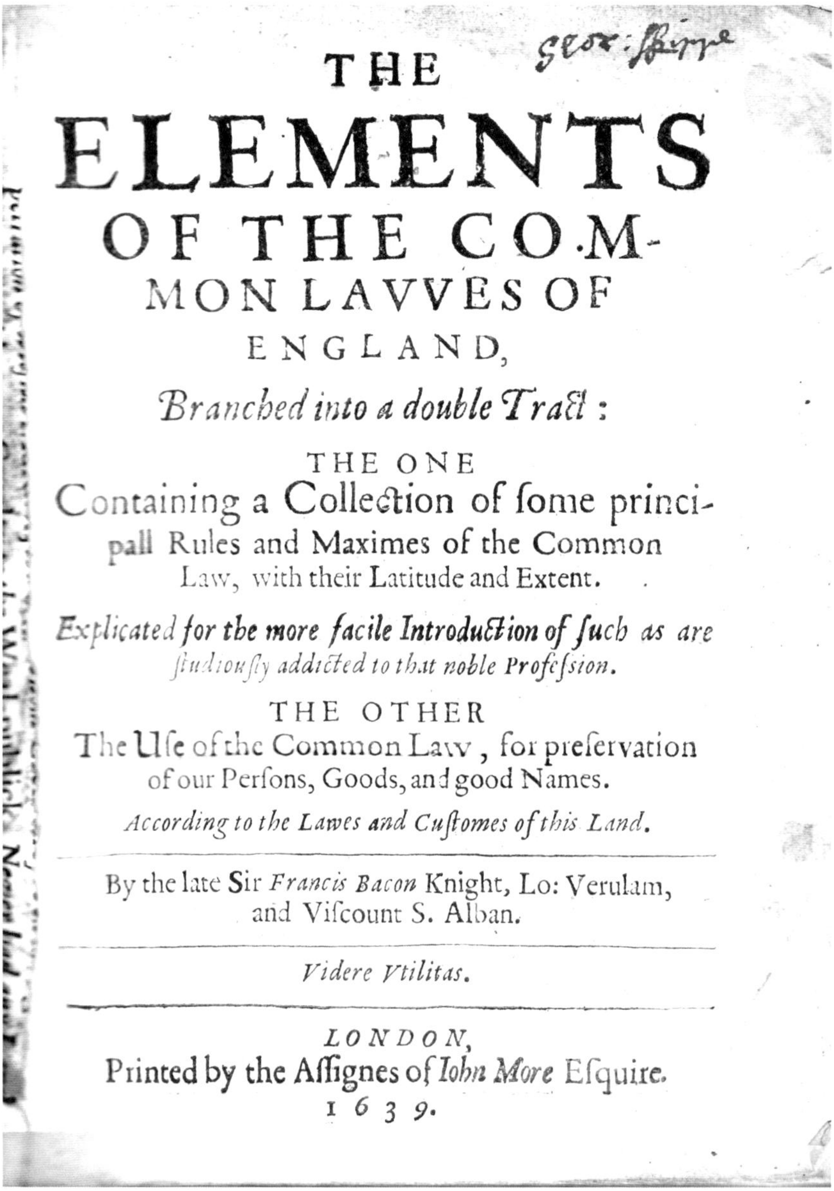

THE
ELEMENTS
OF THE COM-
MON LAVVES OF
ENGLAND,
Branched into a double Tract:
THE ONE
Containing a Collection of ſome princi-
pall Rules and Maximes of the Common
Law, with their Latitude and Extent.
Explicated for the more facile Introduction of ſuch as are ſtudiouſly addicted to that noble Profeſsion.
THE OTHER
The Uſe of the Common Law, for preſervation
of our Perſons, Goods, and good Names.
According to the Lawes and Cuſtomes of this Land.

By the late Sir *Francis Bacon* Knight, Lo: Verulam,
and Viſcount S. Alban.

Videre Vtilitas.

LONDON,
Printed by the Aſſignes of *Iohn More* Eſquire.
1639.

Francis Bacon, *The Elements of the Common Law* (London, 1639); Maxwell, p. 237. See p. 389, note 8, *infra*, and p. 403, note 8, *infra*.

6. Coke, *Institutes*, part 1, p. 36.a (Ch. 5, Of Dower, Sect. 40) (with some slight variations in phrasing), p. 183.b (Ch. 3, Of Joyntenants, Sect. 283) (also with some slight variations in wording). In a marginal note, Quincy also includes references to Coke, *Reports*, part 2, p. 23.b (*Baldwin's Case*) (discussing the interpretation of deeds, and the importance of discerning the parties' intent); Coke, *Reports*, part 6, pp. 36.a–b (*The Bishop of Bath's Case*) (expanding upon the proper interpretation of a lease).

7. Coke, *Reports*, part 8, p. 94.a (*Edward Fox's Case*).

8. Coke, *Reports*, part 8, p. 94.a (*Edward Fox's Case*); Sir Francis Bacon, *Elements of the Common Lawes of England* (1st edition, 1630) (hereafter, "Bacon, *Elements*"), p. 18 (quoting a similarly phrased maxim and explaining that "words are so to bee understood, that they work somewhat, and bee not idle and frivolous"). For further bibliographical information on Bacon's work, see Maxwell, p. 237.

9. Coke, *Reports*, part 4, p. 51.b (*Andrew Ognell's Case*). In a marginal note, Quincy provides an internal reference to his own volume 1, page 92.

175

Maxims etc.

[1] Verba aequivoca & in Dubio posita intelliguntur in digniori & potentiori sensu.[1] 6 Rep. 20.
[2] Verba Chartarum fortius accipiuntur contra Proferentem.[2] 1 Inst 36.a. 183.a. 5 Rep 7. 10 Rep 59 Bacon. 11
[3] Verba debent intelligi secundum subjectam materiam.[3] 1 Inst 36.a. vid. 4 Rep. 12.13 &c.
[4] Quae ad unum finem loquuta sunt, non debent ad Alium detorqueri.[4] Ibid.
[5] Affectio tua Nomen imponit Operi tuo. 1 Inst 49.b.
[6] Vigilantibus, non dormientibus, Jura subveniunt.[5] 2 Rep. 26. 4 Rep. 10. 82. 2 Inst. 690. Coke's Compl. Cop. Sect. 55.
[7] Communis Error facit Jus.[6] D^{r}. & Stud. Diag 1 Chap. 26. 4 Inst 240
[8] Necessitas vincit Legem. Quod necessarium est licitum.[7] 5 Rep. 40. 10 Rep 61.
[9] Necessitas est Lex Temporis. 8 Rep 69.
[10] Consensus tollit Errorem.[8] 5 Rep. 36. 40. 1 Inst 294.a 2 Inst 123
[11] Nemo plus Juris in Alium transferre potest quam Ipse habet.[9] 1 Inst 309.b[10] 4 Rep 24. 6 Rep. 57. 68. 8 Rep 63.

1. A superscript *a* preceding this maxim corresponds with a footnote in the left-hand margin reading "[a]1 Inst.42.a/183.a&b."

2. A superscript *b* preceding this maxim corresponds with a footnote reading "[b]1 Inst 197.a/378.b/8 Rep 144/145. 5 Rep 26."

3. A superscript *x* mark preceding this maxim corresponds with a footnote reading "[x]vid./p. 182. max. 7."

4. This maxim has clearly been inserted at a later time, as it is squeezed interlineally between two other maxims.

5. A superscript *c* preceding this maxim corresponds with a footnote that appears to read "[c]1 West. &c./Part. 2./Sect. 19./Lit 441/1 Inst 262/a&b. 2 Inst 516. 518."

6. A superscript *d* preceding this maxim corresponds with a footnote reading "[d]5 Rep. 40. 41./10 Rep. 39/42. 1 Salk. 33. vid. p. 171 max. 7." Additionally, a superscript crossmark following this maxim corresponds with an interlineal footnote reading "tho' expressly ag^{t}. a Statute. 1 Salk 33." The relevant text in Salkeld, vol. 1, 33, reads, "But it is against the Statute expressly, tho' now *Communis error facit Jus.*"

175

Maxims etc.

[1] Words that are equivocal and doubtfully set down are [to be] understood in their most fitting and powerful sense.[1]
[2] The words of deeds are understood more strongly against the grantor.[2]
[3] Words should be understood according to the subject matter.[3]
[4] Those things which are spoken to one end should not be directed toward another.[4]
[5] Your state of mind imposes a name on your work.[5]
[6] Laws aid the vigilant, not the sleeping.[6]
[7] A common error makes law.[7]
[8] Necessity conquers the law to the extent that it is necessary to permit it.[8]
[9] Necessity is the law of time.[9]
[10] Consensus removes error.[10]
[11] No one can transfer to another more of a right than he himself has.[11]

1. Coke, *Reports*, part 6, p. 20.a (*Gregory's Case*). In a marginal note, Quincy also cites to Coke, *Institutes*, part 1, pp. 42.a–b (Ch. 6, Of Tenant for Life, Sect. 56) (not quoting the maxim, but expressing the same concept: "whensoever the words of a Deed, or of the parties without Deed may have a double intendment, and the one standeth with Law and right, and the other is wrongful and against law, the intendment that standeth with law shall be taken."), pp. 183a–b (Ch. 3, of Joyntenants, Sect. 283) (not quoting the maxim but expressing similar ideas).

2. Coke, *Institutes*, part 1, p. 36.a (Ch. 5, Of Dower, Sect. 40), p. 183.a (quoting a related maxim, "*Quaelibet concessio fortissime contra donatorem interpretanda est*"); Coke, *Reports*, part 5, p. 7.b (*Cases of Leases, Justice Windham's Case*) (stating that "every Deed shall be taken more strongly against the Grantor, and more beneficially for the Grantee" and applying this concept to a lease); Coke, *Reports*, part 10, p. 59.a (*The Bishop of Salisbury's Case*) (quoting a similar maxim, "*ambigua responsio contra proferentem est accipienda*"); Bacon, *Elements*, 11 (quoting and explicating nearly identical maxim). In a footnote, Quincy references Coke, *Institutes*, part 1, p. 197.a (Ch. 4, Of Tenants in Common, Sect. 134) (stating that each man's grant is "taken most strongly against himself"), p. 378.b (Ch. 13, Of Warranty, Sect. 722) (repeating the same proposition); Coke, *Reports*, part 8, p. 145.a (*Davenport's Case*) (stating that "the Grant of every one shall be taken strong against himself, and most beneficially for the Grantee"); Coke, *Reports*, part 5, pp. 26.a–b (*The Countess of Rutland's Case*) (indicating that "it would be dangerous to Purchasers and Farmers . . . if nude Averments against Matter in Writing should be admitted").

3. Coke, *Institutes*, part 1, p. 36.a (Ch. 5, Of Dower, Sect. 40). Adding a *Vid.* notation, Quincy also cites to Coke, *Reports*, part 4, pp. 12.b–20.b (Actions for Slander) (discussing slander actions and quoting a similar maxim on pages 13.b–14.a, "*sermons semper accipiendi sunt secundum subjectam materiam*"). Finally, Quincy footnotes an internal reference to maxim [7] on his own page 182; his intended target may be maxim [8], which seems to be more relevant.

7. A superscript *e* preceding this maxim corresponds with a footnote reading "[e]5 Rep. 40."

8. A superscript *f* preceding this maxim corresponds with a footnote reading "[f]Dr. & Stud/Diag. 1/Chap 16."

9. A superscript *g* preceding this maxim corresponds with a footnote reading "[g]Perkins/Tit. Granti/65."

10. The maxim here states, "*nemo potest plus juris ad alium transferre quam ipse habet.*" Coke, *Institutes*, part 1, p. 309.b. See also Coke, *Reports*, part 4, p. 24.b.

Christopher St. German, *Doctor and Student* (London, 1554), Maxwell, pp. 24–26. See page 393, note 7, *infra*.

4. Quincy makes an *Ibidem* cite here, and it is not clear if he is referencing Coke, *Institutes*, part 1, p. 36.a (discussing words in a deed) or Coke, *Reports*, part 4, pp. 12.b–20.b (*The Lord Cromwell's Case*) (discussing slander actions).

5. Coke, *Institutes*, part 1, p. 49.b (Ch. 7, Of Tenant for Yeares, Sect. 60). The maxim is quoted in the context of a sentence reading, "if the lessor and lessee come upon the ground, of purpose for the lessor to make, and the lessee to take livery, there his entry vests no actuall possession in him untill livery be made."

6. Coke, *Reports*, part 2, p. 26.b (*The Case of Bankrupts*); Coke, *Reports*, part 4, p. 10.b (*Bevill's Case*), p. 82.b (*Sir Andrew Corbet's Case*); Coke, *Institutes*, part 2, p. 690 (Of Offices); Sir Edward Coke, *Compleate Copy-Holder; wherein is contained a learned Discourse of the Antiquity and Nature of Manors and Copy-Holds, with the forme of keeping a Copy-Hold Court and Court Baron* (1st edition, 1630), Sect. 55, pp. 157–58 (quoting the maxim and explaining that "if the Lord receive any such prejudice, it is through his owne default, for not making claime"). The page number was confirmed by reference to the 1641 London edition. For further bibliographical information on Coke's *Compleate Copy-Holder*, see Maxwell, p. 399. In a marginal note, Quincy also cites to William West, *Symboleography*, part 2 (1st edition, 1594), ch. 1 (Fines and Concords), Sect. 19 (Of the division of fines) (discussing the difference between fines with and without proclamation). This text was referenced using the 1601 edition. For further bibliographical information, see Maxwell, p. 487. Quincy's citations continue with Coke, *Institutes*, part 1, pp. 262.a–b (Ch. 7, Of Continual Claim, Sect. 441) (describing a statute of limitations of a year and day for claims regarding fines); Coke, *Institutes*, part 2, pp. 516, 518 (*Modus levandi fines*) (discussing, on the former page, a "two-fold provision full of right and equity" for strangers, whereby they can bring a claim within a year and day of the time when a fine was levied. On the latter page, a similar statute of limitations is discussed.).

7. St. German, *Doctor and Student*, p. 84 (Dialogue I, Ch. 26, A Question made by the Doctor, how certain Recoveries that be used in the King's Court to defeat tailed Land, may stand with Conscience); Coke, *Institutes*, part 4, p. 240 (The Legall Courts within Wales). In a marginal note, Quincy adds citations to Coke, *Reports*, part 5, pp. 40.a–41.a (*Dormer's Case*) (indicating that "the Intent of the Parties is to be observed" in the case of common recoveries, which had become a common practice); Coke, *Reports*, part 10, p. 39.b (*Mary Portington's Case*) (describing how collusion is not presumed in a common recovery when the life tenant vouches the individual holding the "immediate inheritance" through a remainder in tail.), p. 42.b (also discussing a common recovery); Salkeld, vol. 1, p. 33 (*Clay* v. *Sudgrave*) (quoting the maxim). Finally, Quincy includes an internal reference to maxim [7] on his own page 171, which describes custom as the best interpreter of laws.

8. Coke, *Reports*, part 5, p. 40.b (*Dormer's Case*); Coke, *Reports*, part 10, p. 69.a (*The Bishop of Salisbury's Case*) (quoting related maxims, including "*Illud quod alias licitum non est, necessitas facit licitum*"). In a marginal note, Quincy repeats his citation to Coke's fifth volume of *Reports*.

9. Coke, *Reports*, part 8, p. 69.a (*John Trollop's Case*).

10. Coke, *Reports*, part 5, p. 36.a (*Walcot's Case*) (determining that a matter was not a mere "Misprision of the Clerk" but a "Matter of Substance, and the very Point of the Action", and therefore did not fall within the reach of a statute addressing "Want of Form"), p. 40.b (Dormer's Case); Coke, *Institutes*, part 1, p. 294.a (Ch. 8, Of Releases, Sect. 514); Coke, *Institutes*, part 2, p. 123 (*Statutum de Marlebridge*, Ch. 11). In a marginal note, Quincy also references St. German, *Doctor and Student*, pages 52–56 (The First Dialogue, Chapter 16, What is Equity?) (not quoting the maxim but discussing how equity follows the intent rather than the word of the law, and recognizing that exceptions sometimes need to be made in the interest of equity).

Sir Edward Coke (1552–1634). Frontispiece, Edward Coke, *Three Law Tracts* (London, 1764); Maxwell, p. 575. Courtesy, Coquillette Rare Book Room, Boston College Law School.

11. Coke, *Institutes*, part 1, p. 309.b (Ch. 10, Of Attornment, Sect. 551) (quoting similarly phrased maxim); Coke, *Reports*, part 4, p. 24.b (*Copyhold Cases*) (containing a similar, but not identical maxim); Coke, *Reports*, part 6, p. 57.b (*Brediman's Case*) (containing essentially the same maxim as that quoted by Quincy), p. 68.a (*Sir Moyle Finch's Case*) (containing essentially the same maxim); Coke, *Reports*, part 8, p. 63.b (*Swayne's Case*). In a marginal note, Quincy also cites to John Perkins, *Profitable Booke* (1st French edition, 1528, entitled *Incipit perutilis tractatus* . . .), ch. 1 (Grants). Perkins's work dealt primarily with conveyancing, and Quincy cited generally to the section dealing with grants. For further bibliographical information, see Maxwell, p. 485.

176

Maxims. etc.

[1] Quolibet Concessio fortissime contra Donatorem interpretanda est.[1] 1 Inst 36.a. 183.a[2]
5 Rep. 7. 10 Rep 59.
[2] Accessorium non ducit, sed sequitur suum Principale.[3] 1 Inst. 152.a.
[3] Id certum est, quod Certum reddi potest.[4] 1 Inst 45.b. 96.a. 142.a
[4] Omne Majus includit Minus, Cui licet quod Majus, non debet quod Minus est non licere.[5]
4 Rep. 23. 5 Rep. 115. 9 Rep. 49.
[5] Omne Maius trahit ad se Minus.[6] 6 Rep. 43
[6] Quod licitum est pro Minore, & pro Majore licitum est. 8 Rep. 41.
[7] Mala grammatica non vitiat Chartam[7]
1 Inst. 146.b. 6 Rep. 39. 9 Rep. 48.
[8] Nemo debet Rem suam sine facto aut Defectu suo amittere.[8] 1 Inst. 265.a.[9] 8 Rep. 92[10]

1. A superscript *a* preceding this maxim corresponds with a footnote in the left-hand margin referencing "[a]1 Inst 183.b/1 Rep/46."

2. This citation to page 183.a is followed by a superscript *x* corresponding to a note written in a smaller hand on the next line down, reading "[x]How this Max is to be understood."

3. A superscript *b* preceding this maxim corresponds with a footnote referencing "[b]8 Rep. 78." The relevant maxim reads, "*Quod non valet in principali in accessoria seu consequenti non valebit.*" Coke, *Reports*, part 8, p. 78.a.

4. A superscript *c* preceding this maxim corresponds with a footnote referencing "[c]5 Rep. 6./94. 6 Rep/35.36/1 Inst. 45.b. Noy's Max. 65. 1 Roll Abr. 850." Quincy has repeated himself in referencing 1 Inst. 45.b in both the main text and the footnote.

5. Quincy left room to the left of this maxim for later footnotes, but he added no further citations.

6. A superscript circle enclosing an *x* mark precedes this maxim, corresponding with a footnote referencing "[x]Co: Lit:/355.b./2. Inst. 307." Quincy's break from the alphabetical footnoting system suggests that this footnote may have been a later addition.

7. A superscript *d* preceding this maxim corresponds with a footnote referencing "[d]10. Rep/133. 2 Roll/Abr. 146.147.148./2 Cro. 261./3 Cro. 416. 418./Intro. 422."

8. A superscript *e* preceding this maxim corresponds with a footnote referencing "[e]1 Inst/111.b."

9. This may be an error. The correct page number is 263.a. See Coke, *Institutes*, part 1, p. 263.a.

10. The maxim referenced here is worded differently: "*Quod nostrum est sine facto sive defectu nostro amitti seu ad alium transferri non potest.*" Coke, *Reports*, part 8, p. 92.a.

176

Maxims. etc.

[1] Every grant should be interpreted most strongly against the donor.[1]
[2] An accessory does not lead, but follows its own principal.[2]
[3] That is certain which can be made certain.[3]
[4] Every greater thing includes the lesser; anybody who is permitted as to the greater should not be barred as to the lesser.[4]
[5] Every greater thing draws the lesser to itself.[5]
[6] What is permitted for the lesser is also permitted for the greater.[6]
[7] Bad grammar does not void a writing/deed.[7]
[8] No one should lose his property without his own act or failing.[8]

1. Coke, *Institutes*, part 1, 36.a (Ch. 5, Of Dower, Sect. 40) (quoting related maxims, including "*Verba cartarum fortius accipiuntur contra proferentem.*"); p. 183.a (Ch. 3, Of Joyntenants, Sect. 283); Coke, *Reports*, part 5, p. 7.b (*Cases of Leases, Justice Windham's Case*) (stating that "every Deed shall be taken more strongly against the Grantor, and more beneficially for the Grantee"); Coke, *Reports*, part 10, p. 59.a (*The Bishop of Salisbury's Case*) (quoting a related maxim, "*ambigua responsio contra proferentem est accipienda*"). In a marginal note, Quincy adds citations to Coke, *Institutes*, part 1, p. 183.b (Ch. 3, Of Joynetenants, Sect. 283) (discussing the interpretation of ambiguous wording in a recorded grant); Coke, *Reports*, part 1, pp. 46.a–b (*The Case of Alton Woods*) (discussing grants by the king versus those made by a common person. For example, the passage states that a common person as "Tenant in Tail grants *totum statum suum*, it is good during his Life, for his Grant shall be taken most strong against him"). On a side note, Quincy's reference to page 183 of Coke's first *Institutes* includes a footnote reading "How this Max is to be understood"; perhaps Quincy found Coke's discussion of the maxim here most compelling and therefore wished to remember which cited source to emphasize should he deal with the maxim again in the future.

2. Coke, *Institutes*, part 1, p. 152.a (Ch. 12, Of Rents, Sect. 229). In a footnote, Quincy also references a similar maxim in Coke, *Reports*, part 8, p. 78.a (*The Lord Stafford's Case*).

3. Coke, *Institutes*, part 1, p. 45.b (Ch. 7, Of Tenant for Years, Sect. 58), 96.a (Ch. 6, Of Frankalmoigne, Sect. 136), p. 142.a (Ch. 12, Of Rents, Sect. 213). In a marginal note, Quincy also cites to Coke, *Reports*, part 5, p. 6.a (*Cases of Leases*), p. 94.b (*Barwick's Case*) (describing the difference between a lease for life and a lease for years and explaining that, for instance, nothing passes if "a Man makes a Lease for Life to begin at a future Day", the problem being that one "cannot make present Livery to a future Estate"); Coke, *Reports*, part 6, pp. 34.b–36.b (*The Bishop of Bath's Case*) (regarding a dispute over a lease); Coke, *Institutes*, part 1, p. 45.b (Ch. 7, Of Tenant for Years, Sect. 58). Quincy also cites to William Noy, *Treatise of the Principall Grounds and Maximes of the Lawes of this Kingdome* (1st edition, 1641), p. 65 (Ch. 35, Leases) (not quoting the maxim but discussing how a "Lease for years must be for time certain"). The text was located using the star pagination in the 1794 London edition. For further bibliographical information on Noy, see Maxwell, p. 243. Finally, Quincy cites to Rolle, *Abridgment*, vol. 1, p. 850 (not quoting the maxim, but discussing "*Quant le lease ferra dit a commencer*"). *Latin for Lawyers* offers the same translation as that given above. *Latin for Lawyers*, p. 165.

THE

REPORT

OF SIR

EDVVARD COKE Kt.

LATE

LORD CHIEF-JUSTICE

OF

ENGLAND

And one of His MAJESTIES

COVNCIL OF STATE.

OF

Divers Refolutions and Judgements given upon folemn Arguments, and with great Deliberation, and Conference of the moft Reverend Judges, and Sages of the Law; of Cafes in Law which never were Refolved or Adjudged before; And the Reafons and Caufes of the faid Refolutions and JUDGEMENTS.

Faithfully rendred into Englifh.

LONDON,

Printed for *W. Lee*, *M. Walbanck*, *D. Pakeman*, and *G. Bedell*, are to be fold at their Shops in *Fleetftreet*, and at *Grays-Inn*-Gate in *Holborn*, 1658.

Edward Coke, *The Report* (London, 1658), Maxwell; pp. 295–97. Courtesy, Coquillette Rare Book Room, Boston College Law School. This was the first English edition of parts I–XI.

4. Coke, *Reports*, part 4, p. 23.a (*Copyhold Cases*), which contains a maxim worded slightly differently; Coke, *Reports*, part 5, p. 115.a (*Wade's Case*) (quoting related maxims, including, "*omne majus continent in se minus*"); Coke, *Reports*, part 9, pp. 49.a–b (*The Earl of Shrewsbury's Case*) (not quoting the maxim, but discussing how, for example, when the queen grants the office of steward to an earl, "it is implied in Law for Conveniency that he may make a Deputy." Similarly, when a duke is given hunting privileges, "the Law for Conveniency gives him such Attendants as are requisite to the Dignity of his Estate.").

5. Coke, *Reports*, part 6, p. 43.b (*Blake's Case*). In a marginal note, Quincy also cites to Coke, *Institutes*, part 1, p. 355.b (Ch. 12, Of Remitter, Sect. 675) (quoting expanded version of this maxim) and Coke, *Institutes*, part 2, p. 307 (*Statutum de Glocester*, Ch. 5) (quoting nearly identical maxim).

6. Coke, *Reports*, part 8, p. 41.b (*Griesley's Case*).

7. Coke, *Institutes*, part 1, p. 146.b (Ch. 12, Of Rents, Sect. 220); Coke, *Reports*, part 6, p. 39.b (*Henry Finch's Case*) (quoting nearly identical maxim); Coke, *Reports*, part 9, p. 48.a (*Earl of Shrewsbury's Case*) (quoting similar maxim). In a marginal note, Quincy also includes citations to Coke, *Reports*, part 10, p. 133.a (*James Osborn's Case*) (not quoting the maxim, but discussing four types of Latin, including *mala grammatica*); Rolle, *Abridgement*, vol. 2, pp. 146–48 (Obligation) (not quoting the maxim, but discussing who may enter into an obligation, with what words an obligation may be created, etc.); Croke, *Reports*, part 2, p. 261 (*Dobson* v. *Keys*) (stating that "it is but false Latine, which shall not make void a Bond"); Croke, *Reports*, part 3, p. 416 (*Done* v. *Smethier and Leigh*) (discussing a minor grammatical error in a writ, substituting *eos* for *vos*), p. 418 (*The Case of Downs and Hathwait*) (stating that "an Obligation shall not be avoided by vicious writing or incongruity."), p. 422 (*Horn* v. *Barbar*) (debating the proper parsing of the words of an agreement). An alternative translation for *chartam* is "charter". See *Latin for Lawyers*, p. 188.

8. Quincy cites to page 265.a of Coke on Littleton, but his pagination appears to be slightly off. See Coke, *Institutes*, part 1, p. 263.a (Ch. 7, Of Continual Claim, Sect. 442). Quincy also cites to Coke, *Reports*, part 8, p. 92.a (*Fraunces's Case*). Additionally, in a marginal note, Quincy references Coke, *Institutes*, part 1, p. 111.b (Ch. 10, Of Tenure in Burgage, Sect. 167) (not quoting the maxim, but discussing devises).

177

Maxims, etc.

[1] Praestat cautela quam Medela.[1] 2 Inst 299.
1 Inst. 304.b.
[2] De Minimis non curat Lex.[2] 1 Inst 54.a.
2 Inst 306
[3] Interest Rei publicae ne quis Re sua male
utatur.[3] 6 Rep. 37.
[4] Dolosus versatur in generalibus[4] 3 Rep 80
[5] Dona clandestina sunt semper suspiciosa. Ibid.
[6] Clausulae inconsuetae semper inducunt suspicionem[5]
Ibid
[7] Mandata licita[6] strictam Interpretationem
recipiunt, sed illicita latam & extensivam[7]
Bacon 66. 3 Inst 51.
[8] Quando Aliquid Mandatur, mandatur & omne
per quod pervenitur ad Illud.[8] 5 Rep. 115.
vid. 2 Inst. 48. 83.[9]
[9] Crimen non contrahitur nisi nocendi Voluntas
intercedit. Bracton Lib.1. ch 4.[10]
[10] Voluntas non reputabitur pro facto.[11] 3 Inst 69[12]
11 Rep. 98.[13]
[11] Non officit[14] Conatus, nisi sequitur[15] Effectus.
11 Rep. 98. 6 Rep. 42.
[12] Poenae potius moliendae sunt, quam exas-
perandae.[16] 3 Inst 220. Yet Severity of
Punishment is to this End, ut Pena[17] ad Paucos, Metus ad
omnes perveniat; for there is Misercordia etc.[18] Co Lit. 294.

1. A superscript *a* preceding this maxim corresponds with a footnote in the left-hand margin reading "[a]F.N.B. 55/5 Rep. 115./1 Inst 53.b/2 Inst 146."

2. A superscript *b* preceding this maxim corresponds with a footnote referencing "[b]2 Inst 306./1 Inst. 260.b."

3. A superscript *c* preceding this maxim corresponds with a footnote that appears to reference "[c]4 Rep. 277." However, Quincy may have intended "4 Inst. 277."

4. A superscript *d* preceding this maxim corresponds with a footnote referencing "[d]3 Rep 80 &c."

5. Quincy left space in the left-hand margin for this and the preceding maxim, but he ultimately added no further citations.

177

Maxims, etc.

[1] Precaution is preferable to a remedy.[1]
[2] The law does not attend to trivial matters.[2]
[3] It is of interest to the republic[3] that no one uses his property badly.[4]
[4] A deceitful person is occupied with generalities.[5]
[5] Clandestine gifts are always suspicious.[6]
[6] Uncustomary conclusions always introduce suspicion.[7]
[7] Lawful commands receive a strict interpretation, but unlawful ones a broad and extensive interpretation.[8]
[8] When anything is ordered, everything by which it is attained is also ordered.[9]
[9] A crime is not committed unless the intention to injure exists.[10]
[10] The will is not reckoned according to the act.[11]
[11] An attempt is not detrimental unless the effect follows.[12]
[12] Punishments should preferably be softened, rather than exasperated.[13]
Yet severity of punishment is to this end, so that pain reaches few, fear reaches all, for there is mercy, etc.[14]

1. Coke, *Institutes*, part 2, p. 299 (*Statutum de Glocester*, Ch. 5); Coke, *Institutes*, part 1, p. 304.b (Ch. 9, Of Confirmation, Sect. 534). In the margin, Quincy cites to Coke, *Reports*, part 5, p. 115 (*Wade's Case*). The maxim is not quoted therein, and its relevance is not immediately apparent. Quincy may have been drawing a connection with Coke's indication that, "if a Man tenders more than he ought to pay, it is good . . . and the other ought to accept so much of it as is due to him"; alternatively, Quincy may have been interested in Coke's caution that a lessor ought to inspect a lessee's payment for counterfeit coinage or else accept the money "at his Peril." Coke, *Reports*, part 5, p. 115. Quincy also includes marginal citations to Coke, *Institutes*, part 1, p. 53.b (Ch. 7, Of Tenant for Years, Sect. 67) (containing a discussion of waste); Coke, *Institutes*, part 2, p. 146 (*Statutum de Marlebridge*, Ch. 24) (also discussing waste, and indicating that "the Law doth give to every man his proper Action, so as none of them be without due remedy"), and to Fitzherbert, *New Natura Brevium*, p. 55. The ninth edition of Fitzherbert, published in 1793, is too late for our purposes but does contain a discussion of waste on page 55; perhaps this was a reprint of an earlier edition that would have been available to Quincy. Unfortunately, page 55 in the 1704, 1718, 1730, and 1755 editions does not appear to be on point.

2. Although Quincy cites to page 54.a of Coke on Littleton, this maxim does not appear to be located on that page. See Coke, *Institutes*, part 1, p. 54.a. The maxim is quoted on the other page cited by Quincy: Coke, *Institutes*, part 2, p. 306 (*Statutum de Gloucester*, Ch. 5). In the margin, Quincy adds citations to Coke, *Institutes*, part 1, p. 260.b (Ch. 7, Of Continual Claim, Sect. 439) and repeats his earlier citation to page 306 of Coke's second *Institutes*.

3. An alternative translation of *rei publicae* is "state." See, e.g., Peloubet, p. 123.

4. Coke, *Reports*, part 6, p. 37 (*The Dean and Chapter of Worcester's Case*) (containing nearly identical maxim). In the margin, Quincy appears to cite to Coke, *Reports*, part 4, p. 277. However, he likely intended Coke, *Institutes*, part 4, p. 277 (Ch. 63, The Court of the Commission-

6. Both Bacon's and Coke's versions include the word *recipiunt* here. Bacon, *Elements*, p. 66; Coke, *Institutes*, part 3, p. 51.

7. A superscript *e* preceding this maxim corresponds with a footnote extending into the body of the page from the left-hand margin and referencing "[e]3 Inst. 108/HPC. 65. 66./Kelynge/31. Dalton ch 157. p.734."

8. In the left-hand margin, presumably related to this maxim, Quincy has noted "vid. p 172/max 9. p. 182/max 4."

9. This line of text was clearly squeezed in between maxims [8] and [9] at a later time.

10. This is Quincy's sole direct citation to Bracton, which states in relevant part, "*crimen non contrahitur, nisi voluntas nocendi intercedat.*" Henry de Bracton, *De Legibus et consuetudinibus Angliae* (1st edition, 1569) (hereafter, "Bracton, *De Legibus*"), book 1, ch. 4. 136b. The quoted text is located at vol. 2, p. 384 of Samuel E. Thorne's edition (Cambridge, Mass., 1968) (hereafter, Thorne, *Bracton*). The quotation in the original Bracton text is "*Quia crimen non contrahitur nisi voluntas nocendi intercedat.*" My special thanks to Charles Donahue and David Warrington, ever helpful inspiration to me. For further bibliographical information on Bracton, see Maxwell, p. 51.

11. A superscript *f* preceding this maxim corresponds with a footnote referencing "[f]3 Inst. 5./69. 161./ West's Symb/86. *ff*.3./4 Rep. 16."

12. This page contains the opposite proposition, "*Quod voluntas reputabatur pro facto*," indicating that this had anciently been held. Coke, *Institutes*, part 3, p. 69.

13. This version states, "*Voluntas non reputatur pro facto.*" Coke, *Reports*, part 11, p. 98.b.

14. One version of Coke spells this *efficit*. See Coke, *Reports*, part 6, p. 42.b.

15. At least one version reads *sequatur*. See, e.g., Coke, *Reports*, part 11, p. 98.b. For same spelling as Quincy, see Coke, *Reports*, part 6, p. 42.b.

16. A superscript *g* preceding this maxim corresponds with a footnote referencing "[g]HPC. 2./126. 134."

17. Expected spelling is *Poena*. See, e.g., Coke, *Institutes*, part 3, p. 220.

18. This sentence has been squeezed in at the bottom of the page. It is preceded by a small circle with a downward-pointing arrow and may have been intended as a footnote to maxim [12].

ers upon the Statutes of Bankrupts) (discussing, for example, a person who consumes his estate through reckless spending).

5. Coke, *Reports*, part 3, pp. 80.b–81.a (*Twyne's Case*). Quincy cites to page 80, which commences a discussion of a "fraudulent Gift of Goods," although the actual maxim is not cited until page 81.a. His failure to cite to page 81 may be due to a pagination error in his source; for example, the 1727 edition repeats the page number 79 where the number 80 is expected. Quincy repeats this citation to page 80 of Coke in a marginal footnote. An alternative translation for the maxim is, "A deceiver deals in general terms." *Latin for Lawyers*, p. 148.

6. Coke, *Reports*, part 3, pp. 80.b–81.a (*Twyne's Case*). Again, the maxim itself is quoted on the page following that cited by Quincy. This same translation is offered elsewhere. See, e.g., *Latin for Lawyers*, p. 149; Peloubet, p. 60.

7. Coke, *Reports*, part 3, pp. 80.b–81.a (*Twyne's Case*). Quincy's "Ibid" again refers to page 80, although the maxim is quoted on page 81.a.

8. In other words, an agent's act is void when a lawful command is not strictly obeyed. However, when a person commands another to commit an unlawful act, he or she will be considered an accessory to any resulting crime regardless of how loosely the agent adheres to the command. For example, you command me to illegally kill X, but I misunderstand you and kill Y. You will still be regarded as an accessory to my crime. Bacon, *Elements*, p. 66 (quoting and explicating the maxim, which is Bacon's regula 16); Coke, *Institutes*, part 3, p. 51 (Of Murder, Ch. 7). In a marginal footnote, Quincy adds citations to Coke, *Institutes*, part 3, p. 108 (Ch. 47, Larceny or Theft) (discussing felonious takings, such as a man finding his neighbor's horse and, approaching the sheriff under the pretext of ownership, obtaining delivery of the horse by replevin); Sir Matthew Hale, *Summary of the Pleas of the Crown* (1st edition, 1678) (hereafter, "Hale, *Pleas*"), pp. 65–66 (Larceny) (not quoting the maxim but discussing who may commit a felony and explaining, for example, the situation of a woman coerced to murder or theft by her husband). This page number was located using the 1707 London edition. For further bibliographical information on Hale's *Pleas*, see Maxwell, p. 362. Quincy continues his citations with William Kelynge, *Report of Select Cases in Chancery (1730–32), King's Bench, etc. [1731–34]* (1st edition, 1740) (hereafter, "Kelynge, *Select Cases*"), p. 31 (not quoting the maxim but possibly relevant in its discussion of how a testator's intent must conform with the law). For further bibliographical information on Kelynge, see Maxwell, p. 303. Finally, Quincy cites to Michael Dalton, *Countrey Justice, the Practice of the Justices of the Peace out of their sessions* (1st edition, 1618) (hereafter, "Dalton, *Countrey Justice*"), p. 352 (Ch. 157, What Persons are chargeable in Larceny) (discussing the legal excuse of compulsion: "where the Words of the Law are broken by Compulsion, there the Law is not offended"). Quincy cites to page 734 and may have been using a different edition of Dalton; the text quoted here was located on page 352 of the 1742 London edition. For further bibliographical information on Dalton, see Maxwell, p. 227. On a side note, an alternative translation for *Mandata licita* is "lawful authority". *Latin for Lawyers*, p. 189.

9. Coke, *Reports*, part 5, p. 115.b (*Foliamb's Case*). Quincy, apparently at a later time, inserted a reference to Coke, *Institutes*, part 2, p. 48 (*Magna Charta*, Ch. 29) (quoting corresponding maxim, "*quando aliquid prohibetur, prohibetur et omne, per quod devenitur ad illud*"), p. 83 (*Statutum de Merton*, Ch. 3) (also not containing the maxim, but possibly cited for the related proposition that "*quando lex est specialis, ratio autem generalis, generaliter lex est intelligenda*"). In the lefthand margin, Quincy included internal references to page 172 maxim [9] and page 182, maxim [4]. The first reference may actually relate to maxim [11], [12], or [13] on that page, as Quincy may have added maxims after making this cross-reference. The second reference points to a related maxim regarding direct and indirect prohibitions.

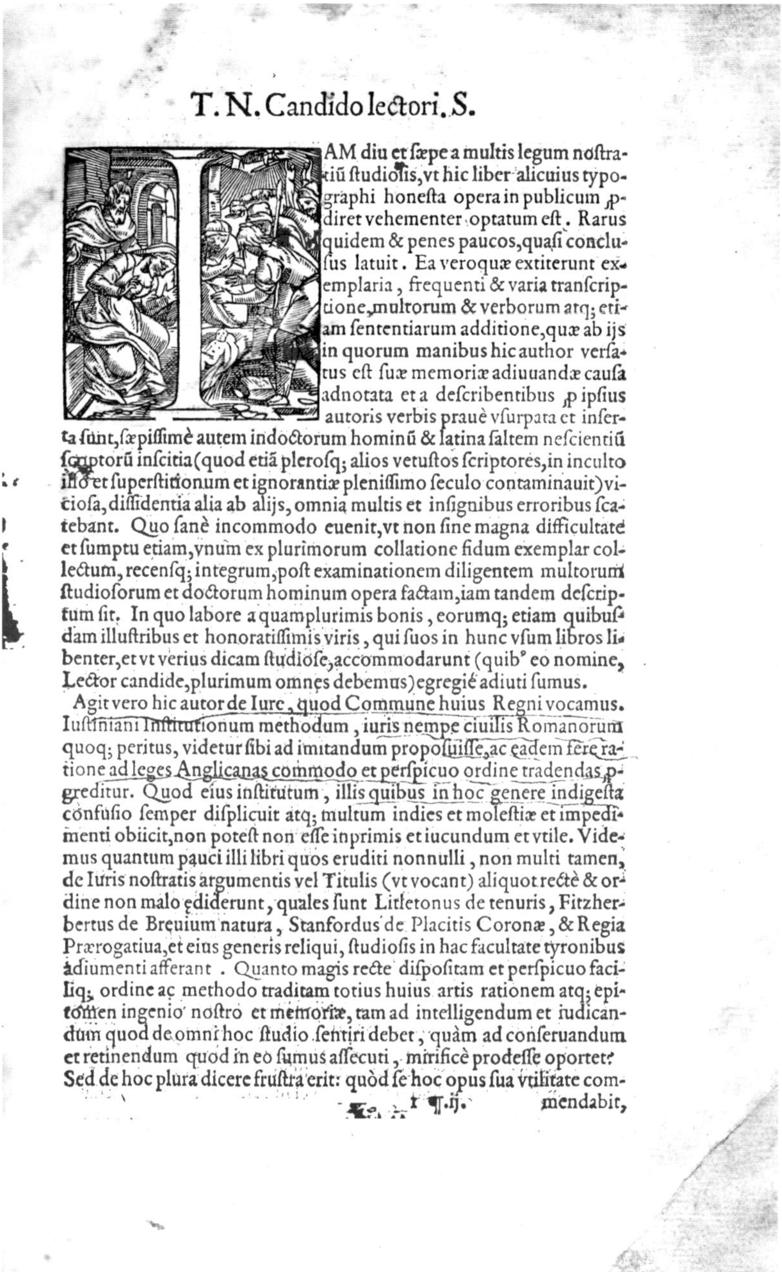

T. N. Candido lectori. S.

IAM diu et ſæpe a multis legum noſtratiũ ſtudioſis, vt hic liber alicuius typographi honeſta opera in publicum ꝓdiret vehementer optatum eſt. Rarus quidem & penes paucos, quaſi concluſus latuit. Ea vero quæ extiterunt exemplaria, frequenti & varia tranſcriptione, multorum & verborum atq; etiam ſententiarum additione, quæ ab ijs in quorum manibus hic author verſatus eſt ſuæ memoriæ adiuuandæ cauſa adnotata et a deſcribentibus ꝓ ipſius autoris verbis praue vſurpata et inſerta ſunt, ſæpiſſimè autem indoctorum hominũ & latina ſaltem neſcientiũ ſcriptorũ inſcitia (quod etiã pleroſq; alios vetuſtos ſcriptores, in inculto illo et ſuperſtitionum et ignorantiæ pleniſſimo ſeculo contaminauit) vitioſa, diffidentia alia ab alijs, omnia multis et inſignibus erroribus ſcatebant. Quo ſanè incommodo euenit, vt non ſine magna difficultate et ſumptu etiam, vnum ex plurimorum collatione fidum exemplar collectum, recenſq; integrum, poſt examinationem diligentem multorum ſtudioſorum et doctorum hominum opera factam, iam tandem deſcriptum ſit. In quo labore a quamplurimis bonis, eorumq; etiam quibuſdam illuſtribus et honoratiſſimis viris, qui ſuos in hunc vſum libros libenter, et vt verius dicam ſtudioſe, accommodarunt (quib⁹ eo nomine, Lector candide, plurimum omnes debemus) egregiè adiuti ſumus.

Agit vero hic autor de Iure, quod Commune huius Regni vocamus. Iuſtiniani Inſtitutionum methodum, iuris nempe ciuilis Romanorum quoq; peritus, videtur ſibi ad imitandum propoſuiſſe, ac eadem fere ratione ad leges Anglicanas commodo et perſpicuo ordine tradendas ꝓgreditur. Quod eius inſtitutum, illis quibus in hoc genere indigeſta confuſio ſemper diſplicuit atq; multum indies et moleſtiæ et impedimenti obiicit, non poteſt non eſſe inprimis et iucundum et vtile. Videmus quantum pauci illi libri quos eruditi nonnulli, non multi tamen, de Iuris noſtratis argumentis vel Titulis (vt vocant) aliquot rectè & ordine non malo ediderunt, quales ſunt Littetonus de tenuris, Fitzherbertus de Breuium natura, Stanfordus de Placitis Coronæ, & Regia Prærogatiua, et eius generis reliqui, ſtudioſis in hac facultate tyronibus adiumenti afferant. Quanto magis rectè diſpoſitam et perſpicuo faciliq; ordine ac methodo traditam totius huius artis rationem atq; epitomen ingenio noſtro et memoriæ, tam ad intelligendum et iudicandum quod de omni hoc ſtudio ſentiri debet, quàm ad conſeruandum et retinendum quod in eo ſumus aſſecuti, mirificè prodeſſe oportet? Sed de hoc plura dicere fruſtra erit: quòd ſe hoc opus ſua vtilitate com-

¶.ij. mendabit,

First page of the first printed edition of Henri de Bracton, *De Legibus et Consuetudinibus Angliae* (London, 1569). See Maxim [9], pp. 400–401, and note 10, p. 402, *supra*. Courtesy, Coquillette Rare Book Room, Boston College Law School.

10. See Thorne, *Bracton*, vol. 2, p. 384. See page 402, note 10, *supra*. Bracton, *De Legibus*, book 1, ch. 4, p. 136[b] (quoting same maxim, with slight variation in wording).

11. Coke, *Institutes*, part 3, p. 69 (Ch. 16, Of Robbery) (citing opposite proposition, which had been held in the past); Coke, *Reports*, part 11, p. 98.b (*James Baggs's Case*) (quoting same proposition, with slight difference in wording). In a marginal note, Quincy also cites to Coke, *Institutes*, part 3, p. 5 (Ch. 1, High Treason) (containing opposite proposition), p. 69 (a repeated citation), p. 161 (Ch. 73, Against Going or Riding Armed) (also citing opposite proposition "by the lawes of the realme of old time"); William West, *Symboleography*, part 1 (1st edition, 1590), p. 86.a (discussing indictments). For further bibliographical information on West, see Maxwell, p. 487. Quincy also cites to Coke, *Reports*, part 4, p. 16 (Actions for Slander) (noting that "Intent of a Man without Act is not punishable by Law").

12. Coke, *Reports*, part 11, p. 98.b (*James Baggs's Case*); Coke, *Reports*, part 6, p. 42.b (*Sir Anthony Mildmay's Case*).

13. Coke, *Institutes*, part 3, p. 220 (Ch. 101, Of Judgements and Execution) (not quoting the maxim but perhaps relevant due to its discussion of how an individual who kills a person in self-defense or in defense of his home shall be acquitted of murder). In a marginal footnote, Quincy includes a citation to Hale, *Pleas*, p. 2 (discussing capital and non-capital offenses), p. 126 (Misprisions) (discussing non-capital offenses), p. 134 (Offences not Capital) (listing a series of non-capital offenses).

14. Coke, *Institutes*, part 1, p. 294.b (Ch. 8, Of Releases, Sect. 514) (discussing attaint and noting, "So odious is perjury in this case in the eye of the Common Law, and the severity of this punishment is to this end, *Ut poena ad paucos, metus ad omnes perveniat*, for there is *Misericordia puniens*, and there is *Crudelitas parcens*").

178

Maxims. etc.

[1] Qui non habet in Aere, luat in Corpore. 2 Inst 173.
[2] Impunitas semper ad Deteriora invitat, & continuum affectum tribuit delinquendi. 4 Rep. 45.[1] 5 Rep. 109.
[3] Minatur Innocentibus, qui parcit nocentibus
4 Rep. 4.[2]
[4] Salus Populi[3] est suprema Lex.[4] 10 Rep. 139.
[5] Delinquens per Iram provocatus, puniri debet Mitius[5] 2 Inst 55.
[6] Quod Quis[6] ob Tutelam Corporis sui fecerit, Jure id fecisse videtur.[7] 1 Inst 162.a. 2 Inst 384. 590. 3 Inst. 56.
[7] Vim vi repellere licet, modo fiat cum moderamine inculpatae tutelae.[8] 2 Inst. 162.a.[9]
[8] Clam Delinquens magis punitur quam palam. 8 Rep 127.
[9] Frustra Legis Auxilium invocat, qui in Legem committit. 3 Inst. 64.
[10] Merito Beneficium Legis amittit, qui Legem ipsum subvertere intendit. 2 Inst 53.
[11] Summa Ratio est, quae pro Religione facit. 5 Rep. 14. 10 Rep. 55. 11 Rep. 50.[10] 1 Inst. 341.a.
[12] Quod fieri non debet, factum valet.[11] 5 Rep. 38.[12]
[13] Mitius imperanti melius paretur. 3 Inst. 23.24.163.

1. The page cited here contains a similar maxim: "*Maleficia non debent remanere impunita, & impunitas continuum affectum tribuit delinquendi.*" Coke, *Reports*, part 4, p. 45.a.

2. Quincy clearly wrote "4 Rep. 4" but may have intended "4 Rep. 45", in which this maxim is found with a slight difference in wording: "*minatur innocentes qui parcit nocentibus*". Coke, *Reports*, part 4, p. 45.a.

3. Quincy appears to have written *Papali* or *Papuli*, but *Populi* was likely his intended word.

4. Underlining in original.

5. A superscript *a* preceding this maxim corresponds with a footnote in the lefthand margin which appears to read, "[a]1 Inst. 217.b/3 Inst 55."

6. Quincy may be abbreviating *Quisque* here. See Coke, *Institutes*, part 2, p. 384.

7. A superscript *b* preceding this maxim corresponds with a footnote reading, "[b]3 Inst 55./56./HPC. 41./42. Dalton/ch. 150. p. 357. 358./Kely. 128." With regard to the Dalton citation, Quincy may have intended pages 337–38. The Kelynge citation is partly obscured by an inkblot on the page number and may be transcribed incorrectly. Although I consulted the original manuscript, I could not absolutely confirm the page number.

178

Maxims. etc.

[1] He who does not have money, suffers in his body.[1]
[2] Impunity always incites toward worse (crimes) and imparts a continuous disposition toward wrongdoing.[2]
[3] He who spares wrongdoers threatens the innocent.[3]
[4] The welfare of the people is the supreme law.[4]
[5] A wrongdoer provoked by anger should be punished more lightly.[5]
[6] That which one does for the protection of his own body is seen to have been done justly.[6]
[7] It is permitted to repel force with force, on condition that it is done by means of blameless defense.[7]
[8] A wrongdoer is punished more in secret than publicly.[8]
[9] He calls upon the assistance of the law in vain who commits injustice against the law.[9]
[10] He justly loses the benefit of the law who endeavors to subvert the law itself.[10]
[11] The highest reason is that which acts for religion.[11]
[12] That which should not be done is valid once done.[12]
[13] One commanding gently is more easily obeyed.[13]

1. Coke, *Institutes*, part 2, p. 173 (*Statutum de Westminster primer*, Ch. 9). An alternative translation is, "What a man cannot pay with his purse, he must suffer in person." *Latin for Lawyers*, p. 229.

2. Coke, *Reports*, part 4, p. 45.a (*Vaux's Case*) (containing a similar maxim); Coke, *Reports*, part 5, p. 109.a (*Foxley's Case*) (quoting first half of the maxim).

3. Coke, *Reports*, part 4, p. 45.a (*Cases of Appeals and Indictments*), containing a nearly identical maxim. Quincy may have erroneously cited to page 4 of Coke.

4. Coke, *Reports*, part 10, p. 139.b (*Keighley's Case*).

5. Coke, *Institutes*, part 2, p. 55 (*Magna Charta*, Ch. 29) (not quoting the maxim, but referring to the writ *de odio et atia*). In a marginal footnote, Quincy cites to Coke on Littleton, but the page number is not written clearly. Quincy also includes a marginal citation to Coke, *Institutes*, part 3, p. 55 (Of Homicide, Ch. 8).

6. Coke, *Institutes*, part 1, p. 162.a (Ch. 12, Of Rents, Sect. 240) (containing similarly phrased maxim); Coke, *Institutes*, part 2, p. 384 (*Statutum de Westminster secundum*, Ch. 12), p. 590 (*De Frangentibus Prisonam*) (quoting nearly identical maxim); Coke, *Institutes*, part 3, p. 56 (Of Homicide, Ch. 8). In a marginal note, Quincy repeats his citation to Coke's third volume of *Institutes* but also cites to Hale, *Pleas*, pp. 41–42 (*Se defendendo*) (not quoting the maxim, but discussing justifiable homicide); Dalton, *Countrey Justice*, pp. 337–38 (Ch. 150, Homicide upon Necessity) (Quincy cites to pp. 357–58, but these fall within Ch. 159. He most likely intended to write pp. 337–38, which contains a discussion of the lawful killing of felons, prison escapees, etc.); Kelynge, *Select Cases*, p. 126 (although the page number quoted by Quincy is not entirely legible, this may be a reference to the discussion on page 126 of false imprisonment.)

8. An *x* mark preceding this maxim corresponds with a footnote reading, "[x]vid/p 181." Quincy records the same maxim, with an additional phrase added, on page 181, maxim [13].

9. Quincy likely intended to refer to the same page in Coke on Littleton. See Coke, *Institutes*, part 1, p. 162.a.

10. Quincy clearly cites to page 50, although the maxim appears on page 70. See Coke, *Reports*, part 11, p. 70.b.

11. A superscript *d* preceding this maxim corresponds with a footnote reading, "[d]2 Lev./184./242."

12. Coke's version reads, "*fieri non debuit, sed factum valuit.*" Coke, *Reports*, part 5, p. 38.b.

7. Quincy cites to Coke's second volume, but the maxim is found in Coke, *Institutes*, part 1, p. 162.a (Ch. 12, Of Rents, Sect. 240). In a marginal footnote, Quincy also provides an internal cross reference to the same maxim on his page 181.

8. Coke, *Reports*, part 8, p. 127.b (*The City of London's Case*).

9. Coke, *Institutes*, part 3, p. 64 (Of Burglarie, Ch. 14).

10. Coke, *Institutes*, part 2, p. 53 (*Magna Charta*, Ch. 29).

11. Coke, *Reports*, part 5, p. 14.b (*The Case of Ecclesiastical Persons*); Coke, *Reports*, part 10, p. 55.a (*The Case of the Chancellors, Masters and Scholars of the University of Oxford*); Coke, *Reports*, part 11, 70.a (*Magdalen College Case*) (Quincy cited to page 50, but the maxim is quoted on 70); Coke, *Institutes*, part 1, p. 341.a (Ch. 11, Of Discontinuance, Sect. 644).

12. Coke, *Reports*, part 5, p. 38.b (*Tey's Case*) (quoting a similar maxim in the context of the payment of fines). In a marginal note, Quincy also cites to Sir Creswell Levinz, *Reports of Cases in the Court of King's Bench and Common Pleas, during the time of Sir R. Foster, Sir R. Hyde and Sir J. Kelyng were Chief Justices: also cases in other courts during that time [1660–96]* (1st edition, 1702), vol. 2, pp. 184, 242. For further bibliographical information on Levinz, see Maxwell, p. 303.

13. Coke, *Institutes*, part 3, pp. 23–24 (Petit Treason, Ch. 2) (quoting the maxim and observing that "lawes justly made for the preservation of the common-weale without extreme punishment or penalty, are more often, and for the most part better obeyed and kept, then lawes and statutes made with great and extreme punishment"), p. 163 (Of Perjury, Ch. 74) (not quoting the maxim, but discussing the lightening of the penalty for perjury from capital and corporal punishment before the conquest to fine, ransom, and preclusion from future testimony because "too severe laws are never duly executed").

179

Maxims. etc.

[1] Plus peccat Author, quam Actor.
5 Rep. 99. 3 Inst. 167.
[2] Culpa est immiscere se Rei ad se non pertinenti[1]
1 Inst. 368.b. 2 Inst. 208. 444.[2] 3 Inst. 91.
[3] Idem est facere, & nolle prohibere, cum
posse.[3] 3 Inst. 158.
[4] Qui non obstat, quod obstare[4] potest
facere videtur.[5] 2 Inst. 146.
[5] Quod prius est, verius est. 1 Inst 347.b
[6] Verba accipienda in mitiore[6] Sensu.[7] 4 Rep. 13.
17.[8] 20. 25. vid 4 Bac: Abr: 505. Cases Time of Holt 39.[9]
[7] Benignior Sententia in Verbis generalibus, seu
dubiis, est praeferenda. 4. Rep. 15.
[8] Sensus verborum ex Causa Dicendi accipiendus est.
4 Rep. 13. 14.
[9] Sermo relatus ad Personam intelligi debet de
Conditione Personae. 4 Rep. 16.
[10] Quod non apparet, non est.[10] 2 Inst. 479.
[11] De non apparentibus, & non Existentibus, Eadem est
Ratio. 4 Rep. 47. 2 Inst. 20.[11]
[12] Multa conceduntur per Obliquum, quae non conceduntur
de Directo. 6 Rep. 47.

1. A superscript *a* preceding this maxim corresponds with a footnote in the left-hand margin reading "[a]2 Inst. 212/213. 2 Roll/Abr. 115."

2. This page number was inserted later with a caret.

3. A superscript *b* preceding this maxim corresponds with a footnote reading, "[b]2 Inst/305." Coke's version ends with *possis*. Coke, *Institutes*, part 3, p. 158.

4. Quincy has crossed out a letter and inserted *r* above with a caret.

5. Although Quincy has left marginal space, no additional citations are footnoted for this or the following maxim.

6. Quincy clearly wrote *mitiore*, but both Coke and Bacon write *mitiori*. Coke, *Reports*, part 4, p. 13.a; Bacon, *Abridgement*, vol. 4, p. 505.

7. A superscript *c* preceding this maxim corresponds with a footnote reading, "[c]Finch./Ch. 2. p. 185/4 Rep. 15 to 20/1 Danver's/Abr p. 80/&c. to 172."

8. On this page, the text notes that "the Words themselves shall be taken *in mitiori sensu.*" Coke, *Reports*, part 4, p. 17.b.

9. This reference to Holt and the preceding reference to Bacon are in a different ink than maxims [6] or [7], and different ink than each other, and were likely inserted at later times.

179

Maxims. etc.

[1] The author sins more than the actor.[1]
[2] It is wrong to meddle with a matter not pertaining to oneself.[2]
[3] It is the same to do as to not prohibit what is possible.[3]
[4] He who does not oppose that which he could oppose is seen to do it.[4]
[5] That which is first is more true.[5]
[6] Words should be understood in the most lenient sense.[6]
[7] The more liberal meaning should be preferred for general, or doubtful, statements.[7]
[8] The sense of words should be understood from the reason for speaking.[8]
[9] A remark related to a person should be understood from the circumstances of the person.[9]
[10] That which is invisible does not exist.[10]
[11] Regarding the invisible and the nonexistent, the reckoning is the same.[11]
[12] Many things are conceded indirectly that are not conceded directly.[12]

1. Coke, *Reports*, part 5, p. 99.a (*Flower's Case*); Coke, *Institutes*, part 3, p. 167 (Ch. 74, Of Perjury).

2. Coke, *Institutes*, part 1, p. 368.b (Ch. 13, Of Warranty, Sect. 701); Coke, *Institutes*, part 2, p. 208 (*Statutum de Westminster primer*, Ch. 25), p. 444 (*Statutum de Westminster secundum*, Ch. 36); Coke, *Institutes*, part 3, p. 91 (Ch. 29, Of Felonie in Jaylers). In a marginal note, Quincy also cites to Coke, *Institutes*, part 2, pp. 212–13 (*Statutum de Westminster primer*, Ch. 28) (defining "maintenance" as "an unlawfull upholding of the Demandant or Plaintife, Tenant or Defendant in a cause depending in suit, by word, writing, countenance, or deed" and describing how the fomenting of complaints or suits in parts of the country other than one's own is "punished with great severity"); Rolle, *Abridgment*, vol. 2, p. 115 (Maintenance) (not quoting the maxim, but discussing the topic of maintenance).

3. Coke, *Institutes*, part 3, p. 158 (Of Monomachia, Single Combate, Duell, Affrays, and Challenges, and of Private Revenge) (quoting nearly identical maxim). In a marginal note, Quincy also cites to Coke, *Institutes*, part 2, p. 305 (quoting a related maxim, "*Qui non prohibet quod prohibere potest, assentire videtur.*").

4. Coke, *Institutes*, part 2, p. 146 (*Statutum de Marlebridge*, Ch. 24).

5. Coke, *Institutes*, part 1, p. 347.b (Ch. 12, Of Remitter, Sect. 659).

6. Coke, *Reports*, part 4, pp. 13.a, 17.b, 20.a (Actions for Slander). Quincy also cites to page 25, but this maxim has not been located therein. Quincy directs the reader to Bacon, *Abridgment*, vol. 4, p. 505 (within the section entitled Slander, and the subsection (K) dealing with "In what Cases uncertain Words are to be construed *in mitiori sensu.*"). Quincy also references "Cases Time of Holt 39", which may be *Report of Cases determined by Holt, [King's Bench], 1688–1710* (1st edition, 1738), but I was unable to confirm this. For further bibliographical information on this collection of cases, see Maxwell, p. 301. In a marginal note, Quincy includes citations to Sir Henry Finch, *Law: or, Discourse thereof* (1st edition, 1613) (hereafter, "Finch, *Dis-*

10. A superscript *f* preceding this maxim corresponds with a footnote reading, "[f]4 Inst. 468/469./3 Inst/46./H.P.C. 8."

11. Coke's version concludes with the word *lex* rather than *ratio*. Coke, *Institutes*, part 2, p. 20.

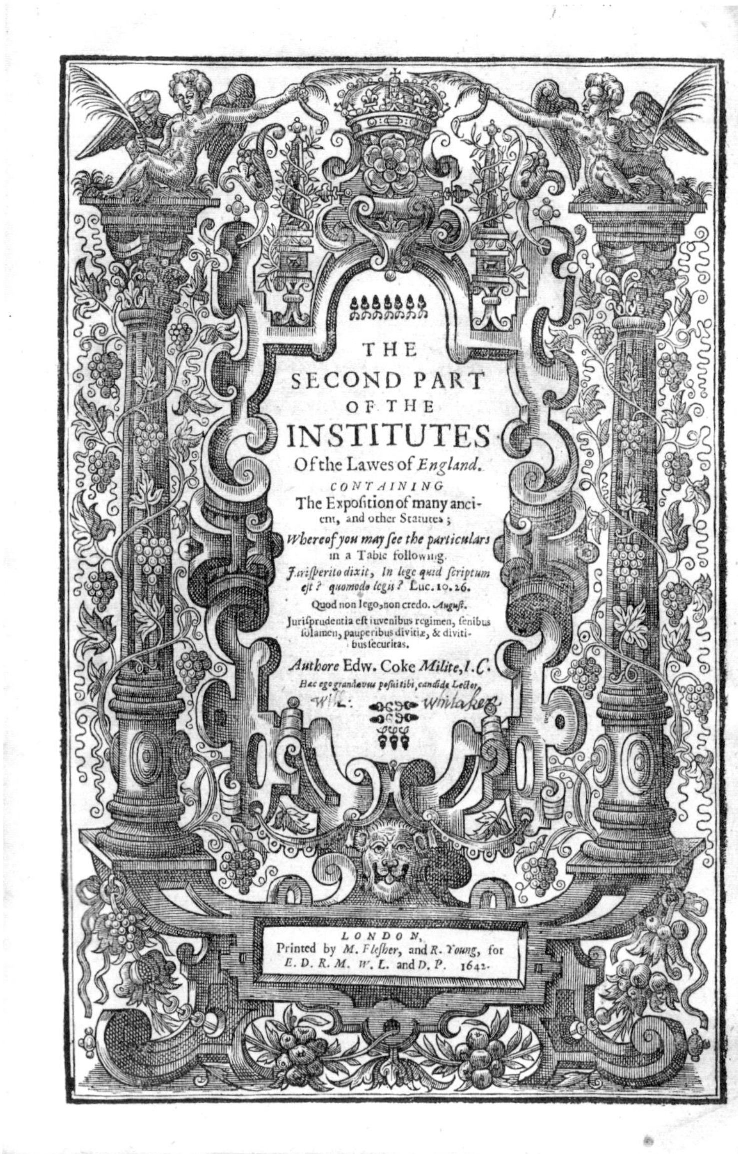

THE
SECOND PART
OF THE
INSTITUTES
Of the Lawes of *England*.
CONTAINING
The Expoſition of many anci-
ent, and other Statutes;
Whereof you may ſee the particulars
in a Table following.
Juriſperito dixit, In lege quid ſcriptum
eſt? quomodo legis? Luc. 10. 26.
Quod non lego, non credo. *Auguſt.*
Juriſprudentia eſt iuvenibus regimen, ſenibus
ſolamen, pauperibus divitiæ, & diviti-
bus ſecuritas.
Authore Edw. Coke *Milite, I.C.*
Hæc ego grandævus poſui tibi, candide Lector.
Will: Whitaker

LONDON,
Printed by *M. Fleſher,* and *R. Young,* for
E. D. R. M. W. L. and *D. P.* 1642.

Sir Edward Coke, *Second Part of the Institutes of the Lawes of England* (London, 1642), Maxwell, p. 546. See p. 413, note 10, *infra*.

course"), (Lib. III, ch. 2, Of trespasses upon the case), pp. 185–86 (discussing slander, and explaining that statements without malice do not give rise to a cause of action). The page number was verified against the 1759 London edition. For further bibliographical information on Finch, see Maxwell, p. 238. Quincy also cites to Coke, *Reports*, part 4, pp. 15–20 (Actions for Slander) (describing the law of slander in detail and quoting the maxim itself on page 20.a). Finally, Quincy cites to Knightley D'Anvers, *General Abridgment of the Common Law* (1st edition, 1705–1737), vol. 1, pp. 80–172; these page numbers have not been confirmed. This translation presumes the word *sunt* after *accipienda*, as the maxim is written in Coke.

7. Coke, *Reports*, part 4, p. 15.b (Actions for Slander).

8. Coke, *Reports*, part 4, p. 13.b (Actions for Slander), with Coke's more expansive version of the maxim extending to page 14.a.

9. Coke, *Reports*, part 4, p. 16.a (Actions for Slander).

10. Coke, *Institutes*, part 2, p. 479 (*Statutum de Westminster secundum*, Ch. 47). Quincy's marginal citation to pages 468–69 of Coke's fourth volume of the *Institutes* is an error; he was probably repeating his earlier citation to volume 2. In the margin, Quincy also cites to Coke, *Institutes*, part 3, p. 46 (Ch. 6, Conjuration, Witchcraft, &c.) (discussing cases of witchcraft or sorcery where an individual threatens to harm another's cattle, goods, or person, but no effect follows); Hale, *Pleas*, p. 8 (Witchcraft) (discussing, among other matters, the use of witchcraft to hurt someone, but without attaining the intended effect).

11. Coke, *Reports*, part 4, p. 47.a (*Cases of Appeals and Indictments*); Coke, *Institutes*, part 2, p. 20 (*Magna Charta*, Ch. 8) (quoting similar maxim).

12. Coke, *Reports*, part 6, pp. 47.a–b (*Dowdale's Case*).

180

Maxims. etc.

[1] Qui semel Actionem renunciavit, amplius repetere non potest.[1] 8 Rep. 59.
[2] Ambiguum Placitum interpretari debet contra Proferentem. 1 Inst 303.b
[3] Probationes debent esse evidentes, perspicuae & faciles intelligi.[2] 1 Inst. 283.a.
[4] Ex Diuturnitate[3] Omnia praesumuntur solemniter Acta.[4] 1 Inst. 6.b. 2 Inst. 362.[5]
[5] Plus valet unus oculatus Testis, quam auriti decem. 4 Inst. 297.[6]
[6] Omnia praesumuntur legitime facta, donec probetur in Contrarium.[7] 1 Inst. 232.b.
[7] Injuria non praesumitur. Ibid.
[8] Odiosa & Inhonesta non sunt[8] praesumenda. 10 Rep. 56. 1 Inst. 78.b.[9]
[9] Stabitur Praesumitioni,[10] donec probetur in Contrarium.[11] 1 Inst. 373.b. 2 Rep. 48. 4 Rep. 71.
[10] Res judicata pro veritate habetur.[12] 1 Inst. 39.a.[13] 2 Inst. 360.[14] 573.[15] 380.[16]

1. A superscript *a* preceding this maxim corresponds with a footnote in the left-hand margin reading, "[a]FNB/428./8 Rep./58. 59;/1 Inst. 138.b/139.a etc./1 Roll. Abr./584./3 Cro. 551."

2. A superscript *b* preceding this maxim corresponds with a footnote reading, "[b]Terms/of y[e] Law./v. Evidence." (underscoring in original). This is probably a reference to Jacob Giles, *New law-dictionary, the interpretation and definition of words and terms used in the law* (London, 1750) (hereafter, "Giles, *New law-dictionary*"), where the definition of evidence includes the maxim, "*Probationes debent esse Evidentes & Perspicuae.*"

3. Coke's version includes the word *temporis* here. Coke, *Institutes*, part 1, p. 6.b.

4. A superscript *c* preceding this maxim corresponds with a footnote reading, "[c]2 Inst./118./Trials per/Pais. 166./220. 232. 233."

5. Reading, in relevant part, "*omnia praesumi debent solenniter [sic] esse acta.*" Coke, *Institutes*, part 2, p. 362.

6. Quincy transposed the page number here, as the maxim is found in Coke, *Institutes*, part 4, p. 279.

7. A superscript *d* preceding this maxim corresponds with a footnote reading, "[d]1 Inst./232.b," a repeat of Quincy's initial citation.

8. Coke includes the words *in lege* here. Coke, *Reports*, part 10, p. 56.a.

9. This page contains a related maxim, "*Nulla impossibilia aut inhonesta sunt praesumenda, vera autem & honesta, & posibilia.*" Coke, *Institutes*, part 1, p. 78.b.

180

Maxims. etc.

[1] He who once retracts an action cannot pursue it further.[1]
[2] One should interpret ambiguous silence against the one offering it.[2]
[3] Proof should be evident, manifest, and easy to understand.[3]
[4] After a length of time all things are presumed to have been done solemnly.[4]
[5] One eyewitness is worth more than ten listeners.[5]
[6] All things are presumed legitimately done, until it is proved to the contrary.[6]
[7] Injury is not presumed.[7]
[8] Hateful and dishonest (acts) are not presumed.[8]
[9] A presumption will stand until it is proved to the contrary.[9]
[10] An adjudicated matter is held as the truth.[10]

1. Coke, *Reports*, part 8, p. 59.a (*Beecher's Case*). In a marginal footnote, Quincy repeats this reference, expanding it to include further related discussion on page 58. Quincy also cites to Fitzherbert, *New Natura Brevium*, p. 428 (regarding the writ of the assize of nuisance; relevance not apparent); Coke, *Institutes*, part 1, pp. 138.b–139.a (Ch. 11, Of Villenage, Sect. 208) (discussing nonsuit and retraxit and quoting the maxim on the latter page); Rolle, *Abridgment*, vol. 1, p. 584 (Default) (not quoting the maxim directly but containing two discussions entitled, respectively, "Retraxit" and "Le effect de ceo"); Croke, *Reports*, part 3, p. 551 (*Dennis* v. *John Payne Sr.*) (discussing a case of retraxit).

2. Coke, *Institutes*, part 1, p. 303.b (Ch. 9, Of Confirmation, Sect. 534).

3. Coke, *Institutes*, part 1, p. 283.a (Ch. 8, Of Releases, Sect. 485). In the margin, Quincy references a definition of "evidence" in a text identified as "Terms of Law," most likely Jacob Giles' law dictionary. See Giles, *New law-dictionary* (defining evidence as "used in the Law for some *Proof*, by Testimony of Men on Oath, or by Writings or Records", and then going on to quote the same maxim, with slight variation in wording, as Quincy) (italics in original).

4. Coke, *Institutes*, part 1, 6.b (Ch. 1, Of Fee Simple, Sect. 1); Coke, *Institutes*, part 2, p. 362 (*Statutum de Westminster secundo*, Ch. 5) (containing similarly worded maxim). In a marginal footnote, Quincy includes a citation to Coke, *Institutes*, part 2, 118 (*Statutum de Marlebridge*, Ch. 9), which does not quote the maxim but states, "The Law doth ever favour possession as an argument of right, and doth incline rather to long possession without shewing any deed, then to an ancient deed without possession." Additionally, the footnote references *Trials per Pais*, presumably referring to Samson Euer, *Trials per Pais: or Law concerning Juries by Nisi Prius, etc.* (1st edition, 1665), although the relevance of the cited pages (pp. 166, 220, 232, 233) is not immediately evident; it is likely that Quincy consulted a different edition than those consulted by me. For further bibliographical information on Euer's work, see Maxwell, 375 (listed under heading of "Duncombe (G.)").

5. Coke, *Institutes*, part 4, p. 279 (Ch. 64, Commissioners for Examination of Witnesses). An alternative translation for *auriti* is "ear witnesses." *Latin for Lawyers*, p. 219.

6. Coke, *Institutes*, part 1, p. 232.b (Ch. 5, Of Estates, Sect. 377). In a marginal footnote, Quincy repeats this citation.

7. Coke, *Institutes*, part 1, p. 232.b (Ch. 5, Of Estates, Sect. 377).

10. A couple of letters are crossed out at the end of this word, and –*ioni* is inserted. The expected word is *praesumptio*. See, e.g., Coke, *Reports*, part 4, p. 71.a (reading, "*Stabit praesumptio donec probetur in contrarium.*").

11. A superscript *e* preceding this maxim corresponds with a footnote reading "[e]1 Inst. 373/a & b."

12. A superscript *f* preceding this maxim corresponds with a footnote in the left-hand margin and extending to the right across the bottom of the page. The footnote references, "[f]1 Inst./ 39.a/167.b/168.a. 2 Inst. 236. Finch. 459."

13. This page contains a related maxim, "*Judicium semper pro veritate accipitur.*" Coke, *Institutes*, part 1, p. 39.a.

14. Here, Coke notes, "*Quia judicia in curia Regis reddita pro veritate accipiuntur*," and "*Interest reipublicae res judicatas non rescindi.*" Coke, *Institutes*, part 2, p. 360.

15. On this page, Coke writes, "*judicia sunt tanquam juris dicta, & pro veritate accipiuntur.*" Coke, *Institutes*, part 2, p. 573.

16. The final page number is written in a darker ink and is out of sequence, likely having been added at a later time. On the referenced page, Coke writes, "*Judicium pro veritate accipitur.*" See Coke, *Institutes*, part 2, p. 380.

8. Coke, *Reports*, part 10, p. 56.a (*The Case of the Chancellor, Masters and Scholars of the University of Oxford*) (nearly identical wording); Coke, *Institutes*, part 1, p. 78.b (Ch. 4, Of Knights Service, Sect. 103) (containing a related maxim).

9. Coke, *Institutes*, part 1, p. 373.b (Ch. 13, Of Warranty, Sect. 109); Coke, *Reports*, part 2, p. 48 (*Magna Charta*, Ch. 29) (discussing how the property of a man accused or indicted of treason or felony should not be seized before attainder, "for when a Subject obtaineth a promise of the forfeiture, many times undue meanes and more violent prosecution is used for private lucre, tending to destruction, then the quiet and just proceeding of Law would permit"); Coke, *Reports*, part 4, 71.a (*Hynde's Case*). In a marginal footnote, Quincy repeats his citation to Coke on Littleton, citing this time to pages 373.a and b.

10. Coke, *Institutes*, part 1, p. 39.a (Ch. 5, Of Dower, Sect. 48); Coke, *Institutes*, part 2, p. 360 (*Statutum de Westminster secundo*, Ch. 5), p. 380 (*Statutum de Westminster secundo*, Ch. 11), 573 (*Articuli Super Chartas*, Ch. 19). All of these pages contain related maxims, with none directly quoted by Quincy. In the margin, Quincy also cites to Coke, *Institutes*, part 2, p. 236 (*Statutum de Westminster primer*, Ch. 37), which may be relevant due to its mention that "the Court *ex officio* ought to inquire of the force; but if they doe not, it is not error, as it hath been adjudged." In a marginal footnote, Quincy repeats two of the citations listed above (Coke, *Institutes*, part 1, p. 39.a; Coke, *Institutes*, part 2, p. 236) but also provides new citations to Coke, *Institutes*, part 1, pp. 167.b–168.a (Ch. 1, Of Parceners, Sect. 248) (stating a similar maxim: "*Judicium est quasi juris dictum*, so called, because so long as it stands in force, *pro veritate accipitur*, [it] cannot be contradicted") and to Finch, *Discourse*, p. 459 (Lib. IV, ch. 45, Of Judgments) (discussing the nature of judgments and noting, "Judgment is the court's final determination of that suit. Upon judgment against the king in a petition, he is presently out of possession . . . In a writ of right the judgment after issue joined is final on either side, not only when it passeth by verdict, or vanquishing of the other's champion, but where the demandant is (a) nonsuit, or the (b) tenant maketh default, or the (c) vouchee after such an issue joined by him, departeth in spite of the court"). Finch, *Discourse*, pp. 459–60.

181

Maxims. etc.

[1] Idem est Nihil dicere, & insufficienter dicere. 2 Inst.
453. 178
[2] Cum Confitente Mitius est agendum. 11 Rep. 30.
4 Inst 66.
[3] In Criminalibus Probationes debent esse Luce
clariores.[1] 3 Inst. 26.[2] 210.
[4] Fatetur Facinus, qui Judicium fugit. 3 Inst.
188. 5 Rep. 109.
[5] Judicandum est Legibus, non Exemplis.[3]
3 Inst. 212. 4 Rep. 33.
[6] Exempla illustrant non restringunt Legem. Co Lit 24.a
[7] Multa in Jure communi contra Rationem Disputandi[4]
pro communi Utilitate introducta sunt.[5] Co Lit. 70.b.
[8] Ratio potest allegari deficiente Lege—But it must be Ratio vera
& legalis[6] & non apparens.[7] Co Lit. 191.a.
[9] Nulla Impossibilia aut Inhonesta sunt
praesumenda, vera autem & honesta, & posibilia
Co: Lit. 78.b.
[10] Nihil quod est inconveniens est licitum.
Ibid 97.b.
[11] Neminem oportet esse sapientiorem[8] Legibus.[9] Ibd: 97.b.
[12] Qui adimit medium dirimit Finem. Ibid 161.a
[13] Qui obstruit Aditum, destruit Commodum. Ibid. 161.a
[14] Vim vi repellere licet, modo fiat moderamine[10] inculpatae Tutelae[11]
non ad sumendam vindictam, sed ad propulsandam
Injuriam.[12] Co: Lit: 162.a.

1. A superscript *b* preceding this maxim corresponds with a footnote in the left-hand margin reading, “[b]Kely/49.50.” Quincy evidently started with *b* and proceeded to *d* with the anticipation of later adding additional citations to other maxims on the page.

2. Coke writes, “*probationes oportent esse luce clariores.*” Coke, *Institutes*, part 3, p. 25. Quincy's page citation appears to be off by one page.

3. A superscript *d* preceding this maxim corresponds with a footnote reading, “[d]3 Cro. 176.”

4. Underlining here and below in original.

5. A superscript *x* mark preceding this maxim corresponds with a marginal note reading “[x]vid Co Lit/232.b. p 171 Max 3.” Quincy records the same maxim, with slight variation, on page 153, maxim [4], but cites there to Justinian's *Digest.*

6. Quincy has crossed out the last letter of this word and inserted an *s* with a caret.

181

Maxims. etc.

[1] It is the same to say nothing and to say too little.[1]
[2] With a confession, it should be pursued more gently.[2]
[3] In criminal cases, proofs should be clearer than light.[3]
[4] He who flees judgment confesses a crime.[4]
[5] One should judge from laws, not from examples.[5]
[6] Examples elucidate, not restrain, the law.[6]
[7] Many things contrary to logical argument were received into the common law for the common good.[7]
[8] Reason can be alleged in a deficient law—but it must be true and legal reason and not (merely) apparent.[8]
[9] Nothing impossible or dishonest should be presumed, but instead what is true, honest, and possible.[9]
[10] Nothing that is unsuitable is permitted.[10]
[11] It is necessary that no one be wiser than the laws.[11]
[12] He who takes away the means frustrates the end.[12]
[13] One who obstructs access destroys a convenience.[13]
[14] It is permitted to repel force with force, on condition that it is done by means of blameless defense, not to take revenge but to fend off injury.[14]

1. Coke, *Institutes*, part 2, p. 178 (*Statutum de Westminster primer*, Ch. 12), p. 453 (*Statutum de Westminster secundo*, Ch. 39).

2. Quincy cites to Coke, *Reports*, part 11, p. 38; while the maxim does not appear to be located on that page, the page does contain a discussion of confession. The maxim is quoted, however, in Quincy's second source: Coke, *Institutes*, part 4, p. 66 (Ch. 5, Court of Star-Chamber).

3. Coke, *Institutes*, part 3, p. 26 (Ch. 2, Petit Treason), p. 210 (Ch. 100, Of False Imprisonment). The former page offers a slight variation on the maxim, while the same wording as that quoted by Quincy is found on the latter page.

4. Coke, *Reports*, vol. 5, p. 109.b (*Foxley's Case*). Quincy also cites to Coke, *Institutes*, part 3, p. 188, but this maxim does not appear to be located on that page. Because *fatetur* is passive, it may be more appropriate to say, "A crime is confessed" or that the fleeing person "manifests a crime."

5. Coke, *Institutes*, p. 212 (Ch. 101, Of Judgments and Executions); Coke, *Reports*, part 4, p. 33.b (*Mitton's Case*).

6. Coke, *Institutes*, part 1, p. 24.a (Ch. 2, Of Fee Tail, Sect. 21).

7. Coke, *Institutes*, part 1, p. 70.b (Ch. 3, Of Escuage, Sect. 96). In a footnote, Quincy also cites to Coke, *Institutes*, part 1, p. 232.b (Ch. 5, Of Estates Upon Condition, Sect. 377), although this maxim does not appear to be located on that page. Quincy may be referring to Coke's discussion of how "by reasoning and debating of grave learned men the darkness of ignorance is expelled, and by the light of legal Reason the Right is discerned and thereupon Judgment given according to Law, which is the perfection of Reason."

7. This maxim appears to have been inserted at a later time, as Quincy has compressed much of it into the left-hand margin of the page.

8. Coke writes *sapentiorem*. Coke, *Institutes*, part 1, p. 97.b.

9. In the left-hand margin, Quincy has drawn a hand with the index finger pointing toward this maxim.

10. There appears to be a small, upward-pointing arrow here, perhaps related to another upward arrow preceding maxim [9].

11. These two words were inserted interlineally with a caret.

12. To the left of this maxim is a marginal note that reads "vid/p 178/172". Quincy recorded the same maxim, in an abridged version, on page 178, maxim [7], and the mention of page 172 may reference maxim [8], which indicates that one need not expose oneself to danger.

8. Coke, *Institutes*, part 1, p. 191.a (Ch. 4, Of Tenants in Common, Sect. 301).

9. Coke, *Institutes*, part 1, p. 78.b (Ch. 4, Of Knights Service, Sect. 103).

10. Coke, *Institutes*, part 1, p. 97.b (Ch. 6, Of Frankalmoigne, Sect. 138).

11. Coke, *Institutes*, part 1, p. 97.b (Ch. 6, Of Frankalmoigne, Sect. 138).

12. Coke, *Institutes*, part 1, p. 161.a (Ch. 12, Of Rents, Sect. 237) (quoting the maxim and indicating that a man who cannot enter and manure his land has been disseised from the land itself).

13. Coke, *Institutes*, part 1, p. 161.a (Ch. 12, Of Rents, Sect. 237).

14. Coke, *Institutes*, part 1, p. 162.a (Ch. 12, Of Rents, Sect. 240). In a marginal note, Quincy also includes a cross-reference to pages 172 and 178 of his maxim collection.

182

Maxims. etc.

[1] Quoties in Verbis Nulla est ambiguitas, ibi Nulla
Expositio contra Verba expressa fienda est. Haw. Abr.
p. 223
[2] Vita Reipublicae Pax est. Co. Lit. 168.a.
[3] Jus accrescendi inter Mercatores pro Beneficio Commercii
locum non habet. Ibid. 182.a.
[4] Quando Aliquid prohibetur fieri ex Directo
prohibetur & per Obliquum.[1] Co: Lit 223.b.
[5] Dormit Aliquando Jus, Moritur Nunquam. Ibid.
279.b.
[6] Dormiunt aliquando Leges, nunquam moriuntur. 2 Inst. 161.
[7] Reipublicae Interest suprema Hominum Testamen-
ta rata haberi. Co Lit 322.b.
[8] Verba relata hoc maxime operantur per Referentiam
ut in eis in esse videntur.[2] Ibid 359.a.
[9] Frustra fit per plura, quod fieri potest per
Pauciora. Ibid 362.b.
[10] Cumunis[3] Opinio is of Authority, & stands with ye Rule of
Law, A Communi[4] Observantia non est recodendum:[5] and
again, Minime mutanda sunt quae certam habuerunt
Interpretationem.[6] Co: Lit: 364.b. 365.a.
[11] Culpa est Rei se immiscere ad se non pertinenti.
vid. p.179. max. 2. ~~Ibid. 368.b.~~[7]

1. An arrow pointing upward corresponds to a footnote in the left-hand margin reading, "vid/p. 172,/max. 9/173/max 8/p 177./max 7." It is not immediately clear why Quincy is cross-referencing his page 172, maxim [9], which refers to fears that afflict men of constancy. It is possible that Quincy added additional maxims after cross-referencing maxim [9], and that the intended maxim therefore is found further down on the page. For instance, maxim [11] refers to the use of an agent for carrying out an action, which is related to the idea of forbidding something to be done indirectly. A similar issue arises with Quincy's internal reference to page 177, maxim [7], as the more relevant maxim on that page appears to be maxim [8]. On this page, it seems plausible that maxim [5] may have been inserted at a later time, thereby changing the sequence, or that Quincy may have overlooked maxims [4], [5], or [6], all of which are brief one-liners, while counting down the page. Quincy's cross-reference to page 173, maxim [8] is more straightforward, as the same maxim is recorded there.

2. A superscript *x* mark corresponds with a marginal note reading, "^{x}vid/p 175./maxs 1. 2. 3." Quincy is cross-referencing three additional maxims related to the interpretation of words. See Quincy's page 175, maxims [1–3].

182

Maxims. etc.

[1] Where there is no ambiguity in the words, then no explanation against the plain words is to be made.[1]
[2] The life of the republic is peace.[2]
[3] A right of increase (i.e. right of survivorship) does not have a place among merchants for the benefit of commerce.[3]
[4] When anything is prohibited to be done directly, it is also prohibited indirectly.[4]
[5] A right sometimes sleeps; it never dies.[5]
[6] Laws sometimes lie dormant; they never die.[6]
[7] It concerns a republic greatly that the final testaments of men be held ratified.[7]
[8] Words to which reference is made in an instrument have the same effect and operation as if they were inserted in the instrument referring to them.[8]
[9] It is pointless to do with more that which can be done with fewer.[9]
[10] The common opinion is of authority, and stands with rule of law. One should not depart from common observance. And again, matters that have had a certain interpretation should be changed as little as possible.[10]
[11] It is wrong to meddle with a matter not pertaining to oneself.[11]

1. Quincy cites to William Hawkins, *Summary of the Crown Law* (1st edition, London, 1728), vol. 1, p. 223. While this maxim is not directly quoted by Hawkins, the text discusses how a defamatory statement identifying only part of an individual's name will nevertheless be classified as libelous if it is clear from the context who is intended to be the target of the remarks. See Hawkins, p. 223 (Sect. 4). For further bibliographical information, see Maxwell, p. 363.

2. Coke, *Institutes*, part 1, p. 168.a (Ch. 1, Of Parceners, Sect. 248).

3. Coke, *Institutes*, part 1, p. 182.a (Ch. 3, Of Joyntenants, Sect. 282). For the translation of *jus accrescendi* as "right of survivorship," see *Latin for Lawyers*, p. 179.

4. Coke, *Institutes*, part 1, p. 223.b (Ch. 5, Of Estates, Sect. 361).

5. Coke, *Institutes*, part 1, p. 279.b (Ch. 8, Of Releases, Sect. 479).

6. Coke, *Institutes*, part 2, p. 161; *Statotum de Westminster primer*, ch. 1.

7. Coke, *Institutes*, part 1, p. 322.b (Ch. 10, Of Attornment, Sect. 586).

8. This translation is taken verbatim from *Latin for Lawyers*, p. 253. Quincy cites to Coke, *Institutes*, part 1, p. 359.a (Ch. 12, Of Remitter, Sect. 684).

9. Coke, *Institutes*, part 1, p. 362.b (Ch. 12, Of Remitter, Sect. 691). This principle is known today as Ockham's Razor.

10. Coke, *Institutes*, part 1, pp. 364.b–365.a (Ch. 13, Of Warranty, Sect. 697).

11. Coke, *Institutes*, part 1, p. 368.b (Ch. 13, Of Warranty, Sect. 701). See maxim [2] on Quincy's page 179 for additional citations for this maxim.

3. The expected word is *comunis* or *communis*.

4. The second *m* was inserted with a caret.

5. The expected word is *recedendum*. See, e.g., Coke, *Institutes*, part 1, p. 364.b.

6. The maxim starting *Minime mutanda sunt* also appears, with slight variation, on p. 153, maxim [5], although Quincy provides no internal reference.

7. Quincy's citation, which appears to have read "Ibid. 368.b" has been eliminated with cross-hatches, likely being replaced with an internal reference once Quincy discovered that he had already quoted the maxim elsewhere in this volume.

ſans felony, mes celuy ſoit en priſon jeſque al venue des Juſtices errants, ou aſsign' a gaole deliverie, & ſe miſt en pais devant eux de bien & male. Et ſi ſoit trove per pais que il le fiſt ſoy defend', ou per miſadventure, donques fra les Juſtices aſſavoier au roy, & le roy luy en fra ſa grace, ſi luy pleiſt. *W.* 1. *cap.* 11. Purview eſt enſement, que nul appell' ſoit abatue ci legierment come avant ad eſte, mes ſi lappellour counte le fait, lan, le jour, le heure, le temps le roy, & la ville ou le fait fuiſt fait, & de quel arme il fuiſt occiſe, ſe eſtoia la appell', & jammes ne ſoit lappell' abatus per default de freſh ſuit puis que home ſue dedeins lan & le jour apres le fait.

Before the making of this Statute, for that men were detained long in priſon before they were called to anſwer, which was ever odious in Law, Writs De odio & atia iſſued out of the Chancery for their relief (as it appeared before in the expoſition upon the Statute of Magna Charta) ſpecially where the fact was either by Miſadventure, or ſe defendendo; and therfore this Act reſtraining thoſe Writs, doth preſcribe a courſe for their ſpeedy calling to anſwer in thoſe two caſes. But now the Writ De odio & atia is revived by the Statute of 42 E. 3. cap. 1. as it appears in the expoſition upon the ſix and twentieth Chapter of Magna Charta. See the Mirror cap. 5. § 5. Magn. Chart. cap. 26, 29. See W. 2. cap. 29. Regiſt. 134.

And where the Statute of Marlbridge had determined, that killing of a man by Miſadventure ſhould not be any offence for the which the delinquent ſhould dye, this Statute maketh the killing of a man ſe defend' in the ſame degree, where by the Common Law he ſhould have dyed for it. Marlb. cap. 26. 21 E. 1. 17. b.

Laſtly, where the Statute of Marlbridge took an order for the parties ſpeedy delivery out of priſon in caſe of Miſadventure, this Act provideth for the ſame both in caſe of Miſadventure and of ſe defendendo.

¶ Per miſadventure ou ſoy defendant, ou en auter manner ſans felony.] Of this matter ſomewhat hath been ſaid in the expoſition upon the Statute of Marlbridge: an Indictment or a Verdict that A. killed B. ſe defendendo is not good, but the ſpeciall matter muſt be ſet down, to the end the Court may adjudge it to be upon inevitable neceſſity; whereof you ſhall read a notable Record in the Parliament Rolls of 3 R. 2. John Imperials caſe; Note the words here, Sans felony, vide Marlbridge ubi ſupra, and in our Books it is ſaid to be no Felony; and the reaſon is, becauſe neither of them is done [...]co animo. Marlbr. cap. 25. 43 Aſſ. p. 3. 3 E. 3 Coron. 302, 354. 15 E. 3. ibid. 116. 2 H. 4. 18. 11 H. 7 23. Fleta lib. 1. cap. 31. Rot. Parliam. 3. R. 2. nu. 18. John Imperials caſe.

If a man kill another in his own defence, if he eſcape, &c. the Town ſhall be amercied, as an ancient mark of the Common Law, that made it Felony.

¶ Soit en priſon jeſque al venue des Juſtices errants ou aſſign' a gaole deliverie.] Hereby it appeareth what expedition ought to be used for avoiding of long impriſonment, viz. untill the next coming of the Juſtices; ſee for this Magna Charta. Magn. Chart. cap. 26. & 29.

And here it is to be obſerved, that the Law of England is a Law of mercie, Lex Angliæ eſt lex miſericordiæ, for three cauſes:

Firſt, that the innocent ſhall not be worn and waſted by long impriſonment, but (as hereby, and by the Statute of Magna Charta appeareth) ſpeedily come to his triall.

Secondly, that priſoners for criminall cauſes, when they are brought to their triall, be humanely dealt withall; for * Severos quidem facit Juſticia, inhumanos * Regula.

 non

Sir Edward Coke, *Second Part of the Institutes of the Lawes of England* (London, 1642), p. 315. See Quincy's concluding maxim, *Lex Angliae est Lex Misericorniae*, Maxim [8], p. 427, *infra*, six lines up from bottom.

183

Maxims. etc.[1]

[1] The Severity of the Common Law, respecting
Felonies was Ut—
Paena ad Paucos, Metus ad Omnes perveniat. For it
is truly said. Etsi—
Meliores sunt quos ducit Amor, tamen plures sunt
quos corrigit Timor. Co Lit. 392.b.[2]
[2] Nemo punitur sine Injuria, facto, seu Defalta; and
Actus Legis Nemini damnosus. 2 Inst. 287.
[3] Ubi Lex est specialis, & Ratio ejus generalis, generaliter
accipienda est ~~2 Inst. 43~~[3] id. p. 172. max.1.
[4] In omni Re nascitur Res quae ipsam Rem ex-
terminat. Ibid. 15.
[5] Ignorantia[4] Judicis saepenumero Calamitas Innocentis
Ibid. 30. 591.[5]
[6] Contemporanea Expositio est fortissima in Lege.
2 Inst. 10. 11. 136. 139. 181.[6]
[7] Omnis Consensus tollit Errorem.[7] 2 Inst. 123

[8] Lex Angliae est Lex Misericordiae.[8] 2 Inst. 315

1. This page has been written on the inside back cover of the volume.

2. Quincy has paraphrased the English text here. See Coke, *Institutes*, part 1, p. 392.b.

3. A citation that appears to read "2 Inst. 43" has been eliminated with cross-hatching. As indicated by the internal reference, Quincy recorded the same maxim on page 172, maxim [1].

4. The letter *n* has been inserted with a carat.

5. This page contains a similar maxim: "*Ignorantia Judicis foret calamitas innocentis.*" Coke, *Institutes*, part 2, p. 591.

6. The maxim is not directly quoted here, but the text discusses how the king, ten years after the passage of an act that made rape punishable in some circumstances by merely fine and imprisonment, decided to make rape a felony once again. Coke observed, "it is *benedicta expositio*, when our ancient Authors, and our yeare books, together with constant experience doe agree". Coke, *Institutes*, part 2, p. 181.

7. The same maxim, sans the word *Omnis*, appears on page 175, maxim [9], with additional sources cited by Quincy.

8. This maxim is written in a larger hand at the bottom of the page, separated from the rest of the maxims above. A fitting end to Quincy's maxim collection.

183

Maxims. etc.

[1] The severity of the common law respecting
felonies was that—
Punishment reaches few; fear reaches all. For it is truly said. Though—
Better off are those whom love leads, nevertheless greater in number are those whom fear corrects.[1]
[2] No one is punished without an injury, deed, or default; and an act of law is damning to no one.[2]
[3] Where the law is specific and its reasoning is general, it should generally be accepted.[3]
[4] In every thing, something arises which eradicates the thing itself.[4]
[5] The ignorance of the judge is oftentimes the misfortune of the innocent.[5]
[6] A contemporary explanation is strongest in the law.[6]
[7] The consensus of all removes error.[7]

[8] The law of England is the law of mercy.[8]

1. Coke, *Institutes*, part 1, p. 392.b (Ch. 13, Of Warranty, Sect. 747).

2. Coke, *Institutes*, part 2, p. 287 (*Statutum de Glocester*, Ch. 1).

3. Coke, *Institutes*, part 2, p. 43 (*Magna Charta*, Ch. 26). See maxim [1] on Quincy's page 172, [pp. 374–75], for additional references for this maxim.

4. I.e., "Everything contains the seeds of its own destruction." Coke, *Institutes*, part 2, p. 15. (*Magna Charta*, Ch. 5), p. 1.

5. Coke, *Institutes*, part 2, p. 30 (*Magna Charta*, Ch. 17), p. 591 (*Statutum de Frangentibus Prisonam*) (containing a similar maxim).

6. Coke, *Institutes*, part 2, p. 11 (*Magna Charta*, Ch. 3), p. 136 (*Statutum de Marlebridge*, Ch. 18), p. 181 (*Statutum de Westminster primer*, Ch. 13) (discussing a similar proposition). Quincy also cites to pages 10 and 139, but the maxim does not appear to be directly quoted there. It is possible that Quincy was consulting an edition with different pagination, or that he was referencing related examples as opposed to quotations of the maxim itself.

7. Coke, *Institutes*, part 2, p. 123 (*Statutum de Marlebridge*, Ch. 11).

8. Coke, *Institutes*, part 2, p. 315 (*Statutum de Glocester*, Ch. 9).

Appendix II

THE COX CHART TO THE QUINCY MANUSCRIPT BOOKS AT THE MASSACHUSETTS HISTORICAL SOCIETY

EDITOR'S NOTE

Daniel R. Coquillette

I HAVE ON NUMEROUS OCCASIONS in these volumes sung the praises of Kevin Willoughby Cox, Harvard Law School, Class of 2006, an exceptional student, research assistant, and colleague. His painstaking analysis of Josiah Quincy Jr.'s manuscripts has been vital to this project. The following "Cox Chart" of the manuscripts not only describes the materials included in these volumes, but much other material, including material not by Quincy at all, but inserted in the manuscript by others. In short, the "Cox Chart" is an invaluable "road map" that will be of obvious value to future scholars.

Call No.	Reel	Manuscript	Pages	Description
P347 ["Southern Journal"]	Reel 3	QP 61	cover	Dull brown cover (original), label indicating South Carolina Journey of Josiah Quincy Jr. original + copy of English Diary
			inside cover, frontis	Table of *Southern Journal*
			1–185	*Southern Journal*
			186–251	Copy of Journey to England
			252–254	Epitaphs of Josiah Quincy Jr.
			255–259	Shenstone excerpts
			260	Newsprint copy of letter from Benjamin Franklin
			261	Epitaph of Josiah Quincy Jr.
			262	Back page of epitaph
			263	Summons of John Draper of Watertown for trespass
			264	Newspaper report of Quincy's departure for London
P347 ["London Journal"]	Reel 3	QP 62	cover	New cover and binding (brown)
			1–146	*London Journal* (original in Quincy's hand)
P347 ["Red Reports"]	Reel 4	QP 55	cover	New cover and binding (brown)
			4 blank pages	
			3–77	Law Reports
			78–82	Numbered blank pages
			4 unnumbered blanks	
P347 ["Volume 1"] ["Law Commonplace"]	Reel 4	QP 56	cover	Original cover of yellowed leather: "Vol. 1 1763 209 [new line] Nescit generosa mens [ignorantiam] [new line] pati 1 Inst.+ 5.10 [illegible]"; spine "Vol. 1" ["nescit . . . generosa mens ignorantiam pati" from Coke, 1 Inst. 6.a (Ch. 1, Of Fee Simple, Sect. 1)]
			1–98	Legal Commonplace Book
			4 blank pages	
			103–107	A copy of "Mr. Prat's" and others' minutes

Notes	*Height*	*Width*	*Breadth*	
Southern Journal [Quincy, *Works*, vol. 3] page numbers end at 210	21.2 cm	17.1 cm	2.8 cm	
London Journal [Quincy, *Works*, vol. 1]	16.9 cm	11.0 cm	1.9 cm	
MHS title: *Law Reports 1762, 1763* *Dougharty* v. *Poor* to *Dom. Rex.* v. *Gay* [Quincy, *Works*, vol. 4]	18.5 cm	12.0 cm	1.1 cm	JQ's vol. 2
Law Commonplace Book [Quincy, *Works*, vol. 2]	20.0 cm	16.1 cm	2.2 cm	JQ's vol. 1

Call No.	*Reel*	*Manuscript*	*Pages*	*Description*
			108–113	Pages torn out
			114–116	Continuation of unknown passage "the affirmative, without any negative expressed or implied"
			117–121	Province of the Massa. Bay [new line] Feb. 1760
			122–141	Hale's Advice on Study of Common Law
			142–143	* vid. Bar Bullfield "the natural duty of a good advocate is . . ."
			144–149	Blank
			150–174	Legis Miscellanea
			175–182	Index
P347 ["Volume 3"] ["Law Reports"]	Reel 4	QP 57	Cover	Original cover of yellowing leather: "Vol. 3, 1764 [illegible] [new line] infelix qui pauca sapit [new line] spernitq. doceri ["wretched is he who knows fews things and is contemptful of being taught"; new line] Co: Lit 232.b" "infelix qui pauca sapit spernitque doceri" Coke, 1 Inst. 232b (Ch. 5, Of Estates Upon Condition, Sect. 377)
			1–2 (1 is inside front)	Quotations
			2–4	Blank
			5–122	Law Reports
			123–124	Blank
			125–129	Law Reports 12/1763, Curia Admiral
			130–150	Blank
			151–157	Queres
			158–160	Blank
			161–163	Latin Maxims
			164–170	Blank
			171–183	Latin Maxims
P347 ["Volume 4"] ["Law Reports"]	Reel 4	QP 58	cover	Original cover of yellowing leather: "Vol. 4"
			0–2	Quotations from literary sources
			3	Blank
			4	Quote from Bacon

Notes	*Height*	*Width*	*Breadth*	
Legis Miscellanea [Quincy, *Works*, vol. 2]				
MHS title: *Reports 1764* *Law Reports* [Quincy, *Works*, vols. 4 and 5] Note, p. 122: "continuation of these reports carried vol. 4 p. 15" case: Russel Armijero *Latin Maxims* [Quincy, *Works*, vol. 2]	20.0 cm	16.1 cm	2.0 cm	JQ's vol. 3
MHS title: *Reports 1765–1769* [Quincy, *Works*, vol. 5]	20.0 cm	16.1 cm	2.1 cm	JQ's vol. 4

Call No.	*Reel*	*Manuscript*	*Pages*	*Description*
			5–10	Legis Miscellanea of Estates
			11–13	Blank
			14–85	Law Reports
			86–87	Blank
			88–100	Law Reports
			101–108	Of Law, Ecclesiastical, Civil, . . .
			109–111	Of the Civil Law
			112	Blank
			113–129	Continuation of Reports, from page 100
			130	Blank
			131–145	Reports: August term 1769
			146–147	Blank
			148–150	copy of letter from Prof. Dickins
			151–156	Maxims (Latin)
			157–160	Blank
			161–184	Miscellaneous writings on Evidence, etc.
P347	Reel 4	QP 54	cover	New cover and binding (brown)
			5 blank pages	Blank
			unnumbered page	page not in JQ script, referencing reports 1761–62
			1 blank page	Blank
			10–32	Law Reports (JQ's numbering 10–32)
			10 blank pages	Blank
P347	Reel 4	QP 60	cover	No orginal writing on spine or cover; label indicating Law Records, Josiah Quincy Jr. 1770
			1 page	text indicating copies of Law Reports belonging to E. Rutledge Esq., handwriting by Josiah Quincy Jr. 1770, Last pages copies from public Documents and Records
			3 pages	Blank
			3 pages	Index of cases (Rutledge's Reports)
			1–64	Copies of reports
			65–66	Blank
			67	Advice on notetaking—don't go too close to edge, since it will be bound in leather

Notes	*Height*	*Width*	*Breadth*
Continuation from p. 122 of vol. 3 *Law Reports* (cont.) Begins with *Hooton* v. *Grovt.* [Quincy, *Works*, vol. 5]			
Not Quincy's handwriting *Latin Maxims* [Quincy, *Works*, vol. 2]			
MHS title: *Law Reports 1771–1772* [Quincy, *Works*, vol. 5] *Simes Wife* ('71) to *Little* v. *Holden* ('72)	20.0 cm	16.1 cm	0.8 cm
Rutledge Reports	23.3 cm	19.5 cm	1.4 cm

Call No.	*Reel*	*Manuscript*	*Pages*	*Description*
			68	Blank
			69–71	Petition of the Assembly of NY to his Majesty
			72–74	Extract of a Representation from the Commissioners to trade and plantation to his Majesty dated Nov. 11 1761
			75–82	Letter from Charles Grath Esquire, Agent for the province of SC to Great Britain
			82–112	More Grath letters
			112–115	Rules and Orders to be Observed by the members of the Commons House of Assembly
			116–119	Blank
			120–158	Cobbler of Agawam
P347	Reel 4	QP 53		Catalog of Josiah Quincy's books
P347	Reel 4	QP 59	cover	Original, very worn brown leather cover, binding deteriorating, nothing written on outside
			1–272	Numbered pages of Compositions Commonplace
			273–329	Blank
			330–361	Index

Notes	Height	Width	Breadth
Catalog of JQ's books			
Political Commonplace Book [Quincy, *Works*, vol. 1]	19.1 cm	16.5 cm	3.7 cm

Appendix III

HARVARD COLLEGE LIBRARY BOOKS BORROWED BY JOSIAH QUINCY JR. 1762–1763

EDITOR'S NOTE

Daniel R. Coquillette

IMAGINE MY EXCITEMENT when I was contacted, on December 10, 2005, by David R. Whitesell, the distinguished Rare Book Cataloger at Harvard's Houghton Library. He told me that the manuscript loan register for 1762–1764 of the Harvard College Library contained a list of all the books Josiah Quincy Jr. borrowed during his senior year, from Sept. 1762–July 1763. According to Whitesell, this is "the earliest surviving circulation record documenting how students and faculty actually used an American college library," and he is preparing a paper on the amazing resource.[1]

What the list tells us about Quincy is both illuminating and almost painfully private. It confirms his broad interest in classics, literature, and history, noted many times above. Quincy had a special interest in international law, evidenced by his borrowing Samuel von Pufendorf's *De jure naturae et gentium libri octo* (Amsterdam, 1688) and Hugo Grotius's *De jure belli ac pacis libri tres* (Amsterdam, 1651). He also borrowed Michel de Montaigne's famous *Essays* (trans. Michael Lord of Montaigne, London, 1613), and Edward Hyde Clarendon's great *The history of the rebellion and civil wars in England* (Oxford,

1. The Harvard College Library burned on the fateful night of January 14–15, 1764, and most of the books were lost. The printed catalogue of 1723, perhaps used by Quincy, is available. See *The Printed Catalogue of the Harvard College Library 1723–1790* (eds. W. H. Bond, H. Amory, Boston, 1996), pp. 3 ff.

1707) books that foretell the young statesman and jurist as well. Finally, there was also evidence of Quincy's dogged ill health and his youthful fears in the medical books he borrowed, and a touching interest in poetry.

Needless to say, I am particularly grateful to David R. Whitesell for this discovery. He also prepared this list, and the learned description of the books, which he generously permits us to reproduce here.

NOTE: The "Catalogue of Books Belonging to the Estate of Josiah Quincy, jun. Esq: Deceas'd (1775)" will be published as Appendix 9 to Volume 5 of this series, *The Reports*. The catalogue of 1775 makes an interesting comparison to the books taken out by the student of 1762–1763, although Quincy's tragically early death makes all of these lists the reading of a young man.[2]

2. The content of a lawyer's library, as evidenced by estate lists, auctions, and other catalogues, is an often overlooked tool for a "greater understanding of the intellectual context of American law." See H. H. Hoeflich, "Auctions and the Distribution of Law Books in Antebellum America," 113 *Proceedings of the American Antiquarian Society* (Worcester, 2005), p. 160.

Harvard College Library Books Borrowed by Josiah Quincy Jr., 1762–1763

David R. Whitesell

Source:
Harvard University Archives, UA III.50.15.60 VT
Library Charging Records 1762–1763

Records of volumes borrowed from the Harvard College Library by Josiah Quincy during his senior year (1762–1763) appear on fol. 14 verso–15 recto of this ledger book. Only seniors were permitted to borrow books—on specified days scheduled approximately three weeks apart during term—and to have no more than three volumes on loan at any one time. Borrowing and return dates in brackets are best guesses added by me. The entire section has been crossed out to indicate that all volumes had been returned. A close transcription follows:

QUINCY

loan date	*author/title entry*	*shelf mark*	*return date*
1762 Sept. 10	Pufendorf de Jure Nat. & Gen.	22.3.1	Nov. 13 [1762]
[Sept. 10]	Grotius de Jure Belli & Pacis	6.5.12	Sept. 24 [1762]
[Sept. 10]	Collegium quartum Disput. &c.	3.6.26	[Sept. 24]
Novr. 13 [1762]	Montaign's Essays	17.3.20	Decr. 4 [1762]
[Nov. 13]	Conferences of ye Virtuosi of France [v. 1]	23.2.17	[Dec. 4]
[Nov. 13]	Clarendon's Hist. of Rebel. [v. 1]	14.1.17	[Dec. 4]
Decr. 4 [1762]	Cowley's Works	23.2.16	Feb. 26 [1763]
[Dec. 4]	Apothegmata	18.6.3	[Feb. 26]
Feb. 26 [1763]	Harris's Lexicon v. 1	26.1.1	April 9 [1763]
[Feb. 26]	Cudworth's Morality	27.6.20	March 19 [1763]
[Feb. 26]	Cornelius in Ecclesiasticum	5.3.7	[Mar. 19]
March 19 [1763]	Montfaucon's Antiq. v. 1	24.1.13	April 9 [1763]
[Mar. 19]	D[itt]o v. 2	24.1.14	[Apr. 9]

loan date	*author/title entry*	*shelf mark*	*return date*
April 9 [1763]	Turner's Syphilus	20.5.26	July 14 [1763]
[Apr. 9]	Aristotelis Opera v. 1	15.1.2	May 7 [1763]
[Apr. 9]	D[itt]o v. 2	15.1.3	[May 7]
May 7 [1763]	Medica statica	20.5.22	July 11 [1763]
[May 7]	The Storehouse of physical Practice	20.3.20	May 28 [1763]
[May] 28 [1763]	Duck's Poems	28.4.3	July 11 [1763]

Following is a list of the works borrowed by Quincy, arranged alphabetically by author, with the exact edition indicated where known. These have been identified by consulting the entries in the printed catalogue of the Harvard College Library (Boston, 1723, and supplements of 1725 and 1735, as reproduced in facsimile in: *The Printed Catalogues of the Harvard College Library 1723–1790.* Edited by W. H. Bond & Hugh Amory. Boston: Colonial Society of Massachusetts, 1996); citations were then verified in other bibliographical sources. Only one of the actual copies read by Quincy still survives at Harvard (Grotius); the others burned in the 1764 fire that destroyed much of the library or were deaccessioned/lost in later years (though Harvard has subsequently acquired copies of most of these editions).

15.1.2–3 Aristotle.
Opera omnia quae extant, Graece & Latine. Lutetiae Parisiorum: Typis Regiis, 1629. 2 vols. (Quincy borrowed both volumes).

23.2.17–18 Bureau d'adresse et de rencontre (Paris, France).
A general collection of discourses of the virtuosi of France, upon questions of all sorts of philosophy. London: Printed for Thomas Dring and John Starkey, 1664–1665. 2 vols. (Quincy borrowed vol. 1 only).

14.1.17–19 Clarendon, Edward Hyde, Earl of, 1609–1674.
The history of the rebellion and civil wars in England, begun in the year 1641 . . . Oxford: Printed at the Theater, 1707. 3 vols., folio (Quincy borrowed vol. 1 only).

23.2.16 Cowley, Abraham, 1618–1667.
The works of Mr. Abraham Cowley. London. [one of many editions published 1668–1700].

27.6.20 Cudworth, Ralph, 1617–1688.
A treatise concerning eternal and immutable morality. London: Printed for James and John Knapton, 1731.

28.4.3 Duck, Stephen, 1705–1756.
Poems on several occasions. London: Printed for the author, 1736.

6.5.12 Grotius, Hugo, 1583–1645.
Hugonis Grotii De jure belli ac pacis libri tres. Editio nova cum annotatis auctoris . . . Amstelodami: Apud Joannem Janssonium, 1651. This copy is now at Houghton Library, call number: Int 940.1*

26.1.1–2 Harris, John, 1667?–1719.
Lexicon technicum: or, an universal English dictionary of arts and sciences. London: Printed for Dan. Brown, Tim. Goodwin, John Walthoe, Tho. Newborough, John Nicholson, Dan. Midwinter, and Francis Coggan, 1708–1710. 2 vols., vol. 1 possibly 2nd ed. (also 1708) (Quincy borrowed vol. 1 only).

18.6.3 Isocrates.
The Godly aduertisement or good counsell of the famous orator Isocrates, intitled Paraenesis to Demonicus: whereto is annexed Cato in olde Englysh meter. London: By William Coplande, 1558.

5.3.7 Lapide, Cornelius Cornelii a, 1567–1637.
Ecclesiasticus Iesu Siracidis expositus accurato commentario R.P. Cornelii a Lapide. Lugduni: Ex Officina Landriana, sumptibus Claudii Du-Four et Claudij Gapaillon, 1634.

17.3.20 Montaigne, Michel de, 1533–1592.
Essayes written in French by Michael Lord of Montaigne. London: Printed by Melch. Bradwood for Edward Blount and William Barret, 1613.

24.1.13–14 Montfaucon, Bernard de, 1655–1741.
Antiquity explained, and represented in sculptures. London: Printed by J. Tonson and J. Watts, 1721. 2 vols. (Quincy borrowed both volumes).

20.3.20 Pechey, John, 1655–1716.
The storehouse of physical practice: beng a general treatise of the causes and signs of all diseases. London: Printed for Henry Bonwicke, 1695.

22.3.1 Pufendorf, Samuel, Freiherr von, 1632–1694.
Samuelis Pufendorfii De jure naturae et gentium libri octo. Amstelodami: Apud Andream ab Hoogenhuysen, 1688.

3.6.26 Rijksuniversiteit te Leiden.
[*Collegium quartum disputatio theologicae in Academia Lugdunum Batavorum.*] Rotterdam, 1627. [This work has yet to be positively identified. The 1723 library catalogue provides an approximate title as well as the place and date of publication.]

20.5.22 Santorio, Santorio, 1561–1636.
Medicina statica: being the aphorisms of Sanctorius. London. [one of 7 editions published between 1676 and 1737].

20.5.26 Turner, Daniel, 1667–1741.
Siphylis. A practical dissertation on the venereal disease. London. [one of 8 editions published between 1717 and 1739].

David R. Whitesell
Rare Book Cataloger
Houghton Library
Harvard University
12/31/2005

INDEX

Note: Page references in italics refer to illustrations or captions. All locations are in Massachusetts unless otherwise indicated. JQ refers to Josiah Quincy Jr.

THIS VOLUME HAS BEEN DESIGNED,
TYPESET IN CASLON TYPES, AND PRINTED AT
THE STINEHOUR PRESS, LUNENBURG, VERMONT

BOUND AT ACME BOOKBINDING,
CHARLESTOWN, MASSACHUSETTS